Grace Livingston Hill Collection #7

Grace Livingston Hill (1865–1947) remains popular more than fifty years after her death. She wrote dozens of books that carry her unique style for combining Christian faith with tasteful and exciting romance.

Isabella Alden (1841–1930), an aunt of Grace Livingston Hill, was a gifted storyteller and prolific author, as well, often using her writing to teach lessons espoused by her husband, Gustavus R. Alden, a minister. She also helped her niece Grace get started in her career as a best-selling inspirational novelist.

Lo, Michael, Grace Livingston Hill
Mickey, a young newsboy, saves the life of heiress Starr Endicott by taking the gunman's bullet himself. To show his gratitude, Delevan Endicott sends the boy off to school where he matures and then returns to the inner city to help his old friends. Through the years he has held Starr in his heart but refuses to intrude on her life. Suddenly he learns she's in danger—a danger she has unwittingly chosen. Can he save her again, and should he?

The Patch of Blue, Grace Livingston Hill
Chris Warren has no idea of listening to the sermon. He's happily day-dreaming about returning to college in the new sports car his father is buying for him. In fact, when his ears catch a few words of the visiting preacher about being thankful in the hard times, he's sorry he's heard even that much. But a sudden bank failure, a gunshot wound, and a family crisis alter Chris's dreams forever, and he finds himself in a place he never expected to be.

The Unknown God, Grace Livingston Hill
It is Brad Benedict's first night in the city, and he has nowhere to go. But when he stoops to pick up the wallet a stranger has dropped, he doesn't think he'll end up in an opera house. And there the majestic music, the haunting words, and the splendid vocalists compel the young man to look at his life and face the truth he's been trying to escape.

Stephen Mitchell's Journey, Isabella Alden
Farmer Mitchell's rheumatism keeps him from taking their produce to sell, so he sends his son, Stephen, in his place. No one ever expects Stephen to meet the greatest challenge of his life, starting him on a journey that will change not only his life but those of his family members, his neighbors, and the surrounding community. A wonderful story of a young man's search for enlightenment and purpose and of people helping people.

Grace Livingston Hill

COLLECTION NO. 7

FOUR COMPLETE STORIES
Updated for today's reader

BARBOUR
PUBLISHING, INC.
Uhrichsville, Ohio

Edited and updated for today's reader by Deborah Cole.

© 2000 by R. L. Munce Publishing Co., Inc.

ISBN 1-57748-825-3

Published by Barbour Publishing, Inc., P.O. Box 719, Uhrichsville, Ohio 44683
http://www.barbourbooks.com

 Member of the
Evangelical Christian
Publishers Association

Printed in the United States of America.

Lo, Michael

Chapter 1

The crowd had gathered at a great stone house on Madison Avenue. An automobile stood before the door. A beautiful little girl, not yet three years old, in white velvet and ermine, with her dark curls framed by an ermine-trimmed hood and silk rosebuds, came out of the door with her nurse for her afternoon ride. The nurse stepped back to the hall for the wrap she'd dropped, leaving the baby alone, her dark eyes shining under the straight dark brows, as she looked gleefully out on the world. At that instant, as if by magic, the crowd assembled.

It might be better to say that just then the crowd focused on the particular house where the baby daughter of the president of a great defaulting bank lived. More or less all morning, men had been gathering, passing the house, looking up with troubled or threatening faces toward the richly laced windows, shaking menacing heads and muttering imprecations. But there had been no disturbance and no concerted crowd until the child appeared.

The police had been more or less vigilant all morning but had seen nothing disturbing. The inevitable small boy had also been in evidence, with his instinct for excitement. Mickey with his papers often found himself in that quarter on bright mornings and would search for the child's starry eyes and dark curls in the windows of this particular house.

But the man with the evil face on the other side of the street, resting his hand against the lamppost and sighting the baby with a vindictive eye, had never been seen there before. Mickey noticed him first. Circling him innocently, he'd heard his imprecations against the rich, caught the whispered oath as the child appeared, and seen the man's ugly look. Alarmed, he crossed to the other side of the street, his eye on the offender, and was the first to see the covert motion, the flash of the hidden weapon, and fear the worst.

"Hi, there! Mickey! Look out!"

An alert voice called from a huddled group of urchins in the front of the crowd, but too late. The boy flashed past without heeding, straight up the stone steps where the child smiled at the crowd. Holding his bundle of papers high, with the late morning sunlight catching his tangle of golden hair, Mickey flung himself in front of the little one. The revolver's sharp crack from the opposite curb was simultaneous with their fall. Mickey's own ragged, neglected little body, receiving the bullet intended for her, went down with her as she fell.

Then all was confusion.

A child's cry—a woman's scream—a police whistle—the crowd's angry roar, like a pack of wild animals that had tasted blood. Stones flew from men whose wrongs had smoldered in their breasts and bred a fury of hate and murder. Women were trampled upon. Two of the plate-glass windows crashed as the flying missiles entered the magnificent home.

The chauffeur attempted to drive the car around the corner but was held up at once. He discreetly got out of the way, leaving the car in the hands of the mob who swarmed into and over it, disfiguring it in their wrath. Then came the noise of exploding tires, ripping of leather cushions, groaning of the machinery as the mob took vengeance on the car to show what they'd like to do to its owner.

Gone into bankruptcy! He! With a great electric car like that and servants to serve him! With his baby attired in a queen's trappings and his house swathed in lace that had taken the eyesight from many poor lace-makers! He! Gone into bankruptcy and slipping away scot-free, while the men he had robbed stood helpless on his sidewalk, hungry and hopeless because the pittances they'd put away in his bank, the result of slavery and sacrifice, were gone! And they were too old, too tired, or too filled with hate to earn it again.

The crowd surged and seethed, snarling, throbbing, desperate—leaderless and more dangerous.

The sight of the child with her dancing eyes and happy smiles, "rolling in luxury," called to mind their own puny darlings, grimy with neglect, lean with want, and hollow-eyed with premature knowledge. Why should one child be pampered and another starved? Why did the bank president's daughter have any better right to those wonderful furs and the exultant smile than their own children? A glimpse into the rooms beyond the sheltering plate glass and drapery showed even greater contrast than they'd dreamed between this home and the bare tenements they'd left that morning, where the children were crying for bread and the wives shivered with cold. Their every breath cried out for vengeance, and with brute instinct they sought to hurt the man through his child, because they had been hurt by the wrong done to their children.

The policeman's whistle had done its work, however. The startled inmates of the house had drawn the child and her preserver within the heavy carved doors and borne them back to safety before the mob could force its way in. Amid the outcry and disorder, no one noticed that Mickey had disappeared until his small band of companions set up an outcry; but even then no one heard.

The mounted police had arrived and were issuing orders. They arrested, handcuffed, and marched away the man who had fired the shot. They ordered the people right and left and rode their horses ruthlessly through the masses. Law and order had arrived, and the downtrodden could only flee.

The square was soon cleared and guarded by a large force. Only the newspapermen came and went without challenge. The threatening groups of men still hovering about withdrew further. The wrecked automobile was patched up and taken to the garage. The street quieted, and by and by workmen came to install temporary protections where the window glass had been broken.

Yet through it all the ragged newsboys stood their ground in front of the house. Until the quiet was restored, they evaded each renewed command of officer or passerby and stayed there, whispering now and again in excited groups and pointing up to the house. Finally a tall policeman approached them.

"Clear out, kids!" he said, not unkindly. "You hear me? You can't stay here any longer."

Then one of them wheeled around. He was the tallest, with a fierce freckled face and flashing black eyes in which the evil passions of four generations looked out upon a world that had always been harsh. He was known as Fighting Buck.

"Mickey's in dare. He's hurted. We kids can't leave Mick alone. He might be dead."

Just at that moment, a physician's runabout drew up to the door, and the policeman fell back to let him pass into the house. Right after him followed the bank president in a closed carriage attended by several men in uniform who escorted him to the door and touched their hats politely as he vanished inside. Around the corners, scowling faces haunted the shadows, and murmured imprecations were scarcely withheld in spite of the mounted officers. A shot was fired down the street, and several policemen hurried away.

"Mickey's in dare. He's hurted. I seen him fall. Maybe he's deaded. We kids wants to take him away. Mickey didn't do nothin'. He jes' tried to save der little kid. Mickey's a good'un. You get the folks to put Mickey out here. We kids'll take him away."

The policeman finally attended to the ragamuffins' pleading. Two or three newspapermen joined the knot around them, and the story was presently written up with all the racy touches writers of the hour knew how to use. Before night Buck, with his fierce black brows drawn in helpless defiance, was adorning the evening papers in various attitudes as the different snapshots portrayed him, and the newsboys, bootblacks, and good-for-nothings standing around him figured for once in the whole city's eyes.

The small band held their place until forcibly removed. Some were barefoot and stood shivering on the cold stones, their grimy faces blue with anxiety and chill.

The doctor came out of the house just as the last one, Buck, was being marched off with a loud protest. He eyed the boy and quickly understood the situation.

"Look here!" he called to the officer. "Let me speak to the youngster. He's a friend, I suppose, of the boy that was shot?"

The officer nodded.

"Well, boy, what's all this fuss about?" He looked kindly, keenly into Buck's black eyes.

"Mickey's hurted—mebbe deaded. I wants to take him away from dare," he burst forth. "We kids can't go off 'n' leave Mickey in dare wid de rich guys. Mickey didn't do no harm. He's jes' tryin' to save de kid."

"Mickey. Is that the boy who took the shot in place of the little girl?"

The boy nodded and looked anxiously into the doctor's face. "Yep. Hev you been in dare? Did youse see Mickey? He's got yaller hair. Is Mickey deaded?"

"No, he isn't dead," said the physician, "but he's pretty badly hurt. The ball went through his shoulder and arm and came mighty near some vital places. I've just been fixing him up comfortably, and he'll be all right after a bit. But he's got to lie very still right where he is and be taken care of."

"We kids'll take care o' Mickey!" said Buck proudly. "He tooked care of Jinney when she was sick, an' we'll take care o' Mickey all right. You jes' brang him out, an' we'll fetch a wheelbarry an' cart him off'n yer han's. Mickey wouldn't want to be in dare wid de rich guys."

"My dear fellow," said the doctor, quite touched by the earnestness in Buck's eyes, "that's very good of you, I'm sure, and Mickey should appreciate his friends. But he's being taken care of perfectly where he is and couldn't be moved. It might kill him to move him, and if he stays where he is he'll get well. I'll tell you what I'll do," he added as he saw the lowering distress in the eyes before him. "I'll give you a bulletin every day. You be here tonight at five o'clock when I come out of the house, and I'll tell you how he is. Then you needn't worry about him. He's in a beautiful room lying on a big white bed and has everything nice around him, and when I came away he was sleeping. I can take him a message for you when I go in tonight, if you like."

Half doubtfully the boy looked at him.

"Will you tell Mickey to drop us down word ef he wants anythin'? Will you ask him ef he don't want us to get him out?"

"Sure!" said the doctor, amused. "You trust me, and I'll make good. Be here at five o'clock sharp and again tomorrow at a quarter to eleven."

"He's only a slum kid!" grumbled the officer. " 'Tain't worthwhile to take so much trouble. 'Sides, the folks won't want um botherin' round."

"Oh, he's all right!" said the doctor. "He's a friend worth having. You might need one yourself someday. What's your name, boy? Who shall I tell Mickey sent the message?"

"Buck," said the child gravely. "Fightin' Buck, they call me."

"Very appropriate name, I'd think," said the doctor, smiling. "Well, run along, Buck, and be here at five o'clock."

Reluctantly the boy moved off. The officer again took up his stand in front of the house, and quiet was restored to the street.

In the great house, meanwhile, consternation reigned.

The nursemaid had reached the door in time to hear the shot and see the children fall. She barely escaped the bullet herself. She was an old family servant and therefore more frightened for her charge than for herself. She had the presence of mind to drag both children inside the house and shut and lock the door immediately, before the seething mob could break in.

The mistress of the house fell in a dead faint as they carried her little daughter upstairs, and a man and a maid followed with the unconscious boy. The servants rushed about, while the housekeeper telephoned the bank president what had happened and sent for the family physician. No one knew yet who was hurt or how much. Mickey had been brought inside because he blocked the doorway, and they needed to shut the door. If it had been easier to shove him out, the nursemaid would probably have done that. But, once inside, humanity bade them look after the unconscious boy's needs. Besides, no one knew yet exactly what part Mickey had played in the morning's small tragedy.

"Where shall we take him?" said the man to the maid as they reached the second floor with their burden.

"Not here, Thomas. Here's no place for him. He's as dirty as a pig. I can't think what come over Morton to pull him inside anyway. His own could have tended to him. Besides, such is better dead!"

They hurried on past the luxurious rooms belonging to the lady of the mansion and up the next flight of stairs. Nora passed by the bathroom door where the full light of the hall windows fell on the grimy figure they carried and uttered an exclamation.

"He's not fit fer any place in this house. Look at his clothes. They'll have to be cut off'n him, and he needs to go in the bathtub before he can be laid anywheres. Let's put him in the bathroom, and you call Morton. She got him in here, and she'll have to bathe him. And bring me a pair of scissors. I'll mebbe have to cut the cloes off'n him—they're so filthy. Ach! The little beast!"

Thomas, glad to be rid of his burden, dropped the boy on the bathroom floor and left to call Morton.

Nora, with little knowledge and less care, took no thought for her patient's life. She was intent on making him fit to put between her clean sheets. She found the tattered garments none too tenacious in their hold to the little half-naked body. One or two buttons and a string were their only attachments. She pulled them off gingerly and, holding them at arm's length, took them to the bathroom window where she pitched them down into the paved court below that led to the kitchen regions. Thomas could burn them or put them on the ash pile. She was certain they'd never go on again and wondered how they'd held together this long.

Morton hadn't come yet, but Nora, discovering a pool of blood under the bare shoulder, lifted him quickly into the white bathtub and turned on the warm water. There was no use wasting time and getting blood on white tiles she'd have to scrub. She wasn't unkind, but she hated dirt. Supporting the child with one arm, she scrubbed him with the other hand. The shock of the water, cold at first, brought consciousness to the boy for a moment in one long shuddering sigh. The eyelashes trembled on the white cheeks, and his eyes opened. He gazed wildly on the strange surroundings, the water, and the vigorous Irish-woman who had him in her power.

He threw his arms up with a struggling motion, gasped as if with sudden pain, and lost consciousness again, relaxing once more into the strong red arm that held him. At this critical moment Morton entered the bathroom.

Morton was a trim, apple-cheeked Scotswoman of about thirty years, with neat yellow-brown hair coiled on top of her head, a cheerful tilt to her freckled nose, and blue eyes set in rosy cheeks. Integrity exuded from her being, flamed from her cheeks, spoke from her stubborn chin, and looked from her trustworthy eyes. She had been with the bank president's baby ever since the star-eyed creature entered the world.

"Och! Look ye at the poor wee'un!" she exclaimed. "Ye're hurtin' him, Nora! Ye shouldn't have bathed him the noo! Ye should've waited the docthur's comin'. Ye'll mebbe kin kill him."

"Ach! Get out with yer soft talk!" said Nora, scrubbing more vigorously. "Did yez suppose I'll be afther havin' all this filth in the nice clean sheets? Get ye to work an' he'p me. Do ye hold 'im while I schrub!"

She shifted the boy into the gentler arms of the nurse and splashed even harder. Then suddenly, before the nurse could protest, she'd dashed foamy suds on the golden head and was scrubbing that with all her might.

"Och, Nora!" cried the nurse in alarm. "You shouldn't 'a' done that! Ye'll surely kill the bairn. Look at his poor wee shoulder a bleedin', and his little face so white an' still. Have ye no mercy at all, Nora? Rinse off the suds at once an' dry him softly. What'll the docthur be sayin' to ye fer all this, I can't think. There, my poor bairnie," she crooned to the child, softly drawing him closer as though he was conscious. "There, my bairnie, it'll soon be over. It'll be all right in a minute, poor wee b'y! There—"

But Nora did her work and made the little lean body glistening white as polished marble, while the heavy hair hung limp like pale golden silk.

The two women carried him to a bed in a large room at the back of the house, not far from the nursery, and laid him on a blanket, with his shoulder stanched with soft linen rags. Morton was softly drying his hair and crooning to the unconscious child, begging Nora to put the blanket over him lest he catch cold, and Nora was still drying his feet, unmindful of Morton's pleading, when the doctor entered with a trained nurse. The boy lay white and still upon the blanket as the two women, startled, drew back from their task. The body, clean now and beautifully shaped, might have been marble except for the delicate blue veins in wrists and temples. In spite of signs of privation and lack of nutrition, the boy showed strength in well-developed muscles, and it went to the heart to see him lying so helpless, with his drenched gold hair and his closed eyes. The white limbs didn't quiver, the lifeless fingers drooped limply, the white chest didn't stir with any sign of breath, and yet the curved lips hadn't altogether gone white.

"What a beautiful child!" exclaimed the nurse involuntarily as she came near the bed. "He looks like a young god!"

"He's far more likely to be a young devil," said the doctor grimly, leaning over him with practiced eyes and listening to the quiet chest. Then he started back.

"He's cold as ice! What have you been doing to him? It wasn't a case of drowning, was it? You haven't been giving him a bath at such a time as this, have you? Did you want to kill the kid outright?"

"Och, the poor wee b'y!" sobbed Morton under her breath, her blue eyes drenched with tears. "He's like to my own wee b'y I lost when he was a baby," she explained in apology to the trained nurse who wasn't, however, regarding her.

Nora had vanished, frightened, to consult with Thomas. Morton brought the things the doctor called for and showed the nurse where to put her belongings. And after everything was done and the boy was comfortable and brought back to consciousness, she stood at the foot of the bed and smiled at him when he opened his eyes.

His eyes were dark blue but wide with brave fear as he glanced about on the strange faces. He looked like a wild bird, whose instincts held him still because he saw no way of flight. He looked from side to side in the room and made a furtive motion to rise from the pillow. And in his glance were the gentle harmlessness and appeal of the winged thing that has been caught.

"Well, youngster, you had a pretty close shave," said the doctor jovially, "but you'll pull through all right! You feel comfortable now?"

"Poor wee b'y!" murmured Morton, her eyes drenched again.

The boy looked from one to another doubtfully. Suddenly he remembered and understood. He looked about the room and toward the door. His eyes turned to the doctor with a question, but his lips formed no words. He looked at Morton and knew her for his baby's nurse. Suddenly he smiled, and that smile seemed to light up the whole room, filling Morton's heart with joy. It seemed to her it was the smile of her own lost baby come back to shine upon her.

"Where's—de little kid?" He searched Morton's face anxiously as he framed the eager question.

"She's safe in her own wee crib takin' her morning nap. She's just new over," answered the woman reassuringly.

Still the eyes weren't satisfied.

"Did she," he began slowly, "get—hurted?"

"No, my bairnie, she's all safe and sound as ever. Your own self saved her life."

The boy's face lit up, as if to say, "Then I'm glad." But not a word did he speak.

"You're a hero, kid!" said the doctor huskily. But the boy knew little about heroes and didn't comprehend.

The nurse bustled up to take her place at the bedside, and Morton and the doctor left, the doctor stepping again into the lady's room below to see if she was feeling quite herself again after her faint.

The nurse leaned over the boy with a glass and spoon. He looked at it curiously. It was a situation entirely outside his experience.

"Why don't you take your medicine?" asked the nurse.

The boy looked at the spoon again as it approached his lips and opened them to speak.

"Is—"

In went the medicine, nearly choking the boy, but he understood and smiled.

"A hospital?" he finished.

The nurse laughed.

"No, it's only a house. They brought you in when you were hurt out on the steps. You saved the little girl's life. Didn't you know it?" she said kindly, her heart won by his smile.

A beautiful look rewarded her.

"Is de little kid—in this house?" he asked slowly, wonderingly.

"Oh, yes, she's here," answered the nurse lightly. "Perhaps they'll bring her in to see you sometime. Her father's very grateful. He thinks it showed wonderful courage for you to risk your life for her sake."

But Mickey understood nothing about gratitude. He only understood that the beautiful baby was in the house and might come there to see him. He settled to sleep with an occasional glad, wistful glance toward the door, as the long lashes sank on the white cheeks, for the first sleep the boy had ever taken in a clean, white, soft bed. The prim nurse, softened for once from her precise attention to duties, stood and looked upon the sleeping child's face, wondering what his life had been and how the future would be for him. She half pitied him that the ball hadn't gone nearer the vital spot and taken him to heaven before he missed the way, so angelic this face appeared in the soft light of the sickroom.

Chapter 2

Starr Endicott, sleeping in her lace-draped crib on her embroidered pillow, knew nothing of the hate and murder that rolled in a wave on the streets outside and had almost blotted out her life. She didn't know that the three notable families whose names were interwoven in her own and whose blood flowed in her tiny veins represented the great hated class of the rich and that those upon whom they'd climbed to this height looked upon them as an evil to be destroyed. Nor did she know that she, being the last and in her name representing them all, was hated most of all.

Starr Delevan Endicott! It was engraved on her tiny pins and locket, on the gold circling her finger, on her brushes and combs. It was embroidered on her dainty garments, coverlets, and cushions, and crooned to her by the adoring Scottish nurse who came of a line that knew and loved an aristocracy. The pride of the house of Starr, the wealth of the house of Delevan, the glory of the house of Endicott—weren't they all hers, this one beautiful baby who lay in her arms to tend and to love. So mused Morton as she hummed.

Oh, hush thee, my babie, thy sire was a knight,
Thy mother a ladie, both gentle and bright—

And what did Morton care that the mother in this case was neither gentle nor bright, but only beautiful and selfish? It made the child dearer that she had her love to herself.

And so little Starr lay sleeping in her crib, and the boy, her preserver, from nobody knew where and of nobody knew what name of fame, lay sleeping also. And presently Delevan Endicott himself came to look at them both.

He came from the turbulent world outside and from his fretting, petted wife's bedside. She had been fussing at him for letting a bank in which he happened to be president do anything that would cause such a disturbance outside her home, when he knew she was so nervous. Not one word about the step that had stood for an instant between her baby and eternity. Her husband reminded her gently how near the baby had come to death and how she should rejoice that she was safe. But her reply had been a rush of tears and "Oh, yes, you always think of the baby—never of me, your wife!"

Sighing, the man had turned from his fruitless effort to calm her and gone to his little daughter. He'd hoped his wife would go with him, but he saw the uselessness of that. The little girl lay with one plump white arm thrown over her head, the curling baby fingers just touching her cheek, flushed with sleep. She looked like a rosebud among the rose and lacy draperies of her crib. Her soft, dark curls and long, dark curling lashes brought out each delicate feature of her face. The father, as he gazed down upon her, wondered how any creature, no matter how wicked, could desire to put out this life. His little Starr, his one treasure!

The man who had tried to do it—could he have intended it, or was it only a random shot? Those who saw judged it intention. The father's quickened heartbeats told him it was, and the thrust had gone deep. How they must hate him, and how they would have hurt his life irretrievably if the shot had done its work. If that other atom of human life hadn't intervened!

Where was the boy who had saved his child? He must see him at once. The gratitude of a lifetime should be his.

Morton divined his thought, as he stepped from the crib after sweeping his lips over Starr's cheek. With silent tread she followed her master to the door.

"The poor wee b'y's in the far room yon," she whispered, and her tone implied that his duty lay next in that direction.

The banker had often noticed this gentle suggestion in the nurse's voice; it reminded him of something in his childhood, and he invariably obeyed it. He might have resented it if it had been less humble, less trustfully certain that of course that was what he meant to do next. He followed her direction now without a word.

The boy had just fallen asleep when he entered and lay as sweetly beautiful as the little beauty he'd left in the other room. The man of the world paused and exclaimed in wonder. He'd been told a little gamin had saved his daughter from the assassin's bullet, but this child's features were as delicately chiseled, his form as finely modeled, his hair as soft as any scion of a noble house might boast. He, like the nurse, felt that a young god lay before him. Mickey had always impressed a stranger thus, even when his face was dirty and his feet bare.

The man stood with bowed head and gazed upon the boy to whom he felt he owed a debt he could never repay.

He recognized the child as representing that great unwashed throng of humanity who were his natural enemies, because by their oppression and by stepping upon their rights when convenient he'd risen to where he now stood and could maintain his position. He had no special feeling for them, but this boy was different! This spirit-child with the form of Apollo, the beauty of Adonis, and the courage of a hero! Could he have come from the hotbeds of sin and corruption? Surely not! He must be of good birth. Inquiry must be made. Had anyone asked the child's name and where he lived?

Then, as if in answer to his thought, the dark blue eyes opened. He found them looking at him and started as he realized it. Yet he couldn't summon words but met the child's steady searching gaze, as if the eyes would see and understand the principles on which the man's life rested. The man felt it and had the sensation of hastily looking at his own motives in the light of this child's look. Would his life bear that burning appealing glance?

Then, unexpectedly, the child's face lit up with his wonderful smile. He'd decided to trust the man.

Never before in his proud and varied experience had Delevan Endicott encountered a challenge like that. It beat through him like a mighty army and took his heart by storm. It was the challenge of childhood to the fatherhood of man. With a strange new impulse the man accepted it and, struggling to find words, could only answer with a smile.

A good deal passed between them before any words were spoken, a good deal the boy never forgot and that the man liked to return to in his moments of self-reproach; for somehow that boy's eyes called forth the best in him and made him ashamed of other things.

"Boy, who is your father?" the man asked huskily at last. He almost dreaded to find another father owning a noble boy like this—and such a father as he would be if it were true he was only a street gamin.

The boy still smiled, but a wistfulness entered his eyes. He slowly shook his head.

"Dead, is he?" asked the man, more as if thinking aloud.

But the boy shook his head again. "No, no father," he answered simply.

"Oh," said the man, and a lump gathered in his throat. "Your mother?"

"No mother, never!" came the solemn answer.

It seemed he scarcely felt that either was a deep lack in his assets. Likely fathers and mothers weren't on the average desirable kindred in his neighborhood. The man reflected and tried again.

"Who are your folks? They'll be worried about you. We should send them word you're doing well."

The boy looked amazed. Then a laugh rippled out.

"No folks," he gurgled. "On'y jest de kids."

"Your brothers and sisters?" asked Endicott puzzled.

"None o' dem," said Mickey. "Buck an' me're pards. We fights fer de other kids."

"Don't you know it's wrong to fight?"

Mickey stared.

Endicott tried to think of something to add to his moral homily but couldn't.

"It's very wrong to fight," he reiterated lamely.

The boy's cherub mouth settled into firm lines.

"It's wronger not to, when de little kids is gettin' hurt an' de big fellers what ought ter work is stole away they bread, an' they's hungry."

It was an entirely new proposition. It was the challenge of the poor against the rich, the weak against the strong, and from the lips of a mere babe.

"I'd fight fer your little kid!" declared the young logician. He seemed to know by instinct this was the father of his baby.

Ah, now he had touched the responsive chord. The father's face lit up. He understood. Yes, it was right to fight for his baby girl, his Starr, his one treasure, and this boy had done it, given his life freely. Was that like fighting for those other unloved, uncared-for, hungry darlings? Were they then dear children, too, of somebody, of God, if nobody else? The boy's eyes were telling him in one long look that the world of children at least was kin, and the father felt that in mere decency of gratitude he must acknowledge so much. Poor hungry babies.

What if his darling were hungry! A sudden longing seized him to give them bread at once. But at least he would shower his gratitude upon this one stray defender of their rights.

He struggled to find words to let the child know this, but the tears in his eyes spoke for him.

"Yes, my boy! You did fight for my little girl. I'll never forget it as long as I live. You saved her life, and that's worth everything to me. Everything, do you understand?"

At last the words rushed forth, but his voice was husky, and those who knew him would have declared him more moved than they'd ever seen him.

The boy understood. A slender brown hand stole out from the white coverlet and touched his. Its outline, long and graceful, spoke of patrician origin. It was hard for the man of wealth and pride to realize it was the hand of the child of the common people, the people who were his enemies.

"Is there anything you'd like to have done for you, boy?" he asked at last because the depth of emotion was more than he could bear.

The boy looked troubled. "I was thinkin', ef Buck an' them could see me, they'd know 'twas all right. I'd like 'em to know how 'tis in here."

"You want me to bring them up to see you?"

Mickey nodded.

"Where can I find them, do you think?"

"Buck, he won't go fur, till he know what's comed o' me," said the boy with confidence in his friend. "He'd know I'd do that fer him."

Then honor and loyalty must exist among the lower ranks of men—at least among the boys. The man of the world was learning a great many things. Meekly he descended the two flights of stairs and went out to his own front doorsteps.

There were no crowds anymore. The police were still on duty, but curious passersby dared not linger long. The workmen had finished the windows and gone. The man felt little hope of finding the boys, but somehow he had a strange desire to do so. He wanted to see that face light up again. Also, he had a curious desire to see these youngsters from the street who could provoke such loving anxiety from the hero upstairs.

Mickey was right: Buck wouldn't go far until he knew how it was with his comrade. He had moved off at the officer's word when the doctor promised to bring him word later, but he didn't intend to let a soul pass in or out of that house all day that he didn't see. So he set his young pickets here and there about the block, each with his bunch of papers, and arranged a judicious change occasionally, to avoid trouble with the officers.

Buck was standing across the street on the corner by the church steps, making a lively show of business now and then and keeping one eye on the house that had swallowed up his partner. He wasn't slow to perceive he was being summoned by a man on the steps and ran eagerly up with his papers, expecting to receive his coin and maybe a glimpse inside the door.

"All about der shootin' of der bank millionaire's baby!" he yelled in his most finished voice of trade, and the father, thinking of what might have been, felt a pang of horror at the careless words from the gruff voice.

"Do you know a boy named Buck?" he questioned as he paid for the paper that was held up to him and searched the unpromising face before him. Then he marveled at the sullen, sly change on the dirty face.

The black brows drew down forebodingly; the dark eyes reminded him of a caged lion ready to spring. The child had become a man with a criminal's face. There was something frightful about the defiant look with which the boy drew himself up.

"What if I does?"

"Only that a boy in here," he said, motioning toward the door, "would like very much to see him for a few minutes. If you know where he is, I wish you'd tell him."

Then came a change more marvelous than before. The whole defiant face became eager, the black eyes danced with question, the brows settled into straight pleasant lines, and the mouth softened.

"Is't Mickey?" he asked earnestly. "Kin we get in? I'll call de kids. He'll want 'em. He allus wants der kids."

He placed his fingers in his mouth, stretched it, and issued forth a sound that might have come from an exulting fiend's mouth, so long and shrill it was. The man on the steps, his nerves already wrought to the snapping point, started angrily. Then suddenly around the corner at a swift trot emerged three ragged youngsters who came at their leader's command swiftly and eagerly.

"Mickey wants us!" explained Buck. "Now youse foller me 'n' don't say nothin' 'less I tell you."

They fell in line behind the bank president and followed, awed, within the portal that unlocked a palace more wonderful than Aladdin's to their astonished gaze.

Up the stairs they slunk, single file, silently and sleuthlike over the polished stairs. They skulked past open doors with frightened defiant glances, the defiance of the poor for the rich, born and bred from hunger, cold, and need of every kind. But they took it all in and for many days gave embellished details of the palace where Mickey lay. It seemed to them that heaven itself could show no grander sights.

In a stricken row against the wall, with sudden consciousness of their ragged caps in hands, grimy hands behind them, they stood and gazed upon their fallen hero-comrade.

They'd perhaps never seen his face clean before. His white robe seemed of unearthly whiteness. It dazzled them. His newly washed hair shone on his head. They saw him gathered into a different world from any they knew. How could he ever be theirs again? How could it have happened in the few hours since Mickey flashed past them and fell martyr to his kindly heart and saved the wicked rich man's child? Buck's brows drew together in his densest frown. He felt that their Mickey was having some terrible change come upon him.

Then Mickey turned and smiled at them and in his familiar voice shouted,

"Say, kids, ain't this grand? Say, I jes' wish you was all in it! Ef you, Buck, an' the kids was here in this yer grand bed I'd be havin' the time o' me life!"

That turned the tide. Buck swallowed hard and smiled his darker smile, and the rest grinned sheepishly. Grandeur and riches hadn't spoiled their prince. He was theirs still and wanted them. He'd sent for them. They gained courage to look around the spotlessly clean room—at the nurse in her crackling dignity; the dish of oranges she promptly handed to them and of which each in awe partook a golden sphere; the bright flowers Morton had placed on a stand by the bed; the pictures hanging on the walls; and then back to the white bed that held their companion. They couldn't get used to the whiteness and cleanness of his face and hands and bright gold hair. It burned like a flame against the pillow, and Mickey's blue eyes seemed darker and deeper than ever before. To Buck the children had given their obedient following and looked to him for protection, but after all he was one like them, only a little more fearless. To Mickey they gave a kind of far-seeing adoration. He was fearless and brave like Buck, but he was something more. In their superstitious fear and ignorance he seemed to them almost supernatural.

They skulked silently down the stairs like frightened rabbits when the interview was over, each clutching his precious orange. Not until the great doors had closed upon them did they utter a word. They had said very little; Mickey had done all the talking. When they'd filed down the street behind their leader and rounded the corner out of sight of the house, Buck gathered them into a little knot.

"Kids, I bet cher Mick don't be comin' out o' this no more. Didn't you notice how he looked jes' like the angel o' the monemunt down at the cemetery?"

The group took on a solemnity that was deep and real.

"Anyhow, he wanted us!" spoke up a curly headed boy with old eyes and a thin face. Mickey had always defended him. He bore a hump on his ragged back.

"Aw! He's all right fer us, is Mick," said Buck, "but he's different. Old Aunt Sal said one day he were named fer an angel, an' like as not he'll go back where he b'longs someday, but he won't never fergit us. He ain't like rich folks what don't care. He's our pard allus. Come on, fellers."

Down the back alley went the solemn procession, single file, till they reached the rear of the Endicott house, where they stood silent. At a signal from their leader, each grimy right hand was raised, and each ragged cap taken off and held high in the air toward the upper window, where they knew their hero-comrade lay. Then they turned and marched silently away.

They were in place before the door whenever the doctor came, and they always went around by the way of the alley afterward for their ceremonial good night, sometimes standing solemnly beneath the cold stars while the shrill wind blew through their thin garments. But as long as the doctor brought them word, or as long as the light burned in the upper window, they felt their comrade hadn't gone yet.

Chapter 3

Heaven opened for Mickey on the day Morton, with the doctor's permission, brought baby Starr to see him.

The baby, in her nurse's arms, gazed down upon her rescuer with the unprejudiced eyes of childhood. Mickey's smile flashed upon her, and she answered with a joyous laugh. The beautiful boy pleased her. She reached out her hands to greet him.

The nurse held her down to the bed. "Kiss the wee b'y—that's a good baby. He took care of baby and saved her life when the bad man tried to hurt her. Kiss the wee b'y and say 'thank you.' "

The saving of her life meant nothing to Starr, but she obediently murmured, "Tank oo!" as the nurse had drilled her to do before she brought her. Then she laid her moist pink lips on cheeks, forehead, eyes, and mouth in turn, and Mickey, in ecstasy, lay trembling with the newness and pleasure of it. No one had ever kissed him before. Kissing was not in vogue in the street where he existed.

Thereafter, every day until he was convalescent, Starr came to visit him.

By degrees he grew accustomed to her presence enough to talk with her freely as child with child. Her words were few and her tongue as yet unacquainted with the language of this world. But perhaps that was better, for their conversations were more of the spirit than of the tongue, Mickey's language, of circumstance, being quite unlike that of Madison Avenue.

Starr brought her wonderful electric toys and dolls, and Mickey looked at them in awe, yet always with a kind of rare indifference, because the child herself was to him the wonder of all wonders.

And every day, when the nurse carried her small charge away after her frolic with the boy, she would always lift her up to the bed and say, "Now kiss the wee b'y, baby Starr, and thank him again fer savin' yer life."

And Starr would lay her soft sweet mouth on his as tenderly and gravely as if she understood her obligation. At such times Mickey would watch her bright face as it came close to his, and when her lips touched his he would close his eyes as if to shut out all else from this sacred ceremony. After Starr and Morton were gone, the nurse would look furtively toward the bed and note the boy's still face, his eyes closed as if to hold the vision and memory longer. At such times her heart would draw her strangely from her formality to touch the boy with a tenderness unnatural to her.

Other times Mr. Endicott would come and talk briefly with the boy, just to see his eyes light and his face glow with that wonderful smile, and think what it would be if the boy were his own. Always Mickey enjoyed these talks, and when his visitor was gone he would think with satisfaction that this was the right father for his Starr. He was glad she had a father. He'd often wondered what it would be like to have a father. Not that he felt a great need for one. He'd taken care of himself since he could remember and felt quite grown-up, and fathers usually drank. But a baby like that needed a father, and he liked Starr's father.

But the dearest thing now in life for him was little Starr's kisses.

To the father, drawn first by gratitude to the boy who had saved his child's life, and afterward by the boy's own irresistible smile, these frequent visits had become a pleasure. There had been a little boy before Starr came to their home, but he had lived only a few weeks. The memory of that golden, fuzzy head, the little fingers, the blue eyes of his son still lingered bitterly in the father's heart. When he first looked upon this waif, the notion seized him that perhaps his own boy would have been like this had he lived, and a strange and unexpected tenderness entered his heart for Mickey. He kept going to the invalid's room night after night, pleasing himself with the thought that the boy was his own.

This notion took such strong hold on the man's heart that he considered adopting the child and bringing him up as his own—this, after he had by the aid of detectives thoroughly searched out all that was known of him and found that no one owned Mickey or seemed to care what became of him except Buck and his small following. Meanwhile the child, well fed, well cared for, happier than he'd ever dreamed of being in his hard life, rapidly convalesced.

Endicott came home one afternoon to find Mickey down in the reception room dressed in black velvet and rare old lace, with his golden hair, which had grown during his illness, tortured into ringlets. An adoring group of ladies had gathered about him, as he stood with troubled, almost haughty mien and gravely regarded their sentimentalities.

Mrs. Endicott had paid no attention to the boy before this, and her sudden interest in him came from a changed view of him as he sat up in a big chair for the first time, playing a game with Starr. His big eyes and beautiful hair attracted her at once, and she lost no time in dressing him up like a doll and making him a show at one of her receptions.

When her husband remonstrated with her, declaring that such treatment would ruin the spirit of any real boy and spoil him for life, she shrugged her shoulders indifferently.

"Well, what if it does? He's nothing but a foundling. He should be glad we were willing to dress him up prettily and play with him a while."

"And what would you do with him after you were finished? Cast him aside?"

"Well, why not?" she said with another shrug. "Or perhaps we might teach him to be a butler or footman if you want to be benevolent. He'd be charming in a dark blue uniform!"

The woman raised her delicate eyebrows, humming a light tune, and her husband turned from her in despair. Was it nothing to her that this child had saved her baby's life?

That settled the question of adoption. His wife would never bring up the boy into anything like manhood. It was different with a girl—she must of necessity be frivolous, he supposed.

The next morning an old college friend entered his office, a plain man with a pleasant face, who hadn't gone from college days to a bank presidency. He was only a plain teacher in a struggling Florida college, and he came soliciting aid for the college.

Endicott turned from puzzling over Mickey to greet this old friend he hadn't seen for twenty years. He was glad to see him. He'd always liked him. He looked him over critically, however, from his successful-New-York-businessman point of view. He noticed the plain cheap business suit, worn shiny in places, the shoes well polished but breaking at the side, the sprinkling of gray hairs. Then his eyes traveled to his friend's kind, worn face, and he couldn't help feeling somehow that the man was happier than he was.

He asked many questions and found pleasure in hearing about the other's family and their happy united efforts to laugh off poverty and have a good time anyway. Then the visitor told of the college, its struggles, its great needs and small funds, how its orange crop, a large part of its regular income, had failed that year because of the frost, and they needed funds to carry on the work that school year. Endicott found his heart touched, though he didn't usually give large amounts to anything.

"I'd be glad to help you, Harkness," he said at last, "but I've got a private benevolence on my hands that will take a good deal of money, I'm afraid. You see we've narrowly escaped a tragedy at our house—." And he launched into the story of the shooting and his indebtedness to Mickey.

"I see," said the professor. "You feel you owe it to the lad to offer him a better life, since he freely risked his life for your child's."

"Exactly!" said Endicott. "I'd like to adopt him and bring him up as my own. But I don't think my wife would feel as I do about it, and I'm not sure I'd be doing the best for the boy. To be taken from one extreme to another might ruin him."

"Well, Endicott, why don't you combine your debt to the child with benevolence and send him down to us for a few years to educate?"

Endicott sat up interestedly.

"Could I do that? Would they take so young a child? He can't be over seven."

"Yes, we'd take him, I think. He'd be well cared for, and his tuition in the prep department would help the institution along. Every little bit helps, you know."

Endicott suddenly saw before him the solution of his difficulties. He entered eagerly into the matter, talking over rates, plans, and so on. An hour later it was settled. Mickey was to take a full course with his expenses prepaid and a good sum placed in the bank for his clothing and spending money. He was to have the best room the school afforded, at the highest price, and study music and art and everything else offered, for Endicott meant to do the handsome thing by the institution. The failure of the bank of which he was president hadn't affected his private fortune.

"If the boy doesn't seem to develop an interest in some of these branches, put some deserving one in his place and put him at something else," he said. "I want him to try everything, to develop the best in him. So we'll pay for everything you've got there, and that will help out some other poor boy perhaps; for of course one boy can't do everything. I'll arrange it with my lawyer that the payments shall be made regularly for the next twelve years, so that if anything happens to me, or if the boy runs away or doesn't turn out worthy, you'll keep on getting money just the same, and someone else can come in on it."

Professor Harkness went away from the office with a smile and in his pocket three letters of introduction to wealthy New York businessmen. Mickey was to go south with him the middle of next week.

Endicott went home that afternoon with a relieved mind, but in his heart he found a surprising reluctance to part with the boy.

When he told Mickey he was sending him to college and explained to him that an education would enable him to become a good man and perhaps a great one, the boy's face was grave. Mickey had never felt the need of an education, and the thought of leaving New York gave him a sensation as if the earth were tottering under his feet. He shook his head doubtfully.

"Kin I take Buck an' de kids?" he asked after a thoughtful pause and with a lifting of the cloud in his eyes.

"No," said Endicott. "It costs a good deal to go away to school, and there wouldn't be anyone to send them."

Mickey's eyes grew wide with something like indignation, and he shook his head.

"Den I couldn't go," he said decidedly. "I couldn't take nothin' great like that and not give de kids any. We'll stick together. I'll stay wid de kids. They needs me."

"But, Mickey—," Endicott said, looking into the large determined eyes and settling down for combat. "You don't understand, boy. It would be impossible for them to go. I couldn't send them all, but I can send you, and I'm going to, because you risked your life to save Starr."

"That wasn't nothin' 't all!" declared Mickey.

"It was everything to me," said the man, "and I want to do this for you. And, boy, it's your duty to take this. It's everybody's duty to take the opportunities for advancement that come to them."

Mickey looked at him thoughtfully. He didn't understand the large words, and duty meant to him a fine sense of loyalty to those who had been loyal to him.

"I got to stay wid de kids," he said. "Dey needs me."

Feeling it was useless to argue against the calmly stated fact, Endicott began again gently, "But, Mickey, you can help them a lot more by going to college than by staying at home."

The boy's eyes looked unconvinced, but he waited for reasons.

"If you become an educated man you can earn money and help them. You can lift them up to better things; build good houses for them to live in; give them work to do that will pay good wages and help them be good men."

"Is you educated?"

Thinking he was making progress, Endicott nodded eagerly.

"Is that wot you does fer folks?" The bright eyes searched his face.

The color flooded the bank president's cheeks and forehead.

"Well—I might—," he answered. "Yes, I might do a good deal for people, I suppose. I don't know if I do much, but I could if I were interested in them."

He paused. He realized the argument was weakened. Mickey studied his face.

"But dey needs me now, de kids does," he said gravely. "Jimmie, he don't have no supper most nights less'n I share, and Bobs is so little he can't fight dem alley kids. Sometimes I gets a flower off'n the florist's back door fer little sick Jane. Her's got a crutch and can't walk much anyhow. And cold nights me an' Buck we sleeps close. We got a box hid away where we sleeps close an' keeps warm."

The moisture gathered in the banker's eyes as he listened to the story. It touched his heart as nothing ever had. He resolved that after this his education and wealth should at least help these slum friends of Mickey to an occasional meal or flower or warm bed.

"Suppose you get Buck to take your place with the kids while you go to school and get an education and learn how to help them better."

Mickey shook his head slowly. "Buck, he's got all he kin do to git grub for hisse'f an' his sister, Jane. His father is bad and kicks Jane and don't get her nothin' to eat. Buck, he has to see after Janie."

"How would it be for you to pay Buck something so he could take your place? I'll give you some money you may do with as you like, and you can pay Buck as much as you think he needs every week. You can send it to him in a letter."

"Would it be as much as a quarter?" Mickey held his breath in wonder.

"Two quarters if you like."

"Oh! Could I do that?" The boy's face fairly shone, and he came and threw his arms about Endicott's neck and laid his face against his. The man clasped him close and would fain have kept him there, for his well-ordered heart was deeply stirred.

Thus it was arranged.

Buck was invited to an interview. But when the silver half-dollar was laid in his grimy palm, and he understood that others would follow and he was to step up into Mickey's place in the community of the children while that luminary went to college to be educated, his face wore a heavy frown. He held out the silver sphere as if it burned him. What! Take money in exchange for Mickey's bright presence? Never!

It took a great deal of explanation to convince Buck that anything could be better "fer de kids" than their own Mickey, now and forever. But he was quick to see where the good lay for Mickey and after a few plain statements from Mr. Endicott no longer demurred. Buck was willing to give up Mickey for Mickey's good but not for his own. But it was a terrible sacrifice. The hard face knotted into a fierce expression when he came to say good-bye. The long scrawny throat worked convulsively; the hands gripped each other savagely. It was like handing Mickey over to a different world from theirs. He confidently promised to return to them as soon as the college completed its mysterious education and live with them as in the past, sleeping in Buck's box alongside him and taking care of the others when the big alley kids grew troublesome. But somehow an instinct taught them he would never return again. They'd had him and would never forget him, but he would grow into a being far above them. They looked vindictively at the rich man who had perpetrated this evil device of a college life for their comrade. It was the old story of the helpless poor against the powerful rich. Even heartbeats didn't count against such power. Mickey must go.

They went to the station the morning Mickey was to depart and stood shivering and forlorn until the train was called. They listened sullenly while Professor Harkness told them that if they wished to be fit to associate with their friend when he came out of college they must begin at once to improve their opportunities. First they must go to school and study hard, and then their friend in college would be proud to call them friends.

They didn't think it worthwhile to tell the kind but ignorant professor that they had no time for school and no clothes to wear if they had the time or inclination to go. Schools were everywhere and free, of course, but it didn't touch them. They lived in dark places and casual crannies, like weeds or vermin. No one cared whether they went to school. No one suggested it. They would have as soon thought of entering a mansion and insisting on their right to live there as to present themselves at school. Why, they had to hustle for a mere existence. They were the water rats, the bad boys, the embryo criminals for the next generation. The problem with any who thought of them was how to get rid of them. But of course this man from another world didn't understand. They merely looked at him dully and wished he would walk away and leave Mickey to them while he stayed. His presence made it seem as if their companion had already left them.

It was hard, too, to see Mickey dressed like the Fifth Avenue boys, handsome trousers and coat, a thick overcoat, a hat on his hair that had always been capless, thick stockings and shining shoes on his feet that had always been bare and soiled with the street grime—and gloves on his hands. This was a new Mickey. "The kids" didn't know him. In spite of their best efforts they couldn't be natural. Great lumps arose in their throats, lumps that never dared arise for hunger or cold or curses at home.

They stood helpless, and Mickey, sensing the trouble, thought to give his comrades some clothing article as a remembrance. Mr. Endicott came upon the scene in time to keep Mickey from taking off his overcoat and enveloping Buck in its folds. He was eagerly telling them Bobs should have his undercoat, Jimmie his hat, and Jane his gloves, and only his stockings and shoes were left for Sam. But he gave them willingly. He saw no reason why he couldn't travel hatless, coatless, barefoot and bare-handed; for hadn't he gone that way throughout his existence? It was a small thing to do for these friends he was leaving for a long time.

The bright face clouded when he was told he couldn't give these things away, that it wouldn't be fair to the kind professor to ask him to carry with him a boy improperly dressed. But he smiled again trustfully when Endicott promised to take the whole group to a clothing house and fit them out.

They bade Mickey good-bye, pressing their grimy noses against the station gate bars to watch their friend disappear from their lives.

Endicott himself felt like crying as he came back from seeing the boy aboard the train, knowing he wouldn't meet the bright smile that night when he went home.

But it wasn't the way of "the kids" to cry when tragedy fell among them. They didn't cry now. When he returned to them, they regarded the banker with lowering brows as the originator of their bereavement. They had no faith in the promised clothing.

"Aw, what's he givin' us!" Buck had breathed under his breath. But to do Buck credit he hadn't wanted to take Mickey's coat from him. When their comrade went from them into another walk in life he must go proudly appareled.

Endicott led the huddled group away from the station to a clothing house and amused himself by fitting them out. The garments weren't of as fine material or elegant a cut as those he'd purchased for Mickey's outfit, but they were warm and strong and wonderful to their eyes. One by one the grimy urchins went into a little dressing room, presently emerging with awe upon their faces to stand before a tall mirror surveying themselves.

Endicott presently bade them farewell and, with a conscience at ease with himself and all mankind, left them.

They issued from the clothing house with scared expressions and walked solemnly a few blocks. Then Buck called them to a halt before a plate-glass show window.

"Take a good look at yersel's, kids," he ordered, "an' we'll go up to the park an' shine around an' see how ther swells feels. Then we'll go down to Sheeny's an' sell 'em."

"Sell 'em! Can't we keep 'em?" demanded Bobs, who had never felt warm in winter in his small life.

"You wouldn't hev 'em long," sneered Buck. "That father o' yourn would hev 'em pawned afore night. You better enjoy 'em a while, an' then git the money. It's safer!"

The children with wisdom born of their unhappy circumstances recognized the truth. They surveyed themselves gravely in their fleeting grandeur and then turned to walk up to the aristocratic part of town, a curious procession. They finished by rounding the Madison Avenue block, marched up the alley, and gave the salute with new hats toward the window where their prince and leader used to be. He was no longer there, but his memory was about them, and the ceremony did their bursting hearts good. Their love for Mickey was the noblest thing that had so far entered their lives.

Jimmie suggested they must let Jane see them before they disposed forever of their elegant garments. So Bobs, minus coat, hat, stockings, and shoes, was sent to bid her to a secluded retreat at the far end of the alley. He hurried back ahead of her tapping crutch to don his fine attire before she arrived.

Little Jane, with sallow face, unkempt hair, and tattered clothing; shivering in the cold twilight, stood and watched the procession of pride as it passed and repassed before her delighted eyes. The festivity might have been prolonged, but the voice of Bobs's father reeling into the alley struck terror to their hearts. They scuttled away to the pawnshop, leaving Jane to hobble back alone to her cellar and wonder how it would feel to wear a warm coat like one of those.

"Say!" said Jimmie as they paused before the shop door and looked reluctantly down at their brief glory. "I wisht we could keep jest one coat fer Janie!"

"Couldn't we hide it some'eres?" asked Sam, and they all looked at Buck.

Buck, deeply touched for his sister's sake, nodded.

"Keep Jim's," he said huskily. "It'll do her best."

Then they filed proudly in and gave up their garments to the human parasite who lived on other men's souls. They came away bearing the one coat they'd saved for Jane, each treasuring a pitiful bit of money which seemed a fortune in their eyes.

Jane received her gift with true spirit, skillfully hid it from her inhuman father, and declared that each boy should have a turn wearing the coat every Sunday at some safe hour; so deep satisfaction reigned among them. Their grandeur wasn't departed after all.

Meanwhile, Mickey, in his luxurious berth in a sleeper, smiled drowsily as he thought of the fine new clothes his friends must be wearing and then fell asleep to dream of little Starr's kisses on his closed eyelids.

Chapter 4

Mickey entered a new world of blue skies, songbirds, and high, tall pines with waving moss and dreamy atmosphere, with plenty to eat and wear and with light and joy and ease.

Yet the world bewildered the boy, and for the first week he stood off and regarded it suspiciously. True, there were no dark cellars or freezing streets, no drunken fathers or frightened children or blows or hunger or privation. But this education he'd come to seek, so he might return to his own world and better it, wasn't a garment one put on and exercised in so many times a day. Nor was it a cup from which one drank or an atmosphere one absorbed. It was a strange, imperceptible thing got at in some mysterious way by a series of vague struggles followed by sudden and almost alarming perceptions.

For a time it seemed to the boy, keen though his mind, that knowledge was granted only to the few, and his was a mind that would never grasp it. How, for instance, did one know how to make just the right figures under a line when one added a long perplexity of numbers? Mickey the newsboy could tell like a flash how much money to return to the stout gentleman who occasionally gave him a five-dollar bill to change on Broadway. But Mickey the scholar, though he knew figures and could study out with labor easy words in his papers, had never heard of adding up figures in the way they did here, long rows of them on the blackboard. He needed private instruction before he could enter classes.

Professor Harkness himself undertook the task and gradually revealed to the child's neglected understanding some of the rudiments that would enable his further progress. The sum paid for his tuition necessitated that the boy advance reasonably, for his benefactor had made it understood he might someday visit the institution and see how he was progressing. Some great pains were taken to enlighten Mickey's darkness.

Nor could the boy understand the discipline that ruled everywhere. He'd always been a law unto himself, his only care being to keep out of the way of those who would interfere with this. Now he must rise with a bell, stay in his room until another bell, eat at a bell, and even play ball when the recreation bell rang. It was hard for an independent spirit to get used to all this, and while he had no mind to be disorderly, he often directly disobeyed the law from sheer misunderstanding of the whole regime.

The boys' dormitory was presided over by a woman who, while thorough in all housekeeping arrangements, had certainly mistaken her calling as a substitute mother for boys. She kept their clothes in order, their rooms aired, their stockings darned, and their lights out at exactly half-past nine. But her grim countenance forbade any familiarity, and she never thought of gaining the confidence of her rough, but affectionate, charges. Mickey never felt like smiling in her presence. He came and went with a sort of high, unconscious superiority that almost irritated the woman, because she wasn't great enough to see the child's unusual spirit and as a consequence didn't win his heart.

But he didn't miss her lack of motherliness, for he'd never known a mother and wasn't expecting it.

The professors he grew to like, some more, some less, always admiring the most those who seemed to deal fairly with their classes—fairness being judged by the code in use among "the kids" in New York. But that was before he knew the president. After that his code changed.

His first interview with that dignitary was on an afternoon when he'd been overheard by the matron using vile language among the boys at the noon hour. She hauled him up with her most severe manner and told him he must answer to the president for his conduct.

As Mickey had no conception of his offense, he went serenely to his fate, walking affably beside her, only wishing she wouldn't look so sour. As they crossed the campus to the president's house, a blue jay flew overhead, and a mockingbird trilled in a live oak nearby. The boy's face lit with joy, and he laughed gleefully. But the matron only looked more severe, for she thought him a hardened sinner defying her authority and laughing her to scorn. After that it was two years before she could believe anything good of Mickey.

The president was a noble-faced, white-haired scholar, with a firm, tender mouth and understanding eyes. He wasn't the kind who won by great athletic prowess; he was an old-fashioned gentleman, well along in years, but young in heart. He looked at the child of the slums and saw the angel in the clay.

He dismissed the matron with a pleasant assurance and took Mickey to an inner office where he let the boy sit quietly waiting a few minutes till he finished writing a letter. If the pen halted and the kind eyes studied the child's beautiful face, Mickey never knew it.

The president asked the boy to tell him what he'd said, and Mickey repeated innocently the terrible phrases he'd used, phrases familiar to him since boyhood, conveying statements of facts that were horrible but nevertheless daily happenings in the corner of the world where he'd brought himself up.

With rare tact the president questioned the boy, until he made sure there was no inherent rottenness in him. Then kindly, but firmly, he laid down the law and explained why it was right and necessary for such a law. He spoke of God's purity. Mickey knew nothing of God and listened with quiet interest. The president talked of education and culture and made matters very plain. When the interview was concluded and the man asked the boy for a pledge of good faith and clean language from then on, Mickey's smile of approval blazed forth, and he laid his hand in the president's readily enough and left the room secretly admiring the man. The whole conversation had appealed to him deeply.

Mickey sought his room and laboriously spelled out with lately acquired clumsiness a letter to Buck:

Dear Buck we mussent yuz endecent langwidg enny moor ner swar.

God donte lyk it an' it ain't educated. I want you an' me to be educate. I ain't gone to, donte yoo ner let de kids.

Mickey

In due time, according to previous arrangement about the monthly allowance, this letter reached Buck. He tracked the doctor for two whole days before he located him and lay in wait till he came out to his carriage, when he got up his nerve to hand over the letter to be read.

The doctor, deeply touched, translated as best he could. Buck's education had been pitifully neglected. He watched the mystic paper in awe as the doctor read.

"Wot's indecent langwidge?" he asked with his heavy frown.

The doctor took the opportunity to deliver a brief sermon on purity, and Buck, without so much as an audible thank you but with a thoughtful air that pleased the doctor, took back his letter, stuffed it into his ragged pocket, and went his way. The man watched him wistfully, wondering whether Mickey's appeal could reach the boy and, sighing, went away to try to make a few things better.

That night "the kids" gathered in front of Jane's window, for she was too weak to go out with them, and Buck delivered a message on ethical culture. Whatever Mickey, their prince, ordered, that must be done, and Buck was doing his level best, although for the life of him he couldn't see the sense in it. But thereafter none of "the kids" was allowed to use certain words and phrases, and swearing gradually disappeared from their conversation. It would have been a curious study for a linguist to observe just what words and phrases were cut out and what allowed to flourish unrebuked; but nevertheless it was a reform, and Buck was doing his best.

With his schoolmates Mickey held a high position from the first. His clothes were good, and he always had a little money to spend. One of Endicott's wishes was that the boy should be like other boys. It meant something among a group of boys, most of whom were the sons of rich fathers. Moreover, he was brave beyond anything they'd seen, could fight like a demon in defense of a smaller boy and didn't shrink from pitching into a fellow twice his size. He could tell all about the New York City baseball and football games, knew the pitchers by name and yet didn't boast uncomfortably. He could swim like a duck and dive fearlessly. He could outrun them all by his lightness of foot and was an expert in gliding away from any hand that sought to hold him back.

His peculiar street slang didn't trouble them in the least, nor his lack of class standing, though that presently became a thing of the past. Mickey, as soon as he understood the way, marched up the hill of knowledge, taking in everything handed to him and assimilating it. It began to look as if no leftover courses in the curriculum might be given to some other deserving youth. Mickey would need them all. The president and the professors became deeply interested in this boy without a past. Everywhere, with everyone, Mickey's smile won his way, except with the matron who hadn't forgiven him because her recommendation of his instant dismissal from the college hadn't been accepted.

The boys hadn't asked many questions about him nor been told much. They knew his father and mother were dead. They thought he had a rich guardian, perhaps a fortune coming someday, but they didn't care. Mickey never spoke about these things, and a strange reticence about him made them dislike to ask him questions, even when they knew him well. He was entered under the name Endicott; on questioning him, Professor Harkness found he could lay no greater claim to any other surname and called him that until he could write to Mr. Endicott for advice. He neglected to write at once and then, the name having become fastened upon the boy, thought it best to let the matter alone since there was little likelihood of Mr. Endicott's coming down to the college, and it could do no harm. He never thought out possible future complications, and the boy became known as Michael Endicott.

But his companions, as boys will, thought the matter over and rechristened him "Angel." So Angel, or Angel Endy, he became, to the end of his college course.

One delight of his new life was his outdoor freedom. A beautiful lake spread its silver sheet at the foot of the campus slope, and here the boy revelled in swimming and rowing. The whole country around was filled with wonder to his city-bred eyes. He attached himself to the natural sciences teacher and took long silent tramps for miles. They penetrated dense hammocks, gathering specimens of rare orchids and exquisite flowers; they stood motionless and breathless for hours watching and listening to some strange wild bird; they became familiar with slimy coiling serpents in dark bogs and green lizards and black velvet spiders; they brought home ravishing butterflies and moths of pale green, gold, and crimson. Mickey's room became a museum of curious, wonderful things, and he an authority on a wide range of topics.

The new life with plenty of wholesome food, fresh air, good sleep, and happy exercise was developing the young body into strength and beauty, even as study and contact with life were developing the mind. Mickey grew up tall, straight, and strong. In all the school, even among the older boys, was none so perfectly developed. In his face were strength, simplicity, and character. With the acceptance of his new moral code according to the president, a look of high moral purpose had grown. No boy in his presence dared use language not up to the standard. No boy with his knowledge dared do a mean or wrong thing. And yet, in spite of this, every boy admired him and was more or less led by him. If he'd been one whit less brave, one shade more conscious of self and self's interests, one bit conceited, this would not have been. But from being a dangerous experiment in their midst, Mickey became known as a great influence for good. The teachers saw it and marvelled. The matron saw it and finally, though grudgingly, accepted it. The president saw it and rejoiced. The students saw it not but acknowledged it in their lives.

Mickey's flame of gold hair grew more golden and flaming with the years. When his ball team played in a nearby town, Mickey was sighted by the crowd and pointed out at once.

"Who's that boy with the hair?" someone would ask a team member.

"That? Oh, that's the Angel! Wait till you see him play!" would be the reply. And he became known among outsiders as the Angel with the golden hair.

At a game a listener would hear, "Oh, see! There'll be something doing now. The Angel's at bat!"

Yet in spite of all this, the boy lived a lonely life. Giving himself continually to those about him, receiving in turn their love and devotion, he yet felt set apart from them. Occasionally some boy's father or mother, or both, or a sister or little brother would come down for a trip through the South. Then that boy would be excused from classes and go off with his parents for perhaps a week, or they'd visit him every day. And Michael would look on and see the love-light beaming in their eyes. That would never be for him. No one had ever loved him like that.

Sometimes he would close his eyes and try to return in memory to the time he was shot and the wonder of the soft bed, the room, and little Starr's kisses. But the years were multiplying now, and room and nurse and all were growing dim. Only Starr's kisses remained, a delicate fragrance of baby love, the only kisses the boy had ever known.

One day, when a classmate had been telling of his father's arrival and what it would mean to him, Michael went into his room and, locking his door, sat down and wrote a stiff schoolboy letter to his benefactor, thanking him for all he'd done for him. It told briefly, shyly, of a faint realization of what he'd been saved from, showed a proper respect and desire to make good, and touched the heart of the busy man who'd almost forgotten about the boy. But it didn't hint of the heart hunger which had prompted his writing.

The next winter, when Michael was seventeen, Delevan Endicott and his daughter, Starr, took a flying trip through the South, stopping for a night and day at the college.

The president told Michael of his expected coming. Professor Harkness had gone north on school business.

The boy received the news quietly enough, with one of his brilliant smiles, but went to his room with a tumult of wonder, joy, and almost fear in his heart. Would Mr. Endicott be as he remembered: kind, interested, and helpful? Would he be pleased with the progress his protégé had made, or would he be disappointed? Would there be any chance to ask after little Starr? She was a baby still in the boy's thoughts; yet of course she must have grown. And so many things might have happened—she might not be living now. No one would think or care to tell him.

Baby Starr! His beautiful baby! He exulted that he'd flung his useless life once between her lovely presence and death! He'd do it again gladly now if that would repay all her father had done for him. Michael the youth was beginning to understand what that meant.

His other friends, Buck, Jimmie, Bobs, and the rest, were still enshrined in his faithful heart, though their memory had dimmed with the years. Faithfully every month the boy had sent Buck two dollars from his pocket money, his heart swelling with pleasure that he was helping those he loved. But only twice had word come back from that far city where he'd left them. In answer to the letter the doctor had translated for them, a brief laborious epistle had come, terse and to the point, written with a pencil stub on the corner of a piece of wrapping paper and addressed by a kind clerk at the post office where Buck bought the stamped envelope. It was the same clerk who usually paid to the urchin his monthly money order, so he knew the address. To indite the letter Buck went to night school two whole weeks before he could master enough letters and words to finish it to his satisfaction. It read:

Deer Mik WE WunT
Buck

The significant words filled the boy's heart with pride over his friend whenever he thought of it, even sometime later. He had faith in Buck. In his mind Buck seemed to be growing and keeping pace with him, and he never dreamed that if Buck saw him now he wouldn't recognize him.

When Mickey had been in Florida several years, another letter came from Buck addressed in the same way, and little better written than the other. Night school had proved too strenuous for Buck; besides, he felt he knew enough for all practical purposes, and it wasn't likely he'd need to write many letters. This occasion, however, called for one.

Dear Mickey,
 Jany is DEAD sHe sayd tell yo hur LUV beeryd hur in owr kote we
give hur ther wuz a angle wit pink wins on top uv the wite hurs an a wite
hors we got a lot uv flowers by yur money so yo needn sen no more
money kuz we ken get long now til yo cum.

                                                                BUCK

After that, though Michael had written as usual every month, for some time no reply came, and the money orders were returned to him as not called for. Buck in his simplicity evidently took it for granted Mickey wouldn't send the money and came no more to the office. At least that was how Michael solved it, and in his heart he vowed to hunt up Buck the minute he was through at college and free to return to New York and help his friends. Meanwhile, though the years had dimmed those memories of his old life, and the days went forward in study, he always kept in view his intention of one day going back to better his native community.

But Mr. Endicott's coming was a great event to the boy. He could scarcely sleep the night before the expected arrival.

Prior to the evening meal, the through train from New York reached the station. Michael was given the privilege of going to meet his benefactor.

Tall and handsome he stood on the platform as the train rushed into the town, his cheeks glowing from excitement, his eyes bright with anticipation, his cap in his hand, and the last rays of the setting sun glowing in his golden hair. When Endicott saw him he exclaimed mentally over his strength and manly beauty, and more than one weary tourist leaned from the open car window and gazed, for something strange and compelling about Michael reminded one of an angel.

Chapter 5

Michael met Mr. Endicott unembarrassed. His early New York life had given him a self-poise that nothing seemed to disturb. But when the father introduced his young daughter, the boy caught his breath and gazed at her with deepening color and intense delight.

She was here then, his Starr! She'd come to see him and looked as he would have her look. He hadn't realized before that she'd be grown up, but of course she would, and the change in her didn't shock his memory. The clear white of her skin with its fresh coloring was the same. New York life hadn't made it sallow. The roses were still in her cheeks. Her eyes were the same, dark and merry, and looked at him straight, unabashed, with the ease of a girl trained by a society mother. Her dark curls were longer, hanging to the slender waist and crowned with a fine wide Panama hat. She gave him a little gloved hand and said, "I'm afraid I don't remember you very well, but Daddy has been telling me about you, and I'm very glad to see you."

She was only a little over twelve, but she spoke with ease and simplicity, and for the first time in his life Michael felt self-conscious. She was so perfect, lovely, finished in expression and movement. She looked at him intelligently, politely curious, and no longer with baby eyes. He couldn't help wondering what she must think of him, and for a few minutes he grew shy before her.

Mr. Endicott was surprised and pleased at the boy's appearance. The passing years had easily erased the tender feelings Mickey the street urchin had stirred in his heart. This visit to the school and college wasn't so much because of the boy, to whom he felt he'd discharged his duty, but because of the repeated invitations of Professor Harkness and the president. It didn't go against him to see the institution he'd from time to time contributed to, with his liberal allowance for the boy's education. It was convenient for him to stop, being on the regular route he'd planned for his southern trip. He'd left his wife at Palm Beach with her fashionable friends and, with Starr as his companion, the father toured the orange belt with a view to investments. It suited him to stop off and receive the thanks of the college; so he stopped. Not that he was a heartless man, but so many things in his world made him forget, and most of us appreciate a little pleasant adulation.

But when Michael stood before him with the deference of more than a son, his heart suddenly leaped back to the day when he'd first gazed upon the little white face on the pillow, when the blue eyes had opened, and Mickey had smiled. Michael smiled now, and Endicott became aware at once of the subtle fascination of that smile. And now the thought presented itself, *What if this were my son! How proud I'd be of him!*

Michael was indeed good to look upon, even to the city critic's eyes. Endicott had left orders with his tailor for a full outfit to be sent to the boy, spring and fall, or suitable plain clothing for a schoolboy, little realizing how unnecessary it was to have dressed him so well. The tailor had taken the measurements sent to him yearly in answer to the firm's letter and kept Michael looking as well as any rich man's son desired to look. Not that the boy knew or realized. The clothes came to him, like his board and tuition, and he took them well pleased and wrote his best letter of thanks each year as Professor Harkness suggested. But he had no idea that part at least of his leadership power with the schoolboys was due to his plain though stylishly cut garments. This fact wouldn't have counted for anything with boys who had been living in Florida for years, for any plain decent clothes were thought fit, no matter how they were cut. But the school's patronage was at least half rich men's sons sent south for a few years to a milder climate for their health. These as a rule, when they came, had exaggerated ideas of the importance of clothes and prevailing modes.

So Michael didn't look like a dowdy country boy to his benefactor but presented a remarkable contrast to many boys Endicott was acquainted with at home. Something about Michael, even as a small lad, commanded marked attention from all who saw him. This attention Endicott and his daughter gave now as they walked beside him in the sunset glow and listened as he pointed out the various spots of interest in the college town.

The institution boasted of no carriage, and the single horse car that traveled to the station belonged to the hotel and its guests. The walk wasn't long, however, and gave the travelers an opportunity to breathe the clear air and feel the evening stillness.

Starr, walking on the inside of the board sidewalk, looked down at the small pink and white and crimson pea blossoms growing everywhere and then up at the tall pines and felt an awe. Her only day at Palm Beach had been so filled with hotels, people, and automobiles that she'd had no opportunity to realize the land's tropical nature. But here in this quiet spot, where the tiny station, the post office, the grocery, and a few scattered dwellings, with hotel lights gleaming in the distance, seemed all there was of human habitation, she suddenly realized the difference from New York.

Michael had recovered his poise as soon as she no longer faced him, though he was profoundly conscious of her presence on her father's other side. But he talked easily and well. Yes, the hotel held five hundred guests and was pretty well filled at this season. Some distinguished people were stopping there. The railroad president's private car had stood on the track for a few hours last week. That car over on the side belonged to a steel magnate. The other one had brought the wife of an inventor. Off toward the sunset were the school and college buildings. No, they couldn't be seen until one passed the orange grove. Too bad there was no conveyance. But the one little car turned off toward the hotel at this corner, and the school's one beast of burden, a mule—Minus, by name, because he wasn't so many things—was lame today and couldn't be requisitioned to bring the guests from the station.

Mr. Endicott felt he was drawing nearer to nature in this quiet walk than he had since he was a boy and visited his grandfather's farm. It rested and pleased him, and he was charmed with his protégé. His frank, simple conversation was free from all affectation or from any hint of his low origin. The man felt already that he'd done a good thing in sending the boy here to be educated. It was worth the little money he'd put into it.

Starr watched Michael shyly from the shelter of her father's side and listened to him. He wasn't like the boys she met in New York. He was fine-looking and possessed both strength and kindness in his face. Above all, his smile and firm chin made her feel he was nobler than most she knew. Something about him made her know he had a greater purpose in life than his own pleasure. Not that she thought this out. Starr had never learned to think. She only felt it as she looked at him and liked him at once. Moreover, she sensed some glamour about the boy, for her father had just told her how he'd saved her life when she was small. She felt a prideful proprietorship in him that made her shy in his presence.

At the college president's gate, on the edge of the campus, the president came out with his apologies. He had been detained on business at the county seat five miles away and drove home with a friend whose horse was slow. He was sorry not to have shown courtesy to their honored guests by meeting them at the station. Endicott walked with the president after the greetings, and Michael dropped behind with Starr and eagerly pointed out to her the buildings.

"That's the chapel, and beyond are the study and recitation rooms. The next is the dining hall and servants' quarters, and over on that side of the campus is our dormitory. My window looks down on the lake. Every morning I go swimming before breakfast."

"Oh, aren't you afraid of alligators?" Starr asked, startled.

Michael looked at her with a tender protectiveness.

"No," he answered without laughing, as other boys would have at her girlish fears, "they never bother us here. Besides, I'm sort of acquainted with them. I'm not afraid of them. Nothing will hurt you if you understand it well enough to look out for its rights."

"Oh!" said Starr, eyeing him in wonder. As if an alligator had rights! What a strange, interesting boy. The idea of understanding an alligator. She was about to ask how understanding the creature would keep one from being eaten up when Michael pointed to the crimson west.

"See!" he said. "The sun is almost down. Don't you love to watch it? In a minute more it will be gone, and then it'll be dark. Hear that evening bird? 'Tit-wiloo! Tit-wiloo!' He sings sometimes late at night."

Starr followed his words and saw the sun slipping like a ruby disc behind the fringe of palm, pine, and oak bordering the lake below the campus. She saw the wild bird dart from the thicket into the clear amber sky above, utter its sweet weird call, and drop again into the fine brown shadows of the living picture. And she watched as the sun slipped lower to the half now, and now less than half.

Breathless they stood and let the two men go on ahead, while they watched the day turn into night. The brilliant crimson poured itself away to her lands, till only a rim of glowing garnet remained; then, like a living thing dying into another life, it, too, dropped away, and all was night.

"Why! How dark it is!" exclaimed Starr as she turned and found she could scarcely see his face. "Where's the twilight? Is anything the matter? I never saw it get dark all at once like this!" She peered around into the strange velvet darkness.

"No, that's all right," Michael assured her. "That's the way we do here. Almost everybody from the North speaks about it at first. They can't understand it. It's the difference in the position of the sun, nearer the equator, you know. I'll show you on the chart in the astronomy room if you like. We haven't any twilight here. It would seem odd. You wouldn't know when night began and day ended. I don't remember it when I lived in New York. Look up there! That's the evening star! It's come out for you tonight—to welcome another—Starr!"

They walked silently through the warm darkness, with Michael touching the young girl's elbow distantly, reverently, to guide her, until they entered the circle of light from the open door, and matron and teachers came out to welcome the young stranger and bring her into the house.

Michael lingered a moment by the door, watching her as she went, her sweet face wreathed in smiles, with the matron's thin arm around her and a new, gentle look upon that one's severe countenance. He watched until they mounted the stairs out of sight.

Outside, he removed his cap and stood looking up at the star, communing with it perhaps about the human Starr that had come back to him out of the shadows of the past.

And she was a star. All who saw her acknowledged it. He marveled as he recalled the change in the matron's face and because of her gentleness to the little girl forgave her all she hadn't been to his motherless boyhood.

Starr came down to dinner in a few minutes radiant in a rosy dress of soft Eastern silk, girdled with a fringed scarf of the same and a knot of coral velvet in her hair. From the string of pearls about her white neck to the dainty point of her slipper she was exquisite, and Michael watched her with open admiration. The long lashes drooped shyly over the girl's rosy cheeks, and she was pleased.

She sat at her father's side to the president's right, with Michael across the table. He bore well Endicott's scrutiny as his keen eyes searched the boy's face throughout the conversation.

That evening passed like a dream, and Michael lay awake again that night anticipating the next day. At last he had some people who in a way he might call his own. They'd cared to come and see him after all the years! His heart swelled with joy and gratitude.

The guests attended chapel exercises with the students the next morning, and Michael saw with pride his companions' eyes turn toward the beautiful young girl and then at him almost enviously. The color mounted into his young face, but he sat so quietly no one would have guessed the tumult running riot in his veins. He felt it was the happiest day of his life.

After chapel, the guests were shown about the college buildings and campus. The president and Endicott walked ahead, Michael behind with Starr, answering her questions.

They'd been through all the classrooms, the gymnasium, the dining hall, servants' quarters, and dormitories. They'd visited the athletic grounds and the tennis courts and walked by the lake, where Michael had taken them out for a short row. Returning, they were met by a professor who suggested they hear some of the classes recite and so turned their steps toward the recitation hall.

"I think you must be very brave," Starr said. "To think you saved my life that way when you were just a little fellow!"

She looked up, her face full of childish feeling.

Michael smiled at her and wondered if any eyes were as beautiful as those before him. The president's daughter was stout and a romp; she never took time to look at the boys. And the professors' daughters were quiet and studious; they paid little attention to the boys.

"I want to thank you for what you did," Starr continued. "Only I can't think of any words great enough to tell you how I feel about it. I wish I could do something to show you how I thank you."

She lifted her eyes again to his. They were entering the school's large hall now.

"Isn't there something you'd like that I could do for you?" insisted Starr, following him into the empty chapel where Mr. Endicott and the president stood looking at a tablet on the wall by the further door.

"Your father has done everything for me," said Michael sunnily, with a sweep of his hand that seemed to include him, his garments, and his mental outfit. He turned his blazing smile upon her, thus speaking more eloquently than words.

"Yes, but that's Papa," said Starr impatiently, softly stamping her dainty foot. "He did that because of what you did for him saving my life. I'd like to do something to thank you for what you did for me. I'm worth something to myself, you know. Isn't there something I could do for you?"

She stood still, looking up into his face anxiously. The two men had passed through the further door and on to the recitation rooms. The girl and boy were alone for the moment.

"You have done something for me. You did a great deal," he said, his voice almost husky. "It was the greatest thing anybody ever did for me."

"I did something for you! When? What?"

"Maybe you don't remember it, but I do. I was getting well from the shot at your house, and your nurse used to bring you up to play with me every day. Always, before you went away, you used to kiss me. I've never forgotten that."

He said it quite simply as if it were a common thing for a boy to say to a girl. But his voice was low as though the depths of his soul were stirred.

The color flooded Starr's cheeks.

"Oh!" she said, embarrassed at the turn in the conversation. "But that was when I was a baby. I couldn't do that now. Girls don't kiss boys, you know. It wouldn't be proper."

"I know," said Michael, his own color heightening now. "I didn't mean that. I wanted you to know how much you'd done for me already. You don't know what it is never to have been kissed by your mother or any living soul. Nobody ever kissed me that I know of but you."

He looked at the little girl with such a grave, sweet expression, his eyes so expressive of the long lonely years without any woman's love, that, child though she was, Starr seemed to understand. Her young soul went forth in pity, and tears sprang to her eyes.

"Oh! That's dreadful! Oh! I don't care if it isn't proper—"

And before he knew what she was about to do, the little girl tilted to her tip-toes, put up her dainty hands, caught him about the neck, and pressed a warm, eager kiss on his lips. Then she sprang away frightened, across the room and through the opposite door.

Michael stood still in bewilderment. The compelling of her little hands, the pressure of her fresh lips lingered with him. Tears gathered in his eyes, but he didn't know it. He stood with bowed head. Nothing so sacred, so beautiful, had ever entered his life. Her baby kisses had been half unconscious. This kiss she gave because she wanted to do something for him. He didn't attempt to understand the joy surging through his heart and pulsing in every fiber of his being. His lonely, unloved life was enough to account for it, and he was only a boy with a brief knowledge of life. But he knew enough to enshrine that kiss in his heart as holy, not even to be thought about carelessly.

When he roused himself to follow her she'd disappeared. Her father and the president were listening to a recitation, but she was nowhere to be seen. She had gone to her room. Michael went alone to a thicket by the lake.

She met him shyly at dinner, with averted gaze and a glow on her cheeks, as if half afraid of what she'd done. But he reassured her with his eyes. His glance seemed to promise he would never take advantage of it. His face wore an exalted look, as if he'd been lifted above the earth, and Starr, looking at him wonder-ingly, was glad she had followed her impulse.

They took a horseback ride to the orange grove that afternoon—Mr. Endi-cott, a professor, Starr, and Michael. The president had borrowed the horses from some friends.

Michael sat like a king on his horse. He'd ridden the college mule bareback every summer, and riding seemed to be as natural to him as any other sport. Starr had been to a New York riding school and was accustomed to taking her morning exercise with her father in the park or accompanied by a footman. But she sat her Florida pony as happily as though he'd been a shiny, well-groomed steed of priceless value. It seemed unusually delightful to her to ride with this nice boy through the beautiful shaded road of arching live oaks richly draped with old gray moss. Michael stopped by the roadside, where the shade was dense, dismounted, and plunged into the thicket, returning in a moment with two or three beautiful orchids and some long vines of yellow jessamine whose perfume filled the air. He wreathed the jasmine about the pony's neck, and Starr twined it about her hat and wore the orchids in her belt.

Starr had never seen an orange grove before, and the trees were loaded with fruit, green and yellow, and set about by blossoms. She tucked a spray of blossoms in her dark hair under the edge of her hat, and Michael looked at her and smiled in admiration. Mr. Endicott, glancing toward his daughter, caught the look and recalled the time when he'd found the two children in his drawing room being made a show for his wife's guests. He sighed half in pleasure, half in foreboding. What a beautiful pair they were, to be sure, and what had the future in store for his little girl?

On the way back they skirted another lake, and Michael dismounted again to bring an armful of great white magnolia blossoms and dainty bay buds to the wondering Starr, and then they rode on slowly through the wooded road.

"I wish you could be here next week," said the boy wistfully. "It will be a full moon then. The best time to ride through this place is on a moonlit evening. The moonbeams make little ladders of the jasmine vines."

"It must be beautiful," said Starr dreamily.

Then they rode for a few minutes in silence. They were coming to the end of the overarched avenue. Ahead of them the sunlight shone clearly like the opening of a great tunnel framed in living green. Suddenly Starr looked up gravely.

"I'm going to kiss you good-bye tonight when we go away," she said softly.

Touching her pony lightly with the whip, she rose out into the bright road, with the boy, his heart leaping with joy, not far behind her.

Before supper Mr. Endicott had a talk with Michael that went further toward making the fatherless boy feel he had someone belonging to him than anything yet.

"I think you've done enough for me, sir," said Michael, respectfully opening the conversation as Endicott came out to the porch where the boy was waiting for him. "I should begin to earn my own living. I'm old enough now," he said, holding his head up proudly. "It's been very good of you all these years—I never can repay you. I hope you'll let me pay back the money you've spent on me, someday when I can earn enough."

Michael had been thinking this speech out ever since the president told him of Endicott's expected visit. But somehow it didn't sound as fine to him when he said it. It had seemed the only right thing to do when he planned it; but as he looked into Mr. Endicott's kind, keen eyes, his own fell in troubled silence. Had his words sounded ungrateful? Had he seen a hurt look in the man's eyes?

"Son," said Endicott after a pause, and the word stirred the boy's heart strangely. "Son, I owe you a debt I never can repay. You gave me back my little girl. I think I have at least a father's right in you at any rate and mean to exercise it until you're twenty-one. You must finish a college course first. When will that be? Three years? They tell me you're doing well. The doctor wants to keep you here to teach after you've graduated, but I thought you might like to come up to

New York and have your chance. I'll give you a year or two in business, whatever seems to be your bent when you're through. Then we'll see. Which would you rather do? Or perhaps you'd prefer to let your decision rest until the time comes."

"I think I'm bound to go back to New York, sir," said Michael, lifting his head. "You know, sir—you said I was to be educated so I might help my friends. I've learned of course that you meant it in the broader sense than just those few boys, for one can help people anywhere; but still I feel as if it wouldn't be right for me not to go back. I'm sure they'll expect me."

"Loyal to your old friends still? Well, that's commendable, but I imagine you'll scarcely find them congenial now. I wouldn't let them hang too closely about you. They might become a nuisance. You have your way to make in the world."

Michael looked at his benefactor with troubled brows. Somehow the man's tone disturbed him.

"I promised," he said simply. Because there had been so little in his affections, Michael had cherished that promise through the years. It stood for principle and loyalty in general.

"Oh, well, keep your promise, of course," said the man easily. "I think you'll find the discharge of it a mere form."

A fellow student came across the campus.

"Endicott," he called, "have you seen Hallowell go toward the village?"

"He just went out the gate," responded Michael pleasantly.

Mr. Endicott looked up surprised. "Is that the name you're known by?"

"Endicott? Yes, sir, Michael Endicott. Wasn't it your wish? I supposed they'd asked you. I had no other name I knew."

"Ah! I didn't know," replied Endicott.

There was silence for a moment.

"Would you—shall I—do you dislike my having it?" asked the boy, delicately sensitive at once.

But the man looked up with something like tenderness in his smile. "Keep it, son. I like it. I wish I had a boy like you. It's an old name and a proud one. Be worthy of it."

"I will try, sir," said Michael.

The guests ate an early supper, and then Michael walked through another sunset to the station with Starr. He carried a small box in which reposed a tiny green and blue lizard for a parting gift. She'd watched the lizards scuttling away under the board sidewalks or changing their brilliant colors to gray like the boards so they might not be observed. She was interested in them and charmed with her gift. This particular lizard Michael had trained to eat crumbs from his hand, and it was tame.

The two said little as they walked along together. Each was feeling what a happy time they'd spent in one another's company.

"I'll write and tell you how the lizard is," said Starr, laughing, "and you'll tell me about the funny and interesting things you're doing, won't you?"

"If—I may," said Michael.

At the station a New York acquaintance of the Endicotts invited them to ride in his private car which was on the side track waiting for the train to pick it up. Michael helped Starr up the steps and carried the lizard into the car as well as the sheaf of flowers she insisted on taking with her.

Some ladies inside welcomed Starr effusively, and Michael, suddenly abashed, laid down the flowers, lifted his cap, and withdrew. A sudden blank had come upon him. Starr was absorbed by people from another world than his. He would have no opportunity to say good-bye—and she'd promised. But then of course he shouldn't expect her to do that. She had been very kind to him.

He was going down the steps now. An instant more and he would be in the track cinders.

A sudden rush, a soft cry, caused him to pause on the car's second step. It was Starr, standing just above him, and her eyes were shining.

"You were going without saying good-bye," she said with reproof in her voice.

Her cheeks were rosy red, but she stood her ground courageously. Placing a soft hand on either cheek as he stood below her, his face almost level with hers, she tilted his head toward her and touched his lips with her own pink ones, delicately as if a rose had swept them.

Simultaneously came the sound of the distant train.

"Good-bye, you nice, splendid boy!" breathed Starr and, waving her hand, darted inside the car.

Mr. Endicott, out on the platform still talking to the president, heard the oncoming train and looked around for Michael. He saw him coming from the car with an exalted look upon his face, his cap off, and the sun sending its golden beams over his hair.

"Son, I'm pleased with you," he said, catching his hand heartily. "Keep it up, and come to me when you're ready. I'll give you a start."

Michael gripped his hand and blundered out some words of thanks. Then the train was there, and Endicott had to go.

The two younger ladies in the car, meanwhile, were plying Starr with questions. "Who's that magnificent young man, Starr Endicott? Why didn't you introduce him to us? I never saw such a beautiful face on any human being."

A moment more and the private car was fastened to the train. Starr, leaning from the window, waved her tiny handkerchief until the train had thundered away among the pines, and nothing was left but the echo of its sound. The sun was going down, but it didn't matter. Sunshine filled the boy's heart. She was gone, his little Starr, but she'd left the memory of her soft kiss and bright eyes, and someday, when he was finished with college, he would see her again. Meanwhile he was content.

Chapter 6

The joy of loving-kindness in his life and a sense that somebody cared seemed to stimulate Michael's mind to greater energies. Whatever he did, whether studying or playing, he did with all his might.

The last year of his stay in Florida, a department of scientific farming was opened on a small scale. Michael presented himself as a student.

"What do you want of farming, Endicott?" asked the president, passing through the room during the teacher's first meeting with his students. "You can't use farming in New York."

In the kind old president's mind was perhaps a hope that the boy would linger with them, for he'd become attached to him in a silent, undemonstrative way.

"I might need it sometime," answered Michael, "and anyway I'd like to understand it. You said the other day that no knowledge was ever wasted. I'd like to know enough at least to tell somebody else."

The president smiled, wondered, and passed on. Michael continued in the class, supplementing the study by reading agricultural magazines and government literature on the subject. Agriculture had had a strange fascination for him ever since a noted speaker from the North had come and told the students that the new field for growth today lay in getting back to nature and cultivating the earth. Michael, as usual, wanted to know if that statement was true, and if so, why.

The three years flew by. Michael won no few honors, and the day came when he'd completed his course and, as class valedictorian, went up to the old chapel for his last commencement in the college.

He sat on the platform looking down on the kind, uncritical audience assembled for the exercises and didn't see a single face come for his sake alone. Many were interested in him because they'd known him through the years and because he bore the reputation of being his class's honor man and the school's finest athlete. But that wasn't like having someone of his own who cared whether he did well or not. He found himself wishing that even Buck might have been there—Buck, the nearest to a brother he ever had. Would Buck have cared that he'd won highest rank? Yes, he'd have been proud of him.

Michael had sent out three invitations to commencement, one to Mr. Endicott, one to Starr, and one addressed to Buck, with the inner envelope bearing the words "For the kids." But no response had come to any of them. He'd received back the one addressed to Buck with "Not Called For" in big pink letters stamped across the corner. It had reached him that morning, just before he stepped onto the platform. He wished it hadn't come till night; it gave him a lonely, almost forsaken feeling. He was "educated" now, at least enough to know what he didn't know, and no one cared.

When Michael sat down after his oration amid a storm of hearty applause, prolonged by his comrades into something like an ovation, someone handed him a letter and a package. A mistake was made at the post office in sorting the mail, and these weren't put in the college box. One of the professors going down later found them and brought them up.

The letter was from Mr. Endicott, containing a businesslike line of congratulations, with a hope for the recipient to come to New York if he still felt like it, and a check for a hundred dollars.

Michael looked at the check in awe, reread the letter carefully, and put both in his pocket. The package was tiny and addressed in Starr's handwriting. Michael saved that till he reached his room. He didn't want to open it before any curious eyes.

Starr's girlish letters had been few and far between, and the last year they'd ceased altogether. She was busy with life—finishing school, dancing school, music lessons, and good times. Michael was a dim, pleasant vision to her.

The package contained a scarfpin of exquisite workmanship. Starr had pleased herself by picking out the prettiest thing she could find. She had her father's permission to spend as much as she liked on it. It was in the form of an orchid, with a tiny diamond like a dewdrop on one petal.

Michael looked on it in wonder, the first suggestion of personal adornment ever to come to him. He saw the reminder of their day together in the orchid; studied the beautiful name, "Starr Delevan Endicott," engraved on the card; then put them carefully back into their box and locked it in his bureau drawer. He'd wear it the first time he went to see Starr. He was very happy that day.

The week after college closed, Michael drove the college mule to the county seat ten miles away and bought a small trunk. It wasn't much of a trunk, but it was the best the town afforded. In this he packed all his worldly possessions, bade good-bye to the president and the professors who hadn't already gone north for their vacations, took a long tramp to his old haunts, and boarded the midnight train for New York.

The boy felt an independence which kept him from letting his benefactor know of his intended arrival. He didn't wish to make him any unnecessary trouble, and though he'd now been away from New York for thirteen years, he felt certain he could find his way about. Some things one may learn even at seven are never forgotten.

When Michael landed in New York, he looked around him with vague bewilderment for a moment. Then he started out with assurance to find a new spot for himself in the world.

He had no baggage but his trunk to hinder him. He'd discovered the trunk could remain in the station for a day without charge. He carried only a handsome raincoat and umbrella, part of the outfit the tailor had sent him that spring, so he picked his way unhampered across Liberty Street, eyeing his former enemies, the policemen, and every little urchin or newsboy with interest. Of course Buck and the rest would have grown up and changed some; they wouldn't likely be selling papers now—but—these were boys such as he'd been.

He bought a paper from a ragged fellow with a pinched face, and a strange sensation came over him. When he left this city he was the newsboy, and now he had enough money to buy a paper—and the education to read it! What a difference! Not that he wanted the paper now, though it might prove interesting later, but he wanted the experience of buying it. It marked the era of change in his life with tremendous contrast. Immediately his real purpose in having an education, to uplift his fellow beings, vague during the years, took form and leapt into vivid concern, as he watched the newsboy's skinny legs scrambling across the muddy street under the horses' feet and between automobiles, in imminent danger of his life.

Michael had thought out what he'd do, and he proceeded to carry out his purpose. He had no idea what a picture of well-groomed youth and manly beauty he presented as he marched down the street. He walked like a king, and New York abashed him no more now than it did before he left. Some spirits are born that way. He walked like a gentleman, unafraid.

He had decided not to go to Mr. Endicott until he found lodging somewhere. An innate delicacy had brought him to this decision. He wouldn't put one voluntary burden upon his kind benefactor. Born and bred in the slums, from where did this feeling come?

Michael threaded his way through the maze of traffic, instinct and vague stirrings of memory guiding him to a quiet shabby street where he found a dingy room for a small price. Dangers that might have beset a strange young man in the city were materially lessened for him because of his wide reading. He'd read about New York whenever he found something in the back of an old magazine, comparing it with his faint memories, until he knew the relation of things to one another pretty well. A stranger less versed might have gotten into most undesirable quarters.

The boy looked around his new home with a strange sinking of heart, after he'd gone out to get something to eat and arranged for his trunk to be sent to his room. It was tiny and not overclean. The faded wallpaper had an ancient floral design. The one window looked out to brick walls, chimneys, and roofs. The city noise clattered in, and the smells and heat made it almost stifling to the boy who had lived thirteen years in the South's sunshine and outdoor freedom.

The narrow bed looked uninviting, the bureau washstand was cheap, and the mirror above it reflected a warped image, disturbing even the least vain. Michael wasn't vain, however, and thought little about himself. But the room with its soiled carpet was depressing. When his trunk was placed between the bureau and the bed there would be scarcely room for the one wooden chair. It wasn't a hopeful outlook. The boy removed his coat and sat down on the bed to whistle.

Life, grim, appalling, specterlike, rose before his mental vision, and he spent a bad quarter of an hour trying to adjust to his surroundings. His previous sunny philosophy struggled with the sudden reality. Then his trunk arrived.

As he opened the trunk a whiff of the South issued forth. He caught his breath with a keen homesickness. His schooldays were over, with the joy of that companion-filled life passed. He hadn't known such aloneness as now in this city.

The last thing he'd put in his trunk was a branch of mammoth pine needles.

The breath of the tree brought back all that meant home to him. He caught it up and buried his face in the plumy tassels.

The tray was filled with flags, pennants, photographs, and college paraphernalia. Eagerly he pulled them out and spread them over the lumpy bed. Then he grabbed his hat and rushed out. In a few minutes he returned with tacks, pins, and a small hammer. In an hour he'd changed the atmosphere of the whole place. Not an available inch of bare wall remained with its dirty wallpaper. College colors, pennants, and flags were grouped about pictures, and over the unwashed window was draped Florida moss. Here and there, apparently fluttering on the moss or about the room, were fastened beautiful specimens of semitropical moths and butterflies in gaudy colors. A small stuffed alligator reposed above the window, gazing down on the scene. A large alligator skin was tacked on one wall. One or two birds' nests fastened to small branches hung here and there.

Michael threw down the hammer and stood back to survey his work, sighing with relief. He felt more at home now with the photographs of his fellow students smiling at him. Opposite was the baseball team, strong and sturdy; to the right the glee club with him as their leader; to the left a group of his classmates, with his special chum in the midst. As he gazed at that kind face in the middle, he could almost hear his voice calling to him: "Come on, Angel! You're sure to win out!"

Michael felt better and hung up his clothes and arranged his effects on clean papers in the rheumatic bureau drawers. These were cramped quarters but would do until he was sure of earning some money, for he wouldn't spend his little savings more than he could help now and wouldn't depend any longer on Mr. Endicott's benevolence.

When his box of books arrived, he would ask permission to put some shelves over the window.

So he cheered himself as he put on his best garments, for he intended to arrive at Madison Avenue about the time his benefactor reached home for the evening.

Michael knew little of New York ways and less of society's habits; the few novels he'd read were his only instructors on the subject. He was going entirely on his dim memories of the habits of the Endicott home during his brief stay there. As it happened, Mr. Endicott was at home when Michael arrived, and the family was dining alone.

The boy was seated in the reception room gazing about him with his usual unconsciousness of self, when Endicott entered bringing Starr. A second time the man was deeply impressed with the fine presence of this boy from obscurity. He didn't look out of place even in a New York drawing room. It was incredible, though of course a large part of it was due to his city-made clothing. Still, that wouldn't account for his ease of manner, graceful courtesy, and instinct for saying the right thing at the right time.

Endicott invited the lad to dine with them, and Starr eagerly seconded the invitation. Michael accepted as eagerly and moments later found himself seated at the elegant table beside a beautiful, haughty woman who stared at him coldly and said nothing to him throughout the meal. The boy looked at her half wonderingly. It almost seemed as if she resented his presence; yet of course that couldn't be. He had the highest idea of this whole family. No one belonging to Starr could have anything but a lovely spirit.

Starr herself seemed to feel her mother's disapproval and spoke little, but she smiled shyly at Michael now and then when her mother wasn't noticing. Starr was sixteen now, slender and lovely as she'd given promise of being. Michael watched her, satisfied.

At last he turned to the mother, in her cold grandeur, and with earnestness and deference in his voice said, his glance still half toward Starr, "She's like you, and yet not!"

He said it gravely, as if it were a great discovery to them both, and he felt sure it was the key to her heart, admitting he admired the beautiful girl.

Mrs. Endicott froze him with her glance.

From the roots of his hair down to the tips of his toes he felt it—her resentment of his daring to express an opinion about her daughter, or even in having an opinion. For an instant his self-possession deserted him, and his face flushed with mingled emotions. Then he saw Starr's look of distress as she struggled to reply for her silent mother.

"Yes, Mama and I are often said to resemble one another strongly," she said with a tremble in her voice that roused the boy's manliness.

He flung off the oppression settling down on him and listened attentively to what Endicott was saying, responding gracefully, intelligently, and trying to convince himself it was his inexperience with ladies that caused him to say something inappropriate. He made no more personal remarks after that.

Endicott took the boy to his den after dinner. Later Starr slipped in, and they talked a little about their beautiful day in Florida together. Starr asked him if he still rode and would like to ride with her in the park the next morning when she took her exercise. It was arranged in her father's presence and with his full consent that Michael should accompany her in place of the groom who usually attended her rides.

Mrs. Endicott came in as they were making this arrangement and called Starr sharply out of the room.

After their withdrawal, Endicott questioned the boy about his college course and living habits. He was pleased to hear Michael was independent enough to secure lodgings before coming to his house. It showed a spirit worth helping, though he told him he should have come straight to him.

Endicott was leaving on a business trip for a week and told Michael to enjoy himself looking around the city during his absence. On his return he should present himself at the office at a certain time when he would put him in touch with something that would start him in life.

Michael thanked him and went back to his hot little room on the fourth floor, happy in spite of heat and dinginess and a certain homesick feeling. Wasn't he to ride with Starr in the morning? He could hardly sleep for thinking of it and of all he had to say to her.

Chapter 7

When Michael arrived at the appointed hour the next morning, he was shown into a small reception room by a maid and waited there a full half hour. Finally he heard garments rustling in the distance and, a moment later, became aware of a cold stare from the doorway. Mrs. Endicott, in an elaborate morning dress, was surveying him through a jeweled lorgnette, her chin tilted, a look of scorn on her face. She must have noted the grace of his movements as he rose to greet her. Yet for some reason this only seemed to increase her dislike.

No welcoming hand was offered in response to his good morning, and no answering smile displaced the woman's severe expression as she confronted the boy, slowly paralyzing him with her glance. No word did she utter.

But Michael possessed great self-control and a keen logical mind. He saw no reason for the woman's rebuking attitude and concluded he must be mistaken. Rallying his smile he asked, "Is Miss Starr ready to ride, or have I come too early?"

Again the silence became impressive as the cold eyes looked him through, before the thin lips opened. "My daughter is not ready to ride—with YOU, this morning or at any other time!"

"I beg your pardon, ma'am," said Michael, now deeply astonished and unable to fathom the woman's strange manner. "Have I misunderstood? I thought she asked me to ride with her this morning. May I see her, please?"

"No, you may not see Miss Endicott! And I consider your coming here at all a great impertinence. Certainly my husband has fully discharged any obligations for the slight service he assumes you rendered many years ago. I've always wondered if you did more harm than good. Of course you were only a child and couldn't do any heroic thing then. Probably if you'd kept out of things the trouble never would have happened, and your meddling simply gave you a wound and a soft bed for a while. In my opinion, far more has been done for you than you deserved, and as far as my daughter is concerned the obligation is discharged."

Michael had stood immovable while the woman uttered her harangue, his eyes growing wide with wonder and dark with a manly shame for her as she went on. When she paused for a moment, she saw his face was white and still like a statue, but something in the depth of his eyes held her in check.

With calm and deference, although his voice rang with honest indignation, Michael spoke. "I beg your pardon, Mrs. Endicott, but I've never felt there was the slightest obligation resting on any of this family for the trifling matter that occurred when, as you say, I was a child. I feel the obligation is entirely the other way, of course, but I can't understand what you mean. How is my coming here at Mr. Endicott's invitation an impertinence?"

The woman looked at him with contempt as if it were scarcely worth the trouble to answer him; yet something about him demanded an answer.

"I suppose you're as ignorant then," she answered cuttingly, "as you seem to be honest. I'll explain. You're not fit company for my daughter. It's strange you don't see that for yourself! A child of the slums, with only shame and disgrace for an inheritance, and brought up a pauper! How could you expect to associate with a gentleman's daughter? If you have any respect for her, you should understand it isn't for someone like you to call on her and take her riding. It's commendable that you've improved what opportunities have been given you, but it's the height of ingratitude in a dependent to take on the airs of an equal. You might as well understand you can't do it. I simply won't have you here. Do you understand?"

Michael stood as if rooted to the floor, horror and dismay growing in his eyes and stupor trickling through his veins, as though the full meaning of her words had been slow to reach his consciousness. Yet outwardly his face was calm, and only his eyes had seemed to change and widen and suffer as she spoke. Finally his voice came to him.

"Madam, I didn't know," he said in a stricken voice. "As you say, I am ignorant."

Then lifting his head with a challenge, as he would whenever he had to face a hard situation, his voice rang clear and undaunted: "Madam, I beg your pardon. I'll not offend this way again. It was because I didn't understand. I wouldn't hurt your daughter in any way, for she's been the only beautiful thing that ever came into my life. But I'll never trouble her again."

The bow with which he left her, marching past her into the hall and out of the door where he'd once laid down his boy life freely for her child, could have been no more gracefully or dramatically effected if he'd been some great actor. It was natural and full of dignity and reproach, and it left the lady feeling smaller and meaner than she'd ever felt in her rose-colored, velvet-lined existence. Somehow the contempt she'd prepared for crushing the lad he suddenly flung from him as a hated garment and walked from her presence, leaving it wrapped about her.

"Well, really!" she gasped at last when she realized he was gone and her eloquence not finished. "Well, really! What right had he to leave like that without my permission? Impertinent to the end! One would suppose he was a grand duke. Such airs! I always told Delevan it was a mistake to educate the masses. They simply don't know their place and won't keep it."

Nevertheless, the woman was shaken. Michael had made her feel as if she'd insulted a saint or a supernal being. She couldn't forget how the light had sifted through the depths of his great eyes as he spoke those last words, and she resented the ease with which he'd left her presence. It was too much like a victor's departure and not like one crushed back into his natural place. She was cross all day.

Starr meanwhile was lingering upstairs waiting for Michael. She was purposely kept busy in a distant room by her mother and wasn't told of his coming.

An hour passed beyond the appointed time, and she grew restless and disappointed, then annoyed and almost angry that he'd so easily forgotten her. But she didn't tell her mother, and the old Scottish nurse who would have been her confidante had been sent on an errand to another part of the city.

Thus, as the days went by, and Michael came no more to the house, the girl thought he didn't want to come, and her disappointment and mortification were succeeded by a haughty resentment, for her mother's teaching had shown some result in her character.

Michael had entered the Endicott mansion a boy with a light heart and a happy vision of the future. He walked out an hour later, a man with a heavy burden on his heart and a blank vision of the future. So much had the woman wrought.

As he walked from the house, his head drooped, and his spirit was troubled within him. He went as one in a terrible dream. His face had the look of an angel newly turned out of paradise and for no fault of his own, an angel who bowed to the supreme mandate, his life crushed within him. People looked at him strangely and wondered as they passed. It was as if sorrow were embodied suddenly, looking through eyes intended for love. For the first time Michael, beloved of his companions for his unselfishness, was thinking of himself.

Yet even so no selfishness was in his thought. It was only as if that which had always given him life and the breath of gladness had suddenly been withdrawn from him and left him panting, gasping in a wide, unexpected emptiness.

Somehow he found his way to his room and locked the door.

Then the great spirit gave way, and he flung himself on the bed. He didn't seem to have an atom of strength left to move or think or even breathe consciously. All his physical powers had deserted him, now in this great crisis when life's foundations were shaken to their depths and nothing seemed to be anymore. He couldn't think it over or find a way out of the horror; he could only suffer it, fact by fact, as it menaced him slowly throughout that day.

Gradually it became distinct and separated itself into thoughts so he could follow it.

First was the fact, like a great knife that severed soul from body, that he might not see Starr or have any more to do with her. So deeply had this interdiction taken hold upon him that it seemed in his agitation he might no longer even think of her.

Next, following in stern, logical sequence, came the reason for this severing of soul: the fact of his lowly birth. Coming as it did, out of a trustful life that had never questioned much about his origin but had sunnily taken life as a gift and thought little about self, with the bluntness of a cruelty, it had cut and hacked in every direction what was left of either soul or body. And it left no hope of putting things together again.

That was how it came as the boy, without a friend in the world to whom he could turn, lay and took it.

Gradually out of the blackness he began to think back to his own beginning.

Who was he? What was he? For the first time in his life, though he knew life more than most boys he'd associated with, he felt shame concerning his own birth, and it scorched its way into his soul.

He might have thought of such a possibility before perhaps, if his very youngest years hadn't been hedged about by a beautiful notion that sprang from the brain of an old Irishwoman in the slums, whose heart was wide as her ways were devious. One day when little Mickey had run an errand for her she said, "Shure, an' then, Mickey, yer an angel sthraight frum hiven an' no misthake. Yer no jest humans like the rist av us; ye must av dhropped doon frum the skoy." And from that it went forth that Mickey was the child of the sky, and that was why no one knew who his parents were.

The notion had guarded the boy's weird babyhood and influenced more than he knew his own thought of existence, until life grew too full to think much on it.

Out of the darkness and murk of the slums Mickey's soul had climbed high, and his ambitions reached up to the limitless blue above him. It had never occurred to him that his upward movements might be restricted. He'd taken others to be as freehearted and generous as he. Heir of all things, he'd breathed the atmosphere of culture as though it were his right. Now he suddenly saw he had no business climbing. He was about to mount a glorious height from which he was sure other heights were visible, when a rude hand brushed him back and dropped him down as though he were some crawling reptile at the bottom of things. And worst of all he might not climb back. He might look up; he might know the way up again. But the honor in him—the only bit of the heights he'd carried back to the foot with him—forbade him to climb to the heights of glory, for they belonged to others, those whom fortune favored and on whose escutcheon was no taint of shame.

And why should some souls be more favored than others? What had he, for instance, to do with his birth? He wouldn't have chosen shame, if shame there was. Yet shame or not he was branded with it for life because his origin was enveloped in mystery. The natural conclusion was that sin had had its part.

Then through the boy's mind tumbled a confusion of questions more or less unanswerable, in the midst of which he slept.

He seemed to have wandered out into the open again with the pines he loved above him and underneath the springy needles with their resinous softness. He lay looking up into the changeless blue that covered the heights, asking the tumultuous questions that throbbed through his heart, asking them of God.

Silently the city noises slunk away and dropped into the ceaseless calm of the South. The breeze fanned his cheek, the pines whispered, and a rippling birdsong touched his soul with peace. A quietness came down on his troubled spirit, and he was satisfied to take the burden laid upon him and bear it. Peace was on him when he awoke, far into the next morning.

The hot June sun steamed into his stuffy room and fell across the bed. He was sodden and heavy with the heat and the oppression of his garments. His head ached, and he felt as nearly ill as he'd ever felt. The specter of the day before confronted him in its torturing baldness, but he faced it now and looked it squarely in the eyes. It wasn't conquered yet, not by any means. The sharp pain of its newness was as great, and the deep conviction was still there that because of wrong this burden was laid upon him. But his soul had adjusted to the inevitable as it hadn't at first.

The boy lay still looking out upon a new life in which everything had to be readjusted to the idea of him and his new limitations. Before this he had thought no height wasn't his for the climbing. Now the heights were his, but he wouldn't climb because his presence might mar the heights themselves. It was wrong, unfair, that things should be so; but they were so, and as long as sin and wrong existed in the world they would be so.

He must look upon life as he'd looked upon every contest through his education. There were always hard things to be borne, but that only made the conquest greater. He must face this thing and win.

And what had he lost that had been his before? Not the beautiful girl, his heart's idol all these years. She was still there, alive and well, and more beautiful than ever. His devotion might yet stand between her and harm if need arose. True, he'd lost the hope of companionship with her, but that had been a day's growth. He'd never had much of it before or expected it when he came north. It would have been a glory and joy beyond expression, but one could live without those things and be true. Some reason for it all existed somewhere in the infinite, he was sure.

The ordinary boy wouldn't philosophize in this way, but Michael had never been an ordinary boy. His soul had always been open to the universe and optimistic in the most trying surroundings. He'd come out of the hardest struggle his soul had yet met, but he'd come out a man. The lines about his mouth weren't there the day before and spoke of strength and self-control. New depths were in his eyes as of one who'd looked down and seen things unspeakable, having to number himself with the lowly.

While he lay there trying to take in the change that had come to him, he suddenly thought of his childhood companions, the little waifs like him who came from the earth's refuse. They'd loved him. He recalled slowly, laboriously, incidents from his early history. Many were dim and uncertain, but little kindnesses stood out. A bad cut on his foot once and how Buck had bathed it and bound it in dirty rags, doing double duty with the newspapers for several days to save his friend from stepping. A bitter cold night back as far as he could remember when he'd had bad luck and come among the others supperless and almost freezing. Buck had shared a crust and found a warm boiler room where they crawled out of sight and slept. Other incidents, more blurred in his memory, but enough to recall how loyal the little gang had been to him. He saw once more their faces when they heard he was going to college, blanched with horror at the separation, lighting with pleasure when he promised to return!

The years, how they'd changed and separated! Where were they, these who really belonged to him? What had the years done to them? And he had a duty to them. How had he been in the city all these hours and not even thought of looking for those loyal souls who stood by him faithfully when they were mere babies? He must go at once. He'd lost his head over attempting to reach things that weren't for him, and this shock had come to set him straight.

Gravely he rose at last, these thoughts surging through his brain.

The heat, the stifling air, his recent struggling, and the exhausting stupor made him reel dizzily as he stood. But his mettle was up now, and he set his lips and went about making himself neat. He longed for a dip in the crystal waters of the college lake. The tiny washbowl in his room proved a poor substitute with its tepid water and diminutive towel.

He went out and breakfasted carefully and then, with his map in his pocket, started out to find his old haunts.

Chapter 8

Thirteen years in New York had brought many changes. Some of the well-remembered landmarks were gone, with new buildings in their places. A prosperous-looking saloon, palatial in its entrance, marked the corner where he used to sell papers. It had been a corner grocery store. Saloons! Always and everywhere were saloons! Michael looked at them wonderingly. He'd forgotten them in his exile, for the college influence had barred them from its vicinity.

The boy Mickey had been familiar with saloons, looking upon them as a necessary evil, where drinking fathers spent the money that should have bought their children food. He'd been in and out of them selling his papers, warming his feet, and getting a crust now and then from an uneaten bit on the lunch counter. Sometimes there had been glasses to drain, but Mickey with his observing eyes had early decided he would have none of the stuff that sent men home to curse their children.

College influence, while little had been said on the subject, had filled the boy with horror for saloons and drunkards. He stood appalled now as he turned at last into an alley where familiar objects, doorsteps, cellars, met his gaze, with grog shops along the way and taking command of every corner.

A strange feeling came over him as long-forgotten sights awoke his memory. Was this really the place, and was that opening beyond the third step the blind alley where Jane used to live? Things were so much dirtier, so much worse in every way than he remembered them. He hurried on, not noticing the attention he was attracting from the wretched children in the gutters, though he scanned them eagerly, with the wild idea that Buck and the rest might be among them.

Yes, the alley was there, dark and ill-smelling as ever, and in its dim recesses on a dirty step a woman's figure hunched—a figure he knew at once. Who was she? What had they called her? Sally? Aunt Sal?

He hurried up to where she sat looking at him. Her gray hair straggled down on her dirty cotton dress open at the neck over shriveled yellow skin; soiled old hands hung over slatternly garments; stockingless feet were stuck into a tattered pair of men's shoes. Nothing seemed changed since he saw her last, except the hair had been black then and the skin not so wrinkled. Aunt Sally had always been good-natured, even when she was drunk; her husband was always drunk also when he came home, but never good-natured. The boy recalled these things as he stood looking down at the wreck of a woman before him.

The bleary eyes looked up unknowing, half resentful of his intrusion.

"Aunt Sally!" cried the boyish voice. "Aren't you Aunt Sally?"

The woman looked surprised. "I be," she said thickly, "but wot's that to youse? I beant no hant o' yourn."

"Don't you remember Mickey?" he asked almost anxiously, for now the feeling had seized him that he must make her remember. He must find out if he could whether anything was known of his origin. Perhaps she could help him.

Perhaps, after all, he might trace his family and find at least no disgrace upon him.

"Mickey!" the woman repeated dully. She shook her head. "Wot's Mickey?"

"Don't you remember Mickey, the little boy who sold papers and brought you water sometimes? Once you gave me a drink of soup from your kettle. Think!"

A dim perception entered the sodden eyes.

"Thur was a Mickey long ago," she mused. "He had hair like a h'angel, bless the sweet chile. But he got shot an' never come back. That war long ago."

Michael took off his hat, and the little light in the dark alley seemed to catch and tangle in the gleam of his hair.

The old woman started as though she'd seen a vision. "The saints preserve us!" she cried aghast, shrinking back into her doorway with raised hands. "An' who be yez? Yeh looks enough like the b'y to be the father of 'im. He'd hair loike the verra sunshine itself. Who be yez? Spake quick. Be ye man er angel?"

Something in the woman's tone went to the lonely boy's heart, even while he recoiled from the repulsive creature before him.

"I'm just Mickey, the boy, grown a little older," he said gently, "and I've come back to see the place where I used to live and find the people I used to know."

"Y've lost yer way thin, fer shure!" said the woman, slightly recovering her equilibrium. "The loikes uv youse nivver lived in dis place. Fer ef yous ain't angel, you's gintulmun, an' no gintulmun ivver cum from the loikes o' this. An' besoides, the b'y Mickey, I tel'd yez, was shot an' nivver comed back no more. He's loikely up wid de angels where he b'longs."

"Yes, I was shot," said Michael, "but I wasn't killed. A good man sent me to college, and I've just graduated and come back to look up my friends."

"Frinds, is it, ye'll be afther a findin'? Thin ye'd bist look ilsewhar, fer thur's no one in this alley fit to be frinds with the loikes uv you. Ef that's wot they does with b'ys at co-lidge, a pity 'tis more uv um can't git shot an' go there. But ef all youse tell is thrue, moi advice to yez is, juist bate it as hoird as ivver yez kin out'n yere, an' don't yez nivver set oies on this alley agin. Ye'd better stay to co-lidge all the days uv yer loife than set fut here agin, fer juist let 'em got holt uv yez an' they'll spile yer pretty face. Look thar!" she pointed toward a wreck of humanity that reeled into the alley. "Would yez loike to be loike that? My mon come home loike that ivvery day of his loife, rist his bones, an' he nivver knowed whin he died."

Maudlin tears rolled down the poor creature's cheeks, for they could be no tears of affection. Her man's departure from this life could have been only a relief. Michael recoiled from the sight with a sickening sadness. Nevertheless, he meant to find out if this woman knew anything of his old friends or of his origin. He rallied his forces to answer her.

"I don't have to be like that," he said. "I've come to look up my friends, and I want you to tell me if you know anything about my parents. Did you ever hear anything about me? Did anybody know who I was or how I came to be here?"

The old woman tried to gather her scattered faculties, but she shook her grizzled head. "I ain't nivver laid oies on yez before, an' how cud I know whar yez cum from, ner how yez cam to be here?"

He perceived it would require patience to extract information from this source. "Try to think," he said more gently. "Can you remember if anyone ever belonged to the little boy they called Mickey? Was there ever any mother or father or—anybody that belonged to him at all?"

Again she shook her head. "Nivver as Oi knows on. They said he just comed a wee babby to the coourt a wanderin' with the other childer, with scarce a rag to his back, an' a smile on him like the archangel, and some said as how he nivver had no father ner mother, but dthrapped sthraight frum the place where de angels live."

"But did no one take care of him or ever try to find out about him?"

"Foind out, is it? Whist! An' who would tak toime to find out whin ther's so miny uv their own. Mickey was allus welcome to a bite an' a sup ef any uv us had it by. There wuz old Granny Bane with the rheumatiks. She gave him a bed an' a bite now an' agin, till she died, an' afther that he made out to shift fer hisse'f. He was a moighty indepindint babby."

"But had he no other name? Mickey what? What was his whole name?"

The old woman only stared stupidly.

"Didn't he have any other name?" There was almost despair in his tone.

Another shake of the head. "Just Mickey!" Her eyes grew dull again.

"Can you tell me if any other people living here now used to know Mickey? Any other men or women who might remember?"

"How kin Oi tell?" snarled the woman impatiently. "Oi can't be bothered."

Michael stood in troubled silence, while the woman turned her head to watch a neighbor coming down the street with a basket in her hand. Her visitor seemed to interest her no longer. She called out some rough ribaldry to the woman, who glanced up fiercely and deigned no further reply. Then Michael tried again.

"Could you tell me about the boys who used to go with Mickey?"

"No, Oi can't," she answered crossly. "Oi can't be bothered. Oi don't know who they was."

"There were Jimmie and Sam and Bobs and Buck. Surely you remember Buck—and little Janie. Janie who died after Mickey went away?"

The bleared eyes turned full upon him again. "Janie? Fine, Oi remimber Janie. They had a white hurse to her, foiner'n any iver cum to the coourt before. The b'ys stayed up two noights selling to git the money fur it, an' Buck he stayed stiddy while she was aloive. Pity she doied."

"Where's Buck?" demanded Michael with a sudden twinge of his heartstrings that seemed to bring back the old love and loyalty to his friend. Buck had needed him perhaps all these years, and he hadn't known.

"That's whot the police would like fer yez to answer, I'm thinkin'!" laughed old Sal. "They wanted him bad fer breakin' into a house an' mos' killin' the lady an' gittin' aff wid de jewl'ry. He beat it dat noight, an' ain't none o' us seen him these two year. He were a slick one. He were awful smart at breakin' an' stealin'. Mebbe Jimmie knows, but, Jimmie, he's in jail, serving his time fer shootin' a man in the hand durin' a dhrunken fight. Jimmie, he's no good. Never wuz. He's jest like his foither. Bobs, he got both legs cut aff, bein' runned over by a big truck, and he doied in the horspittle. Bobs, he were better dead. He'd uv gone loike the rist. Sam, he's round these parts mostly nights. Ye'll hey to come at noight ef yez want to see him. Mebbe he knows more 'bout Buck'n he'll tell."

Sick at heart, Michael put question after question but got no more information, and the old woman showed signs of impatience again. Carefully noting what she said about Sam and getting a few facts as to the best time and place to find him, Michael turned and walked sadly out of the alley. He didn't see old Sal's alert eyes following him nor the keen expression on her face as she stretched her neck to see which way he turned as he left the alley. As soon as he was out of sight, she shuffled down from her doorstep to the corner and peered after him through the morning sunshine. Then she went slowly back to her doorstep.

"Now whut in the divil could he be a wantin' wid Buck' an' Sammie?" she muttered to herself. "All that story 'bout his bein' Mickey was puttin' it on my eye. I'll giv warnin' to Sammie t'night, an' ef Buck's in these pairts he better git out West some'res. The police uv got onto 'im. But hoiwiver did they know he knowed Mickey? Poor little angel Mickey! I guv him the shtaight about Bobs an' Jimmie, fer they wuz beyant his troublin', but he'll niver foind Sammie from the directin' I sayed."

Michael, sad, horror-filled, conscience-stricken, found a restaurant and ate his dinner, thinking meanwhile what he could do for the boys. Could he visit Jimmie in prison and make his life more comfortable in little ways? Could he plan something for him when he came out? Could he help Sam? The old woman had said little about Sam's condition. Michael thought he might likely by this time have built up a nice little business. Perhaps he had a prosperous newsstand in some frequented place. He looked forward eagerly to meeting him again. Sam had always been a silent child dependent on the rest, but he was one of the little gang, and Michael's heart warmed toward his former comrade. He surely wouldn't find him so loathsome and repulsive as old Sal. She made him heartsick. Just to think of drinking soup from her dirty kettle! How could he have done it? Yet he knew no better life then, and he was hungry and a child.

So Michael mused and with a great heart hunger to know what had become of Buck. Could he and Sam together plan some way to find Buck and help him out of his trouble? How could Buck have done anything so dreadful? And yet even as he thought it he remembered that "pinching" hadn't been a crime in his childhood days, not unless one was found out. How had these principles, or lack of principles, been replaced gradually in his own life without his realizing it? It was strange and wonderful. Practically now he, Michael, had been made into a new creature since he left New York and so gradually and pleasantly he hadn't realized it.

Yet, as he marveled, a thought shot through him that perhaps it hadn't been a good thing, this making him into a new creature, with new desires and aims and hopes that could never be fulfilled. Perhaps he'd have been happier, better off, if he'd never been taken out of that environment and brought to appreciate another one where he didn't belong and could never stay, since that old environment was the one where he must stay whether he would or not. He put the thought from him as unworthy at once; yet its sharpness lingered and with it a vision of Starr's face as he'd seen her two nights before in her father's home, before he knew the door of that home was shut upon him forever.

Michael passed the day wandering about the city, trying to piece together his old knowledge with the new and know the city in which he'd come to dwell.

It was nearing midnight, when Michael, by old Sal's advice and utterly fearless in his ignorance, entered the court where he had spent his babyhood.

The alley was dark and murky in the humid summer night. But unlike the morning hours it was alive with a writhing, chattering, fighting mass of humanity. Doorways overflowed. The narrow alley itself seemed fairly thronging with noisy, unhappy men and women. Hoarse laughs mingled with rough cursing, pierced with an occasional scream. Stifling odors lurked in cellar doorways and struck one full in the face unawares. Curses seemed to be the setting for all conversation, whether angry or jolly. Babies tumbled in the gutter, and older children fought over some garbage scrap.

Appalled, Michael halted and almost turned back. Then, remembering this was where he'd come from—where he belonged—and that his duty, his obligation, was to find his friends, he went steadily forward.

There sat old Sal, a belligerent gleam in her sodden eyes. Four men on a step opposite, with a candle between them, were playing cards. Sal muttered a word as Michael approached, and the candle was extinguished. It looked as if one had carelessly knocked it onto the pavement, but the glare flickered into darkness, and Michael could no longer see the men's faces. He wondered if one of them was Sam. But when he rubbed his eyes and looked again the four men were gone, and two children occupied the step, holding a sleeping baby between them and staring at him in open-mouthed admiration.

The weird blinking light of the distant streetlamp, the noise and confusion, the odors and curses filled him anew with a desire to flee, but he wouldn't let himself turn back. Never had Michael turned from his duty out of fear or dislike of anything.

He tried to enter into conversation with old Sal again, but she ignored him. She'd taken "a wee drapth" and was alert and suspicious. In fact, the whole alley was alert for this elegant stranger who was none of theirs and must have come to spy on someone. He wanted Sam; therefore Sam was hidden well and at that moment playing a crafty game in the back of a cellar on top of an old beer barrel, by the light of a wavering candle, well guarded by sentinels along the way. Michael could have no more found him than a needle in a haystack the size of New York.

He wandered for two hours through the alley, seeing sights long since forgotten, hearing words unspeakable, following suggestions of interested bystanders, always coming back without finding Sam. He hadn't yet understood he wasn't intended to find Sam. He had taken these people into his confidence as he'd always taken everyone into his confidence, and they were playing him false. If they had lived on Fifth Avenue, he wouldn't have expected them to be interested in him and his plans and desires. But these were his very own people, at least the "ownest" he had in the world, and among them he'd once moved freely, confidently. He saw no reason why they'd have changed toward him, though he felt the antagonism in the atmosphere as the night wore on, even as he felt it in the Endicott house the day before.

Heartsick and baffled, at last he took his way slowly, looking back many times and leaving many messages for Sam. He felt as if he simply couldn't return to even so uncomfortable a bed as the one in his new lodgings without finding some clue to his old comrades.

Standing at the corner of the alley opposite the saloon's flaunting lights, he looked back at the swarming darkness of the alley, and his heart filled with a great wave of pity, love, and sorrow. Almost at his feet in a dark shadow of a doorway a tiny white-faced boy crouched fast asleep on the stone threshold. He thought of little Bobs and his own barren childhood, and a mist came before his eyes as he looked up at the sky where the very stars seemed small and far away.

"Oh, God!" he said under his breath. "Oh, God! I must do something for them!"

And then, as if the opportunity came with the prayer, there reeled into view three or four men and a woman.

The woman was talking in a high frightened voice and protesting. The men caught hold of her roughly, laughing and flinging out coarse jests. Then another man came stealing from the darkness of the alley and joined the group, seizing the woman by the shoulders and speaking words too vile for repetition. In terror the girl turned, for Michael could see, now she was nearer, that she was only a young girl and pretty. Instantly he thought of Starr, and his soul rose in mighty wrath that any man would treat any girl as he'd seen these do. Then the girl screamed and struggled to get away, crying, "It ain't true! Lem'me go! I won't go with you—"

Instantly Michael was upon them, his powerful arms and body dashing the men right and left. And because of the suddenness of the attack coming from this unexpected quarter—for Michael had stood somewhat in the shadow— and because of the cowardliness of all bullies, for the moment, he prevailed against all four, long enough for the girl to slip like a wraith from their grasp and disappear into the shadows.

Then when the men, dazed from surprise, though not seriously hurt, discovered their prey was gone and a stranger from the higher walks of life had frustrated their plans, they fell upon him in their wrath.

Michael, brave always and well trained in athletics, parried their blows for an instant. But the man who had come from the shadows, whose face was evil, stole up behind and stabbed him in the shoulder. A sudden faintness made him less able to defend himself. He felt he was losing his senses, and the next blow from one of the men sent him reeling into the street where he fell heavily, striking his head against the curb. A loud cry of murder was heard in a woman's shrill voice, the padded rush of the villains into their holes, the distant ring of a policeman's whistle, and then all was as quiet as a city night could be. Michael lay white and still with his face looking up to the faint pitying moon so far away and his beautiful hair wet with blood flowing out on the pavement. There he lay on the edge of the world that was his own and would not own him. He had come to his own, and his own received him not.

Chapter 9

Michael awoke in the hospital with a bandage around his head and a stinging pain in his shoulder whenever he tried to move.

Back in his inner consciousness there sounded the last words he had heard before he fell, but he couldn't connect them with anything at first: "Hit him again, Sam!"

Those were the words. What did they mean? Had he heard them or merely dreamed them? And where was he?

A glance about the long room with its rows of white beds, each with an occupant, answered his question. He closed his eyes again to be away from all those other eyes and think. Sam! He'd been looking for Sam. Had Sam then come at last? Had Sam hit him? Had Sam recognized him? Or was it another Sam?

But something was wrong with his head, and he couldn't think. He put up his right arm to feel the bandage, and the pain in his shoulder stung again. Somehow to his feverish fancy it seemed the sting of Mrs. Endicott's words to him. He dropped his hand feebly, and the nurse gave him something in a spoon. Then, half dreaming, he fell asleep, with a vision of Starr's face as he'd seen her last.

Three weeks he lay on that narrow white bed and learned to face the battalion of eyes from the other narrow beds around him; to distinguish the quiet sound of the marble-lined room from the rumble of the unknown city without. And when the rumble was the loudest, his head ached with the thought of the alley and the horrible sights and sounds that seemed written in letters of fire across his spirit.

He learned to look upon the quiet monotonous world of ministrations as a haven from the world outside into which he must presently go, and in his weakened condition he shrank from the new life. It seemed filled with disappointments and sorrow.

But one night a man in his ward died and was carried silent and covered from the room. Some of his last moaning utterances had reached his fellow sufferers' ears with a vision of his life and home, and his mortal agony for the past, now that he was leaving it all.

That night Michael couldn't sleep, for the court, the alley, and the whole sunken humanity were pressing upon his heart. It seemed his burden that he must give up his life's hopes to bear. And there he had it out with himself and accepted whatever should come to be his duty.

Meanwhile the wound on his head was healed, the golden halo had covered the scar, and the cut in his shoulder, which had been only a flesh wound, was doing nicely. Michael was allowed to sit up and then to be about the room for a day or two.

In those days of his sitting up, when the sun crept in for an hour each day and reached his hair, the other men of the ward began to notice him. He seemed to them set apart, one lifted above what held them to sin and earth. His countenance spoke of strength and self-control, two things many of them lacked, either through constant sinning or constant fighting with poverty and trouble. So, as he began to get about, they sent for him to come to their bedsides. As they talked, one and another poured out his separate tale of sorrow and woe, till Michael felt he could bear no more. He longed for power to help, to put these wretched men on their feet again to lead a new life, to crush some of the demons in human form who were grinding them down to earth. Oh, for money and knowledge and authority!

One man had lost both legs in a defective machine he was running in a factory. He was a skilled workman with a wife and three children. But he was useless now at his trade. No one wanted a man with no legs. He might be better dead. Damages? No hope of that. He'd accepted three hundred dollars to sign a release. He had to. His wife and children were starving, and they must have the money then or perish. There was no other way. Besides, what hope had he in fighting a great corporation? He was a poor man, a stranger in this country, with no friends. The company had been plenty willing to swear it was the man's fault.

Another had tried to asphyxiate himself by turning on the gas in his wretched little boardinghouse room. He'd lost his position because of ill health, and the firm wished to put a younger man in his place. He almost succeeded in taking himself out of this life.

Next to him was one horribly burned by molten metal he'd been compelled to carry without adequate precautions. It was a cheaper method of handling the stuff, and men cost less than machinery. You could always get more men.

The man across from him was wasted away from insufficient food. He'd been out of work for months, and what little money he could pick up in odd jobs had gone mostly to his wife and children.

And so it was throughout the ward. On almost every life sin—somebody's sin—had left its mark. One or two cheery souls, though poor, were blest with friends and a home of some kind and were looking forward to a speedy restoration, but these were the exception. Nearly all the others blamed someone else for their unhappy condition, and in nearly every case someone else was undoubtedly to blame, even though in most cases each individual had been somewhat responsible.

All this Michael gradually learned, as he began his practical study of sociology. As he learned story after story and formulated the facts of each, he came to three conclusions: First, there wasn't enough room in the city for these people to have a fair chance at life's beautiful things. Second, the people with the good things were getting them all for themselves and didn't care a straw whether others went without. Third, somebody should be doing something about it, and why not he?

Of course it was absurd for a mere boy just out of college, with scarcely a cent to his name—and not a whole name to call his own—to think of attacking the problem of the people single-handed. But still he felt he was called to do it and meant to try.

He had no idea whether anybody else had seen it this way or not. He'd read a little of city missions and charitable enterprises, but they scarcely reached his inner consciousness. His impression gathered from such desultory reading had been that the effort was sporadic and ineffective. And so, in his gigantic ignorance and egotism, yet with his sensitivity to the inward call, Michael set himself to espouse the cause of the people.

Wasn't he one of them? Hadn't he been born there that he might be one of them and know what they had to suffer? Weren't they his kindred so far as he had any kindred? Hadn't he been educated and brought into contact with higher things so he might know what these other human souls might be if they had the opportunity? If he'd known more he would have added "and if they would." But he didn't; he supposed all souls were as willing to be uplifted as he'd been.

Michael went out from the hospital feeling that his lifework was before him. The solemn pledge he'd taken as a child to return and help his former companions became a voluntary pledge of his young manhood. He knew little about the matter, but he felt much, and he was determined to do, wherever the way opened. He had no doubt the way would open.

"Now, young man, take care of yourself," said the doctor in parting from his patient a few days later, "and, for the land's sake, keep away from back alleys at night. When you know a little more about New York, you'll learn it's best to keep far away from such places. Don't fool around thinking you can convert any of those blackguards. They need to be blown up, every one of them, and the place obliterated. Mind, I say, and keep away from them."

Michael smiled and thanked the doctor and walked unsteadily down the hospital steps on feet that were strangely wobbly for him. But he didn't intend to obey the doctor. He had been turning the matter over in his mind and had a plan. And that night about ten o'clock he went back to the alley.

Old Sal was sitting on her doorstep, a little more intoxicated than the last time, and the young man's sudden appearance beside her startled her into an Irish howl.

"The saints presarve us!" she cried, tottering to her feet. "He's cum back to us agin, shure he has! There's no killin' him! He's an angel shure. B'ys, rin! Bate it! The angel's here again!"

There was a sound of scurrying feet, and the place seemed to clear suddenly of the children that had been underfoot. One or two scowling men, or curious women in whose eyes the light of life had died and been left unburied, peered from dark doorways.

Michael stood quietly until Sal's howling had subsided, and then he spoke in a clear tone.

"Can you tell me if Sam has been around here tonight? Is he anywhere near here now?"

There was no answer for a minute, but someone growled out that he might and then he might not have been. Someone else said he'd just gone away, but they didn't know where. Michael perceived it was a good deal as it had been before.

"I've brought a message for him, a letter," he said, and he spoke so that anyone nearby might hear. "Will you give it to him when he comes? He'll want to see it, I'm sure. It's important. I think he'll be glad to get it. It contains good news about an old friend of his."

He held out the letter courteously to old Sal, and she looked at its white crispness as though it had been a message from the lower regions calling her to judgment. A letter, white, square-cornered and clean, with clear, firm inscription, had never come before her gaze. Old Sal had never learned to read. The writing meant nothing to her, but the whole letter represented a mystic communication from another world.

Instinctively the neighbors gathered to look at the letter, and Sal, seeing herself the center of observation, reached forward a dirty hand wrapped in a corner of her apron and took the envelope as though it had been hot, eyeing it fearfully.

Then, bowing and touching his hat to her as though she'd been a queen, Michael turned and walked out of the alley.

Old Sal stood watching him, a kind of wistful wonder in her bleary eyes. No gentleman had ever tipped his hat to her, and no man had ever done her reverence. From her childhood she'd been brought up to forfeit the respect of men. Perhaps she'd never realized she might have been anything but what she was and that men might have honored her.

The neighbors, too, were awed for the moment and stood watching in silence.

Then, when Michael turned the corner out of sight, Sal exclaimed, "Now that's the angel, shure! No gintlemin would iver uv tipped his 'at to the loikes of Sal. Saints presarve us! That we should hev an angel in this alley!"

When Michael reached his lodging, he found that he was trembling so from weakness and excitement that he could scarcely drag himself up the three flights to his room. So had his splendid strength been reduced by trouble and the fever that came with his wounds.

He lay down weakly and tried to think. Now he'd done his best to find Sam. If Sam didn't come in answer to his letter he must wait until he found him. He wouldn't give up. So he fell asleep with the burden on his heart.

The letter was as follows:

Dear Sam,

You can't have forgotten Mickey who slept with you in the boiler room and with whom you shared your crusts. You remember I promised when I went away to college I'd come back and try to make things better for you all? And now I've come and am anxious to find the fellows and see what we can do together to make life better in the old alley and make up for some of the hard times when we were children. I've been down to the alley but can get no trace of you. I spent the best part of one night hunting you, and then a slight accident put me in the hospital for a few days; but I'm well now and am anxious to find you all. I want to talk over old times and find out where Buck and Jim are and hear all about Janie and little Bobs.

I'm leaving this letter with Aunt Sally, hoping she'll give it to you. I've given my address below and would be glad to have you come and see me at my room. If you prefer I'll meet you wherever you say, and we'll go together and eat something to celebrate.

Hoping to hear from you very soon, I am as always,

Your brother and friend,
Mickey

A few days later the postman brought a begrimed envelope addressed in pencil to the door. Michael with sinking heart opened it. It read:

MicKY ef yo be reely hym cum to KelLys karner at 10 tumoroW nite. Ef you are mIcK youz thee old whissel an doante bring no une wit yer Ef yO du I wunt be thar.

SAM

Seated on his lumpy bed Michael puzzled this out, word by word, until he made fairly good sense of it. He was to go to Kelly's corner. How the words stirred his memory. Kelly's corner was beyond the first turn of the alley, at the extreme end of an alley within an alley, and had no outlet except through Kelly's saloon. Only the "gang" knew the name, "Kelly's corner," for it wasn't really a corner at all, only a pocket or hiding place so titled by Buck for his own and "de kids'" private purpose. If Michael had been inclined to be a coward since his recent usage in the alley, he'd have kept away from Kelly's corner. Once in there alone with enemies, no policeman's club or hospital ambulance would ever come to help. The things that happened at Kelly's corner never got into the newspapers.

Memory and instinct made this clear to Michael, and if he needed no other warning, those words in the letter about not bringing anyone with him were sufficient to make him wise.

Yet Michael never so much as thought of not keeping the appointment. His business was to find Sam, and it mattered as little to him now that danger stood in the way as it had the day he flung his neglected body in front of Starr Endicott and saved her from the assassin's bullet. He would go, of course, and alone. Neither did it occur to him to leave his name and whereabouts at the police station to be searched for in case he didn't turn up in a reasonable time. It was all in the day's work, and Michael thought no more about the possible peril he was facing than he'd thought of broken limbs and bloody noses before a football scrimmage.

Something else in the letter stirred old memories. The whistle! Of course he hadn't forgotten that, although he hadn't used it much among his college companions. It was a strange, weird, penetrating sound between a call and whistle. He and Buck had made it up as a signal. When Michael went to college he'd held it sacred as belonging to his old friends, and never, unless alone in the woods where only the birds and the trees could hear, had he let its echoes ring. Sometimes he'd startled the mockingbirds with it, and once he let it ring into the midst of his astonished comrades in Florida when he was hidden from their view and they didn't know who made the sound. He tried it now softly, and then louder, until he knew he could still give it.

The next night at precisely ten o'clock Michael's ringing step sounded down the alley—firm, decisive, secure. Such assurance Daniel must have had as he faced the lions, and so went the three Hebrew children into the fiery furnace.

"It's him! It's the angel!" whispered old Sal, who was watching. "Oi tould yez he'd come fer shure!"

"He's got his nerve with him!" murmured a girl with bold eyes and a coarse kind of beauty, as she drew further back into the shadows. "He ain't comin' out again so pretty, I guess. Not if Sam don't like. Mebbe he ain't comin' out 'tall!"

"Angels has ways, me darlint!" chuckled Sal. "He'll come back al roight— ye'll see!"

On walked Michael, down the alley to the narrow opening that to the uninitiated wasn't an opening between the buildings, and slipped in the old way. He'd thought it out in the night. He was sure he knew just how far beyond Sal's house it was. On into the fetid air of the close dark place, the air struck him in the face like a hot, wet blanket.

All was still when he reached the point known as Kelly's corner. It had been so as he remembered it—the place of plots, the hatching of murders and robberies. Had it so changed that it was still tonight? He hesitated for an instant. Should he wait a while or knock on some door? Would it be any use to call?

But the instinct of the slums was upon him again, his birthright. It seemed to drop upon him from the atmosphere, a sort of stealthy patience. He would wait. Something would come. He must do as he had with the forest birds when he wished to watch their habits. He must stand still unafraid and show he was harmless.

So he stood three, perhaps five minutes. Then softly at first and gradually growing clearer, he gave the call he'd given years before, a barefoot, hungry child in that spot many times.

The echo died away. Nothing made him know a group of curious alley dwellers huddled at the mouth of the trap in which he stood, watching with eyes accustomed to the darkness, to see what would happen—to block his escape if escape should be attempted.

Then out of the silence a sigh seemed to come, and out of the shadows one shadow unfolded and came forward till it stood beside him. Still Michael didn't stir but softly, through half-open lips, breathed the signal once more.

Sibilant, rougher, with a hint of menace as it issued forth, the signal was answered this time, and with a thrill of wonder the mantle of the old life fell upon Michael once more. He was Mickey—only grown more wise. Almost the old vernacular came to his tongue.

"Hi! Sam! That you?"

The figure in the darkness seemed to stiffen with sudden attention. The voice was like, and yet not like, the Mickey of old.

"Wot youse want?" questioned a voice gruffly.

"I want you, Sam. I want to see if you look as you used to, and I want to know about the boys. Can't we go where there's light and talk a little? I've been days hunting you. I've come back because I promised. You expected me to come back someday, didn't you, Sam?"

Michael was surprised to find how eager he was for the answer to this question.

"Aw, what ye givin' us?" responded the suspicious Sam. "D'youse s'pose I b'lieve all that gag about yer comin' here to he'p we'uns? Wot would a guy like youse wid all dem togs an' all dem fine looks want wid us? Youse has got above us. Youse ain't no good to us no more."

Sam scratched a match on his trousers and lit an old pipe he held between his teeth. But as the match flared up and showed his own face, a lowering brow, shifty eyes, a swarthy, unkempt visage, sullen and sly, the eyes weren't looking at the pipe but up at the face above him which shone out white and fine in the little gleam in the dark court. The watchers crowding at the opening saw his face and almost imagined soft shadowy wings behind him. Thus with old Sal's help Michael got the name again, "the Angel." And thus he became "the angel of the alley."

"Sam!" he said, and his voice was very gentle, although he was conscious of two more shadows of men behind him and perhaps more lurking in the dark corners. "Sam, if you remember me you'll know I couldn't forget, and I do care. I came back to find you. I've always meant to come, all the time I was in college. I've had it in mind to come back here and make some of the hard things easier for"—he hesitated—"for us all."

"How did youse figger youse was goin' to do that?" Sam asked, his eyes narrowing on Michael, as he purposely struck another match to watch the effect of his words.

Then Michael's smile lit up his face, and Sam, however much he may have pretended to doubt, knew in his heart this was the same Mickey of old. There was no mistaking that smile.

"I'll need you to help me figure that out, Sam. That's why I was so anxious to find you."

A curious grunt from behind Michael warned him the audience was being amused at Sam's expense. Sam's brows were lowering.

"Humph!" he said, ungraciously striking a third match in time to watch Michael's face. "Where's yer pile?"

"What?"

"Got the dough?"

"Oh," said Michael, "no, I haven't got money, Sam. I've only my education."

"An' wot good's it, I'd like to know. Tell me those?"

"So much good I can't tell it in one short talk," answered Michael steadily. "We'll have to get better acquainted, and then I hope I can make you understand how it's helped. Now tell me about the others. Where's Buck?"

There was a dead silence.

"It's hard to say!" Sam muttered at last.

"Don't you know? Haven't you any idea, Sam? I'd so like to hunt him up."

The question seemed to have produced tension in the atmosphere. Michael felt it.

"I might, an' then agin' I might not," answered Sam in the tone that barred further questions.

"Couldn't you and I find him and—and—help him, Sam? Aunt Sally said he was in trouble."

Another match was scratched and held close to his face while Sam's narrow eyes seemed to pierce his very soul before he answered with an ugly laugh.

"Oh, he don't need none o' your help, you bet. He's lit out. You don't need to worry 'bout Buck. He kin take car' o' hisse'f every time."

"But won't he come back sometime?"

"Can't say. Hard to tell."

"And Jim?" Michael's voice was sad.

"Jim, he's doin' time."

"I'm sorry!" said Michael.

A strange hush came over the dark group. Now why should this odd chap be sorry? No one else cared, unless it might be Jim, and Jim was caught. It was nothing to them.

"Now tell me about Janie—and little Bobs—." The questioner paused. His voice was low.

"Aw, cut it out!" snarled Sam irritably. "Don't come any high strikes on their account. They're dead, an' you can't dig 'em up an' weep over 'em. Hustle up an' tell us wot yer wantin' to do."

"Well, Sam," said Michael, trying to ignore the natural repulsion he felt at his onetime friend's last words, "suppose you take lunch with me tomorrow at twelve? Then we can talk over old times. I'll tell you about my life, and you must tell me what you're doing."

Sam was silent from sheer astonishment. Take lunch? Never in his life had he been invited out to lunch. Nor had he any desire for an invitation now.

"Where?" he asked after a silence so long Michael began to fear he wasn't going to answer.

Michael named a place not far away. He'd selected it that morning, It was clean, yet not too clean. The fare was far from princely, but it would do. And the locality was none too respectable. Michael was enough of a slum child still to know his guest would never go with him to a respectable restaurant;

moreover, he wouldn't have the wardrobe or the manners. He awaited Sam's answer breathlessly.

Sam gave an odd little laugh as if taken off guard. The place named seemed so harmless, and the whole matter of the invitation took on the form of a great joke.

"Well, I might," he drawled. "I won't make no promises, but I might, an' then again I might not. It's jes' as it happens. Ef I ain't there by twelve sharp you needn't wait. Jes' go ahead an' eat. I wouldn't want to spoil your digestion fer my movements."

"I'll wait!" said Michael. "You'll come, Sam. I know you will. Good night!"

And then he did an extraordinary thing. He put out his clean, strong hand, warm and healthy in the keenness of love, found the hardened grimy hand of his onetime companion, and gripped it in a hearty grasp.

Sam started back with the instant suspicion of attack and then stood ashamed and still. The grip of that firm, strong hand, the touch of brotherhood, a touch such as had never come to his life before since he was a little child, completed the work the smile had begun, and Sam knew the real Mickey was before him.

Then Michael walked swiftly down that narrow passage, at the opening of which the human shadows scattered silently and fled, to watch from other furtive doorways, down through the alley unmolested and out into the street again.

"The saints preserve us! Wot did I tell yez?" whispered Sal. "It's the angel all right, fer shure."

"I wonder wot he done to Sam," murmured the girl. "He's got his nerve all right, he sure has. Ain't he beautiful!"

Chapter 10

Michael went early to his lunch party. He was divided between wondering if his strange guest would appear and, if he did, what he should talk about and how he would pilot him through the embarrassing experience of the meal. One thing he was determined upon. He meant to find out if possible whether Sam knew anything about his, Michael's, origin. It was scarcely likely, and yet Sam might have heard some talk by older people in the neighborhood. His one great longing was to find out and clear his name of shame, if possible.

Another thing troubled Michael. He wasn't sure he'd know Sam even if he came. The glimpse he'd caught the night before when the matches were struck wasn't illuminating. He had a dim idea Sam was below medium height, with a thin, sallow face, small, narrow eyes, slouching gait, and a head not wide enough from front to back. He had a feeling Sam couldn't see all that should be seen. Sam didn't understand about education. Could he ever make him understand?

Sam came shuffling along at ten minutes after twelve. His sense of dignity wouldn't have allowed him to be on time. Besides, he wanted to see if Michael would wait as he'd said. It was part of testing him—not to prove he was really Mickey, but to see what stuff he was made of and how much he'd meant what he said. Michael was there, standing anxiously outside the eating house. He didn't enjoy the surroundings or the attention he was attracting. He was too well dressed for that locality, but these were his oldest clothes. He would have considered them shabby at college. He was getting worried his plan had failed. Then Sam slouched along, his hat drawn down, his hands in his pockets, wearing an air of indifference that almost amounted to effrontery. He greeted Michael as if they'd had no previous arrangement and met by chance. Nothing about his manner showed he'd come late to test him, but Michael knew intuitively it was so.

"Shall we go in now?" said Michael, smiling happily. He was glad Sam had come, repulsive in appearance though he was, hard of countenance and unfriendly in manner. He felt he was getting on a little in finding and helping his old friends and perhaps learning more of his own history.

"Aw, I donno's I care 'bout it!" drawled Sam, as if he hadn't intended going in all along and hadn't been anticipating the "feed" all morning.

"Yes, you better," said Michael, putting a friendly hand on Sam's shoulder. If he felt a repugnance to touching the tattered, greasy coat, he controlled it, remembering how he'd once worn garments far more tattered and filthy. His desire to uplift made him forget everything else.

It wasn't that Michael was so filled with love for this miserable creature who used to be his friend or so desired to renew old associations after long years of separation. It was the terrible need, the conditions, that appealed to his spirit because of what had once been done for him. It had come upon him without his knowledge, with the revival of old scenes and memories. But as with workers for humanity, it had gone so deeply into his soul as to make him forget there was even such a thing as sacrifice.

They passed into the restaurant: Michael in his well-made clothing and with his strikingly handsome face and gold hair attracting at once every eye in the place; Sam with an insolent air of assurance to cover a sudden embarrassment of pride at the company he was in.

Michael gave a generous order and talked pleasantly as they waited. Sam sat in low-browed silence, watching him furtively, almost disconcertingly.

When they reached the course of three kinds of pie and a dab of dirty-looking pink ice cream professing to be fresh strawberry, Michael looked keenly at his guest and asked, "What're you doing now, Sam? In business for yourself?"

Sam's eyes narrowed until they were almost eclipsed, though a steel glitter could be seen beneath the colorless lashes. A mask, impenetrable as lead, seemed to settle over his face, which had been gradually relaxing during the meal into a half-indulgent grin of interest in his odd host.

"Yas, I'm in business fer myself," he drawled at last, after scrutinizing the other's face to be sure of no underlying motive for the question.

"Newsstand?" asked Michael.

"Not eggs-act-ly!"

"What line?"

Sam finished his mince pie and began on the pumpkin before he answered. "Wal, there's sev'ral!"

"Is that so? Got more than one string to your bow? That's a good thing. You're better off than I am. I haven't looked around for a job yet. I thought I'd get at it tomorrow. I wanted to look you fellows up first before I got tied down to anything where I couldn't get off when I wanted to. Perhaps you can put me onto something. How about it?"

Michael hadn't once thought of going to Endicott for the position and help offered him, since the setting down he'd received from Mrs. Endicott. The time appointed for his going to Endicott's office was long since passed. He hadn't even turned the matter over in his mind since that awful night of agony and renunciation. Mrs. Endicott had told him her husband "had done enough for him," and he realized this was true. He would trouble him no more. Sometime perhaps the world would turn around so he could repay Endicott's kindness that he might not repay in money, but until then Michael would keep out of his way. It was the one little rag of pride he allowed himself from the shattering of his hopes.

Sam narrowed his eyes and looked Michael through, then slowly widened them again, with an expression of real interest.

"Say! Do you mean it?" he asked doubtfully. "Be you straight goods? Would you come back into de gang an' not snitch on us ner nothin'?"

"I'm straight goods, Sam, and I won't snitch!" said Michael quickly. He knew he could hope for no fellow's confidence if he "snitched."

"Wal, say, I've a notion to tell yeh!"

Sam attacked his ice cream. "How would a bluff game strike you?" he asked as the last mouthful of cream disappeared. He reached for the fresh cup of coffee the waiter had just set down.

"What sort?" asked Michael, wondering what he was coming on in the way of revelation, but resolving not to be horrified at anything. Sam mustn't suspect until he could understand the difference education had made in the way of looking at things.

"Wal, there's diffrunt ways. Cripple's purty good. Foot all tied up in bloody rags, arm an' hand tied up, a couple o' old crutches. I could lend the clo'es. They'd be short fer yeh, but that'd be all the better gag. We cud swap, an' I'd do the gen'lman act a while." He looked covetously at Michael's handsome brown tweeds. "Den you goes fom house to house, er you stands on de corner—"

"Begging!" said Michael aghast. His eyes were on his plate, and he was trying to control his voice, but something of his horror crept into his tones.

Sam felt it and hastened on apologetically. "Er ef you want to go it one better, keep on yer good cloes an' have the asthma bad. I know a feller what'll teach you how an' sell you the whistles to put in yer mouth. You've no notion how it works. You just go around in the subbubs tellin' you've only been out of the 'orspittal two days an' you walked all this way to get work an' couldn't get it, an' you want five cents to get back—see? Why, I know a feller—course he's been at it fer years an' has his regular beats—folks don't seem to remember—and he can work the ground over 'bout once in six months er so, and he's made high's thirty-eight dollars in a day at asthma work."

Sam paused triumphant to see what effect the statement had on his friend, but Michael's face was toward his coffee cup.

"Seems sort of small business for a man!" he said at last, his voice steady with control. "Don't believe I'd be good at that. Haven't you got something that's real work?"

Sam's eyes narrowed. "Ef I thought you was up to it," he murmured. "You'd be great with that angel face o' yourn. Nobody'd ever suspect you. You could wear them clo'es, too. But it's work all right, an' mighty resky. Ef I thought you was up to it—"

He continued to study Michael, and Michael, with innate instinct, felt his heart beat in discouraged thumps. What new deviltry was Sam about to propose?

"You used to be game, all right!" murmured Sam. "You never used to scare easy. Wal, I'll tell you," he said in answer to Michael's questioning eyes which searched his sharp wizened face.

"You see, it's a reg'ler business, an' you hev to learn. But I'd give you pinters—all you'd need to know. I'm pretty slick myself. There's tools to open things, an' you hev to be ready to 'xplain how you come thur an' jolly up a parlor maid per'aps. It's easy to hev made a mistake in the house er be a gas man er a plumber wot the boss sent up to look at the pipes. But night work's best pay after you get onto things. Thur's houses where you ken lay your han's on things goin' into the thousands an' lots ov um easy to get rid of without anybody findin' out. There's Buck—he used to be great at it. He taught the gang. The day he lit out he bagged a bit o' glass wuth tree tousand dollars, 'sides a whole handful of fivers an' tens wot he found lyin' on a dressin' table pretty as you please. Buck, he were a slick one at it. He'd be pleased to know you'd took up the work—"

Sam paused and eyed Michael with the first friendly gleam he'd shown in his eyes, and Michael, with his heart in a tumult of emotions and the quick color flooding brow and cheek, held himself in check. He mustn't speak too hastily. Perhaps he hadn't understood Sam's meaning.

"Where is Buck?" Michael looked Sam straight in the eye. The small pupils seemed to contract and shut out even his gaze.

"They ain't never got a trace of Buck," he said.

"But don't you know?" Something in Michael's look demanded an answer.

"I might, an' I might not."

Michael was still for several seconds watching Sam, each trying to understand the other.

"Do you think he'll come back where I can see him?" he asked at length.

"He might, an' he might not. 'T depends. Ef you was in th' bizness, he might. It's hard to say. 'T depends."

Michael watched Sam again thoughtfully.

"Tell me more about the business," he said at last, his lips compressed, his brows drawn into a frown of intensity.

"Thur ain't much more t' tell," said Sam, still sullen. "I ain't sure you're up to it."

"What do you mean by that?"

"Ain't sure you got de sand. You might turn faint and snitch." Sam leaned forward and spoke in low rapid sentences. "Wen we'd got a big haul, 'sposen you'd got into de house an' done de pinchin', and we got the stuff safe hid, an' you got tuk up? Would you snitch? Er would you take your pill like a man? That's what I'd want to be sure. Mickey would 'a' stood by the gang, but you—you've had a edicashun! They might go soft at college. I ain't much use fer edicated persons myself. But I'll give you a show ef you promise stiff not to snitch. We've gotta big game on tonight up on Madison Avenue, an' we're a man short. Dere's dough in it if we make it go all right. Rich man. Girl goin' out to a party tonight. She's goin' to wear some dimons wuth a penny. Hed it in de paper. Brung 'em home fom de bank this mornin'. One o' de gang watched de feller come out o' de bank. It's all straight so fur. It's a pretty big haul to let you in de first try, an' you'll hev to run all de risks. But ef you show your game we'll make it a bargain."

Michael held himself tensely and fought the desire to choke the fellow. He tried to remember he was the same Sam who had once divided a crust with him and whom he'd come to help and reflected that he might have been as bad himself if he hadn't been taken from the terrible environment of the slums and shown a better way. He knew that if for one fraction of a second he showed his horror at the evil plot or tried to stop it, all hope of reaching Sam, Buck, or the others was ended—and with it all hope of finding any stray links to his own history. Besides, though honor was strong in him and he'd never "snitch" on his companions, it would certainly be better to find out as much as possible about the scheme. There might be other ways of stopping such things besides "snitching."

Then suddenly his heart almost stopped beating. Madison Avenue! Sam had said Madison Avenue and a girl! What if they were planning to take Starr's jewels? He knew very little about such matters except what he'd read. It didn't occur to him that Starr wasn't yet "out" in society; that she would be too young to wear costly jewels and have her costume put in the paper. He only knew his heart was throbbing again painfully and that the fellow before him seemed too vile to live longer on the same earth with little, exquisite Starr.

He was quite still when Sam had finished. His face was white with emotion, and his eyes were blazing blue flames when he raised them to look at Sam. Then he became aware that his answer was awaited.

"Sam, do you mean burglary?" He tried to keep his voice low and steady as he spoke, but he felt as if he'd shouted the last word. The restaurant was almost empty now, and the waiters had retired behind the scenes amid a clatter of dishes.

"That's about as pretty a word as you can call it, I guess," said Sam, drawing back with a snarl as he saw the light in Michael's eyes.

Michael looked him through, and if a glance can burn, then surely Sam's soul shrank scorching into itself. But it was so brief that the brain keen only to earthly things hadn't analyzed it. Michael dropped his glance to the table again and began playing with his spoon and trying to get calm with a deep breath as he used to when he knew a hard spot in a ball game was coming.

"Well, why don't you speak? You 'fraid?" he said with a sneer a devil from the pit might have given.

Then Michael sat up calmly. His heart was beating steadily now, and he was facing his adversary.

"No! I'm not afraid, Sam, if there were any good reason for going. But you know I never could feel comfortable in getting my living off somebody else. It doesn't seem fair to the other fellow. They've got a right to the things they own, and I haven't. And because I might be smart enough to catch them napping and sneak away with what they prize doesn't make it right, either. Now that girl probably thinks a lot of her diamonds, you see, and it doesn't seem quite the manly thing for a big strong fellow like me to get them away from her, does it? Of course you may think differently, but I'd rather do some good hard work that would keep my muscles trim than to live off someone else.

"There's a pretty gray moss that grows where I went to college. It floats along a little seed blown in the air first and lodges on a tree limb and begins to fasten itself into the bark and grow and suck life from the big tree. It doesn't seem much at first, and it seems as if the big tree might spare enough juice to the little moss. But wait a few years and see what happens. The moss grows and drapes itself in long festoons all over that tree, and the first thing you know, that tree has lost its green leaves and stands up stark and dead with nothing on its bare branches but that old gray moss which has to die, too, because it has nothing to live on any longer. It never learned to gather any juice for itself. They call the moss a parasite. I couldn't be a human parasite, Sam. You may feel differently about it, but I really couldn't."

Michael's eyes had grown dreamy and lost their fire as he remembered the dear South and dead sentinel pines with their waving gray festoons against the blue sky. As he talked he saw the great outdoors again where he'd wandered so many years free and happy, free from humanity's burdens that pressed sorely now. A great longing to fly back to it all, away from the sorrow and degradation and shame, filled his heart, leaped into his eyes, caught and fascinated the attention of the listening Sam, who understood little of the peroration. He'd never heard of a parasite. He didn't know he'd always been a human parasite. He was merely astonished and fascinated by the passion and appeal in Michael's face as he spoke.

"Say!" he said in a tone almost of admiration. "Is that wot edicashun done fer you?"

"Perhaps," said Michael pleasantly, "though I think I always felt a bit that way, Sam. I just didn't know how to say it."

"Wal, you allus was odd!" muttered Sam half apologetically. "I couldn't see it that way myself, as you say, but o' course it's your fun'ral! Ef you kin scratch up enough grub bein' a tree, why, that's your lookout. Moss is good 'nough fer me fer de present."

Michael beamed his wonderful smile on Sam. "Perhaps you'll see it my way someday, Sam, and then we can get a job together!"

There was so much comradery in the tone and so much brilliancy in the smile that Sam forgot to be sullen.

"Wal, mebbe," he chuckled, "but I don't see no edicashun comin' my way dis late day, so I guess I'll git along de way I be."

"It isn't too late yet, Sam. There's more than one way of getting an education. It doesn't always come through college."

After a little more talk, in which Sam promised to find out if Michael could visit Jim in his temporary retirement from the law-abiding world and Michael promised to visit Sam in the alley again at an appointed time, the two separated.

Then Michael went forth to reconnoiter and to guard the Endicott house.

With no thought of any personal danger, Michael laid his plans. Before sundown he was on hand, having considered all visible and invisible means of ingress to the house. He watched from a suitable distance all who came and went. He saw Mr. Endicott come home. He waited till the evening drew near when a luxurious limousine stopped before the door, assured himself only Mrs. Endicott had gone out. A little later Mr. Endicott also left the house. Starr hadn't gone out. He felt he needed doubly to watch now as she was alone with only the servants.

Up and down he walked. No one passed the Endicott house unwatched by him. None came forth or went in without his noting it.

The evening passed, and the master and mistress of the house returned. One by one the lights went out. Even the servants' rooms were dark at last. The night deepened, and the stars thickened overhead.

The policeman's whistle sounded through the quiet streets, and the city seemed to be sinking into a brief repose. It was long past midnight, and still Michael kept up his patrol. Up this side of the street, down that, around the corner, through the alley at the back where "de kids" had stood in silent respect toward his window years ago, back to the avenue again and on around. With his cheery whistle and steady ringing step he awakened no suspicion, even when he came near a policeman. Besides, no lurkers of the dark would steal out while he was so noisily in the neighborhood.

And so he watched the night through, till morning broke and sunshine flooded the window of the room where Starr, unconscious of his vigil, lay sleeping.

Busy milk wagons were making their rounds, and sleepy workmen with dinner pails slung over their arms were striding to their day's work through the morning coolness, as Michael turned his steps toward his lodging.

Broad morning was upon them, and deeds of darkness could be no more. The night was over. Nothing had happened. Starr was safe. He went home and to sleep well pleased. He might not companion with her, but it was his privilege to guard her from unsuspected evils. That was one joy that couldn't be taken from him by the taint upon him. Perhaps his being a child of the slums might yet help guard her life from harm.

Chapter 11

The first week in September Michael, passing through a crowded thoroughfare, came face-to-face with Mr. Endicott.

The days had passed into weeks, and Michael hadn't gone near his benefactor. He'd felt he must drop out of his old friend's life until he could show his gratitude for the past. Meanwhile he hadn't been idle. His winning smile and clear eyes had been his passport, and after a few preliminary experiences he'd secured a position as salesman in a large department store. His college diploma and a letter from the college president were his references. He wasn't earning much, just enough to pay his absolute expenses and a bit over. But he was gaining experience.

This Saturday morning of the first week of September he'd come to the store as usual but found that because of a firm member's sudden death the store would be closed for the day.

He was wondering how to spend his holiday and wishing he might get out and breathe the open air under waving trees and listen to the birds and water and wind. He was half tempted to squander a few cents and go to Coney Island or up the Hudson, anywhere to get out of the grinding, noisy, tempestuous city. Its sin and burden pressed on his heart night and day because of that from which he'd been saved and yet couldn't save others.

Then out of a doorway rushed a man toward a waiting automobile and almost knocked Michael over in his progress.

"Oh! It's you, young man! At last! Well, I'd like to know what you've done with yourself all these weeks and why you didn't keep your appointment with me."

"Oh!" said Michael, pleasure and shame striving together in his face. He could see the man wasn't angry and was relieved to find him.

"Where are you going, son?" Endicott's tone had already changed from gruffness to kindly welcome. "Jump in and run down to the wharf with me while you give an account of yourself. I'm going down to see Mrs. Endicott off to Europe. She's taking Starr over to school this winter. I'm late already, so come on."

Michael seemed to have no choice and stepped into the car, which whirled through the maze of humanity and machinery toward the regions where the oceangoing steamers harbored.

His heart was in a tumult at once, both of embarrassed joy to be with the man who'd done so much for him and of eager anticipation. Starr! Would he see Starr again? That thought was uppermost in his mind. He hadn't yet realized she was going away for a long time.

All spring he'd kept guard over the house in Madison Avenue. Not all night, of course, but hovering about there now and then, and nightly for two weeks after he'd talked with Sam. Always he walked that way before retiring and looked toward the window where a soft light burned. Then they'd gone to the seashore and the mountains, and the house had put on solemn shutters and lain asleep. Michael knew from a stray paragraph in the society column of the daily paper he happened to read.

Toward the end of August, he'd made a round through Madison Avenue every night to see if they'd returned home, and for a week the shutters had been down and the lights burning as of old. It was good to know his charge was back safely. And now he was to see her.

"Well! Give an account of yourself. Were you trying to keep out of my sight? Why didn't you come to my office?"

Michael looked him straight in the eye with his honest, clear gaze that showed no sowing of wild oats, no dissipation or desire to escape friendly espionage. He decided in a flash that this man should never know the blow his beautiful, haughty wife had dealt him. What she said was true, and he would give the real reason why he hadn't come.

"Because I thought you'd done for me far more than I deserved already, and I didn't wish to be any further burden to you."

"The dickens you did!" exclaimed Endicott. "You good-for-nothing rascal! Didn't you know you'd be more of a burden running off like that without a trace so I could hunt you up, than if you'd done as I told you? Here I've been worrying unnecessarily about you. I thought you'd fallen among thieves or gone to the dogs. Don't you know it's unpardonable to run off from a man who's told you he wants to see you? I thought I made you understand I had more than a passing interest in your welfare!"

The color came into the fine, strong face and a pained expression in his eyes.

"I'm sorry, sir. I didn't think of it that way. I thought you felt some kind of an obligation. I never felt so, but you said you did, and I thought if I got out of your way I wouldn't trouble you anymore."

"Trouble me! Why, son, I like to be troubled once in a while by something besides getting money and spending it. You never gave me a shadow of trouble, except these last weeks when you disappeared and I couldn't do anything for you. You've somehow crept into my life, and I can't get you out. I don't want to. But, boy, if you felt that way, what made you come to New York at all? You didn't feel that way the night you came to my house to dinner."

Michael's eyes owned this was true, but his firm lips showed he would never betray the real reason for the change.

"I—didn't—realize—sir!"

"Realize? Realize what?"

"I didn't realize the difference between my station and yours, sir. There was nothing during my years in school to make me know. I'm a child of the slums"—unconsciously he drifted into words from Mrs. Endicott's speech—"and you belong to a fine old family. I don't know what terrible things are in my blood. You have riches and a name beyond reproach." He saw the words in an article he'd read the evening before and felt they fitted the man and the occasion. He didn't know he was quoting. They'd become part of his thoughts.

"I might make the riches if I tried hard," he held up his head proudly, "but I could never make the name. I will always be a child of the slums, no matter what I do!"

"Child of the fiddlesticks!" interrupted Endicott. "Wherever did you get that rot? It sounds as if you've been attending society functions and listening to their twaddle. It doesn't matter what you're the child of, if you've a mind to be a man. This is a free country, son, and you can be and climb where you please. Tell me—where did you get all these ideas?"

Michael looked down. "In a number of places."

"Where?"

"For one thing, I've been down to the alley where I used to live."

The eyes were looking into his now, and Endicott felt a strange swelling of pride that he'd had a hand in the making of this young man.

"Well?"

"I know what you've taken me from—I can never be what you are!"

"Therefore you won't try to be anything? Is that it?"

"Oh, no! I'll try to be all I can, but—I don't belong with you. I'm of another class—"

"Oh, bosh! Cut that out, son! Real men don't talk like that. You're a better man now than any of the pedigreed dudes I know of. As for taints in the blood, I could tell you about some of the sons of great men who have taints as bad as any child of the slums. Young man, you can be whatever you set out to be in this world! Remember that."

"Everyone doesn't feel that way," said Michael with conviction, though he was conscious of great pleasure in Endicott's hearty words.

"Who, for instance?" said Endicott, looking at him sharply.

Michael was silent.

"Who?" asked the insistent voice once more.

"The world!"

"The world is brainless. You can make the world think what you like, son. Remember that! Here we are. Would you like to come aboard?"

But Michael stood back.

"I'll wait here," he said gravely. He realized Mrs. Endicott would be there. He mustn't intrude, not even to see Starr. Besides, she'd made it a point of honor for him to keep away from her daughter. He had no choice but to obey.

"Very well," said Endicott, "but see you don't lose yourself again. I want to see you about something. I'll not be long. It must be nearly time for starting." He hurried away, and Michael stood on the edge of the throng looking up at the great floating village.

It was his first view of an oceangoing steamer at closer range, and everything about it interested him. He wished he might have gone aboard and looked the vessel over. He'd like to know about the engines and see the cabins and especially the steerage he'd read so much about. But perhaps he'd have another opportunity. He'd go to Ellis Island, too, and see the emigrants as they entered the country, seeking a new home where they'd been led to expect to find comfort and plenty of work. Finding none, most of them landed inevitably in the city slums, where the population was already congested and where vice and disease preyed upon them. Michael had been spending enough time in the alleys of the metropolis to be deeply interested in the city's problems and deeply pained by its sorrows.

But he wasn't thinking altogether of the masses and the classes as he stood in the sunlight and gazed at the great vessel about to plow its way over the waters. He was realizing that somewhere within those many windowed cabins was a bright-faced girl, the only one of womankind in the earth his tender thoughts had hovered about. Would he catch a glimpse of her face before she left for the winter? She was going to school, her father said. How could they bear to send her across the water from them? A whole winter was a long time, and yet it would pass. Thirteen years had passed since he left New York, and he was back. It wouldn't be as long as that. She would return and need him perhaps. He would be there and ready when he was needed.

The lips were set firmly, with the patient, fearless lines of a soldier in the boy's face, and rugged strength showed forth. If he'd been born in aristocratic circles he would have been the idol of society, the spoiled of all who knew him. Even now those in sight were staring at him, and more than one pair of marine glasses from the first cabin deck were pointed at him; but he stood deep in his thoughts and utterly unconscious of his attraction.

It was only a moment before the first warning came, and people crowded on the wharf side of the decks, while others hurried down the gangplank. Michael watched the confusion with eagerness, his eyes searching the decks for Starr.

When the last warning was given, as the gangplank was about to be hauled up, Mr. Endicott hurried down, and Michael suddenly saw her face in the crowd on the deck above, with her mother's haughtily pretty face just behind her.

Without realizing what he was doing, Michael moved through the crowd until he stood close behind Starr's father. Then all at once he became aware that her eyes were upon him, and she recognized him.

He lifted his hat and stood in reverent attitude, his eyes glowing eloquently, his face paying her tribute as plainly as words could have. The noonday sun burnished his hair with its aureole flame, and more than one of the passengers called attention to the sight.

"See that man down there!" exclaimed a woman behind Mrs. Endicott. "Isn't he magnificent! He has a head and shoulders like a young god!" She spoke as if her acquaintance with gods was wide, and her neighbors turned to look.

"See, Mama," whispered Starr, glowing with pleasure. "They're talking about Michael."

Then the eyes turned sharply and recognized him. "You don't mean to tell me that upstart has dared to come down and see us off. The impudence! I'm glad your father had enough sense not to bring him on board. He'd probably have come if he'd let him. Come away, Starr. He simply shall not look at you that way!"

"What! Come away while Papa is standing there watching us out of sight? I simply couldn't. What would Papa think? And, besides, I don't see why Michael shouldn't come if he likes. I think it was nice of him. I wonder why he hasn't been to the house to explain why he never came for that horseback ride."

"You're a silly, ignorant girl, or you'd understand he has no business coming to our house, and he knows it. I want you to stop looking in that direction at once. I simply won't have him devouring you with his eyes that way. I'd like to go back and tell him what I think of him. Starr, stop, I tell you!"

But the noise of the starting drowned her words, and Starr, her cheeks like roses, was waving a handkerchief and smiling and throwing kisses. The kisses were for her father, but the smiles, the glances, and the waving bit of cambric were for Michael, and they all traveled through the air together, drenching the bright uncovered head of the boy with sweetness. His eyes gave her greeting and thanks and parting all in one in that brief moment, and her graceful form and dainty vivid face were engraved on his memory in quick sweet blows of pain, as he realized she was going from him.

Slowly the great vessel glided out upon the waters and grew smaller and smaller. The crowd on the wharf was breaking away and hurrying back to business or home or society. Still Michael stood gazing, with that illumined expression on his face.

Endicott, a mist on his own glasses at parting from his beloved baby, saw the boy's face as it were the face of an angel and was half startled, turning away embarrassedly as though he'd intruded upon a soul at prayer; then he looked again.

"Come, son!" he said huskily. "It's over! We better be getting back. Step in."

The ride to the office was a silent one. Somehow Endicott didn't feel like talking. There had been some annoying differences between him and his wife, and a strange belated regret that he'd let Starr go away for a foreign education was eating into his heart. Michael, on his part, was reliving the passing of the vessel and the blessing of the parting.

Back in the office, however, all was different. Among the familiar walls and gloomy desks and chairs, Endicott was himself and talked business.

"What are you doing with yourself? Working? What at? H'm! How'd you get there? Like it? Satisfied to do that all your life? You're not? Well, what's your line? Any ambitions? You should have got some notion in college of what you're fit for. Have you thought what you'd like to do in the world?"

Michael hesitated, then looked up with his clear, direct, challenging gaze.

"Two things," he said. "I want to earn money and buy some land in the country, and I want to know about laws."

"Do you mean you want to be a lawyer?"

"Yes."

"What makes you think you'd be a success as a lawyer?"

"Oh, I might not be a success, but I need to know law. I want to try to stop some things that shouldn't be."

"H'm!" grunted Endicott disapprovingly. "Don't try the reform game; it doesn't pay. But if you feel that way you'll probably be all right to start. That'll work itself off and be a good foundation. There's no reason why you should not be a lawyer if you choose, but you can't study law selling calico. You might get there someday, if you stick to your ambition. But you'd be pretty old before you were ready to practice if you started at the calico counter and worked your way up through everything you came to. Well, I can get you into a law office right away. How soon can you honorably get away from where you are? Two weeks? Well, just wait a minute."

Endicott called up a number on the telephone by his side, and there followed a conversation, brief, pointed, but in terms Michael could barely follow. He gathered that a lawyer named Holt, a friend of Mr. Endicott's, was being asked to take him into his office to read law.

"It's all right, son," said Endicott as he hung up the receiver and whirled around from the phone. "You're to present yourself at the office as soon as you're free. This is the address—." He hurriedly scribbled something on a card and handed it to him.

"Oh, thank you!" said Michael. "But I didn't mean to have you take any more trouble for me. I can't be dependent on you any longer. You've done so much for me."

"Bosh!" said Endicott. "I'm not taking any trouble. And you're not dependent on me. Be as independent as you like. You're not quite twenty-one, are you? Well, I told you you were my boy until you were of age, and I suppose there's nothing to hinder me doing as I will with my own. All I've done for you so far has paid well, and I feel the investment was a good one. You'll get a small salary for some office work while you're studying, so after you're twenty-one you can be on your own if you like. Till then I claim the privilege of giving you a few orders. Now that's settled. Where are you stopping? I don't intend to lose sight of you again."

Michael gave him the street and number. Endicott frowned.

"That's not a good place. I don't like the neighborhood. If you're going to be a lawyer, you must start in right. Here, try this place. Tell the woman I sent you. One of my clerks used to board there."

He handed Michael another address.

"Won't that cost a lot?" asked Michael, studying the card.

"No more than you can afford," said Endicott, "and remember, I'm giving orders until your majority."

Michael beamed his brilliant smile at his benefactor.

"It's like a real father!" said the boy, deeply moved. "I can never repay you. I can never forget it."

"Well, don't!" said Endicott. "Let's turn to the other thing. What do you want land for?"

Michael's face sobered instantly.

"For an experiment I want to try," he said without hesitation, and then his eyes lit up. "I can do it now, soon, perhaps, if I work hard. You see, I studied agriculture in college."

"The dickens you did!" exclaimed Endicott. "Why did you do that?"

"Well, it was there, and I could, and I wanted to know about it."

"H'm!" said Endicott. "I wonder what some of my pedigreed million-dollar friends' sons would think of that? Well, go on."

"Why, that's all," said Michael, laughing happily. "I studied it, and I want to try it and see what I can do with it. I want to buy a farm."

"How would you manage to be a farmer and a lawyer both?"

"Well, I thought there might be a little time after hours to work, and I could tell others how—"

"Oh, I see; you want to be a gentleman farmer," said Endicott, laughing. "I understand that's expensive business."

"I think I could make it pay, sir," said Michael, shutting his lips with his firm challenge. "I'd like to try."

Endicott looked at him quizzically for a minute and then, whirling around in his office chair, he reached out his hand to a pigeonhole and took out a deed.

"I've a mind to let you try," said Endicott, chuckling as if it were a good joke. "Here's a little farm down in Jersey. It's swampy and thick with mosquitoes. I understand it won't grow a beanstalk. There are twelve acres and a tumbledown house on it. I had to take it in settlement of a mortgage. The man's dead, and there's nothing but the farm to lay hands on. He hadn't even a chick or a child to leave his debt to. I don't want the farm and can't sell it without a lot of trouble. I'll give it to you. You may consider it a birthday present. If you'll pay the taxes I'll be glad to get it off my hands. That'll be something for you to be independent about."

He touched a bell, and a boy appeared.

"Take this to Jowett and tell him to have a deed made out to Michael Endicott and attend to the property transfer, nominal sum. Understand?"

The boy said, "Yes, sir," and disappeared with the paper.

"But I can't take a present like that from you after all you've done for me," gasped Michael, a granite determination showing in his blue eyes.

"Nonsense," said Endicott. "Other men give their sons automobiles when they come of age. May I not give you a farm if I like? Besides, it's of no account. I want to get rid of it, and I want to see what you'll make of it. I'd like to amuse myself seeing you try your experiment."

"If you'll let me pay you for it little by little."

"Suit yourself after you've become a great lawyer," said Endicott laughing, "but not till then—remember. There, cut it out, son! I don't want to be thanked. Here's the description of the place and directions how to get there. It isn't many miles away. If you've got a half holiday, run down and look it over. It'll keep you out of mischief. There's nothing like an ambi█████keep people out of mischief. Run along now—I haven't another minute to spare. But mind you turn up at Holt's office this day in two weeks and report to me afterward how you like it. I don't want to lose sight of you again."

Another man entered on business, cutting short the interview, and Michael, bestowing an agonizingly happy grip on Endicott's hand and a brilliant smile, took his directions and hurried out into the street.

Chapter 12

W ith the precious paper in his hand, Michael hurried to the Des-
Brosses Ferry. Would there be a train? It was almost two o'clock.
He'd had no lunch, but what of that? He had in his heart what
made mere eating seem unnecessary. The experiences of the past two hours
had lifted him above earthly things. And a farm, a real farm! Could it be true?
Had his wish come true so soon? He could scarcely wait for the car to carry
him or the boat to puff its way across the water. He felt as if he must fly to
see his new possession. And Mr. Endicott had said he might pay for it sometime when he got to be a great lawyer. He had no doubt he would get there if
such a thing were possible, and, anyhow, he meant to pay for that ground.
Meanwhile it was his. He wasn't a poor nobody after all. He owned land and
a house.

His face was a mingling of delightful emotions as he stood by the ferry rail
and let his imagination leap ahead of him. The day was perfect. It had rained the
night before, and everything, even the air, seemed newly washed for a fresh trail
at living. The sunlight shimmered on the water, and every wavelet sparkled like
a jewel. Michael forgot for the moment the sorrow and misery of the crowded
city he was leaving behind him. For this afternoon at least, he was a boy again
wandering off into the open.

His train was being called as he stepped from the ferry. He hurried aboard
and was soon speeding through the open country, with glimpses of the sea, as
the train neared the beach. They passed beautiful resorts, private villas, great
hotels, and miles of cottages set in a green terrace with glowing autumn flowers in boxes or bordering the paths.

Michael watched everything with interest. This was the land of his new possession. Whatever was growing here would likely grow on his place if properly planted and cared for. Before this, flowers had had little part in his farming
scheme, but as soon as he saw the brilliant display he resolved to have some
also. And flowers would sell as well as, if not better than, vegetables if properly marketed.

That vivid hedge of scarlet and gold—he thought they were called dahlias—
would take up little room and make his new place beautiful. Farther on, one
great white cottage spread its veranda wings on either side to a tall fringe of
pink, white, and crimson cosmos. Then a rambling gray stone piece of quaint
architecture, with low sloping roofs of mossy green and velvet lawn creeping
down even to the white beach sands, was set about with flaming scarlet sage.
It was a revelation to the boy who had never seen the like.

Nature in its wildness and original beauty had been in Florida; New York
was all pavements and buildings with a window box here and there. He as yet
knew nothing of country homes in their luxury and perfection, except from

magazine pictures. All along he was picking out features he meant someday to transfer to his farm.

After three he reached the station and walked a good fifteen minutes to the farm, but every step was a delight.

Pearl Beach, they called the station. The beach was half a mile from the railroad, and an odd straggling town, mostly cottages and a few stores, hovered between railroad and beach. A river, broad and shallow, wound about the village and lost itself in the ocean's wideness.

Here and there a white sail flew across its gleaming center, and fishermen in little boats sat at their idle task. What if his land should touch this bonny stream!

Too eager to wait for investigation, he stopped a passing stranger and questioned him. Yes, the river was salt. It had tides with the sea, too. They had great fishing and sailing, and some preferred bathing there to the ocean. Yes, Old Orchard Farm was on its bank. It had a river frontage of several hundred feet, but it was over a mile back from the beach.

The stranger wanted to linger and gossip about the death of the former owner of Old Orchard and its probable fate now that the mortgage had been foreclosed, but Michael, with a happy light in his eyes, thanked him courteously and hurried on. He felt like a bird set free. He breathed in the strong salt air with delight.

And the city's burden came to him again, the city with all its noise and folly and sin; with its smells and heat and lack of air; with its crowded, suffering, awful humanity, herded together like cattle and living in conditions worse than the beasts of the fields. If he could only bring them out here, some of them at least, and show them what God's earth was like! Ah!

His heart beat wildly at the thought! It wasn't new. He'd harbored it ever since his first visit to the alley. It was his great secret, his much-hoped-for experiment. This little farm would open the way. Money would be needed, of course, and where would it come from? But he could work. He was strong. He would give his young life for his people—save them from their ignorance and despair. At least he could save some; even one would be worthwhile.

So he mused as he hurried on, eyes and mind open to all he saw.

No fence stood in front of Old Orchard Farm. A white road bordered with goldenrod and wild asters met the scraggly grass that matted and tangled itself beneath the gnarled apple trees. A grassy rutted wagon track curved itself between the trees up to the house set far back from the road. A passing man identified the place for Michael.

The house was of weather-beaten unpainted clapboards, its roof of curled and mossy shingles, doubtless leaking, and patched here and there. A crazy veranda ambled across the front. Inside he found a long, low room with an old-fashioned chimney place wide enough to sit in; a square south room that must have been a dining room because of the painted cupboard with empty shelves gazing between half-open doors; and a small kitchen, not much more than a shed. In the long room a staircase twisted up to the four rooms under the leaky roof. It was all empty and desolate, except for an old cot bed and a broken chair. The floors had a sagging, shaky appearance. The doors quaked when opened. The windows were cobwebby and dreary. Yet it looked to the new householder's eyes like a palace. He saw it in light of future possibilities and gloried in it. That chimney place. How would it look with a great log burning in it and a rug and rocking chair before it?

What would Aunt Sally, perhaps, say to it when he got it fixed up? Could he ever coax her to leave her dirty doorstep and her drink and come out here to live? And how would he manage it all if he could? There would have to be something to feed her with and buy the rug and the rocking chair. And first of all there would have to be a bathtub. Aunt Sally would need to be purified before she could enter the portals of this ideal cottage, when he'd made it as he wanted it to be. Paint and paper would make wonderful transformations, for he'd often helped remodel the college rooms during summer vacations. He'd watched the workmen and finally taken a hand. This habit of watching and helping had taught him many things. But where were paper and paint and time coming from? Ah, well, leave that to the future. He would find a way. Yesterday he didn't have the house or the land for it to stand on. It had come, and the rest would follow in their time.

He went happily about planning for a bathroom. They would need water power. He had seen windmills on other places he passed. That was perhaps the solution, but windmills cost money. Still—all in good time.

A tumbledown barn and chicken house stood in the back near a scraggly attempt at a garden: a strawberry bed overgrown with weeds, a sickly cabbage lifting its head bravely, a gaunt row of currant bushes, another of raspberries. A broken fence was just beyond that, with a stretch of soggy bog land to the right. Then the farm trailed off into desolation, ending in a charming grove of thick trees down by the river's bank.

Michael surveyed it carefully, noted the exposure of the land, kicked the sandy soil to examine its unpromising state, walked all around the bog, and tried to remember what he'd read about cranberry bogs. He wondered if the saltwater came up here—was it good or bad for cranberries? And he wondered if cowpeas grew in Jersey and if they'd do for a fertilizing crop as they did in Florida. Then he walked through the lovely woods, smelling the breath of pines. They weren't like the giant pines of the South but were sweeter and more beautiful in their form.

He went down to the river's brink and looked across. Not a soul was in sight, and nothing moved except a distant sail fleeing out to the sea. He remembered what the man had said about bathing and, yielding to an irresistible impulse, was soon swimming out across the water. To propel himself with strong, graceful strokes through the water gave him a new lease on life. A bird shot up into the air with a wild sweet note, and he felt like answering to its melody. He whistled softly in imitation of its voice, and the bird answered, and again and again they called across the water.

But a look toward the west where the water was crimsoning already with the setting sun warned him his time was short. He swam back to the sheltered nook where he'd left his clothes, and improvising a towel from his handkerchief he dressed rapidly. The last train left at seven. If he didn't wish to spend the night in his new, uninhabitable abode, he must make good time. It was later than he'd thought, and he wanted to go back to the station by way of the beach if possible, though it was out of his way. He must stand on the shore once, look out across it, and know how it looked near his own house.

He hurried through the grove and across the farm to the eastern edge. Looking beyond the broken fence that marked the bounds of the bog and over the waste of salt grass, he could see the white waves tumbling to get past one another. He took the fence at a bound, made good time over the uncertain footing of the marsh grass, and was soon standing on the broad smooth beach with the open stretch of ocean before him.

It was the first time he'd ever stood on the seashore, and the awe that filled him was great. But beyond any other sensation came the thought that Starr, his beautiful Starr, was out there on that vast ocean, tossing in a tiny boat. For now the great steamer that had seemed so large and palatial had dwindled in his mind to a frail toy, and he was filled with a nameless fear for her. His little Starr out there on that fearful deep, with only that cold-eyed mother to take care of her. A wild desire to fly to her and bring her back possessed him, a thrilling, awesome something he'd never known before. He stood speechless before it.

Then he looked up and said aloud, "Oh, God, I love her!"

He faced the thought with solemn joy and pain for an instant, then turned and fled from it down the purpling sands, fleeing, yet carrying his secret with him.

All the way home the new thought surged over him: He loved her, and she could never be his. It was beautiful, but it was agonizing. He recalled how beautiful she was as she waved farewell. And some of her smiles were for him, he was sure. He knew the kisses were for her father, and yet they were blown freely his way, and she looked pleased at his presence. He saw the same look in her eyes she wore that day in the college chapel when she threw precaution to the wind and put her arms about his neck and kissed him. His young heart thrilled with a deep joy over the memory of it. It was wonderful that she'd done it, when he was what he was, a child of the slums! The words seemed burned upon his soul now, part of his life. He wasn't worthy of her, not worthy to receive her favor.

Yet he closed his eyes, leaning his hand against the window frame as the train hurried along, and saw again the bright lovely face, the dainty fingers blowing kisses, the lips wreathed in smiles, and knew some of the farewell was surely meant for him. He forgot the beautiful villas along the way, forgot to watch for the lights or care how the cottages looked at evening. Whenever the track veered toward the sea and gave a glimpse of gray sky and yawning ocean with an occasional point of light to make the darkness blacker, he seemed to know and, opening his eyes, strained to look across it. Out there in the blackness somewhere was his Starr, and he might not go to her or she come to him. That gray, impassable sky and sea of impossibility would always lie between them.

As he neared New York, however, these thoughts dropped from him. Standing on the ferryboat, with the city's million twinkling lights and the looming blackness of buildings towering against the illumined sky, the people called to him. Over there in the darkness, swarming in the fetid atmosphere of a crowded court, were thousands like him—yes, for he was one of them. He belonged there. They were his kind, and he must help them!

Then his mind went to the farm and his plans, and he entered back into the grind of life and assumed its burden with the sweet pain of his secret locked in his heart.

Chapter 13

S am, have you ever been in the country?"

Michael asked the question. They were sitting in a small, dreary room he could afford to rent in a house on the edge of the alley. Not that he'd moved there! He couldn't have endured life if he'd had to spend it in that atmosphere. He still kept his little fourth-floor back in the dismally respectable street. He hadn't gone to the place Endicott recommended, because he found the difference he'd have to pay would enable him to rent this room near the alley. For his purposes this seemed necessary now.

The weather was growing too cold for him to meet with his new old acquaintances of the alley outside, and it was little better indoors even if he could have endured the dirt and squalor of those apartments that would have been open to him. Besides, he had a great longing to show them something brighter than their own forlorn houses.

A settlement house a few blocks away hadn't drawn the dwellers in this particular alley. They were sunken too low, perhaps, or the settlement workers had found more hopeful quarters in which to work, for the city was wide and deep and dark. Michael knew little about the settlement house. He'd read of such things and had glanced shyly toward its workers now and then. But as yet he knew none of them, though they'd heard of the "angel-man of the alley" and were curious to check him out.

But Michael's enterprise and ways of working were his own. He had reached back into his childhood years and found out from his inner consciousness what he'd needed then, and now he was going to try to give it to some other "kids" as forlorn and friendless as he'd been. He couldn't do much, but what he could do he would and as soon as possible.

So he'd rented this tiny room and purified it. He'd compelled Sam to help him. And that compelling was almost a modern miracle, wrought by radiant smiles and a firm grip on Sam's shoulder when he told him what he wanted done.

Together they'd swept and scrubbed and scraped the dirt from that room.

"I don't see what you're makin' sech a fuss about dirt fer!" grumbled Sam as he arose from his knees after scrubbing the floor for the fourth time. "It's what we're all made of, dey say, an' nobuddy'll know de diffrunce."

"Just see if they won't, Sam," Michael said as he polished off the door he'd been cleaning. "See there—how nice that looks! You didn't know that paint was gray, did you? It looked brown before; it was so thick with dirt. Now we're ready for paint and paper!"

With soap and water they'd worked night after night till very late, and Sam actually let a well-planned, promising raid go by because he was so interested in what he was doing and was ashamed to tell Michael of the plan.

Sam had never helped paper a room; in fact, he'd probably never seen a room with clean, fresh paper on its walls, unless in some house he'd entered unlawfully. When this one was arrayed at last in its newness, he stood back and surveyed it in awe.

Michael had chosen paper the color of sunshine, for the court, the alley, the room, and even the souls of the people were dark. They must have light and brightness if he would win them to better things. Besides, the paper was only five cents a roll, the cheapest he could find in the city. Michael had learned during college vacations how to put it on. He made Sam wash and wash his hands before he handled the delicate paper.

"De paper'll jest git dirty right away," Sam said, grumbling, though he washed his hands and his eyes glowed as they used to when a child at a rare "find" in the gutter.

"Wot'll you do when it gits dirty?" demanded Sam.

"Put on some clean," said Michael. "Besides, we must learn to have clean hands and keep it clean. I wish we had some curtains. They had thin white curtains at college."

"Are you makin' a college fer us?" Sam asked, sharply.

"Well, in a way, perhaps. You know I want you to have all the advantages I had as far as I can get them."

Sam only whistled and looked perplexed, but he was doing more serious thinking than he'd ever done.

So the two had worked and planned, and now tonight the work was about finished. The walls reflected the yellow of the sunshine, and the woodwork was painted white enamel. Michael had just put on the last gleaming coat.

"We can give it another coat when it looks a little dirty," he'd remarked to Sam.

"Dey better hev dere han's clean," Sam, frowning, had replied.

The floor was painted gray. There was no rug. Michael felt its lack and meant to remedy it as soon as possible, but rugs cost money. A small coal stove was set up and polished till it shone, and a fire was laid ready to start. They hadn't needed it while they were working hard. The furniture was a wooden table painted gray with a cover of bright cretonne, two wooden chairs, and three boxes. Michael had collected these furnishings carefully and economically, for he had to sacrifice many small comforts to get them.

On the walls were two or three good pictures fastened by brass tacks and some of the gray moss and pine branches from Michael's room. In the central wall appeared one of Michael's beloved college pennants. Those who entered the room understood it to be the symbol of what made the difference between them and "the angel," and they looked at it reverently.

At the windows two lengths of snowy cheesecloth, crudely hemmed by Michael, were tacked up in pleats with brass-headed tacks and tied back with narrow yellow ribbons. This had been the last touch, and Sam sat looking thoughtfully at the stiff angular bows when Michael asked if he'd ever been in the country.

"Sure!" said Sam scornfully. "Went wid de Fresh Air folks wen I were a kid."

"What did you think of it?"

"Don't tink much! Too empty. Nothin' doin'! Good 'nough fer kids. Never again fer me."

Three months had passed since Michael had made his memorable first visit to Old Orchard Farm. For weeks he'd worked shoulder to shoulder every evening with Sam, and as yet no word of that plan nearest his heart had been spoken. This was his first attempt to open the subject.

That Sam had developed a certain respect and fondness for him he was sure, though it was never expressed in words. Always he either objected to any plan Michael suggested or was extremely indifferent and wouldn't promise to be on hand. He was almost always there, however, and Michael had realized Sam was proud of his friendship and at least somewhat interested in his plans to better the court.

"Other things in the country make up for the city's stir," said Michael thoughtfully.

This was the first unpractical conversation he'd tried to hold with Sam. He'd been leading him up through the various stages from dirt and degradation, by means of soap and water, then paper and paint, and now they'd reached the doorway of nature's school. Michael wanted to introduce Sam to the great outdoors. For, though Sam had lived all his life outdoors, it had been a world of brick walls and stone pavements, with little sky and almost no water. Not a green thing in sight, not a bird or a beast except of burden. The first lesson waited in a paper bundle under the table. *Will Sam take it?* Michael wondered as he rose and brought it out, unwrapping the papers carefully, while Sam watched and pretended to whistle, not to show too much curiosity.

"What things?" he asked at last.

"Things like this," answered Michael, setting out on the table an earthen pot containing a scarlet geranium in bloom.

It glowed forth its brilliant torch at once and gave just the touch to the clean room Michael had hoped it would. He stood back, surveying it proudly, and then looked at Sam to see if the lesson had been understood. He expected to see a scornful expression on the hardened sallow face of the slum boy, but instead Sam was gazing openmouthed, with unmitigated admiration.

"Say! Dat's all right!" he exclaimed. "Where'd you make de raise? Say! Dat makes de paper an' paint show up fine!"

Then he rose from the box he'd been sitting on and went and stood before the flower.

"Say! I wisht Jim cud see dat!" he exclaimed after a long silence, and something in his face brought the quick moisture to Michael's eyes.

It was only a common red geranium bought for fifteen cents, but it had touched with its miracle of bright life the young burglar's hardened soul and opened his vision to higher things. And in that moment his heart turned to his old companion who was uncomplainingly taking the punishment which rightfully belonged to the whole gang.

"We'll take him one tomorrow," said Michael in a voice husky with feeling. It was the first time Sam had voluntarily mentioned Jim, and he'd seemed so loath to take Michael to see him in jail that Michael had ceased to speak of the matter.

"There's another one like this where I bought this one. I couldn't tell which to take; they were both pretty. We'll get it the first thing in the morning before anybody else snaps it up, and then when could we get in to see Jim? Would they let us in after my office hours, or would we have to wait till Sunday? You look after that, will you? I might get off at four o'clock if that's not too late."

"Dey'll let us in on Sunday ef you ask, I reckon," said Sam, much moved. "But it's awful dark in prison. It won't live, will it? Only one streak o' sun shines in Jim's cell a few minutes every day."

"Oh, I think it'll live," said Michael hastily, a strange choking sensation in his throat at the thought of his onetime companion shut in a dark prison.

Of course, he deserved to be there. He'd broken the laws, but then no one had ever made him understand how wrong it was. If someone had only tried, Jim might never have done what put him in prison.

"I'm sure it'll live," he said again cheerfully. "I've heard geraniums are hardy. The man told me they would live all winter in the cellar if you brought them up again in the spring."

"Jim'll be out again in de spring," Sam said softly. It was the first sign of anything like emotion in Sam.

"Isn't that good!" said Michael heartily. "I wonder what we can do to make it pleasant for him when he comes back to the world. We'll bring him to this room, of course, but in the spring this'll be getting warm. And that makes me think of what I was talking about a minute ago. There's so much more in the country than in the city!"

"More?" questioned Sam.

"Yes, things like this to look at. Growing things you get to love and understand. There's a river that sparkles and talks as it runs. Trees that laugh and whisper when the wind plays in their branches. And wonderful birds, live breaths of air with music inside that make splendid friends when you're lonely. I know, for I made lots of bird friends when I went away from you all to college. You know, I was pretty lonely at first."

Sam looked at him with keen wonder and a lighting of his face that made him almost attractive and sent the cunning in his eyes slinking out of sight. Had this fine greathearted creature really missed his old friends when he went away? Did he really need them still with his education—and—difference? It was food for thought.

"Then there's the sky, so much of it," went on Michael, "and so wide and blue, with soft white clouds sometimes. They make you feel rested when you look at them floating through the blue and never seeming tired—not even when there's a storm and they have to hurry. And there's the sunset. Sam, I don't believe you ever saw the sunset, not right, anyway. You don't have sunsets here in the city; it just gets dark. You should have seen one I saw not long ago. I mean to take you there someday, and we'll watch it together. I want to see if it'll do the same thing to you it did to me."

Sam looked at him in awe, for Michael wore his exalted look. And when he spoke like that Sam feared perhaps he was, as old Sal said, more angel than man.

"Then there's the earth, covered with green—plenty to lie in if you want to— and it smells so good. And there's so much air—enough to breathe your lungs full and nothing disagreeable in it, no ugly smells or sounds. And things are growing everywhere. Oh, Sam! Wouldn't you like to make things like this grow?"

Sam nodded and reached out hesitantly to touch the velvet of a green leaf.

"You'll go with me, Sam, to the country sometime, won't you? I've got a plan, and I'll need you to help me carry it out. Will you go?"

"Sure!" said Sam in quite a different voice from any reluctant assent he'd ever given. "Sure, I'll go!"

"Thank you, Sam," said Michael, more moved than he dared show. "And now that's settled I want to talk about this room. I'm having five kids here tomorrow early in the evening. I told them I'd show them how to whittle boats, and we're going to sail them in the scrub bucket. They're about the age you and I were when I went away to school. Perhaps I'll teach them a letter or two of the alphabet if they seem interested. They should know how to read, Sam."

"I never learned to read—" muttered Sam half belligerently.

"That so?" said Michael, as if it were a matter of small moment. "Well, what if you were to come in and help me with the boats? Then you could pick it up when I teach them. You might want to use it someday. It's good to know how, and a man learns things quickly, you know."

Sam nodded.

"I don't know's I care 'bout it," he said indifferently, but Michael saw he intended to come.

"Well, after the kids have gone—I won't keep them late—I wonder if you'd like to bring some of the fellows in to see this?"

Michael glanced around the room.

"I have some pictures of alligators I think they might like to see. I'll bring them down if you say so."

"Sure!" said Sam, trying to hide his pleasure.

"Then tomorrow morning I'm going to let the woman who lives in the cellar under Aunt Sally's room bring her sewing here and work all day. She makes buttonholes in vests. It's so dark in her room she can't see, and she's almost ruined her eyes working by candlelight."

"She'll mess it all up!" grumbled Sam. "An' she might let other folks in, an' they'd pinch the picters an' the posy."

"No, she won't do that. I've talked to her about it. The room is to be hers for the day, and she's to keep it looking just as nice as it did when she found it.

She'll only bring her work over and go home for her dinner. She's to keep the fire going so it will be warm at night, and she's to try it for a day and see how it goes. I think she'll keep her promise. We'll try her anyway."

Sam nodded as to a superior officer who nevertheless was awfully foolish. "Mebbe!"

"Sam, do you think it would be nice to bring Aunt Sally over now a few minutes?"

"No," said Sam shortly, "she's too dirty. She'd put her fingers on de wall first thing—"

"But, Sam, I think she should come—and first. She's the one who helped me find you—"

Sam looked sharply at Michael and wondered if he suspected how long that same Aunt Sally had frustrated his efforts to find his friends.

"We could tell her not to touch things, perhaps—"

"Wal, you lemme tell her. Here! I'll go fix her up an' bring her now." And Sam hurried out of the room.

In a few minutes he returned with Aunt Sally. But it was a transformed Aunt Sally. Her face had been scrubbed in a circle out as far as her ears, and her scraggy gray hair was twisted in a tight knot at the back of her neck. Her hands were several shades cleaner than Michael had ever seen them, and her shoes were tied. She wore a small three-cornered plaid shawl over her shoulders and entered cautiously as if afraid to come. Her hands were clasped high across her breast. She'd evidently been severely threatened against touching anything.

"The saints be praised!" she exclaimed warmly after she'd looked around in silence. "To think I'd ivver see the loikes uv this in de alley. It lukes loike a palace. Mickey, ye're an angel, me b'y! An' a rale kurtin, to be sure! I ain't seen a kurtin in the alley since I cummed. An' will ye luke at the purty posy a blowin' as foine as ye plaze! Me mither had the loike in her cottage window when I was a leetle gal! Aw, me pure auld mither!"

And suddenly, to Michael's amazement and Sam's disgust, old Sal sat down on the one chair and wept aloud, with the tears streaming down her seamed, sin-scarred face. Sam was for putting her out at once, but Michael soothed her with his cheery voice, making her tell of her old home in Ireland and the kind mother she'd loved, though it was long years since she'd thought of her.

With rare skill he drew from her the picture of the Irish cottage with its thatched roof, peat fire, and well-swept hearth; the table with the white cloth; the cat in the rocking chair; the curtain starched stiffly at the window; the bright posy on the deep window ledge; and, last, the little girl with clean pinafore and curly hair who kissed her mother every morning and trotted off to school. But that was before the father died and the potatoes failed. The schooldays were soon over, and the little girl with her mother came to America. The mother died on the way over, and the child fell into evil hands. That was the story, and as it was told Michael's face grew tender and wistful. Would that he knew so much of his history as that!

But Sam stood by dumbstruck, trying to imagine this old woman as the bright rosy child she told about. Sam was passing through a sort of mental and moral earthquake.

"Perhaps someday we'll find another little house in the country where you can go and live," said Michael. "But, meanwhile, suppose you go and see if you can't make your room look like this one. You scrub it up, and perhaps Sam and I will come over and put some pretty paper on the walls for you. Would you like that? How about it, Sam?"

"Sure!" said Sam rather grudgingly. He hadn't much faith in Aunt Sally and didn't see what Michael wanted with her anyway, but he was loyal to Michael.

Irish blessings mingled with tears and garnished with curses in an extra-ordinary way were showered upon Michael.

At last, when he could stand no more, Sam said, "Aw, cut it out, Sal. You go home an' scrub. Come on now!" And he bundled her off in a hurry.

Late as it was, old Sal lit a fire and by the light of a tallow candle got down on her stiff old knees and began to scrub. It seemed nothing short of a miracle that her room could ever look like the one she'd just seen; but if scrubbing could do anything toward it, scrub she would. She hadn't thought of scrubbing her room for ten years. She hadn't seemed to care. But tonight, as she worked with her trembling, drink-shaken hands, the memory of her childhood home was before her vision, and she worked with all her might.

So the light and cheeriness of the little white room in the dark alley began to work. It was named "the angel's quarters," and to be invited within its charmed walls was an honor all coveted as time passed. And that was how Michael began the salvation of his native alley.

Chapter 14

Michael had been with the new law firm three months and was getting accustomed to the violent contrast between the day spent in the atmosphere of low-voiced, quiet-stepping, earnest men, who moved about in their environment of polished floors, oriental rugs, leather chairs, and walls with leather-covered law books, and the evening spent down in the alley where his bare white and gold room made the only tolerable spot in the neighborhood.

He was still occupying the fourth-floor back at his original boardinghouse and had seen Mr. Endicott briefly three or four times, but nothing had been said about his lodgings.

One morning he came to the desk set apart for him in the law office and found a letter lying there for him.

"Son," it said, "your board is paid at the address given below, up to the day you are twenty-one. If you don't get the benefit it will go to waste. Mrs. Semple will make you quite comfortable, and I desire you to move to her house at once. If you feel any obligation toward me, this is the way to discharge it. Hope you are well. Yours, Delevan Endicott."

Michael's heart beat faster with varied emotions. It was pleasant to have someone care, and of course if Mr. Endicott wished it so much he would manage somehow—perhaps he could get some night work or copying to do—but he'd never let him bear his expenses.

He hurried off at the noon hour to find his benefactor and make this plain with due gratitude. He found, however, that it wasn't so easy to change the man's mind, once made up. Endicott wouldn't hear of any change in arrangements. He had paid the board for the remaining months of Michael's minority and maintained his right to do so if he chose. Neither would he let Michael refund him any of the amount.

So Michael moved, bag and baggage, and found the change good. The regular, well-cooked meals increased his appetite, which had been going back on him for some time under his economical regime, and the larger room with better outlook and more air, to say nothing of a comfortable bed with adjoining bathroom, and plenty of heat and light, made life seem more worthwhile. Besides, he now came in pleasant contact with other boarders, and a large parlor with easy chairs boasted an old-fashioned square piano which still retained much of its original sweet tone.

Mrs. Semple had a daughter, Hester, an earnest, gray-eyed girl with soft brown hair and a firm chin, who had taken an art course at Cooper Institute and painted very good pictures which didn't sell. Hester played the piano—not very well, but well enough to make it enjoyable to a lonely boy who'd known no music in his life except the birds or his own whistle. She played hymns on Sunday after church while they waited for dinner to be ready, and evenings after supper she played other things—old ballads and tender melodies from old masters simplified for her ability. Michael sometimes lingered a half hour before hurrying to the alley, joining his rich natural tenor with her light, pretty soprano. Sometimes Will French, a young fellow who was in the same law office and also boarded at Mrs. Semple's, stayed a while and sang bass. It made it seem more as if Michael were living in a home.

All this time, Michael was carrying on his quiet work in the alley, saying nothing about it to anybody. In the first place, he felt shy about it because of his personal connection with the place. Not that he wished to hide his origin from his employers, but he felt he owed it to Mr. Endicott, who had recommended him, to be as respectable as possible. And so long as they neither knew nor cared it didn't matter. Then it never occurred to Michael he was doing anything remarkable with his little white room in the darkness of the sin stronghold.

Night after night, he gathered his newsboys and taught them whittling, basketry, reading, arithmetic, and geography, with a little philosophy and botany thrown in unawares. Night after night, the older fellows dropped in, one or two at a time, and listened to the stories Michael told—of college life and games they were interested in or nature and his experiences in finding an alligator or a serpent or watching some bird. He never realized he was preparing in the school of experience to be a magnificent public speaker. With an audience as difficult as any he could have found in the whole city, he managed to hold them every time.

And the favorite theme often was agriculture. He would bring a new little plant to the room, set it up, and show it to them, and then talk about soil conditions and how plants were being improved. He would usually take time at noon to read some article on agriculture and review it for their benefit.

They heard all about Burbank and his wonderful experiments in making plants grow and develop, and as they listened they gathered around the blossom Michael had just brought to them and gazed with wonder at it. A flower was a strange enough sight in that court, but when they heard the stories it became filled with new interest. For a while they forgot their evil plotting and were lifted above themselves.

Another night he talked on fertilizers and how one crop would sometimes give out something another crop needed later. Gradually, because he talked about things he was interested in, he gave these sons of ignorance a dim knowledge of and interest in the culture of life and the tilling of the ground, preparing them for what he'd hardly dared put into words even to himself.

One day he took Sam down to Old Orchard. It was the week before Christmas. They'd made their second visit to Jim the week before, and he'd spoken of the spring when he would get out into the world again. He seemed to be planning to get even with those who had confined him for his wrongdoing. Michael's heart was filled with anxiety for him.

Something about Jim appealed to Michael from the beginning. He'd first seen him standing behind his cell grating, a great unkempt hulk of a fellow with fiery red hair and brown eyes that roved restlessly through the corridor. He would have been handsome except for his weak chin. Jim had melted almost to tears on seeing the scarlet geranium they brought him on that first visit, and he seemed to care more about his old comrade "Mickey's" appearance than Sam had.

Jim was to get out in April. If only he had someplace to go!

Michael and Sam talked about it on the way down. Sam seemed to think Jim would find it pretty hard to leave New York. Sam himself wasn't much interested in Michael's continued hints about going to the country.

"Nothin' doin' " was his constant refrain when Michael tried to tell him how much better it would be if some of the city's congested part could be spread out into the country—especially for the poor people who would have a greater opportunity for success in life.

But Sam was impressed with the wideness of the landscape on his first long trip out of the city. As Michael unfolded to him the story of the gift of the farm and his own hopes for it, Sam left off his scorn and gave replies that showed he was thinking about it.

"Say!" he said suddenly. "Ef Buck was to come back, would you let him live down to your place an' help do all them things you're plannin'?"

"I surely would. Say, Sam—do you or do you not know where Buck is?"

Sam gazed thoughtfully out of the window. Then he looked down at his feet and nodded his head slowly.

"I thought so!" said Michael eagerly. "Sam, is he in hiding for something he's done?"

Sam nodded his head again, even more slowly and cautiously.

"Sam, will you send him a message from me?"

Another nod.

"Tell him I love him," Michael breathed the words eagerly. His heart remembered kindness from Buck more than anything else in his sad childhood. "Tell him I want him—I need him! Tell him I want him to make an appointment to meet me somewhere so we can talk over this plan of mine. I want him to go in with me and help me make that farm into a fit place to take people who haven't the right kind of homes, where they can have honest work and good air and be happy! Will you tell him?"

And Sam nodded his head emphatically.

"An' Jim'll help, too, ef Buck goes. That's dead sure!" Sam volunteered.

"And, Sam, I'm counting on you!"

"Sure thing!" said Sam.

Michael tramped all over the place with Sam, showing him everything and telling all his plans. He was very familiar with his land now. He'd planned the bog for a cranberry patch and already negotiated for the bushes. He'd trimmed up the berry bushes in the garden himself during his holiday trips and arranged with a fisherman to dump a few shellfish haulings on one field where he thought that kind of fertilizer would be effective. He'd determined to use his hundred-dollar graduation present in fertilizer and seed. It wouldn't go far, but it would be a beginning. The work he'd have to get some other way. He would have little time to put toward it himself until late in the summer probably, and a great deal should be done in the early spring. He would have to be content to go slow, of course, and must remember that unskilled labor was always expensive and wasteful; still, it would likely be all he could get. Just how he would feed and house even unskilled labor was a problem yet to be solved.

It was a day of many revelations to Sam. For one thing, even the bare snowy stretch of wide country had taken on a new interest to him since Michael had been telling all these wonderful things about the earth. Sam's brain, which up to this time had never busied itself with anything except how to get other men's goods from them, had suddenly awakened to the wonders of the world.

He spotted a colony of cocoons on the underside of leaves and twigs. "Say, ain't dem some o' de critters you was showin' de fellers t'other night?"

And Michael fell upon them eagerly. They happened to be rare specimens, and he knew from college experience that such could be sold to advantage to the museums. He showed Sam how to remove them without injuring them. A little farther on they came to a wild growth of holly, loaded with berries and burnished thorny foliage, and near at hand a mistletoe bough with tiny white transparent berries.

"Ain't dem wot dey sell for Chris'sum greens?" Sam's city eyes picked them out at once.

"Of course," said Michael delighted. "How did I miss them before? We'll take a lot back with us and see if we can get any price for it. Whatever we get we'll devote to making the house livable. Holly and mistletoe should have a good market about now. That's another idea! Why not cultivate a lot of this stuff right in this tract of land? It seems to grow without any trouble. See! There are lots of little bushes. We'll encourage them, Sam. And say, Sam, if you hadn't come along I might never have thought of that. You see, I needed you."

Sam grunted in a pleased way.

When they reached the house, it looked even more desolate in the snowy stretch of setting than with the grass about it. Michael's heart sank.

"I don't know if we can ever do anything with the old shack," he said, shaking his head. "It looks worse than I thought."

" 'Tain't so bad," said Sam cheerfully. "Guess it's watertight." He peered through the dusty windowpane where he'd cleared a spot with his coat sleeve. "Looks dry inside. 'Twould be a heap better'n sleepin' on de pavement fer some. Dat fire hole would take in a lot o' wood, an' I guess dere's plenty round de place without robbin' de woods none."

Michael led him to the seashore and bade him look. He wanted to see what effect it would have upon him. The coast swept wild and bleak in the cold December day, and Sam shivered in his thin garments. A look of awe and fear came into his face. He turned his back on it.

"Too big!" he said sullenly, and Michael understood that the sea in its vastness oppressed him.

"Yes, there's a good deal of it," he admitted, "but after all it's sort of like the geranium flower."

Sam turned back and looked.

"H'm! I don't see nothin' like!" he grunted despairingly.

"Why, it's wonderful! It's beyond us! We couldn't make it. Look at that motion! See the white tossing rim of the waves! See that soft green-gray! Isn't it just the color of the little down on the geranium leaf? See the silver light playing back and forth, and look how it reaches as far as you can see. Now doesn't it make you feel a little as it did when you first looked at the geranium?"

Sam looked in vain. "Not fer mine!" he shrugged. "Gimme the posy every time."

They walked in silence along the beach toward the flowing of the river, and Sam eyed the ocean furtively as if he feared it might run up and engulf them suddenly when they weren't looking. He'd seen the ocean from wharves, of course, and once stole a ride in a pilot boat out into the deep a little way. But he'd never been alone with the whole sea at once as this seemed. It was too vast for him to comprehend. Still, in a misty way, he knew what Michael was trying to make him understand, and it stirred him uncomfortably.

They hired a little boat, and Michael with strong strokes rowed them back to the farm, straight into the sunset. The sky was purple and gold that night and empurpled the golden river, whose ripples blended into pink and lavender and green. Sam sat huddled in the boat's prow facing it all. Michael had planned that. The oars dipped quietly, and Sam's small eyes widened and took it all in. The sun slipped lower in a crimson ball, and a flood of crimson light broke through the purple and gold for a moment and left a thin, clear line of flame behind.

"Dere!" exclaimed Sam, pointing excitedly. "Dat's like de posy. I kin see that all right!"

Michael rested on his oars and looked back at the sunset, well pleased with this day's work.

They left the boat at a little landing where its owner had promised to get it and walked back through the wood, gathering holly branches and mistletoe. When they reached the city, Michael found a good market for it and received enough for what he'd brought to more than cover the price of the trip. Best of all, Sam was as pleased with the bargain as if it were for his personal benefit.

When they parted, Sam wore a mistletoe sprig in his ragged buttonhole, and Michael carried holly branches back to his boarding place. Most of this he gave to Hester Semple to decorate the parlor with, but one fine branch he kept and carried to his room and fastened over his mirror.

After gazing at it, he selected a spray containing several fine large berries, cut it off, and packed it carefully in a tiny box. This without name or clue to sender, he addressed in printing letters to Starr. Mr. Endicott had asked him to mail a letter to her as he passed by the box the last time he'd been in the office, and without his intention the address had been burned into his memory. He hadn't expected to use it, but there could be no harm, surely, in sending the girl this bit of Christmas greeting out of a world of possible people. She would never know he sent it, and perhaps it would please her to get a piece of Christmas holly from home. She might think her father had sent it. It didn't matter, and it helped him think he might send this much of his thoughts over the water to her. He thought about how she would look when she opened the box. But whether she was pleased or not he could only surmise, for she would never know to thank him. Ah, well, it was as near as he dared hope for touching life's happiness. He must be glad for what he might have and try to work and forget the rest.

Chapter 15

Now about this time the law firm where Michael worked became deeply interested in their new boy. He studied hard and seemed to know what he was about all day. They saw signs of extraordinary talent in him. Once or twice, thinking to make life pleasant for him, they invited him to their club or to some evening's entertainment, and always Michael had courteously declined, saying he had an engagement for the evening. They casually questioned Will French, the other student, who was a happy-go-lucky and in the office because his father wished him to study something and not because he wanted to. Will said Michael went out every evening and came in late. Mrs. Semple had remarked she often didn't know whether he came in at all until she saw him at breakfast.

This report and a weariness about the eyes some mornings led the firm's senior member to look into Michael's affairs. The natural inference was that Michael was getting into social life too deeply, perhaps wasting the hours in late revelry when he should have been sleeping. Mr. Holt liked Michael and dreaded seeing signs of dissipation appear on that fine face. He asked Will French to make friends with him and find out if he could where he spent his evenings. Will agreed and at once entered on his mission with a zeal beyond all baffling.

"Hello, Endicott!" called Will, as Michael reached the front door on his way to his mission that same evening. "Where're you going? Wait, can't you, and I'll walk along with you? I was going to ask if you wouldn't go to a show with me this evening. I haven't anything on for tonight, and it's slow."

As he spoke he seized his coat and hat, which he'd purposely left in the hall, and put them on.

"Thank you," said Michael, as they went out together. "I'd be glad to go with you, but I have something that can't be put off."

"Well, go tomorrow night with me, will you? I like you and think we should be friends."

Will's idea was they'd get to talking at a show and he could find out a good deal. He thought it must be a girl. He'd told the senior Holt it was a girl, of course, and he wouldn't take long to spot her. It must be either a girl or revelry to take the fellow out every night in the week so late.

"Well, I'm sorry," said Michael, "but I'm afraid I have an engagement every night. It's rather a permanent job I'm engaged in. What do you do with your evenings?"

Will described parties and entertainments he had been invited to and nice girls he knew, hinting he might introduce Michael if he was so inclined. Michael talked on, leading his unsuspecting companion further from the subject of his own evenings. Finally they came to a corner, and Michael halted.

"I turn here," he said. "Which way do you go?"

"Why, I turn, too," said Will, laughing. "That is, if you don't object. I'm out for a walk, and I don't care much what I do. If I'm not welcome, just tell me and I'll clear out."

"Of course you're quite welcome," said Michael. "I'm glad to have company, but the quarter I'm walking to isn't pleasant for a walk, and indeed you mightn't like to return alone even early in the evening if you walk far. I had an unpleasant encounter myself once, but I know the ways of the place now, and it's different."

Will eyed him curiously. "Am I allowed to ask where we're going?" he asked in a comical tone.

Michael laughed. "Certainly. If you're bound to go, I'll have to tell you all about it. But I strongly advise you to turn back now, for it isn't a savory neighborhood, and I don't believe you'll care for it."

" 'Where thou goest I will go,' " replied Will, mocking. "My curiosity is aroused. I'll certainly go. If it's safe for you, it is for me. My good looks aren't nearly as valuable as yours or so noticeable. And since I have no valuables in the world, I can't be knocked down for booty."

"You see, they all know me," explained Michael.

"Oh, they do! And can't you introduce me? Or don't you like to?"

"I suppose I can, if you really want me to, but I'm afraid you'll turn and run when you see them. They're not very—handsome. They're not what you're used to. You wouldn't want to know them."

"But you do."

"I had to," said Michael desperately. "They needed something, and I had to help them!"

Up to now Will was sure Michael had fallen into the hands of sharpers. But something in his tone made him turn and look, and he saw Michael's face uplifted in the streetlight, glowing with an earnestness that surprised and awed him.

"Look here, man," he said. "Tell me who they are and what you're doing anyway."

Michael told him a few words, saying little about himself or his first reason for being interested in the alley. There were a few neglected newsboys, mere kids. He was trying to teach them a few things, reading and figures and a little manual training. Something to make life more than suffering and sin.

"Is it settlement work?" Will asked, puzzled and interested.

"No, there's a settlement, but it's too far away and has too big a district to reach this alley. It's just my own little work."

"Who pays you for it?"

"Who pays me?"

"Yes, who's behind the enterprise? Who forks over the funds and pays you for your job?"

Michael laughed long and loud. "Well, now, I hadn't thought about pay, but I guess the kids do. You can't think how they enjoy it all."

"H'm!" said Will. "I think I'll go along and see how you do it. I won't scare 'em out, will I?"

"Well, now I hadn't thought of that. In fact, I didn't suppose you'd care to go all the way, but if you think you do, I guess it'll be all right."

"Not a very warm welcome, I must say," laughed Will, "but I'm going just the same. You get me in, and I'll guarantee not to scare the crowd. Have any time left over from your studies for amusement? If you do I might come in on that. I can do tricks."

"Can you?" said Michael, looking at his unbidden guest doubtfully. "Well, we'll see. I'm afraid you'll be disappointed. It's very informal. Sometimes we don't get beyond the first step in a lesson. Sometimes I have to stop and tell stories."

"Good!" said Will. "I'd like to hear you."

"Oh, you wouldn't enjoy it, but there are a few books there. You might read if you get tired looking around the room."

And so Michael and his guest entered the yellow and white room together. Michael lit the gas, and Will blinked in amazement.

Coming through the alley to the room had taken away Will's exclamatory powers and exhausted his vocabulary. The room in its white simplicity, immaculately kept and constantly in touch with fresh paint to hide any stray finger marks, stood out in startling contrast with the regions round about it. Will took it all in, paint, paper, and pictures. The tiny stove glowing warmly, the improvised seats, the blackboard in the corner, and the bits of life in the geranium, butterfly cocoons, and birds' nests. Then he looked at Michael, tall and fine and embarrassed, in the center of it all.

"Great Scott!" he exclaimed. "Is this an enchanted island, or am I in my right mind?"

But before he received an answer they heard clattering young feet and a tumult outside the door. Then the boys entered, eager, panting but decorous, some with clean faces, most of them with clean hands or moderately so, all with their caps off in homage to their prince. Michael welcomed them as if he stood in a luxurious drawing room on Fifth Avenue, and these were his guests.

He introduced them, and Will greeted them chummily. They stood off from him at first with suspicion, huddled together in a group near Michael. But later, when the chalkboard lesson was over and Michael was showing a set of pictures, Will sat down in a corner with a string from his pocket and began showing two of the boldest some tricks. This took at once. When he added a little sleight of hand, pulling pennies from their hair, pockets, and hands, and letting them keep them after the game was over, they were ready to accept him into their inner circle at once.

But when Sam, unaccountably late that night, sidled in alone, he looked at the stranger with belligerence. Michael introduced him as his friend, and Sam's eyes glinted with a jealous light. Sam didn't like Michael to have any friends of that sort. This new man wore shiny boots, fine new clothes, and well-brushed hair and manipulated a smooth handkerchief with fingers as white as any gentleman's.

To be sure, Michael was like that. But he belonged to them, and his clothes made him no worse. Who was this intruder? A gentleman? All gentlemen were natural enemies to Sam.

"Come outside," said Sam to Michael gruffly, ignoring the white hand Will held out cordially.

Michael saw something was on his mind. "Will, can you amuse these kids a minute or two while I step out? I won't be long."

"Sure!" said Will heartily. He hadn't had such a time in months, and what a story he'd have to tell the senior partner in the morning.

"Ever try to lift a fellow's hand off the top of his head? Here, kid, sit in that chair and put your right hand flat on the top of your head. Now, sonny, you lift it off. Pull with all your might. That's it—"

Michael's eyes shone, and even Sam grinned surreptitiously.

"He'll do," he said to Sam as they went out. "He was lonesome this evening and wanted to come along with me."

Lonesome! A fellow like that! It gave Sam a new idea to think about. Did people with money and education and used to living in clothes like that get lonesome? Sam looked more kindly back at Will as he closed the door.

Alone in the dark cold entry, where the wind whistled up from the river and every crack seemed to conduct a blast, Sam and Michael talked in low tones.

"Say, he's lit out!" Sam's tone conveyed dismay as well as apology.

Michael guessed at once whom he meant. "Buck?"

Sam grunted assent.

"When?"

"Day er so ago. I tuk yer word to 'im, but he'd gone. Lef' word he had a big deal on, an' ef if it came troo all right 'e'd send fer us. You see it wan't safe round 'ere no more. The police was onto his game. Thur wan't no more hidin' fer him. He was powerful sorry not to see you. He'd always thought a heap o' Mickey!"

"How long had he known I was here?" Michael's face was grave in the darkness. Why hadn't Buck sent him word? Made some appointment?

"Since you first cum back."

"Why—oh, Sam, why didn't he let me come and see him?"

"It warn't safe," said Sam earnestly. "Sure thing, it warn't! 'Sides—"

"Besides what, Sam?"

" 'Sides, he knowed you had edicashun, an' he knowed how you looked on his way o' livin'. He didn't know but—"

"You mean he didn't trust me, Sam?"

Sam felt the keen eyes upon him even in the darkness. "Naw, he didn't tink you'd snitch on him ner nothin', but he didn't know if you'd tink you had to do some tings what might kick it all up wid him. You'd ben out o' tings fer years, an' you didn't know de ways o' de city. 'Sides, he ain't seed you like I done—"

"I see," said Michael. "I understand. It's a long time, and of course he only knows what you've told him, and if there was danger—but, oh, Sam, I wish he could go down to Old Orchard. Did you ever tell him about it and my plans?"

"Sure ting I did. Tole 'im all you tole me. He said 'twar all right. Ef he comes out on dis deal he'll be back in a while, an' he'll go down dere ef you want him. He said he'd bring a little wad back to make things go ef dis deal went troo."

"Do you know what the deal is, Sam?"

"Sure!"

"Is it dis. . .is it"—he paused for a word that would convey his meaning and yet not offend—"is it. . .dangerous, Sam?"

"Sure!" admitted Sam solemnly as though it hurt him to pain his friend.

"Do you mean it will make more hiding for him?"

"Sure!" emphatically grave.

"I wish he hadn't gone!" There was sharp pain in Michael's voice.

"I wisht so, too!" said Sam with a little choke. "Mebbe 'twon't come off after all. Mebbe it'll git blocked. Mebbe he'll come back."

The anxiety in Sam's tone touched Michael, but another thought struck him.

"Sam," he said, plucking at the other's sleeve in the darkness, "tell me—what was Buck doing—before he went away? Was it all straight? Was he in the same business with you?"

Sam breathed heavily but didn't answer. At last with difficulty he answered a gruff "Nope!"

"What was it, Sam? Won't you tell me?"

"It would be snitchin'."

"Not to me, Sam. You know I belong to you all."

"But you've got new notions."

"Yes," admitted Michael, "I can't help that, but I don't go back on you, do I?"

"No, you don't go back on we'uns, thet's so. But you don't like we'uns doin's."

"Never mind. Tell me, Sam. I think I must know."

"He kep a gamin' den—"

"Oh, Sam!" Michael's voice was stricken, and his great athletic hand gripped Sam's hard skinny one, and Sam in the darkness gripped back.

"I knowed you'd feel thet way," he mourned as if the fault were all in his telling. "I wisht I hadn't 'a' tole yer."

"Never mind, Sam. You couldn't help it, and I suppose I wouldn't have known the difference myself if I hadn't gone away. We mustn't judge Buck harshly. He'll see it the other way in time."

Sam straightened perceptibly. Something in this speech put him in the same class with Michael. He'd never had qualms of conscience concerning gambling, but now he found himself arrayed against it almost unawares.

"I guess mebbe!" he said comfortingly and then sought to change the subject. "Say, is dat guy in dere goin' along to de farm?"

"Who?"

"Why, dat ike you lef' in de room. Is he goin' down 'long when we's go?"

"Oh, Will French! No, Sam. He doesn't know anything about it yet. I may tell him sometime, but he doesn't need that. He's studying to be a lawyer. Perhaps someday if he gets interested he'll help do what I want for the alley and all the other alleys in the city—make better laws and see that they're enforced."

"Laws!" said Sam in a startled voice. "What laws?" Laws were his natural enemies.

"Laws for better tenement houses, more room and more windows, better air, cleaner streets, room for grass and flowers, pure milk and meat, less crowding and dirt. Understand?"

It was the first time Michael had gone so deep into his plans with Sam, and he longed now to have his comradeship in this hope, too.

"Oh, sure!" said Sam, relieved he hadn't mentioned laws about gambling dens and pickpockets.

Sam might be willing to reform his own course in Michael's brilliant wake, but as yet he hadn't reached the point where he cared to see vice and dishonesty swept off the globe.

They went slowly back to the white room to find Will French leading a chorus of youngsters in the latest popular melody while they kept time with an awkward shuffle of their ill-shod feet.

"Cut it out, kids," Sam growled. "You scratch de floor."

Will French subsided with apologies. "I never thought of the floor, Endicott. Say, you should have a gymnasium and a swimming pool here."

Michael laughed.

"I wish we had, but I'd start on a bathroom. We need that first of all."

"Well, let's get one," said Will eagerly. "That wouldn't cost so much. We could get some people to contribute a little. I know a man with a big plumbing establishment. He'd do a little something. I mean to tell him about it. Is there anyplace it could be put?"

Sam followed them, listening, wondering, as they stepped into the hall to see the little dark hole which might with ingenuity be converted into a bathroom. While he leaned back against the doorjamb, hands in his pockets, he studied the newcomer's face.

"Guess dat guy's all right," he reassured Michael as he helped him turn the lights out a little later.

Will was waiting on the doorstep, whistling a new tune to his admiring following. He'd caught "de kids."

"I say, Endicott," he said as they walked up the noisy midnight street and turned into the avenue. "Why don't you get Hester to go down there and sing sometime? Sunday afternoon. She'd go. Ask her."

And that night was the beginning of outside help for Michael's mission. Hester fell into the habit of going down Sunday afternoons, and soon she had an eager following of sad-eyed women and eager little children, and Will French spent his leisure hours hunting up tricks and games and puzzles for the kids.

Meanwhile, the account he'd given Holt and Holt of the way Michael spent his evenings was not without fruit.

About a week after Will's first visit to the alley, the senior Mr. Holt paused beside Michael's desk one afternoon before leaving the office and laid a bit of paper in his hand.

"French tells me you're interested in work in the slums," he said in the same tone he used to give Michael an order for his daily routine. "I'd like to help a little if you can use that." He left before Michael had fully comprehended what he'd said. The young man looked down at the paper and saw it was a check made out to him for one hundred dollars!

With a quick exclamation of gratitude he was on his feet and out in the hall after his employer.

"That's all right, Endicott. I don't get as much time as I'd like to look after the charities, and when I see a good thing I like to give it a boost. Call on me if you need money for any special scheme. And I'll mention it to some of my clients occasionally," said the old lawyer, pleased with Michael's gratitude.

He did, and the clients responded. Every little while a ten-dollar bill or a five, and now and then a check for fifty, would find its way to Michael's desk—for Will French, thoroughly interested, kept Holt and Holt well informed concerning what was needed.

Chapter 16

Before winter was over Michael put in the bathroom, bought a plow and other farm implements, and secured the services of a man who lived near Old Orchard to do some early plowing and planting. He bought seeds and fertilizer, enough at least to start his experiment, and toward spring he took advantage of a holiday, and with Sam and a carpenter went down to the farm and patched up the old house.

After that a few cots, some boxes for chairs and tables, some cheap comforters for cool nights, some dishes and cooking utensils from the ten-cent store, and the place would be ready for his alley-community when he dared bring them down. A canvas cot and a wadded comforter would be luxury to any of them. The only question was, would they be contented out of the city?

Michael had read many articles about taking the poor of the cities into the country, and he knew experience had shown they were in most cases miserable to get back again. He believed this might be different with the right conditions. In the first place, they must have an environment full of new interest to replace the city's rush, and then they must have some great object they would be eager to attain. He felt, too, that they should be prepared beforehand for their new life.

To this end he had spent two or three hours a week the last six months with five or six young fellows Sam had called in. He had brought the agricultural papers to the room and made much of the illustrations. The boys as a rule couldn't read, so he read to them, or rather translated into their own slangful English. He told them what wonders had been attained by farming the right way. As these fellows had little idea of farming in any way, or little knowledge of farm products except what came to them through the markets in their very worst forms, he carried in cabbages, apples, and other fruits and vegetables for their inspection.

One night he brought several gnarled, green-skinned, sour, speckled apples. He called attention to them very carefully. Because an apple was a treat, however poor it might be, he asked them to notice the flavor as they ate. Then he produced some magnificent specimens of apples, crimson and yellow, with polished skins and delicious flavor, and set them in a row on the table beside more little speckled apples. They looked like a sunset beside a ditch. The young men gathered around the beautiful apples, touching their shiny streaks as if they might be painted and listening to the story of their development from the ugly specimens they had just been eating. When the perfect apples were cut up, each one enjoyed the delicious fruit with new understanding.

Other nights, with Will and Hester's help, Michael demonstrated potatoes and other vegetables, with regular lessons on how to get the best results with these products. Hester served a tasty refreshment from roasted potatoes, cooked just right, and showed the difference between the soggy potatoes full of dry rot and those grown under the right conditions. Occasionally a cup of coffee or some delicate sandwiches accompanied a demonstration of lettuce or celery or cold cabbage in the form of slaw, and the light refreshments served with the agricultural lessons became a pleasant feature of Michael's evenings. More and more young fellows dropped in to listen to the lesson and enjoy the plentiful "eats" as they called them. When they reached the lessons on peas and beans, the split-pea soup and rich bean soup were well appreciated.

Not that all took the lessons with equal enthusiasm, but toward spring Michael felt that his original five with Sam as their leader would do fairly intelligent work on the farm. They were told the story often, until they were eager to know if they might be among the pioneers in the work.

Will French faithfully reported the condition of the work, and more friends and clients of the office would stop at Michael's desk, chat with him briefly about the work, and always leave something to help it along. Michael's eyes shone, and his heart beat high with hopes in these days.

But he still had further work to do before his crude apprentices were ready to be sent out into the wilds of nature.

Michael began one evening to tell them of the beauty and wonder of the world. He used a cocoon to illustrate, and for three evenings they watched with bated breath the strange little roll, almost doubting Michael's veracity, yet full of curiosity. Then one night it burst its bonds and floated up into the white ceiling, its pale green, gorgeously marked wings captivating their hearts in a way no years could ever make them forget. It was the miracle of life, and they'd never seen or heard of it.

Another night he brought a singing bird in a cage and pictures of wild birds. He taught them the ways of the birds they would see in New Jersey, how to tell their songs apart, where to look for their nests—all the odd things a bird lover knows and that Michael through roaming about the woods knew by heart. The bird in its cage stayed in the yellow and white room and, strange to say, thrived, becoming a joy and wonder to visitors and a marvel to those who lived in the court. Its continuous brilliant song burst forth from a heart that seemed too full of happiness and must bubble over into music. The kids and even the older fellows felt a proprietorship in it and liked to stand beneath the cage and call to it as it answered "peep" and watched them through the gilded bars.

One night, with the help of Will French, who had some wealthy friends, Michael borrowed a large picture of a sunset and told them about the sunlight and its effects on growing things and the wonder of its departure for the night.

By this time they would listen in awed silence to anything Michael said, though the picture was perhaps one too many for most of them. Sam, however, heard with approval and afterward laid his finger reverently on the picture's crimson, purple, and gold. Sam understood, for he'd seen the real thing. Then he turned to the others.

"Say, fellers, it's aw-right. You wait till yer see one. Fine ez silk an' twicet as nateral."

So the work went on. Spring was coming and with it the end of Jim's "term" and the beginning of Michael's farm experiment.

Meanwhile Michael was working hard at his law and studying half the night when he returned from the alley work. If he hadn't had an iron constitution and thirteen years of healthy outdoor life, with plenty of sleep and exercise and good food, he couldn't have stood it. As it was, the hard work was good for him, for it kept him from brooding about himself and his hopeless love of the little girl far across the water.

Some weeks after Christmas a brief note from Starr had come, with his name written in her hand and the address in her father's.

Dear Michael,

I'm almost sure I'm indebted to you for the lovely holly sprig that reached me on Christmas. I've tried to think who the sender might be, for I didn't know the writing, or rather printing. But today it fell down from over the picture where I had fastened it on the wall, and I noticed for the first time "A Happy Christmas" in the tiny letters of the message cut or scratched on the underside of the stem. The letters reminded me of you and the charming surprises you used to send me long ago from Florida when I was a little girl. Then all at once I was sure you had sent the holly, so I'm sitting right down to write and thank you for it.

You see, I was very lonesome and homesick that Christmas morning, for most of the girls in the school had gone home for Christmas. Mama had meant to come and take me to Paris for the holidays, but she wrote she wasn't well and couldn't come, so I knew I'd have to be here by myself. I was feeling very sad even with the presents Mama sent me, until I opened the box and saw the dear holly berries that cheered me up and made me think of home. I kept it on my desk all day so the bright berries would make me feel Christmassy.

And just before dinner that night, what do you think happened? Why, my dear daddy came to surprise me, and we took the loveliest trip together, to Venice, Florence, and Rome. It was beautiful! I wish you could have been along and seen everything. I know you'd have enjoyed it. I mustn't take the time to write about it because I should be studying. This is a very pleasant place and a good school, but I'd rather be at home, and I'll be glad when I'm finished and allowed to come back to my own country.

Thanking you ever so much for the pretty Christmas reminder, for you see I'm sure you sent it, and wishing you a belated Happy New Year, I am

Your friend,
Starr Delevan Endicott

Michael read and reread the letter, treasured the thoughts and visions it brought him, pondered whether he might answer, and decided he had no right. Then he put it away with his own heartache, plunging into his work with redoubled energy and taking an antidote of so many pages of Blackstone when his thoughts lingered on forbidden subjects. So the winter fled, and spring came stealing on apace.

Chapter 17

As Michael had no definite knowledge of either his exact age or birth month, no day could be set for his coming of age. His own memory of how many summers and winters he had passed showed he was about seven years old at the time of the shooting. If that was correct it would make him between nineteen and twenty at the time of his graduation.

On the first day of July following his first winter in New York, Michael received a brief letter from Mr. Endicott, containing a check for a thousand dollars, with congratulations on his majority and a request that he call at the office the next day.

Michael, eager, grateful, overwhelmed, was on hand at the appointed minute.

The wealthy businessman, whose banking affairs had long since righted themselves, turned from his multifarious duties and rested his eyes on the young fellow, listening half-amused to his eager thanks.

The young man in truth was a sight to rest weary eyes.

The winter in New York had put new lines on his face and deepened the wells of his blue eyes. They were the work of care and wit and suffering but had made a man's face out of a boy's fresh countenance. Power showed in the fine brow, strength in the firm, well-molded chin, and both kindness and unselfishness in his pleasant lips. The city barber had been artist enough not to cut the glorious hair too short, while yet giving it the latest clean-cut curve behind the ears and on the neck. By instinct Michael's hands were well cared for. Endicott's tailor had looked out for the rest.

"That's all right, son," Endicott cut Michael's sentence short. "I'm pleased with the way you've been doing. Holt tells me he never had a more promising student in his office. He says you're cut out for the law, and you're going to be a success. But what's this they tell me about you spending your evenings in the slums? I don't like the sound of that. Better cut that out."

Michael began to tell in earnest protesting words of what he was trying to do, but Endicott put up an impatient hand.

"That's all very well, son. I've no doubt they appreciate your help and all that, and it's been commendable of you to give your time. But now you owe yourself and the world something. You've got to turn out a great lawyer and prove to the world that people from that district are worth helping. That's the best way in the long run to help those people. Give them into somebody else's hands now. You've done your part. When you get to be a rich man you can give them something now and then if you like, but it's time to cut out the work now. That sort of thing might be popular in a political leader, but you've got your way to make. It's time you gave your evenings to culture and to going out into society. Here's a list of concerts and lectures for next winter. You should go to them all. I'm sorry I didn't think of it this winter, but perhaps it was as well not to go too deep at the start. You should waste no more time, though. I've applied for season tickets for those things on that list, and you'll receive them in due time. An art exhibit or two will have good things to see. You've got to see and hear everything if you want to be a thoroughly educated man. I said a word or two about you here and there, and I think you'll receive some invitations worth accepting pretty soon. You'll need a dress suit, and I sent word to the tailor about it this morning when it occurred to me—"

"But," said Michael, amazed and perturbed, "I don't belong in society. People don't want someone like me there. If they knew they wouldn't ask me."

"Bosh! Didn't I tell you to cut that out? People don't know, and you've no need to tell them. They think you're a distant relative of mine if they think anything about it, and you're not to tell them you're not. You owe it to me to keep still about it. If I guarantee you're all right, that should suit anybody."

"I couldn't go where people thought I was more than I was," said Michael, head up, eyes shining, his firmest expression on his mouth, but trouble in his eyes. It was hard to go against his benefactor.

"You got all those foolish notions from working down there in the slums. You've got a false idea of yourself and a false notion of right and wrong. It's high time you stopped going there. After you've been to a dance or two and a few theater suppers, and you're acquainted with some nice girls who'll invite you to their house parties, you'll forget you ever had anything to do with the slums. I insist you give up that work at once. Promise me you won't go near the place again. Write them a letter—"

"I couldn't do that!" said Michael, his face expressive of anguish fighting with duty.

"Couldn't! Nonsense. There's no such word. I want you to do it. Haven't I proved my right to make that request?"

"You have," said Michael, dropping his sorrowing eyes slowly and taking out the folded check from his pocket.

"You have the right to ask it, but I have no right to do what you ask. I've begun the work, and it wouldn't be right to stop it. Indeed, I couldn't. If you knew what it means to those fellows—but I can't keep this if you feel that way! I was going to use it for the work—but now—"

Michael's pauses were eloquent. Endicott was deeply touched, but he wouldn't show it. He was used to having his own way, and it irritated him, while it pleased him somehow, to have Michael so determined. As Michael stopped talking he laid the check on the desk.

"Nonsense!" said Endicott. "This has nothing to do with the check. That was your birthday present. Use it as you like. What I've given I've given and won't take back even if I have nothing more to do with you from this time forth. I have no objection to your giving away as much money as you can spare to benevolent institutions, but I do object to your wasting your time and reputation in such low places. It will injure you eventually. I want you to take your evenings for society and lectures and concerts—"

"I'll go to the concerts and lectures gladly," said Michael gravely. "I can see they'll be fine for me, and I thank you very much for the opportunity. But that won't hinder my work. It begins always rather late in the evening, and there are other times—"

"You've no business staying out in places like that after the hour decent amusements close."

Michael refrained from saying he'd noticed society ladies returning from balls and entertainments several times on his way home.

"I simply can't have it if I'm to stand behind you."

"I'm sorry," said Michael. "You won't ever know how sorry I am. It was so good to know I had somebody who cared a little for me. I'll miss it very much. It's been almost like having a real father. Do you mean you'll have to give up the—fatherliness?"

Endicott's voice shook with mingled emotions. This young upstart, who professed to be so grateful and for whom he'd done so much, wouldn't actually run the risk of angering him—for the sake of a few wretched beings and a sentimental feeling he belonged in the slums and should do something for them!

"It means I won't do anything I planned to do for you, if you persist in refusing my reasonable request. Listen, young man—"

Michael noticed with pain that he'd dropped the customary "son" from his conversation, and it gave him an odd sensation of having been cut off from the earth.

"I planned—"

The keen eyes searched the face before him, and the man's voice took on an insinuating tone—the tone he used when he wished to buy up some political pull, that never failed to buy his man. Yet even as he spoke he felt that here was a man he couldn't buy.

"I planned to do a good many things for you. You'll be through your studies soon and be ready to set up for yourself. Had you thought ahead enough to know whether you'd like a partnership in some old firm or whether you want to set up for yourself?"

Michael's voice was grave and troubled, but he answered at once. "I'd like to set up for myself, sir. There are things I must do, and I don't know if a partner would feel as I do about them."

"Very well," said Endicott with satisfaction. He could only be pleased with the straightforward, decided way in which the boy was going ahead and shaping his own life. It showed he had character. There was nothing Mr. Endicott prized more than character—or what he called character.

"When you get ready to set up for yourself, and I don't think that will be so many years off from what I hear, I'll provide you an office, fully furnished, in the city's most desirable quarter and start you off as you should be started in order to win. I'll introduce you to some of my best friends and send lucrative business your way, with great corporations that will bring you into immediate prominence. Then I'll propose your name for membership in two or three good clubs. Now I'll do those things because I believe you have it in you to make good, but you'll need the boosting. Every man in this city does. Genius alone can't work you to the top, but I can give you what you need, and I mean to do it. But I feel that you should comply with the conditions."

There was a deep silence in the room. Michael was struggling to master his voice, but when he spoke it was husky with suppressed feeling.

"It's a great plan," he said. "It's just like you. Thank you, sir, for the thought, with all my heart. It grieves me more than anything I ever had to do to say no to you, but I cannot do as you ask. I cannot give up what I'm trying to do. I feel it would be wrong for me. I feel it is imperative, sir!"

"Cannot! You're like all the upstart reformers, filled with conceit. You think no one else can do the work but you! I'll pay someone to do what you're doing! Will that satisfy you?"

Michael shook his head slowly.

"No one could do it for pay," he said with conviction. "It must be done from—perhaps it's love—I don't know. But no one was doing it, and I must, for they are my people!"

As he said this the young man lifted his head with his angel-proud look that defied a universe to set him from his purpose, and Endicott, while he secretly revelled in the boy's firmness and purpose, yet writhed that he couldn't control this strength as he would.

"Your people! Bosh! You don't even know that! You may be the son of the richest man in New York for all you know."

"The more shame mine, then, if he left me where you found me! Mr. Endicott, have you ever been down in the alley where I used to live? Do you know the conditions down there?"

"No, and I don't want to go. And, what's more, I don't want you to go again. Whatever you were or are, you should see that you're mine now. Why, how do you know you weren't kidnapped for a ransom and the game went awry? There are a thousand possible explanations for your presence there. You may have been lost—"

"Then haven't I a debt to the people I lived with?"

"Oh, poppycock!" exclaimed the man angrily. "We'd better close the conversation. You understand how I feel. If you think it over and change your mind, come back and tell me within the week. I sail Saturday for Europe. I may not be back for three or four months. If you don't make up your mind before I go, you can write to me here at the office, and my secretary will forward it. You've disappointed me beyond anything I could have dreamed. I'm sure when you think it over you'll see how wrong you are and change your mind. Until then, good-bye!"

Michael arose dismissed, but he couldn't go that way.

"I won't change my mind," he said sadly, "but it's terrible not to have you understand. Won't you let me tell you about it? Won't you let me explain?"

"No, I don't want to hear any explanations. There's only one thing for me to understand, and that is that you think more of a set of vagabonds in an alley than you do of my request!"

"No! That's not true!" said Michael. "I think more of you than of any living man. I don't believe I could love you more if you were my own father. I would give my life for you this minute."

"An old word somewhere says, 'To obey is better than sacrifice.' Most people think they'd rather be great heroes than do simple everyday things demanded of them. The test doesn't always prove they would."

Michael's head went up almost haughtily, but great tears were in his eyes. Endicott dropped his own gaze from that sorrowful face. He knew his words were false and cruel. He knew Michael wouldn't hesitate a second to give his life. But the man couldn't bear to be withstood.

"If you feel that way I cannot take this!" Michael held out the check sadly, proudly.

"As you please!" snapped Endicott. "There's the wastebasket. Put it in if you like. It isn't mine any longer. You may spend it as you please. My conditions have nothing to do with what is past. If you don't prize my gift to you, by all means throw it away."

With a glance that would have broken Endicott's heart if he hadn't been too stubborn to look up, Michael slowly folded the check and put it back in his pocket.

"I do prize it," he said, "and I prize it because you gave it to me. It meant and always will mean a great deal to me."

"Hmph!"

"Perhaps I should tell you one more thing," Michael said hesitantly. "The farm. I'm using it in my work for those people. Perhaps you won't approve of that."

"I have nothing further to do with the farm. You bought it, I believe. You wanted to pay for it when you were earning enough money. That time hasn't come, so nothing more need be said. It's your farm, and you may use it as a pleasure park for pigs if you like. I don't go back on my bargains. Good afternoon."

Endicott turned to the phone, took up the receiver, and called up a number. Michael saw the conversation was ended. Slowly, with heavy step and heavier heart, he left the office.

New lines of sadness were etched on Michael's face that day. And when he went down to the alley that evening he was so gentle with the kids that they looked at him more than once with a new kind of awe and wonder. It was the gentleness of sacrifice for them, bringing with it the pain of love.

Old Sal, who came over to "look in" that evening, as she put it, shook her head as she stumped back to her rejuvenated room with its gaudy flowered wall, bit of white curtain and flowerpot in the window, all the work of Michael and his follower Sam.

"I'm thinkin' he'll disuppeer one o' these days. Ye'll wake up, an' he'll be gahn. He's not of this worrld. He'll sprid his wings an' away. He's a man-angel, thet's wot he is!"

Michael went home that night and wrote a letter to Mr. Endicott that would have broken a heart of stone, telling his inmost thought, showing his love and anguish in every sentence, and setting forth simply and unassumingly the wonderful work he was doing in the alley.

But though he waited anxiously day after day he received no reply. Endicott read every word of the letter and fairly gloated over the boy's strength, but he was too stubborn to let it be known. Also he rather enjoyed the test to which he was putting him.

Michael watched the outgoing vessels on Saturday, looked up the passenger lists, went down to the wharf, and tried to see him before he sailed. But for some reason he couldn't get in touch with him.

Standing sadly on the wharf as the vessel sailed, he caught sight of Endicott. Though he was sure he had been seen, he received no sign of recognition and turned away heartsick, feeling as if he had for conscience's sake stabbed one who loved him.

Chapter 18

Those were trying days for Michael. The weather had turned suddenly warm. The office was sometimes stifling. The daily routine got on his nerves, he who never knew he had nerves. He ached that Starr was gone from him—forever—and now he had by his own word cut loose from the man who was like a father to him—forever! He saw no hope in the future.

About that time, too, another sorrow came to him. He was glancing over the paper one morning on his way to the office, and his eye fell on the following item:

LONE TRAIN BANDIT HURT IN FIGHT AFTER GETTING LOOT
Captured by Conductor After Rifling Mailbags on Union Pacific Express

Topeka, Kan., July 20—A daring bandit was captured last night after he robbed the mail car on the Union Pacific train that left Kansas City for Denver at ten o'clock.

The train, known as the Denver Express, carrying heavy mail, was just leaving Kansas City when a man ran across the depot platform and leaped into the mail car through the open door. The clerk in charge faced the man, who aimed a revolver at him. He was commanded to bind and gag his five associates, and he obeyed. The robber went through the registered pouches, stuffing the packages into his pockets. Then he commanded the clerk to untie his comrades.

At Bonner Springs, where the train stopped briefly, the robber ordered the men to continue their work so as not to attract the attention of persons at the station. When the train reached Lawrence, the robber dropped from the car and ran toward the rear of the train. The conductor summoned two Lawrence policemen, and all three followed. After a quick race and a struggle, during which his arm was broken, the robber was captured. He appears to be an old offender New York police have been searching for in vain for the past ten months. He is known in the city's lower districts as "Fighting Buck" and has a list of offenses against him too numerous to mention.

Michael didn't know why he'd noticed the article or read it through to the finish. He didn't care to read that kind of thing; yet lately all crime and criminals held a sorrowful fascination for him. "It's what I might have done if I'd stayed in the alley," he would tell himself when he heard of some terrible crime being committed.

But when he reached the end of the article and saw Buck's name his heart seemed to stand still. Buck! The one old comrade he'd loved the most, who had loved and sacrificed for him; to whom he'd written and sent money; whose brain was brighter and heart was bigger than the others'; for whom he'd searched in vain and found only to lose before he saw him; whom he'd hoped yet to find and save. Buck had done this and was caught. And a government offense, too—robbing the mailbags! It would mean long, hard service. It would mean many years before Michael could help him to the right kind of life, if ever.

He asked permission to leave the office that afternoon and took the train down to the farm where Sam had been staying for some weeks. He read the article to him, hoping Sam would say there was some mistake and would know Buck was safe. But Sam listened, his countenance lowering. When the reading was finished he swore a great oath, such as he'd never uttered in Michael's presence, and Michael knew the story must be true.

Nothing could be done now; the law must have its course. But Michael's heart was heavy with the weight of what might have been if he could have found Buck sooner. The next day he secured permission to begin his vacation at once and, in spite of his presence being needed at Old Orchard, took the train for Kansas. He felt he must see Buck at once.

All during the long dismal ride, Michael's heart was beating over and over with the story of his own life. "I might have done this thing. I would have dared and thought it brave if I hadn't been taught better. I might be even now in jail with a broken arm and a useless life. The story of my crime might be bandied through the country in the newspapers if it hadn't been for Mr. Endicott—and little Starr! And yet I've hurt his feelings and alienated his great kindness by refusing his request. Was there no other way?"

Always his conscience answered, "There was no other way!"

Michael, armed with a letter from the senior Holt to a powerful member of Western municipal affairs, found entrance to Buck in his miserable confinement possible. He dawned upon his onetime friend, out of the cell's darkness, as an angel of light. Indeed, Buck, waking from a feverish sleep on his hard cot, moaning and cursing with the pain from his arm, started up and looked at him with awe and horror! The light from the corridor caught the gold in Michael's hair, and Buck thought some new terror had befallen him, and the death angel was summoning him to a final judgment for his misdeeds.

But Michael met his old friend with tenderness and a few phrases that had expressed their childish loyalty. Weakened by fever and pain, and above all his defeat and capture, Buck broke down and wept, and Michael wept with him.

"It might have been me instead of you, Buck. If I'd stayed behind, I'd have done all those things. I see it clearly. I might have been living here and you out free. Buck, if it could give you my chance in life and help you see it all as I do, I'd gladly lie here and take your place."

"Mickey! Mickey!" cried Buck. "It's me own Mickey! You was allus willin' to take de rubs! But, Mickey, ef you'd hed de trainin' you'd hev made de fine robber! You'd hev been a peach an' no mistake!"

Michael had found a soft spot in the warden's heart and succeeded in doing some little things for Buck's comfort. He hunted up the chaplain and secured a promise from him to teach Buck to read and write and to read to Buck all letters he received, until he could read them himself. He sent a pot of roses with buds in full bloom to perfume the dark cell, and he promised to write often.

Buck could only say over and over, "Oh, Mickey! Mickey! Ef we wos oney kids again! Oh, Mickey, I'll git out o' here yit an' find ye. Ye'll not be ashamed o' me. Ef I oney hadn't a bungled de job. It was a bum job, Mickey! A bum job!"

Michael saw little use in talking to Buck about his sin. Buck had nothing to build on in morals. To be loyal to his friends and do his "work" so he wouldn't get caught were the only articles in his creed. To get ahead of the rich, to take from them what was theirs if he could, regardless of life or consequences, that was virtue. The rich were enemies; they must outwit him or lose. If they died, it was "all in the day's work" and their loss. When his turn came he'd take his medicine calmly. But Buck's trouble now was that he'd "bungled the job." He'd disgraced his profession. Things had been going against him lately, and he was "down on his luck."

Michael left the West feeling the time allotted him with Buck was too short for what he wanted to do for him; yet he felt it was worth the journey. Buck appreciated his sympathy, even if he didn't have an adequate sense of his sinfulness. Michael had talked and pitied and tried to make Buck see, but in vain, and Michael went home to hope and write and try to educate Buck through sheer love. It was all he saw to do.

About this time, Michael began receiving money in small sums anonymously through the mail. "For your work," the first was labeled, and the remittances that followed had no inscriptions. They weren't always addressed in the same hand, and he never knew the writing. Sometimes there would be a ten-dollar bill, sometimes a twenty and often more, and they came irregularly, enclosed in a thin, inner envelope of foreign-looking paper.

Michael wondered if Starr could have sent them, but that was impossible, for she knew nothing of his work, and they were always postmarked New York. He discovered that such thin foreign-looking envelopes could be bought in New York, and after that he abandoned trying to solve the mystery. It was probably some eccentric, kind person who didn't wish to be known. He accepted the help gladly and broadened his plans for the farm accordingly.

Sam and his five friends had gone down early in the spring, bunking in the old house and enjoying the outing immensely. Under Sam's captaincy and the tutelage of an old farmer Michael had found, who couldn't work much himself but could direct, the work had gone forward.

Michael came down Saturdays and such ends of afternoons as he could get. Many mistakes were made through ignorance, and no less than five times the whole gang went on strike until Michael returned to settle some dispute between the new scientific farming he'd taught them and some old superstition or clumsy practice of the farmer's. But on the whole they did tolerably good work.

The farm community had been meanwhile increasing. Michael picked them up in the alley, or they came to him and asked to be taken on for a trial. They'd heard of the experiment through Sam or one of the boys who had returned to the city for a day on some errand.

One glorious summer morning Michael took ten small newsboys down to pick wild strawberries for the day, and they came back dirty, tired, strawberry streaked, and happy, loudly praising Old Orchard as if it were a heaven. After that Michael had no trouble transplanting anyone he wished to take with him.

He found a poor wretch lately moved with his family to one of the crowded tenements in the alley. He was sodden in drink and going to pieces fast. Michael sobered him up, found he used to be a master carpenter, and quickly transplanted him to Old Orchard, family and all.

Under the skilled carpenter's hand, tents and, later, one-room shacks or bungalows sprang up. Michael bought lumber and found apprentices to help, and the carpenter repaired barns, outhouses, and fences or built shacks, whenever the head of affairs saw fit to need another.

The only person in the whole alley Michael invited in vain to the farm was old Sally. She steadily refused to leave her brightly papered room, curtained window, and geranium. It symbolized "ould Ireland" to her, and she felt afraid of Michael's new place. It seemed like a door to heaven, from which she felt barred by her life, and some nameless terror in her thoughts. She wasn't ready to leave her bit of life and take chances even for Michael. And so she sat on her doorstep and watched the alley dwellers come and go, listening with interest to each new account of the farm, but never willing to see for herself. Perhaps the secret of her hesitation went deeper than superstition. She had learned Old Orchard had no rum shop around the corner. Old Sally couldn't risk it, so she stayed at home.

But the carpenter's wife was glad to cook for the men during the busy days of planting and weeding and harvesting, and the community grew. Two or three other men came down with their families and helped the carpenter build little houses, with a tiny garden in back and a flower bed in front. They could see the distant sea from their tiny porches and the river winding its salty silver way around. It was a great change from the alley. Not all could stand it, but most of them bore the summer test well. When winter set its white distance upon them, chilled the flowers to slumber, and stopped the labor, the testing time would come, and Michael was thinking about that.

He began hunting out helpers for his purposes. He found a man skilled in agricultural arts and secured his services to hold a regular school during the winter for the men. He found a poor student at Princeton who could run up on the train daily and give simple lessons in reading and arithmetic. He impressed it upon Sam and the other young men that unless they could read for themselves enough to keep up with new discoveries, other farmers would get ahead of them and grow bigger potatoes and sweeter corn. He talked eagerly with them about what they were going to do and how the place was going to grow, until he felt as if they owned the earth and meant to show the world how well they were running it. In short, he poured his own spirit of enthusiasm into them and made the hard summer of unaccustomed labor one great game.

When the proceeds from their first simple crops came in from selling products they didn't need, Michael carefully divided it among his workmen. At his wish they went in a body, and each started a bank account at the town's national bank. It was an absurdly small amount, but it made the workers feel like millionaires. Word of the successes reached the city, and more people came down, until by fall thirty-eight men, women, and children were living on the farm.

Of course that made little appreciable difference in the alley's population, for as soon as one family moved out another moved in, and there was plenty of room for Michael's work to go on. Nevertheless, thirty-eight souls were on the way to a better knowledge of life, with clean, wholesome surroundings and a chance to learn how to read and work.

The carpenter was set to build more tiny houses for the next summer's campaign. The tents were folded away. The spring wheat was in. The fall plowing and fertilizing were completed and whatever else should be done to a farm for its winter sleep. Half a dozen cows were introduced into the settlement, and a roomy chicken house and run were built. Sam set about studying incubators and teaching his helpers. Then when the cranberries were picked, the community settled down to its study.

The Princeton student and the agricultural student grew deeply interested in their motley school and found a young woman who traveled down every afternoon for compensation and taught a kindergarten. Many of the prematurely grown-up mothers came with delight and profit and incidentally learned how to be better, cleaner, wiser mothers. The young woman of her own accord added a cooking school for the women and girls.

Once a week Michael brought someone from New York to amuse these poor childish people. And so the winter passed.

Once a wealthy friend of Mr. Holt asked to see the place. After going around the farm and making himself friendly by roasting chestnuts around the open fire in the "big house," as the original cottage was called, he returned to New York praising Michael. A few days later he mailed Michael the deed of the adjoining farm of one hundred acres, and Michael, radiant, realized his dreams for his downtrodden people were coming true. There would be room enough now for many years to come for the people he needed to bring down.

Of course this hadn't been done without discouragements. Some in the community had proved unmanageable, or unwilling to work; some had run away or smuggled in whiskey. There had been two or three incipient fights, and more than double the number of disappointing enterprises, but the work was going on.

And still no word came from Mr. Endicott.

Michael was holding well with his employers, who were beginning to talk to him of a partnership with them when he was finished. He had far outstripped French in his studies and seemed to master everything he touched with an eagerness that showed great intellectual appetite.

He still kept up his evening work in the room in the alley, though he divided his labors somewhat with Will French, Hester Semple, and others who heard of the work and offered their services. It had almost become a little settlement or mission in itself. The one room had become two and a bath, then the whole first floor with a small gymnasium. Will French led enthusiastically in this, and Hester had done many things for the little children and women. The next people for Michael's farm were always being prepared and were spoken of as "eligibles" by the workers.

Hester Semple had proved a valuable assistant, ready with suggestions, tireless, and as fervent as Michael. Night after night, the three toiled and came home happily together. The association with the two was sweet to Michael, whose heart was famished for friends and relations who "belonged." But Michael never thought to look on Hester in any other light than friend and fellow worker.

Will and Michael were coming home from the office one afternoon, talking eagerly of the progress at the farm.

"When you get married, Endicott," said Will, "you must build a handsome bungalow or something for your summer home, down there on the knoll overlooking the river where you can see the sea in the distance."

Michael grew sober at once. "I don't expect ever to be married, Will," he said after a pause, with one of his faraway looks and his chin up.

"The dickens!" said Will, stopping in his walk. "She hasn't refused you?"

"Refused me? Who? What do you mean?"

"Why, Hester. She hasn't turned you down, old chap?"

"Hester! Why, Will, you never thought—you don't think she ever thought—?"

"Well, I didn't know," said Will, embarrassed. "It looked pretty much like it sometimes. There didn't seem much show for me. I've thought lately you'd settled it and were engaged sure."

"Oh, Will," said Michael in a tone that showed his soul was moved to its depth.

"I say, old chap!" said Will. "I'm fiercely sorry I've butted into your affairs. I never dreamed you'd feel like this. Since I have, though, will you give me a good send-off with Hester? Sort of bless-you-my-son, and tell me you don't mind if I go ahead and try my luck."

"With all my heart, Will. I never thought of it, but I believe it would be great for you both. You seem sort of made for each other."

"It's awfully good of you to say so," said Will, "but I'm afraid Hester doesn't think so. She's taken up with you."

"Not at all!" said Michael eagerly. "Not in the least. I've never noticed it. I'm sure she likes you best."

So from that night Michael almost always had some excuse for staying later at the room or for going somewhere else for a while so he'd have to leave them partway home, and Hester and Will from then on walked together more. Thus Michael took his lonely way, cut off from even this friendly group.

And summer and winter made the second year of the Old Orchard community.

Then the following spring Starr Endicott and her mother came home, and things began to happen.

Chapter 19

Starr was eighteen and very beautiful when she returned. Society was made at once aware of her presence.

Michael, whose heart was alert to know of her and find out where Mr. Endicott was, saw the first notice in the paper.

Three times Endicott crossed the water to visit his wife and daughter during their stay abroad, and every time Michael knew and anxiously awaited some sign of his return. He'd read the society columns for two years now solely to see any news of the Endicott family, and he was growing wondrously wise in society's ways. He had also come to know society a little in another way.

Shortly after his last interview with Endicott, Emily Holt, daughter of the senior member of the Holt and Holt firm, had invited Michael to dine with her father and her. Following this had come an invitation to a house party at the Holts' country seat. This came in the busy season of the farmwork, but Michael, eager to please his employers, took a couple of days off and went. He enjoyed the good times to the full. He renewed his tennis, at which he'd been a master, and his rowing and riding, in both of which he excelled. Also, he met some pleasant people who accepted him for the splendid fellow he appeared and didn't ask who he was. Men of his looks and bearing didn't come their way every day, and Michael was good company wherever he went.

In the evenings, though, Michael was at a loss. He couldn't dance or make small talk. He was too intensely in earnest for society's ways, and they didn't understand. He could talk about books he'd read and what he thought, but they were great thoughts and not good form for a frivolous company to dwell upon. One didn't want an economics problem or a deep philosophical question thrust upon one at a dance. Michael became a delightful but difficult proposition for the girls present, each one undertaking to teach him how to talk in society, but each failing. At last Emily Holt set out to give him gentle hints on light conversation and found herself deep in a discussion of Wordsworth's poems, about which she knew nothing and in which Michaël's weary soul had been steeping itself lately.

Emily retired in laughing defeat finally and advised her protégé to take a course on modern novels. Michael, always serious, took her at her word and proceeded to do so, but his course ended after two or three weeks. He found them far from his taste, most too vividly portraying his alley's sins in high life. Michael had enough of that in real life and felt he couldn't stand the strain of modern fiction, so he returned to Wordsworth and found soothing mental stimulus.

Other invitations followed; some he accepted, and some he declined. Still, the handsome, independent young Adonis was in great demand despite his peculiar habit of always being in earnest about everything. Perhaps they liked him and ran after him more because of his inaccessibility and because he was doing something in the world. For it was being whispered about among those who knew—and perhaps Emily Holt originated it—that Michael would be brilliant in doing worthwhile things someday.

The tickets Endicott promised had arrived in due time, and anxious to please his benefactor, even in his alienation, Michael faithfully attended concerts and lectures and enjoyed them fully. He borrowed from his sleep, rather than from his work or study. And so he grew in knowledge and love of the arts.

Matters stood thus when Starr appeared on the scene. The young girl made her debut that winter, and the papers were filled with her picture and the activities given in her honor. She dined and danced day and night, and no debutante ever received the critics' higher praise for beauty, grace, and charm.

Michael read them all, carefully cut out and preserved a few pleasant things written about her, looked at the pictures, and turned from the pomp and pride to the snapshot of her on horseback in the park with her groom, which she sent to him when she was a little girl. That was his alone, but these others belonged to the world in which he had no part.

From all this society Michael now held aloof. He received many invitations, for he was growing more popular every day; but he declined them all. His honor kept him from going anywhere Starr was sure to be. He had a right, of course, and it would have been somehow pleasant for her to see he was welcome in her world. But her mother's biting words always appeared before his mental vision as she put him down from her glorified world into shame and sin and sorrow. He felt that Starr was so far above him he mustn't hurt her by coming too near. And so in deference to his vow when his unworthiness was first presented to him, he stayed away.

As Starr heard more of his conquests in her world, she wondered and was piqued that he didn't come near her. And one day, meeting him by chance on Fifth Avenue, she greeted him graciously and invited him to call.

Michael thanked her with his quiet manner, while his heart was in a tumult over her beauty and her smiles that blossomed out in the old childish ways—only more beautifully, it seemed to him. He went in the strength of that smile many days, but he didn't call.

The days passed into weeks and months, and still he didn't appear, and Starr, hearing more of his growing inaccessibility, determined to show the others she could draw him out of his shell. She humbled her Endicott pride and wrote him a charming note asking him to call on an afternoon when she and her mother held court. But Michael, though he treasured the note, wrote a courteous but decided refusal.

This angered Starr so much she decided to cut him out of her good graces entirely. And indeed her social activities scarcely gave her time for remembering old friends. In occasional odd moments when she thought of him at all, it was with a vague disappointment that he too, with all her other childhood things, hadn't turned out to be what she had thought.

But she met him face-to-face one Sunday afternoon walking on the avenue with one of many young men who eagerly attended her. He was slender and handsome, with dark eyes and hair and a reckless mouth. Jaded lines had already formed around his eyes and lips. His name was Stuyvesant Carter. Michael recognized him at once from his picture in the papers the week before as leader with Starr of the cotillion. Seeing him with her in the sunny afternoon was like a cloud of trouble looming on a perfect day. He searched the man before him to the depths and then looked at the beautiful, innocent, happy face.

Michael was walking with Hester Semple, who in her broadcloth tailored suit and black plumed hat looked pretty and distinguished walking beside him. His own garments always seemed to set him off as if designed especially for him, and many watched him as he passed by.

Had it been a moment later, or even three minutes before, Will French would have been with them, and Michael would have been obviously a third member of the party, for he was careful in these days to let them both know he considered that they belonged together. But Will had stopped a moment to speak to a business acquaintance, and Hester and Michael were walking slowly ahead until he rejoined them.

"Look!" said Hester excitedly. "Isn't that the pretty Miss Endicott whose picture's in the papers so much? I'm sure it must be, though she's ten times prettier than her pictures."

But Michael was already looking with all his soul in his eyes.

As they came opposite, he lifted his hat with such marked deference to Starr that Stuyvesant Carter looked at him insolently, with a careless motion of his own hand toward his hat. But Starr, with brilliant cheeks and her eyes looking straight at Michael, continued her conversation with her companion and never by a flickering eyelash recognized her former friend.

Hester was so taken up with looking at the society beauty that she never noticed Michael's lifted hat until they were passed. Then Will French joined them breezily.

"She's a peach, isn't she?" he breathed as he took his place beside Hester, and Michael dropped behind. "But I suppose it'll rub off. They say most of those swells aren't real."

"I think she's real!" declared Hester. "She has sweet eyes and a charming smile. The color on her cheeks wasn't painted on. I just love her. I'd like to know her. She certainly is beautiful and doesn't look a bit spoiled. Did you ever see such eyes?"

"They aren't half as nice as a pair of gray ones I know," said Will, looking at them as they were lifted smiling to his.

"Will, you mustn't say such things—on the street—anyway—and Michael just behind. Why, where is Michael? Oh, he's dropped behind and is walking slowly. Will, does Michael know Miss Endicott? I never thought about their names being the same. But he lifted his hat to her—and she simply stared blankly at him as if she'd never seen him before."

"The little snob!" said Will indignantly "I told you they were all artificial. I believe they're some kind of relation or other. Come to think of it—I believe old Endicott introduced Michael into our office. Maybe she hasn't seen him in a long time and has forgotten him."

"No one who has known Michael could ever forget him," said Hester with conviction.

"No, I suppose that's so," said Will, looking at her wistfully.

After this meeting Michael kept more aloof from even small entrances into society and gave more of his time to study and to work among the poor.

So the winter passed in a round of festivities, transplanted for a few weeks to Palm Beach, back to New York, then to Tuxedo Park for the summer—and Michael knew but had no part in it. Now she had cut him out of her life herself, and he might not even cherish her bright smiles and words of the past. She didn't wish to know him. It was right and best—but agony!

Michael grew pale that year and looked more like the man-angel than ever as he came and went in the alley. Old Sally from her doorstep, drawing nearer to her own end, saw it first and called daily attention to Michael's spirit look as he passed.

One evening early in spring, Michael was starting home weary and unusually discouraged. Sam had gone down to the farm with Jim to prepare for the spring work and find out how things were going and what was needed from the city. Jim was developing into a tolerably dependable fellow except for his hot temper, and Michael missed them from the alley work, for the rooms were crowded now every night. True, Hester and Will were faithful, but they were so much taken up with one another these days that he didn't like to trouble them with unusual cases, and he had no one with whom to counsel. Several things had been going awry, and he was sad.

Hester and Will were ahead, walking slowly as usual.

Michael locked the door with a sigh and turned to follow them, when he saw in the shadows on the other side of the court two figures steal from an opening between the houses and move along toward the end of the alley. Something in their demeanor made Michael watch them. As they neared the end of the alley toward the street they paused a moment, and one figure stole back. He thought he recognized her as a girl cursed with more than the usual amount of beauty. She disappeared into the dark tenement, but, after looking back, the other kept on toward the street. Michael quickened his steps and reached the corner at about the same time, crossing as the other man passed the light and looking full in his face.

To his surprise he saw that the man was Stuyvesant Carter!

With an exclamation of disgust and horror, Michael stepped in the man's path and blocked his passage.

"What are you doing here?" he asked in tones that would have made a brave man tremble.

Stuyvesant Carter glared at him, drew his hat down over his eyes, and snarled: "Get out of my way, or you'll be sorry! I'm probably doing the same thing you're doing here!"

"Probably not!" said Michael. "You know you can mean no good to a girl like the one you were just with. Come down here again at your peril! And if I hear of you having anything to do with that girl, I'll have the whole thing made public."

"Indeed!" said Carter. "Is she your girl? I think not. And who are you anyway?"

"You'll find out if you come down here again!" said Michael, his fingers fairly aching to grip the gentlemanly villain before him. "Now get out of here at once, or you may not be able to walk out."

"I'll get out when I like!" sneered the other, nevertheless backing away through the opening given him. After reaching a safe distance, he added tauntingly, "And I'll come back when I like, too."

"Very well—I'll be ready for you, Mr. Carter!"

Michael's tones were clear and distinct and could be heard two blocks away in the city night. Hearing his real name spoken fearlessly in such an environment, Carter slid away as if he'd suddenly been erased from the scene.

"Who was dat guy?" asked a small voice at Michael's elbow.

Hester and Will were far down the street in the other direction and had forgotten Michael.

Michael turned and saw one of his smallest "kids" crouching in the shadow beside him.

"Why, Tony, are you here yet? You should have been asleep long ago."

"Was dat de guy wot comes to see Lizzie?"

"See here, Tony—what do you know about this?"

Tony proceeded to unfold a tale that made Michael's heart sick.

"Lizzie, she's got swell sence she went away to work to a res'trant at de sheeshole. She ain't leavin' her ma hev her wages, an' she wears fierce cloes, like de swells!" finished Tony solemnly as if these were the worst of all he'd told.

So Michael sent Tony to his rest and went home with a heavy heart, to wake and think through the night what he should do to save his bright beautiful Starr from the clutches of this human vampire.

When morning dawned Michael knew—he would go to Mr. Endicott and tell him the whole story. Starr's father could and would protect her better than he could.

As early as he could he hurried to carry out his purpose. But on arriving at Mr. Endicott's office he was told the gentleman had sailed for Austria and would be absent some weeks, even months, perhaps, if his business didn't mature rapidly.

Michael asked for the address, but when he reached his desk again and tried to frame a letter to convey the truth convincingly to the absent father, who couldn't read it for more than a week at least and would then be thousands of miles away, he gave it up as useless. Something more effectual must be done quickly.

First he must have facts. He couldn't do anything until he knew without a doubt that what he feared was true. If he could have told Mr. Endicott, all would have been different; he could investigate if he saw fit. Michael might have left the matter in his hands. But he couldn't tell him.

If he could go to some other male family member with the warning, he must be very sure of his ground before he spoke. If there were no such male friend or relative he must do something else—what? He shrank from thinking.

So, with the sources open to a keen lawyer, he took steps to ferret out the life and doings of Stuyvesant Carter and, needless to say, unearthed a lot of information so sickening he felt almost helpless before it. It was appalling—and more so because of the man's rank and station. If he had been raised in the slums one might have expected it—but this!

The second day, Michael, haggard and worn with the responsibility, started out to find that useful male Endicott relative. There seemed to be no such person. The third morning he came to the office determined to tell the whole story to the senior Mr. Holt and ask his advice and aid in protecting Starr. But to his dismay he found the man had been taken seriously ill with heart trouble, and it might be weeks before he could return to the office.

Deeply grieved and baffled, the young man tried to think what to do next. The junior Mr. Holt had never encouraged confidences and wouldn't likely help in this matter. He must do something himself.

And now Michael faced two alternatives. Only two people could he tell the story to: Starr and her mother!

Tell Starr all he knew he could not. To tell her anything of this story would be gall and wormwood! To drop a hint that would blacken another man's character would place him in an awkward position. To think of doing it was like tearing out his heart for her to trample upon.

Yet Michael would rather face a thousand bristling cannons in battle than meet the mother on her own ground and tell her what he had to tell, while her steel-cold eyes pierced him through with scorn and unbelief. He felt he would fail if he went to her.

At last he wrote a note to Starr:

Dear Miss Endicott:
 Can you let me have a brief interview at your convenience and as soon as possible? I have a favor to ask of you which I earnestly hope you will grant.

Sincerely yours,
Michael

He sent the note off with fear and trembling. He had carefully considered every word, and yet it haunted him that he might have written differently. Would she grant the interview? If she didn't what should he do?

The next day he received a ceremonious note on creamy paper crested with a silver star monogrammed in blue.

Miss Endicott will receive Mr. Endicott tomorrow morning at eleven.

A shiver ran through him as he read and then consigned the elegant communication to his wastebasket. It wasn't from his Starr. It was from a stranger. Yet the subtle perfume stealing from the envelope reminded him of her. On second thought he drew it forth again and put it in his pocket. After all she'd granted the interview, and this paper was part of her daily life; it had come from her, and she had written and sent it to him. It was precious.

Starr had been more than usually thoughtful when she read Michael's note. It pleased her that at last she'd brought him to her feet, though not for the world would she let him know. Doubtless he wished her influence for some position he would have asked of her father if he'd been at home. Starr knew nothing of the alienation between her father and Michael. But Michael should pay for his request, in humility at least. So she sent her cool stab.

But Michael didn't look humiliated as he entered the library where Starr had chosen to receive him. His manner was grave and assured, and he made no sign of the tumult it gave him to see her thus in her own home again where the luxury enhanced her womanliness and charm.

He came forward to greet her as if she hadn't cut him dead the last time they met, and Starr, as she regarded him, was struck with wonder over the exalted beauty of manhood that was his unique inheritance.

"Thank you for letting me come," he said. "I won't intrude long upon your time—"

Starr had a strange fearful sensation he would slip away from her again before she was willing.

"Oh, that's all right," she said graciously. "Won't you sit down? I'm always glad to do a favor for a childhood friend."

She had rehearsed that sentence many times in her mind, and it was meant to convey reproach and indifference. But as she fluttered into a great leather chair she felt her voice was trembling, and she'd miserably failed in what she'd meant to do. She felt strangely ashamed of her attitude, with those two clear eyes looking straight at her. It reminded her of how he'd looked when he told her in the Florida chapel long ago that nobody but she had ever kissed him— and she had kissed him then. Suppose he was going to ask her to do it again! The thought made her cheeks rosy, and her society air deserted her. But of course he wouldn't do that. It was a crazy thought. What was the matter with her anyway, and why did she feel so unnerved? Then Michael spoke.

"May I ask if you know a man by the name of Stuyvesant Carter?"

Starr looked startled and then stiffened slightly.

"I do!" she answered graciously. "He's one of my intimate friends. Can he do something for you that you'd like my intercession?"

Starr smiled graciously. She thought she understood the reason for Michael's call now and was pleased to think how easily she could grant his request. The idea of introducing them was stimulating. She was pondering what a handsome pair of men they were and so different from each other.

But Michael's clear voice startled her again out of her complacence.

"Thank God there isn't!" he said, and his tone made Starr sit up and put on all her dignity.

"Indeed!" she said with asperity, her eyes flashing.

"Pardon me, Miss Endicott," Michael said sadly. "You don't understand my feeling!"

"I certainly do not." Starr had inherited her icicle sentences from her mother.

"And I cannot explain," he went on sadly. "I must ask you to take it on trust. The favor I've come to ask is this—that you won't have anything further to do with that young man until your father's return. I know this may seem strange to you. But, believe me, if you understood, you wouldn't hesitate to do what I've asked."

Michael held her with his look and earnest tones. She couldn't speak from sheer astonishment at his audacity. Then she froze him with a look copied from her mother's haughty manner.

"And what reason can you give for such an extraordinary request?" she asked at last, when his look compelled an answer.

"I cannot give you a reason," he said gravely. "You must trust me that this is best. Your father will explain to you when he comes."

Another pause and then Starr asked, "And you really think I'd grant such a ridiculous request which implies a lack of trust in the character of one of my warmest friends?"

"I most earnestly hope you will," answered Michael.

In spite of her hauteur she was impressed by Michael's manner. His grave tones and serious eyes told her heart that here was something extraordinary; at least she gave Michael credit for thinking there was.

"I certainly won't do anything of the kind without good reason for it." Starr's tone was determined and cold.

"And I can give you no reason beyond telling you he isn't the kind of man a friend of yours should be."

"What do you mean?"

"Please don't ask me. Please trust me and give me your promise. At least wait until I can write your father."

Starr rose with a look of her father's stubbornness now in her pretty face.

"I wish to be told," she demanded angrily.

"You wouldn't wish it if you knew," he answered.

She looked at him steadily for a full moment, then tossed her head and said, "I must decline your request, Mr. Endicott. You'll excuse me. I have a luncheon engagement now."

She stood aside for him to go out the door.

He rose with pleading still in his eyes. "You'll write to your father and tell him what I've said? You'll wait until you hear from him?"

"It's impossible, Mr. Endicott." Starr's tone was freezing now, and he could see she was very angry. "Mr. Carter is my friend!" she flung at him as he passed her into the hall.

Another anguishing night brought Michael face-to-face with the necessity for an interview with Starr's mother.

Taking his cue from the hour Starr had set for his call, he went a little before eleven o'clock and sent up the card of the firm with his name written below, for he doubted he would obtain an interview if the lady thought he might be there on his own business.

Mrs. Endicott probably didn't recognize the former "Mickey" under the title written below his most respectable law firm's name. Any representative of Holt and Holt was to be recognized, of course. She came down within a half hour, graciously with lorgnette in hand, until she reached the center of the reception room where he was put to await her. Then Michael arose, almost from the same spot where she had addressed him nearly four years before, the halo of the morning shining through the window on his hair. With a start and stiffening of her form, she recognized him.

"Oh, it's you!" Her tone argued ill for Michael's mission, but with grave and gentle bearing he began.

"Madam, I beg your pardon for the intrusion. I wouldn't have come if there'd been another way. I tried to find Mr. Endicott but was told he'd sailed—"

"You needn't waste your time and mine. I'll do nothing for you. As I told you before, if I remember, I think far too much already has been done for you, and I never felt you had the slightest claim on our bounty. I refuse to hear any hard-luck stories."

Michael's face was a study. Indignation and shame struggled with a sudden sense of the ridiculous. What he did was laugh—a rich, clear, musical laugh that stopped the lady's tirade better than anything else could have.

"Well! Really! Have you come to insult me?" she said angrily. "I'll call a servant." She stepped toward the bell.

"Madam, I beg your pardon," said Michael, grave at once. "I intended no insult and haven't come to ask a favor. I came because of a serious matter, perhaps a grave danger to your home, which I thought you should know about."

"Indeed! Well, make haste," said Mrs. Endicott, half mollified. "My time is valuable. Is someone planning to rob the house?"

Michael looked straight in her face and told her briefly a few facts, delicately worded, forcefully put, which would have convinced the heart of any true mother that the man before her had only pure motives.

Not so this mother. The more Michael talked, the stiffer, haughtier, more hateful grew her stare. Then he paused, not wishing to overwhelm her with his facts.

"How could you possibly know these things," she remarked, "unless you were in the same places where you claim Mr. Carter has been? But, oh, I forgot! Your former home was there, and so you must have many friends among—ah—those people!" She punctuated the last two words with a contemptuous look through the lorgnette.

"But, my dear fellow," she went on in her patronizing manner, "you should never trust those people. Of course you don't understand that, having been away from them so many years among respectable folks, but they really don't know what the truth is. I doubt there's any foundation for all you've been telling me."

"Madam, I've looked into the matter and know every word I've told you is true. Two of the city's most noted detectives have been investigating. I wouldn't have come if I hadn't had indisputable facts to give you."

Mrs. Endicott arose, still holding the lorgnette to her eyes, though she showed the interview was drawing to a close.

"Then, young man," she said, "I must tell you the things you've been saying are not considered proper to speak of before ladies in respectable society. I remember your low origin and lack of breeding and forgive what I would otherwise consider an insult. Further, it isn't considered honorable to investigate a gentleman's private life too closely. All young men sow their wild oats and are probably none the worse for it. In fact, if a man hasn't seen life he isn't worth much. It's his own affair and not your business. I must ask you not to say anything of this to anyone. Not a word! My husband would be deeply outraged to know a friend of his daughter's, a man of refinement and position, had been the object of scandal by one who should honor anyone he honors. I can't spare any more time this morning."

"But, madam! You certainly don't mean you won't investigate this matter for yourself? You wouldn't let your daughter accept such a man as her friend?"

The lorgnette came into play again, but its stare was ineffectual upon Michael's pale, earnest face. His deep eyes lit with horror at this monstrous woman who seemed devoid of mother love.

"It's none of your business what I mean. You've done what you thought was your duty by telling me. Now put the matter entirely out of your mind. Desist at once!"

With a final stare, she swept out of the room and up the broad staircase. Michael, watching her until she was out of sight, left the house with bowed head and burdened heart to write a letter to Starr's father. The letter would have performed its mission where his other efforts had failed, but because of a sudden and unexpected change of address it just missed him at every stopping place, as it traveled its silent, unfruitful way about the world after him, never getting anywhere until too late.

Chapter 20

Starr was very angry when Michael left her. There was perhaps more hurt pride and pique in her anger than she'd have owned. He hadn't succumbed to her charms; he hadn't seemed to notice her as other men did; he had even lost the look of admiration he used to wear when they were boy and girl. He'd refused to tell her what she had a great curiosity to know.

She was sure that if Michael would tell her what he had against Stuyvesant Carter she could explain it. Her head was almost turned by now with the adoration she'd received. She thought she knew almost everything Stuyvesant Carter had ever done. He was a fluent talker and had spent many hours detailing incidents and anecdotes of his eventful career to her. He had raced a good deal and still had several expensive racing cars. There was nothing very dreadful about that except it was dangerous. He used to gamble a great deal, but he promised he'd never do it again because she thought it unrefined. Of course it wasn't as if he didn't have plenty of money, and her mother had told her all young men did those things. No, not her father, of course, for he'd been unusual, but times were different now. Young men were expected to be a little wild. It was the influence of college life and a progressive age, she supposed. It didn't do any harm. They always settled down and made good husbands after marriage. Michael didn't understand these things. He'd spent many years in Florida with a dear old professor and a lot of good little boys and was unacquainted with the world's ways.

Thus she reasoned, though Michael's warning troubled her. Finally she decided to go to the best source of information and ask Carter himself.

So three days after Michael's visit, when Carter dropped in to ask her to go to the opera that evening instead of something else they'd planned, she laughingly questioned him.

"What in the world can you ever have done, Mr. Carter, that would make you unfit company for me?"

She asked the question lightly, though her eyes watched his face closely as she waited for the answer.

The blood rolled in dark waves over his handsome face, and his brows grew dark with anger, half hiding the start of almost fear with which he regarded her.

"What do you mean, Starr?" He looked at her keenly and couldn't tell if she were in earnest or not.

"Just that," she said, half mocking, half serious. "Tell me what you've been doing that would make you unfit company for me? Someone has been trying to make me promise to have nothing to do with you, and I want to know what it means."

"Who's been doing that?" Dangerous lights flickered in the dark eyes, lights that showed the brutality of the coward and the evildoer.

"Oh, a man! But if you look like that I won't tell you anything more about it. I don't think I like you now. You look as if you could eat me. You make me think there must be something to it."

Quick to take the warning, the young man brought his face under control and broke into an artificial laugh. Suddenly he understood, and fear entered his heart. There was nothing like being bold and taking the bull by the horns.

"I'll wager I can explain the riddle for you," he said airily. "I lost my way the other evening coming home late. There had been some mistake, and my car didn't come to the club for me. I started on foot, leaving word for it to overtake me." He lied as he went along. He'd had a short lifetime of practice and did it easily. "I was thinking about you and how soon I dared ask you a certain question, when all at once I noticed things seemed unfamiliar. I turned to go back but couldn't tell which way I'd turned at the last corner—you see what a dangerous influence you have on me—and I wandered deeper into things. It wasn't a very savory neighborhood, and I wanted to get out as soon as possible. I suspected it wasn't even safe down there alone at that hour of the night. I was hesitating under a streetlight close to a dark alley, trying to decide the quickest way out and what I should do to find a policeman. Suddenly, out of the dark, loomed a great tall brute with the strangest-looking yellow hair and a body that looked as if he could play football with the universe. He charged me with having come down there to visit his girl.

"Well, of course the situation wasn't very pleasant. I tried to explain I was lost and had never been down in that quarter before and didn't even know his girl. But he wouldn't listen to anything and began threatening me. Then I took out my card and handed it to him, unwisely, of course—but then I'm wholly unused to such situations. I explained to him who I was and of course I wouldn't want to see his girl, even if I'd be so mean and all that. But that fellow wouldn't take a word of it. He threw the card on the sidewalk, ground his heel into it, and used all sorts of evil language I can't repeat. Finally, after I thought he was going to put me in the ditch and pummel me, he let me go, shouting after me that if I ever came near his girl again he'd publish it in the newspapers. Then of course I understood what a foolish thing I'd done in giving him my card. But it was too late. I told him as politely as I knew how that if he'd show me the way to get home I'd never trouble him again. He finally let me go."

Starr's eyes were all this time searching his face. "Was the man intoxicated?"

"Oh, I presume so, more or less. They all are down there, though I'd say he wasn't of the slums himself. He was well dressed and probably angry I'd discovered him in such haunts."

"When did this happen?"

"About a week ago."

"Why didn't you tell me about it before?"

"Oh, I didn't want to distress you. Besides, I've had my mind too full of other things. Starr, darling, you must have seen all these weeks how much I love you and how I've only been waiting for the opportunity to ask you to be my wife."

Starr was in a measure prepared for this proposal: Her mother had instructed her that the alliance was wholly acceptable, even desirable. She herself was quite taken up with this handsome admirer who flattered her hourly and showered attentions upon her until she felt quite content with herself, the world and him. Starr had a spice of daring that liked what she thought to be Carter's wildness and energy, and she'd made up her mind to accept him.

One week later the society papers announced the engagement, and the world was in a flutter over the many functions immediately set up in their honor.

Michael, at his desk in the busy office, read and bowed his head in anguish. His bright, beautiful Starr, to be sacrificed to a beast like that! Would that he might save her again to life and happiness!

For the next few days Michael went about in a state that almost bordered on the frantic. His pale face looked drawn, and his eyes burned like live coals. People turned to look after him on the street and exclaimed, "Why, look at that man!" Yet he seemed more like an avenging angel dropped down for some terrible errand than like a plain, ordinary man.

Mr. Holt noticed it and spoke to him about it. "You should drop work and take a good vacation, Endicott. You're in bad shape. You'll break down and be ill. If I were in your place I'd cancel the rent of that office and not try to start out for yourself until fall. It'll repay you in the end. You're taking things too seriously."

But Michael smiled and shook his head. He was to open his own office the following week. It was ready with its simple furnishings, in marked contrast to the rooms that would have been his if he'd acceded to his benefactor's request. But Michael had lost interest in office and work alike, and the room seemed now only a refuge from men's eyes where he might hide with his great sorrow and try to study out some way to save Starr. Surely her father would do something when he received his letter! It was long past time for an answer. But then perhaps he was already doing something, though he was unwilling to afford Michael the satisfaction of knowing it.

He gave much thought to sending a cablegram, telling the story to the father while telling nothing to the world, but abandoned the idea.

Sam came up from the farm and saw Michael's face and was worried.

"Say, pard, wot yer bin doin' t' yersef? Better come down t' th' farm an' git a bit o' fresh air."

The only two people who didn't notice the change in Michael's appearance were Hester and Will. They were too much engrossed in each other by this time to notice even Michael. They usually left the rooms in the alley earlier than Michael and went home by themselves.

They left him thus one night about three weeks after Starr's engagement had been announced. Michael stayed in the room for an hour after everyone else had gone. He was expecting Sam to return. Sam had been up from the farm several times lately, and this time without any apparent reason he had lingered in the city. He hadn't been to the room that night except for ten minutes early in the evening when he mumbled something about a little business and said he would be back before Michael left.

Michael sat for a long time, his elbow on the table, his head in his hands. He'd thought of a way that might prevent Starr from throwing away her happiness. The morning paper had hinted of plans for a speedy wedding. It was rumored that Miss Endicott would marry as soon as her father reached home. Michael was desperate. The father might arrive too late for him to speak with him. He'd begun to know it was hard to convince people of the evil of those they'd chosen as friends. It would take time.

There was a way. He might have the whole story published in the papers. A public scandal would doubtless delay if not stop this alliance, but a public scandal that touched Mr. Carter would also touch and bring into publicity the girl whose life was almost linked with his. Not until the last resort would Michael bring about that publicity. That such a move on his part would beget him the eternal enmity of the entire Endicott family he didn't doubt, but that factor didn't figure in Michael's calculations. He wasn't working for himself in this. Nothing that ever happened could make things right for him, he felt, and what was his life, or good name even, beside Starr's happiness?

Wearily, at last, his problem unsolved, he got up and turned out the lights. As he was locking the door, his attention was arrested by two figures standing between him and the streetlight at the end of the alley. It was a man and a woman, and the woman seemed to be clinging to the man and pleading with him.

Such sights weren't uncommon in the alley. Some poor woman often thus appealed to what used to be good in the man she married, to get him to stay away from the saloon or give her a little of his money to buy food for the children.

More than once in such instances Michael had successfully added his influence to the wife's and convinced the man to go quietly home.

He put the key hastily in his pocket and hurried toward the two.

"You won't never go back to her!" he heard the woman cry fiercely. "You promised me—"

"Shut up, will you? I don't care what I promised," said the man in a guarded voice Michael felt sure he'd heard before.

"I won't shut up! I'll holler ef you go, so the police'll come. You've got a right to stay with me. You won't do me wrong, ner you won't go back to that stuck-up piece. You're mine, I say, and you promised!"

With a curse the man struck her a cruel blow across the mouth and tried to tear her clinging hands away from his coat, but they only clung more fiercely.

Michael sprang to the woman's side like a panther.

"Look out!" he said in clear tones. "You can't strike a woman!" His voice was low and calm and sounded as it had on the ball field when he was giving directions to his team at some crisis in the game.

"Who says I can't?" snarled the man, and now Michael was sure he knew the voice.

Then the wretch struck the woman between her eyes, and she fell heavily to the ground.

Like a flash Michael's arm went out and felled the man. In the same breath, from the shadows sprang Sam's slender, wiry figure flinging itself upon the man on the ground who with angry imprecations was struggling to his feet. His hand had gone to an inner pocket as he fell, and in a moment more came a flash of light, and Michael felt a bullet whiz by his ear. Nothing but the swerving of the struggling figures saved it from going through his brain. In that instant it occurred to Michael that was what had been intended. The conviction that the man had also recognized him gave strength to his arm as he wrenched the revolver from the would-be assassin's hand. Nobody knew better than Michael how easy it would be to plead "self-defense" if the fellow got into trouble. A man in young Carter's position with wealth and friends galore needn't fear wiping an unknown fellow out of existence, whose friends with few exceptions were toughs and jailbirds and ex-criminals.

As he gave Carter's wrist the twist that sent the revolver to the ground beside the unconscious woman, Michael heard the hurried footsteps of the law officer accompanied by a curious motley crowd who had heard the pistol shot and come to see any new excitement life offered. He suddenly realized how bad matters would look for Sam if he were found in the embrace of one of society's pets who would surely tell a tale to clear himself regardless of others. Michael had no care for himself. The police about that quarter knew him well and were acquainted with his work. They looked upon him with almost more respect than they did the priests and deaconesses who went about their errands of mercy; for Michael's spirit look of being more than man and the stories attached to his name in the alley filled them with a worshipful awe. There was little likelihood of trouble for Michael with the officers he knew. But Sam was another proposition. His past life hadn't been virtuous, and lately he'd been in New Jersey so much he was little known and would be suspected of causing the trouble. Besides, the woman lay unconscious at their feet.

With a mighty effort Michael now reached forth and plucked Sam, struggling fiercely, from his antagonist's arms and put him behind him in the doorway, standing firmly in front. Carter, thus released, sprawled in the road; then taking advantage of the momentary release he struggled to his feet and fled in the opposite direction from which the officers approached.

"Let me go! I gotta get 'm!" muttered Sam, pushing fiercely to get by Michael.

"No, Sam, stay where you are and keep quiet. You'll gain nothing by running after him. You'll only get into trouble yourself."

"I don't care what happens to me!" said Sam. "I'll kill him. He stole my girl!"

But Michael stood before him like a wall.

"Yes, Sam, my poor fellow, I know," said Michael gently, sadly. "I know, Sam. He stole mine, too!"

Sam subsided as if he'd been struck, a low awful curse upon his lips, his face pale and baleful.

"You, too?" The yearning tenderness went to Michael's heart like sweet salve, even in the stressful moment. They were brothers in sorrow, and their brotherhood saved Sam from committing a crime.

Then the police and crowds swept up breathless.

"What does all this mean?" panted a policeman, touching his cap respectfully to Michael. "Someone been shooting?"

He stooped and peered into the pale face of the still-unconscious woman and then looked suspiciously toward Sam standing sullenly behind Michael.

"He's all right," said Michael with a smile, throwing an arm across Sam's shoulder. "He only came in to help me when he saw I was having a hard time. The fellow made off in that direction." Michael pointed after Carter, whose form had disappeared in the darkness.

"Any of the gang?" asked the officer as he hurried away.

"No!" said Michael. "He doesn't belong here!"

One officer hurried away accompanied by a crowd; the other stayed to look after the woman. He touched the woman with his foot as he might have tapped a dying dog to see if any life remained. A low growl like a fierce animal came from Sam's closed lips.

Michael put a warning hand on his arm. "Steady, Sam, steady!" he murmured and went himself and lifted the girl's pretty head from its stony pillow.

"I think you'd better send for the ambulance," he said to the officer. "She's had a heavy blow on her head. I arrived just in time to see the beginning of the trouble—"

"Ain't she dead?" asked the officer indifferently. "Best get her into her house. Don't reckon they want to mess up the hospital with such cattle as this."

Michael caught the fierce gleam in Sam's eyes. A second more would have seen the officer lying beside the girl in the road and a double tragedy to the night's record, for Sam was crouched and moving stealthily like a cat toward the officer's back, a look of almost insane fury upon his small, thin face. Michael's steady voice recalled him to sanity, as many times in the midst of a game he'd put self-control and courage into his teammates' hearts.

"Sam, could you come here and hold her head a minute, while I try to get some water? Yes, officer, I think she's living, and she should be taken to the hospital as soon as possible. Please give the call at once."

The officer sauntered off to do his bidding. Michael and Sam began working over the unconscious girl, and the crowd stood idly waiting until the ambulance rattled up. They watched with awe as the woman's form was lifted in, and Michael and Sam climbed up on the front seat with the driver and rode off. Then they drifted away to their beds, and the street settled into the brief night respite.

The two young men waited at the hospital an hour until a white-capped nurse came to tell them Lizzie had recovered consciousness, and there was hope of her life. Then they went out into the late night.

"Sam, you're coming home with me tonight!" Michael put his arm affectionately around Sam's shoulders. "You never would come before, but you must come tonight."

And Sam, looking into the other's face, saw something in Michael's suffering eyes that made him yield.

"I ain't fit!" Sam murmured as they walked along. It was Sam's first hint that he wasn't every whit as good as Michael, and Michael with rare tact had never by a glance let Sam know how much he wished to have him cleaner and more suitably garbed.

"Oh, we'll make that all right!" said Michael, thankful that at last the time had come for presenting the neat garments he'd purchased some weeks before as a gift for Sam.

The dawn was hovering in the east when Michael led Sam up to his room and, throwing wide the door of his private bathroom, told Sam to take a hot bath; it would make him feel better.

While Sam was thus engaged Michael bundled up Sam's old garments and, stealing to the back hall window, landed them neatly on top of the ash barrel in the court below. Sam's clothes might see the alley again by way of the ash man, but never on Sam's back.

Late that same morning Sam, clothed and in a new and righter mind than ever in his life, walked down with Michael to breakfast and was introduced as "my friend Mr. Casey" to the landlady, who was hovering about the now-deserted breakfast table. He looked every inch a respectable citizen. Not handsome and distinguished like Michael, of course, but proper as a guest at Mrs. Semple's breakfast table.

Michael explained that an accident had detained them late the night before. Mrs. Semple gave special orders for a nice breakfast to be served to Mr. Endicott and his friend and said it wasn't any trouble at all.

People always thought it was no trouble to do things for Michael.

While they ate, Michael arranged with Sam to take a trip out to see Buck.

"I was expecting to go this morning," he said. "I'd made my plans. They write me that Buck's getting uneasy and they wish I'd come. But now"—he looked at Sam—"I think I should stay here a while. Could you go in my place? I must attend to some things here."

Sam's face grew dark with sympathy. He understood.

"I'll keep you informed about Lizzie," went on Michael with delicate intuition, "and anyway, you couldn't see her for some time. I think if you try you could help Buck as much as I. He needs to understand that breaking laws is all wrong, that it doesn't pay in the end and there has to be a penalty—you know. You can make him see things in a new way if you try. Will you go, Sam?"

"I'll go," said Sam.

Michael knew he'd do his best. Sam's changed viewpoint might have more effect on Buck than anything Michael could say. For it was an open secret between Sam and Michael now that Sam stood for a new order of things and the old life, so far as he was concerned, had been put away.

So Sam was taken safely away from the danger spot, and Michael stayed to face his sorrow and the problem of how to save Starr.

Chapter 21

The papers the next morning announced that Mr. Stuyvesant Carter, while taking a shortcut through the city's lower quarter, had been cruelly attacked, beaten, and robbed and barely escaped with his life.

He was lying in his rooms under a trained nurse's care and recovering as rapidly as could be expected from the shock.

Reading it the next morning after seeing Sam off to Kansas, Michael lifted his head with that quiet show of indignation. He knew the message must have been telephoned to the paper by Carter himself shortly after he escaped from the police. He saw just how easy it was for him to give out any report he chose. Money and influence would buy even the public press. It would be little use to try to refute anything he chose to tell about himself.

The days following were to Michael one long blur of trouble. He haunted Mr. Endicott's office in hopes of getting news of his return, but they told him the last letters had been very uncertain. He might come quickly or might be delayed a month or even longer, and a cablegram might not reach him much sooner than a letter, as he was traveling from place to place.

After three days of this agony, knowing the enemy would soon be recovering from his bruises and be about again, he reluctantly wrote a note to Starr.

> *My dear Miss Endicott,*
>
> *At the risk of offending you, I feel I must try again to save you from what I feel can only be great misery. The young man we were speaking of has twice to my knowledge visited a young woman of the slums within the last month and has even since your engagement been maintaining an intimacy with her which can only insult you. Though you may not believe me, it gives me greater pain to tell you this than anything I ever had to do before. I've tried every way I know to communicate with your father but have thus far failed. I hope that if you won't take my word for it, you'll at least find some trustworthy intimate family friend you can confide in, who'll investigate this matter for you and give you his candid opinion of the young man. I can furnish such a man with information as to where to get the facts. I know that what I've said is true. I beg for the sake of your future happiness that you'll discover for yourself.*
>
> *Michael*

To this note, within two days, he received a condescending reply.

> *Michael,*
>
> *I'm very sorry you've used means so low to accomplish your end, whatever that may be. It's beyond me to imagine what possible motive*

you can have for all this ridiculous calumny you're trying to cast on one who's shown a noble spirit toward you.

Mr. Carter has fully explained to me his presence at that girl's home, and because I don't like for anyone to think evil of the man I'm to marry, I'm taking the trouble to explain to you. The young woman is a former maid of Mr. Carter's mother, and she's deeply attached to her. She does up Mrs. Carter's fine laces, and Mr. Carter has twice been the bearer of laces to be laundered, because his mother was afraid to trust such valuable pieces to a servant.

I hope you'll now understand the terrible things you've tried to say against Mr. Carter are false. Such things are called blackmail and bring terrible consequences in court, I'm told, if they become known, so I must warn you never to do anything like this again. It's dangerous. If my father were at home he'd explain it to you. Of course, having been in that out-of-the-way Florida place for so long you don't understand these things. But for Papa's sake I wouldn't like you to get into trouble in any way.

I must say one more thing: Mr. Carter tells me he saw you down in that questionable neighborhood and that you are yourself interested in this girl. When this is the case it seems strange you should have thought so ill of him.

Trusting you'll cause me no further annoyance in this matter,

S. D. Endicott

When Michael had read this, he bowed himself on his desk as one stricken unto death. To read such words from the one he loved better than his own soul was terrible! And he might never let her know these things said of him were false. She would probably have the idea always that his presence in that alley was shameful to him. So far as his personal part in the danger to her was concerned, he was from now on powerless to help her. If she thought such things of him—if she'd really been made to believe them—then of course she could credit nothing he told her. Some higher power than his would have to save her if she was to be saved.

To do Starr justice she was very much stirred by Michael's note and after a night of wakefulness and thought had taken the letter to her mother. Not that Starr turned naturally to her most unnatural mother for help in personal matters usually, but she seemed to have no one else. If only her father were home! She thought of cabling him, but what could she say in a brief message? How could she make him understand? And then the world was always standing by to peer over one's shoulder when one sent a message. She couldn't hope to escape the public eye.

She considered showing Michael's note to Morton, her faithful nurse, but Morton, wise in many things, wouldn't understand this matter and would be powerless to help her. So Starr went to her mother.

Mrs. Endicott, shrewd to perfection, masked her indignation under a proper show of horror and told Starr of course it wasn't true; but equally of course it must be investigated. She gave her word she'd do so immediately, and her daughter needn't think further of it. Then she sent at once for Carter, holding a brief consultation with him, and at the end called Starr and cheerfully gave the version of the story she wrote to Michael.

Stuyvesant Carter could be very alluring when he tried, and he chose to try. The stakes were a fortune, a noble name, and a very pretty girl he was as much in love with at present as he'd ever been, in his checkered career, with any girl.

Moreover his nature held revenge long. He delighted turning the story on the man who pretended to be so righteous and dared give him orders about a poor, worthless slum girl. He set his cunning intellect to devise a scheme for catching his adversary in his own net. He found a powerful ally in the mother of the girl he was to marry.

For reasons of ambition Mrs. Endicott desired an alliance with the Carter house, and she was determined nothing should upset her plans for her only daughter's marriage.

She knew that if her husband returned and heard any hint of the story about Carter, he would at once end any relations between him and Starr. It would be mortifying to have the arrangements balked after things had gone so far. And there was that hateful Mrs. Waterman, setting her cap for him so odiously everywhere, even since the engagement had been announced. Mrs. Endicott would risk nothing. Therefore she planned with the young people for an early marriage. She was anxious to have everything so cut-and-dried and matters gone so far that her husband couldn't upset them when he returned. Finally she cabled him asking him to set a positive date for his homecoming as the young people wished an early wedding. He cabled back a date not so far off, for in truth, though he'd received none of Michael's warnings, he was uneasy about his daughter's engagement. Carter had seemed all right, and he saw no reason to demur when his wife wrote that the young people had come to an understanding; but he hadn't thought the marriage would be soon. He was troubled at losing the one bright treasure of his home, when he'd just got her back again from her European education. He felt it was unfortunate that imperative business had called him abroad almost as soon as she returned. He was in haste to be back.

But when his wife followed her cable message with a letter speaking of an immediate marriage and setting a date only four days after his arrival, he cabled her to set no date until his return, which would be as soon as possible.

Mrs. Endicott had planned well, however. The invitations had been sent out that morning. She thought it unnecessary to cable again but wrote: "I'm sorry, but your message came too late. The invitations are out now and arrangements going forward. I knew you wouldn't want to stop Starr's plans, and she seems to have her heart set on being married at once. Dear Stuyvesant finds it urgent to take an ocean trip, and he cannot bear the thought of going without his wife. I don't see how things could be held off now. We'd be the laughingstock of society, and I'm sure you wouldn't want me to endure that. And Starr, dear child, is childishly happy over her arrangements. She's only anxious to have you properly home in time, so do hurry and get an earlier boat if possible."

Over this letter Mr. Endicott frowned and looked troubled. His wife had always taken things in her own hands when she would. But concerning Starr they'd never agreed, though he'd let her have her way about everything else. It was like her to get this marriage fixed up while he was away. Of course it must be all right, but so sudden! And his little Starr! His one little girl!

Then, with his usual abrupt action, he put the letter in his inner pocket and hurried his business as much as possible to take an even earlier boat. And he finally succeeded by working night and day and leaving several important matters to go as they would.

The papers at last announced that Mr. Delevan Endicott, abroad for three months on business, had sailed for home and would reach New York nearly a week before the date set for the wedding. The papers also were filled with elaborate foreshadowings of what that event would likely mean to society.

And Michael, knowing he must suffer and endure to the end of it, if perchance he might yet save her in some miraculous way, read every word and knew the day and hour of the boat's probable arrival. He planned to meet the boat himself. If possible he'd go out on the pilot and meet his man before he landed.

Then the silence of the great deep fell about the traveler, and the day passed with the waiting one in the city and preparations hurried forward by skilled workers. The Endicott home was filled with comers and goers who brought silks and satins and costly laces and jewels from around the world.

Over the machinery she set going, Mrs. Endicott presided with the calmness and positive determination of one who had a great purpose in view and meant to carry it out. Not a detail escaped her vigilant eye; not an item was forgotten of the million necessities the world expected and she must have forthcoming. Anything to make the wedding unique, artistic, or perfect must be carried out. This was her highest opportunity to shine, and Mrs. Endicott intended to make the most of it. Not that she hadn't shone throughout her worldly career, but she knew that with her daughter's marriage, her own life would reach its zenith point and then decline. This event must be remembered in the annals of the future so long as New York married and was given in marriage. Starr's wedding must surpass all others in wonder, beauty, and elegance.

So she planned, wrought, carried out, and day by day the gleam in her eyes indicated she was nearing triumph.

It didn't disturb her when the steamer was overdue one day and then two. Starr, even amid the festivities in her honor, found time to worry about her father, but the wife only found cause for congratulations. She felt her crucial time was coming when her husband reached home. If Michael had carried out his threats, or if breath of the stories concerning Carter's life reached him, there would be trouble against which she had no power.

Not until the third morning with still no news of the vessel did Mrs. Endicott feel uneasy. It would be awkward to have to delay the ceremony, and of course it wouldn't do to have it without the bride's father when he was hurrying to be present. If he would arrive just in time so much the better, but late—ah—that would be dreadful! She tightened her lips and looked like a Napoleon saying, *There shall be no Alps!* In like manner she would have said if she could, *There shall be no sea if I wish it.*

But her anxiety was only manifested by closer vigilance over her helpers as hourly the preparations glided to their finish.

Starr grew nervous and couldn't sleep, hovering from room to room in the daytime looking out the windows or telephoning the steamship company for news. Her fiancé found her unsatisfactory, and no plans he proposed for her diversion pleased her. Dark rings appeared under her eyes, and she looked at him with a troubled expression sometimes when she should have been laughing in the midst of pleasures.

Starr deeply loved her father, and some vague presentiment of coming trouble seemed to shadow life. Now and then Michael's face with its great, true eyes and pleading expression came between her and Carter's face, blurring its handsome lines, and then indefinite questions haunted her. What if those terrible things Michael had said were true? Was she sure? At such times she saw a weakness in the lines about Carter's eyes and mouth.

But she was unused to studying character and had no guide to help her in her lonely problem of choosing, for already she'd learned that her mother's ways and hers weren't the same, and her father didn't come. When he came it would be all right. It had to be, for there was no turning back now. The wedding was two days off.

Michael, in his new office, acknowledged to himself he couldn't work. He'd done all he could and awaited a report of that vessel. When it landed he hoped to be the first man on board; in fact, he'd arranged to meet it before it landed. But it didn't come! Would it be prevented until the day was put off? Would that improve matters? And could he accomplish anything with Mr. Endicott if he had time? Wasn't he foolish to try? Mr. Endicott was already angry with him for another reason. His wife and Starr and that scoundrel Carter would tell all sorts of stories. Of course he would believe theirs over his! He groaned aloud sometimes, alone in his office, and wished he could fling himself between Starr and evil once for all—give his life for hers. Gladly he'd do it if it would do any good. Yet there was no way.

And then came news. The vessel had been heard from many miles out at sea, with a propeller broken and laboring along at great disadvantage. But if all went well she would reach her dock at noon the following day—eight hours before the wedding!

Starr heard, and her face blossomed into smiles. All would go well. She telephoned the steamship company later, and her fears were allayed by their assurances.

Mrs. Endicott heard the news with relief. Her husband would scarcely have time to find out anything. She must prevent his seeing Michael before the ceremony.

The young man heard, and his heart beat wildly. Would there be enough time to save Starr?

Noon the next day came, but the steamer hadn't landed, though the news from her was good. She would be in before night, for sure. Mr. Endicott would be in time for the wedding, but that and no more. He sent reassurances to his family, and they were going forward happily in the whirl of last things.

But Michael in his lonely office hung up the telephone receiver with a heavy heart. There would be no time to save Starr. Everything was against him. Even if he could get speech with Mr. Endicott, which was doubtful now, would the man listen at this the last minute? Of course his wife and daughter and her fiancé could easily persuade him all was well and Michael a jealous fool!

As he sat thus with bowed head before his desk, he heard footsteps along the stone floor of the corridor outside. They halted at his door, and hesitating fingers fumbled with the knob. He looked up frowning and was about to send any chance client away, explaining he was too occupied now to be interrupted, when the face of the woman opening the door caught his attention.

Chapter 22

It was Lizzie, with her baby in her arms—the girl he had defended in the alley, whose face he'd seen lying white and unconscious in the moonlight, looking ghastly enough with the dark hair flung back against the harsh stone pillow.

The face was white now but softened with motherhood. The bold, handsome features had taken on a gentleness, though passion and unrest glowed and burned in her dark eyes.

She stood looking at Michael after she closed the door and held the baby close as if she feared someone might be there wanting to take it from her.

As Michael watched her, fascinated, cut to the heart by the suffering in her eyes, he was reminded of an exquisite Madonna he'd seen in an exhibit not long ago. The draperies had been dainty and cloudlike, and the face refined in its beauty, but the eyes had held the same sorrowful mother-anguish. It passed through his mind that this girl and he were kin because of a mutual torture. His face softened, and he felt a great pity for her.

His eyes wandered to the upturned face of the baby wrapped in the shabby shawl against its mother's breast. It was a beautiful sleeping face, with a look of the spirit world from which it had recently come, a little stranger soul.

Why had the baby come? To make one more of the swarming mass of sinful wretches crowding the alley? Would those cherub lips half-parted now in a seraphic smile live to pour forth blasphemous curses as he'd heard from even very small children in the alley? Would that tiny seashell hand, resting so trustingly against the coarse cloth of its mother's raiment, looking like a rosebud gone astray, live to break open safes and take their contents? Would the soft round body, whose tender curves showed pitifully beneath the thin old shawl, grow up to lie in the gutter someday? The problem of the people had never come to Michael so forcibly, so terribly as in that moment before Lizzie spoke.

"Be you a real lawyer?" she asked. "Kin you tell what the law is 'bout folks and thin's?"

Michael smiled and rose to give her a chair as courteously as if she'd been born a lady.

"Sit down," he said. "Yes, I'm a lawyer. What can I do for you?"

"I s'pose you charge a lot," said the girl, glancing around the room. "You've got thin's fixed fine as silk here. But I'll pay anythin' you ast ef it takes me a lifetime to do it, ef you'll jest tell me how I kin git my rights."

"Your rights?" questioned Michael sadly. Poor child! Had she any rights in the universe that he could help her get? The only rights he knew for such as she were room in a quiet graveyard and a chance to be forgotten.

"Say, ain't it against the law fer a man to marry a woman when he's already got one wife?"

"It is," said Michael, "unless he gets a divorce."

"Well, I ain't goin' to give him no divorce, you bet!" said the girl fiercely. "I worked hard enough to get a real marriage, an' I ain't goin' to give up no fash'nable swell. I'm's good's she is, an' I've got my rights, an I'll hev 'em. An' besides, there's baby!" Her face softened and took on a love-light, and immediately Michael was reminded of the Madonna picture again. "I've got to think o' him!"

Michael marveled to see the girl revelling in the little helpless burden who had added to her sorrow.

"Tell me about it." His voice was gentle. He recalled suddenly that this was Sam's girl. Poor Sam, too! The world was a terrible tangled mess of trouble.

"Well, there ain't much to tell that counts—only he kep' comp'ny with me, an' I wouldn't hev ennythin' else but a real marriage, an' so he giv' in, an' we had a couple o' rooms in a respectable house an' hed it fine till he had to go away on business, he said. I never b'leeved that. Why, he was downright rich. He's a real swell, you know. What kind o' business cud he have?" Lizzie straightened herself proudly and held her head high.

"About whom are you talking?" asked Michael.

"Why, my husband, 'course, Mr. Sty-ve-zant Carter. You ken see his name in the paper real often. He didn't want me to know his real name. He hed me call him Dan Hunt fer two months, but I caught on, an' he was real mad fer a while. He said his ma didn't like the match, an' he didn't want folks to know he'd got married; it might hurt him with some of his swell friends—"

"You don't mean to tell me Mr. Stuyvesant Carter married you!" said Michael incredulously.

"Sure!" said Lizzie proudly. "Married me jest like enny swell; got me a dimon ring an' a silk-lined suit an' a willer plume an' everythin'." She held up a grimy hand on which Michael saw a showy glitter of jewelry.

"Do you have anything to show for it?" asked Michael, expecting her to say no. "Do you have any certificate or paper to prove you were married according to law?"

"Sure!" said Lizzie triumphantly, drawing forth a crumpled roll from the folds of her dress and smoothing it out before his astonished eyes.

There it was, a printed wedding certificate, in blue and gold with a colored picture of two clasped hands under a white dove with a gold ring in its beak. Beneath was an idealized boat with silken sails bearing two people down a rose-lined river of life; and the whole was bordered with orange blossoms. It was one of those old-fashioned affairs country ministers gave their parishioners in years gone by and can still be found in some dusty corners of a forgotten drawer in country bookstores. But Michael recognized at once that it was a real certificate. He read it carefully. The blanks were filled in, the marriage date she gave was there, and the bridegroom's name, though evidently written in a disguised hand, could be deciphered as "Sty. Carter." Michael didn't recognize the names of the witnesses or the officiating minister.

"How do you happen to have Mr. Carter's real name here when you say he married you under an assumed name?" he asked, moving his finger over the blurred name that had evidently been scratched out and written over again.

"I made him put it in after I found out who he was," said Lizzie. "He couldn't come it over me thet-a-way. He was awful gone on me then, an' I cud do most ennythin' with him. It was 'fore she cum home from Europe! She jes' went fer him an' turned his head. Ef I'd a-knowed in time I'd gone an' tole her, but land sakes! I don't s'pose 'twould a done much good. I would a-ben to her before— only I was fool 'nough to promise him I wouldn't say nothin' to her ef he'd keep away from her. You see I needed money awful bad fer baby. He don't take to livin' awful good. He cries a lot, an' I hed to hev thin's fer 'im, so I threatened him ef he didn't do sompin' I'd tell her, an' he up an' forked over, but not till I promised. But now they say the papers is tellin' he's to marry her tonight, an' I gotta stop it somehow. I got my rights an' baby's to look after, promise er no promise. Kin I get him arrested?"

"I'm not sure what you can do until I look into the matter," Michael said gravely. Would the paper he held help or not, in his mission to Starr's father? And would it be too late? His heavy heart couldn't answer.

"Do you know these witnesses?"

"Sure," said Lizzie. "They're all swells. They come down with him when he come to be married. I never seen 'em again, but they was real jolly an' nice. They gave me a bokay of real roses an' a bracelet made like a snake with green glass eyes."

"And the minister? Which is his church?"

"I'm sure I donno," said Lizzie. "I never ast. He come along an' was ez jolly ez enny of 'em. He drank more'n all of 'em put together. He was awful game fer a preacher."

Michael's heart sank. Was this a genuine marriage? Could anything be proved? He questioned the girl carefully and then sent her on her way, promising to do all in his power to help her and arranging to let her know as soon as possible if she could do anything.

That was a busy afternoon for Michael. The steamer's arrival was forgotten. His telephone rang vainly on the desk to a silent room. He was out tramping over the city searching for the witnesses and minister who had signed Lizzie's marriage certificate.

Meanwhile the afternoon papers came out with a glowing account of the wedding that was to be, headed by pictures of Starr and Mr. Carter, for the wedding was a great event in society circles.

On her way back to the alley, confident Michael, the angel of the alley, would do something for her, Lizzie heard the boys crying the afternoon edition of the paper and was seized with a desire to see if her husband's picture would be in again. She could ill spare the penny she spent for it, but what was money in a case like this? Michael would do something for her, and she would have more money. Besides, if worse came to worst she would go to the fine lady and threaten to make it all public, and she would give her money.

Lizzie had had more advantages than most of her class in the alley. She'd worked in a seashore restaurant several summers and could read a little. From the newspaper account she gathered enough to rouse her half-soothed frenzy. Her eyes flashed fire as she went about her dark tenement room making the baby comfortable. His feeble wail and sweet eyes looking into hers only fanned the fury of her flame. She determined not to wait for Michael but to go on her own at once to that girl who was stealing her husband, her baby's father, and tell her what she was doing.

With the cunning of her kind, Lizzie dressed herself in her best: a soiled pink silk shirtwaist with elbow sleeves, a spotted and torn black skirt that showed a tattered orange silk petticoat beneath its ungainly length, a wide white hat, with soiled and draggled willow plume of Alice blue, and high-heeled pumps run over on their uppers. If she'd only known she looked ten times better in the old shawl she wore to Michael's office—but she took great satisfaction in being able to dress appropriately when she went to the swells.

The poor baby she wrapped in his soiled best and pinned a large untidy pink satin bow on the back of his dirty blanket. Then she started on her mission.

Now Starr had just heard her father's vessel would dock in a little over an hour, and her heart was light and happy. All her misgivings seemed to flee away, now that he was coming. She flew from one room to another like a wild bird, trilling snatches of a song and looking prettier than ever.

"Aw, the wee sweet bairnie!" murmured the old Scottish nurse. "If only her man will be gude to her."

Some special bit of Starr's attire for the evening hadn't arrived. She was in a twitter of expectancy about it, to be sure it pleased her. When she heard the bell she rushed to the head of the stairs and halfway down to see if it had come, and the servant opened the door to Lizzie and her baby.

One second more and the door would have closed hopelessly on poor Lizzie, for no servant in that house would have admitted such a creature to their lady's presence a few hours before her wedding. But Starr, poised halfway on the landing, called, "What is it, Graves—someone to see me?"

"But she's not the sort of person—Miss Starr!" protested Graves with the door only open a crack now.

"Never mind, Graves—I'll see her for a minute. I can't deny anyone on my wedding day, you know, and Father almost safely here. Show her into the little reception room." She smiled a ravishing smile on the devoted Graves.

So with many qualms of conscience and misgivings as to what the mistress would say if she found out, Graves ushered Lizzie and her baby to the room indicated, and Starr fluttered down to see her. So it was Starr's own doing that Lizzie came into her presence on that eventful afternoon.

"Oh, what a sweet baby!" exclaimed Starr. "Is he yours?" Lizzie's fierce eyes softened.

"Sit down and tell me who you are. Wait—I'll have some tea brought for you. You look tired. Won't you let me give that sweet baby a little white shawl of mine? I'm to be married tonight, and I'd like to give him a wedding present," she said merrily, and Morton was sent for the shawl and another servant for the tea, while Starr amused herself by making the baby crow at her.

Lizzie sat in wonder. She almost forgot her errand, watching this sweet girl in her lovely attire making much of her baby.

But when the tea had been brought and the soft white wool shawl wrapped around the smiling baby, Starr said again, "Now please tell me who you are and what you've come for. I can give you only a minute or two more. This is a busy day, you know."

Lizzie's brow darkened.

"I'm Mrs. Carter!" she said, drawing herself up with conscious pride.

"Carter?" said Starr politely.

"Yes, I'm the wife of the man you're goin' to marry tonight, an' this is his child. I thought I'd come an' tell you 'fore 'twas too late. I thought ef you had enny goodness in you you'd put a stop to this an' give me my rights, an' you seem to hev some heart. Can't you call it off? You wouldn't want to take my husband away from me, would you? You can get plenty others, an' I'm jest a plain workin' girl, an' he's mine anyhow, an' this is his kid."

Starr had started to her feet, her eyes wide, her hand fluttering to her heart.

"Stop!" she cried. "You must be crazy to say such things. My poor girl, you've made a great mistake. Your husband is some other Mr. Carter. My Mr. Carter is not that kind of man. He's never been married—"

"Yes, he has!" interposed Lizzie fiercely. "He's married all right, an' I got the c'tif'ct all right, too—only I couldn't bring it this time cause I lef' it with my lawyer. But you can see it ef you want to, with his name all straight. Sty-Vee-Zant Carter, all writ out. I see to it he writ it himself. I kin read meself pretty good, so I knowed."

"I'm very sorry for you," said Starr sweetly, though her heart was beating violently in spite of trying to be calm and get rid of this wretched imposter without making a scene before the servants. "I'm very sorry, but you've made a great mistake. I can't do anything for you now. But later when I return to New York, if you look me up, I'll try to do something for the baby."

Lizzie stood erect in the middle of the room, her face slowly changing to a stony stare, her eyes fairly blazing with anger.

"De yer mean ter tell me yer a-goin' t' marry my husban' ez ef nothin' happened? Ain't yer ter ast him ef it's true ner nothin'? Ain't yer goin' t' find out what's true 'bout him? 'R d' ye want 'im so bad ye don't care who yer hurt or wot he is, so long's he makes a big splurge before folks? Ain't you a-goin' ter ast him 'bout it?"

"Oh, why, certainly," said Starr. "I'll ask him, but I know you're mistaken. Now really I have to say good afternoon. I haven't another minute to spare. You must go!"

"I won't stir a step till you promise you'll ast him straight away. Ain't you got no telyphone? Well, you kin call him up an' ast him why he didn't never speak to you of his wife Lizzie and where he was the evenin' of Augus' four. That's the date of the c'tif'ct! Tell him you seen me, an' then see wot he says. Tell him my lawyer is a-goin' to fix him ef he goes on. It'll be in all the papers tomorrer mornin' ef he goes on. An' you kin say I won't never consent to no divorce; they ain't respectable, an' I got to think o' that on baby's account."

"If you'll go quietly away now and say nothing about this to anyone, I'll tell Mr. Carter all about you," said Starr, her voice trembling with an effort at self-control.

"D' ye promus you will?"

"Certainly," said Starr with dignity.

"Will ye do it straight off?"

"Yes, if you'll go at once."

"Cross yer heart?"

"What?"

"Cross yer heart ye will? Thet's a sort o' oath t' make yer keep yer promus," explained Lizzie.

"A lady needs no such thing to make her keep her promise. Don't you know ladies always keep their promises?"

"I wasn't so sure!" said Lizzie. "You can't most allus tell—'t's bes' to be on the safe side. Will yer promus me yer won't marry him ef ye find out he's my husband?"

"Most certainly I won't marry him if he's already married. Now go, please, at once. I haven't a minute to spare. If you don't go at once I can't have time to call him up."

"You sure I kin trust you?"

Starr turned on the girl such a gaze of mingled dignity and indignation that her eye quailed before it.

"Well, I s'pose I gotta," she said, dropping her eyes before Starr's righteous wrath. "But no weddin' bells fer yer tonight ef yer keep yer promus. So long!"

Starr shuddered as the girl passed her. The whiff of unwashed garments, stale cooking, and undefinable tenement odor sickened her. Must she let this creature have a hold even momentarily upon her last few hours? Yet she knew she must; she wouldn't rest until she'd been reassured by Carter's voice and the explanation he would surely give her. She rushed upstairs to her private phone, locking the door on even her old nurse, and called up the phone in Carter's private apartments.

Without admitting it to herself, she had been troubled all afternoon because she hadn't heard from Carter. Her flowers had come—magnificent in their costliness and arrangement—and everything he was to attend to was done. But no word had come from him. It was unlike him.

She knew he'd given a dinner the evening before to his old friends who were to be his ushers and that the festivities would have lasted late. He probably hadn't arisen very early, but it was drawing toward the wedding hour now. She intended to begin dressing at once after phoning him. It was strange she hadn't heard from him.

After much delay an unknown voice answered the phone and told her Mr. Carter couldn't come now. She asked who it was but got no response, except that Mr. Carter couldn't come now. The voice had a muffled, thick sound. "Tell him to call me then as soon as possible," she said, and the voice answered, "Awright!"

Reluctantly she hung up the receiver and called Morton to help her dress. She preferred to get the matter out of the way before she went about the pretty ceremony and with an ill grace and troubled thoughts submitted herself to her nurse's hands. The coarse beauty of Lizzie's face haunted her. It reminded her of an actress Carter had once openly admired. She found herself shuddering inwardly every time she recalled Lizzie's harsh voice and uncouth sentences.

She paid little heed to dressing and let Morton do as she would, starting nervously when the phone bell rang or anyone tapped at her door.

A message came from her father finally. He hoped to be with her in less than an hour, and no word had come from Carter! Why didn't he know she would be anxious? What could have kept him from his usual greeting to her—and on their wedding day!

Suddenly, in the midst of Morton's draping of the wedding veil she was trying in various ways to see how to put on at the last minute, Starr started up from her chair.

"I cannot stand this, Mortie. That will do for now. I must telephone Mr. Carter. I can't understand why he doesn't call me."

"Oh, but the poor man is that busy!" murmured Morton as she hurried obediently out of the room. "Now mind you don't muss that beautiful veil."

But after a half hour of attempting to reach Carter, Starr suddenly appeared in her door, calling for her faithful nurse again.

"Mortie!" she called excitedly. "Come here quick! I've ordered the electric. It's at the door now. Put on your big cloak and come with me! I've got to see Mr. Carter at once, and I can't get him on the phone."

"But, Miss Starr!" protested Morton. "You've no time to go anywhere now, and look at your pretty veil!"

"Never mind the veil, Mortie. I'm going. Hurry. I can't stop to explain. I'll tell you on the way. We'll be back before anyone misses us."

"But your mama, Miss Starr! She'll be very angry with me!"

"Mama mustn't know. And anyway I must go. Come—if you won't come with me I'm going alone."

With these words Starr grasped a great cloak of dark green velvet, threw it over her white bridal robes, and hurried down the stairs.

"Oh, Miss Starr, darlin'," moaned Morton, looking hurriedly around for a cloak. "You'll spoil yer veil sure! Wait till I take it off'n ye."

But Starr had opened the front door and was already getting into the luxurious car that stood outside.

Chapter 23

Michael, as he searched, kept crying in his heart, *Oh, God! Do something to save her! Do something to save my little Starr!*

The prayer prayed itself without apparent thought or volition on his part, as he went from place to place, searching out what he needed to know. At last toward six o'clock, his chain of evidence led him to the door of Stuyvesant Carter's apartments.

After some delay the door was opened a little by a servant who stared at him blankly but finally admitted that the three men whose names he mentioned were inside. He also said Mr. Carter was in but couldn't be seen.

He closed the door on the visitor and went inside to see if any of the others would come out. An altercation ensued in loud, unsteady tones. At last the door opened again, and a fast-looking young man who admitted himself to be Theodore Brooks slid out and closed it carefully behind him. The air that came with him was thick with tobacco smoke and heavy with liquor, and Michael's one glimpse into the room showed a strange radiance of some peculiar light that glowed into the dusky hall.

The heavy-eyed youth braced against the wall looked into Michael's face with an impudent laugh.

"Well, parson, what's the grouch? Are you the devil or an angel sent to bring retribution?"

He ended with a silly laugh that told the young lawyer's experienced ear that the young man had been drinking heavily. And this was the man whose name was signed as Rev. Theodore Brooks, D.D., on the tawdry marriage certificate Michael held in his hand. His heart sank at the futility of the task.

"Are you a minister?" asked Michael.

"Am I a minister?" drawled young Brooks. "M–my–m–m–m'nster! Well, now, that gets my goat! Say, boys, he wants t' know 'f I'm a m–min'ster! Minster of what? Min-ster plen–p'ten'sherry?"

"Did you ever perform a marriage?" asked Michael sharply to stop the loud guffaw reechoing through the apartment's polished corridors.

"P'form a m'riage, d' ye say? No, but I'm goin' t' perform 't a marriage tonight 'f the dead wakes up in time. Goin' t' be bes' man. Say, boys! Got 'im 'wake yet? Gettin' late!"

Michael in despair took hold of the other's arm and tried to explain what he wanted to know. Finally he succeeded in bringing the matter into the fellow's comprehension.

"Wedding, oh, yes, I 'member, peach of a girl! Stuyvy awfully fond of her. No harm meant. Good joke! Yes, I borr'wed Grand'f'ther Brooks's old gown 'n' ban's. Awf'lly good disguise! No harm meant—on'y good joke—girl awf'lly set on getting married. Stuyvy wanted t' please 'er—awfully good joke!"

"A ghastly joke, I should say, sir!" said Michael sternly.

And then the door was flung open by hands from inside, loud angry voices protesting while another hand sought unavailingly to close the door again. But Michael came and planted himself in the open door and stood like an avenging angel calling to judgment. The scene revealed to him was too horrifying for words.

A long banquet table stood in the midst of the handsomely furnished room. Amid the scattered remains of the feast—napkins under the table, upset glasses still dripping their ruby contents down the damask tablecloth, broken china, scattered plates and silver—stood a handsome silver coffin, within which, pallid and deathlike, lay the handsome form of the evening's bridegroom. Around the casket in sconces burned tall tapers, casting their spectral light over the scene.

Distributed about the room—lounging in chairs, fast asleep on the couches, lying under the table, fighting by the doorway, one standing on a velvet chair raising an unsteady glass of wine and attempting a drinking song—were ten young men, the flowers of society, the expected ushers of the evening's wedding.

Michael, with his pale face, his golden hair aflame in the flickering candlelight, his eyes full of shocked indignation, stood for a moment surveying the scene and all at once knew his prayer was answered. There would be no wedding that night.

"Is this another of your ghastly jokes?" he turned to Brooks who stood by as master of ceremonies, undisturbed by the stranger's presence.

"That's just what it is," stuttered Brooks, "a j–j–joke, a p–p–p–pract'cal joke. No harm meant, only Stuyvy's hard to wake up. Never did like gettin' up in the mornin'. Wake 'im up, boys! Wake 'im up! Time to get dressed for the wedding!"

"Has anyone sent word to Miss Endicott?"

"Sent word to Mish Endicott? No, I'd 'no's they have. Think she'd care to come? Say, boys, that's a good joke. This old fellow—don't know who he is—devil 'n' all his angels p'raps—he s'gests we send word to Mish Endicott t' come t' th' fun'ral."

"I said nothing of the kind," said Michael fiercely. "Have you no sense of decency? Go and wash your face and try to realize what you've been doing. Have someone telephone for a doctor. I'll go and tell the family." Michael strode out of the room to perform the hardest task ever.

He didn't wait for the elevator but ran down the stairs, trying to steady his thoughts and realize the horror through which he'd just passed.

As he started down the last flight he heard the elevator door clang below. As it shot past him he glimpsed white garments and a face with eyes he knew. He stopped short and looked upward. Was it—could it be? No, of course not. He was foolish. He turned and compelled his feet to hurry down the rest of the stairs. But at the door his worst fears were confirmed, for there stood the electric car, and the Endicott chauffeur's familiar face assured him someone of the family had just gone to the ghastly spectacle upstairs.

In sudden panic he turned and fled up the stairs. He couldn't wait for elevators now. He wished for a protecting angel's wings, that he might reach her before she saw that horrible sight.

Yet even as he started he knew he must be too late.

Starr stopped startled in the open doorway, with Morton, protesting, apprehensive, behind her. The soft cloak slid down the satin of her gown and left her revealed in all her wedding whiteness, her eyes like stars, her beautiful face flushed. Then the eyes rested on the coffin and its deathlike occupant, and her face went white as her dress, while horror grew in her eyes.

Brooks, more nearly sober than the rest, saw her first and hastened to do the honors.

"Say, boys, she's come!" he shouted. "Bride's come. Git up, Bobby Trascom. Don't yer know ye mustn't lie down when there's a lady present—Van—get out from under that table. Help me pick up these things. Place's a mess. Glad to see you, Mish Endicott." He bowed low and staggered as he recovered himself.

Starr turned toward him. "Mr. Brooks," she said in a tone that sobered him somewhat, "what does it mean? Is he dead?"

"Not at all, not at all, Mish Endicott," he tried to say gravely. "Have him all right in plenty time. Just a little joke, Mish Endicott. He's merely shlightly intoxicated."

But Starr heard no more. With a stifled cry and a groping motion of her white-clad arms, she crumpled into a white heap at her horrified nurse's feet. As she fell Michael appeared at the door, like the rescuing angel he was, and with one withering glance at the huddled group of men he gathered her in his arms and sped down the stairs, faithful Morton puffing after him. Neither of them noticed a man who got out of the elevator just before Starr fell and, walking rapidly toward the open door, saw the whole action. In a moment more Mr. Endicott stood in the door surveying the scene before him with stern, wrathful countenance.

Like a dash of cold water, his appearance brought several participants in the disgraceful scene to their senses. A few questions and he had the whole shameful story: the stag dinner growing into a midnight orgy; the foolish dare and its reckless acceptance by the already intoxicated bridegroom; the drugged drinks; and the practical joke carried out by brains long under the influence of liquor. Carter's men who had protested had been bound and gagged in the back room. The jokers had found no trouble in securing the necessary tools to carry out their joke. Money will buy anything, even an undertaker for a living man. The promise of secrecy and the generous fees brought all they needed. Then when the ghastly work was completed and the unconscious bridegroom lying in state in his coffin amid the debris of the table, they drowned the horror of their deed in deeper drinking.

Mr. Endicott turned from the scene, his soul filled with loathing and horror.

He'd reached home to find the house in a tumult and Starr gone. Morton, going out the door after her young mistress, had whispered to the butler their destination and that they would return at once. She suspected it would be best for someone to know.

Mr. Endicott ordered the runabout and hastened after them, arriving a moment or two later. Michael had just vanished up the apartment stairs as he entered the lower hallway. The vague indefinite trouble that had filled his mind concerning his daughter's marriage to a man he little knew, except by reputation, crystallized into trouble, clear and distinct, as he hurried after his daughter. Something terrible must have come to Starr, or she would never have hurried away almost alone at such a time.

The electric car was gone by the time Mr. Endicott reached the lower hall again, and he was forced to go back alone as he came, without further explanation than what he could see. But he had time in the rapid trip to become profoundly thankful the disgraceful scene he'd left had occurred before and not after his daughter's marriage. Whatever circumstances might excuse the reckless victim of his comrades' joke, the fact remained that a man who could fall victim to such a joke was not the companion for his daughter's life—she who had been guarded at every possible point and loved as the apple of his eye. He dared not think yet about the perpetrators of this gruesome sport. No punishment seemed too great for such. And she, his little Starr, had looked upon that shameful scene and seen the man she expected to marry lying as one dead! It was too awful! And what had it done to her? Had it killed her? Had the shock unsettled her mind? The journey to his home seemed longer than his whole ocean voyage. Oh, why hadn't he let business go to the winds and come back long ago to shield his little girl!

Meanwhile, Michael, his precious burden in his arms, had stepped into the waiting car, motioning Morton to follow and sit in the opposite seat. The delicate Paris frock trailed unnoticed underfoot, and the veil's rare lace fell back from the white face. But neither Michael nor the nurse thought of satin and lace now, as they bent anxiously over the girl to see if she still breathed.

All the way to her home Michael held the lovely bride in his arms, feeling her weight no more than a feather, thankful he might bear her away from the danger that had threatened her life. He wished he might carry her to the ends of the earth and never stop until he had her safe from all harm. His heart thrilled wildly with the touch of her sweetness, even while he bent over her to watch for returning consciousness.

But she didn't become conscious before she reached the house. His strong arms held her as gently as though she'd been a baby as he stepped carefully out and carried her to her own room, laying her upon the white bed, where two hours before the delicate wedding garments had been spread for her to put on. Then he stood back, looked reverently on her dear face, and turned away. In the hall he met her mother, and her face was fairly disfigured with sudden recognition of him.

"What! Is it you have dared come into this house? The impertinence! I'll report your doings to my husband. He'll be very angry. You're at the bottom of this whole business! You'll be dealt with as you deserve!"

She hissed the words after him as Michael descended the stairs with bowed head and closed lips. It didn't matter now what she said or thought of him. Starr was saved!

He was about to go into the world again, away from her, from even knowing how she came out of her swoon. He had no further right there. His duty was done. He'd been allowed to save her when she needed him!

But as he reached the door it opened, and Mr. Endicott hurried in.

He paused for an instant.

"Son! It was you who brought her home!" he said, as if that conviction had just been revealed to his perturbed mind. "Son, I'm obliged. Sit here till I come. I want to speak with you."

The doctor came with a nurse, and Michael sat and listened to the distant voices in her room. He gathered from the sounds that Starr was conscious, was better.

Until then no one had thought of the wedding or the guests who would be gathering. Something must be done. So, as the organ sounded forth the wedding march—for by some blunder the bride's signal was given to the organist when the Endicott car drew up at the church—Michael, bareheaded, hat in hand, walked gravely up the aisle. Unconscious of the eyes and the astonished whispers of "Who is he? Isn't he magnificent? What does it mean? I thought the ushers were to come first?" he stood calmly in the chancel and faced the wondering audience.

If an angel had come from heaven and interfered with their wedding they couldn't have been more astonished. As he stood beneath the soft lights in front of the wall of living green and blossoms, with his pale face and dignity, they forgot to study the fashion of his coat and sat awed before his beautiful face. For tonight Michael wore the look of transport with chin uplifted, glowing eyes, and countenance that showed the spirit shining through.

The organist looked down and instinctively hushed his music. Had he made some mistake? Then Michael spoke. Doubtless he should have gone to the minister who was to perform the ceremony and given him the message, but Michael little knew the ways of weddings. It was the first he'd ever attended, and he went straight to the point.

"Because of the sudden, serious illness of the groom," he said, "it will be impossible for the ceremony to go on at this time. The bride's family asks that you'll kindly excuse them from further intrusion or explanation this evening."

Inclining his head slightly to the breathless audience, Michael passed down the aisle and out, and the organist, by tremendous self-control, kept on playing softly until the excited people who had drifted usherless into the church got themselves out into their carriages.

Michael walked out into the night, bareheaded still, his eyes lifted to the stars shining far above the city, and said softly, reverently, "Oh, God! Oh, God!"

Chapter 24

Following hard upon the interrupted wedding came other events. These helped hush matters and gave the world a plausible reason why the ceremony didn't come off as soon as the groom was convalescent from what was easily attributed to the many banquets and entertainments preceding a society wedding.

During that eventful night, while Starr lay like a crushed lily torn from its stem, her mother, after a stormy scene with her husband, in which he made it plain what kind of man she wanted her daughter to marry, and during which she saw the fall of her greatest social ambitions, was suddenly felled by a stroke.

The papers next morning told the news as sympathetically as a paper can tell one's innermost secrets. It praised the ability of the woman who had so successfully arranged for what had promised to be the greatest wedding of the season, if not of all seasons, and upon whose overtaxed strength the last straw had been laid in the bridegroom's illness. It stated that of course the wedding would be delayed indefinitely, as nothing could be thought of while the bride's mother lay in such a crucial state.

For a week daily bulletins of her condition were published in more and more remote corners of the paper, until the ripple made in the stream of life passed, and no further mention was made except when they sent for some famous specialist, took her to the shore to try the sea air, and brought her home again.

But all the time the woman lay locked in rigid silence. Only her cold eyes followed whoever entered her room. She gave no sign of knowing what they said or caring who came near. Her husband's earnest pleas, Starr's tears, drew from her no expression that could even be imagined from a fluttering eyelash. Nothing but that stony stare, that almost unseeing gaze, followed wherever one moved. It was a living death.

And when one day the release came and the eyes were closed forever from this world, it was a sad relief to both husband and daughter. Starr and her father stole away to an old New England farmhouse where Mr. Endicott's elderly maiden sister still lived in the old family homestead. She was a soft-spoken woman with plain gray dresses and soft white laces at wrists and neck and ruched about her sweet old face above her silver hair.

Starr hadn't been there since she was a child, and her sad heart found her aunt's home restful. She stayed there through the fall and until after the first of the year, while her father came and went as business dictated, and the Endicott home on Madison Avenue remained closed except for the caretakers.

Meanwhile Carter had discreetly escorted his mother to Europe and was supposed by the papers to be returning almost immediately. Not a breath of gossip, strange to say, stole forth. Everything seemed arranged to quiet any suspicion that might arise.

Early in the fall he returned to town, but Starr was still in New England. No one knew of the estrangement between them. Their immediate friends were away from town still, and everything seemed natural in the order of decency. Of course people couldn't be married at once after a death in the family.

No one but the two families knew of Carter's repeated attempts to reconcile with Starr; of his feeble endeavor to explain; of her continued refusal to see him and the decided letter she wrote him after he had written her the most abject apology he knew how to frame. Nor did anyone else know of her father's interview with the young man, wherein he was told some facts about himself more plainly than anyone even in his boyhood ever dared tell him. Mr. Endicott agreed to keep silence for Starr's sake, provided the young man created no gossip about the matter, until the intended wedding was forgotten and other events had taken the minds of society from their particular case.

Carter, for his sake, didn't care to let the story get abroad and sullenly acceded to the command. He didn't, however, think it necessary to make himself entirely miserable while abroad, and some more than once spoke his name in company with that of a young and dashing divorcee. Some even thought he returned to America sooner than he intended in order to travel on the same steamer she was taking. But those whispers hadn't yet crossed the water, and even if they had, such things were too common to cause much comment.

Then, one Monday morning, the papers were filled with horror over a terrible automobile accident, in which a party of seven, of whom the young divorcee was one and Stuyvesant Carter was another, went over an embankment sixty feet in height, the car landing upside down on the rocks below and killing every member of the party. The paper also stated that Mr. Theodore Brooks, intimate friend of Carter's, who was to have been best man at the wedding some months previous, postponed because of the sudden illness and death of the bride's mother, was in the party.

Thus ended the career of Stuyvesant Carter, and thus the world never knew exactly why Starr Endicott did not become Mrs. Carter.

From the moment he left after delivering his message in the church, Michael saw no more of the Endicotts. He longed to call and inquire for Starr; to get some reconciling word from her father; to ask if there wasn't some little thing he might be trusted to do for them. But he knew his place wasn't there, and his company wasn't desired. Neither would he write, for even a note from him could seem to Starr a reminder of the terrible things she'd witnessed, that is, if anybody told her he had brought her home.

One solace alone he allowed himself. Nightly as he went home late he would walk far out of his way to pass the house and look up at her window; and always it comforted him to see the dim radiance of her soft night-light. Behind those windows she lay asleep, the dear girl he was permitted to carry to her home and safety, when she had almost reached the brink of destruction.

About a week after the fateful wedding day, Michael received a brief note from Starr.

My dear Mr. Endicott:

I wish to thank you for your trouble in bringing me home last week. I cannot understand how you were there at that time. Also I'm deeply grateful for your kindness in making the announcement at the church.

Very sincerely,
S. D. E.

Michael felt the covert question in that phrase: "I cannot understand how you were there at that time." She thought, perhaps, that to carry his point and stop the marriage he had had a hand in that miserable business! Well, let her think it. It wasn't his place to explain and could matter little to her what she believed about him. As well to let it rest. He belonged out of her world and would never try to force his way into it.

And so with the pale face lingering from the hard days of tension, Michael went on, straining every nerve in his work. He kept the alley room open nightly even during hot weather and stayed in constant touch with the farm, which was now fairly on its feet and almost earning its own living. Contributions still kept coming to him quietly here and there, though, and helped in the many new plans growing out of the many new necessities.

The carpenter had built and built, until bungalows of one or two and three rooms dotted about the farm for rent at a low price to the workers. It had become a community by itself, spoken of as "Old Orchard Farms" and well-respected in the neighborhood. In truth the motley company Michael and Sam gathered there had done far better in the way of law and orderliness than either had hoped. They seemed to take pride in letting nothing that could hurt "the boss's" reputation as a landowner be charged to them. If by chance any sordid being came into their midst who couldn't see matters in that light, the rest promptly taught him better or put him out.

And now the whole front yard was aflame with brilliant flowers in their season. The orchard had been pruned and trimmed and grafted, and in spring showed forth in pink and white splendor. At all seasons the grassy drive wound its way up to the old house, through a vista of green or brown branches.

Michael had thought for some time of rebuilding the old house—for what he didn't know. He didn't hope to use it except as a transitory dwelling; yet he wanted to have it as he dreamed it out. It might be needed someday, and now was the time to get it ready. So one day he took an architect down to stay overnight and get an idea of the surroundings, and a few weeks later he had a plan for how the old house could be made into a beautiful new house and yet keep the original outlines. The carpenter, pleased with doing something really fine, undertook the work and was moving it forward rapidly.

The main walls were to be built around with old stone bought from the ruins of a desolated barn. Some of the stone was rusty, golden, and green in lovely mellow tones; some was gray with age and mossy in places; and now and then a dead black stone strengthened the whole coloring. There would be wide, low windows everywhere, letting the sunlight in, with some nestled in the sloping roof to be stained green like the moss that would grow on them someday. A piazza would extend across the entire front with rough stone pillars and a stone-paved floor up to which the orchard grass would grow in a gentle terrace.

Sam and his helpers were already starting rose vines to train about the trellises and pillars. Sam had elected to call it Rose Cottage. Who would ever have suspected Sam of having poetry in his nature?

The great stone fireplace with its ancient crane and place to sit inside was to be retained and built about with more stone. The partitions between the original sitting room and hall were to be torn down, making one living room with the fireplace as center, a window at one side looking toward the sea, and a deep seat with bookcases in the corner. Heavy beams would be put in the ceiling to support it, and fine wood used in the wainscoting and paneling, with rough soft-toned plaster between and above. The floors would be smooth, well-fitted hardwood boards.

A gable would be added on the morning side of the house for a dining room, all windows, with an ocean view on one side and the river on the other. Upstairs would be four bedrooms and a bathroom, with white wainscoting halfway up and delicately vined or tinted papers above.

Michael enjoyed going down to look at the house and watch the progress, as the whole community did. They called it "the boss's cottage," and after work at night men, women, and children stopped by to see what had been done during the day. In it they saw their highest dreams coming true for the man they loved because he'd helped them to a future of possibilities. Each one wondered if he would ever get to the place where he could build himself a house like that and resolved secretly to try for it; always the work went better the next day after the visit.

But, after all, Michael would turn from his house with an empty ache in his heart. What was it for? Not for him. It wasn't likely he would ever spend happy hours there. He wasn't like other men. He must take his happiness in making others happy.

But one day, as he watched the laborers, he suddenly wanted Starr to see it, to know what she would think of it and if she'd like it. Sometime, in the changing of the world, she might chance that way, and he would have an opportunity to show her the house he built—for her! Not that he'd ever tell her the last. She must never know she was the only one in the world he could ever care for. That would seem a great presumption in her eyes. But there would be no harm in showing her the house, and he would make it now as beautiful as if she were to occupy it, with the hope that she might one day see and approve it.

As the work neared its completion, he watched more carefully, matching tints in rooms and always bringing some new idea or finding some bit of furniture that would fit into a certain niche. In that way he cheated the lonely ache in his heart and made believe he was happy.

And another winter drew its white mantle about its shoulders and prepared to face the blast.

It was a bitter winter for the poor, for everything was high, and unskilled labor was poorly paid. Sickness and death lurked in the milk supply, the food supply, the unsanitary tenements about the alley, which, because it hadn't been so bad as some other districts, had been left uncondemned. Yet it was bad enough, and Michael's hands were full keeping his people alive and trying to keep some of them from sinning. For always where misery exists, so does more sinning.

Old Sal sat shivering on her doorstep with her tattered shawl about her shoulders or peered from her muslin-curtained window to see the dirty white hearse, with its pink-winged angel atop, pass slowly in and out with some little fragment of humanity. She knew her turn would come one day to leave it all and go. Then she turned back to her little room which had become the only heaven she knew and solaced herself with the contents of a black bottle!

Chapter 25

During the years of his labor in the alley Michael had become better known among workers for the poor, and he found strength in their brotherhood, though he kept mainly to his own corner and had little time to visit other fields. But he'd formed pleasant distant friendships and met prominent men interested in reforms of all sorts.

He was hurrying back to his boarding place one evening late in January, thinking again of how to reach the masses and help them live in decency so they might stand some chance of being good as well as being alive.

At the crossing of another avenue he met a man whose eloquence as a public speaker was only equaled by his tireless work among men.

"Good evening, Endicott," he said cordially, halting. "I wonder if you're not the very man I want. Will you do me a favor? I'm in great straits and no time to hunt up anybody."

"Anything I can do, sir. I'm at your service," said Michael.

"Good! Thank you! Are you free this evening for an hour?"

"I can be," said Michael, smiling. The other man's hearty greeting and warm "thank you" cheered his lonely heart.

"Well, then, you'll take my place at Madison Square Garden tonight, won't you? I've just had a telegram that my mother's very ill, perhaps dying, and I must go at once. I'm on my way to the station now. I thought Patton would be at his rooms and help me out, but they tell me he's out of town on a lecture tour."

"Take your place?" said Michael, aghast. "That I could never do, sir! What were you going to do?"

"Why, there's a mass meeting at Madison Square Garden. We're trying to get more playgrounds and roof gardens for poor children, you know. I was to speak about the tenement district and give people a general idea of the need. I'm sure you're well acquainted with the subject. They're expecting some men who can give generously if they're touched the right way. You're very good to help me out. You'll excuse me if I hurry on. It's almost train time. I want to catch the six o'clock express west."

"But, sir, I couldn't do that. I'm not a public speaker—I never addressed a large audience in my life! Isn't there someone else I could get for you?"

While he was speaking, a vision of the church filled with the fashionable world, waiting for a wedding that didn't materialize, came strangely to his thoughts.

"Oh, that doesn't make the slightest difference in the world! You know the subject from A to Z, and I don't know another available soul tonight who does. Just tell them what you know. You needn't talk long; it'll be all right anyway. Just smile your smile, and they'll give all right. Good night, and thank you from my heart! I must take this cab." He hailed a passing cab and sprang in-side, calling out above the city's noise, "It's at eight o'clock. Don't worry! You'll come out all right. It'll be good practice for your business."

Michael stood still in the middle of the crowded pavement and looked after the departing cab in dismay. He felt utterly inadequate to fill the situation and tried to think of someone else. There seemed no one used to speaking who knew the subject. The few who knew were either out of town or at some distance. He didn't know how to reach them in time. Besides, Michael wouldn't shirk a situation no matter how trying it was to him. It was one of the first principles he was taught in football, and before he reached his boarding place, his chin was up, his lips set.

Will French coaxed it out of him after dinner and laughed and slapped him on the shoulder. Will was engaged to Hester now and was outrageously happy.

"Good work, old fellow! You've got your chance. Now give it to 'em! I don't know anybody who can do it better. I'd like to bring a millionaire or two to hear you. You've been there—now tell 'em! Don't frown like that, old fellow. You've got the chance of your life. Why don't you tell 'em about the tenement in the alley?"

Michael's face cleared. "I hadn't thought of it, Will. Do you think I could? It isn't exactly on the subject. I understood from him I was to speak of the tenement in relation to the playground."

"The very thing," said Will. "Didn't he tell you to say what you knew? Well, give it to 'em straight, and you'll see those rich old fellows open their eyes. Some of 'em own some of those old rickety shacks and probably don't know what they own. Tell 'em. Perhaps the old man who owns our tenement will be there! Who knows?"

"By the way," said Michael, his face alight, "did I tell you Milborn told me the other day they think they're on the track of the real owner of the tenement? The agent let out something the last time they talked with him, and they think they may discover who he is, though he's hidden himself well behind agents for years. If we can find out who he is, we may help him understand the great need for him to make a few changes."

"Yes, a few changes!" said Will, sneering. "Tear down the whole rotten death trap and build a new one with light and air and a chance for human beings to live! Give it to 'em, old man! He may be there tonight."

"I believe I will," said Michael thoughtfully, and he went up to his room and locked the door.

When he came out again, Will, waiting to accompany him to the meeting, saw in his eyes the look of the dreamer, the man who sees into the future and prophesies. He knew Michael wouldn't fail in his speech that night. He gave a knowing look to Hester as she came out to go with him, and Hester understood. They walked behind him quietly or speaking in low tones. They felt the pride and anxiety of the moment as much as if they were going to make the speech. The angel in the man had dominated them also.

Now Starr had come down with her father for a week's shopping the last time he ran up to his sister's, and on this particular evening she had claimed her father's society.

"Can't you stay at home, Daddy dear?" she asked. "I don't want to go to Aunt Frances's 'quiet little evening' one bit. I told her you needed me tonight since we have only a day or two before I go back."

Aunt Frances was Starr's mother's sister and as the servants of the two families agreed, "Just like her, only more so." Starr had never been quite happy in her company.

"Come with me for a while, daughter. I'm sorry I can't stay at home all evening, but I promised I'd drop into a charitable meeting at Madison Square for a few minutes. We won't need to stay long, and if you're with me it'll be easier to get away."

"Agreed!" said Starr and got ready quickly.

So the roll of martial music poured forth from the fine instruments secured for the occasion, and the evening's leaders and speakers, with the presidents of this society or that army or settlement or organization for the relief and benefit of the poor, filed onto the great platform. And Starr and her father occupied prominent seats in the vast audience and joined in the enthusiasm that spread like a wave before the great American flag that burst out in brilliant electric lights of red and white and blue.

Michael entered with the others, as calmly as though he'd spent his life preparing for the public platform. There was fire in his eyes, the fire of passion for the people of the slums who were his kin. He looked over the audience with a throb of joy to think he had such a mighty opportunity. His pulses weren't stirred, because he had no self-consciousness. His subject was to live before the people; he was nothing at all. He had no fear about telling them, if that was all they wanted. Sentences burning with the blood of souls had been pouring through his mind since he'd decided to talk of his people. He was only in a hurry to begin lest they wouldn't give him time to tell all he knew! Could he ever tell it? It was endless as eternity.

With a strange stirring of her heart, Starr recognized him. She felt the color stealing into her face. She thought her father must notice it and glanced at him, but he was deep in conversation about some banking business. So she sat and watched Michael during the opening exercises and wondered how he came to be there and what his position was. Did lawyers get paid for doing something to help along charitable institutions? She supposed so. He was probably given a seat on the platform for his pains.

Yet she couldn't help thinking how fine he looked sitting there in the center, the place of honor, it seemed. He was taller than the others, sitting or standing, and his fine form and bearing made him quite noticeable. Starr could hear women about her whispering to their escorts: "Who is he?" Her heart gave strange little throbs that she knew. It seemed odd to her that seeing him now took her back to that morning in Florida when she'd kissed him in the chapel.

The memory seemed sweet and tender, and she dwelt upon it, while she watched him gazing calmly over the audience, rising and moving to let another pass him, bowing and smiling to a noted judge who leaned over to grasp his hand. Did young lawyers like that get to know noted judges? And wherever did he get his grace? Rhythm and beauty were in his every motion. Starr had never had such an opportunity to observe him before, for in the sea of faces she knew hers would be lost, and she might watch him at will.

"Daddy, did you know Michael was up there?" she asked after awhile when her father's friend returned to his seat.

"Michael? No, where? On the platform? I wonder what in the world he's doing there? He must be mixed up in this thing somehow. I understand he's stuck at his mission work. I tried to stop him several years ago. Told him it would ruin his prospects, but he was too stubborn to give up. So he's here!"

Mr. Endicott searched out Michael and studied the face keenly, looking in vain for any marks of degradation or fast living. The head was lifted with its conquering look; the eyes shone forth like jewels. *Michael was a man, a son— to be proud of,* he told himself and breathed a heavy sigh. That was one time his stubbornness hadn't conquered, and he found himself glad it hadn't.

The opening exercises were mere preliminary speeches and resolutions, mixed with music and the introduction of the city's mayor and one or two other notables who said a few apathetic words commending the work and retired on their laurels.

"I understand this Dr. Glidden who's to speak is quite eloquent," said Starr's father as the president got up to introduce the evening speaker. "The man just talking with me says he's worth hearing. If he's tiresome we'll slip out. I wonder which one he is? He must be the man with the iron-gray hair over there."

"Oh, I don't want to go out," said Starr. "I like it. I never was in a great meeting like this. I like to hear them cheer."

Her cheeks were rosy, for in her heart she found she longed to stay there and watch Michael a little longer.

"I'm sorry to tell you our friend and advertised speaker was called away by the sudden and serious illness of his mother and left for the West on the six o'clock express," said the chairman.

Sounds of disappointment swept over the audience, and some men reached for their hats.

"Well, now that's a pity," whispered Endicott. "I guess we better go before they slip in some dry old substitute. I've been seen here—that's enough."

But Starr laid a hand on her father's arm.

"Wait a little, Daddy," she said softly.

"But he's sent a substitute," went on the chairman, "a man he says is a hundred times better able to talk on the subject than he. He spoke to me from the station phone just before he left and told me he felt you'd all agree he did well to go when you heard the man he sent in his place. I have the pleasure of introducing to you Mr. Michael Endicott, who will speak to you this evening on the needs of the tenement dwellers—Mr. Endicott."

Amid the silence that ensued after the feebly polite applause Michael rose. For an instant he stood, looking at the audience, and a strange subtle thrill ran over the assembly.

Then Michael, measuring the spacious hall, flung his clear, beautiful voice out into it and reached its uttermost bounds.

"Did you know that in this city now are 71,877 totally dark rooms? Some of them are connected with an air shaft twenty-eight inches wide and seventy feet deep, and many have no access to even a dark shaft. And did you know these rooms are the only place in the world for thousands of little children, unless they stay in the street?"

The sentence shot through the audience like a deliberate lightning bolt, crashing through the hearers' hearts and tearing away every vestige of their complacency. The people sat up and took notice. Starr trembled—she didn't know why.

"There's a tenement with rooms like this—a dumbbell tenement, it's called—in the alley where, for no reason I know, I was born."

"Oh!" The sound swept over the listeners in a great wave like a sob of protest. Men and women raised their opera glasses and looked at the speaker again. They asked one another who he was and settled down to hear what more he had to say.

Then Michael told of three dark little rooms in "his" tenement where a family of eight, accustomed to better things, had been forced by circumstances to make their home and where tuberculosis germs had been growing in the dark, until the whole family was infected. He spoke of a ten-year-old girl, living in one of these rooms, pushed down on the street by a playmate, an accident thought nothing of in a healthy child; but in this child it produced tubercular meningitis, and after two days of agony the child died. He told of a delicate girl, who with her brother were the sole wage earners of the family, working all day and sewing far into the night to make clothes for the brothers and sisters, who had fallen prey to the white plague. He told instance after instance of sickness and death from the terrible conditions in this one tenement.

Then a refined-looking woman in the audience, who had dropped in with her husband on the way to some other gathering, drew her mantle about her shoulders with a shiver and whispered: "Really, Charles, it can't be healthy to have such terrible things in the city where we live. Germs could get out and float around to us. Such low creatures should be cleaned out of a decent community. Do let's go now. I can't listen to another word. I won't enjoy the reception."

But the husband sat frowning and listening to the end of the speech, granting her whisper the single growl: "Don't be a fool, Selina!"

On Michael went, taking his audience with him through room after room of "his" tenement, showing them horrors they'd never dreamed. He gave them an occasional glimmer of light when he told of a curtained window with fifteen minutes of morning sun, where a little cripple watched for her sunbeam and pushed her pot of geraniums along the sill to benefit from its brief shining. He brought laughter from the audience over the wit of some poor creatures in trying situations, showing a sense of humor wasn't lacking in "the other half." And he set them weeping over a baby's funeral.

He told them how hard the workers were trying to improve the terrible conditions; how cruelly slow this tenement's owner was even to cut windows into dark air shafts; how so far it had been impossible to discover the name of the building's true owner, because he had for years hidden behind agents who held the building in trust.

The speech closed in a mighty appeal to the people of New York to rise up and wipe out this curse of the tenements and build in their places light, airy, clean, wholesome dwellings, where people might live and work and learn life's lessons aright, and where sin could find no dark hole in which to hatch its loathsome offspring.

As Michael sat down amid a burst of applause given few speakers, another man stepped to the front of the platform. The cheers were hushed somewhat, only to swell and burst forth again, for this man was one of the city's great minds and always welcome on any platform. He'd been asked to make the final appeal for funds for the playgrounds. It was considered a great stroke of luck by the committee to secure him.

"My friends," he said when the hush came at last and he could be heard, "I appreciate your feelings. I'd like to spend the remainder of the night applauding the man who has just finished speaking."

The clamor showed signs of breaking forth again.

"This man has spoken from his heart. And he knows what he speaks about, for he's lived in those tenement rooms, like the children for whom he pleads. I'm told he's given every evening for four years out of a busy life, just opening into great promise, to help his people. Listening to him has reminded me of Lanier's wonderful poem 'The Marshes of Glynn.' Do you recall it?

Ye spread and span like the catholic man who hath mightily won
God out of knowledge, and good out of infinite pain,
and sight out of blindness, and purity out of a stain.

Let us get to work at once and do our duty. I see you don't need urging. My friends, if such a man as this, a prince among men, can come out of the slums, then the slums are surely worth redeeming."

The audience thundered and clamored, and women sobbed openly, while the ushers hurried about collecting the eager offerings. Michael had won the day, and everybody was ready to give. It helped get the burden of such conditions off their consciences.

Starr sat through the whole speech with glowing cheeks and wet lashes. Her heart throbbed with wonder and personal pride in Michael. Somehow the years between seemed to drop away, and she saw before her the boy who had described the Florida sunset and filled her with childish admiration over his beautiful thoughts. His story appealed to her. The lives of the little ones he'd been telling about were like his poor neglected existence before her father took him up—the little lonely life offered freely to save her own.

She forgot all that had passed between: her anger at his not coming to ride; after her return from abroad, his not calling or accepting her invitations; her rage at his interference in her affairs. Her persistent folly now seemed unspeakable. She was ashamed of herself. The tears streamed unnoticed down her cheeks.

When the speeches were over and the applause had subsided, Starr turned to her father, her face aglow, her lashes still wet. Her father had been silent and absorbed. His face was inscrutable now. He could mask his emotions even to those who knew him best.

"Daddy dear," whispered Starr, "couldn't we buy that tenement and rebuild it? I'd love to give those children happy homes."

Endicott turned and looked at his treasured child, her lovely face eager now. She had infinite faith in her father's ability to purchase anything she wanted. The father himself was deeply stirred. He looked at her searchingly at first, then tenderly, but his voice was almost gruff.

"H'm! I'll see about it!"

"Couldn't you let Michael know now, Daddy? I think it would be such a help to him to know his speech has done some good." The voice was sweet and appealing. "Couldn't you send him word by an usher?"

"H'm! I suppose I could." Endicott took out his fountain pen and a business card and began to write.

"You don't suppose, Daddy, that the owner will object to selling? There won't be any trouble about it that way, will there?"

"No, I don't think there'll be any trouble."

Endicott slipped the card into an envelope he found in his pocket and, calling an usher, asked him to take it to the platform to Michael. What he had written was this:

I suppose you've been talking about my property. Pull the tenement down if you like and build a model one. I'll foot the bills.

                                                                    D. E.

When Michael, surprised at receiving a communication on the platform, tore the envelope open and read, his face fairly blazed with glory. Starr was watching him, and her heart gave an odd throb of pleasure at the light in his eyes. The next instant he was on his feet and, with a whispered word to the chairman, came to the front of the platform. He raised his hand and brought instant silence.

"I have good news. May I share it with you? The owner of the tenement is in this house and has sent word he'll tear it down and build a model one in its place!"

The ring in Michael's voice and the light on his face equalled a dozen votes of thanks. The audience rose to its feet and cheered.

"Daddy! Oh, Daddy! Are you the owner?" Astonishment, reproof, excuse, and forgiveness mingled in Starr's voice.

"Come, Starr," said her father abruptly, "we'd better go home. This is a hot, noisy place, and I'm tired."

"Daddy dear! Of course you didn't know how things were!" said Starr sweetly. "You didn't, did you, Daddy?"

"No, I didn't know," said Endicott evasively, "that Michael has a great gift of gab! Would you like to stop and have an ice somewhere, daughter?"

"No, Daddy, I'd rather go home and plan how to make over that tenement. I don't believe I'd enjoy an ice after what I've heard tonight. Why do some people have so much more than others to start with?"

"H'm! Deep question, child. Better not trouble your brains with it."

Starr saw that her father, though deeply moved, didn't wish to discuss the matter.

The next day Michael called at Endicott's office but didn't find him in and wrote a letter out of his joyful heart, asking permission to call and thank his benefactor and talk over plans. The following day he received a curt reply.

Son—Make your plans to suit yourself. Don't spare expense within reason. No thanks needed. I did it for Starr. You made a good speech.

Michael choked down his disappointment over this rebuff. He wasn't forgiven yet. He might not enter into communion again, but he was beloved. He couldn't help feeling that, because of the "Son" that began the communication. And the grudging praise his speech received was more to Michael than all the adulation people had showered upon him since the meeting. But Starr! He did it for Starr! She wanted it! She was perhaps there! How else would she have known? The thought thrilled him. Oh, if he might have seen her! But then perhaps he couldn't have told his story, so it was just as well. But Starr was interested in his plans! How wonderful for her to work with him even in this indirect way. Oh, if someday—!

But here Michael shut down his thoughts and went to work.

Chapter 26

Late in January Michael was taking his nightly walk homeward by way of the Endicott home. He was convinced Starr was still away from home, for he'd seen no lights now for several weeks in the room he knew was hers. But there was always the chance she might have returned.

He was nearing the house when he saw from the opposite direction a man turn the corner and with halting gait walk slowly toward the house and pause before the steps. Something familiar in the man's attitude caused Michael to hasten his steps, and coming closer he found it was Mr. Endicott looking up the steps of his home as if they were a difficult hill he must climb.

Michael stopped beside him, saying good evening, the thrill of his voice conveying his joy in the meeting.

"Is that you, son?" asked the older man, swaying slightly toward him. "I'm glad you came. I feel strangely dizzy. I wish you'd help me in."

Michael's arm went about the other's shoulders at once, and his ready strength almost lifted his benefactor up the steps. He opened the night latch with the key handed him and, without waiting to call a servant, helped Mr. Endicott up to his room and to his bed.

The man sank back wearily with a sigh and closed his eyes, then suddenly roused himself.

"Thank you, son, and will you send a message to Starr that I cannot come tonight as I promised? Tell her I'll likely be all right tomorrow and will try to come then. You'll find the address at the head of the telephone list in the hall. I guess you'll have to phone for the doctor. I don't feel like myself. Something must be wrong. I think I've taken a heavy cold."

Michael hurried to the phone and called the physician, begging him to come at once, for he could see Mr. Endicott was very ill. Then his voice trembled as he gave the message to Western Union over the phone. It seemed almost like talking to Starr, though he sent the telegram in her father's name.

The message sent, he hurried back to the sick man, who seemed to have fallen into a stupor. His face was flushed and hot, the veins in his temples and neck throbbing rapidly. In all his healthy life Michael had seen little of illness, but he recognized it now and knew it must be a violent attack. If only he knew something to do until the doctor arrived!

Hot water used to be the universal remedy for all diseases at college. The matron always had someone bring hot water when anyone was ill. Michael went downstairs to find a servant, but they must all be asleep, for he'd been unusually late in leaving the alley that night.

He found that the bathroom would supply hot water, however, so he undressed his patient, wrapped him in a blanket, and placed his feet in hot water. But the patient showed signs of faintness and couldn't sit up. A footbath under such conditions was difficult to administer. The unaccustomed nurse got his patient into bed again with difficulty and was wondering what to do next when the doctor arrived.

Michael watched the doctor's grave face as he examined the sick man. He knew his intuition was right. Mr. Endicott was seriously ill. At last the doctor stepped out of the room and motioned Michael to follow him.

"Are you a relative, young man?" he asked, looking at Michael keenly.

"No, only someone who's very much indebted to him."

"Well, it's lucky for him if you feel that indebtedness now. Do you know what's the matter with him?"

"No," said Michael. "He looks pretty sick to me. What is it?"

"Smallpox!" said the doctor. "And a case at that." He noted there was no blanching of panic in the young man's face, no hint of movement to leave the room. The man wasn't a coward anyway.

"How long have you been with him?" he asked abruptly.

"Since I telephoned you," said Michael. "I happened to be passing the house and saw him trying to get up the steps alone. He was dizzy, he said, and seemed glad to have me help him."

"Have you ever been vaccinated?"

"No," said Michael indifferently.

"The wisest thing for you would be to get out of the room at once and let me vaccinate you. I'll try to send a nurse to look after him as soon as possible. Where's the family? Not at home? The servants will probably scatter as soon as they learn what's the matter. A pity he wasn't taken to the hospital, but it's hardly safe to move him now. He's a very sick man, and there's only one chance in a hundred of saving him. You've run some big risks, taking care of him this way."

"Any bigger than you're running, doctor?" Michael smiled gravely.

"H'm! Well, it's my business, and I don't suppose it's yours. People are paid for those things. Come and get out of this room, or I won't answer for the consequences."

"The consequences will have to answer for themselves, doctor. I'm staying here till somebody better comes to nurse him."

Michael's eyes didn't flinch as he said this.

"Suppose you take the disease?"

Michael smiled one of his brilliant smiles. "Why, then I will, but I'll stay well long enough to take care of him until the nurse comes."

"You might die!"

"Of course."

"Well, it's my duty to tell you you'd probably be throwing your life away, for there's only a chance he won't die."

"Not throwing it away if I helped him suffer a little less. And you said there's a chance. If I didn't stay, could he miss that chance?"

"Probably."

"Can I do anything to help or ease him?"

"Yes."

"Then I stay. I should stay anyway until someone comes. I couldn't leave him this way."

"Very well, then. I'm proud to know a man like you. There's plenty to be done. Let's get to work."

The hour that followed was filled with instructions, and Michael had no time to think what would become of work or anything. He only knew this was the present duty and went forward in it step by step. Before the doctor left, he vaccinated Michael and gave him careful directions on how to take all necessary precautions for his own safety. But he knew from the lofty look in the young man's face that these were secondary considerations. The patient's needs came first.

The doctor roused the servants, told them what had happened, and tried to persuade them to stay quietly in their places, assuring them he'd see they ran no risks if they obeyed his directions. But they all panicked and gathered their effects, like the Arabs of old who folded their tents and stole away in the night. Before morning Michael and his patient were alone in the house.

Early in the morning the doctor called. He hadn't secured a nurse yet. Could Michael hold the fort a few hours longer? He'd relieve him sooner if possible, but experienced nurses for contagious cases were hard to get just now. There was a great deal of sickness. He might get one this morning, but it was doubtful. He had telephoned everywhere.

Of course Michael would hold the fort.

The doctor gave explicit directions, asked questions, and promised to call as soon as possible.

Michael, alone in the great silence that the occasional babble of a delirious person emphasizes in an otherwise empty house, began to think of things that must be done. Fortunately a telephone was in the room. He wouldn't have to leave his patient alone. He called Will French and told him in a few words what had happened; laughed pleasantly at Will's fears for him; asked him to look after the alley work and attend to one or two matters connected with the office work which couldn't be put off. Then he called Sam at the farm, for Michael had long ago found it necessary to have a telephone put in at Old Orchard.

The sound of Sam's voice cheered his heart. After Michael explained briefly his present position as nurse for the head of the Endicott house who lay sick with smallpox, Sam responded with a "Fer de lub o' Mike!"

When Michael had finished his directions to Sam and received his partner's promise to do everything as Michael would have done it, Sam broke out with: "Say, does dat guy know what he's takin' off'n you?"

"Who? Mr. Endicott? No, Sam, he doesn't know anything. He's delirious."

"Ummm!" grunted Sam, deeply troubled. "Well, he better fin' out wen he gets hisself agin, er there'll be sompin' comin' to him."

"He's done a great deal for me, Sam."

"Ummm! Well, you're gettin' it back on him sure thing now. Say, you t' care o' yerse'f, Mickey! We all can't do nothin' w'th'ut yer. You lemme know every day how you be."

"Sure, Sam!" responded Michael, deeply touched by the choking in Sam's voice. "Don't worry. I'm sound as a nut. Nothing'll happen to me. The doctor vaccinated me, and I won't catch it. You look after things for me, and I'll be on deck again someday, all the better for the rest."

Michael sat back in the chair after hanging up the receiver, his eyes glistening with moisture. To think the day had come when Sam cared like that! It was a miracle.

Michael returned to the bed to look after his patient. After doing everything the doctor had said, he decided to reconnoiter for some breakfast. There must be something in the house to eat even with the servants gone, and he should keep up his strength.

It was late in the morning, nearly half-past ten. The young man hurried downstairs and began to search the pantry. He didn't want to be away long from the upper room. Once, as he was looking in the refrigerator for butter and milk, he thought he heard a sound at the front door. But then all seemed still, so he hurriedly put a few things on a tray and carried them upstairs. He might not be able to come down again for several hours. But when he reached the top of the stairs he heard a voice, not his patient's, but a woman's voice, sweet and troubled.

"Daddy! Oh, Daddy dear! Why don't you speak to your little girl? What's the matter? Can't you understand me? Your face and your hands are so hot—they burn me. Daddy dear!"

It was Starr's voice, and Michael's heart stood still with the thrill of it—and the instant horror of it. Starr was in the room of death with her father. She was exposed to the terrible contagion—she, the beautiful treasure of his heart!

He set the tray on the hall table and hurried to the door.

She sat on the side of the bed, her arms about her father's unconscious form and her head buried in his neck, sobbing.

For an instant Michael was frozen with horror at her danger. If she'd wanted to take the disease she couldn't have found a more certain way.

The next instant his senses returned and without thinking he sprang forward and caught her up in his arms, bearing her from the room and setting her down at the bathroom door.

"Oh, Starr! What have you done!" he said, a catch in his voice like a sob.

Starr, frightened, struggling, sobbing, turned and looked at him.

"Michael! Why are you here? What's wrong with my father?"

"Go wash your hands and face quickly with this antiseptic soap," he commanded, alert now and dealing out the things the doctor had given for his own safety. "And here! Rinse your mouth with this quickly, and gargle your throat! Then go and change your things as quick as you can. Your father has the smallpox, and you have been in there close to him."

"The smallpox!"

"Hurry!" ordered Michael, handing her the soap and turning on the hot water.

Starr obeyed because people did when he spoke in that tone, but her frightened eyes sought his face for some reassurance.

"The smallpox! Oh, Michael! How dreadful! But how do you know? Has the doctor been here? And how did you happen to be here?"

"I was passing last night when your father came home, and he asked me to help him in. Yes, the doctor was here and will come again soon and bring a nurse. Now hurry! You must get far away from this room!"

"But I'm not going away!" said Starr stubbornly. "I'm staying by my father. He'll want me."

"Your father would be distressed beyond measure if he knew you were exposed to such a terrible danger. He'd much rather you go away at once. Besides, he's delirious, and your presence can't do him any good now. You must take care of yourself, so that when he gets well you'll be well, too, and can help him back to health."

"But you're staying."

"It doesn't matter about me," said Michael. "There's no one to care. Besides, I'm a man and strong. I don't think I'll take the disease. Now please take off those things you wore in there and get something clean that hasn't been in the room and go away from here as quickly you can."

Michael had barely persuaded her to take precautions when the doctor arrived with a nurse and the promise of another before night.

He scolded Starr for her foolishness in going into her father's room. He had been the family physician ever since she was born, knew her well, and took the privilege of scolding when he liked. Starr succumbed meekly. But one thing she wouldn't do, and that was leave the house while her father remained in critical condition. The doctor frowned and scolded but finally agreed to let her stay. And indeed it was perhaps the only choice, for she had undoubtedly been exposed to the disease and was subject to quarantine. There seemed to be no place she could safely go where she could be comfortable, and the house was large enough for two or three parties to remain in quarantine in several detachments.

There was another question. The nurses would have their hands full with their patient. Someone must stay in the house to look after things, see they needed nothing, and prepare meals. Starr, of course, knew nothing about cooking, and Michael's experience was limited to roasting sweet potatoes around a college bonfire and cooking eggs and coffee at the fireplace on the farm. But a good cook to stay in a plague-stricken dwelling would be difficult to find, so the doctor decided to attempt the willing services of these two. Starr was established in her own room upstairs, which could be shut away from the front part of the house by a short passageway and two doors, with access to the lower floor by means of the back stairs. And Michael made a bed of the soft couch in the reception room, where he'd twice passed through trying experiences. Great curtains kept constantly wet with antiseptics shut away the sickroom and adjoining apartments from the rest of the house.

Michael was to place such supplies as were needed at the head of the stairs, just outside the curtains, and the nurses would pass all dishes through an antiseptic bath before sending them downstairs again. The electric bells and telephones in the house enabled them to communicate without danger of infection.

Starr was at once vaccinated, and the two young people received many precautions and orders with medicine and a strict regime. Even then the doctor shook his head. If those two beautiful faces should have to pass through that dread disease, his heart would break. Whatever skill and science could do to prevent that should be done.

So the house settled down to a daily routine—the busy city humming outside, but no more a part of them than if they were living in a tomb. The warning card on the door sent the neighbors scurrying off in a panic to Palm Beach or Europe, and even the strangers passed by on the other side. The grocery boy and the milkman left their orders hurriedly on the front steps, and Michael and Starr might almost have used the street for an exercise ground—so deserted it had become.

But they didn't need to go farther than the front door, for they had a lovely side and backyard, screened from the street by a high wall, where they could walk when they weren't too busy with their work—which for their unskilled hands was laborious. Nevertheless, the orders were strict, and every day they went out for a couple of hours at least. To keep from getting chilled, Michael invented games when tired of walking, and twice after a new snowfall they went out and threw snowballs, coming in with glowing faces and shining eyes, to change wet garments and hurry back to their kitchen work. But this was after the first few serious days were passed, and the doctor had given them hope that if all went well the patient had a good chance of pulling through.

They settled into their new life like two children who had known each other a long time. All the years between were as if they hadn't been. They made their blunders, were merry over their work, and grew into each other's companionship. Their cooking ideas were primitive, and if they couldn't have ordered things from caterers, they and the nurses might have starved. But with telephoning the nurses for directions and studying the recipes on the boxes of cornstarch and farina and oatmeal and the like that they found in the pantry, they were learning day by day to do a little more.

And then one blessed day the dear nurse Morton walked in and took off her things and stayed. Morton had paid a long-delayed visit to her old father in Scotland that winter. But when she saw in the papers the notice of the calamity that had befallen the house of her past employer, she packed her trunk and took the first steamer back to America. Her baby and her baby's father needed her, and nothing could keep Morton away after that.

Her coming relieved the situation, for though she'd never been a fancy cook, she knew all about good old-fashioned Scottish dishes, and from the first hour took up her station in the kitchen. Comfort and order reigned at once, and Starr and Michael had time on their hands not spent in eating, sleeping, working, or exercise.

Then they read together, for the library was filled with treasures of literature, many of which Michael had never had access to except through public libraries. But a book in hand is more satisfying when one has a bit of leisure in a busy life. Starr had been reading more than ever this winter with her aunt and enjoyed the pleasant companionship of a book together.

Then some hours Starr played softly and sang, for the piano was far from the sickroom and couldn't be heard upstairs. Indeed, if it hadn't been for the anxious struggle going on up there, these two would have had a beautiful time.

For, unknown to them, they were growing daily to delight in each other's presence. Even Michael, who had long ago laid down the lines for his life and never expected to be more to Starr than friend and protector, didn't realize where this intimate companionship was leading. When he thought of it at all, it seemed a precious solace for his years of loneliness, to be enjoyed fully and treasured in the barrenness that must surely follow.

Upstairs the fight continued daily, until at last one morning the doctor told them it was won, that the patient, though very much enfeebled, would live and slowly regain his strength.

That was a happy morning. The two caught each other's hands and whirled around the dining room when they heard it, and Morton came in with her sleeves rolled up and her eyes like two blue lakes blurred with raindrops in the sunlight.

The next morning the doctor looked the two over before he went upstairs and set a limit to their quarantine. If they kept on doing well they would be reasonably safe from taking the disease. It would be a miracle, almost, if neither took it; but it looked as if they'd be all right.

Now they had been so absorbed in one another that they'd thought little about taking the disease themselves. If either had been in the house with nothing to do but brood, it might have been the sole topic of thought. But their healthy busy hours had helped the good work on.

One bright morning, while waiting for the doctor to come, Michael was glancing over the morning paper, and Starr was trying a new song that had just arrived in the previous evening's mail.

Suddenly Michael exclaimed in dismay, and Starr, turning on the piano stool, saw him staring out the window, his face pale and drawn.

"What is it?" she asked in quick, sympathetic tones.

Michael turned to look at her vivid beauty, his heart thrilling with the sound of her voice, and suddenly felt the gulf between them. What he'd read in the paper had shaken him from his dream and brought him back to the reality of what he was.

The paper reported Buck's escape from jail. Michael was greatly troubled for Buck and instantly recalled he belonged in Buck's class and not in Starr's charmed circle here.

He looked at the girl with serious, tender eyes that seemed less intimate than in these weeks. She sensed the difference at once.

He showed her the item.

Starr's face softened with sympathy, then expressed indignation. "He was one of those people in your tenements you've been trying to help?" she asked, trying to understand his look. "He should have been ashamed to get into jail after you were helping him. Wasn't he a worthless fellow?"

"No," said Michael in quick defense, "he never had a chance. And he wasn't just one of those people; he was the one. He was the boy who took care of me when I was a little fellow. He shared everything he had—a hard crust, a warm cellar floor. I think he loved me—"

Something in Michael's face and voice warned Starr to tread lightly.

"Tell me about him," she said softly.

So Michael, his eyes tender, his voice gentle, because she cared to know, told her of Buck. When he finished, her eyes were wet with tears, and she looked so sweet he had to avert his own eyes to keep from taking the lovely vision into his arms and kissing her. It was a strange, wild impulse and frightened him. Suppose someday he forgot himself and let her see how he dared love her? That must never be. He must watch himself. Her sweet friendship to him must never be broken by his word, look, or action.

And from that morning his manner changed, subtly, intangibly—but changed.

They read and talked together, and Michael opened his heart to her as never before about the alley, his farm community, and his hopes for his people. Starr listened and entered eagerly into his plans, yet felt the change, and her troubled spirit didn't know what it was.

Chapter 27

All this while Michael communicated daily with Sam, as well as Will French, who with Hester's help had kept the alley rooms going, though they reported the leader was sorely missed.

Sam reported daily progress with the house and about two weeks before Michael's release from quarantine announced its completion, even to papering the walls and oiling the floors.

A fire had been burning in the furnace and fireplaces for several weeks, so the plaster was thoroughly dry. Michael planned for Starr and her father to go straight to the farm as soon as they were free to leave the house.

To this end Hester and Will were given daily commissions to purchase this or that article of furniture, until at last Michael felt the house would be habitable for Starr and her precious invalid.

During the winter Michael had purchased rugs and charming, suitable furniture for the house he was building. He'd already selected the important things and knew he could trust Hester's taste for the rest. For some reason he'd never said much to Starr about Hester or Will, perhaps because they had always seemed to belong to one another and thus set apart from his life.

But one morning Starr entered the library where Michael was telephoning Hester about some last purchases she was making and overheard these words: "All right, Hester, you'll know best, but I think you better make it a dozen instead of half. It's better to have too many than too few, and we might have company."

Now, of course, Starr couldn't know dishes were being discussed. In fact, she didn't stop to think what they were talking about; she only knew he called this other girl "Hester." She suddenly realized that during these weeks, although she addressed him as Michael, he avoided using any name for her, except on one or two occasions, substituting pronouns whenever possible. She hadn't noticed this before, but when she heard that "Hester" in his pleasant tones, she wondered. Who was Hester? And why was she Hestered so carelessly as though he had a right? Was Michael engaged to her? Why hadn't she thought of it before? Of course it would be natural. This other girl had been down in his dear alley, working shoulder to shoulder with him all these years, and he must love her.

Starr's bright morning suddenly clouded over with darkness, and though she tried to hide it even from herself, her spirit was heavy with something she didn't understand.

That evening Michael came into the library unexpectedly. He'd been out in the kitchen helping Morton open a box that was stuck. He found the room dark but thought he heard a soft sound like sobbing in one corner.

"Starr!" he said. "Starr, is that you?"

He didn't know he'd called her by her name, though she knew very well. She kept still an instant and then rose from the crumpled heap in the corner of the leather couch where she'd dropped in the dark to cry out the strange ache of her heart. She thought Michael was safely in the kitchen for a while.

"Why, yes, Michael!" she said in a broken voice, though struggling to make it natural.

Michael stepped to the doorway and turned on the hall lights so he could see her figure standing in the shadow. Then he stepped over to her, his whole heart yearning over her, but with great control.

"What's the matter—dear?" He breathed the last word almost under his breath. He didn't realize he'd spoken it aloud.

It seemed to envelope her with a deep tenderness, breaking her partial self-control. She sobbed again before she could speak.

Oh, if he only dared take that dear form into his arms and comfort her! But he had no right!

Michael stood still and struggled with his heart, standing near her, yet not touching her.

"Oh, my dear!" he breathed to himself, in love and self-restraint.

But she didn't hear the breath. She was struggling on her own, remembering that Hester girl and her own duty. She mustn't let him see how she felt, not for anything in the world. He was kind and tender. He had always been. He'd denied himself to stay with them in their need because of his gratitude toward her father for all he'd done for him. He breathed that "dear" as he would have to any tenement child in trouble. Oh, she understood, even while she let the word comfort her lonely heart. But why had she been left to trifle with a handsome scoundrel? Why hadn't she been worthy to win the love of a great man like this one?

At last, in her sweet voice she burst forth: "Oh, Michael, you've been so good to me—to us, I mean—staying here all these weeks and not showing any impatience when you had great work to do. I've just been thinking how horrid I was to you last winter—the things I said and wrote to you—and how I treated you when you were trying to save me from an awful fate! I'm so ashamed— and so thankful! I realized tonight what I owe you, and I can't ever thank you. Can you forgive me for the horrid way I acted and for passing you on the street that Sunday without speaking to you—I'm so ashamed! Will you forgive me?"

She put out her hands with a pathetic motion toward him in the room's half light, and he took them in his warm ones and held them, his whole frame thrilling with her sweet touch.

"Forgive you, little Starr!" he breathed. "I never blamed you—"

And there's no telling what might not have happened if the doctor hadn't arrived just then to complete arrangements for their going to the farm.

When Michael returned from letting the doctor out, Starr had fled upstairs to her room. When they met the next morning the bustle of preparation was upon them, and each cast shy smiling glances toward the other. Starr knew she was forgiven, but she also knew a wall stood between them that hadn't before, and her heart ached with the knowledge. Nevertheless, it was a happy morning, and one couldn't be miserable in Michael's company, with her father recovering rapidly and the prospect of going with him into the beautiful outdoors in a few hours.

Michael prepared to go with a look of solemn joy. Solemn because the wonderful companionship he'd had alone with Starr would soon end. Joyful because he could be with her still and know she'd escaped the terrible disease. Besides, he might always serve her, and they were friends now, not enemies—that was a great deal!

Old Orchard stood on tiptoe that lovely spring morning when the party came down. The winding road to the cottage was arched with bursting bloom, for the apple trees had decorated for the occasion and made a canopy of pink and white for Starr to pass beneath.

Not a soul was in sight as they drove up to the cottage, except Sam, standing respectfully to receive them in front of the piazza, and Lizzie, vanishing around the corner of the cottage with her boy toddling after—Lizzie had come down to be a waitress at Rose Cottage for the summer. But every soul on the farm was watching at a safe distance. Sam, without breathing a word, had conveyed to them all that those coming as their guests were beloved of Michael, their angel-hearted man. They stood in silent, adoring groups behind a row of thick hedges and watched them arrive, glorying in the beauty of the one they called in their hearts "the boss's girl."

The room stood wide and inviting to receive them. A fire of logs burned on the great hearth, and a deep leather chair sat before it, with a smaller rocker at one side and a sumptuous leather couch for the invalid on the other side, where the light of the flames wouldn't strike the eyes, yet the warmth would reach him. Soft greens and browns were blended in the silk pillows piled on the couch and on the seats that appeared here and there about the walls as if they grew by nature. The bookcase was filled with Michael's favorites—Will French had seen to this—and a few books were scattered on the big table where a green shaded lamp of unique design, a magazine, and a chair at just the right angle suggested a pleasant evening hour. Two or three pictures adorned the walls; Michael had selected these as he learned more about art from his study at the exhibits.

"Oh!" exclaimed Starr. "How lovely! It's a real home!"

It will probably be Michael and Hester's someday, she thought. But she wouldn't let shadows spoil her good time now, for it was her good time, and she had a right to it. She, too, was happy that she and Michael were friends— the kind of friends that can never be enemies again.

The invalid sank into the couch cushions with a pleased light in his eyes. "Son, this is all right. I'm glad you bought the farm."

Michael turned with a look of love to the only father he'd ever known. It was good to be reconciled with him and know he was on the road to health once more.

The doctor who had come down with them looked about with satisfaction.

"I see you're fixed," he said to Endicott. "I wouldn't mind being in your shoes myself. Wish I could stay and help you enjoy yourself. If I had a pair of children like those, I'd give up work and buy a farm alongside and settle down for life."

The days at the farm passed in a charmed existence for Starr and her father. Everything they needed seemed to come as if by magic. Starr's every wish was anticipated, and Lizzie waited upon her devotedly, never by even a look trying to win recognition. Starr, keen in her remembrances, knew and appreciated this.

After the first two days Michael was back and forth in the city. His business, growing steadily before his temporary retirement from the world, had piled up and was awaiting his attention. His work in the alley called loudly for him every night. Yet he came down to the farm often and spent his Sundays there.

One Saturday evening about three weeks after arriving at the farm, they were all seated cozily in the cottage living room. The invalid was resting on the couch in the shadow, with Starr seated close beside him, the firelight glowing on her face, her hand in her father's. Michael sat by the table with a fresh magazine he was about to read to them when a knock came at the door. Opening the door, Michael found Sam standing on the piazza, and another dark form huddled behind him.

"Come out here, can't yer! Buck's here!" whispered Sam.

"Buck!" Michael spoke the word with a joyful ring that thrilled Starr's heart with sympathy as she sat listening, her ears alert with interest.

"I'm so glad!" said Michael's vibrant voice again, with real welcome. "Come in, Buck. I have a friend here who knows all about you. No, don't be afraid. You're safe. What? Well, we'll turn the light out and sit in the firelight. You can go over in that corner by the fireplace. No one will see you. The shades are down."

Michael's voice was low, and he stood inside the doorway.

There was dissent in a low whisper outside, and then Sam's voice growled, "Go in, Buck, ef he says so." And Buck reluctantly entered, followed by Sam.

Buck was dressed in an old suit of Sam's, with his hands and face washed and hair combed. Sam had imbibed ideas and wasn't slow to impart them. But Buck stood dark and frowning against the closed door; his eyes, like black coals in a setting of snow, darted about the room in restless vigilance. His body wore the habitual air of crouching alertness. He started slightly when anyone moved or spoke to him.

Michael went quickly over to the table and turned down the lamp.

"You won't mind sitting in the firelight, will you?" he said to Starr in a low tone, and her eyes told him she understood.

"Come over here, Buck," said Michael, motioning toward the sheltered corner of the other side of the fireplace from where Starr was sitting. "This is one of my friends, Miss Endicott, Mr. Endicott. Will you excuse us if we sit here and talk a few minutes? Miss Endicott, you remember my telling you about Buck?"

Starr, with sudden inspiration, stood up and crossed to where the dark-browed Buck stood frowning and embarrassed in the chimney corner and put out her hand to him. Buck looked at it in dismay and didn't stir.

"Why don't yer shake?" whispered Sam.

Then with a grunt of astonishment Buck put out his rough hand and for the first time held a lady's hand in his. The hunted eyes looked up startled to Starr's. And somehow Starr, with her smile and her eyes and her gentle manner, unknowingly conveyed a thought from Browning's poem to Buck! Poor, neglected, sinful Buck!

All I could never be,
    All men ignored in me,
This, I was worth to God, whose wheel the pitcher shaped.

And Michael, looking on, knew what she'd done and blessed her in his heart.

Buck sat down in the chimney corner, half in shadow with the lights from the great log flaring over his face. The shades were drawn, the doors closed. He was surrounded by friendly faces. For a few minutes the eyes ceased roving around the room and rested on Starr's sweet face as she quietly held her father's hand. It was a sight Buck's eyes had never rested upon in his whole checkered existence, and for the moment he let the sweet wonder of it filter into his dark, scarred soul with blessed healing. Then he looked from Starr to Michael's face nearby, joyous at Buck's coming, anxious with the outcome, and for a moment the heavy lines in forehead and brow that Buck had worn since babyhood softened with a tender look. Perhaps 'tis given once to even the lowest soul to see, no matter how far fallen, just what he might have been.

They had been sitting thus for about fifteen minutes, talking quietly. Michael intended to take Buck upstairs soon and question him, but first he wanted time to think what to do. Then suddenly a loud knock startled them all, and as Michael rose to go to the door there followed the resounding clatter of the tongs falling on the hearth.

A voice with a knife edge to it cut through the room and made them shiver.

"Good evening, Mr. Endicott! I'm sorry to trouble you, but I've come on an unpleasant errand. We're after an escaped criminal, and he was seen entering your door a few minutes ago. Of course I know your good heart. You take 'em all in, but this one is a jailbird. You'll excuse me if I take him off your hands. I'll try to do it as quietly as possible."

The big, blustery voice ceased, and Michael, looking at the sinister gleam of metal in the hands of the men accompanying the county sheriff, knew the crisis was upon him. The man, impatient, was already pushing past him into the room. It was no use resisting. He flung the door wide and turned with the saddest look Starr had ever seen on a man's face.

"I know," he said, his voice filled with sorrow. "But—he was one I loved!"

"Wasted love, Mr. Endicott. Wasted love. Not one of 'em worth it!" growled the big man walking in.

Then Michael turned and faced the group around the fireplace and, looking from one to another, paled with amazement, for Buck wasn't among them!

Starr sat beside her father in the same attitude she'd held throughout the last fifteen minutes, his hand in hers, her face turned, startled, toward the door and something inscrutable in her eyes. Sam stood close to the fireplace, the tongs he'd just picked up in his hands and a look of sullen rage on his face. Nowhere in the whole room was a sign of Buck, and there seemed no spot where he could hide. The dining room door was in the opposite wall, and behind it could be heard the cheerful clatter of clearing the table. If Buck had escaped that way there would have been an outcry from Morton or the maid. Every window's shade was closely drawn.

The sheriff looked suspiciously at Michael whose blank face showed he had no part in making way with the outlaw. The man behind him looked sharply around and finished with a curious gaze at Starr. Starr, rightly interpreting the scene, rose to the occasion.

"Would they like to look behind this couch?" she said, moving quickly to the other side of the fireplace over toward the window, with a warning glance toward Sam.

Then while the men searched in vain around the room, in the chimney closet and behind the furniture, she stood beside the corner window.

Michael had arranged for the windows to have springs worked by pressing a button like some car windows, so a touch would send them up at will.

Only Sam saw Starr's hand slide under the curtain and unfasten the catch at the top—then quickly down and touch the button in the windowsill. The window went up noiselessly, and in a moment the curtain was moving out, puffed by the soft spring breeze, and Starr had returned to her father's side.

"I can't understand it," Michael said. "He was here a moment ago!"

The sheriff, nosing about the fireplace, turned and stepped over to the window, sliding up the shade and peering out into the dark orchard.

"H'm! That's where he went, boys. After him, quick! We should have posted a watch at each window as well as at the back. Thank you, Mr. Endicott! Sorry to trouble you. Good night!" And the sheriff clattered after his men.

Sam quickly pulled down the window, fastened it, and gazed with almost worshipful understanding at Starr.

"Isn't that fire getting pretty hot for such a warm night?" said Starr, pushing back the hair from her forehead and bright cheeks. "Sam, suppose you get a little water and pour over the log. I think we won't need any more fire tonight anyway."

And Sam hastened to obey, his mouth stretching in a broad grin as he went out the door.

"She'd make a peach of a burglar," he remarked to himself as he filled a bucket with water and hurried back to the fire.

Michael, in his strait between law and love, was deeply troubled and had followed the men out into the dark orchard.

"Daddy, I think you'd better get up to your room. This excitement has been too much for you," Starr said.

But Mr. Endicott demurred. He had been interested in the drama enacted before him and wanted to sit up and see the end of it. He was inclined to blame Michael for bringing such a fellow into Starr's presence.

But Starr laughingly bundled him off to bed and sat for an hour reading to him, her heart in a flutter to know how things came out. She wondered if Sam understood and put out the fire and if she could safely give him any broader hint.

At midnight, Michael lay awake with a troubled spirit, wondering if he might have done anything for Buck if he'd only done it in time—and been right to do.

Cautiously a man stole out of the orchard's darkness until he stood close to the old chimney. Then softly on the midnight summer air came a peculiar sibilant sound, clear, piercing, yet blending with the night and leaving no trace of its origin. One couldn't tell where it came from. But Michael, keeping his vigil, heard and rose up on his elbow. Was Buck calling him? It came again, softer this time but distinct. Michael sprang from his bed and threw on his garments. That call should never go unanswered!

Stealthily, in the moonlight, a dark figure stole forth from the chimney top, climbed down on the ladder that had been tilted against it, helped lay the ladder back in the deep grass and, joining the figure on the ground, crept toward the river where a boat waited.

Buck lay down in the bottom of the boat, covered with a piece of sacking, and Sam took up the oars when a long, sibilant whistle like a night bird floated through the air. Buck started up and turned suspicious eyes on Sam.

"What's that?"

"It's Mickey, I reckon," said Sam reverently. "He couldn't sleep. He's huntin' yer!"

Buck lay down with a sound like a moan, and the boat took up its silent glide toward safety.

"It's fierce ter leave him this a-way!" muttered Buck. "Youse tell him, won't yer, an' her—she's a ly-dy, she is. She's all right! Tell her Buck'll do ez much fer her someday ef he ever gits the chance."

"In doin' fer her you'd be doin' fer him, I spekullate," said Sam after a long pause.

"So?" said Buck.

"So," answered Sam. And that was how Sam told Buck of Starr's identity.

Now Starr, from her darkened window beside the chimney, had watched the whole thing. She waited until she saw Michael come slowly, sadly back from his fruitless search through the dawning mist alone, with bowed head, and her heart ached for the problem filling him with sorrow.

Chapter 28

S tarr was coming to the city on the early morning train with Michael to shop for summer clothes. She was leaving in a few days to be bridesmaid at the wedding of an old school friend who lived out West, and she told herself she wanted the pleasure of this trip to town with Michael. She treasured each beautiful day filled with precious experiences, like jewels to be strung on memory's chain, with a vague unrest lest some future event might snatch them from her forever.

She wished she had refused her friend's pleading, but the friend had delayed the wedding until Starr could leave her father, and her father had also insisted she have the rest and change after the winter's ordeal. So Starr seemed to have to go, much as she preferred to stay. She had vowed to herself that she would return at once after the wedding despite the family's pleas to stay all summer with them. She sensed that the days of her companionship with Michael might be short, and she must make the most of them. It might never be the same again. She wasn't even sure her father would remain all summer at the farm as Michael urged.

This morning she was happy about going with Michael. The sea seemed to sparkle with a thousand gems as the train swept along. Michael told her of his first coming to see the farm and pointed out the flowers along the way. She assured him Old Orchard was far prettier than any of them, now that the roses were beginning to bud. It would soon be Rose Cottage indeed!

Then the talk fell on Buck and his brief visit.

"I wonder where he can be and what he's doing," said Michael, sighing. "If he only could have stayed longer for me to talk with him. I believe I could have persuaded him to a better way. But it's a mystery how he got away with those men watching the house."

Starr, her cheeks rosy, her eyes shining mischievously, looked up at him. "Didn't you suspect where he was hiding?"

Michael looked at her with a sudden start and smiled into her eyes. "Why, no. Did you?"

"Of course. I knew all the time. Do you think it was dreadful for me not to tell? I couldn't bear to have him caught before you'd had a chance to help him and when he was so good to you as a little boy. Besides, I saw his face, that terrible, hunted look. There wasn't anything really wrong in my opening that window and throwing them off the track, was there?"

"Did you open the window?"

Starr nodded saucily. "Yes, and Sam saw me do it. Sam knew all about it. Buck went up the chimney right through that hot fire. Didn't you hear the tongs fall down? He went like a flash before you opened the door, and one foot was still in sight when that sheriff came in. I was so afraid he'd see it. Was it wrong?"

"I suppose it was," he said sadly. "The law must be maintained. It can't be set aside for one fellow who's touched one's heart by some childhood action. But right or wrong I can't help being glad you cared to do something for poor Buck."

"I think I did it mostly for—you," she said softly, her eyes still down.

For answer, Michael reached out his hand, took her small gloved one lying in her lap, and pressed it for an instant. Then, as if a mighty power were forcing him, he laid it gently down again and drew his hand away.

Starr felt the pressure of that strong hand and its message through long days afterward, and more than once it gave her courage and cheer. Come what may, she had a true friend.

They spoke no more till the train swept into the station and they'd hurried through the crowd and were standing on the front of the ferryboat. The water sparkled before them, and the whole, stirring city spread before their gaze, with the light from the cross on Trinity Church steeple sending its glory in their faces.

"Look!" said Michael, pointing. "Do you remember the poem we were reading the other night—Wordsworth's 'Upon Westminster Bridge'? Doesn't it fit this scene perfectly? I've often thought of it when I was coming across in the mornings. To look over there at the beauty, one would never dream of all the horror and suffering within those streets. It's beautiful now. Listen! Do you remember it?"

Earth has not anything to show more fair:
   Dull would he be of soul who could pass by
A sight so touching in its majesty:
   This City now doth like a garment wear
The beauty of the morning; silent, bare,
   Ships, towers, domes, theatres, and temples lie
Open unto the fields and to the sky;
   All bright and glittering in the smokeless air.
Never did sun more beautifully steep
   In his first splendor valley, rock, or hill;
Ne'er saw I, never felt, a calm so deep!
   The river glideth at its own sweet will:
Dear God! the very houses seem asleep;
   And all that mighty heart is lying still!

Starr gazed long at the picture before her, while her companion spoke the beautiful lines word by word.

Michael's hat was off, and the morning sunlight lay on his hair and cheek and brow. Her heart swelled within her as she looked, and tears filled her eyes. She dared not look longer lest she show her deep emotion. The look of him, the words he spoke, and the whole wonderful scene would linger in her memory as long as life should last.

Two days later Starr started west, and life seemed empty for Michael. She was gone from him, but still she would come back. Or would she? How long could he hope to keep her if she did? Sad foreboding filled him, and he worked with strained nerves, for now he knew that right or wrong she was heart of his heart, part of his consciousness. He loved her better than himself, and he saw no hope in forgetting. Yet never would he ask her to share the dishonor of his heritage.

The day before Starr was expected back at Old Orchard, Michael picked up the morning paper and with growing horror read:

BANDIT WOUNDED AS FOUR HOLD UP TRAIN
EXPRESS MESSENGER PROTECTS CASH DURING DESPERATE GUNFIGHT IN CAR

Fort Smith, Ark.—Four bandits bungled the holdup of a Kansas City passenger train, between Hatsfield and Mena, Ark., early today. One was probably fatally wounded and captured, and the others escaped after a battle in which the express messenger exhausted his ammunition and was badly beaten.

When the other robbers escaped, the wounded bandit eluded the conductor and made his way into the sleeper, where he climbed into an empty berth. But he was soon traced by the drops of blood from his wound. The conductor and a brakeman hauled him out and battled with him in the aisle amid passengers' screams. The bandit aimed his revolver at the conductor and fired, but his wrist twisted suddenly, sending the bullet into his own body instead of the conductor's. The wounded bandit received the bullet in his left breast near the heart and will probably die. The express messenger is in the hospital at Mena and may recover.

If the bandit's bullet had gone as intended it would probably have wounded one or two women passengers, who at the sound of trouble had jumped from their berths into the aisle and were directly in the bullet's path.

The captured bandit may prove to be the escaped convict "Buck," who was serving a long sentence in the state penitentiary and for whom the police have been searching in vain for the last three months.

Michael was pale and trembling when he finished reading the story. Was this then Buck's end? Must he die like that? Disgrace and sin and death, with no chance to make good? Michael bowed his head on the table before him, his heart too heavy to think it out. That evening a telegram arrived from Arkansas.

A man named Buck is dying here and calls incessantly for you. If you wish to see him alive, come at once.

Michael took the midnight train. Starr had telegraphed her father she would reach Old Orchard in the morning. It was hard to go when she was just returning. Michael wondered if it would always be so now.

Buck roused at Michael's coming and smiled feebly.

"Mickey! I knowed you'd come! I'm done for, pardner. I ain't long fer here, but I couldn't go 'thout you knowin'. I'd meant to git jes' this one haul an' git away to some other country where it was safe. Then I was goin' to try'n keep straight like you'd want. I would a'got trough all right, but I seen her—the pretty lady—your girl—standing in the aisle right ahin' the c'ndct'r, jes' es I wuz pullin' the trigger. I knowed her right off, an' I couldn't run no resks. I ain't never bin no bungler at my trade, but I had to bungle this time 'cause I couldn't shoot your girl! So I turned it jes' in time an' took it mese'f. She seen how 'twas 'ith me that time at your house, an' she he'ped me git away. I sent her word I'd do the same for her someday. Bless her—an' now—you tell her we're square! I done the bunglin' fer her sake, but I done it fer you too, pard—little pard—Mickey!"

"Oh, Buck!" Michael knelt beside the bed and buried his face in the coverlet. "Oh, Buck! If you'd only had my chance!"

"Never you mind, Mickey! I ain't squealin'. I knows how to take my dose. An' mebbe they'll be some kind of collidge whar I'm goin', an' I kin get a try at yet—don't you fret, little pard—ef I git my chancet I'll take it fer yer sake!"

The life breath seemed spent with the effort, and Buck sank slowly into unconsciousness and so passed out of a life that had been against him.

After doing the last little things permitted him, Michael sadly returned home.

He reached the city in the morning and spent several hours putting to rights his business affairs. By noon he found himself so weary he took the two o'clock train down to the farm. Sam met him at the station. Sam somehow sensed when to meet him, and the two gripped hands and walked home together across the salt grass. Michael told in low, halting tones what Buck had said. Sam kept his face turned the other way, but once Michael glimpsed it and was sure tears were on his cheeks. To think of Sam shedding tears for anything!

Arriving at the cottage, Sam told him he thought Mr. Endicott was taking his afternoon nap upstairs and Miss Endicott had gone to ride in an auto with some fancy woman who'd called for her.

Being weary and yet unwilling to risk waking Mr. Endicott by going upstairs, Michael asked Sam to bolt the dining room door and give orders not to disturb him for an hour. Then he lay down on the leather couch in the living room. The windows were open around, and the sweet breath of the opening roses stole in with the summer breeze, while the drone of bees and the song sparrow's pure notes lulled him to sleep.

Chapter 29

Michael had slept perhaps an hour when he was roused by voices—a sharp, hateful one with an unpleasant memory in it and a sweet, clear one that went to his soul.

"Sit down here, Aunt Frances. No one's about. Papa's asleep, and Michael hasn't returned yet from a trip out West. You can talk freely."

"Michael, Michael!" sniffed the voice. "Well, that's what I came to talk to you about. I didn't want to say anything where the chauffeur could hear. He's too curious and might tell the servants. I wouldn't have it get out for the world. Your mother would have been mortified about all this, and I can't see what your father is thinking about. He never did seem to have much sense where you were concerned!"

"Aunt Frances!"

"Well, I can't help it. He doesn't. Now take this matter of your being down here, and the thought of your calling that fellow Michael—as if he were a cousin or something! Why, it's disgusting! I hoped you'd stay out West until your father was well enough to go away somewhere with you. But now that you've come back I think you should leave here at once. People will talk, and I don't like it. Why, the fellow will presume on it to be intimate with you—"

Michael suddenly realized he was listening to a conversation not intended for his ears, and yet he couldn't get out of hearing without passing the door in front of which the two women were seated. Both the dining room door and the stairs were on the other side of the room from him, and he would risk being seen by either or both of them if he attempted to cross to them. The windows were screened by wire nailed over the whole length, so he couldn't get out through them. He could only lie still and pretend to be asleep if they discovered him afterward. It was embarrassing but not his choosing.

There was a slight stir outside. Starr had risen and stood with her back to the doorway.

"Aunt Frances! What do you mean? Michael is our honored and respected friend, our protector—our host. Think what he did for Papa! Risked his life!"

"Stuff and nonsense! Risked his life. He took the risk for his own reasons. He knew how to worm himself into the family again."

"Aunt Frances! I won't hear you say such things. Michael is a gentleman, well educated, with the highest ideals and principles. If you knew how self-sacrificing and kind he is!"

"Kind, yes, kind!" sniffed the aunt. "What will you think about it when he asks you to marry him? Will you think he's kind to offer you a share in the inheritance of a nobody—a charity—dependent—a child of the slums? If you stay here you'll have all New York gossiping about you, and then when you're in disgrace—I suppose you'll turn to me to help you out of it."

"Stop!" cried Starr. "I won't listen to another word. What do you mean by disgrace? There could be no disgrace in marrying Michael. The girl who marries him will be the happiest woman in the world. He's good and true and unselfish to the heart's core. But there's no danger of his ever asking me to marry him, Aunt Frances. I'm sure he loves another girl and is engaged to marry her, and she's a nice girl too. But if it were different, if he were free and asked me to marry him, I would be as proud and glad as if a prince of the highest realm had asked me to share his throne with him. I'd rather marry Michael than any man I ever met, and I don't care in the least whether he's a child of the slums or a child of a king. I know what he is, and he's a prince among men."

"Oh, really! Has it come to this? Then you're in love with him already, and my warning comes too late, does it? Answer me! Do you imagine yourself in love with him?"

"Aunt Frances, you have no right to ask me that question," said Starr steadily, her cheeks red, her eyes bright.

Michael was sitting bolt upright on the couch now, forgetful of his eavesdropping, fairly holding his breath to listen and straining his ears that he might not lose the slightest word. He was devouring the dear little form in the doorway with his eyes, and her words fell on his tired heart like raindrops in a thirsty land, bringing forth the flowers of hope into lovely bloom.

"Well, I do ask it!" snapped the aunt. "Come, answer me—do you love him?"

"That, Aunt Frances, I shall never answer to anybody but Michael. I must refuse to hear another word on this subject."

"Oh, very well, good-bye. I'll leave you to your silly fate, but don't expect me to help you out of trouble if you get into it. I've warned you, and I wash my hands of you."

The angry woman flounced out to her waiting car, but the girl stood still in the doorway.

"Good afternoon, Aunt Frances," she said with dignity. "I shall never ask your help in any way."

Starr watched the car out of sight, tears welling into her eyes and rolling down her cheeks. Michael sat breathless on the couch and tried to think what to do, while his very being was rippling with the joy of her words.

Then she turned and saw him, and he stood up and held out his arms.

"Starr, my little Starr! My darling! Did you mean all you said? Would you really marry me? I've loved you always, Starr, since the first time I saw you as a tiny child. I've loved your soft baby kisses and those you gave me later when you were a little girl and I was an awkward boy. You never knew how dear they were or how I would go to sleep at night dreaming about those kisses on my face. Oh, Starr! Answer me? Did you mean it all? And could you ever love me? You said you would answer that question to no one else but me. Will you answer it now, darling?"

For answer she came and stood inside his arms, her face all tears and smiles, and he folded her within his strong clasp and, stooping, whispered softly,

"Starr, little darling—my life—my love—my—wife!"

Three weeks later, when the roses were bursting with bloom over the porch at Rose Cottage and June was everywhere with her richness and beauty, Starr and Michael were married on the piazza under an arch of roses. A favored few of society's cream motored down to Old Orchard to witness the ceremony, and despite her ugly predictions and threats Aunt Frances was among them, smiling and dominating.

"Yes, so sensible of her not to make a fuss with her wedding, when her father is getting back again. Of course she could have come to my house and been married. I begged her to—naturally she shrank from another wedding in connection with the old home—but her father seemed to dread coming into town, so I advised her to go ahead and be married here. Isn't it a charming place? So rustic and simple and quite artistic in its way. Michael had done it all, planned the house and everything, of course, with Starr's help. You know it's quite a large estate, belonging to Michael's great-grandfather once, several hundred acres, and he's used part of it for charitable purposes—has a farm school or something for poor slum people and is teaching them to be decent. I hope they'll be duly grateful. See those roses? Aren't they perfectly dear?"

Thus she chattered to those in the car with her all the way to the farm. To see her going about among the guests and smiling and posing to Michael when he came near, you would have thought she had made the match and never dreamed it was only because Michael, out of his great, forgiving heart, had said, "Oh, forgive her and ask her down. She's your mother's sister, and you'll be glad you did afterward. Never mind what she says. She can't help her ideas. It was her unfortunate upbringing, and she's as much to be pitied as I for my slum education."

The pretty ceremony under the roses was over, and Starr had gone upstairs to change the simple embroidered muslin for her traveling dress and motor coat. Michael and Starr were to take their honeymoon in their own new car, a wedding gift from her father, and Endicott himself was to go to his sister's by rail in Will French's company, to stay during their absence and be picked up by them on their homeward route.

Michael stood among his friends on the piazza giving last directions to Will, who was to look after his law business during his absence. Will was eager to tell his friend how he and Hester planned to be married in the fall and set up housekeeping in a five-room flat that might have been a palace from the light in Will's eyes. Hester was talking with Lizzie, who had edged near the porch with her boy hiding shyly behind her, but the smile Hester threw in Will's direction now and then showed she well knew his subject of conversation.

The whole community had gathered in the orchard in front of the rose arch to watch the wedding ceremony, and many still lingered to see the beloved bride and groom depart.

Suddenly, during Will's eager description of the flat and its prospects, Michael noticed Sam's shy look as he waited anxiously for notice.

"Excuse me, Will. I must see Sam a minute," said Michael, hurrying over to where the man stood.

"Say, Mickey," said Sam shyly, grasping Michael's hand, "me an' Lizzie sort o' made it up as how we'd get tied, an' we thought we'd do it now whiles everybody's at it, an' things is all fixed. Lizzie wanted me to ask you ef you s'posed she'd mind ef we'uns stood thur on the verandy whur yous did, arter you was gone?"

Sam looked at him as if he'd asked for half of Michael's kingdom and scarcely expected to get it, but Michael's face was filled with glory as he clasped his comrade's rough hand heartily.

"Mind! She'd be delighted, Sam! Go ahead. I'm sorry we didn't know it before. We'd have liked to give you a present, but I'll send you the deed to the little white cottage at the head of the lane, the one that looks toward the river and the sunset, you know. Would you two like to live there?"

Sam's eyes grew large with happiness, and a mist came over them as he held tight to the hand enclosing his own and choked and tried to answer.

Amid a shower of roses and cheers, Michael and Starr rode into the sweet June afternoon, alone together at last. And when they had gone beyond the town and were on a stretch of quiet woodsy road, Michael stopped the car and took his bride in his arms.

"Dear," he said as he tenderly kissed her, "I've just been realizing what might have happened if Buck hadn't seen you in time and taken the shot himself—that I might not have you, my life, my dear, precious wife!"

Then Starr looked up with her eyes dewy. "Michael, we must try to save a lot of others for his sake."

And Michael smiled and pressed his lips to hers again, with deep, sweet understanding.

When they were riding along again, Michael told her what Sam asked and how another wedding was to follow theirs.

"Oh, Michael!" exclaimed Starr. "Why didn't you tell me sooner! I wish we'd stayed to see them married. Couldn't we turn around now and get there in time if you hurry?"

"We'll try," said Michael, reversing the car.

In an instant more it was shooting back to Old Orchard, arriving just as Sam and Lizzie were shyly taking their places, hand in hand, under the roses, in as near imitation of Michael and Starr as their unaccustomedness could compass.

Jim discovered the car coming up the orchard lane.

"For de lub o' Mike!" he exclaimed aloud. "Ef here don't come Mickey hisse'f and her! Hold up dar, mister preacher. Don't tie de knot till dey gits here!"

And a cheer arose loud and long and echoed through the trees and over the river to the sea. Three cheers for the love of Michael!

Sam and Lizzie bloomed forth with smiles, and the ceremony went forward with alacrity now that the real audience was present.

An hour later, having done their part to make the wedding festivities as joyous as their own had been, Michael and Starr started out again into the waning day, a light on their faces and joy in their hearts.

Starr, her heart full, laid her hand on Michael's and said with shining eyes, "Michael, do you know—I found a name for you. Listen: 'And at that time shall Michael stand up, the great prince which standeth for the children of thy people: and at that time thy people shall be delivered, every one that shall be found written in the book.' Michael, you are my prince!"

And Michael, as he stooped and kissed her, murmured, "My Starr."

The Patch of Blue

Chapter 1

C hristopher Walton closed the hymnbook, put it in the rack, adjusted his mother's wrap on her shoulders as she sat down, arranged the footstool at her feet, then sat back and prepared to get through the boredom of the sermon time.

Chris had no idea of trying to listen to the sermon. He never even pretended to himself that he was listening. He carried his tall, good-looking self to church regularly because his father and mother required the household to attend church, but his soul was as far away as possible from the dim religious sanctuary light. Nobody suspected of course that behind his handsome, polite exterior the world was rushing on in his thoughts.

It would have been astonishing if that world could have suddenly appeared in church. It would have created quite an uproar. Sometimes it was a football game with the grandstand rooting wildly and he himself scoring a glorious touchdown. Sometimes it was a party he'd attended the night before, with lively music stealing through his thoughts. Sometimes it was his own life plans, when he saw himself alternately writing a book that would set the world on fire or becoming a central figure on the stock exchange floor or a wealthy stockbroker who could give great sums to charity and education.

But none of these things figured in his thoughts this morning. His mind was full of college. Three weeks more and he expected to be gone from this pew, back to college life. He drew a breath of secret satisfaction as he remembered a college student could do as he pleased about attending divine service. If he had important lessons to study or wasn't feeling up to the mark, he could stay away. There would be no compulsion. Oh, there was no real compulsion at home. Nobody would have forced him to go if he'd taken a stand against it perhaps. Yet his father's expectation and his mother's grieved look were as good as law to him, and he'd have felt uncomfortable and out of harmony with his family if he attempted to cut church here. And Chris loved his family. He enjoyed pleasing his father and mother even though it was sometimes a bore.

His father was getting old, he reflected with a pang. His hair was deeply silvered. Heavier lines were coming into his kind face. Chris was still a little anxious over the look in his face at the breakfast table as he finally yielded to their pleas to stay at home this morning and nurse the blinding headache that made it impossible for him to eat his breakfast.

Chris settled back comfortably in his father's place at the head of the cushioned pew and reflected on what a pleasant family he had. Nothing must ever be allowed to happen to his family! He paid them each brief tribute. Such a sweet mother, natural pink in her cheeks and a delicate refinement and peace about her. His sister, Elise, pretty and stylish and smart. She was off at a weekend house party today, and he missed her from her corner of the pew. They'd always been good comrades. He would miss her when he returned to college.

College! Ah, now he was off! It would be his senior year. It was going to be great! Dad had been wonderful about it. He'd arranged for him to take one of the best rooms in the dorm. And it was practically settled that Walt Gillespie was to be his roommate in place of that dub Chad Harmon. They were to have a suite, two bedrooms, and a spacious sitting room between. Of course many students couldn't afford an outfit like that. And Mother had given up one of her finest Oriental rugs, the one he'd always admired the most, for his floor. Of course she would have a new one in its place, but he knew she loved this blue one. Yet she wanted him to have it; she said they wanted his last year to be the best of all.

Then Dad was making a generous donation to their new fraternity building, and it was hinted that Chris would be suggested for president of their chapter next semester. Dad had been awfully generous with money, too—said he wanted him to have everything during his college life because one went to college only once. Dad had been pleased that he'd been popular in his old fraternity. Of course it was Dad's influence that had gotten him in here at the first. They were a terribly exclusive bunch. It was wonderful having a father who was well off and able to put one into the front ranks of things.

And then, the crowning joy of all, Dad was going to let him have a car, one of the very best, to take with him. He'd picked it out, and it was coming tomorrow morning. He was to take it out alone and try it out thoroughly before the final deal was made. But it was practically bought already, for he was sure he'd find nothing wrong with it. It was a great car.

The shining new car in all its flashing chromium and deep blue body rolled slowly down the aisle past his pew and let him study it as the minister rose in the pulpit to introduce a visiting preacher that morning. Chris was so interested in his car that he hardly heard what was going on and scarcely noticed the stranger on the platform.

Chris was thinking how he would take Gilda Carson out for a ride tomorrow after he'd had a good long tour by himself. Gilda was always boasting about Bob Tyson's car and how he'd taken her here and there. But Bob Tyson's car wasn't worth mentioning in the same breath with his new one. Gilda would boast about his now, he was sure.

Not that he cared so much what Gilda thought or did. She wasn't especially his girl, but hearing her always talking about Bob's wonderful car was a bit irksome. Well, there wouldn't be anything wrong with his new car. Such a purring engine, freewheeling, adjustable seats, marvelous shock absorbers, and, above all, speed! The car was doing eighty and even ninety now, up and down the stately church aisles, and Chris sat with a saintlike expression on his face and watched it. He almost wondered why the people didn't turn and look after it in admiration.

Suddenly a new voice broke into his meditations. The minister had introduced the stranger.

He was announcing his text now—two texts. "Oh, give thanks unto the LORD for He is good!" and "How can we sing the LORD's song in a strange land?"

Chris recognized the first text as part of the responsive reading they'd just had, but the second seemed a little out of the ordinary, and he wondered idly what it could have to do with the first. The opening words of the preacher's sermon arrested his attention for an instant.

"It's easy enough to thank God when everything is going well and we have all we want. The true test of a thankful heart is to sing praise when things are going wrong. When we've lost our money or friends or are disappointed in our dearest ambitions, or when we're in a strange, unhappy environment, then we cry out, 'How can we sing the LORD's song in a strange land?'"

That was about all Chris heard of that sermon, and he only wondered a moment about it before he drifted back into his own thoughts. He averred to himself that it was ridiculous to expect anybody to be thankful for sorrow and disaster, for poverty, sickness, and loss. The minister seemed to be mentioning someone who said he was grateful for every trouble he'd ever had and through his disappointments had learned to praise the Lord for them. Well, that was absurd. No one could thank the Lord for unhappiness.

He was thankful his life was laid in pleasant surroundings, and he paused long enough to give a quick thanksgiving for his home, his parents, his pleasant environment, the happy college days that still lay before him, his new car—and then he was off again anticipating his senior year at college and what he had to do before he went back. He tabulated different items mentally on his fingers, things he mustn't forget. Not the least among them was trying the new car tomorrow, and presently the car was rolling up and down the aisle again before his happy vision, and the minister with his absurd message about being glad for unhappiness was utterly forgotten.

He had arranged a full program for the next few days by the time the closing hymn was finally announced, and he found the place for his mother and arose with relief to join in the hymn of praise. He noticed with a vague annoyance that a line in the hymn conveyed that same illogical suggestion about giving thanks for trouble that the minister had suggested in the beginning of his sermon. But he raised his voice a little louder at the refrain of praise and steadily thought of all the joys of his life with true thanksgiving. He certainly was grateful the lines had fallen to him in such pleasant places, and just now he was most grateful the service was over and he would soon be free to return to the delightful details of everyday living.

Out in the summer day he drew a breath of relief and talked eagerly to his mother about the new curtains she was selecting the next day for his college room. He had definite ideas of what he wanted, built on a college room of a famous athlete he'd seen last spring.

Chris was glad his father's headache seemed better and the dinner table was a cheerful place, with everything he liked best to eat. His father seemed a bit grave and silent, but he attributed that to the headache, for he responded smiling to anything that was said. Chris tried to persuade himself he'd imagined those lines of care on his father's face. He talked eagerly of his new car, and his father seemed pleased and promised to take a drive with him if he'd come down to the bank between eleven and twelve o'clock the next day.

Monday morning Chris came whistling down the stairs with a glad light in his eyes. His mother stood in the hall below him, and he paused at the foot of the stairs to touch a light kiss on her forehead. Such a pretty little mother! But he knew just what she was going to say, and he wished to forestall it. She was a peach of a mother but always afraid of things, and he was so full of his own joy this morning that he felt a little impatient toward her fears.

"Oh, Chris, you'll be careful, won't you?" she implored, as he'd known she would.

"Sure, Muzzie. I'm always careful. What's the idea? You act as though I'd never driven before."

"But a new car, Chris—that's different. You don't know how it will act. And a new kind you've never driven before. That freewheeling. I'm afraid of it. You don't know how to work it. They tell me it's quite different from other driving. I wish you'd take a serviceman along with you the first day or two."

Chris laughed. "Well, I like that! A serviceman! Why, Mud, you know Uncle Eben's car was just like this one, and I drove it for him all the time he was here, every day for two weeks. But, Mother, seriously, you must stop worrying about me. I'm not a kid anymore. I'm a man. This is my last year at college—remember. And, besides, there isn't a car made that I can't drive. Why do you suppose I've hung around Ross Barton's garage all these years if not for that? I'm considered a good driver. Why don't you go along with me and prove it? I'll give you a good ride and leave you wherever you say. Then you'll have more confidence in me."

"Oh, I can't, Chris. I have a committee meeting here at the house this morning. But you won't be late for lunch, will you? You know I'll be worried."

The boy stopped and silenced her with a kiss on her soft cheek.

"Now, look here, Mother," he said earnestly. "You've got to stop worrying. You're just making trouble for yourself. Besides, I'm stopping at the bank at eleven for Father, and you know he'll come back on time. You've got him well trained. Sure you don't want to go along for a spin? Well, come on out and look at the car anyway. Did you see it yet from the window? Look!"

He flung the front door open.

"There! Isn't that a winner! Isn't it the neatest car you ever saw? Long, clean sporty lines. Dad was great to do this for me. Having this car'll make all the difference in the world in my college life."

His mother smiled indulgently with a wistful look in her eyes and patted his arm.

"Your father feels you deserve it, Chris," she said lovingly. "We want you to get the greatest enjoyment possible out of your last year in college."

She stood in the open doorway and watched him drive away, thinking what a happy lot she had with such a son. Then she turned with a slight sigh of anxiety, and yet a smile, and went back to her pleasant sheltered life, thinking how good God had been to her.

Chris drove out into the clear September morning, his face alight with satisfaction, down through the pleasant street of the pretty suburb where he was born. He wanted first of all to ride around the old familiar streets and get used to the idea that this wonderful car was his.

As he thrilled to the touch of the new wheel, he remembered that first old Ford he bought for ten dollars. He'd tinkered with it for three weeks before it would run. He'd been so happy with it then, till the kind policeman who'd known him all his life stopped him because he was too young to drive and had no license. But he never dreamed then that only a few short years more and he'd be driving one of the best cars made and thrilling that it was his own.

It was practically his own now. Dad would see to the red tape of the purchase tomorrow morning. He'd promised. And then he'd drive it back to the home garage, and it would be his. It made him feel a man to think of it. He suddenly remembered his first express wagon and how serious life had looked to him as he'd taken it out that first morning after Christmas on the street and showed it to his playmates. And his first bicycle! Dad had always been so good to him, getting him everything he wanted. How he loved that wheel!

But, boy! It was nothing like this first car! This was great! Skimming along with the top down and the wind in his hair—there was nothing like it!

He was skirting the edge of the grove outside town now where they had the high school picnics. The trees were golden, with here and there a vivid coral one. They were early in turning. The yellow leaves against the blue autumn sky filled him with ecstasy. He wished he had someone to talk to who would understand; yet he felt he couldn't put into words what he was feeling. College and the car and the glorious day all mixed up in his soul. Boy! It was great!

He whirled back into town again and traversed the streets, going slowly by his own house and waving to his mother, whose face he could see at the window, just to give her confidence in his driving. His mother waved back to him. She was a great mother! She was a pretty good sport, fearful as she was. Some mothers would have made a terrible kick at their sons' going off to college with a high-powered car. Mothers were always afraid of accidents.

There was Natalie Halsey. He would pick her up and take her for a spin. She had her arms full of packages and might be glad of the lift. He'd never had much to do with Natalie, although they'd been in the same class in high school. She was a quiet, shy girl, always hurrying home right after school and never going to any parties or high school affairs, a bit shabby, too, and with very few friends among the high school clique. Did he hear her father had died this summer? He wasn't quite sure. It would be better not to mention it. He hadn't seen Natalie for a year or two. He couldn't remember when it was.

He drew up alongside the girl and called out pleasantly, "Hello, Natalie, want to ride? I'm going your way."

Natalie turned with a delighted smile and surrendered her heavy packages as he sprang out and took them from her.

"That will be wonderful!" she said, turning a tired smile upon him, and he wondered why he'd never noticed before what blue eyes she had. "I was just wondering whether I could get these things home. I twisted my arm yesterday, and it aches so I could hardly hold on to everything."

"You shouldn't try to carry such loads," reproved Chris in a grown-up tone. "Why didn't you have them sent?"

"Well, the chain stores don't deliver," said Natalie frankly, "and we can't afford to go to any other."

She laughed as if it were a joke, and he looked at her with a wondering pity. He'd never realized before that decent people had to consider such trivial matters. It embarrassed him. He changed the subject and took the one uppermost in his mind: college.

"You're going back to college this fall, I suppose? I forget where you went."

Natalie laughed again, this time wistfully.

"No such luck for me," she said. "I went two years to the university, but last year Mother was too sick to leave, and this year—well—I shouldn't complain," she added brightly. "I've just got a job, and I'm very fortunate in these hard times."

"A job!" said Chris in dismay and looked at her. Why, she seemed just a kid out of high school! So slender and frail-looking!

"You know my father died last spring," added Natalie sadly. "I needed a job badly."

"Oh, I'm sorry!" said Chris. He felt he was bungling things. He recalled suddenly that Natalie hadn't been at the commencement exercises three years ago. Someone had been sick. Her essay had received honorable mention, but someone else had read it. Poor kid! She must have been having a rotten time.

"I just got the job," confided Natalie almost eagerly. "I'm to be cashier at the chain store on the corner of Park Avenue. I'm so pleased."

The ring to her voice told of anxiety and need, and Chris looked at her wonderingly, pityingly.

"Oh, I say," said Chris, as they neared her home. "Wouldn't you like to take a little spin? You don't have to go in yet, do you? I've just got this new car, and I'm trying her out. Want to go?"

"Oh, I'd love to," said Natalie breathlessly, "but I've got to get right home. My mother's been sick again, and I've left her alone this morning. It was only a bad case of flu, but she's weak, and I don't like to leave her long. My sister had to go on an errand. But the car is wonderful, and I thank you for this much of a ride. I'll remember it a long time."

He helped her out and carried her packages to the door of the plain little house, suddenly noticing the contrast between this home and his. There was something touching and lovely in the way Natalie thanked him. Her voice was sweet and womanly. He felt a deep discomfort because this pretty, frail girl had to work in a grocery store and make change for all kinds of people.

The discomfort lasted as he spun away into the bright September day again. He half wished he hadn't picked Natalie up and found out the unhappiness in her life. He couldn't do anything about it, of course.

He whirled into another street, and Betty Zane was coming around the corner.

"Hello, Betts!" called Chris. "Want t' ride in my new buggy?"

"Oh, boy! Do I?" replied Betty, clambering in without waiting for him to get out and help her, and they drove away.

Betty was pretty and stylish and a chatterbox. She admired the car and in the same breath told of one as wonderful that Bruce Carson had just bought. Betty had much gossip to tell of the different members of the old high school class and gave many hints about parties she might be induced to go to with the boy who asked first. She talked of college and what she expected to do there; decried the fact that Chris wasn't attending a coeducational college where they might continue their acquaintance; openly said she'd like more rides in his wonderful new roadster; and left him reluctantly when it was time for him to go for his father.

Chris had quite forgotten Natalie and her difficulties when he rode downtown toward his father's bank. His mind was full of what Betty Zane had told him. When he closed his eyes he could see the bright red speck of Betty's little sharp painted lips and the dancing sarcastic eyes. He still heard some of her flattery ringing in his ears. He knew some of the things she said were bold, things his mother wouldn't have liked. But of course Betty was modern. Mother would have to learn that girls weren't as when she was young. Then why should he suddenly think of Natalie? She was more like the girls of his mother's day. But then that was probably because she'd had no chance in life, no good times. She was old-fashioned, poor thing! But she was nice. Too bad she couldn't have had a better chance!

Then he turned downtown and made his way through increasing traffic toward his father's bank.

Within half a block of the bank he came to a traffic light. As he waited for it to change, he noticed an unusual traffic jam and stretched his neck to discover the cause.

Then he saw a long double line of people blocking the sidewalk in front of the bank and surging out into the street, right in the way of traffic. What could it mean?

The light flashed green, and Chris moved on a few paces nearer the scene of confusion. There must have been an accident. There were so many people and cars, he couldn't see what was the matter. Then as he drew nearer he saw ugly menacing faces in the crowd and heard a rough voice.

"There he is, the son of the president, ridin' around in a five-thousand-dollar car, while we have to sweat fer our money!"

Then a kind of growl passed over the crowd like a roll of muffled thunder, and suddenly a little thickset man in the crowd picked up a brick from a pile along the curb where the road was being mended and hurled it straight at Chris. It crashed through the beautiful glass of the windshield, barely escaped hitting him in the temple, and glanced off through the open window at his left. Chris was too much astonished to be frightened at first.

But the shattering glass had fallen among the crowd and cut hands and faces here and there, a bit got into someone's eye, and all was confusion. Fists were shaken in his face, angry threats were hurled at him, and Chris was hard put to know what to do, for the car was tight in traffic and he couldn't move it.

Then suddenly he heard his policeman friend's voice at his left.

"Better get out of here quick, Chris," he said in a guarded voice. "Start yer engine. I'll make a way fer ya."

The mounted law officer rode fearlessly into the crowd, hitting this way and that with his club, till the mob separated enough for Chris to go through, escorted by two or three burly policemen who appeared out of the throng. They battled an opening through to the side street that led to the alley behind the bank. But as they turned the corner Chris heard the report of a shot, and a bullet whistled by his ear straight through what was left of the windshield. Then he knew he'd had a close call.

As he reached the alley behind the bank where he had meant to turn in, the mob surged from the other end of the block coming toward him.

"Get inta that back doorway there quick and lock it after ya," said the friendly policeman riding close. "I'll look after yer car. Be spry there."

Chris slid from the car, and another officer slipped in behind him. Chris sprang to the doorway, but the door was locked. He began to beat on the door, and the mob with yells of delight surged toward him. He put his shoulder to the heavy door, but he couldn't even shake it. They were all but upon him, when suddenly without warning the door gave way, and he fell across the threshold!

Chapter 2

C hris never knew exactly what happened for the next minute or two. Someone kicked him as he lay there across the threshold, and a cruel blow from a heavy club hit his arm. Someone shouted, "Kill him!" And then he heard a policeman's whistle and wild confusion. Someone had caught him from within the door and was pulling him inside the building. Someone else caught his feet from without and pulled. His shoe came off in the struggle. Something hit him on the head with a dull thud. There were wild yells and a sudden blank.

The door was shut when he came to, and he was inside. Anxious faces hovered about him. He couldn't distinguish them, but he tried to straighten up from the hard couch where he was lying. He recognized the back room of the bank building, a storeroom for old records and files.

"I'm all right!" he said unsteadily as he tried to stand up, thinking of his father somewhere in the building. Then a memory of his mother came and brought him back to his senses. His mother mustn't hear about this. All her worst fears would be justified. She would never feel safe about him again.

Then came with a pang the thought of his beautiful car. Where was it? Was it ruined? Oh, what had happened anyway? Why was all that mob out there, and what was going on? Had there been an accident? And had they mistaken him for someone else? He was still dazed from the blows on his head.

Someone brought him a glass of water, and he drank it slowly, trying to remember just what had happened. His blood was beginning to boil over the indignity done to him and his car. He was becoming furious with himself for not jumping into that crowd and seizing the fellow who had thrown that brick. What was the matter with him anyway that he'd weakly submitted to being led away by the police? He should have done some heavy tackling to show that crowd where to get off. Why be a star football player if one couldn't act in a time of emergency? Of course it had taken him by surprise, but he should have done something anyway. He turned toward the door to go out yet and get somebody, but even as he turned, things went black before his eyes, and he caught himself from falling by the headrest.

"Better lie down again," advised an anxious voice he vaguely identified as a cashier in the bank. Then another put out a kind hand and tried to lead him to the couch, but the motion brought him back from the confusion of his mind again.

"No, I'm all right now. Thank you," he said, blinking at them. "Where's Dad? I'd like to see Dad."

They looked at one another and whispered, and one of them stepped to the door and tapped. Another whispered conversation and he came back.

"Your father's in consultation, but he'll see you in about ten minutes," he said gravely.

Chris sank down on the hard couch again and began to take stock. It was then he missed his shoe.

"Say, did that hyena get my shoe?" he asked with a shade of his old grin coming back to his face.

"He sure did!" responded a cashier, looking gravely out of the grating above the door. "What's left of it is out there in the alley, I guess, but you wouldn't want to wear it. I have an extra pair in the closet. I'll get them. Maybe they'll serve you for the time till you can do better."

He brought the shoes, and Chris had recovered sufficiently to laugh at their fit. He stood up, trying to regain some of his old assurance and poise. Then someone opened the door to his father's office and beckoned him, and he had to throw his energy into walking steadily through that door. He mustn't frighten his father. He felt a good deal shaken up, but he was all right.

"You're lucky you came off as well as you did," murmured the cashier as he closed the door behind him.

Then Chris walked into his father's presence and stood in dismay. For the bank president was sitting at his beautiful mahogany desk with his head down on his arms on the desktop and a look of despair about him.

"Dad! What's the matter?" Chris cried in alarm, quickened out of his daze by his beloved father's stricken appearance.

Slowly the father lifted his head, struggled upright in his chair and looked at him with such a ghastly, haggard face his son was more alarmed than ever. Why, his hair seemed to have silvered more in the few hours since breakfast, and those deep lines in his face were terrible to see.

"What's the meaning of all this, Dad? Are you sick? Oh, Dad!"

His father passed a trembling hand over his forehead and eyes and struggled to make his voice steady.

"No, son, I'm not sick. I'll be all right. It's—just—been a shock."

"But—what is it, Dad?" And then with dawning comprehension he went on, "What's the meaning of all that crowd outside in the street? Has something happened? There hasn't been a run on the bank? Dad—has there?"

He saw by the look in his father's face it was true and sought to find the right word of encouragement.

"But it can't be anything serious, can it, Dad? Our bank? Your bank?"

"It's serious, son," answered his father huskily. "It couldn't be more so. A traitor's been at work inside our ranks."

"Oh, Dad! But don't look that way. It'll be righted somehow."

"Yes, it'll be righted," agreed the sad voice, humiliated to the depths. "It'll be righted for the depositors, I trust. At least they won't lose much, we hope, perhaps nothing in the end. But it means utter ruin for us! For your mother and you and me! For your uncle Ben and Mr. Chalmers and the Tryons."

Chris looked perplexed. "But I don't understand why you—"

"No, you don't understand, son. It's too astounding. You couldn't understand. But, son, it means that we as officers and directors must give up everything to satisfy our depositors. It means that even our house and furniture must go, every-thing that will bring in anything. It means that your mother and I will have no home and no income, and I'm too old to begin again, Chris. It couldn't be done!"

He ended with a groan, and Chris staggered across the room and laid his hand on his father's silvered head that was down upon his arms again.

"Never mind, Dad," he found himself saying bravely, over the terrible lump that had come in his throat. "You've got me. I can carry on."

The father's answer was another groan, and then he lifted his head, and the boy saw tears in his father's eyes.

"You don't understand yet, Chris. It means I can't send you, my only son, back to college! It means I can't buy you the car I promised or do the other things for you and your sister I've always meant to do. And how are you going to carry on without a college diploma in these days? I can't do a thing for you. I! To have failed!"

"There, Dad! Don't feel that way!" said the boy, patting his father's arm awkwardly. "What's the difference? I don't mind. I shouldn't have had a car yet anyway. I—it—"

Suddenly he knew he mustn't tell his father what had happened to him and the car as he was coming in. If he was going to be a man and help his father now, that was one thing he'd have to take care of himself without his father's help. Whatever he was liable for that had been damaged he'd pay himself. Perhaps it would be covered by insurance—he didn't know. But he closed his lips tight and resolved to tell nothing about it. His father had enough to bear.

"Look here, Dad!" he began again. "Can't you get out of this place and go home? Does Mother know anything about what's happened?"

"I trust not," said the man hoarsely, his whole frame shaken by a convulsive sob. "Not yet."

"Well, there, what's the use in taking it so hard? There'll be some way out. Doesn't Mother own our house? Can't you keep that?"

The gray head was shaken solemnly.

"She owns it," he said wearily. "I put it in her name long ago. But only for her need in case of my death. We talked it all over then, about men who did that to protect themselves when they knew they were about to fail. Mother said then, and I know she'll stick by it now, that she wouldn't think of keeping a house when others felt we were in debt to them. It wouldn't be honorable, son. We've got to do the straight thing even though we're penniless."

Chris was silent a moment, taking it all in. Then he answered bravely, "Sure thing, Dad. Of course we have!"

Somehow the father felt a little thrill of comfort from the way the boy said that "we," including himself in the sacrifice. The father put out his hand and grasped his boy's hand.

"Thank you for that, son. You're going to stand by, and that'll help a lot. I feel I'm awfully to blame not to have discovered sooner what was going on, but we'll work it out, somehow, together! You've helped me a lot already, boy!

Now I'm going out there and speak to the crowd."

"Oh, no, Dad!" cried Chris in quick alarm. "Listen! You mustn't. I've been out there. I know what it's like. The people are seeing red just now. It wouldn't be safe. Wait till tomorrow, Dad. Wait till you've made some statement in the papers. Wait till the people have cooled off a little."

"No, son! I'm going now. I've got to face the thing, or I couldn't live with myself overnight. People out there are in distress. Widows and orphans, who trusted me with their all. They've been telephoning all day till I'm nearly crazy. Mrs. Manders, the widow of my old friend. Mrs. Beyers, that poor little old paralytic, and those two Johnson sisters sewing their fingers to the bone making clothes for people and putting it all in here for a rainy day. Oh! It's a burden too great to be borne! But I must tell them I'll do my best."

"Oh, but not yet, Dad! Not today!"

"Yes, today! Now! I couldn't go home and face my wife with it undone. She'd expect it of me. She'd want it. Don't worry, son. I've sent for a band of police to stand about in the crowd in case there are some lawless ones. They're always around when there's any excitement."

"You don't understand, Dad. You mustn't go out now. It would be suicidal."

"Yes, I understand. And I must go. You stay here, lad!"

"No, Dad, if you're going out I belong with you!" protested Chris.

"Listen, son—there's no danger. But if there is, I'd rather you were safe in here, to take care of Mother."

"No, Dad, she'd want me to stand by you!" declared Chris, linking an arm in his father's.

So they stood when Mr. Chalmers, a director, tapped at the door and entered.

"They've come, Mr. Walton," he said respectfully, almost deprecatingly, "but I wish you'd change your mind! The chief says he'll do his best, but he wishes you wouldn't go today."

"Thank you," said the bank president, lifting his distinguished-looking head in a way that meant he couldn't be persuaded. "I'm ready." Then he looked down at Chris whose young head was thrown back with that same look of determination and, smiling gravely, added, "We're ready."

Mr. Chalmers opened his lips with a glance at Chris to protest, and another director, Mr. Tryon, in the doorway said, half under his breath, "Oh, do you think that's wise?" Then they closed their lips and stood back with respect in their eyes for the father and son. In each one's eye was that which made it necessary for them to go and to stand together.

The wild-eyed crowd, milling together, battled for first place next to the great bronze grating of the doors. Turning feverish glances toward the entrance, calling out threats now and then, almost crushing the few frightened, determined women who had joined the mob, they were suddenly amazed by the unexpected opening of the doors.

Those immediately in front were pushed into the marble entranceway, falling at the feet of the advancing two, the father and the son.

Two cashiers had opened the doors, swinging them back noiselessly behind the noisy, unnoticing crowd, who had stood there for five hours beating on that door and screaming out threats. They were now so busy with their own madness that they didn't see the opening doors.

An instant the crowd blinked and wavered, as the four bullies who had occupied first place in the doorway rolled backward on the floor. Then four others were quick to mount over them and clamber on, wild for their rights and their money.

But two officers with clubs beat back the throng and brought them to their senses, and the crowd drew closer and cried out for a hearing and their money. The women were pleading now with clasped hands and tears rolling down their cheeks. It was a wild scene, and Chris's heart stood still with the horror and sadness of it as he stood in the doorway until the fallen men could be removed from their way. For the first time in his few short years, he sensed a little of the sorrow and helplessness of a great part of the world. He'd never thought before of his fellowmen who weren't as fortunate as he. Now he began to see and understand, and his heart swelled painfully with the greatness of misery and the thought that indirectly, perhaps, his beloved father and therefore he, too, had caused it. For the first time he realized why that stone was flung through his beautiful new windshield a few short minutes before and why someone cried what he hadn't recalled until now: "There he is, the son of the president, riding around in a five-thousand-dollar car!" He could see how they felt, and he was filled with a new kind of shame.

Then out they stepped, the president of the bank with his only son, and a wild cry burst from the mob. One moment they stood there side by side. Then the bank president raised his hand, and the mob hushed for one breathless moment. And while the silence hung in space, before it broke into chaos, Christopher Walton senior spoke.

"Friends," he said, and his voice was steady and clear so that it was heard to the outer edge of the crowd.

Then from across the street came a missile, swift and hard and sure, aimed straight for the brave man's face. Chris saw what was coming and drew his father aside just a hair's breadth. The ball of slime and mud hit the grill of the door before which he stood and glanced off, only spattering his face. But even then he didn't waver. He merely took out his white handkerchief and wiped away the mud from his cheek and eyes and then lifted his hand again for silence.

The sheer bravery of the act silenced the crowd again, and while it lasted he spoke.

"Friends, I'm here to tell you you'll get back every penny of your savings just as soon as possible. I personally pledge to give up all I have, my home and personal property, and I know the directors will do the same. This thing has come about through a circumstance just as surprising and heartbreaking to us as to you, and to the last cent we have we'll make good. We ask you to go quietly to your homes, and within a few days, as soon as it's physically possible to find out the extent of our trouble and our resources, we shall communicate with every one of our depositors and let them know how soon they may expect their first installment of what is coming to them. We ask your cooperation, and it's to our mutual benefit to work together."

He paused an instant and glanced down at his son standing so straight and tall beside him, almost reaching his father's height. Then he added, with the first smile that had lightened his sorrowful features all day: "My son is here beside me to say that if anything happens to his father before this promise is made good, he stands ready to see that it's fulfilled. Isn't that so, Chris?"

"It sure is, Dad," answered the son with a clear ring in his voice.

Then the crowd, always ready to be swayed either way, broke into a cheer, and some of the women wept.

Only on the outer edge of the crowd, where the policemen were quietly hand-cuffing a dark-browed youth with slime on his hands, was there a low, menacing undertone, like a growl of distant thunder.

Then a hand drew the father and son within the sheltering doors again, and most of the crowd turned and drifted hesitantly away.

Sometime later a closed car drove up around the corner of the alley behind the bank and took the Waltons and two of the bank directors to their homes. And the region about the bank and the streets where they had to pass was well patrolled.

Mrs. Walton was highly excited when they finally arrived home.

"Where have you both been?" she cried. "I've been so worried. I thought I'd go crazy."

"Oh," said the elder Walton sympathetically, "that was because so many people were calling up constantly. I'm so sorry. I never dreamed you'd be worried yet, and I didn't want to tell you until it was necessary, not until I could come home and explain it myself. My dear, we've been through terrible times this morning."

He passed a frail hand over his furrowed forehead and looked at her with weary eyes. Chris, watching him, seemed to see him suddenly grow old before his eyes. He saw his mother put her hand hastily over her heart in quick pre-monition, and while his father explained about the run on the bank, it all swept over him what it would mean to his mother to lose her home and be poor. That was tough on Mother! His pretty little mother! It suddenly came to him that he must somehow stand between her and this great calamity.

Then amazingly he saw her face relax, her fears drop away, her face grow calm, and almost a smile come out on her lips.

"Oh, is that all?" she said with great relief. "I thought you must have had some awful sickness or a stroke, or you would have to have a terrible operation."

Suddenly Chris began to laugh.

"Oh, Mother," he cried, "excuse me, but—why!—you're only afraid of things you imagine and get up out of nothing! When it comes to real things, Muz, you've got the nerve. I'll say you're a real little hero!"

"But, Mary," said the father anxiously, "you don't understand. It means we'll have to give up our house and all the beautiful things you've gathered through the years—rugs, jewels, pictures—"

"Of course!" said the mother nonchalantly. "Why speak about such trifles? We've been poor before. Besides, don't you remember what the minister said on Sunday—that we must thank God for the hard things that come into our lives as well as for the nice things? There's probably some wise reason in all this, and maybe we'll see it soon. Come on now—let's go to dinner. It's waited long enough. And it's a good dinner, beefsteak and mushrooms. If we won't be able to afford such things anymore we can at least enjoy this one—unless, Christopher, you think we should give this dinner to some creditor?" she asked with a twinkle.

Christopher senior took his wife in a tender embrace and smiled, his whole anxious face relaxing.

And Chris junior murmured as he turned away to brush aside a strange blurring that came into his eyes: "Say, Mother, you're something! Who'd ever think you'd take it like that?"

"But I'm getting old, Mary," said the banker. "It's not as if I could begin all over again."

"So am I," said Mother cheerfully. "But Chris is young, and an old head and a young head together are more than twice as good as just a young head making young mistakes. Come, hurry and carve that steak!"

And surprisingly they sat down at that belated dinner laughing.

If the prowler in the shrubbery outside the dining room window heard that laughter, it perhaps only added fuel to the fire in his angry heart that wanted his money, wanted it tonight, and meant to get it somehow soon.

Not until Chris got up to his own room a couple of hours later, for they'd lingered talking it out and clinging together for reassurance, did he suddenly realize what this change of circumstances would mean to him. On the bed lay a pennant in flaming colors bearing the name of his college. He'd bought it today to give to Gilda to put on her wall, and now he wasn't going back to college!

He was filled with fear over this fact as he finally put out his light and opened his window, and he failed to see the figure with the menacing white face lurking in the hedge beyond the rhododendrons. He got into his bed and began to look his misfortunes in the face, and not till those still deep dark hours toward morning did he fall into a light sleep.

And then, suddenly, a shot rang out, almost in the room, and he sprang out of bed in alarm!

Chapter 3

When Natalie Halsey entered the house after watching Chris drive off, she tiptoed down the dark hall and cautiously opened the door into the kitchen to lay down her packages on the kitchen table. Then she peered through the half-open door into the front room which was temporarily converted into a bedroom during her mother's sickness. The house boasted of only four rooms, two upstairs and two down, with a little lean-to shed for a laundry.

"Yes?" said a quick, alert voice from the shadows of the sickroom, and Natalie threw the door open wide and gave a cheery laugh.

"I can't move without your hearing me, can I, Mother!" she said, coming in and pushing up the shades at the window to let the day's brightness in. "I hoped you'd have a good long sleep while I was gone. You scarcely slept a wink all night, and you simply have to make it up, or you'll have a relapse. Didn't you get a nap this morning?"

"Oh, yes," said the invalid, "I think I did, but I kept one ear open for your coming." She gave a funny, brave laugh as if it weren't important. "I'm really not tired. I'm quite rested. And I've decided to get up today and go to work. I've got to finish that hemstitching for Mrs. Baker."

"Now, Mother, look here! You've got to behave!" said Natalie firmly. "You're not getting up until the doctor says so, and not even then unless you're good. As for that old hemstitching, I may as well tell you Janice finished it weeks ago and took it to Mrs. Baker, and she was wonderfully pleased with it and paid for it right away. So you needn't think or work yet a while."

The mother gave her a startled look.

"The dear child!" she said tenderly. "Was that what she was doing so quietly when I was supposed to be asleep? And I thought she was studying."

"Oh, she studied, too," said Natalie.

"But—" The mother's eyes had a worried look. "The money must be all gone. I can't see how you've kept things up—and gotten me luxuries, too. I know you two have just starved yourselves."

"Do we look starved?" chirped Natalie. "Mother, quit worrying, and I'll tell you some good news. I've got a job! Not just a snatch of work, but a real job with a regular salary and hours. I start Monday morning at eight o'clock sharp! Now will you be good?"

"Oh, Natalie! Child! Where is it?"

"Well, maybe you won't like it so well, but it's really good pay, easy hours, quite respectable and nice. Just think how wonderful it will be not to worry from one six months to another. And then not know whether the dividend we should get from our one-and-only is really coming or not."

"Tell me, dear! What is it?"

"Well, it's cashier in the chain store. Now, Mother, don't look that way. It's a lovely store, clean and light and airy, and the nicest manager. He treats me like a queen. He's having my little glass den painted up new for me and getting me a comfortable stool. He's married and kind, and he says his wife told him it made all the difference in the world what kind of stool the cashier had, whether she got tired and cross or not."

Mrs. Halsey made a sound like a moan.

"Oh, Natalie, my baby! To think of your working in a store with a lot of rough men! Oh, how badly your father would feel if he knew we'd come to that! He was so particular about his dear girls."

"Nonsense, Mother!" said Natalie a bit sharply because of the sudden lump that came in her throat and threatened tears. "Father would be glad I had the chance of such a nice place. They're not rough men anyway. They're just nice pleasant boys who work so hard they haven't time to look at anybody. It's mostly ladies I'll have to do with. People who come shopping. I'll be sort of shut away in a little glass room, and people come to the window with their checks and money. I think it'll be fun, Mother. You know I always could make change accurately, and anyway there's a machine to do it. It will be nothing but fun."

"You're a brave girl," said her mother, wiping away a few tears with a feeble hand.

"There, now, Mother dear, stop those tears this minute. This is nothing to be sad about. Be glad. Why, Mother, I thought you taught me God takes care of us and nothing He doesn't allow can come to His people. Don't you think He can take care of me as well in a chain store as in a fine parlor?"

"Oh, yes," sighed the sick woman. "Of course, but—"

"But it's not the way you'd like it? Is that it, Mother? Well, say! Don't you think He loves me as much as you do? Come, Mother. Cheer up. We're on the road to wealth. Can't you rejoice with me?"

"Oh, yes," said the mother, fetching a little smile. "You're a good girl."

"No, I'm not particularly good. Don't make the mistake of overestimating my worth," said Natalie. "I'm normal as a human girl. I envied Gilda Carson this morning. She was out with a lovely hound on a chain. But I wouldn't keep mine on a chain if I had him. I'd teach him to run alongside and never stray or bark at other dogs. Say, Mother, you don't know how I came home now, do you? Did you hear me arrive? I came home in a wonderful new car, with a perfectly good handsome young man. I wish you'd been at the window to see how fine I was. He asked me to take a ride, too. But I knew I had to get the soup on for dinner so I declined."

"A young man?" said the mother fearfully. "Oh, Natalie, who?"

"Oh, you needn't sigh like that, Mother. He was perfectly all right. He has the name of being as good as he is good-looking. It wasn't a tramp or a drummer or anybody wild from down at the Flats. It was the son of our bank president, if you please. Christopher Walton, with a fine new car his father has given him to take back to college."

"Natalie! How did he happen to ask you?"

"Oh, he rode alongside the sidewalk and asked me if he could give me a lift. I had some groceries, and I suppose I may have looked overburdened," said Natalie, taking half the joy out of her unexpected ride by this facing of facts. "He's always been noted for his kindness."

"That was—nice of him," said the mother thoughtfully. "That's the kind of young man you might naturally have had for a friend if everything had gone well with us and your father had lived. Of course he wouldn't think so now, though. He wouldn't know from present appearances that your father was as good as his."

"Oh, Mother, don't talk that way!" said Natalie with sudden impatience. "We all had Adam for a remote grandfather anyway. What's the difference about family?"

"Because—dear child, you don't understand. Class means a lot to most people. It probably does to him. Most young men in his station in life would only look on one in yours as someone to condescend to."

Natalie was silent for a moment.

"Well, suppose he did?" she said with a matter-of-fact tone. "I had a nice ride, and he talked to me as if I was any nice girl. He used to be in my class in high school, you know. It wasn't anything so notable, just a few blocks in a pretty car, but it was fun, and I'm glad I had it."

"Yes, of course," the mother hastened with belated pleasure to state, "so am I. How I wish you had a car of your own."

"Oh, now, Mother, what would we do with a car of our own here in this street? Where would we keep it? On the front porch or out in the old forsaken chicken coop?"

At last Natalie got her mother to laugh a little. Then she suddenly sobered.

"Dear child!" she said with a quiver in her voice. "Something else about this makes me troubled. I wouldn't want you to get interested in a handsome young man who might offer you a ride now and then, mean nothing by it, and then break your heart."

Natalie sat down in the rocking chair and broke out laughing, perhaps to help her hold back the tears which were very near the surface this morning. For in spite of her brave words and cheery manner, things were looking pretty serious for her. She didn't mean to tell her mother only thirty-seven cents of the hemstitching money remained after she'd purchased the necessities she'd just brought home and that they'd had to ask the landlord to let the rent run until her first week's pay before he might expect an installment on it. Poor child! She'd been up and down several times in the night trying to soothe her mother to sleep, rubbing her back with steady, patient hands, bathing her aching forehead with witch hazel, and getting her a glass of milk. The strain was beginning to tell on her. To tell the truth, it had been a bit hard to contrast her life with that of some of her class members she'd glimpsed on the street that morning, and her brave spirit had faltered several times.

So now she laughed to hide her tears and put on a comical manner.

"Oh, Mother dear! What a silly 'fraidy-cat you are! Do you take me for an absolute fool? Don't you know I have no intention of falling for any boy, no matter how fine or how plain he may be? I'm going to hold Mother's hand and stay at home and make life happy for you. Perhaps Janice will marry, and when I get old I'll make bibs and dress dolls for her children. But I'm cut out for a grand old maid. I'm not going to break my heart for anybody. Now! Will you be good? It's time for your beef tea, and if you find any more causes to worry I'll send for the doctor! So there!"

So with coaxing and play she cheered her mother to a real smile, fed her beef tea, and chattered on about how she was going to make over her old green serge for a school dress for Janice, till the day settled into a peaceable groove of homely duties.

Then Janice breezed in announcing she had an order for a dozen handkerchiefs and three pairs of pillowcases to hemstitch, and the sun shone in the parlor bedroom.

Later when the mother was taking an afternoon nap and the sisters were doing up the brief kitchen work and having a cheery confabulation together about how they were going to make both ends meet, Natalie confided to her sister the story of her ride and her mother's fears.

"Mums is afraid I'm going to lose my heart at once, of course," she laughed.

"Well," said Janice thoughtfully, "I shouldn't think it would be a hard thing to do, Natty. I think he's wonderful. Not a single one of your high school class is as good-looking or as polite and considerate. And he's smart, too."

"Oh, sure!" agreed Natalie out of a heart that had held those same opinions through four lonely high school years and three hardworking empty ones since. "That goes without saying. Why look lower than the best? That's why I'm getting ready to be a cheerful spinster. I couldn't possibly aim for the highest, so why aim at all? Oh, Jan! For pity's sake, let's talk about something practical. Do you realize I've got a job and if we can get through till next Saturday I'll have a pay envelope? But how to get through till then is the problem. Suppose you take stock. Can we do it? We still have thirty-seven cents in the treasury, but Mother's wee dividend doesn't come in for another six weeks yet. How about it? Could we live on beans for a day or two and leave the thirty-seven cents for Mother's extras? We can charge beef for beef tea for a week if it comes to a pinch."

"Sure we can," said Janice gallantly. "I've got two pounds of rice, a box of gelatin, half a pound of sugar, and some junket tablets hidden away in case of emergency, and there's still a quarter in my once-fat pocketbook. We'll manage. With all this you brought in today we'll live like kings. That meat will make a wonderful soup, and we'll eat the meat, too, and then sandwiches and hash! Oh, sure! And you got a stalk of celery. You extravagant thing! That'll just put pep into any meal."

"He threw that in," said Natalie, laughing.

"Oh, he did!" said Janice, looking at her sister sharply. "Well, I guess Mother'll have something else to worry about. Which will it be, Natty, a bank president or a grocery man, that I'll have for my best brother-in-law?"

"Oh, stop your nonsense!" said Natalie good-naturedly. "Come on and let's clean this cupboard shelf and find out to a grain how much we have left. I imagine by next week Mother can be up a little while each day, and perhaps the next week you could go back to school. Then we'll have to work out a regular schedule of housework, so you won't have too much on your hands while I'm in the store."

So they scrubbed the cupboard shelves and set out their meager food supply, apportioning the items for each day and jubilant they could get through to the first payday.

"A shredded wheat biscuit apiece, six days," counted Natalie, "not counting tomorrow. We have enough oatmeal for tomorrow morning."

"His sister is very nice, too," mused Janice, measuring out the rice and carefully putting it in a clean glass jar.

"What?" said Natalie, turning toward her sister. "Whose sister?"

"Chris Walton's sister," said Janice, her eyes on a tiny bag of raisins. "If an egg and a little milk could be spared, we could have rice pudding for Mother's birthday. She could eat that surely. You know Friday is her birthday. We really should have some chicken broth. How about my going out and raiding our neighbor's hen coop?"

"Is she indeed?" said Natalie. "What's her name? How do you know she's nice?"

"Who? The hen I'm going to raid? Now how could I possibly tell what her name is till I've met her?" said Janice in an aggrieved tone.

"I was speaking of the bank president's daughter," said Natalie in a dignified tone. "But if you wish to be trivial it doesn't matter. What's a stolen hen among friends?"

"Why," said Janice, giggling, "she's in my class in school, and her name's Elise. I think she's nice because she never has any runs in her stockings and she doesn't use a lot of makeup. We don't have much to do with each other, of course—how could we? She has her own friends. But she smiled at me the other day when we passed in class. I like her. I think you can usually tell, don't you? Even if you don't know people very well. She never makes me feel the runs in my stockings the way Gilda Carson does or how much too short my old blue dress is getting, and—anyhow, I like her."

"Well, that's nice," said Natalie irrelevantly. "So do I, if she smiled at you." She suddenly bestowed a resounding smack on her sister's cheek.

"How about stewing these eight prunes?" said Janice, rubbing off her sister's kiss and grinning. "Maybe Mother would like a taste, and they've been here a long time. Not that I like them," she finished with a grimace. "When you get to be a bank presidentess or a lady grocer, whichever it is, please let's not have prunes. I'm ashamed to look a prune in the face—I've hated so many of them."

"No, my dear, we'll never have another prune when I attain either of those great estates. We'll have grapefruit served in cracked ice or honeydew melon with lemon juice or black grapes from South Africa—on one provision, however, and that is that you cut out that nonsense and never speak of it again. Even in fun I don't like it, Jan," she added seriously. "If I ever meet Chris Walton again I'd be ashamed to think we'd ever talked such nonsense. Promise me, dear, you won't!"

"You dear funny serious darling!" said the younger sister in a burst of admiration. "Of course not, if you don't want me to. I was only kidding anyway. But seriously, Nat, I do wish you had some nice friends like that and some good times like other girls."

"I have all the good times I want," said Natalie, shutting her lips firmly. "Haven't I the chance to go to Bible school? You don't know how glad I am of that. I've wanted it ever since that first time I went. I'm so glad it doesn't cost anything. I love every minute. You're sure you don't mind giving up Monday evenings?"

"Why should I mind, dearest dear? Where would I go? To the opera or to Gilda Carson's dance at the country club, or did you suppose a host of boyfriends might be waiting outside the door to bear me to the movies or some other entertainment? No, rest your conscience, serious sister—I'll only be falling asleep over my hemstitching or stealing an hour at a magazine story."

"Oh, Jan, I wish you had some good times! I mean for you to, when I get on a little further."

"Oh, certainly, we'll all have good times," chanted Janice, waving the dish towel. "Now, if you don't mind, I'll retire to my hemstitching and earn a few honest pennies for a rainy day without prunes."

Softly laughing, the two girls scurried upstairs to get their sewing, walking quietly lest they awaken their mother. They had good times together, these two girls so almost isolated from their own kind. They were perhaps closer to one another than most sisters because hard work and poverty had separated them from the girls who would have been their natural mates if their father's fortune hadn't been swept away when they were very young, and sickness and death hadn't changed their environment. They chatted quietly as they worked, talking over all the people they'd met and the details that made up their days. Natalie asked questions about Janice's school friends, recalling incidents of their older brothers and sisters, and Janice inquired about the chain store and her sister's new position.

At last Janice folded away her hemstitching. "It's getting too dark for you to work on that green serge any longer, Natalie, and I can't see to pull the threads. We can't afford to get glasses so we better stop. What's for supper? I'm hungry."

"Toast and tea and a cup of junket for Mother," said Natalie, folding the skirt widths she'd just pieced cleverly so it wouldn't show. "There's enough codfish left for you and me," she added firmly, "creamed codfish on toast with a dish of dried apple sauce apiece and warmed-over cocoa. We simply have to hoard every crumb till next Saturday. Can you stand it, Jan?" she looked at her sister anxiously.

"Sure thing," said Janice bravely, almost blithely. "Aren't I husky enough to survive a week of codfish and applesauce? I might even give up the applesauce if you'd ask me, especially the dried part. I'm not partial to dried apples. But they're not nearly as scratchy to the tongue as dried peaches. I detest them."

"We're eating the codfish tonight so we can have a meatball apiece tomorrow."

"Noble sacrifice!" giggled Janice. " 'On to the codfish! Let joy be unconfined! No sleep till morn while youth and beauty meet—' Is that how it goes?"

"Stop your nonsense!" said Natalie smiling. "You'll wake Mother."

"Mother's awake. I heard her stirring as I came by the door. I'm going to light her lamp now. Is her toast ready?"

So they gathered about the mother with a tempting tray, tempting as to the delicacy of its preparation if not filled with rare food, and the three of them settled down, a brave trio, trusting God and cheering one another in the tender ways at their command.

Chapter 4

The sound of a falling body downstairs brought Chris swiftly to his senses. He sprang into action, but his mother was there before him. He found her kneeling at the foot of the stairs, stooping over his father who lay huddled there with blood on the floor beside him and on the breast of his bathrobe.

"Call Doctor Mercer!" she said in a low, strained voice.

Chris hurried to the telephone, his heart beating wildly. What had happened? Was his father shot through the heart? Oh, dear, what had happened? He thought he'd always see his mother in her delicate blue robe kneeling beside his stricken father, her soft gray curls falling over her slender shoulders and that courageous look in her eyes. How pretty his mother must have been when she was a girl! That was a strange thought to come at such an awful time; yet it flung itself at him as he took down the receiver.

He was back in the hall in an instant. "He's on the way. Can't I lift him up?"

"No, we'll wait till the doctor comes. Get a glass of water!"

He sprang for the water, noting as he passed the dining room window that it was pushed halfway up from the bottom.

"What was Dad doing down here?" he whispered as he brought the water.

"He heard a noise and came down to investigate," murmured the mother. "I tried to make him wait and telephone for the police, but he wouldn't."

Then there was a sound at the door. The doctor had arrived, with a policeman just behind him wanting to know what had happened. The next half hour was a confusion of horror to Chris. Policemen coming and going silently, murmured directions, fingerprints on the windowsill, footprints outside the window; a quick, low gasp of pain from the stricken man as he regained consciousness under the doctor's ministrations; anxious waiting during the search for the bullet which had entered somewhere around the lungs; bandages; subtle pungent odors filling the house; the swift arrival of a trained nurse from the hospital; a bed brought downstairs; and his father moved to it. It seemed like one awful nightmare that couldn't be true. His father! And yesterday everything was so wonderful and he was so thankful nothing dreadful was in his life!

Strange how that unnatural sermon from Sunday should come back to him now—that one sentence, rather, from the sermon, that he'd heard above his joyful thoughts—that suggestion that people should be thankful for the hard things that came to them. Bosh! How could they? What good could come from an experience like this one? How could one believe terrible experiences were sent in love to anyone?

Things settled down into quiet at last. That fearful probing for the bullet was over. It was found in a serious spot close to the lung. His father lay sleeping under opiates with the white-capped nurse in charge and silence reigning. The mother was going about with white face and bright, brave eyes, preparing in the kitchen something the doctor had ordered.

"It's a very serious situation," the doctor told Chris, "but if all goes well he has an even chance of pulling through. You'll have to be a man and take the burden from your mother, son."

Chris straightened his young shoulders and nodded gravely. He felt as if the burdens of the universe had suddenly settled upon him. He felt as if the ground under him was sinking and everything he'd ever known and trusted was toppling about him. But he bowed the doctor out, taking his directions, helped the nurse arrange a curtain to keep the light from her patient's eyes, helped his mother in the kitchen, and then persuaded her to lie down and save her strength for later when she might be needed. At last he was free to go to his own room and change his bathrobe and slippers for more suitable clothing.

He stood in the middle of his room and looked about him dazed. Looked at his watch and stared about again. Was it only three short hours since he heard that shot? Why, ordinarily at this hour he'd still be sleeping. It was only six o'clock in the morning; yet that house had seemingly passed through a whole day's work!

Was it only yesterday morning he was so happy getting his things in shape for packing? There on his desk lay a pile of letters he'd sorted out to burn. And there were the piles of new undergarments his mother had marked yesterday and laid on the window seat for him to put in his trunk. College! He couldn't go now. And that car? Where was it? He should hunt up the police and find out what they did with it. He hadn't thought of it since.

Softly he tiptoed down to the telephone booth in the back hall and finally got in touch with the police station. They assured him the car was safe, what was left of it, and his heart sank. His next duty would be to communicate with the owner. Would he be liable for the damage, or would the insurance cover it? He knew very little about insurance rules. A five-thousand-dollar car—its beautiful glitter defaced! Another five thousand dollars to add to the hundreds of thousands, perhaps, that his father owed. Well, he'd look after that anyway. Somehow he would find a job. He must! He must be a man now and take cares upon himself. Maybe his father would never recover. Even if he lived he might always be an invalid. He had to face that possibility.

Yesterday he was facing another happy year of college life, football, basketball, baseball, fraternities, honors, all that college life meant. Today he might as well be an old man and be done with it. He had debts and a family dependent on him. He dropped his head down on the telephone stand and sighed. If he hadn't been ashamed he would have cried. He could feel the tears in his eyes and throat. He swallowed hard and fought them back. He was a man. He had to be! And Dad, his wonderful dad, was lying in there in the living room between life and death. Dad might not get well. What did it matter whether he went to college or not? If Dad ever got well he wouldn't care whether he owned a sports car or not!

Presently he roused himself to telephone the car agency, ask anxious questions about insurance and disclose the car's whereabouts. He was relieved when they said they would take care of it and let him know later about the insurance. He left the telephone with a sigh, tiptoed to the living room door, and looked in. The nurse came and spoke to him in a noiseless voice, telling him to go to bed and snatch some sleep. Chris dragged himself upstairs and threw himself across his bed. The sun was high, flinging its rays across the room, but he didn't notice it. He was too weary in soul and body and dropped asleep as soon as his head touched the pillow.

Long days and anxious nights followed when the world's affairs were practically forgotten in the more vital question of whether the husband and father would live or die, and Chris felt he was aging a year an hour. College was a thing of the past, and he stuffed away all the pennants and athletic articles in a dark closet and tried to forget there was such a thing as being a boy with a carefree life. Yet there wasn't much actually to do. Hang around the halls; listen for the slightest sound from the sickroom; run errands for the nurse or doctor, sometimes in a wild hurry that the beloved father's life was slipping away no matter what they did. Once he had to go to the train to meet a famous specialist who was coming in consultation. That was a terrible day that seemed ages long.

As Chris recalled the afternoon when he and his father had stepped out of the bank door and stood together before that angry mob, it seemed years past. Yet he was sometimes conscious of a thrill of pride in his father. If Dad had to go out of life, he was glad he had this last brave act to remember. Sometimes when he closed his eyes to try to sleep he could see the noble look on his father's face as he opened his lips to speak and stood there controlled and quiet when the mud was thrown in his face. At such times his blood would boil over the indignity till it seemed he must go out and hunt for the criminal who did it and throttle him. Then he'd get up and pace back and forth in his room like a caged lion until, remembering his father downstairs might hear, he would force himself to lie down again.

Affairs at the bank seemed a distant, vague interest. Every day someone would call up and ask after the president and give some hint of how matters were going. Chris knew a bulletin had been sent to depositors giving them hope of an installment in the near future. He knew his mother had signed over all properties in her name or in a joint account. He knew vaguely that other directors had done the same and there was hope of putting the bank back someday on some kind of working foundation. But he seemed to have drifted so far from it that it didn't interest him. His heart seemed frozen, dead. His universe had turned to stone. He wondered why God could let a catastrophe like this come to his father and mother, such wonderful Christians. And he'd never done anything so bad that he should be treated like this! It almost looked as if his father and mother had put their trust vainly in God.

One day on the street Chris was hurrying along with medicine the nurse had sent him to get, and a man, passing, looked pleasantly at him. The lean, kind face was vaguely familiar. Somehow, though, he sensed a former impression of antagonism. He glanced back and suddenly remembered this was the man who had preached that sermon about being thankful for the hard things as well as the good things that came into one's life. Chris stabbed him in the back with a black scowl and passed on.

"Good guy that is! Knows a lot about it! Like to lose all he's got, wouldn't he? Like to have his father dishonored and shot and lying between life and death for weeks. Like to give up his chance of getting anywhere in the world because he couldn't finish his college education. You bet he'd be thankful for all that handed out to him in one day, wouldn't he?"

Chris swung belligerently into his own door and shut it behind him; yet he couldn't shut out the memory of that kind glance. An impression of deep lines of sorrow remained with him, though the man didn't look old.

Gradually as the days passed, the tension in the sickroom subsided. The burden on their hearts wasn't as heavy. The father seemed to be improving a little, and hope sprang up.

Then, one morning, a telephone call came from Walt Gillespie's sister. Walt was coming home for a few hours and wanted to see Chris. Could he take lunch with him? He wanted to consult him about something.

Chris was whistling softly under his breath as he got ready. It was good to have the cloud lifted, even briefly, to feel that things weren't quite as hopeless in the sickroom and that he might go out a few hours without that dread feeling clutching at his heart that death might enter during his absence. It would be good to see Walt again, even though he'd been gone from home a short time. It gave him a warm pleasant feeling that Walt wanted to see him and a thrill to hear how things were going at college. It was a salve for his hurt pride that even though he wasn't coming back to college, they valued his opinion enough to consult him about something.

As he walked down the street, he began to wonder what Walt could want. Probably to discuss some questionable men who were up for consideration by the fraternity. It might be Dick Bradford. If so he was absolutely against him. He was yellow. You couldn't depend on him.

As he approached the Gillespie home he suddenly realized he was on foot instead of driving the handsome new car he'd talked with Walt so much about. It may have been this thought which obsessed him as he went up the steps; or did Walt, as he came down the stairs and met him in the hall, have the slightest shade of kind condescension about him as he greeted him? He must be mistaken. Walt was never that way with him—with anybody. Walt and he had been buddies since they were little kids. No, he was just sensitive.

Yet he felt it again up in Walt's room, when they were reviewing the history of the last few weeks in college, Walt telling about the new boys, the fraternity's prospects, the faculty changes. Especially what was being done in the fraternity. Walt had been made president! A sudden pang shot through Chris. There had been strong hints that he was to be made president this semester.

Then he rose to the occasion and put out a cordial hand for the old-time grasp!

"Congratulations, pard!" he said eagerly, his ready smile beaming forth. "That's great!"

Walt accepted his eagerness a bit languidly as befitted one in a higher position and went on to tell of the men who had been pledged.

With studied casualness Walt announced, "And, oh, yes, we're taking in Dick Bradford. That'll be a help."

Chris froze at once. Dick Bradford! Walt knew what he thought of Dick Bradford. Then Walt hadn't come to consult him about that. It was settled. He felt the condescension in his former comrade's manner now and closed his lips quickly in a firm line.

Then he opened them to say with decision, "You'll be making a great mistake, Walt. He's yellow. I thought I told you what happened last spring—"

But Walt waved him aside. "He's got personality, Chris. No man in the new bunch can match him for that, and we need men with personality, outstanding men, who can represent us anywhere and make a good impression. We feel we've done a good thing in securing him. In fact we almost lost him to the Deltas. They had him all but pledged."

"He's a typical Delta," said Chris with his old haughty manner that used to bring Walt to terms in the old days.

But Walt simply lifted his chin a shade higher and smiled superciliously. "You always did have it in for Dick, but your advice is a bit late. Dick was pledged last night, and we feel he's the right man. He has charm, you know. And now, kid—"

Chris frowned with a sudden quick chill at his heart. This wasn't the old kindly "kid" of his childhood; it was a condescending tone, a term of diminution. It was as if they'd suddenly changed places and the admiring deference Walt had always paid him had suddenly been demanded of him. Did becoming fraternity president for a semester do this to Walt? Would it have done that to him?

But Walt was talking fluently now. "We got together last night, some of us who're in the heart of things, and decided it wasn't fair to your college for a man like you to drop out at the end this way."

He spoke as if Chris had dropped out through sheer wantonness. Chris looked up at him in astonishment.

"We feel it's due the college and our class that you should finish. You had a fine record throughout, both athletics and studies, and neither the class nor the teams can afford to lose you at this stage. We feel you should come back and finish."

Chris lifted his chin and looked at his old comrade coldly. This wasn't even the old tone of sympathy and love he felt he had a right to expect from Walt. He was talking as if he were an officer who had a right to rebuke him.

"In short," went on Walt, putting on an official manner, "we felt something should be done for you. So we've looked around and found several ways of helping out. With an athletic scholarship we can fix things so you'll have practically nothing to pay. Of course you couldn't occupy the suite we'd expected to take together." Walt's eyes were on the floor now, fitting the toe of his well-polished shoe into the pattern of the Oriental rug. "You wouldn't expect that. And, anyhow, Dick has taken over your share in the apartment so that would be impossible even if you could afford it. But there's a vacant room on the fourth floor, and I think you could be fairly comfortable there. Of course it's among the freshies, but that would be part of the concession, I believe, from the college, some duties up there—"

He paused suddenly and looked up, worried by Chris's stony silence as he received his offer.

Chris was sitting there with his haughtiest manner, his head thrown up, his eyes angry, looking at his friend as if he'd suddenly become an alien enemy.

Walt fidgeted uneasily. He knew that look on Chris's face but had never had it turned on him before. He hastened to speak in a different tone.

"Why, what's the matter, old man? You don't understand. I'm offering you a chance to finish your college course. I've come down on purpose. The frat sent me. They're behind me, and they'll be behind you. And the college wants you."

"Sorry!" said Chris stiffly. "It's impossible."

"But look here, Chris," said Walt, getting nervous. He had thought this would be put through so easily. "You don't understand. It won't cost you a cent. It's a free gift! The college feels you're worth it to them! They haven't a man who can come up to you in athletics, and they really need you."

"That's gratifying, I'm sure," said Chris. He assumed his most dignified manner and shut his lips with that finality that made his former playmate remember other occasions and understand this would be a battle.

He settled down to argue. He still had several good reasons why Chris should come back with him today to college.

"Why, I've had this ready to propose for a week, but I wouldn't do it until your father was out of danger," he said in a conciliatory tone that helped a lot toward soothing Chris's wounded pride.

"My father isn't out of danger yet," said Chris. "He's better, but we have to take very good care of him."

"Oh, certainly! Of course!" said the other young man a bit impatiently. "But a nurse can do that! He'd get well twice as quick if he knew you were back in college getting what's coming to you. Why, I've had my sister on the qui vive watching the bulletins from the doctor, and she wired me the minute he said your father was better."

"That wouldn't make any difference," Chris said and suddenly knew he was right. "It will be a long time before my father's well, and I'm needed right here. I have responsibilities. And you're mistaken about Dad. I'm sure now under the circumstances that Dad would expect me to stand by."

But Walt Gillespie didn't give up. He argued it this way and that. It presently appeared that another fraternity member had come down with him, an alumnus, and was to be at lunch, and Chris had it to go over again.

But Chris didn't weaken. As the argument went on, he only grew stronger in the knowledge of what he had to do. A vision came vividly to his mind of that angry mob in front of the bank the day he stood by his father and promised to see that his covenant with the people was made good. It convinced him his place was here at home helping his father make good and cheering and helping his mother.

Later, when he was alone, the tempting things they offered would come back to him and stab him with longing to go. For before they were done with him, the jobs they'd secured for him, the fourth-story dormitory, and the condescension were scrapped; and the beautiful suite with Walt for roommate was even offered free, with the promise to put Dick Bradford elsewhere. He found satisfaction of course in thinking they wanted him so badly. It healed his wounded pride when the dignified alumnus humbled himself to tell Chris he was the only man they knew who could come in now and carry the fraternity through a certain crisis.

But when it was over, Chris could only say it was impossible, that he had other obligations which came first.

Of course, on the way home, after seeing Walt and the alumnus off on the 2:50 train, he thought perhaps he'd been a fool to refuse such an offer. Perhaps his father would blame him for taking things in his own hands this way. Yet the knowledge remained, in the back of his mind, that he should stay and work and help pay back his father's debt if possible—at least help him in his present need.

A deep gloom settled upon him as he turned toward home. He had an opportunity to finish his last college year—which any fool would tell him he needed before he would be worth much in the business world—and yet it was blocked by honor.

But when he entered the house and found his father's condition hadn't been as good that day, he forgot all about college again as anxiety fell on his weary young shoulders.

Chapter 5

One morning the doctor came out of the sickroom with a triumphant look on his face.

"Well, sir," he said to Chris, "your father's going to get well. I didn't tell you before because I wasn't sure he wouldn't have a setback; but he's come through his worst danger now. The lung is clear, and he's on the way to health again. From now on you won't need to keep so still when you walk through the hall, and in a few days he'll be up and around. But don't worry him about business. Not till he's strong. Not a word. I've told him I won't have it."

But the sick man seemed strangely apathetic toward worldly affairs. Somehow in that darkened chamber he had caught a vision of something bigger than earthly things, and he lay back and rested.

One night shortly before Thanksgiving Chris came in from the crisp outside air and went as usual to see his father, who had now been promoted to a chair.

Mr. Walton looked up and smiled. "Sorry, boy, about the college, but—maybe there'll be a way yet."

"Oh, Dad!" cried Chris, summoning a brightness he didn't feel. "Don't worry about college! I'm all right. Just so you get well—that's all we care about."

"You're a fine son!" said the father tenderly. "And, with God's help, I'm going to get well. The doctor promises me that if I do well I can return to the bank by December 15. So you see I'm getting better. And, son, Mother and I have been talking about the house and think the sale should be put through as soon as possible for our creditors' sake."

"The doctor said you mustn't talk about business yet," said the son, a lump rising in his throat.

"I won't, but I didn't want you unprepared if someone comes to look at the house. The doctor said it wouldn't do me any harm. In fact it's a relief to feel I'm doing something to make up to my creditors. You won't mind?"

"Of course not!" said Chris, swallowing hard.

He thought of Walt's visit and his pleas to return to college. He hadn't told his mother. He knew he was needed at home for a long time yet. He felt proud of himself for refusing the offer, though, and for remaining silent about it. And he admitted to himself that he felt some bitterness toward the world and toward God, too, for handing him "such a raw deal," as he phrased it.

But the next day Chris began looking for a job in earnest. Before that he didn't think he should be away from the house for more than a few minutes at a time in case he was needed. He knew unemployment was a problem and that older men than he with families dependent upon them were looking in vain for jobs. But he didn't think he'd have a hard time finding a good-paying job. After all, why wouldn't any of a dozen large firms want to hire him? He didn't expect to be a bank president at first, of course, but he did expect several places to open up to him at a good salary because he was Christopher Walton junior.

He'd considered taking a position as a bond salesman, a bank cashier, an assistant in a real estate office looking toward a partnership, or even something in insurance. They all appealed to him in various ways. Or a management position in one of the large oil corporations might be the thing. Of course he expected six months' training in anything before he would be put in a responsible position with a worthwhile salary.

Chris wasn't conceited; rather he was judging probabilities by his old standards, as the son of the town's leading bank president. He had no idea what it meant to be a bank president whose bank had closed its doors and left hundreds of people destitute. Despite the fact he'd promised to give up everything and stand by his creditors, he was still a failure. And Chris had yet to discover that nobility sometimes begets contempt. Later on he wondered if some people wouldn't have respected his father more if he'd kept his millions and lived on in his big house, with servants and cars galore. He found that some men respected money more than honesty and bowed to those who had it. His young, indignant soul had many experiences to pass through before he found peace.

So Chris started out early the next morning to find his "position," as he called it, expecting to announce his success to his father on his return. First he visited the city's three best-known bond houses, the heads of which were his father's personal friends. The head of the first was in conference and declined to see him that day. The head of the second was hurrying out but informed him coolly they had no openings now. They were thinking of dismissing two men, rather than taking on any. Perhaps in the spring. How was his father? He glanced at his watch, and Chris knew the interview was over.

The third one told him they hadn't enough business to warrant taking on new men, and even if they did Chris should finish college before applying for such a job. He suggested that money could be borrowed for his last college year. When Chris told him he'd been invited to finish college under scholarships but was needed at home, the man shook his head and told him it was foolish to decline that offer; his father would never allow that when he was well again.

The young man was silent as he left, realizing there might be some truth in what the man said. He couldn't tell him how desperate they would be and how he must work to help his father and mother.

All that day he tramped from place to place, marking each one off his list as he left, growing more disheartened and bewildered as he plodded on. His bright prospects were diminishing rapidly.

It didn't help to meet Gilda Carson stepping into Bob Tyson's car. She was home from college for Thanksgiving and gave him a half smile, as if she scarcely knew him. No lighting of the face or calling out to him to be sure and come over that evening. Just a cool bow, and she was off, smiling at Bob as they drove away together.

He frowned and walked half a block beyond his destination, telling himself he didn't care what Gilda did or what Bob Tyson thought. Yet he knew he did.

His pride had been hurt. He'd never thought Gilda was worth bothering about, but he'd enjoyed taking the prettiest girl in school about and having her to himself whenever he chose. And for her to freeze him out this way because his father had lost his money! Well, he would do the same, he told himself.

He thought of the fellows off in college. If they were back home, things would be different. He wouldn't feel so alone. They never high-hatted as girls did. If Walt Gillespie were home he'd show them a thing or two. Walt was his best friend. Of course he'd seemed a bit lofty when he told him about being the frat president and then about Dick Bradford. As a matter of fact, Walt hadn't written since he'd gone back to school. College life kept him busy, of course, and he never was keen on writing letters. But if Walt had stayed home instead, Chris knew he wouldn't have left him without a word. He might have sent him a postcard at least, about a game or the frat or some other news.

He came home that night with his young face almost haggard and gray lines about his eyes and mouth. His mother watched him anxiously across the table but asked no questions. She knew without asking that he'd been out job hunting with no success.

The next morning Chris, his jaw set, started out to look among some less prominent firms. Before night he would find something. He would force himself in somewhere. It was ridiculous to think no one wanted him. He had tried only one day.

About ten o'clock he passed the station and saw Betty Zane stepping down from the train with her suitcase, home for Thanksgiving from her coeducational college.

"Hello, Chris! Can you take me home in your lovely new car?" she called, a mocking tone in her voice.

Betty Zane knew he had no new car now, as she must have known all that had happened since she'd left two months earlier. If no one else had, her kid sister Gwendolen would have informed her. Betty wanted him to admit he had no car. She was like that. She used to pin a butterfly to her desk in school and enjoy watching the poor fluttering wings. Chris remembered Gilda's freezing bow the day before and gave Betty his best imitation of it.

"Nothing doing," he answered abruptly. "I'm out on business. There's the taxi."

Betty stared at him, then turned her back and walked huffily away.

Chris hurried away, even more unhappy because he knew he should be ashamed of himself. And he remembered it was the day before Thanksgiving!

Oh, he was thankful Dad was getting better and Mother wasn't breaking under the strain. But even that had a sting in it, for what prospect had Dad but bitterness and disappointment? How could they ever be happy again? Dad wouldn't keep that cheery look long after he returned to business. It was fine his good name would be cleared and no one would have to suffer for the bank's troubles, but just wait till the excitement subsided. Dad would suffer, and so would Mother, and it was up to him to do something about it. He must get a real, paying job.

At home he found his father and mother rejoicing that the family car they'd had for only four months was sold at a good price. Dad had family prayers as usual, reading a chapter about the Lord's goodness and actually thanking Him that the car was sold so well! He couldn't understand their feeling, for he felt so indignant at the loss of their car that he could hardly bend his knees to kneel with them. *Thank God for that?* Chris thought. *No!*

As they stood up after prayer Mr. Walton added, with a puzzling ring to his voice, "I heard today of a possible customer for the house. If that's true we may soon be on an honest basis."

"Honest?" Chris asked with a questioning look on his face.

"Yes, son, I shrink every day from coming out of a house like this when many depositors—people who trusted me to take care of all they had—have almost no food or shelter."

Chris sensed that his parents were intent on one thing: paying their debts. Possessions meant nothing to them as long as a single creditor had anything against them.

He almost asked, "But where shall we go, Dad, if the house is sold?" and then thought better of it in view of the courage and honor both parents were displaying.

With the house going, too, Chris felt as if he were standing on a tiny speck of land in the midst of a wild ocean, watching the land crumble under his feet. College had gone yesterday, the car today, and perhaps tomorrow the house where he was born. And where were their friends? Would they go, too, until he and his family stood alone in an alien world?

Chapter 6

Not until the week after Thanksgiving did the buyer come to look at the house. Chris had begun to hope he was a myth and no one would come.

He was a large, pompous man who used coarse language and wore a huge diamond on his fat little finger.

He had seven children who swarmed through the house, touching Mrs. Walton's delicate embroideries, staring into her private room, yelling at one another from one story to another, and even attempting to be what Chris called "smart" with him. They discussed the furnishings, laughed at some items as funny and old-fashioned, were curious about the rich tapestries the Waltons had counted among their finer treasures, and asked endless questions.

As Chris progressed from cellar to attic, showing them the rooms at his mother's request, his indignation grew. Why did they have to put up with this treatment from such low, common people? It was bad enough they were buying the house. If they wanted it, let them take it and keep still. If not, let them go! He had no patience with his mother's sweet smiles and gentle manners. He knew it was as hard for her as for him. Yet she kept her strength and sweetness. How could she? These people acted as if the house belonged to them already.

One daughter with too much lipstick said she hoped he'd call on her often. It would be nice for someone to come who knew the house well, and he'd likely be homesick and would enjoy coming back. He looked at her coldly and said nothing. He waded deep into the waters of humiliation that day.

It was rumored the father was a bootlegger and had made a great sum of money he didn't know how to spend. He was delighted with the house and offered to buy the pictures, hangings, furniture, and even the precious works of art the owners had purchased abroad. They wanted the house as soon as the Waltons could move. They didn't question the price and even offered to pay a bonus if they could take possession in two weeks.

Chris, curling his lip in disgust, looked to his father for a quick refusal. But he saw only relief on his face and realized his father wanted more than anything release from debt and help for his depositors. So he kept silent instead of protesting. After all the price was good, and a bonus would help. They were paupers now, he must remember, and couldn't be picky.

Those were bitter days for Chris, tramping the streets all day, sometimes far into the evening and sometimes walking miles into the country to reach a man who had influence.

Then came the question of where they would go. Chris wondered about a pleasant boardinghouse or a hotel apartment. But the next night when he came home and heard his parents' plan, he thought his cup of humiliation had overflowed.

A small rundown house stood on a back street—the same street where the washerwoman lived—with kitchen windows looking out on the railroad. It fell into Mr. Walton's hands through the death of a man without family; he owed him a long-standing debt and had given him a judgment note against the house. Much to Chris's horror, his family planned to move in the next week and vacate their family estate, turning it over to the bootlegger's family.

Elise had been summoned home from her aunt's where she stayed while her father was ill. Elise in her pretty blue dress, with her pale golden curls and blue eyes—she'd never looked so lovely to her brother as when he thought of her living on Sullivan Street next to their washerwoman!

Chris had guarded his words carefully during the weeks his father was recovering, but suddenly one sentence about Elise and his mother living next to the washerwoman slipped out. Chris saw the look of pain in his father's eyes.

"But," said Elise cheerfully, "she won't be our washerwoman anymore, Chris. We can't afford one—we have to do the wash ourselves. It'll be fun!"

Mr. Walton let out a sigh.

"Now don't worry, Daddy!" said Elise. "Mother and I will enjoy it, won't we, Mother? I can learn to cook and keep house. This is only a game, so just smile!"

And her father, in spite of himself, smiled and murmured, "Maybe it'll be for only a little while."

That night Chris bought a paper and spent two hours studying the want ads. As he finally got into bed he remembered the man who had preached that foolish sermon his last time at church. There was no way he could be thankful for what had been handed out to him now. Mother and Elise in a place like Sullivan Street! He had to get a job. Even if it wasn't high up, he still had to get one! He didn't call it a position anymore. He might even be a little thankful if he had a few dollars coming in. No creditor would take his money, he decided—not till he was making enough to put Mother in a comfortable position anyway.

The next morning he started out early and answered three ads, but he found a long line of discouraged-looking applicants waiting at each. A fourth place had named an hour for applicants to arrive, so he used the time between to step around to Sullivan Street and found it even worse than he'd feared.

The house had once been whitewashed, but scarcely enough of the original remained to identify it. Peering through the dirty windows, he counted five rooms and a lean-to kitchen. Four dirty limp cords were fastened from stakes in the hard ground to the top of the front window sash; four brown, dried-up morning glory vines twined about them, waving in the chill November breeze. To Chris those four vines represented his family of four, coming down to Sullivan Street from the glory of their ancestral home. The dead leaves rasped back and forth against a broken windowpane; the scratching sound sent a lump into the boy's throat.

Dashing around the narrow path to the tiny backyard, mostly paved with ashes, he found a tattered clothesline stretched from the corner of the house to the fence and back. He could just imagine his beautiful young sister hanging up the family wash in a chill wind like today's. The tightness in his throat grew.

He hurried to the next place on his list, trying to forget the dismal future, was told they wanted only college graduates, and turned away with more bitterness in his heart.

He should be thankful for this? Not at all! Where was his father's God anyway? He surely couldn't be real. It reminded him of the day he discovered there was no Santa Claus and the sick feeling he had as a child then. What else could happen?

The next few days were Chris's toughest. His mother and father were determined to move to the Sullivan Street house. Even their first glimpse hadn't discouraged them from it.

He watched them walking down the street like common folks, the first time they had been out since the car was sold. Chris followed, dropping his eyes and hoping they wouldn't meet anyone they knew.

"It looks hopeless," Mr. Walton said, with a hint of a sigh. "If I didn't remember what wonders you can work with simple things I might give up. But we can be happy there for a while, can't we, Mary? Perhaps something will change, and we'll get into a better neighborhood soon."

"We can be very happy!" said Mrs. Walton, smiling brightly at her husband. "A little paint will work wonders. We can save on butter and other things and buy the paint, and Chris and I can put it on. I'll do the inside and Chris the outside. I bought a pair of overalls for the chauffeur and never gave them to him. They'll do for Chris, and we have a ladder, don't we?"

Either the picture of him in overalls on a ladder painting that Sullivan Street house or the cheerfulness of his mother's voice brought sudden tears to Chris's eyes. He hadn't felt like crying since he was a little boy.

Mother hadn't been discouraged with the inside of the house, either. She reminded them of the coal range in the cellar at home and how good it was they had never sold it. They were out of date now, and no one would want to buy it. But it would practically heat the house in mild weather and was wonderful to cook with. One could broil a beefsteak over hot coals to such perfection that a gas-broiled steak would blush with shame.

She was sure her mother's red sofa in the attic, though shabby and old-fashioned, would fit in between the side windows that looked out on the alley. A stand, her father's old pine desk, and a few overstuffed chairs would do well, too. Memories had kept them in the attic all these years instead of sending them to the dump. But now she seemed happy they could find some use again.

The next day, after another morning spent hunting in vain for a job, Chris came home for lunch to find his mother had gone down to "the other house," as the maid who was staying till after they were moved put it. As if it could be called a house! He hurried down and found her washing windows, her sleeves rolled up, an old sweater pinned around her and her face as eager as a child's.

The wife of the president of Fidelity Bank washing windows in late November in a cold house!

Chris escorted his mother home at once, so fast she was almost out of breath, and scolded her the entire way, but she only smiled. He returned to the house after lunch and finished the windows, leaving them streaked but dust-free. Then he looked around in dismay at the ugly walls and dirty floors. How could his dear mother bear it?

After that Chris hurried home, gathered up his camera, tennis rackets, and a set of golf clubs and sold them to a secondhand store. Then he found a man who whitewashed houses and hired him to scrub the whole house early in the morning. At least his mother wouldn't have to come into that filthy den with the grime of former tenants about her.

He abandoned his job search until the move was completed. Then Chris and his sister set to work packing, he with a frown darkening his handsome face and Elise giggling at his bungled efforts. His indignation grew, for he saw no joke in the family tragedy. Their whole lives were wrecked. How could Mother and Elise laugh about it? They were just alike.

Then he would glance at his father, smiling from his invalid chair, under doctor's orders not to help, a look of peace on his face. What kept his father so serene? He knew he grieved that his wife and daughter must work so hard and that his son couldn't go to college; yet the lines of care weren't etched as deeply on his forehead now as some weeks before the bank closed its doors. Was he relieved just because he was doing his best toward paying the depositors? No, it must be more than that.

In spite of himself Chris knew his father's faith must make the difference. But he could never believe in a God Who would do such things to trusting people. Chris hardened his heart each time he heard his father pray, for he somehow always began with a word of thanksgiving. The young man couldn't understand it. His sister was only a child, of course. She enjoyed every new thing, even moving into a dinky little house on a backstreet, like a child playing with her dollhouse. His mother was simply glad his father was up and around again. Neither Mother nor Elise had any sense of what this terrible change in the family fortune would mean! But his father understood and still bore up.

With fresh paint and paper on the walls and the few pieces of old furniture scattered about, somehow Chris had to admit the little place took on a certain air. The oak sideboard and table and chairs from the servants' kitchen helped. Even the draperies from the nursery when he was little—bright cretonnes with tiebacks, long since packed in an old chest in the attic and only pulled out for home charades when they needed costumes—seemed to turn the Sullivan Street shanty into a comfortable nest in the midst of a desolated world.

That first night they had supper in the new home.

Elise and her mother, in plain cotton dresses, were in the tiny kitchen fixing supper, and a savory smell was already pervading the house. Anna, the departing maid, had cooked a stew that morning in the old house before the last load of things from the attic came over. She had also fried doughnuts and baked two mince pies between her other duties as a surprise for Mrs. Walton. Chris had carried them over and hidden them early that morning.

Elise was setting the table, humming a cheery tune. Mr. Walton was sitting in the faded Morris chair beside the attic table, reading the evening paper, just as if he were in his library in the leather chair next to the carved desk and alabaster lamp. Chris looked in wonder. Did his father notice the difference or even care?

His sister's voice summoned him from his thoughts.

"It's only a couple of blocks or so up the avenue, Chris," said Elise, noticing the frown gathering on her brother's brow. "I'd go, but Mother needs me. One loaf of bread will do. And dinner will be ready when you come back. It's one of those chain stores, the second block on the right. I bought a cake of soap there yesterday. You can't miss it."

"Why? Will I see the rest of the soap out watching for me?" he asked, slinging his cap on the back of his head. "I thought you made an A in English. Why would the fact that you bought a cake of soap there yesterday keep me from missing the store?"

"Quit your kidding and hurry, please. I'm making popovers, and they need to be eaten as soon as they're done."

Chris, stepping into the brisk night air, felt like an exile in an evil world again. The cheerful atmosphere in the little house, though it half angered him, made the outside world seem more unfriendly. How dark Sullivan Street was. The city should put in more lights. His indignation grew as he hurried along. It seemed now as if he had been angry ever since the bank closed.

He found the chain store bright and busy with people inspecting this vegetable or buying that pound of cheese or box of crackers or sack of potatoes. He watched a woman, list in hand, piling up her groceries on the counter and crossing to the meats. He glanced around curiously. He hadn't been in a grocery store since he was little. The hired help had always ordered the food over the telephone. Not even his mother had mingled with the common people like this. He had to admit that everything looked clean and appetizing. And what was that fragrance? It smelled like oranges. And then he caught a pleasing whiff of freshly brewed coffee.

But no one noticed him, and he was used to deference. Of course, no one knew him in this section of the city, and he felt some relief in that. He watched as the people hovered over the fresh produce, almost as if they were selecting a new car or a Christmas present. What difference did it make which bunch of carrots they bought? Then bright red cranberries in a basket caught his eye, and he wondered at their beauty.

Finally Chris, growing impatient, approached an aproned clerk helping a stout lady accumulate a great quantity of items on the counter. While she was deciding which cereal to choose from the top shelf, he could ask the clerk to get his loaf of bread.

But the clerk looked up, smiled, and shook his head. "I'm sorry, but I'm busy now. You'll need to wait. Someone will be free soon."

Chris stepped back, the color flooding his face. He didn't need to stay here. Surely other stores would sell bread! But then his recent lowly estate flashed before him, and he slunk into the nearest corner. There he was, hemmed in by brooms and bargain cans of peaches, watching sullenly for a free clerk, when he suddenly heard low words whispered behind him.

"That's 'm," said the voice. "He's the ol' man's only son. Some baby! Yeah, right behind you. No, he don' know me. I was in grammar when he was in high. He woul'n't know me from a bag of beans. An' anyhow he al'ays was an awful snob! No, I woul'n't speak t' him. I woul'n't want t' be consider'd high 'n' mighty. I hate snobs!"

Chris could feel the back of his neck getting warm. At that moment the clerk wheeled around to him.

"Now, sir, what can I do for you?"

"A loaf of bread, please," he said in a voice that sounded unnatural to him. He didn't recall ever buying a loaf of bread. He wondered if there was a certain way of asking for it.

He frowned after the two whispering girls who had been behind him. They were at the meat counter now, giggling and chewing gum. The one with red hair and freckles looked vaguely familiar. She might have been the kid who ran through a football game once at school and made everyone furious. Her opinion didn't matter. But had the whole school regarded him as a snob?

He had always considered himself to be his father's respectful son. A snob looked down on other people. Well, perhaps he had, but he didn't think they knew. It was a breach of etiquette to let others know they were despised, and he realized, with a twinge, that he must have failed.

At last, loaf of bread in hand, Chris hastened with his check and money to the cash window, hoping to get out before he encountered the whisperers. And there before him, peering out at him from behind the glass, was a familiar pair of eyes and a shy smile.

Chapter 7

Natalie Halsey! Her friendly face seemed like a pleasant oasis in this otherwise unfriendly environment.

"Hello!" he said, his own face lighting up with relief. "Is this where you hang out? I didn't know it was in this neighborhood."

"Yes, this is where you picked me up in your new car the other day and took me home. I'm so grateful you got me home so soon. Mother had had a bad spell just before I left and was getting nervous about my being gone so long. She might have had a relapse if I'd been much longer."

"Really!" he said, startled yet pleased to be commended for something after hearing those unpleasant whispers.

"You're home from college for the Thanksgiving holiday, aren't you? Or— that would be over now, wouldn't it? It must be a weekend then."

"No such luck!" he said, a dark cloud passing over his face. "I didn't get to college."

"Oh, that's right," said Natalie. "Someone said you were at home, but I wasn't sure. Are you working somewhere? Of course you'll enjoy that, too. It's nice to be doing something real."

He looked at the sweet face before him, noticing weary lines and a shadow under the eyes, and felt a sudden tenderness for her and anger at himself. She was doing something real. She'd found it herself, and he couldn't get anything!

"I wish I were," he said. "I've walked all over this town, and nobody wants me. You don't know of a good job, do you?"

"Oh! Why, yes, I do. But—you wouldn't want this job."

"Try me and see."

Chris thought of the room shut in by cretonne curtains and his beautiful mother in that tiny kitchen getting supper. He must get something!

"But," Natalie said hesitantly, "it's only—it's not along the lines—you're used to."

"My lines are at the bottom of the ladder now," Chris said, his lips set, his chin up, "in case you haven't heard. I'm groveling, if you know what that means. If you have any jobs like that, lead me to 'em!"

Just then a woman slipped between them to change a five-dollar bill, and two others followed with their checks to be paid, and Chris had to step back. He watched as Natalie's slender fingers counted off the soiled bills and then the dimes and nickels, admiring how quickly she did it.

"It's only here in this store," she said after the other customers had walked away. "You wouldn't want to work here, would you, in a place like this?"

"I don't know why not," said Chris, swallowing hard at a surprised lump in his throat. "Is there a chance here, do you think? I must get a job."

"We're losing a man today," said Natalie. "He got a telegram that his father has died, and he must go back to Wisconsin and stay with his mother and get a job there. Our manager's quite disturbed about it. He needs someone right away, but he's very particular. I don't know if he's found anyone yet, and he must by Monday. If you could come back at a quarter to nine—we stay open till nine on Saturday nights—I could speak to him about it. There might be a chance. But it's only a starting position."

More customers walked up then, all talking at once and passing their checks and money through the cash window to Natalie.

"I'll be back," Chris said decidedly.

Outside, the stench of pork and cabbage and fish frying in old grease met him. Pah! What a neighborhood! And he would be a common grocer's clerk and sell cheese and rat traps and pickled pigs' feet to those gossipy women— instead of being his college football team's halfback, the frat president, and a banker's son! He pictured himself in that crowded store weighing sugar and cutting cheese and bringing up great cases of cereal and canned stuff. Girls like the two whisperers would think they could say smart things and tease him. How his mother would hate it! How he would hate it!

At the same time he felt a certain elation that perhaps he had a job in sight. Besides, hadn't he heard one could be promoted in these stores? Of course he wouldn't remain a clerk long. If he'd inherited any of his father's business ability he could get ahead quickly. And if he didn't like the chain store line, he could save up a little money and get into another line. But people had to eat no matter how hard times were. The food business might not be a bad idea, after all.

He decided not to say anything about it at home until he knew more. After all, the job wasn't his yet. Natalie had only promised to speak to the manager. Someone else may have it, or the manager might think him a snob, too. It seemed as if anything could happen in this strange new world.

Chris had almost reached home when he remembered he hadn't thanked Natalie for her kindness. He had never done anything for her, except give her a ride home. Well, he would go back later and check on the job, anyway. He wouldn't want to turn down any job, no matter how unsatisfactory. It was only a grocery, but perhaps he could earn a little and help out at home while looking for something better.

He came whistling through the door of the little house, and even his sister noticed the change from when he had left scowling.

At last they gathered around the table, spread with a coarse tablecloth and the old dishes used in the kitchen at their old home. Somehow it didn't seem as mournful as Chris had expected, and for a long time afterward he remembered his father's blessing.

"Father, we remember that Your Son had nowhere to lay His head sometimes when He was on the earth. Thank You for this comfortable, quiet home You've given us and for this evening meal. Show Your glory through it. Amen."

Chris, quiet and thoughtful during the meal, went to the kitchen for a pitcher of water and more popovers from the oven, to save his mother and sister the trip.

"We have much to be thankful for," he heard his father say from the other room. "Mary, what wonderful children we have. I haven't heard a murmur out of either one of them."

"Why, Daddy, we're having the time of our lives," said Elise.

"Same here!" Chris added, turning his face away as he set the pitcher on the table. He didn't feel quite honest in saying it, but he couldn't bear not to be a good sport when his father and mother were taking it so well.

He helped Elise clear the table and wash the dishes, and at about half-past eight he grabbed his hat and started for the door.

"Oh, I thought we'd all go to bed early," Mrs. Walton said, looking at him anxiously.

"I won't be long, Mother. I'm going to see a man about a job I heard of. I can't get him any other time, and it might turn out to be something."

"Well, come home as soon as you can. This is a strange neighborhood, and we aren't sure yet what kind of people live here. I'll worry—"

"No, you won't worry, Mother," said Chris quickly. "You've been a good sport, and you're not going to worry anymore."

She smiled as she watched him go. He knew she was weary and that despite her brave smiles and cheerful manner she'd had a difficult day. He felt a twinge of pain for thinking so much about his own disappointment.

But as he neared the store he hesitated. How could he go in there and ask for a job a girl had recommended? A poor girl who scarcely knew him either? Shouldn't he go back and get his father to write a letter or contact the head of these stores or do something to place him on a regular footing and give him a worthwhile salary?

Then suddenly he recalled those two girls' words about his being a snob and felt he would rather work his way into favor than try to hang on to old influences. So he lifted his chin and walked through the door.

A few last-minute customers were making their purchases, and Natalie behind her glass window was busy, too, counting change and closing up her cash register for the night. She smiled at him briefly, as he waited by the door. As soon as she was free, he went over and spoke to her in a low voice.

"Wouldn't you prefer I come in Monday morning and talk with the manager myself? I don't want to keep you. And these other people look so tired that I hate to bother them now."

"Oh, no," said Natalie smiling, "he expects you. I told him you were coming. I didn't say much. I thought you'd rather do your own talking. I just said I knew a man who wanted work and had told him to come around. He seemed relieved. He's worried all day about it, but he had no time to go out and look up anybody. The district manager went to New York yesterday, so he can't call on him for an extra man. He's over there opening those crates. Now's as good a time as any to talk to him—only a few customers are left. His name is Foster."

Chris summoned his nerve and walked over to the man in the white linen coat and apron. Why, he didn't look much older than he was!

"Are you Mr. Foster?" he asked, trying to remember he was asking a favor, not granting one, by being willing to work in that store. "I heard you needed a man. Would I do?"

Foster looked at Chris and smiled. "Help me put these cans on the shelves, and let's see how you can work. After that we'll talk."

Chris flung his cap on top of a barrel and started stacking the cans in orderly rows on the shelves, silently loading up his arms from the crates and walking back and forth quickly. Foster scarcely seemed to notice him except for an occasional direction, and they worked away as if they'd always done this. Chris even pushed himself to see how quickly he could put the cans in order and return for another load.

When the crates were empty Foster stopped. "That's all. You seem to have enough pep. Take those empty crates to the cellar, the door over to your right, smash them with the ax you'll see at the foot of the stairs, and pile them with the other wood against the wall. Then we'll talk." ·

When Chris came back upstairs, the customers were gone and the front door closed. Natalie was putting on her hat and coat.

Foster pulled out a pen and notebook and asked his name, age, and experience. Was he a stranger to the town? Was he willing to obey orders?

Chris answered briefly, studying his new employer. He seemed to be an alert young man without conceit. Chris liked him immediately.

"All right," said Foster, "you report Monday morning at eight o'clock. You understand I haven't authority to hire you permanently. But I'll try you out for a week and report to my boss when he gets back next week. If you work out I'll be glad to have you. You did a good job tonight. Good night. See you Monday," he added, grasping Chris's hand in a firm shake.

Chris held the door for Natalie, and they walked down the street together.

"You must've said some nice things about me, for him to hire me so quickly. I appreciate it. If I get the job I'll have you to thank."

"Oh, I only told him you were all right, steady, and dependable. He knew my grandmother and my father and knows I wouldn't say it if it weren't so. I told him we were in the same school and you always had good marks."

"Well, I won't forget it," Chris said with a smile. "Say, let me carry that package. Sorry I haven't a car anymore to take you home."

"Oh, I'm used to carrying things," she said laughing. "It's no problem. We're coworkers now, and a working girl has to carry her own packages."

"Not if a gentleman is about," said Chris, taking the heavy carton from her despite her protests.

"You'll have your own packages to carry soon. Employees get a discount, and sometimes on Saturday nights they let us have perishable items for almost nothing. I save a lot that way carrying things home."

"I suppose you do," said Chris thoughtfully. "I never thought about saving on things like that. I'll have to take lessons from you, though my mother used to tell us stories of how they lived on very little when she was a girl."

"She'll know then. It doesn't take long to learn to save. But really you mustn't go out of your way for me. Please let me take it now. This is my corner."

"It isn't out of my way. You didn't know I lived on the next street to yours, did you?"

"No, I didn't," she said, a look of sympathy on her face. "I knew you had to leave your home, and I'm sorry about that. I always enjoyed looking at it. I saw your beautiful mother coming outside one day. She seemed perfect there. I liked to think of her living in such lovely surroundings. My mother had a nice home, too, when she was young."

Chris's heart warmed toward her because she admired his mother and was sad about his lost home. There seemed somehow a bond between them.

"I guess it's hard for a girl," he said, searching for the right words, "to grow up—not having everything she wants."

"Oh, I don't know," said Natalie, laughing again. "We've had some wonderful times. When Father was alive we enjoyed what we had, much more it seemed than some people who have everything. But it was always nice to hear Mother tell about the hardwood floors and Oriental rugs and lovely things they had in her home when she was a girl. Of course, when we didn't have things we usually made them if we could."

"It's a rotten deal for a girl like you to have to do that!"

She looked at him surprised. "Oh, no! I don't think so."

"You don't?" It was his turn to be surprised.

"Not at all. Nothing God allows to come to His children is a rotten deal. He loves us and knows what we need most. He wouldn't let it come to us if it wasn't for our best."

"You believe He sends such things then?"

"He lets them come. Everything must first pass through His hands."

A sweet trustfulness in her voice filled him with sudden reverence toward her.

"Of course some of the hard things test us, but He permits them, and what He permits must be best for us."

"What good could come out of your being poor and working for your living and carrying packages too heavy for you?"

"Well," said Natalie, smiling, "perhaps it keeps me from being a snob. I would have been an awful snob if I'd had a lovely home and all the nice things some girls have."

"You?" said Chris, and then he laughed. "I overheard two snub-nosed, lip-sticked flappers call me a snob this afternoon in the store. They were in grammar school when we were in high."

"I know who you mean. But they only thought so because you weren't fresh with them the way some of the other boys were. You never were a snob. You were always kind and pleasant to everybody. Look how you picked me up and took me home with all my packages in your beautiful new car."

"But why shouldn't I?"

"That's it," said Natalie. "You're a gentleman. You never were a snob. Now

Bob Tyson wouldn't have done that. He wouldn't even have seen me as he whizzed by."

"Well," said Chris, "it's comforting you didn't think I was a snob. But I'm not so sure I wasn't about to become one, come to think of it. Your example of my courtesy wasn't a fair one, because I saw you were a lady. I'm not so sure I'd have picked up those two girls even if they had a whole truckload to carry. So you think the raw deal that's been handed out to me is to teach me something? You think I should be thankful for it? Losing my home and my college diploma and my car and everything that makes life worthwhile?"

"You haven't lost your home," said Natalie quickly, "or your family. You still have a place to live, and I'm pretty sure it's a real home even if it isn't as big and elegant as the old one was. And maybe there are bigger and better things in life than college diplomas."

Chris looked at her keenly for a moment. "Say, you talk like the man who preached in our church the last Sunday before the crash. He said we should be thankful for everything that's handed out. But I don't know anybody who ever took it to heart."

"Oh, yes, I heard him, too. He runs the mission on Water Street. Did you ever go down there? It's very interesting."

"No," said Chris, "but I think if he had a little of the hardness he's talking about he'd sing a different tune. I can't see singing praise when the earth is reeling under you."

"Oh, he knows," she said, a sudden sadness in her eyes. "He lost his wife and two children to smallpox in China where he's a missionary. He's only back on a year's furlough because of a serious operation he had to have. He's going back in a couple of months to take charge of a leper hospital and doesn't expect to return to this country. He knows what it is to praise God in trials. He calls it 'singing in the rain.' "

"I guess I'd better keep quiet," Chris said, looking down thoughtfully. "I'm not in the same league with a man like that."

"He would say he's an ordinary man with a great God. God can do great things with people who believe Him and let Him."

They had reached Natalie's door by now, and Chris handed her the packages.

"Good night," he said quietly, tipping his cap. "You've given me something to think about. And thank you more than I can say for what you've done for me."

Chapter 8

Natalie's mother looked at her anxiously as she came in, noticing the bright color in her cheeks and the light in her eyes.

"Did someone come home with you, dear?" she asked guardedly.

Natalie turned and smiled at her mother as she set her packages on the kitchen counter.

"Why, yes, Mother," she said. "I don't know how I'd have managed all these if he hadn't. My arm's ached all day where I twisted it last night wrestling with that window with the broken cord. See what I've brought, Mother—celery! Isn't that great? It was frosted on the outside and turned brown, so it doesn't sell well. But the heart of it is as sweet as can be. I tasted some, and it's wonderful. We can make apple salad and meat salad and celery soup, besides eating the best of it plain."

"It wasn't one of the store men, was it, Natalie?" asked her mother, wiping her hands on the roller towel and coming over to look at the celery. "I wouldn't encourage them to get too friendly if I were you. It isn't wise. If you let one of them come home with you another might want to, and you don't know what they're all like. Even if we have to go without, I wouldn't bring so much you can't carry it yourself. Of course, Janice might come sometimes and meet you at closing."

"Oh, Mother!" exclaimed Natalie, kissing her mother. "Don't worry. All the boys in the store are pleasant and nice. That's the only kind they hire there. And they all have their own girls. You don't need to worry about me. They don't want to go with me. They tell me about their girls every chance they get. They tell me where they went the night before and ask my advice about what to get them for Christmas. I'm a regular old maid auntie in the store, so I'm perfectly safe. Nobody thinks of me there as a girl; I'm just the cashier. But this wasn't one of them. At least he isn't yet, though he's going to be Monday. It was Chris Walton."

"Chris Walton! Again!" said the mother with alarm in her voice. "Oh, Natalie, I'm afraid you'll get interested in him! Why does he keep coming around you?"

Janice appeared in the front room doorway then. "What do you mean, Natty— Chris Walton working in the store? Your store? Why there? You'd think his father could get him a different job in some bank or lawyer's office or something, wouldn't you? Mother, did you hear what Natalie said? Chris Walton is going to work in the chain store."

"Is that what you said, Natalie? How strange!"

"Isn't it?" agreed the daughter. "I couldn't believe he would. He's always seemed so exclusive and remote. But he came into the store this afternoon to buy bread, and—"

"Has he been coming there to meet you?" interrupted the mother, quick to spot any possible danger to her daughter.

"No, of course not, Mother," said Natalie, frowning. "How silly! Why, he didn't even know I was there till he came up to pay his check, and then he stopped a minute and said he was looking for a job. He hasn't gone back to college, Mother, though it's his senior year. He said he'd walked all over the city and couldn't find anything to do anywhere, and he laughingly asked if I knew of a job. Of course I told him we had an opening in the store, just that day. It was Tom Bonar's job—you know, the one with the red hair. He got a telegram that his father had died, and he had to go back to Wisconsin right away and stay with his mother. Mr. Foster was upset about it all day because he didn't know where to turn for the right man. I didn't think Chris would even consider it, but he seemed so earnest that I had to let him know about it. And he jumped at the chance. He had a good attitude about it, too. Said he was at the bottom of the ladder ready to do anything. So he came back at closing time, and Mr. Foster tried him out a little and said he could start Monday."

"Oh, dear child, I hope you won't get interested in him. He'll be in the store all day, and you'll see him a lot."

"Why shouldn't she get interested in him, Mother?" broke in Janice. "He's a prince! I should think you'd be glad she could have such a friend."

"But he won't stay there," said the mother. "He'll get something more important soon and return to his own social class, and Natalie will be hurt."

"Oh, Mother!" cried Natalie. "Please don't always think of me in terms of matrimony. I have no desire to fall in love or get married or break my heart. Chris is a nice fellow I knew a little in school, and there's nothing wrong with his carrying my packages home once in a while, although I'll manage not to need it. I guess you've brought me up decently, Mother, and I hope you can trust me—and God. Besides, I don't wear my heart on the outside where every passing thing can break it. He was only grateful to me for telling him about the job tonight. He probably won't have time to look at me again. We're busy people in that store, Mother. We haven't time for nonsense. But here's something. I had a chance to tell him about God on the way here."

When she'd finished telling of her conversation with Chris, Mrs. Halsey kissed her daughter on the forehead.

"Forgive me, dear, for worrying. You and Jan are all I have, and I keep fluttering about you like an old hen over her chickens. I guess I can trust my girl to be careful, and I'm glad you could talk with him that way. I've heard his father and mother are devoted to God and to one another. His father is an elder in our church, but of course I've never known them personally. And you can't tell these days what a son is by his father."

"I also told him about our mission and the Bible school. Maybe he'll go sometime. He seemed interested. Now I suppose you'll worry about that. But if Jan fixes her lessons so she can go Monday nights with me, we'd be together, and I doubt he would walk home with us. He's just an old schoolmate being polite. For pity's sake, don't make me so self-conscious about him, or I'll have to get another job."

"I won't, dear," said Mrs. Halsey quickly. "I shouldn't have spoken at all. I'm just afraid for you and regret you can't have the right companionship."

"I should worry about companions!" said Natalie. "I've got Jan, haven't I? What's better than a good sister? Is that cocoa on the stove? Look—it's boiling over! My, I'm hungry. These late Saturday hours and the rush at dinnertime make me feel like a starving street child. Oh, you've got toast and eggs for me! Can't you both sit down and eat something, too?"

"We saved our oranges from this morning, and yours, too," Janice said. "Remember—you didn't eat yours at breakfast."

Then the three sat down to a simple meal in the neat white kitchen and had as good a time as if they'd been three girlfriends, chatting and planning.

But just before they went to bed Mrs. Halsey said, "Natalie, I'm sorry I said what I did. I don't want you to think I don't trust you, and I'm glad of how you're using your influence with that young man. We'll pray he gets to know the Lord."

"Why, sure! We can claim that promise 'Where two of you shall agree.' He'd be a powerful influence if he knew the Lord. He's a member of the church like most of the other young people who go, but it seems as if he doesn't believe anything much. He talked as if it were all guesswork and might as well be any other religion as Christianity. I doubt I'll have another chance to speak about it to him. He'll probably go his own way after tonight. But we can pray, and that will reach him without his knowing we have anything to do with it."

"Dear child!" said the mother with a loving look at her elder daughter.

Meanwhile Chris was nearing his own door and, suddenly remembering he had a job, began to whistle cheerfully. His mother was hanging up the clean dish towels on a string line above the range and smiled. She had scarcely heard him whistle since the crash.

"Well," announced Chris, "I think I've landed a job at last. It won't be manager of Standard Oil Company or president of the Rockefeller Foundation, but I guess it'll provide at least enough salt for our meals."

Mr. Walton glanced up from the evening paper, and Mrs. Walton hurried in just then from the kitchen. Elise stood in the doorway behind her.

"What is it?" asked his sister.

He took a deep breath and let out the words quickly: "Errand boy in the chain store!" He waited for their reaction.

"A grocery?" said his sister.

"Good work, son!" said his father quickly.

"That's a nice, clean business," said his mother with interest.

"I'm proud of you, Chrissy!" Elise said, smiling to cover her surprise.

Chris drew another deep breath, this time of relief.

"Well, don't get too set on it," he said sheepishly. "They're only trying me out Monday. They may not keep me. I may prove too good for 'em!"

After that they had family worship, with Mr. Walton giving thanks for Chris's prospects, and then they went to bed upstairs in the funny rooms, where even a bed and a small bureau seemed too crowded. They called back and forth through the thin partitions and joked about the strangeness, but the hominess was pleasant.

Chris lay there thinking about his family and how well they took his grocery job. He knew Elise might even be kidded about it by her classmates in school. He felt deeply thankful as he realized how well and normal his father was. In fact, now that he thought about it, his father seemed more cheerful than he had for the past year or so. Probably the bank's affairs had been growing more complicated and burdensome, and now it was good to be down at rock bottom and try to climb up bravely again.

Overall Chris felt happier than he had since their trouble came and wished them all a cheerful good night. His thoughts then turned to Natalie. What an unusual girl she was—not shy as she seemed in school. He wished he'd known her before when he could show her some nice times. It would have been fun to give her rides and take her to class parties. He didn't recall seeing her at any. Probably the girls had snubbed her, too.

Then he thought of the odd things she'd said about God and being thankful for the hard times in her life. He didn't know another girl who would talk like that. He wondered how she got that way and was amazed at how well she had answered everything he'd said. Well, perhaps there was something in it. Dad seemed to have something to lean on. He couldn't understand what it was, but he vaguely wished he knew.

Then he thought of his old high school friends in college. Not one had written him a line about the frats or how the last football game had gone—not even a cheering word or regret he wasn't with them. Of course, they came after him that time. But when they couldn't carry him off in triumph to be their hero again, that was the end. True, he hadn't written to them, but that was different; he didn't think he had anything to write about. And then it came to him: They had parted ways. Life had swept them into separate worlds. He wondered if he would ever hear from them again.

Chapter 9

Natalie closed the front door of her home and started down the street for work on Monday morning. She noticed a man standing at the street corner, his hat pulled down over his eyes and a watch in his hand.

A look of annoyance crossed her face. This was the third time in recent weeks that same man had stood there, watching her come out of the house, almost as if he were waiting for her, timing her. He always gave her an ugly, familiar look as she passed, though she pretended not to notice him. She shrank from encountering him. He was large and rough-looking, and she felt almost afraid of him, although it seemed absurd during the day on a busy street.

Impulsively she turned and walked around the block to escape him. But when she reached the avenue he was standing at the next corner, in the same position, this time with an amused look on his face.

She turned her head the other way and acted as if she hadn't seen him. Something about his face made her shudder. Perhaps he wasn't watching her, and she was only imagining it.

Then, as if to answer her thought, the man spoke. "Hello, girlie! Can't get away from me, can ya?"

Her heart beat wildly. For an instant she wanted to run, but her feet felt like lead. It occurred to her that she must control herself and not let him know she was frightened. She'd made a mistake in going out of her way. He must have seen her hesitate at her own door and then turn the other way to avoid him. She wouldn't do that again. She would hold up her head and walk by him as if he weren't there. Perhaps she should warn Janice. It would be terrible if he bothered her little sister on the way to school.

She forced herself to walk steadily down the avenue, but she was trembling so she could scarcely stand up.

She tried to put the man out of her thoughts. She wouldn't look back to see if he was following her. He was probably just a common man with low standards. She had nothing to fear. Besides, policemen were about, and she could call one if he attempted to follow her. She might report it to the one who often came into the store. It was just as well to have a man like that cleared out of a neighborhood. It really wasn't safe for a fifteen-year-old girl like Janice to have to pass such a man. Of course, Janice would have to learn to take care of herself, too, but she felt ages older than her sister and that she must protect her. Above all she mustn't let her mother find out that man had spoken to her. It would frighten her so she'd always be anxious when either of them was away from home.

Natalie started thinking about the dresses she was planning for Janice, one for now and one for her commencement next spring. She wondered how much she could save each week from her meager salary. She hadn't minded missing the school activities at her commencement, but she hated for Jan to. Her little sister loved good times and had so few of them. She'd been so sweet about staying out of school while Mother was sick, and now that Mother was well enough to be alone all day, she could have more freedom. Work would come soon enough. And now that Mother didn't need extra food and medicine and a doctor all the time, some could be set aside for a spring wardrobe for Jan. She always had to wear made-overs because she was the smallest one in the family. For once she should have a dress, perhaps two, which she might pick out for herself in the store and try on.

Suddenly the man burst into her thoughts again. What if he hung around and frightened Mother? It was silly to think that, and what could she do but pray?

"God, please take care of Mother and Janice," she prayed, "and protect them—protect us all." Her heart grew quieter, her nerves steadier.

As Natalie approached the store she remembered Chris. Would he show up to work, or would he back out after thinking it over? It didn't seem real that Chris Walton, the banker's son, the most popular boy in high school—and in college, she'd heard—would come to work that morning in the store as she was, to measure sugar and potatoes and bring up kegs of mackerel from the cellar. Probably when his people found out they put a stop to it. His refined mother would doubtless do something about it. She'd want him in a profession.

But Natalie was glad Chris had been willing to do good honest work. It fit the ideal she'd formed of his character through four years of high school. And she didn't like to change her ideals of people she admired. Her standards were high, and not many measured up to them. So far he had. She wouldn't likely have much to do with him. Their lives were so far apart. Even if he worked in the store for a while, he'd find something else more in line with a profession, and this stint would only be used as a stepping-stone to something more suitable. But if he came, she hoped he'd do well while he was there. She liked to think a few noble young men existed. It made the world seem more worthwhile to live in.

Of course he'd been kind to her, and now he was grateful she'd told him about the position; but she mustn't presume upon that. She must remain quiet and aloof. Introducing him to the manager had been ordinary kindness. Anyone would do that. She didn't expect him to pay her any attention, and she certainly didn't want him to think she did. In fact, she must get away every evening before he did, so it wouldn't look that way. And he mustn't think he had to carry her packages home. He'd be so tired by evening, anyway, that he would want to get home quickly and wouldn't have time for her. So she needn't worry about that.

But Chris was waiting outside the store when Natalie arrived, so they talked for a minute or two. It was pleasant for him to be so friendly. All the girls had admired him, and she couldn't blame them. She had always liked to hear him recite in school because he seemed to enjoy it and know what he was talking about. She'd seldom gone to a school game because she had to hurry home to help her mother right after school. But she would sometimes watch the boys practicing in the field on her way home. She singled out Chris as a strong player and noticed how he led the others and they deferred to him.

Well, she would enjoy this pleasant contact with someone who could have been a friend under other circumstances. But she mustn't let her head get turned by it. He was Chris Walton, and she was Natalie Halsey, born into different worlds and stations. Of course her family had been good, too, but the world had forgotten that, though the families of the earth were one after all! But then she knew what people thought of a poor girl permitting a friendship with a young man in a higher social class, and she didn't intend to put herself in such a position. So as soon as the store opened she retired to her glass den and started working with her cash register and books, while Chris stood back by a counter and watched the day in the store unfold.

It fascinated him to be part of this busy new world. Almost at once people swarmed in for coffee and butter and yeast cakes, for a loaf of bread and a box of Aunt Jemima's prepared buckwheat, for cereals and dried beef and glasses of jelly for lunches.

In half an hour business slowed a bit, and the manager set him to work. He gave him a linen coat and an apron and showed him how to pick over a barrel of potatoes and put them up in paper sacks, so many pounds to a sack. They would have a special sale on potatoes that day. And when he'd measured the potatoes he had to look over a barrel of lettuce and pick out the perfect heads. Strange, bitter thoughts came to him occasionally as he remembered the other boys in his class in college now, walking about with college caps, whistling on the campus as they went from one class to another, wearing their fraternity pins, and planning their pleasant careers for the future, while he sorted decaying vegetables.

But for the most part Chris was interested in what he had to do, eager to do it thoroughly, and curious to see how quickly he could do it. He was too busy to contemplate the fate that had thrown him into a chain grocery instead of college.

Now and then he glanced over at the glass den where Natalie worked, making change, smiling pleasantly at the customers, a crowd always around her window. How patient and sweet she looked. Her delicate face shone out, too fine for such surroundings. Of course the store was nice and clean, the people were decent and respectable, and her work wasn't unpleasant. But somehow she looked more like a lady to be waited on than one waiting on others. She possessed a quiet refinement. What was that nursery rhyme Elise used to sing, "Sit on a cushion and sew a fine seam, and feed upon strawberries, sugar, and cream."

So Chris's thoughts moved in and out all day between the cabbages he brought up from the cellar and the empty crates and cans he carried down to the cellar. He was an errand boy as he'd said, taking orders moment by moment, never finished with one activity before another was handed him. By noon he was so hungry he devoured the hot coffee and sandwiches the manager had sent in for his helpers from the pie shop up the street because he couldn't spare any of them then to go out and get it for themselves.

They ate the food quickly, one at a time, standing in the backroom where supplies were kept, leaning against the big refrigerator or sitting on the cellar stairs or an empty crate, and hastened back to work. Chris wondered that they had so much business all the time. He hadn't guessed a grocery store would be so active. Someone always seemed to want something. By night he was weary and sore in every muscle. Some muscles he didn't know he had—and he'd thought all his muscles were perfectly fit. This seemed much more strenuous than playing football, perhaps because it was new and he was excited and anxious to please.

He heard that day that the district manager would be in around midweek, and his fate would probably be decided then. The district manager might have someone else lined up for that place, and Chris, being a substitute, would have to step out.

That made it a game for Chris, and he worked harder than ever. He might not have picked out the grocery business for his life's work, but he didn't want to be put out of anything he undertook. He wanted to be so good they would beg him to stay, even if he was leaving on his own for a better position.

The other workers were friendly among themselves but regarded Chris with suspicion and considered him an outsider. They may have learned something of his former estate, so he felt he had to win their confidence. They answered him abruptly, gave him only the information required to do his job, and left him to find out everything else for himself. They let him search for an item in the cellar instead of telling him how close it was to him and were as unpleasant as possible without fighting openly.

Chris found it baffling at first, and then he grew indignant. He wanted to take them out and thrash them one by one. Instead he fumed inwardly over their insolence and childish taunts.

On Chris's third day three young women, dressed for an afternoon tea, breezed into the store, holding their dainty chiffons and handsome fur coats back from the barrels and boxes. In loud voices and affected manners, they demanded to see Christopher Walton.

Chapter 10

Chris had been cleaning the cellar all day. The boxes and supplies kept down there were to be rearranged, so everything in the cellar had to be moved and cleaned. He'd never done anything like it, except washing the windows in the Sullivan Street house, but he was working hard to finish before night. He'd borrowed a pair of overalls that didn't fit him, and his hair was sticking out all over. He was wringing out a wet mop when the man from the meat counter yelled down the cellar stairs.

"Hey, Walton! Some dames up here wanna see ya! Make it snappy!"

Chris dropped his mop in dismay and looked upstairs. "I can't come!" he shouted at the man's disappearing heels.

"Make it snappy!" was the only reply. "The boss hates a mess o' ladies around in the way. This ain't no social tea!"

Chris stomped up the stairs, wiping his wet hands on his overalls and raking his fingers through his hair. He wanted to catch a glimpse from the back of the store first and see if this was a practical joke. If the boss had sent for him he'd go, of course; otherwise he'd retreat to the cellar and pretend not to have heard. Surely his mother or Elise wouldn't come to bother him there.

But Irene Claskey, Ethel Harrower, and Anna Peters hadn't waited at the front of the store. There they stood, outside the storeroom into which the cellar stairs led. By the time he'd reached the top of the stairs it was too late to turn around.

"Hello, Chris! Congratulations!" Irene squealed, throwing her hands in the air.

"So it's true! You've got a job!" Ethel exclaimed. "How long will it last?"

"Oh, Chris, you're a scream. Whose overalls are those? Did you borrow them from your butler?" That last came from Anna.

And then they laughed so loudly that everyone in the store turned to stare.

Chris glared at the girls, his chin in the air. He groaned inwardly when he saw the manager coming toward him with a smile.

"Did you want something?" Chris asked the girls in a stern, impersonal manner, as if he were addressing a customer.

"Sure, we want something!" Irene said, smiling over Chris's discomfiture. "We're having a high school reunion next Saturday night at the Rabbitt Inn on Horndale Pike, and we want you to take a bunch of us up there."

"I don't have a car!" said Chris, the color rising in his face.

"Oh, we know that!" Ethel chimed in. "But we can get a car if you'll drive it. Dad said you're a good driver, and he'd trust our car with you. We have to start at five o'clock, and we're meeting at my house—"

"Nothing doing!" Chris interrupted. "Sorry, but I have to work. Good afternoon!" He vanished down the stairs, shutting the door behind him.

The customers glanced at the girls and, with knowing smiles, returned to their shopping. The girls stared after Chris and then giggled and marched out of the store, poking and pulling at the produce and making rude remarks.

Chris stayed in the cellar the rest of the afternoon. He wasn't about to go upstairs and be kidded by anyone. He swept and mopped and scrubbed until he made the cellar look like a parlor. Each crate was arranged in logical order, and each row was labelled with a number on the beam overhead and the same number chalked on each container. Anything could be found quickly. Of course, Chris had worked with only half of his well-trained mind; the other half had been enraged over his humiliation. Fools, he called those girls, taking out his anger on the cellar floor until it was clean enough to eat on.

When everyone else had gone home, the manager came downstairs and looked around in wonder. Chris listened silently to the praise for how he'd cleaned and arranged things. Finally he burst forth.

"I'm sorry those girls made such a scene, Mr. Foster. I've scarcely seen them since school, but I guess they wanted to play some kind of joke on me. I got really frustrated."

"Oh, that's all right, Chris," said Foster. "I understand. Some girls like to do that. Don't worry. You've done a good job this afternoon. Forget the other. You took care of 'em all right, and I was glad to see it. You didn't let them get to you. They hurried away after you left them."

"Thank you, sir. It's great of you to take it that way. One thing's certain. I don't want anything more to do with those girls. Never did have much, but we were in the same class in school."

"Well, they don't act like ladies, that's for sure," said Foster. "There are plenty of young women who do, though. Miss Halsey is one, for instance. She may not wear furs or traipse around to parties, and she may have to work for her living, but she sure outshines those three. She's a fine girl."

"Yes, she is," Chris said, with a thrill of pleasure at hearing Natalie commended.

"Well," said Foster, "guess it's time for us to quit tonight. You've made this cellar look like a palace! You'll make a go of it here—I can see that already. Well, good night!"

Chris walked home that night with a lilt to his step. His manager had praised him and even hinted that his job was almost a sure thing. He was surprised to find he cared so much.

He'd almost forgotten about the unpleasant incident with the girls until he realized he hadn't seen Natalie all day except at a distance. She hadn't waited for him and may have had heavy packages to carry home. In his only glimpse of her she looked pale and tired. Perhaps her mother had taken a turn for the worse and she'd sat up all night with her. He felt uneasy at the thought.

Then he wondered if Natalie had seen those girls. Of course she must have. No one could have missed them. That fiendish Irene had seen to that. Did Natalie think that was the kind of girl he liked? Did she hear their invitation and think he would drive those girls to that infamous roadhouse on Horndale Pike! He certainly didn't want Natalie—or anyone—to think he was intimate with those girls.

Of course he'd known Irene Claskey and Anna Peters since kindergarten, but Ethel Harrower was a fairly new arrival in town without any particular social standing. Only Irene and Anna had taken her up. She used too much rouge and lipstick and smoked a lot in public. It gave him an unpleasant feeling to think Natalie supposed her to be his friend. Was that why Natalie had hurried home?

He would try to get out early the next morning and speak to her in the store before customers starting coming, though it had been his policy, and apparently hers, too, to keep some distance. Well, perhaps he could catch up to her on the way. He didn't know what he would say; he was too well bred to jump in and blast those girls. But he wanted Natalie to know where he stood with them. Well, it wasn't long till tomorrow. Anyhow he was glad at what Mr. Foster had said. He would tell Natalie that. She would be pleased, too.

So he came whistling again up the walk to the little clapboard house that looked so desolate on the outside and yet was so cheery inside.

His father glanced up at the sound. "Our boy's coming through in good shape, Mary."

"I knew he would, didn't you?" she said smiling.

They had a delightful supper that night despite the simple provisions. Mrs. Walton was bringing out her old recipes for plain, wholesome food that was cheaply bought and derived its savory taste and smell from seasoning, careful preparation, and slow cooking. Perhaps because it was different from what they'd eaten for years, its simplicity charmed the family. They had bean soup made with tomatoes, potatoes, and celery tops—a "mess of pottage," Mrs. Walton called it—and brown bread, baked apples and cream, and even bread pudding with a dash of chocolate. It all tasted delicious to them, especially after working hard.

Elise, too, had found a job, caring for two children after school, and she came in tired and hungry from riding them up and down the street in their wagon. Moreover, she was happy about earning fifty cents to help the family in their calamity.

After supper, while Elise was clearing away the dishes, Chris told in an off-hand way what the manager had said to him.

A look of joy spread over his father's face, and tears came to his eyes. "Son! That's great! I—I'm so proud of you. You've won a bigger battle this week than you ever faced in school or on the football field. You're learning to conquer yourself. You're doing well at something you don't like and under trying circumstances. Don't think I haven't understood—"

"But, Dad," interrupted Chris, "I—you—"

"You couldn't hide it from us, son. Your mother and I knew how hard it was for you to give up college and go to work. It's hard work, too, and you're not used to it. We dreaded it for you more than you could for yourself. We had great ambitions for you, Chris. You know that. You're our only son, and we dreamed you would achieve great things. But I've learned through these problems that we can't grow strong without being humble. We can't do great things when we put ourselves first. You've gained a great victory this week. I hope it will continue. You can achieve even greater things. You'll have setbacks, and you'll find it's hard to conquer self sometimes. But if you've learned to put yourself aside and do well what's hardest for you, you've reached a great place in life. Only one thing is higher than that, and that's to let the Lord Jesus come into your life and take self's place with His love. If you can learn those two things I'll know why God let this reversal come to us. There must be some reason why we should thank Him for it, and now I begin to see what it could be."

Chris looked at his father in amazement, the color stealing into his cheeks. He suddenly felt like a failure in his father's eyes.

"Why, Dad," he said huskily, "I didn't know—I never—thought—you felt that way."

"Well, I do, son, and your mother feels that way, too. Go on and win what's most important in life. Let Christ come into your life with His power and love, and we'll be so happy we can't contain ourselves."

Chris thought about his father's words when he went up to bed later. He'd said much the same as Natalie. In fact, that minister had said similar words about thanking God for hard things. The minister, Dad, and Natalie—all saying the same thing! Would God—if He really existed—have sent these things into his life for a reason? This God wouldn't have thought enough of him to turn a great bank's affairs upside down and alter other people's lives, just to change the way he related to himself, to others, and to God Himself. Or would He? Most of the professors and students at college felt that if God existed at all, He was only an impersonal force. Well, it was worth thinking about. Somehow the idea didn't make him angry, either, as it had a week ago.

He fell asleep thinking of what Natalie had told him about the missionary's life and bitter disappointments and of her face when she said, "What He permits must be best for us." And there was that other phrase she used regarding the missionary: "He's only an ordinary man with a great God." The last thing he remembered was the earnestness in Natalie's eyes as she said it. First thing in the morning he would tell her what Mr. Foster said. She got the job for him; she had a right to know he was getting along well with the manager.

He hurried through his breakfast and left so he could walk with her to the store. But when he passed her corner he saw only a man slouched against a lamppost, his hat down over his eyes, glancing furtively up and down the street.

Foster had just unlocked the door for Natalie as Chris reached the store, and although it was early she slipped into her glass den at once, with only a distant smile for Chris, and went to work as if she were very busy.

Chris felt his spirits drop. Why was Natalie acting like that? Was it because those girls had come in and asked for him? Was she ashamed of him because he'd had such visitors and didn't want to be associated with him? Well, if she felt that way he wouldn't bother her. He lifted his head and walked over to Foster for his day's orders, but his heart was sore.

All day long he measured sugar and rice into small quantities and packed them in paper bags, working in silence. The other men kidded him about the "dames," as they called them, but he kept on, his face without expression.

He tried to dwell on his father's words to him the night before and picture his mother's satisfied smile. But he'd mixed them up in his thoughts with Natalie and her words to him so that he got little help from that. He stayed out of her sight, thus reinforcing her feeling that she should stay out of his.

For indeed those girls had affected Natalie more than she realized. She decided she was right not to have anything to do with Chris, at least of her own accord. He belonged in the same social class with the girls. She'd never admired their arrogance, but most of the town considered them high on the social scale and would regard her as an outsider. She would never let Chris Walton say she chased him after getting him a job in the same store where she worked. She would go her own way as she had in school. He would soon forget she existed, just as he had in school.

The free and easy way those girls had marched into the store and demanded to see him, talking to him in that loud, familiar way, had made her see the difference between them. He probably liked the girls. They were part of his crowd in school and knew him better than she did. She'd idealized someone again, as she always did, and taken it hard when she found out the person was human. If only she could not like people so much and make them better than they were, she would save herself some pain.

So Natalie stayed in her glass den, ate her sandwich at noon without going outside, and sat late at her work in the evening until she was sure Chris was gone. No one inside the store or out could ever say she'd chased an aristocrat!

Chris had slipped out the back door, after hovering in the shadows of the backroom, his hat in his hand, to see if Natalie would leave. She didn't even look up. Well, he wouldn't trouble her further. The darkness of the street matched the darkness in his heart. The previous night's joy was past, and now he didn't care whether he pleased Foster or not. Fate or God or somebody was playing a mean trick on him. Or perhaps Natalie was.

He passed the end of Natalie's street and noticed the same man slouched at the corner. Could he be a friend of Natalie's? Was she going out with him? Chris knew the answer was no. When he turned onto Sullivan Street, he glanced back and saw the man look down the street and then start walking slowly toward the store.

A sudden panic seized Chris. The man may have been waiting for Natalie, and now he was going after her. He didn't like his looks. Chris hesitated a second, then walked quickly across the avenue, ran a block down Sullivan Street, and rounded the corner of the street that ended behind the chain store. He reached the back of the store and slipped through the alley just beyond.

Chapter 11

Chris paused a moment and peered around the corner of the building. He was satisfied he'd reached there a full block ahead of the other man who was apparently in no hurry. Yes, he could see a figure lounging under a streetlight at the next corner, glancing now and then back up the street. He wasn't too late. Inside the store he could see Natalie putting on her coat and walking toward the door. Foster was in the back arranging cans on the counter for tomorrow. Two other men had stayed to help him.

He drew a deep breath. Should he walk up and speak to her or follow her at a distance ready to protect her if she needed it? Or at least he could watch and discover whether she met this fellow as an acquaintance? She had a right to choose her own friends.

Yet, even as he considered this, his feet seemed to carry him to the door as Natalie came out, her arms full of packages.

As naturally as if he'd always done so, he stepped up to her and took her packages.

"Well, you've come at last!" he said, trying to laugh naturally as if she hadn't avoided him all day. "I thought maybe you brought your dinner and overnight bag and meant to stay till tomorrow and save walking home."

"Oh!" she said, her eyes lighting up and her cheeks turning pink. "But I thought you went home long ago! I was waiting—that is, I thought—"

"All right, say it! You were waiting till I got away so you wouldn't have to walk home with me. It's best to be frank even among friends. I wouldn't want to intrude. If you want to know the truth I did start home—got up to the corner. I was pretty sure you didn't want to be around me after those girls came in the store yesterday. And I didn't intend to bother you anymore if you felt that way. But when I reached the corner of your street I saw a rough-looking man standing on the corner where you had to pass, as if he were waiting, and I couldn't let you go there alone. So I sprinted around and down the alley and came after you. But if I've made a mistake and he's a friend of yours, just say the word and I'll leave you now."

"Oh!" cried Natalie. "I don't feel that way at all! I'm so glad you came! He tried to speak to me last night, and I was so frightened I could hardly get inside the house. And I didn't dare tell Mother. She wouldn't have let me come to work today. I've seen him out there three mornings."

She caught her breath, and he could see the tears welling up in her eyes. He felt the indignation rising within him, but his voice sounded calm and protective.

"Well, if that's the case let's cut through the alley and go up around the far block and avoid him. I'm here to look out for you. If that dirty sucker shows his face around you, I'll let him know where to get off. Don't worry."

He slid his arm within hers, putting her on his right side and guiding her through the dark alley and up another block where they couldn't be seen.

"Now," Chris said, "why didn't you speak to me all day?"

"Why, I did speak to you. I said good morning!" she said, half laughing.

"Like an icicle you did!" said Chris grimly. "What did I do to you? Did you think I staged that scene in the store yesterday? Did you think I made a date with those girls to get the spotlight on me in front of the boss and spoil my chances of keeping the job? Those girls did that just to get me in trouble. I never have liked that Peters girl, and Irene is always showing off. Besides, she only wanted to get back at me for refusing to take her to a roadhouse one night. She wanted to rub it in that I don't have a car now. Wanted me to be their chauffeur. Did you hear what she said?"

"I certainly did, and—I didn't think any of those things about you—really. I just thought that I—that you—"

"You just thought you didn't want to be seen with me after all that publicity," he said, watching her face for a reaction. "I understand, and I don't blame you, but you don't need to look quite so much like an icicle. I won't bother you if you don't want to be friends."

"Oh!" said Natalie, the tears spilling over onto her cheeks. "I didn't think any such thing. After I saw those girls dressed up—and I knew they belonged to the crowd you used to go with—I knew they wouldn't recognize me if they saw me and wouldn't speak to me if they did. It made me realize I'm not in your—social class, and I didn't want you to think I expected you to walk home with me and carry my packages. I hate it when girls do things like that. I wasn't brought up that way!"

They had reached a quiet block of houses with no one else about, and their steps slowed.

"I didn't mean for you to feel that way, Natalie," Chris said, a new tenderness in his voice, "as if anybody could ever think you were like that! Why, Natalie, I think you're wonderful!"

He had a sudden desire to kiss her, but such wasn't his habit. His mother had brought him up to reverence girls, and he felt a deep reverence for this girl. So he drew her arm closer within his, grasped her hand, and searched for new words to clarify his feelings.

Natalie struggled to regain her composure. "Thank you," she said simply. "It's nice to know you're friendly and haven't misunderstood me."

"Sure!" he said. "Why—I think you're wonderful!" he repeated. "You're the kind of person I want for a real friend. I've been thinking a lot about what you said about God and how everything must pass through Him before it gets to us. How could I misjudge you after that? You've done a lot for me. Not just introducing me to the job—I'm grateful for that, of course—but you've helped rekindle my trust in somebody, something—God, I guess. I almost lost it when everything happened. But you've lost many more things than I have, and you're waiting and believing in Him. It made me think, and I've been much happier since. I'm not sure I understand things any better, but I feel better. At college almost no one believed anything. You also helped me see myself."

"How do you mean, see yourself?" asked Natalie.

"Well, you helped me see I was arrogant. I may as well call it by its right name," he said. "You helped me see I was a conceited snob, and God, if there is a God Who cares about such things, probably had to let me go through this before I got too calloused."

"Well," Natalie said, looking at him and smiling, "you're the kind of person I thought you were, and I'm glad. I hate to be disappointed in people. It's great for you to speak out and be so frank with me. And thanks for being so friendly and helpful, too. I haven't had time to make many friends here."

"Well, I'm glad about it, too, and I hope we'll be good friends. What are you doing tonight? Could we go someplace and talk about it more? I've been mixed up about everything, and you seem to understand pretty well."

"Oh!" said Natalie, hesitating a moment and wondering what to do. "This is my night to go to Bible school—if Mother's well enough for me to go."

"May I go with you? I'm not crazy about you walking around town in the dark with a man like that tagging after you. May I come for you? What time?"

"Oh, would you go there?" she asked, a look of wonder on her face. "You'd like it, I'm sure. The man I told you about speaks tonight. It's at eight o'clock. But I hate for you to take your time looking after me. Maybe your family won't like it."

"Why not?" asked Chris, looking at her questioningly.

"I'm not in your social class, you know," she said gravely.

"Neither am I anymore," said Chris laughing, suddenly realizing it didn't hurt him as it had. The fact that they could both laugh over it seemed to draw them closer.

They arrived at her door, and she reached out to take her packages. But he held onto them.

"There are too many for you. May I carry them inside for you? That sack is potatoes—after filling nine million bags today, more or less, I know what they feel like. You shouldn't carry stuff this heavy."

"Oh, I'm quite strong," said Natalie, laughing and reaching for them again.

"No, please—I'm taking them in, if you don't mind," insisted Chris.

Natalie had a vision of her mother in a big apron getting supper and Janice setting the table, with horrified expressions on both their faces. She could feel her cheeks glowing red in the dark to think that now her mother would worry again. But something in Chris's cultured, pleasant voice caused her to surrender, and with a quick prayer that all might be well inside she opened the door into the tiny hall.

Mrs. Halsey was taking bread pudding out of the oven, and the scent of cinnamon wafted down the hall.

"My, that smells good!" he said, walking through the hall into the kitchen at the end where the door stood open. He crossed to the table and set the packages down, then turned toward the astonished mother, taking off his cap.

"Good evening!" he said with a smile. "You don't know me. I'm the delivery boy from the chain store. I hope you don't mind my lack of ceremony. I had to put these down before I could take off my hat."

"Mother, this is Chris Walton," said Natalie, appearing behind him with shining eyes and glowing cheeks.

Mrs. Halsey was at once cordial. "You've been very kind," she said, studying the young man's face. "I've told Natalie she shouldn't bring so much at once or impose on your good nature."

"Oh, that's nothing," said Chris. "I live near here and am glad to be of use. How cozy you look here. Is that the pudding that smells so good?"

"Won't you stay and help us eat it?" Mrs. Halsey asked, smiling.

"Oh, I wish I could, but I've got the butter for supper in my pocket, and I expect Mother is flattening her nose against the windowpane this very instant watching for me. Sorry. That looks like a real pudding, and I'd like to sample it. Perhaps you'll ask me again sometime?"

"Why, of course," Mrs. Halsey said, "if you really care to come."

"That's settled then," said Chris, turning to Natalie. "There, Natalie, don't forget to arrange that soon, or I'll have to remind you. Now I must hurry, or I'll get in trouble for not bringing the butter sooner. I'll come back to go to that school with you, Natalie—at seven thirty, did you say?"

"Oh, it isn't necessary to start before a quarter of eight. It's only a short distance," said Natalie, not daring to look at her mother.

"I suppose you've forgotten me," Janice said, suddenly appearing in the doorway, algebra book and pencil in hand.

Chris turned, bewildered.

"This is my sister, Janice," said Natalie. "I guess you haven't met her before."

"You're not by any chance the little girl with the red tam I used to pull to school on her sled my last year in high school? Those look like her eyes."

"The very same," said Janice, dimpling. "It's been several years since I rode on a sled—or anything else for that matter."

"Sorry I don't have a bus to take you out in, but I don't even own a wheelbarrow anymore. But, say, you've grown up fast! You must be in high school now. Doesn't that make us seem ancient, Natalie? And it seems like yesterday when I pulled you on your sled to school. Well, I'd better go, or this butter will melt. See you later!"

As Chris turned the corner onto the avenue, he noticed a figure in the shadows on the opposite side of the street, pausing now and then to glance up and down the street. He was glad he'd decided to go with Natalie to the Bible school.

Janice raised the question as the door closed behind him. "How did that happen, Natalie? I thought you had eschewed the society of gentlemen forever and were going to hold Mother's hand."

"Oh, Janice, you make me tired!" said Natalie irritably. "It wasn't my fault. I waited to bring home those potatoes before they were sold tomorrow, and when I came out of the door he was standing outside. He hadn't gone at all. I tried to make him understand I could carry my own packages, but it was no use. He was almost offended at me—said he wouldn't bother me if it annoyed me. I had to let him come. And I can't help it that he's going to Bible school, can I? It was entirely his idea."

Mrs. Halsey looked at her usually placid daughter in surprise. "Why, Natalie dear, I never meant for you to feel that way," she said anxiously. "I'm sorry. Please forget it, dear. I just couldn't bear for a rich man's son to look down on you or for you to get interested in someone who might be beneath you, morally or spiritually—or who meant nothing by his attentions. I should have trusted you, though. He seems like a nice young man and not a bit spoiled by his wealth."

"But he isn't wealthy anymore, Mother," said Natalie. "They're living on Sullivan Street near the railroad, next to the woman who used to wash for them. They've given up everything they had and are as poor as we are, I guess, from what I hear."

"Well, dear, I was wrong to judge anyone by money or position. I liked him very much in that brief minute or two. And if you want to invite him to come here, do as you think best. He'll be welcome. But guard your heart, Natalie, and don't get caught up in dreaming. You're my wonderful girl, and I can't bear for anything to hurt you."

Natalie turned away, pressing her hands against her hot cheeks, as she suddenly remembered the tone in which Chris had said, "I think you're wonderful!"

Then Janice, eyeing her sharply, began to chant in a comical tone,

You may go and nibble, nibble, nibble,
   At the cheese, cheese, cheese;
Little mouse, you may nibble
   If you please, please, please,
But be careful, little mouse,
   Of the cunning little house,
For you may someday find out
   That it's a trap, trap, trap!

Janice had a clear, sweet voice, and the mocking words rang out through the kitchen. Natalie, her nerves frayed, sat down in a chair and began to laugh hysterically as Janice's soprano rose in an improvised chorus.

Oh, my cunning little mouse,
   Oh, my darling little mouse,
Oh, you wonderful, wonderful, wonderful
   little mouse!

Then Natalie suddenly straightened up and looked at her mother and sister. "Look here, you two dears. You've got to stop this now, once and for all. I won't be teased this way. I'm not about to throw my heart out in the street for every young man to trample over. Besides, when a girl trusts her life to the Lord for leading, He won't let her go the wrong way and give her thoughts to the wrong one, will He?

"Chris is polite and kind, and of course I like that. But I don't have any funny notions, and you don't need to think I have. If the Lord has someone for me to fall in love with someday, He'll likely show me without a question when the time comes. But for now I'm just a girl, and when anybody is friendly and seems to have the right ideas, I don't know why I shouldn't be friendly to a certain extent, too, without passing through the inquisition.

"Now, if you don't think I'm right about that, I'll go upstairs and stay there. And when Chris comes back you can send him away with any excuse you like for my not going with him. But I won't stand for all these anxieties and fears any longer. It takes the joy out of life. If you don't want me to speak to him I won't, but I don't want to hear any more about it."

"The worm has turned!" Janice uttered solemnly into the silence that followed Natalie's outbreak.

Then they all burst forth into merry laughter.

Finally the mother came and put her arms around Natalie and kissed her. "You're right, dear. I had no idea we were persecuting you. Forgive me. He's a fine young man, and if you can help him know the Lord Jesus it'll be wonderful. I'm with you and trust you every step of the way. It's a great thing when a mother can say that of her child. Now let's have supper. It's getting late."

"And I'm with you, too!" Janice added. "I'm so much with you that I'm going to study my algebra this evening and not go to Bible school till next week. How's that for sacrifice?"

Natalie stopped in the middle of the kitchen. "You'll do no such thing! I'll help you with your algebra after we come home. But I'm determined you'll start in this class at the beginning of the first lesson. We're starting the book of Hebrews, and it's important to hear the introduction, or you won't get the same interest. If you stay at home I'll stay, too."

"All right, captain! I'll go!" said Janice cheerfully. "I want to sacrifice myself in any way possible to keep peace in this household."

Then Natalie turned toward her, laughing, and the two girls chased each other around the little house, from kitchen to living room, to hall and back to kitchen again, till they suddenly realized their mother was doing all the work, and they stopped to help put dinner on the table.

The girls had never gone out with a young man, so they all ate their dinner with excitement. Even Janice, a young schoolgirl, felt elated, and the mother seemed as pleased as any of them.

"You'd better put on your other dress, Natalie," said her mother, as they gathered up the dishes. "You run up and dress, and I can do these few dishes as well as not."

"No," said Natalie, "I'm not dressing up just because a boy I used to go to school with is going along. If he doesn't like me the way I am he needn't go. It's a plain school, and people don't dress up to go there. I'll do these dishes. You fixed dinner, and I can see you're tired."

In the end they all did the dishes, the mother sitting down and wiping the silver, and they finished quickly. Then Natalie changed her blouse and wore her Sunday hat, but neither of them said anything about it. Indeed they didn't have time, for they could hear Chris's step on the walk and his clear whistle and then the sound of his knock on the door.

"Seems like being regular people, doesn't it?" said Janice softly under her breath as she started for the door. "The Halsey family is going out among 'em!"

And as they started off with their escort, Mrs. Halsey sighed that a simple activity like going to a religious meeting could bring such delight. How little youthful pleasure her dear girls had had in their lives! If their father had only lived—!

Then she slipped up to her room and knelt a long time by her bed, asking for wisdom to guide and guard her children, so she would know what the Lord wanted her to do and wouldn't get her own will in the way of the Lord's leading.

Chapter 12

At the Bible school that night, Chris heard a man speak as if he were personally acquainted with Jesus Christ, had talked with Him face-to-face and received his instructions from a Bible that seemed real, not just a collection of mystical sayings handed down from long ago. Chris was deeply stirred.

Under this teacher, words, phrases, and even verses and chapters he'd had a verbal acquaintance with since his childhood suddenly acquired new, wonderful meaning. He gazed around at the other people who were listening, Bibles and notebooks open on their laps, their eyes fixed on the speaker. Not one looked doubtful. Their faces seemed to reflect an inner light. Even Natalie and her young sister had the same rapt look. How did this man discover these wonderful things? Were they merely interpretation? No, he didn't seem to be twisting the words, for he read them as they were printed. Natalie had found the place and handed him a Bible. He could follow along, and, lo, the familiar story was there. Yet it meant as clearly as print what the teacher said it meant. That was obvious. And all the teacher did was explain the meaning of a Greek word and have them turn to several other references.

The teacher said that Scripture must be interpreted by itself, comparing Scripture verse with Scripture verse, and that was how it worked out and made things clear. Why, some passages Chris had learned by heart when he was a child in primary class; but no one had ever explained them to him, so they'd been just a lot of words to him.

He learned for the first time, in casual reference, that the Bible was written according to a marvelous numerical structure. Each book and verse and even each word was worked out mathematically and so perfectly that one could distinguish between two copies of ancient manuscripts that differed slightly and identify the original, because the incorrect one wouldn't conform to the numerical structure. He learned that this could be proved and studied only in the Hebrew and Greek, and a sudden desire to study those languages was born in him. He'd like to be able to prove that thing. If it was true, it upset his college professors' doubts. In fact, the teacher stated that no scholar had written a single paragraph in imitation of this numerical structure and made good sense out of it; no other book had as yet been found to be written this way; and this same law of numbers governs every department of creation. The conclusion was that the God Who created the earth also authored the Book.

He caught a slight vision of the symbolism throughout the Bible, the significance of numbers and the significance of the meaning of proper names in the Bible. He heard references to certain truths that clarified sentences he'd considered vague.

When the lesson finally closed with prayer, leaving its imprint on his heart, he was sad it was over. The talk seemed to last only a few minutes, but in actuality an hour had passed. Chris wanted to ask a lot of questions, but he'd sooner have cut off a small piece of his tongue than admit it.

The teacher stood at the door as they went out. He grasped Chris's hand in a warm, quick shake and called him brother, with a bright look that seemed to come from strength filled with both joy and sorrow.

Out in the night again a silence fell on the three. At last Janice spoke: "I think he's wonderful, don't you, Natalie?"

"We're studying a wonderful book," said Natalie thoughtfully, "and he knows it well."

"I'd like to know something," said Chris, more in a tone of thinking aloud than expecting an answer. "He kept talking about 'saved ones.' What did he mean? Who did he mean? How can people tell whether they're saved or not?"

"Oh!" said Natalie, looking at him earnestly. "You can, of course! Don't you know you're saved?"

"Why, no," said Chris, "of course not. Nobody knows till after they're dead, do they? And anyhow—saved from what?"

"Why, saved from the consequences of sin—guilt and death."

"I've never felt I was such a great sinner," said Chris, lifting his chin a bit.

Natalie was silent a moment. "We're all great sinners," she said quietly.

"I don't see that," said Chris. "What have you done that's so awful? What have I done? Little things, of course, but I've always tried to live a pretty decent life."

"Of course, the great sin—the only sin, after all, that is terrible—is not believing in Him. Rejecting Him when He did so much for us. The Bible says that in God's sight 'all have sinned, and come short of the glory of God.' "

"I've heard that line all my life, but I never saw why so much emphasis was put on sin. Most respectable people live pretty good lives. I never had any real desire to be bad. I can't feel I'm a great sinner, and I don't see why I should try."

Natalie was praying silently for the right answer and finally spoke hesitantly: "People never do feel they're sinners till they've had a vision of Jesus, do they? When you see Who He is, then you begin to realize how far short you've fallen."

"Oh!" said Chris blankly. Then after a moment he added, "How could you do that? He isn't here. You can't see a person who isn't here."

"Yes, you can," she said, smiling. "You can find Him in His Word. And you can find Him in prayer. The Holy Spirit has promised to reveal Him to us if we ask Him. But you've got to come believing. Faith is the key that unlocks the Word and makes us see things we couldn't understand without it."

Chris looked at her wonderingly. "How could someone believe something they didn't believe—something they weren't convinced was true?"

"Belief is an act of the will," Natalie explained, "not an intellectual conviction. It's something you deliberately will to do. It's taking God at His word and letting Him prove to you that what He promises is true. That's how it was put in Bible school last week, and I've proved it's true."

"You have?" he eyed her curiously as they walked along the dark street.

"Oh, yes! Ever since I knew I was saved."

"There it is again," said Chris, with slight irritation in his voice. "You say it the way he did tonight, as if it were some sort of charm. What does it mean? What do you have to do?"

"Oh, you don't have to do anything," she assured him. "Just accept it. Believe it. Salvation is a free gift, and you only need to take it. The moment you accept it you know you're saved, and nothing can take you out of His hand, for you're His. You're under His care, and He can present you faultless—without spot or wrinkle or anything like it—'before the presence of His glory.' That's not because you are without fault. It's because He is faultless and lives within us and has given us the right to wear His righteousness. It's only through His righteousness in us that we can be faultless." Natalie was talking earnestly, filled with wonder that she was given an opportunity to say these things.

"I still don't understand," said Chris. "How does believing a thing make you know you're saved?"

"Well," said Natalie thoughtfully, praying for the right words again, "if you were a prisoner, condemned to die, and you were told that someone else had taken the death penalty for you and you might go free, you would only have to accept his death for yours and believe what you were told. He's said that the minute you accept His grace and believe His Word you're born again and are one of His saved ones. He also says that whoever believes has 'everlasting life, and shall not come into condemnation; but is passed from death unto life.' "

"But I don't see how believing a thing could make a difference in how you feel."

"Well, you couldn't see, because faith makes it possible for you to see. It's the key that unlocks the mystery, and you can't find out until you try it yourself. Nobody can make you see it. You have to take that key of belief and unlock it for yourself. You do it in other things. Why not trust God as well as people? Suppose you need something at the store and you ask the manager about it; he says he'll get it right away, and then you don't worry about it anymore. You trust him. Yet you don't really know he'll do it. You haven't proved him, but you take it for granted he'll keep his word. You decide to believe him until he disproves himself. Why not take God at His word?"

Chris was silent. At last he said, "But I'm a church member, you know. Doesn't that make it all right?"

"No," said Natalie, smiling and shaking her head. "He didn't say, 'If you join the church you're saved—passed from death to life.' He said whoever believes."

They had reached the house now, and Janice went inside while Chris and Natalie paused at the door.

"Won't you—come in?" asked Natalie hesitantly, wondering what her mother would think.

"No," said Chris, "it's getting late, and we have to be up early. But—I'd like to know more about this. We'll talk about it another time. Perhaps I'll join that class. I like that bird. He's sincere—you can see that. Well, good night!" And he left abruptly.

"Odd," he said to himself as he walked home, "I never knew she was a girl like that! How different she is from the other girls I knew in school! Imagine any of them talking about how to be saved or even caring about it!"

Why hadn't he known her before? he wondered again. Why hadn't he sought her out and taken her places instead of some of the girls he had?

Oh, the other girls weren't all silly, of course. Janie Anderson, Marguerite Manning, and Roxanna White were sensible, fine girls. He'd taken them different places. But no girl had ever stirred him as this sweet person who sat beside him tonight listening to that unusual message. He'd especially enjoyed watching her lovely, earnest face as she listened.

As he walked up to his door, he felt that a strong tie had been formed between them that evening. Of course they were both young, and it wasn't time yet to think of more serious things. But he felt that the friendship with Natalie Halsey had come into his life to stay. Here was a person with something more than froth, more even than a good education, pleasant manners, and a desire to please. Life had sifted and tested her early. Her face bore marks of experience that hadn't hardened her but had brought a lovely peace on her brow and a charming light in her eyes. He felt a longing to understand and have the same secret she possessed.

Chapter 13

The days that followed were full of hard work, but somehow Chris found it pleasant. His coworkers were still a little belligerent, being jealous of any word the manager spoke to him, and stood ready to criticize or sneer behind his back. But Mr. Foster liked him and said nice things occasionally about his work, for he was selling now with the rest and understood the stock as well as anyone. And in a moment of leisure he could glance at Natalie behind her glass window, making change, smiling to the women customers, courteous to the men, and sending a tiny flash from her eyes to him across the store now and then when no one was watching.

They were careful not to let their friendship be known. It seemed too indefinite, almost too sacred to be dragged through the store and joked about as it inevitably would be. None of the other employees knew Natalie recommended Chris, he discovered. She went her quiet way among them, smiling at each one but remaining aloof. The manager spoke respectfully to her, and they all called her Miss Halsey, not Natalie.

Every night they would meet in some agreed-upon place around the corner or after the others had left and walk home together, with him carrying whatever packages she had. The coarse-looking man who had troubled her earlier seemed to have disappeared. He no longer stood at the street corner when Natalie started out mornings, and she was greatly relieved.

The weeks passed swiftly.

"Mother, I think Chris has a girl," said Elise one evening when they were waiting for Chris to come home for dinner. Sometimes he was unaccountably later than necessary.

"Oh!" said Mrs. Walton, looking up a little anxiously. "Do you think so? I supposed he would sometime, but—he seems so young."

"He's no younger than I was when I fell in love with you, Mary," Mr. Walton said, glancing up from his paper.

"Well, that was different," said Mrs. Walton, smiling. "You were—I was—that is—"

"Exactly so," her husband said with a twinkle. "I was just thinking that myself."

"What makes you think he has a girl, Elise?" asked her mother.

"Well, I've seen him walking with her twice very slowly, when I went down for Daddy's paper. It's just after the store closes, and he was carrying a bunch of extra packages."

"Oh, I hope it's not Anna Peters," said the mother, with concern in her voice.

"No, it isn't Anna! Chris can't bear her. He says she's bold."

"She is!" agreed the mother.

"It's a girl around here."

"Around here!" Mrs. Walton said, clearly alarmed.

"Yes, I think she lives over on Cromar Street. I thought I heard his voice the other night as I was crossing at the corner. If it's the house where he was standing, her sister's in my class at school. And the girl used to be in Chris's class in high school."

"Who is she?"

"She's one of the Halsey girls. I think her name is Natalie. Her sister is Janice. Janice seems nice enough, but no one knows her very well. She always has to hurry home. Her mother's been sick. She wears made-over dresses."

"That's nothing against her," said the mother sharply. Her own daughter would probably come to that very soon.

"Well, she's pretty, but the girls don't invite her to things much."

"Better get acquainted, Elise, and bring her around," Mr. Walton suggested. "It would be nice to know what the family's like. Of course there may be nothing serious in carrying someone's packages. Chris is a gentleman, and it would be natural to walk with someone who lived near here. But, Mary, if Chris is getting acquainted with someone you'd better find out who she is and invite her here. That will make the friendship safer then. Chris is young, and of course the girls have always liked him. It's natural he'll want friends."

"I will," said Mrs. Walton, sighing.

Just then Chris came whistling up on the porch, a look of joy on his face.

The next afternoon after school Elise caught sight of Janice as she was leaving and hastened after her.

"Janice!" she called. "Wait for me a minute!"

Janice stopped in surprise. She was used to hurrying away as soon as school closed and not talking with the girls. Her mother had needed her so long that it had become second nature to her, even when the need for haste wasn't as urgent. The other girls seldom included her in parties or activities. She'd played with them in the primary grades and knew them all, but she was no more one of them now than her sister had been in high school.

So now she waited, gravely surprised. What could Elise Walton want? Probably some message from the teacher—maybe about the essay she was to write for Friday's class. Or perhaps it was to tell her of the class banquet; they sometimes invited her to it, though they knew she never accepted because she couldn't pay the two dollars.

She stood, half impatient, until Elise caught up with her. From a distance she'd admired Elise, especially her clothes, exquisite and perfect in every detail and with distinctive touches about them. Janice was glad to get a closer view of them so she might copy some small features in her own made-over garments.

"I wondered," Elise said, gasping for breath and falling into step with her as if they'd always been close friends, "if you wouldn't take pity on me and explain that algebra problem you did on the board this morning. You did it so beautifully and quickly! But the period was almost over as you finished, and I didn't have time to see what you did. Where did you get that quotient? I simply can't figure it out. I've been working for the last ten minutes on it. You see, we have another one almost like it in our lesson for tomorrow."

"Of course I'll show you," said Janice in surprise. "But you're always faster at algebra than I am. You wouldn't have any trouble getting it if you took a little time."

"But I haven't time!" said Elise with an embarrassed laugh. "You see, I'm in a hurry today because Mother and I are going to try papering a room. We've never done one before, and I don't know how it will come out. But I'm so excited about it that I don't know what to do. It's my brother's room, and we want to surprise him with it. Have you ever hung paper?"

"I certainly have!" exclaimed Janice, a little haughtily. "We always do ours. My sister's a clipper at it. She can put it on as smooth as the skin on your face. But she's busy all day now. She works in the chain store up on the avenue."

"Oh!" gasped Elise. "Which sister is that?"

"I have only one sister," she said, smiling. "There are only three of us, Mother and Natalie and I, since Father died."

"Oh, I didn't know your father died," said Elise, a look of sympathy on her face. "How hard that must have been. My father almost died a few weeks ago. We didn't know for a long time whether he would get well or not."

"Yes, I know," the girl said. "Mother read about it in the papers. He's the president of the bank, and we were interested—" She stopped suddenly.

"Oh, no! Were you some of the people who lost money through us? I'm so sorry—"

"Oh, don't worry," she said, smiling. "We didn't have much there to lose. Mother had just taken out most of it to make the last payment on our house."

"How fortunate!" said the other girl. "But Father says he hopes everybody will get back what they lost in a little while. When he gets stronger he's going to try to do something about it. But I hope you'll get yours back soon."

"Oh, I don't think enough was there to matter," Janice said again, wishing she hadn't mentioned it. "What's this about the problem? Do you mean the one about the pumps? See—you divide the quotient by nine."

And Janice opened her book, and the two girls walked slowly along with their heads together over the algebra.

"Oh, yes, of course, how silly of me!" said Elise at last. "My, I'm glad I asked you. Now it won't take ten minutes to get my work finished for tomorrow, and I can go at the papering right away before dark. The man who sold us the paper told us a little about putting it on, but I'm scared to death about the ceiling. He told us to get a new dust brush and smooth it ahead down the middle of a strip of paper. But he warned me it was hard to keep it on and hard to make it go straight. I'm afraid I'll make a mess of it."

Janice laughed. "It's hard till you get used to it. The first time I put paper on the ceiling it came down behind my shoulders as fast as I put it on, and when I got to the end of the strip I was all wound up in it. Oh, I was a mess!"

The two girls laughed over this, and Elise made a wry face.

"I expect I'll make a mess of the whole thing, but I've got to try. My mother was going to do it herself, but I can't let her get up on chairs and stepladders and break her hip or something. She put on some wallpaper once when she was a young married woman."

"Mine didn't, because she didn't have to then. They were well off, but she had to later when we lost all our money. Natalie and I have been brought up to do everything we could. If we didn't make things, we didn't have them. But it's kind of fun to make things and do things like papering, don't you think?"

"Maybe!" Elise said, laughing. "I'll tell you better when I get this paper on the wall. I wish you could come in and sort of coach me."

"I wish I could, too," said Janice, "but I've got to hurry home. Mother's been doing some fine sewing for a woman, and she wants it before five o'clock, so I must take it. But if there's anything else I can do to help later, I'd love to."

"Thank you. I may call on you yet. By the way, why don't you come over and visit me sometime? We're near neighbors, aren't we?"

"Yes, we are," said Janice consciously, as if she'd considered the matter before but hadn't expected it to be recognized. "I'd love to sometime, if I can get the time. You see—well, we're pretty busy, all of us, most of the time. Since my sister got the position in the chain store, I have to take her place getting dinner and doing a good deal of the housework. Mother's been sick and can't do the housework and sew, too, and we need the money from her sewing."

"Well, we're busy at our house, too," said Elise frankly. "I'm taking care of some kids three times a week, so now I'm proud to say I rank in the laboring class, too. I guess I've been pretty useless most of my life, but I'm trying to make up for it now as well as I can. You don't realize when you don't have to work what a difference it makes. But, honestly, I think it's kind of fun."

A serious look crossed Janice's face. "I guess it's fun sometimes to put up with things and try to make ends meet. But when someone you love is very sick and you don't have enough money to buy fruit and other necessities, or when someone dies and things get mixed up it isn't much fun."

Elise looked at her thoughtfully.

"I like you," she said suddenly. "I wish we could be friends. I don't know why we haven't been before."

"I've always liked you," said Janice, smiling, "but I never had time to be friends with anyone. It's nice to know you want to be friends, though, and I'd love it."

"Well, let's go to school tomorrow together," Elise suggested. "What time do you start? I'll wait in the house till I see you pass our corner."

"All right!" said Janice, her eyes lighting up. "I'd love that! I've never had anyone to walk to school with since Natalie finished high school."

"Well, you have now," said Elise, reaching out and squeezing Janice's hand. "It's going to be nice. I'm glad!"

The two girls parted, and Janice hurried home.

"Mother, what do you think?" she asked as she burst into the house. "Elise

Walton ran after me and asked me to help her with her algebra, and she wants to be friends. Do you suppose her brother made her do that? She was really pleasant and lovely about it, as if she meant it."

"Then I wouldn't question it, dear," said her mother, glancing up wearily from her sewing. "Did you like her?"

"Oh, yes! And she isn't the least bit snobbish. She and her mother are papering a room this afternoon. She says her mother used to do it when she was first married. I was telling her about putting it on ceilings and how careful you had to be."

Mrs. Halsey looked up in surprise. "Are they as hard pressed as that? I've heard that Mr. Walton has been quite honorable about giving up his property, but I didn't think they'd have to do such things for themselves. It must be very hard for them."

After a moment she added, "I wonder if they have a roller to make the seams smooth. Suppose you take ours with you and go around that way when you take Mrs. Graves's evening dresses home. It certainly would be easier for them to have one, and if they own one it can't do any harm to be neighborly."

So Janice hunted up their roller and started on her errand.

Elise had found her mother up in the room they were to paper, wearing an old dress, with her sleeves rolled up and a scaffolding composed of the ironing board, the kitchen table, and two chairs. She had just finished cutting the last length of ceiling paper as Elise burst into the room.

"Mother! I've been looking for you! You haven't broken your promise and started, have you? Oh, Mother! You carried up that table by yourself!"

"No, I didn't. Chris ran home a little while ago to get his overcoat instead of his sweater. The store is sending him into town on an errand, and he was afraid he'd be cold. He brought the table up for me. And look in my room and see what a nice pasting table I fixed up with the two cutting tables and some boards I found in the cellar. No, I didn't carry them up, either. I got that little Jimmy next door to bring them for me when he came home for lunch, and I gave him ten cents and a red apple to pay for doing it. Hurry up, and let's get at this. The paste is all ready."

Elise changed into an old dress and joined her mother. "Well, Mother, I scraped up a friendship with the sister of Chris's girl."

"Oh, my dear! I don't know that I'd call anyone Chris's 'girl' on such a slight foundation. Surely if she meant anything special to Chris he'd say something about it to your father and me."

"I wonder!" said Elise.

"I'm quite sure he would," said the mother as if she wished to convince herself.

"Well, anyhow, I liked her a lot—the sister, I mean. I guess she's been lonely. She didn't say so, but she seemed very glad I wanted to be friends."

"Is she—refined, dear? I don't mean, of course, that we should despise her if she isn't—but—well, you know what I mean. I wouldn't like Chris to be interested in bold, forward girls—or coarse ones."

"She's not any of those things, Mother. She's really nice. I'm sure you'd call her refined. She has a low, sweet voice and looks straight at you quietly and waits for you to speak instead of rushing in as if she knew it all."

"Well, that sounds good. But you don't know about the sister, do you? This one is the youngest. The other one may be different."

"Yes, I found out about the other one. I don't suppose you'll like it, but—well—she works in the chain store!"

The mother turned and faced her daughter, an anxious look on her face. "Oh! Well, that might explain the packages. Chris may be only showing kindness to a fellow worker. But—it's so easy for people thrown together that way to get interested in each other when they're not truly congenial. I'd hate for Chris to spoil his life by getting attached to a common girl. But it does seem as if he'd have sense about it. I'm sure he has fine ideals."

"Of course, Mother. He has. I wouldn't worry. And—it may not be anything but a little kindness, as you say. I don't see, Mother, why you can't trust things like that to God. You trust a lot of other things just as big."

Mrs. Walton glanced at her daughter with surprise. Elise wasn't one to speak much of God.

"I suppose I should," she said, smiling. "I forget sometimes when a new danger looms that life isn't all in our own hands to plan for. Dear, wasn't that a knock at the door? Can you run down, or shall I?"

But Elise was already on her way. She opened the door, and there stood Janice with the roller.

"Mother thought you might not have a roller and would like to use ours," she said, half embarrassed before this girl she'd held in awe so many years.

"Oh, how wonderful! It was sweet of you to think of it. No, of course we never even knew there was such a tool. How do you use it? Won't you come in just a minute and show me? Come upstairs and meet my mother. She'd love it. No, I won't keep you but a second, but I do want you to know my mother. Then you can show us how to use this cute thing."

Janice consented reluctantly to go upstairs.

"It's Janice Halsey, Mother," called Elise as they climbed the high, narrow stairs. "She's brought us a roller to use on the seams of the paper. Wasn't that lovely? Her mother sent it over."

"Oh, a roller!" said Mrs. Walton, coming to the head of the stairs. "How nice! I used to have one years ago. I don't know what became of it. Janice, I'm glad to meet you, and it was very kind of you to think of us. Won't you thank your mother for me?"

Janice stayed only a few minutes, and when she was gone Elise came back and started working in earnest.

"Didn't you like her, Mother?" she asked.

"Yes, very much," said the mother, turning from the window where she'd been watching the departing girl. "Of course one can't judge a person in a minute or two, but she seems well bred. I was watching her walk. She moves with a natural grace. Now that Anna Peters swaggers."

Elise laughed. "Oh, Mother, you're so funny when you don't like someone."

"Well, don't ever let me catch you walking that way!" said her mother. "Now this Janice seems to be a lady. Her mother must be one, too."

"Janice says her mother never had to work," said Elise thoughtfully. "Isn't it odd how people and circumstances change when they get ready, and you can't do anything about it. You must have to do the best you can."

"I suppose, dear, that God plans it all," said her mother.

"Well, if you believe that, why do you worry?"

Mrs. Walton was silent a moment and then smiled at her daughter. "I shouldn't, should I? Well, I don't mean to, but sometimes I forget what a great God we have. Now, dear, shall we get to work? I'm glad for you to know that sweet child, and someday perhaps we'll go and see the mother. I just hope the older sister is as sweet."

A few days later a man entered the store and bought a pound of cheese and a box of crackers. Chris waited on him and couldn't help but notice a long scar across one cheek. He noticed also that he walked slowly about the store, stared at the cash window, and hurried up to it when Natalie was free. Then the man pushed his check and the money in, made some remark, and laughed in a coarse manner.

Chris heard the coarse laughter and could feel his anger rising. But he had to turn to his next customer, a lady who wanted to inspect every orange he put in the bag for her. When he glanced up again the man was sauntering out the door, with an ugly look back at Natalie. She had shrunk behind her window with a troubled expression on her face.

Chris wondered what was familiar about the droop of the man's shoulders as he left, and not until later in the day did he remember the man on the street corner and compare the two. Had that man returned and hunted up Natalie to annoy her? He felt some anxiety the rest of the afternoon. But it was a busy day, and Chris couldn't stop to think much.

The manager let most of the men leave early that night. Chris was in the cellar piling up boxes that had been thrown downstairs in a hurry that afternoon. He didn't like his orderly basement to be in a mess for the next morning.

"Walton," Mr. Foster called downstairs, "they're all gone but Miss Halsey, and I think she's almost through. She has three cents too much in her balance sheet and is trying to find out her mistake, but I think it won't take her long. Would you two mind closing up the store tonight? I promised my wife I'd meet her and take her out tonight."

"Sure, Mr. Foster! I'll be glad to!" Chris called back, proud that he was trusted to close up. The manager didn't usually let anyone else do that.

He heard the manager say good night to Natalie and go out the door. He put the last box in place and, picking up some scattered excelsior, snapped out the light and walked upstairs.

He was wearing old shoes with soft, pliable soles that made no sound. He enjoyed the thought of glimpsing Natalie before she saw him. Her pleasant countenance always filled him with wonder—that such a lovely, unspoiled girl existed.

Then he stepped into the store and came within sight of Natalie's glass den. There before him stood a tall man wearing a black mask over his face, pointing a revolver at Natalie!

Chapter 14

For an instant Chris stood paralyzed with horror. He knew instinctively that Natalie wouldn't throw up her hands and hand over her cash register. She wouldn't think of herself and would fight to the last hope.

And there was no hope. He could see the man didn't care what he did or whom he hurt. It seemed incredible that this would happen, at half past six in the evening on a street that an hour earlier would have been crowded with passersby, in a store that five short minutes before would have been protected by a large force of men. Every one of them gone, and he was the only one left! Doubtless the bandit, or bandits, knew that—there were probably at least two. They must have thought he was gone, too. He'd been in the cellar for some time, and the store would seem empty to someone peering in from the street. He mustn't let them know he was there until he could do something to protect Natalie and the cash in the register and the safe. He knew a larger amount of money than usual was in the safe, brought in that afternoon after the bank closed.

And now Natalie must open that safe, and quickly, too. Would she? He was afraid she might refuse. Indeed she seemed to be doing so now. She was sitting up straight and pale behind her glass window, her eyes round with fear as she stared at that ugly, menacing gun. But she hadn't raised her hands.

"Put 'em up, girlie, and don't touch that telephone," the man snarled. "Up with 'em an' you march out here. Open that safe in the backroom and quick about it! Up with 'em! I ain't got time to waste. I'll count three, see? An' ef they ain't up when I gets to three, I'll shoot! And when I shoot, I shoot! I don't mind layin' out a pretty one like you. I shoot t' kill! One—!"

The store was so quiet that Chris felt as if his heart had stopped. He had to do something before it was too late. Could he get out and call for help? He had no weapon. He couldn't hope to handle a man with a gun single-handed.

"Two!"

The word landed like a bullet deep into Chris's heart. Natalie hadn't stirred or even lifted her hands. Her mouth was set firmly, and she was white as death.

He glanced around and saw beside him a large basket of hard green apples. He recalled his boyhood years when he practiced pitching baseballs. Could he hit that gun and knock it out of the man's hand? And if he did would it go off and kill Natalie? But even before that memory an earlier practice came to his lips, learned at his mother's knee in babyhood: "Oh, God, help me save her!"

Silently he seized an apple, crouched, and swung his arm.

"Oh, God!" Suddenly he knew he believed there was a God.

The hard green missile whizzed through the air like a bullet. Chris heard a crash and an explosion, but he couldn't stop to see what happened. Another apple whizzed by and struck the man on the temple. He had started for the door, but it dazed him, and he looked back. Just then Chris hurled another apple full in his nose, with another in his eyes.

"Oh, God! Oh, God! Help me!" prayed Chris in his heart, aiming another apple at the enemy.

Suddenly the man crumpled to the floor. Could only apples knock a man out? He plunged across the room and was upon him with a wrestling hold he'd learned in high school. The man struggled and kicked him, then struck a blinding blow across Chris's eyes. The room seemed to spin, with bright stars shooting about, but still he kept hold of the man's throat.

Where was Natalie? He couldn't see her. What voice did he hear? And how did all these people get into the store?

He opened one eye and saw brass buttons leaning down to him. Of course! Police headquarters was just down the street, but why did they come? They must have heard the gun go off. Oh! Was Natalie killed?

Someone loosened his hold on the man's throat and, helping him to his feet, wiped the blood from his nose and patted him on the shoulder.

"Good work, boy!" the man said.

Chris could hear handcuffs click as the police pulled the struggling man up from the floor.

"Where is she?" Chris cried.

"Where's who? What? You mean the one who telephoned us? Why, who was she?"

"Natalie! The cashier!"

They jerked the door of the glass den open, and there lay Natalie on the floor, with the telephone across her hand and her mouth beside the instrument. But the girl didn't move.

Chris was down on his knees at once, picking her up as if she were a baby and bringing her out into the store.

"He must have shot her after all!" he groaned.

"No such thing!" said a man in the crowd, coming closer. "She's just fainted. I saw the gun fall and go off in the corner. I was comin' by the store an' saw that first apple come flyin' an' hit that guy just as pretty! Man, that was some pitchin'! I couldn't make out what was goin' on. At first I thought the men here was kiddin' each other with the manager gone. I thought they was wastin' good apples an' ought t' be reported, till I heard that gun go off in the corner by the door, almost next t' me. An' then right away I heard the p'lice whistle, and they come flyin' down the street. I knew somethin' was doin'. But, say! How'd you get ont' it?"

"Call came over the wire: 'Chain store holdup!' That was all," said the police chief. "A woman's voice—guess she did it." He nodded toward Natalie. "Boys, get some water! Bring her to. She's some brave little girl!"

Chris had laid her gently on the floor and now put water to her lips, took a clean handkerchief from his pocket, and bathed her face. Presently she opened her eyes and stared in amazement at the crowd.

"Oh, are you all right, Chris?" she murmured.

"Sure!" said Chris, drawing a breath of relief. "Don't talk now. Wait. I'm heating you up some coffee. Some was left over from what the men had at noon. No, don't get up till I bring it."

More people were gathering now. A woman from the apartment over the drugstore across the street said she was sitting at the window watching for her husband's train to come in and saw the whole thing. She said the store was light enough for her to see the apples come flying across the room, maybe even a bushel of them.

A small boy who scarcely ever missed a thrill like that testified he heard the gun go off and arrived while the apples were flying. He said he saw the tall man get hit in the nose and go down.

The confusion quieted down after a few minutes. Chris brought Natalie coffee and made her drink it. When she could sit up they sent for a taxi, though she wanted to put her cash register in the safe first.

Chris took her home but insisted he was coming right back. "I was put in charge. I'll come back and stay here till I can get Mr. Foster on the telephone. He probably won't be back at his house till late this evening, but I'd feel better staying here till I get word from him."

He was holding his handkerchief to his bruised cheek now, but he was happy, looking across at Natalie who had her hat and coat on.

"I should stay, too," she protested. "Mr. Foster left me here, too, and told me what to do about the money."

"No, Miss Halsey. You need some rest after that bout. You're some brave lady, but it ain't fer a woman to go through them things and try t' sit up on a hard stool all evenin' till yer boss comes. You go home an' get some rest, or you won't be on hand t'morro'. An' you'll be needed then, see?" said the young policeman who had ordered the taxi.

"Yes, you two did good work," said another policeman, coming up. "We been watchin' that guy about three weeks. He's been hangin' round suspicious-like, but we couldn't get ennythin' on 'm, an' now we caught 'm in the act, with plenty o' witnesses. 'Course I ain't sure, but he looks t' me like one o' them guys that's got 'is mug in the rogues' gallery. If it's so, you two did better'n you expected. Don't worry, lady. We'll stick around an' guard this store real careful tonight. You rest till tomorrow."

So Chris put Natalie carefully into the taxi, as if she were a priceless treasure, and climbed in after her.

Chapter 15

For an instant they looked at one another in the darkness, then his hand sought hers and clasped it.

"Oh, you were wonderful!" said Natalie softly, leaving her hand in his. "I was conscious long enough to see the first two apples hit the mark, and then I felt myself going down and had enough sense to grab the telephone and take it with me."

"Thank God you're safe!" said Chris. "I was so worried when I came up from the cellar! I prayed, Natalie, and I'll never doubt Him again! The whole time I was firing apples at that creep I was asking God to help me!"

"Oh, Chris!" said Natalie, putting her other hand over their clasped ones, never realizing what she was doing. "That's the best thing of all. I've prayed so much that you'd believe!"

"You prayed for me, Natalie?" he asked wonderingly.

"Oh, yes, I've been praying for you ever since the day you talked about getting a raw deal. I'm so glad you believe Him. Why, I'd have been willing to go through much more terrible things for you to see that. It's been the deepest desire of my heart."

"Natalie, darling—!" Chris reached over and drew her close, wrapping his arms about her reverently. "You're wonderful! I love you. I thank God for saving you from that man's gun. Oh, Natalie, I thought he'd killed you!"

He pulled her face close to his, and she could feel the tears on his cheek. She caressed his wet eyelids softly with her fingers, and then Chris lifted his head and put his lips on hers. Such a thrill of joy passed through him as he had never known on earth. Was love like this?

Suddenly he sat up straight, his arms still about her, and spoke eagerly. "Natalie, dear—I suppose I have no business talking about love—in my position. A clerk in a chain store on a starvation salary, with family responsibilities and a burden of debt to help out with. But, oh, if you'll just say you think you might sometime in the future care for me, I'll work hard and get somewhere as soon as possible so I can discharge the responsibility and take care of you, too. Do you think you could ever care?"

He held her away and searched her face anxiously, as the taxi whirled around the corner onto Cromar Street.

"Oh!" said Natalie, catching her breath. "I care now—with all my heart! It may sound awful, but I think I've cared ever since you were a boy in school and I would listen to you recite!"

Then she hid her confusion against his coat, and they clung together.

The taxi stopping in front of Natalie's home at last brought them back to reality.

Chris helped her out, and they made quite a promenade of the walk from the street to the porch, twelve feet by actual measurement.

"But I've got a family, too, and responsibilities," said Natalie suddenly. "I couldn't—"

"Well, of course we couldn't now," said Chris, slipping his arm about her and holding her close to his side. "But with God's help we'll get where we can. I'll get to the place where I can take care of my responsibilities and yours, too, and then you won't have to work in a store any longer. A store—our store—is all right, of course," he added loyally, "but it isn't the place for the woman I love. I want you taken care of, my darling! And now you should go right in and get to bed. You're trembling. Shall I go in and tell your mother what's happened?"

"No," said Natalie, "not tonight. She doesn't need to know about that man— at all, maybe. She doesn't go out much. She wouldn't be likely to hear it. If she knew, she'd be frightened every time I went to the store. And—about us—well, perhaps we'd better wait a little for that. She likes you a lot, but—it might seem sudden to her. We'll wait and talk it over a few days first, shall we?"

"I'd like that," said Chris. "It's like having our own secret a few minutes longer. But I mean for everyone to know it the first minute I'm in a position to take care of you. And I think we should tell your mother very soon."

Then suddenly he stooped and kissed her softly again.

"I'm only a poor girl, you know," she said. "I've been in another class from yours almost all my life."

"Thank God for that!" said Chris. "If you hadn't been you might not love me now. Oh, darling, I'm the happiest person alive! And to think God had this in store for me. Why, Natalie, I'm glad of every hard thing that's happened to me. It brought me this beautiful love out of the darkness. If I'd gone back to college this last year I might never have known you, except as a quiet little girl in my high school class! And I was so angry I had to give up college. What's college beside a love like this?"

They might have talked all night if Janice hadn't walked with brisk steps down the narrow hall inside and flung the door open.

"What are you two doing out there in the cold?" she asked. "Nice night for a tête-à-tête, isn't it? There's a northeaster blowing forty knots an hour, and you two aren't even aware of it. There'll be snow before morning, and Natalie took the old ratty fur off the neck of her coat this morning, too. Come on in where it's warm. If you two want to talk secrets, Mother and I will stay in the kitchen, and you can have the front room."

Chris and Natalie looked up, the color spreading over their cheeks.

"Thank you! I'm just going," said Chris. "I have to get back to the store for a while. I brought Natalie home. She was—a little tired. At least—she should be! She's—worked hard today."

"I heard a car stopping out here at the door a few minutes ago. What was it?" asked Janice, looking curiously from one to the other.

"Oh, that was a taxi," said Chris. "You see, I thought your sister was pretty tired, and there was a taxi—and so—"

"Are you sick, Natalie?" asked Janice anxiously, lowering her voice so it wouldn't reach the kitchen.

"Not at all," said Natalie. "It was just an idea. I'll tell you about it, Jan, when we get up to bed. It was—nothing."

"Is she sick?" asked Janice, looking straight at Chris.

"No, not a bit," said Chris, smiling and facing her clear eyes. "I think she's had a hard day and should get to bed soon. That's honest, little sister—so don't worry. I must go at once."

Janice smiled. "All right, big brother. I'll see that she gets to bed at once. Any tonic or anything needed?"

"No, just a glass of milk and something hot to eat, and—I wouldn't worry Mother if I were you. She'll be all right."

He smiled a wonderful radiance at Natalie, and Janice lost none of the radiance as she watched him.

"I still have my senses," said Janice caustically.

Chris took a reluctant leave, and Janice swung the door shut.

"He's getting very chummy! 'Little sister' and 'Mother,' indeed! Sounds almost like one of the family." She smiled at Natalie. "Come on in and eat supper. We thought you were never coming. We're only having creamed codfish—but it's delicious, if I do say so—and we have plenty of fluffy boiled potatoes to eat with it and cranberry sauce for dessert. Mother made that, so you know it's all right. And Mother's interest money has come, and it's five whole dollars more than it was last time. So there!"

Janice was cheerful, but she glanced at her sister and decided she must go to bed early.

Chris returned to the store so joyful he scarcely knew what he was about. He found himself a hero in the eyes of the policemen, who hung around the store and talked the attempted burglary over so many times it seemed like a great bank robbery by the time they were finished.

About half past eleven the telephone rang. Foster had arrived home and found the police chief's message that something had happened at the store. His breath was coming in short gasps as he asked questions.

The chief was still there and took the call. The story had lost none of its spice in its retelling, and Foster got a vivid description of the whole attempted robbery with full details and plenty of credit for Natalie and Chris.

Then the manager spoke to Chris and was thankful almost to tears for what Chris had done. If the robbery had succeeded when he left the store in someone else's care, he'd be blamed for it and would probably lose his management position. And that would mean losing all he'd gained in five hard years of work in the store, from clerk on up. He said he was coming right up even though it was late. He wanted to take Chris by the hand. He wanted to be on the spot and hear the whole account again. No, he couldn't wait till morning; he was coming right away. Would Chris wait? It wouldn't take him long to get there in his car.

They had quite a session in the store at midnight. All the police force that could be spared for a few minutes from preventing other illegal incidents were assembled. In fact they'd spent most of the evening hovering about and trying to make a hero out of Chris. By the time Foster arrived, Chris was almost bored with it.

"I didn't do anything much," he said. "I couldn't do anything else! It was"— he was going to say "luck," but he hesitated and finished with—"a miracle I hit that gun and that it didn't go off in Miss Halsey's face instead of on the floor. I was terrified as soon as I'd done it in case that had happened. I should have sent out a big alarm and scared the fellow away! But, well, I couldn't see letting him get away and try it on us again."

So they praised him and slapped him on the back and rallied around him till far after midnight.

Early in the evening he'd telephoned home that he was detained at the store. But his mother hadn't been able to sleep till he came.

She called to him softly as he came up the stairs: "You all right, Chris?"

"Sure, Mother!" he said, pushing open the door and stepping in to kiss her. Then he slipped out again without a word about what had kept him.

When Chris got to his own room, he was so excited he didn't think he'd ever sleep. After months of sadness, doubt and darkness, hard work and bitterness, here was so much joy at once he couldn't take it all in.

But above Foster's kind words, the policemen's praise, and the knowledge that he'd saved the store from loss, in his heart rang the sweetness that Natalie loved him and a deep thanksgiving to God for letting him save her life.

And she loves me! he sang in his heart. *I know everybody would think I was a fool and a cad to tell a girl I loved her when I haven't a cent to offer her. But with God's help I will have, and she understands. We'll keep our own counsel and talk to God about it, and I'm sure the time won't be long when I can have the privilege of taking care of my dear girl.*

Then for the first time in several years he knelt beside his bed and prayed, thanking God for the way He'd led him and even for the sorrow He'd allowed, which had brought such joy into his life.

After that he lay down but couldn't sleep for thinking how sweet Natalie had looked when she told him how she'd cared for him even when they were in high school. And he thrilled to the memory of her soft lips. Oh, Natalie was wonderful! And she would be his someday! Life had suddenly taken on glory— even hard work was glorious!

Chapter 16

The family read about it the next morning in the paper as they sat at breakfast, just before Elise left for school and after Chris had swallowed a bite or two and rushed away. He hadn't waited for the rest to come down. He said he had to be at the store early.

The other workers met him with marked deference and respect, going out of their way to be nice to him. It made him feel like laughing. He was a hero—for throwing a few green apples at a man's head instead of aiming a baseball at a mark. He laughed to himself as he set out the fresh vegetables. What a little thing it took to make a hero, and why had he ever cared so much about it?

About ten o'clock the district manager arrived, and then the hero business began again. The district manager had some stately words to say about the company's indebtedness to him. It was quite public, for customers would pick out heads of lettuce and oranges, pausing and looking at Chris, and ask to hear the story again from the quiet salesman who wished he'd been in Chris's boots last night. Of course, none of them had the reputation as pitcher that Chris had enjoyed in school, and each knew he wouldn't have done half as well in nabbing the burglar and saving the cashier's life.

Then the district manager and Foster called Chris and Natalie into the backroom and shut the door. The district manager told Natalie the company was quite pleased with her service in saving the company's money and having presence of mind. They were increasing her salary and giving her a platinum wristwatch with a suitable engraving to commemorate the event. He then turned to Chris and told him the company had been watching him with interest since he'd started working there. They'd already decided to promote him with a salary increase in the near future, but last night's good work had prompted them to promote him at once. The assistant manager was moving to the coast, and the company had decided to put Chris in his place. They wanted him to learn as much as possible from Mr. Foster with a view toward taking a management position himself someday. And of course the salary increase would be substantial.

Chris was overwhelmed. He tried to thank the two men, but the words kept getting stuck in his throat. Then he and Natalie stood quietly with their eyes full of gratitude. Chris's heart was swelling with pride.

That noon he took Natalie over to the tearoom for lunch to celebrate. It was their first real chance to talk it over alone, for last night they were too engrossed with each other. But they could only sit and exclaim and beam at one another.

"You were wonderful!" said Natalie, her eyes filling with tears in spite of her effort to keep them back. "You saved my life! He was going to shoot! I could see it in his face."

Chris looked at her with something in his eyes that brought the color to her cheeks. And after a moment he said, "God was good, Natalie! And I'm so glad now that I didn't get to college and was put here to help save you. I suppose someone else would have saved you, if I hadn't been here, but I'm glad I got to. And come to think of it, Natalie, if the bank hadn't closed and Dad hadn't lost his money, I might never have known you."

They didn't eat much in that half hour, but they returned to their duties radiant.

That night Chris's family met him with praise and excitement.

"So, son," said his father, standing up and walking to his side where he took hold of his hand, "you've made a hero of yourself. Got your picture in the paper and everybody calling up to tell me how fine you are."

"Picture in the paper!" said Chris. "How did they do that?"

"Oh, they raked up that old football snapshot, the one of you in your torn sweater and mud on your face, the one the girls in school used to carry around in their schoolbooks," said his sister with dancing eyes. "Some brother I've got. Look! It's in the evening paper!"

"Oh, say!" said Chris. "What a fuss about throwing a few apples!"

"That's not all!" said Mr. Walton. "Mr. McLaughlin called this morning and offered to take you into the Title and Trust Company and train you to become a banker. Title and Trust is a sound old company. How about it, son? Want to be a banker?"

"Nothing doing, Dad. They wouldn't have me when I needed it, and now I'm in line for management of the chain store someday. I wouldn't give it up for any old job in a bank. I'd be years getting a pittance, and then some. Then there's another thing—a grocery is a good solid business. You can't have a run on a grocery. People have to eat. I'm sticking by the chain store. It's a great institution. Someday maybe I'll be the head of the whole company."

"But, Chris dear, a banker is always so respected. Your father—"

"I know, Mother. It's a respectable business, but so is the grocery business. Besides, one banker is enough in the family at a time. And, Mother, I didn't notice that respect saving our home when we got in a tight place. Dad was one in a thousand, of course, and everybody understood that and trusted him. But I didn't see it getting him by any better than if he'd been a grocer. I'm putting in my lot with the chain store if you don't object."

"Of course not, son," his father said quickly. "Not if you've thought it over carefully and decided that way. I'm proud to have a son like you, and the grocery business is good and honorable and as much needed as a bank."

"Another thing, Mother, I—we—that is, I've about decided I want to prepare to do some real Christian work, and that takes money."

They stared at Chris in wonder, the color deepening on his face as he looked down at his plate.

"You see, we—that is, I've come to see things in a different way lately. I used to think what you believed was mostly bunk. Oh, I know I went to church and all, but I didn't think it was fair when you and Dad believed so firmly in God and yet lost all you had. But now I see it differently, and I want to study the Bible and prepare to be of some use in the church and among people. I don't know how to tell you—" He searched about for words, aware of his sister's bright eyes on him.

"You see, we—that is, well, there's a girl I'd like you to invite to dinner or something!" he blurted out at last.

"Chris!" cried his mother. "You're not trying to tell us you want to get married. Not yet!"

Chris laughed. "What do you think I am, Mother—crazy? Of course not. She's just a wonderful girl, and I want you to know her."

"And you aren't engaged, either?" she asked, a sharp tone of anxiety in her voice.

"Not exactly engaged, Mother. What do I have to get engaged on? I've got a family to look out for, and she has, too. We have to work hard, both of us for a while yet. But we like each other a lot, Mother, and I want you to know her."

"Is she the girl whose life you saved, Chris?"

Chris looked his mother in the eye, his color rising a bit. "Yes, Mother, if you call it that, though I'm not so sure she didn't save mine instead, calling up the police just in time."

She studied his face again. Then she smiled brightly. "I'll go see her tomorrow, Chris."

"Thanks, Mother—a lot. You'll like her. She's wonderful, and she's your kind!" He stooped and kissed her tenderly.

"Well, I hope for your sake she is," she said with a sigh.

Chris sat down in his chair again. "There's another thing. You might as well hear the whole story at once."

They looked startled, but he didn't give them time to worry.

"It's this. I've got to the place where I can say I'm glad, from my own standpoint, that all this trouble happened to us. I can see that going back to college isn't always the best a person can begin life with, and that whatever God permits is always best. It's Natalie's doings. She's a wonderful Christian, and she's helped me see it, too. She's had a lot of hard things in her life and says she's glad for them; they've helped her know God better and not be as selfish. And—well—she's got me thinking that, too. And now I know I'm saved, and I want God to have His way in my life. And—we're going to study the Bible at a class that's been started down at the Water Street Mission. I just thought I'd like you to know the whole thing."

His father was standing beside him now, with shining eyes, and his mother came over and laid her lips tenderly on his hair.

"That's the best news you've ever given me, son," Mr. Walton said, a pleased look on his face. "It's better than health or wealth or anything else in life—to know you belong to Christ and are learning to follow His will. I've believed God was working out His best when He allowed us to experience sorrow and humiliation and poverty, but I didn't see why. Nor did I expect to until I went Home. But He's let me see now—bless His holy name! And we'll love the little girl, too, for helping."

"Yes, dear!" agreed the mother.

"Well, then, that's all right!" exclaimed Chris. "I should have known you'd take it like this, but I hated to tell you. I wasn't sure you'd understand."

"It's a wonderful thing to understand," his father said, "for I'd rather have you know the Lord than be the richest banker who ever lived."

So presently Chris hugged them, pinched his sister's cheek to make her look less solemn, and hurried away to the next street to call on Natalie.

But he called on Natalie's mother first. He found her sitting in the front room finishing a bit of sewing while the girls washed the supper dishes. He went over and took her work gently out of her hands and laid it on the table as she looked wonderingly at him, almost a premonition in her eyes.

"Now, Mother Halsey," he said as tenderly as he'd have spoken to his own mother, "I've come to confess to you. I don't know what you'll say to me, and I'm sorry if you don't like it, but it's done, and you should know about it. You see, last night I told Natalie I loved her. I didn't mean to do it so soon—not till I had a settled position and plenty of money to take care of her as she should be cared for. But—well—I—told her, and I found out she cares, too, and I thought you should know it. I don't want to do anything underhanded. Do you mind very much, Mother Halsey?"

Natalie's mother looked at the earnest young man waiting eagerly for her answer, her lip trembling and tears filling her eyes. But she said with a warm smile, "You dear boy!" Then she put up her two hands and, drawing him toward her, kissed him on each cheek.

Then she brushed away the tears with her handkerchief and smiled again.

"I should be very glad and proud," she said. "I am. Of course it's a little sudden, and you're both young, and I was afraid of a rich young man at first. I didn't know how dear you were—"

"But I'm not rich, Mother Halsey," Chris laughed joyously. "I'm as poor as a church mouse. That's what makes it so bad for me to have told Natalie how I feel when I can't do a thing about it yet. But if you'll trust me I'll work hard and try to get to a place where I can give her the kind of home she should have."

"Oh, I meant you were accustomed to riches. I was afraid you'd be spoiled. But you're not! You're all and more than I could possibly desire in a man for my dear girl. And I'm proud of you besides. Oh, I've read the paper. You and Natalie thought you'd kept last night's events from me, and Janice helped, too. But the boy who came to fix the gas stove told me and showed me a paper. He knew who Natalie was and who you were, and I know all about it, and I'm proud of you both. Of course I didn't expect this—not so soon anyway. But I guess you had a right—and I can understand."

"You're a peach, little new mother," said Chris, "and I hope I won't disappoint you. The only thing is that I wish I could get Natalie out of that store right away, though of course I'd miss seeing her. But I'd like to relieve her and all of you at once of all care and work."

"Well, that's dear of you. But of course Natalie must go on working, and you mustn't expect to have all you want right away. It won't hurt either of you to work and win your way ahead, and I'm glad Natalie has joy in her life. She's never had much chance to have a good time—"

"Now, Mother!" protested Natalie from the kitchen doorway. "I've always had a happy life."

"Yes, you've been a good girl and said so," said the mother, smiling ruefully.

"No, but, Mother, I have!" insisted Natalie. "I've been happy in my home and family. I've had you and Father and my wonderful sister."

"Yes, she would add that," said Janice, joining them as she wafted a dish towel over the dinner plates. "She's some sister, I tell you, big brother!"

"You said it!" added Chris. "I'm so happy I could shout!"

"But," warned the mother, "you may have a long road ahead full of disappointment and waiting, you know."

"We know," said Natalie, smiling, "and we don't care. We have each other now, and those other things won't matter so much."

"And it's not going to be so frightfully long, either, Mother Halsey, if I can make it short by hard work, see? And I guess it makes some difference, too, that we both belong to God now," he added quietly.

"It certainly does," said the mother with shining eyes. "It makes all the difference in the world to me. I couldn't have given my child to a man who didn't know the Lord, rich or poor. Natalie told me about that last night, and I was glad. I couldn't help seeing how things might be going and would have been troubled for my girl to be with you much longer if you didn't belong to the royal family."

He flashed her a bright smile as she slipped out of the room, leaving him with Natalie.

"Oh, I'm glad I belong!" he said as Natalie sat down beside him on the couch. He took her hand reverently and bent over to lay his lips on it.

But out in the kitchen Janice was complaining. "I don't see why they need to have the door shut. We're entirely in sympathy with them. Aren't they going to be chummy anymore? I surely wouldn't begin that way."

"Well, dear, suppose you let them talk things over first. We'll make some fudge, and the smell of it will call them out soon. Natalie brought home fresh chocolate tonight. Suppose you start it while I finish this seam, and then I'll help stir it."

Soon the fragrance of cooking chocolate slipped under the crack of the front room door and brought the two back to reality from the earthly heaven they'd been planning for the future. They came out then with shining eyes and helped beat the fudge.

After Chris was gone that night, Janice turned back with a sigh. "Well, I guess it'll be nice after all, having a brother-in-law. He seems to fit in anywhere, and, besides, my arm always aches stirring fudge!"

Chapter 17

It was a bright day the following spring when Chris brought his father down to the bank in an old secondhand Ford he'd bought for a song. The Fidelity Bank and Trust Company had opened its doors again to the public and was rewarded by a long line of depositors waiting to put back into the bank the money they had recently received from it.

The bank had paid back every cent of its indebtedness and was on its feet again for business with a clean record.

It was nothing short of a miracle that had made this possible, and the one used to work this miracle was Christopher Walton senior, the honored president. For he was unanimously elected president again, even against his protest. The bank felt it couldn't do without his influence and good judgment. They recognized it was mainly through his wisdom and efforts that the bank's affairs were reconstructed.

Two things had conspired to make possible this miracle of the business world. Three men, warm friends of Mr. Walton's who were in Europe when the bank's doors closed, had returned and come to the bank's aid with a large sum of money. This, plus the fact that Mr. Walton was able to turn over at a good figure a huge block of real estate in which much of the bank's assets had been tied up, had restored the people's confidence, and the bank was in a fair way to be stronger than ever.

Mr. Walton's personal fortune was gone, but he had his friends and his business and his neighbors' confidence again.

"And someday," said Chris junior, as they talked it over one night, "you might even be able to buy back our home—that is, when I get to be owner of the chain stores." His eyes twinkled. "I love that place, and so does Natalie. I'd like to have it back and see you and Mother in it again. I heard the other day that the chump who bought it is getting restless again and seeking fairer pastures. He says the people in this town are high-hats, and he thinks he'll go to Europe and buy an old palace somewhere in Italy. When he does I mean to see if we can buy it back—that is, if it's all right with God," he added softly. "What He wants goes with me from now on."

Mr. Foster had been transferred to managing the district, and Chris was now manager of the store. He was as pleased as if he'd been made president of the United States, perhaps even more, for he had developed a genuine love for his store and the goods he handled. His efficiency had been commended more than once by headquarters.

"Dad, I've been thinking," he said after a minute. "The house next to us here is on the market at a very low price, and I'm talking with the agent about financing it. He thinks it can be done at a price I could probably carry. What would you think about it? It's a double house, you know, and has possibilities.

We could fix it up, and if Natalie and I found it possible to get married soon, we could take this side and let Natalie's mother and Jan have the other side, and then we families would all be together. At least that would do for the present till we could get back the old home."

"I think it would be lovely!" said Mrs. Walton, her eyes shining. "That won't be like losing you. Oh, Chris, you're a dear boy!"

"Well, Mother, that was Natalie's suggestion. She loves you, and her mother does, too."

"And I love them both and Janice, too," the mother added, "and so do your father and Elise. I think we'll be content, whether we get the old house back or not. I might be just as satisfied to stay here. It's cozy, and we're happy together."

That was the beginning of the talk, but things moved rapidly on, and it wasn't long before the house next door was getting a new coat of paint outside and in. Natalie was shopping for some pretty bargain curtains, and evenings were exciting times when everybody had to come over to the new house and see the latest thing that had been done to it.

One day Betty Zane's young sister asked Elise, "Say, is it true your brother's going to marry that Halsey girl?"

"Yes," said Elise coldly, "it is." Her tone didn't invite further comment, but her smile showed she was entirely satisfied with his choice.

"Mercy," said Betty, "did she work in a store? I'd think you would feel terrible about it."

"Yes, she worked in a store," said Elise, "and so does my brother, but we're delighted about it. We love her dearly and are glad he's marrying her. She's choice. Good-bye! I'm going this way today." And Elise swept around the corner a bit haughtily.

But some weeks later Betty Zane and Anna Peters were walking down the street together.

"Did you know," began Betty, "that Chris Walton and Natalie Halsey are being married this evening? The wedding's in the church, and only a few intimate friends are invited. But they say the owner of the chain stores is coming and has given Natalie a whole silver service. Aren't things strange? Chris Walton working in a grocery store and then getting to be manager. But I can't understand his marrying that poor Halsey girl."

"I heard she came from a fine old family," said Anna.

"Well, what's that when you don't have a rag to wear on your back? I wonder what on earth she'll get married in? Probably something old or made over."

"Well, yes, it's old, and it'll be made over a little," said Anna. "Our dressmaker is doing it. But she says it's gorgeous. It's her mother's wedding dress, ivory satin, and a thread lace veil that must have cost a fabulous price. Natalie's almost her mother's size. The dress hardly has to be changed at all, just taken in a little on the shoulders. But, say! She might have invited us, don't you think? Her old schoolmates! They say she has some gorgeous presents from the people in the stores. I'd like to see them. I think it was mean of her not to ask us."

"Well," Betty said, "I don't see why she should. We never acted as if she existed when she was in school. But I suppose now that Mr. Walton is back in the bank and everything's going well we'll have to take her up."

"I don't see why," said Anna. "They're still going to live down on that Sullivan Street. Isn't it strange, when they don't have to anymore? I don't see why they'd expect us to call on them."

"Well, if you ask me," chimed in Betty's younger sister, tagging along behind them, "I don't believe they know or care what you do. They live in a world of their own and like it. I've been talking with Janice Halsey lately, and she says they all go down to that Water Street Mission and study the Bible. I think they're all odd."

"Yes," said Anna, sighing, "I guess that's it. They're peculiar people. They don't seem to mind in the least that they lost all their money and had to live in that unfashionable district. And imagine staying there when they don't have to! I met Chris the other day, and he was whistling away and smiled at me like a ray of sunshine, though I know he can't bear me. They seem happier than they were when they were rich. And those Halseys do, too."

"I know," said Betty. "I don't understand it. They're happy without things, and I've got a lot, and sometimes I'm bored. Yet they go around looking as if they'd just inherited a fortune and belonged to some royal family."

Five blocks away, at that moment, Chris was placing a delicate wedding ring on Natalie's finger.

"I've been thinking, dear," he said softly, "how good God has been to us, to take me out of the life I thought was so wonderful and put me where I might know you. Oh, my darling!"

The Unknown God

Chapter 1

The night was cold and dark. A fine mist was falling, and freezing as it fell, covering everything with a glare of ice. The streetlamps made vain attempts to light up their corner of the dark world, only succeeding in throwing a feeble flicker here and there on the treacherous pavements, revealing occasional glazed patches of dirty snow in sheltered corners. Even the electric lights which flung their brightness into the night here and there could not give a cheerful air to the city. The streetcar drivers, muffled from head to foot, stood solemnly at their posts, as though performing the world's funeral service. Their gaunt beasts, without enough spirit left to shiver back at the chilling atmosphere enfolding their heavy bodies, strained at their heavy load and slipped on the icy stones. All gave one more touch of dreariness to the scene.

It was not a night when someone would have chosen to take a walk for pleasure. Yet one young man was out with the intention of getting some amusement if possible. He was a stranger in the city, having drifted there that very day and for want of money had engaged himself to work in the first position he could find, which happened to be in the shop of a tobacconist. The work was not altogether to his liking. He was capable of better things. But better things did not present themselves, and he needed money, so he tried to make the best of this.

But it was a poor best he could make out of it so far. He had to go to a boardinghouse, and the cheapest he could find was very cheap in comforts as well as name. He was obliged to take a room with another young man, which he didn't like. The room looked dirty, too, and this newcomer was used to a clean room.

His mother had been his former landlady; and though she was weary and overworked, still she had contrived to keep things tolerably clean, even if it was a cheap boardinghouse, with an air of unmistakable forlornness and poverty about it.

Her son had never paid his board then and consequently attended theaters and entertainments as often as he chose. It had never occurred to him to pay board to his mother. He gave her money, now and then, a little, when she was in a tight place and mustered courage to ask for it. But he enjoyed his evenings at the theater, and a young man should have amusement.

Perhaps as a result of his late hours, he had a habit of sleeping late mornings. He was often behind time at the store, which at last brought down upon him the reproaches of his employer. At this he had grown angry, taken his wages, and bought a ticket to the city, and here he was.

He thought of it all now as he walked slowly along the city street. He wasn't exactly sorry yet, though his situation was looking uncomfortable. He hadn't analyzed the matter and therefore didn't realize that his love of amusement was perhaps at the bottom of the whole trouble. Indeed, he was on his way to find amusement now, though he didn't have a cent in his pocket for buying a ticket to anything. He wasn't familiar enough with the city to know in what direction to go. But his instincts told him, and he presently found himself in the region of the large theaters.

An unusually bright flood of light attracted his attention to a large building, and he quickened his steps. Other people were going in the same direction. As he neared the corner, he saw a procession of bobbing umbrellas and people carefully picking their way along the slippery sidewalk. Something very attractive must be going on here, he felt sure. He joined the crowd and pressed nearer the door. Over the heads of the people, he caught a few glimpses of large letters, just a word or two, "Bernhardt" and "La Tosca."

His heart warmed within him. He had seen Sarah Bernhardt before and knew that *La Tosca* was considered one of her best parts.

"Now, Brad Benedict, this is just your luck," he muttered to himself as he stood back on the steps and let the crowd surge by him. "I wish I hadn't paid for that miserable week's board in advance. I might have found someplace where they wouldn't require that."

This young man, Bradley Benedict, as he stood there in the partial darkness scowling at his fate, had anything but an attractive look. Yet, seen in a strong light, his face wasn't a poor one. He had a good forehead, if the rest of his face hadn't been so utterly out of harmony with such a thought. It wasn't a weak face but rather reckless one. A good thought, or sometimes a glance at his mother, had been known to alter his expression, until he had almost a look of goodness and beauty. But he had a quick temper and a headstrong will.

By his side stepped an old gentleman, leaning forward in the light, fumbling with some coins, evidently trying to find one of the right value to pay for an evening paper he had just bought and which a small newsboy was holding impatiently up to him. Three ladies, who seemed to belong to the old gentleman, waited a little apart. Suddenly, with a nervous move, the old gentleman dropped his wallet at the feet of the young man, scattering coins this way and that. Young Benedict possessed much good nature in his makeup, and he instantly stooped to help the old gentleman. But when the wallet was finally righted and the newsboy paid, the old man seemed disturbed and still searched the dark steps eagerly.

"There's an odd bit of coin missing that I picked up in my travels. I wouldn't lose it for a good deal," he said in a troubled tone.

Brad began the search once more and after some minutes rescued the coin from a crack into which it had slipped.

The old gentleman's thanks were profuse, and he seemed to be looking the young man over to see if it would do to offer to pay him for the service performed. But Brad had worn his best clothes when he came off on this expedition to a strange city, and the old man decided it wouldn't do. Suddenly a new thought struck him.

"Do you have a ticket in here, young man?" he asked.

"No," growled Brad, recalling his misfortune once more.

"Well, I've an extra one our party won't use. Take it if you want it. Hope you'll enjoy it. I'm obliged to you for your service."

He pressed the ticket into Brad's hand and was gone. The young man didn't wait long but followed his benefactor up the steps and into the hall, very much pleased with the sudden change in his fortunes.

He presented his ticket and was shown to his seat, which proved to be a good one, but not near the seat of the old gentleman. Of that he was glad. He felt more self-respect here, as if he had paid his own way in. He settled himself and began to look about. The opera house was a fine one, with much of interest to be seen. But his attention was almost immediately directed to the stage. It presented a remarkable appearance to the eyes of this young man who was so accustomed to attending the theater. Seats were built up in semicircular tiers which nearly covered it, and the curtain was raised. What in the world did it mean? While he looked, several hundred people filed in, musicians with their great instruments and ladies in beautiful dresses, and seated themselves.

It certainly was something new under the sun. He wasn't aware that Bernhardt performed with any chorus, but perhaps *La Tosca* introduced new features.

Presently two young women came in, dressed more in the theater style than any of the others, followed by two young men in full evening dress, with another handsome young man a little in the rear. At sight of them the audience broke into applause.

"Who are they?" Benedict ventured to ask the young man at his side.

"The soloists and the leader," replied his neighbor in a tone which made the questioner feel like a greenhorn and resolve to keep, his mouth closed.

Above the hum of talk arose the soft murmur and twang of the different instruments as their owners tightened a string here and there. The scene and the sounds were much like the opening of any performance, with the exception of the well-filled stage. He tried to think that another stage was still beyond this one and that presently the curtain, which represented a road winding off to green hills, with lovely woods on either side, would roll up and disclose it. But he came to the conclusion, after a little study, that this was impossible.

He looked the audience over. It was much like the audience of a high-class opera. The boxes near the stage were filled with people, many of them in full dress and ablaze with diamonds. He had heard that Bernhardt drew the elite. He watched the different people as they came in. Some wore quiet dress; but the large majority of those who took seats in the parquet and dress circle carried their wraps in their hands, or thrown loosely about their shoulders, and wore no hats. As he watched, an old lady with white hair drawn into many wearying puffs and crimps, with a long white opera cloak enveloping her stout figure, rolled by him, followed by her footman with most decorous bearing. A man with a tall crush hat, an eyeglass, and a fur-trimmed overcoat reaching from his hat brim to his toes, followed and made much display in seating himself and arranging his belongings to his satisfaction.

As young Benedict was absorbed in looking at these—to him—odd specimens of humanity and making mental comments on them, a soft, sweet strain suddenly broke upon his ear, so low and tender it could scarcely have been distinguished if the audience hadn't hushed just then to let the beautiful music flow over it. He didn't remember ever watching a fine orchestra before. It was very interesting, and to a certain extent the wonderful sweetness of the music thrilled him.

He glanced angrily at a group of latecomers in the aisle who were waiting for this to be over so they might be seated and were heartless enough to whisper. And it fell sharply on his ear when some irate individual upon whom the door had been closed rapped loudly several times for admittance. He glared at an usher and wondered why such things weren't stopped. The music had certainly found a little entranceway into his soul, although he was looking for something very much to his taste. While this was going on, he wanted to hear it.

He drew a long breath as the music died away. Music had never made him feel so strange before, and he didn't understand it.

There was a moment's pause, during which people rustled into seats, and then a rich, sweet tenor sang clear and distinct the words "Comfort ye my people, saith your God." In all his experience of operas and theaters, Bradley Benedict had never heard one that commenced this way. He wished he knew the idea of this *La Tosca*. Could it be a religious play? No, for he had heard it spoken of in anything but a reverent tone.

Chapter 2

Perhaps sarcasm was behind it all. Maybe the curtain would rise in a moment, and a great chorus would break in above this sweet voice and drown it, and there would be cheers and laughter and something jolly. But this thought grated. He didn't want the sweet voice stopped. Something in these words appealed to him. They were so distinctly spoken he could understand. And yet, though he heard, his mind took in only that first sentence of the solo: "Comfort ye my people, saith your God."

Comfort. He knew what that meant. He dimly remembered how in his little boyhood, when he fell or hurt his finger, his mother would drop everything and gather him up in her arms and say, "Mother will comfort you."

He suddenly felt how utterly desolate he was here in this strange city and that he would like to be a boy again, with his mother to comfort him. To be sure, it was long years since that mother had had time or strength to think of comforting her son. And if she had, she would about as soon have thought of offering comfort to the president of the United States as to him, for she wouldn't have expected it to be received with anything but scorn. But the grown-up boy dimly remembered the comfort and shelter of those arms long ago and had a faint desire to feel them about him once more.

"Comfort my people, saith your God," the song rang on.

Did God care to comfort people? What would be such comfort if a mother's were so good? What was God? It was a new picture to this darkened mind, the picture of a God comforting beloved people, and the outlines were dim because there was too much brightness in it for these eyes so long unused to the light.

"Every valley shall be exalted, and every mountain and hill made low, the crooked straight, and the rough places plain," sang on the same voice, and Brad didn't understand it. He looked for the curtain to rise and explain it all. Instead, the chorus rose and burst forth in one grand prophetic strain: "And the glory of the Lord shall be revealed, and all flesh shall see it together; for the mouth of the Lord hath spoken it."

The singers took up the sentence and shouted it back and forth at one another with a gladness in their voices that made this one listener feel they were speaking of something which brought them pleasure. In some way a little thrill of satisfaction passed through his own heart, so used to respond with emotion to what was put before him in song or act or story. This certainly was a different theater.

A deep bass voice now took up the song in solemn accents: "Thus saith the Lord of hosts. Yet once a little while, and I will shake the heavens and the earth, and the sea and the dry land, and I will shake all nations. . . . The Lord whom ye seek shall suddenly come to his temple, even the messenger of the covenant, whom ye delight in."

Would these people dare to produce all this in scenery and acting? Would they try to have an earthquake and a storm at sea? Would they try to represent the coming of the Lord? This young man was shocked at the thought.

His idea of God had never been definite. He had been to Sunday school when he was a small boy. But the teacher didn't approve of trying to teach much of sacred things to little children, so he had a general idea that he must be good or a great and terrible Being would do something awful to him. When he graduated from this class, the teacher required him to learn a lesson, and he thought it stupid, so he stayed away. His mother, poor thing, hadn't known much of God or at least hadn't tried to teach him. He had heard God's name mostly taken in vain; indeed, he hadn't been altogether careful of how he used it upon occasion. Why should he? It meant little to him. And yet the thought that this terrible song about the Lord's sudden coming was about to be represented, jarred him—frightened him, perhaps.

He looked about on the audience to see if anyone felt as he did, but they all looked calm. One lady was intently studying the scrap of a butterfly bonnet on the head of her neighbor in front; and the eyeglass man had his neck twisted to get a better view, through his opera glasses, of someone in a private box. Brad wondered vaguely how they could be so indifferent. Did people know what this was to be? He'd heard that many people objected to the play *La Tosca,* and perhaps it was as he feared.

But the grand voice went calmly on, speaking the terrible words: "But who may abide the day of his coming; and who shall stand when he appeareth? For he is like a refiner's fire."

Young Benedict heard no more for some time. His heart was stirred wonderfully. This was awful. He wished the old man on the street hadn't dropped his wallet or given him the ticket. He wished he were out in the cold and sleet this very minute. He would get out of this. It was a terrible place; how people stood it he didn't understand. But everything was still; everyone was listening. He didn't want to make a stir and draw all eyes to him. Perhaps when this solo was finished there would be a pause, when he could get out. Meanwhile, he tried to stop his ears from hearing these terrible words. Nevertheless, they sounded all the clearer in his heart, and he began to wonder how he could stand before this God Whom he knew not.

The young man, his neighbor, looked at him curiously as he wriggled in his seat, glancing back toward the door, and a good woman at his other side offered him her fan. But his discomfort grew. He looked down at his boots, trying to forget the hall and all about him, to think of what he would do tomorrow and to lay plans for his future career. The people in the hall seemed to troop silently away for a while, and the seats seemed empty, leaving him alone with the voice. And swiftly the acts of his past life gathered about him in shadowy forms and looked down upon him trembling, as the voice died away in the words "For he is like a refiner's fire."

The contralto had taken up the song, but the change of voice didn't arrest the young man's attention. He seemed under a spell. He heard none of the words of the solo except the closing—so soft and sweet that it fell like a blessing on the hushed roof: "Emmanuel, God with us." It left a tender touch in the air as it died away, and its gladness was almost too deep for utterance in the singer's voice. Yet this must be the God about whom the question had been asked: "Who shall stand when he appeareth?"

To some, then, the thought "God with us" brought nothing but wonderful joy! What a God this was!

The joyful chorus took up the strain: "O thou that tellest good tidings in Zion, get thee up into the high mountain."

Brad looked up. The shadows slunk behind, and the audience was there again. It was impossible not to be lifted up by this burst of joy and melody, though the young man didn't understand in the least what it was all about. There seemed no sense or connection. Yet he dimly perceived the story running through the whole, as one who listens to a tale in an unknown tongue and, understanding not one single sentence, will yet catch at the sense from the speaker's voice or motions or from the lighting of the eyes, so subtle are the ways that spirits have of communicating thoughts to one another.

"Arise, shine, for thy light has come, and the glory of the Lord is risen upon thee." And this listener felt his soul try to rise and be glad with the rest. But the bonds of its ignorance and blindness were so great that it sank back again in despair. He felt the cold, chill shadows creep over the earth and darkness so dense it could be felt hiding every face, as the bass told the story.

Then gradually a corner of this heavy blackness lifted, and a little light crept into the sky as the voice went on: "The people that walked in darkness have seen a great light." And an eager anxiety came in his heart to see that light and stand in the full rays of its brightest glory, even as he had sometimes longed to be the great, rich, successful hero of some play to which he had listened for an evening.

But something was different about this feeling that swayed him. It was so dim and indefinite and faraway, and only part of him seemed to long for this, while the other part of him was angry and irritated at the thought and wished to get away. Why didn't he go? But the chorus was rising again. He would go as soon as they were through; the room was too still now.

Softly as an angel might have sung above a sleeping baby, the music began. The great company of sopranos hushed their sweet notes till they sounded far away in the clouds. Then coming nearer, tenderly, exultantly, as if tears might be in the voices—tears of joy—came the words: "For unto us a child is born."

And the basses took it up in the same faraway tone, as though it floated from an upper world almost: "Unto us a Son is given."

Still a third time the altos sang the strain, and a fourth time the tenors took it up. They were all glad. Was this poor, bound soul of his to have no part in the joy? And what was it all about? A child born! A Son given! Why should they all care about that?

"And the government shall be upon his shoulders; and his name—shall be called"—sang the whole company. And then they paused an instant for the orchestra to catch up and gather strength to bring out the words that followed—wonderful words, like great, polished precious stones of many colors and greatest brilliancy, which shone in the setting of this golden music as if placed there by a master workman.

"Wonderful!"

Bradley Benedict sat up straight, his hands clinched and his breath coming through his tightly closed lips. He had never heard a word spoken or sung like that before.

"Counselor!"

A great wave seemed to sweep over him and roll away, leaving him breathless.

"The mighty God!"

Every syllable seemed to strike a great blow at his heart and go through him, and a fear came stealing over it. But there was something like a benediction in the next: "The everlasting Father!"

Now, in spite of fear, came a longing for his mother again. He didn't remember his father's love.

"The Prince of Peace!" sang the great company, who seemed to have been coming on and on, until now they were here in their full power, and the chorus sat down amid loud applause. The voice of it seemed harsh and out of place to the heart that had just been so stirred by the grandeur of the music. He wished the people had kept still.

And now the orchestra broke away as though the heavenly company had just come down to sing this one song and announce to earth this one great thing and was hastening back to join the praise in heaven.

Very sweet the strains were, and Brad listened as he had never listened to any music in his life before. He didn't know it and was annoyed when a lady behind him sneezed a funny little catlike sneeze just in the midst of it, which set two young girls in front to giggling.

This music seemed to suggest all that had been left out of his life—clear skies, sunny days, and the hushed, sweet peace of green fields far away from city life. He had never known he cared for these things, but now they stood like beautiful, inviting pictures. He could even hear the murmur of the night wind as it whispered among tall branches and softly touched tired grass and sleeping flowers, humming a little in tune with a twinkling brook which wound about not far away. The birds all seemed asleep; he thought he heard one twitter as he stirred. The world, the noisy world, seemed a long way off from this quiet place, where all were waiting for some great thing to happen.

The meadows weren't all alone with the birds. He, Bradley Benedict, the new hand at rolling tobacco, was there. He was awfully conscious of his own presence in that holy place the music was picturing. Others were waiting, too. Indeed, he wasn't sure if the whole world weren't waiting with him to see what would happen.

Now the soprano was singing in simple, clear recitative about the shepherds abiding in the fields, keeping watch over their flocks by night. Brad could see the night sky, with its dotting of stars and the glory that suddenly shone; could see the angel when he came and the shepherds' faces. The story was new to him. Scarce any inkling of it had ever been revealed to him as to many others. His childish idea of that day had been measured by the amount of property he acquired in sticks of candy, sleds, and balls.

When the tender air of "He shall feed his flock like a shepherd" floated through the room, something was so infinitely lovely and loving in this One described that his heart went out in longing. And when the soprano took up the song, with "Come unto him, all ye that labor and are heavy laden, and he will give you rest," tears were almost in his eyes. He could scarcely control himself, and he had a strong conviction that if that One they were singing about stood up there where he could see Him, he would have to go. He wouldn't be strong enough to resist.

The intermission had come. The young leader turned, bowing to the audience, then sank into his chair, throwing back his hair and wiping his forehead with his handkerchief. Brad might leave now. Why didn't he take this opportunity? Others were going out. The stout old lady with the white hair and white cloak was lumbering out, with her dignified footman gravely following, bearing robes and shawls. She looked bored. The young man had lost his desire to get out. But half mechanically he reached down for his hat, until a remark of a pretty girl nearby attracted his attention to the leader.

"He looks awfully tired, doesn't he? My! He must be smart to have drilled them so well."

"Yes, and he's so smooth," murmured her companion. "But it's a dreadfully long program, I think. He should leave out some."

Brad's eyes went to the leader, who looked not much older than he. The face was noble, pure, and intellectual. He could only admire it. What was this young man?

Why did he give such a strange performance? Brad had long ago made up his mind that Sarah Bernhardt would not appear this evening. He had made some mistake. But to what had he come? Did this young man feel and believe all the singing he had been leading? Or was it mere poetry?

No, Brad decided it was something higher than mere sentiment. He made up his mind that the young man felt the joy of belonging to that everlasting Father. If he didn't, how could he have made those people sing it with such triumphant voices, as if they were the angels themselves come down to tell the story?

But the intermission was over, and he hadn't gone yet, although his hat was in his hand.

The chorus had begun once more.

"Behold the Lamb of God, that taketh away the sins of the world."

He began to long to have his own sins taken away and wondered how it could be done, and when the sad contralto voice started to sing he listened eagerly.

"He was despised and rejected of men; a man of sorrows and acquainted with grief." And then the chorus sang: "Surely he hath borne our griefs and carried our sorrows. He was wounded for our transgressions; he was bruised for our iniquities: the chastisement of our peace was upon him, and with his stripes we are healed. All we like sheep have gone astray."

"Have gone astray," echoed the alto. And the bass and tenor answered, "We have gone astray; we have turned every one to his own way."

Yes, we have turned every one to his own way, answered the listening heart that now thought of it for the first time. He had turned to his own way when he left his old employer and his mother and came off here to this strange city to seek his fortune, which was proving so hard to find. He began to see many other things he had done and left undone. How he had turned to his own way.

"And the Lord hath laid on him the iniquity of us all."

There was something almost terrible in the sweetness of this concluding sentence. What claim had he upon the great Lord that his iniquity should be laid upon Him? During the first part he had been terrified and discomfited because, in the light of the prophecies, he had been made to see his own heart more clearly than he had ever seen it before. Now, when his own worthlessness and sin stood out so blackly, here was a pitying One ready to take the whole. He began to understand the story better, which at first had seemed so incomprehensible. But what was the tenor singing?

"Thy rebuke has broken his heart. He is full of heaviness. He looked for some to have pity on him, but there was no man, neither found he any to comfort him. Behold, and see if there be any sorrow like unto his sorrow."

He bowed his head in his hands, regardless of the curious and scornful neighbor. What did it mean? There must be love to make such sorrow, and all for him—that is, for the world, and he realized he was included. Could there be in this young man's heart at that moment a little thrill of real love for an unknown God Who had borne sorrow for him, with none to comfort Him? With none to comfort Him! Again that strange little thrill in his heart! Here was the link between him and this God. Hadn't he longed for comfort that very night? His mind went back to the first words of the evening: "Comfort ye my people, saith your God." God Who had been without comfort or pity in His own great sorrow yet wanted the people who had caused this sorrow to be comforted! It was wonderful. It wasn't strange that that word, one of His names, had rung out so clear and strong and bright in the music. "Wonderful!" Such a God as this was indeed wonderful!

When he raised his head again, the chorus was singing: "Lift up your heads, O ye gates, and be ye lifted up, ye everlasting doors, and the King of glory shall come in."

And the great question which seemed to be asked by many of all nations and ages, "Who is the King of glory?" was the same question he had asked himself at the beginning of the evening. Who was this God? The answer swelled and soared as from millions of voices besides those belonging to the visible chorus on the platform: "The Lord of hosts, he is the King of glory."

Some little idea of the power and majesty meant to be conveyed by these words entered this newly aroused mind, and he pondered the thought that such a mighty God should care for him.

He was absorbed in the idea for some time and did not take in what followed, until suddenly, with one accord, quietly and respectfully, the whole audience rose to their feet! Benedict got up, too, just as the first great "hallelujah" of that magnificent chorus burst upon his ears. Astonished at all that had gone before, worn out with the usual emotions that had been swelling within his heart, trembling from excitement so he could scarcely stand, he listened as the hallelujahs were flung on every side with prodigal hand, like respondent rockets in a great celebration. His heart swelled as the words of adoration were poured forth from those hundreds of trained throats: "King of Kings, and Lord of Lords! Hallelujah!" He felt that he could never go back to his old life and be the same again.

He was dimly conscious that another intermission followed this, during which time a great many of the diamonded and eyeglassed sort rustled out, and their places were quietly and gladly filled from the throng which had paid for standing room at the back of the house.

Of the third part which followed, he remembered only the first solo, that wonderful sentence, the climax of our trust, which contains our hope for life eternal.

"I know that my Redeemer liveth, and that he shall stand at the latter day upon the earth; and though worms destroy this body, yet in my flesh shall I see God. For now is Christ risen from the dead, the firstfruits of them that sleep."

Oh, to know that! To feel that wonderful surety! He looked at the white-robed singer with awe, feeling almost the possibility that she might vanish from their sight into the heavens when this song was over. It never entered his mind that she might not feel it all, for how else could she sing so to other hearts?

The closing triumphal chorus he heard as in a dream. But he echoed the "blessing and honor, glory and power, for ever and ever" with a glad "Amen" in his heart, keeping in his mind the words "I know" and resolving that they should be his own someday if ever he could find out how to make them his.

He went out into the dark and wetness.

Chapter 3

The rain had almost ceased; the wind was keener and sharper, and the pavements had become treacherous glass indeed. The throng ahead of him slipped and tottered, and some actually fell. They had almost to crawl along. But Bradley Benedict heeded none of these things. He was back in the opera house still, face-to-face with the Man of Sorrows.

He scarcely noted which way he was going until a hand was laid upon his shoulder, and a voice, too familiar to please him, shouted, "Hello! Which way you goin', and where've you been?"

It was the young man who was to be his roommate, on his way from a cheap theater. He knew the look of the place. He had been to such often before and taken delight in them; but tonight his heart turned from it with revulsion. He felt as if he had lived years since he entered the opera house that evening.

"I'm going home," he answered his companion shortly, and even as he spoke he felt what a misnomer that word was when applied to the squalid lodging house. He wished he were going home to his mother; and then and there he resolved to go just as soon as he could earn enough.

"H'm!" said the other man. "Well, you'd better turn around and plod along in the other direction if you expect to get there without going around the world. Come on!" He turned his unwilling friend about and walked along by his side.

"Where've you been?" he asked Benedict again, as soon as they were out of the crowd.

"In there," said Benedict, pointing toward the opera house with a sort of friendly feeling for the building where he had passed through such a strange experience. A glow he couldn't understand was in his heart.

"There!" exclaimed the other in a surprised voice. "You must have a heap of cash. It costs a penny to get in there. What's on tonight? Bernhardt? Let me see. No. Why, it was an oratorio night, wasn't it?" He glanced up at his companion with astonishment and a look of almost respect. "Is that the set you belong to?" he added.

Benedict replied simply by a nod. He had never known exactly what an oratorio was before. But now that he considered the matter, it certainly must have been what he had been listening to.

It was a silent walk the rest of the way to the boardinghouse. Brad's mind was too full of things to care to talk much, and the young man by his side found he had no conversation ready for the sort of companion who took his amusement at the oratorio *Messiah*. Now and then he glanced curiously at him as they shuffled along over the ice. A keen, strong wind had arisen and afforded sufficient excuse for them to retire behind their coat collars and keep silence.

Bradley Benedict was turning over in his mind this thought: Would this strange new feeling stay with him, or would it go away and leave his life the same empty void, without purpose or promise, that it had been only a few hours before? He realized now that it had been a bad and worthless life and wondered why he had never known it before.

Sleep didn't come to this young man as soon as to his roommate. The air of the room was breathless, and mingled with the smell of tobacco was a strong odor of fried onions, lingering probably from the boardinghouse supper. His evening with refined people, listening to wonderful music and thinking higher thoughts than had ever entered his mind before, seemed to have quickened his sensibilities to these little things. He felt almost stifled. He arose, went to the window, and threw up the sash. The cold air poured in and made him shiver, but he threw his coat about his shoulders and looked out.

The city was quieting into its after-midnight stillness now. The breeze had blown a small space in the heavy sky for the moon to shine faintly through, which the hurrying clouds were rapidly trying to cover again. One tiny star threw out a few flickering, straggling beams between clouds. The earth looked very dark, except where the lights of the city shone through glass. It was intensely cold. The sky grew black again as the clouds gained a temporary victory over the moon and the one star.

Brad felt alone—alone with God—and "Who shall stand when he appeareth?" came to his mind. Then the moon struggled through the clouds once more, and he thought of the words: "The people that sat in darkness have seen a great light." How many scraps of song could he remember? He felt the same desires which had moved him when he first heard the words—the longing to be able to sing the joyful songs; to feel secure; to have this Friend, this Comforter.

Suddenly, as if in answer to his soul's cry, there seemed to come over the wicked city a soft, sweet voice singing the words with tender pathos: "Come unto me, all ye that labor and are heavy laden, and I will give you rest."

He listened until the voice died away on the night, and then in the darkness he bowed his head and came and found rest.

Mrs. Benedict sat by the remains of a meager fire in the grate of the parlor. The room was deserted by all the boarders now, and she was free to sit here in peace for a few minutes. It was late, and she was so weary she had scarcely enough strength to take her up the stairs to her sleeping room. She had thought earlier in the day that the most delightful thing that could happen to her would be to drop into a bed and stay there and never have to get up again. She had gone through the day looking forward almost eagerly to the time when she could throw her burdensome, tired-out body on the bed and relax her over-strained muscles for a little time. But now she sat, trying to warm herself from the few weak-looking coals still left in the grate and gain strength to go up to her room.

It had been a more than usually wearisome day. The cook had been undeniably drunk and not able to do a stroke of work. The slouchy second girl, who was her only other assistant, had been out late the night before and had done nothing all day but dawdle about and yawn. One of the young men boarders, whom she had hoped would turn out to be a "permanent," had left that morning. Another had departed, leaving a used-up pair of suspenders and a hat with the crown jammed in, to pay his last month's board. She had decidedly failed in her meek efforts to coax three others into paying something toward past arrears. And the rent collector had called and told her he couldn't wait much longer.

Besides all this, she had neuralgia in one cheek and eye—and her boy was gone away. That was the climax. Her boy! She had thought about it and cried about it until she had no more strength left for either.

As she sat looking absently into the coals, where smoldered the stumps of two or three boarders' cigars, a tear trickled weakly down her cheek, scarcely gathering strength enough as it went to fall in a good honest splash in her lap, but instead spreading itself out in a wet spot among the wrinkles. Her hair was rough and gray; one lock had escaped from the pin that tried to hold it in a hard knot at the back of her head and hung now in a discouraged way about her face. The eyes were faded blue, and the skin was so wrinkled you couldn't guess what the contour of the face might have been in earlier days. She looked like a sad picture of despair.

The room itself was a desolate enough place. Mrs. Benedict had been obliged to relax her vigilance for cleanliness during the trials of the past few days. As a result, the disorder that reigned made it even more Sahara-like than usual. The ashes had spread themselves about on the hearth and gathered a small collection of toothpicks and cigar stumps. A fine, soft dust was over the mantel, broken here and there by the marks of some boarder's elbow.

An emaciated, hollow-chested, haircloth sofa was placed against the wall, and a table stood on the other side of the room, hidden by a faded red-and-black flannel spread and holding a few *Fireside Companions*. A weary-faced clock on the mantel, a few cane-seat chairs in various stages of dilapidation, and a depressed-looking rocker completed the furniture in the room. The floor was covered with a large-figured, much faded and darned red-and-green ingrain carpet, helped out in front of the door and fireplace by pieces of dreary oilcloth from which the paint had long ago departed. On the walls hung a few family groups and portraits, Mrs. Benedict's marriage certificate, and a cross made of hair flowers, all framed in oval or square black frames.

The marriage certificate occupied the place of honor over the sofa, with a full-length portrait of "Braddie," as she called her son, hanging on one side. He wore baggy plaid trousers and a coat and carried a hat, much too large for him, stiffly in one hand. The hair was long and thick, and the face chunky and expressionless, for the photograph was a poor one and old. But his mother gazed at him, remembered her little boy as he used to be, and sighed a great, deep sigh.

Then she turned her tear-dimmed eyes to the picture hanging on the other side. It was a man, presumably, though the picture which must have been taken long ago had faded so that little was distinct except some black hair and a coat. The light from the smoky lamp was turned low, however, and there was no bright fire to help out the features. But the lonely heart looking at them knew how the face had looked, and the weak tears gathered and coursed down between the wrinkles thick and fast. It was a hard world, and she was so tired!

A sharp ring of the doorbell broke the stillness of the room, and she looked toward the hall a moment in surprise. Yes, she had locked the door for the night before sitting down. Surely all the boarders were in. The clerk at Mason's had come in half an hour ago, and he was always the last one. But she arose mechanically and went to answer the bell.

She unfastened the lock and threw back the door, holding the lamp in one hand in front of her eyes, so that she was completely blinded. While the darkness rushed in and the lamplight staggered out to take its place, she was conscious of somebody standing beside her. It was a strong man like her Braddie. He shut the door, took the lamp from her hand, and then, taking her in his arms, uttered one word: "Mother!"

She was so tired and glad and so confused as to whether this was really Braddie or Braddie's father come back to earth again. She hadn't been held for twenty years.

To his old employer Bradley Benedict said the next morning, "I've found God, Mr. Bolton, and I've come home to take care of my mother and prove to you that I'm trying to live a different life, if you'll take me back and try me."

Two or three years afterward it was announced that the oratorio *Messiah* would be rendered in the largest church of the place in which the Benedicts lived. Brad immediately took two tickets and selected the best seats the house offered. Then he said, "Mother, the oratorio *Messiah* is to be here next week, and I want you to hear it. It's what saved me and brought me home to begin life again."

And Mrs. Benedict, not in the least knowing what an oratorio was but glad to please "her Braddie," donned her plain black silk, combed her white hair to its smoothest, and went. She sat and watched her tall boy proudly through the whole evening and told him at the close it was a nice concert, as good as any she and his father ever went to. But of the music she heard little, and she wondered in her heart what it could possibly be in that singing which had anything to do with Bradley's coming home.

Things have changed since Bradley Benedict came home that night. The boarders are gone, and the family, now three, has moved to a small, cozy house. The old furniture has given place to bright, cheery belongings, and Mrs. Benedict is renewing her youth under the loving care of her son and his dear Mary.

O ye disciples of Fashion and Art, as I passed by and beheld your devotions, I found an altar, in this oratorio *Messiah,* set up by you "To the Unknown God." Whom therefore ye ignorantly worship, Him could this unlearned young man declare unto you. For God, "that made the world and all things therein, and hath made of one blood all nations of men for to dwell on all the face of the earth, and hath determined the times before appointed, and the bounds of their habitation; that they should seek the Lord, if haply they might feel after him, and find him, though he be not far from every one of us."

Stephen Mitchell's Journey

by Isabella Alden

Chapter 1

An Uphill Start

Now don't drive fast, Stephen. It looks like this is going to be another warm day, and the horses had a hard pull of it yesterday. And mind you don't leave that load with anybody but Baker. He's the one I made the bargain with."

"Suppose he isn't there?" asked Stephen, sitting on the seat of the old farm wagon.

"He'll be there fast enough, so don't deliver them potatoes or cabbages to anybody but him," said the older man, standing ready to open the gate. "I ain't going to have any squabbles with him. He will as like as not say they never come at all, if he doesn't happen to see them unloaded. If he isn't on hand when you get there, you hang around till he comes, if you have to stay till night."

"And, Stephen, don't forget to stop in the village and ask Mis' Bascome for that pattern Fanny promised me weeks ago for Sarah Jane. She's about tired of waiting for it." This came from a woman's voice in the doorway.

While that voice was still speaking, an upper window was raised, and a curly, reddish head appeared, whose owner shouted down more directions.

"Steve, would you stop at the store and get me some green braid to match this piece?"

"Oh, land!" said Stephen gruffly. "I don't know a green braid from a blue braid. How am I going to match anything?"

"The clerk will help you," Sarah Jane said as she tossed the braid down. "I'd think you might do that much, when you're the only one who gets a chance to go to town."

"I don't like to go to the store," he growled. "I don't mind the grocery or the blacksmith or any of them things, but that dry goods store I despise. That fellow behind the counter thinks he knows everything. I wish Sarah Jane would do her own errands."

"She would in a minute if she had a chance," said the mother, "but you know she doesn't get to town once in an age. If there'd been room with the load, she might have gone this morning."

"Well, there ain't room," said the man at the gate, speaking briskly. "It's a heavy uphill road, and the horses are old, and Steve and the potatoes and cabbages is about all they can manage. You tend to them things, Steve. Keep track of your money, and don't do no fooling around with it. You'll have to pay a quarter to get in at the gate, even if you don't stay half an hour. I call that cheatin' to make you pay to sell your produce, but no use growlin'. Poor folks have to take what they find in this world. Get started now—the sun's climbing higher every minute."

As the wagon rattled down the rocky road, the old man closed the gate and with a weary sigh turned and limped toward the house, muttering against the rheumatism that held him prisoner.

You have now been introduced to the Mitchell family—father, mother, Sarah Jane, and Stephen. As for the farmhouse, it would be easy enough to describe, if that were worthwhile—a long, dilapidated building, gray with age and neglect, with a shutter here and there hanging by a hinge and an occasional broken pane of glass. It might have been pretty and bright, full of life and cheer, but that must have been a long time ago.

Often on a summer evening, Farmer Mitchell sat tilted back in his armchair, his gray head against the wall, his eyes fixed on his great, bony, wrinkled hands. Mrs. Mitchell, sitting not far from him in a little, old-fashioned rocker, was darning some glaring rent in Steve's limited wardrobe or setting a huge patch somewhere.

"I've worked hard," he used to say, putting his hands together so that fingers and thumbs matched and then looking down upon them, while he spoke in a half-tremulous, half-querulous tone. "There ain't a neighbor around here but what will tell you that. I've worked early and late, planned and struggled, if ever a man did, and what does it amount to? A mortgage on the farm, with the interest eating up every dollar we can raise—a hand-to-mouth living from day to day, expecting tomorrow to bring an end to it.

"That's about how it goes—everything rundown, of course. House needs painting. Barn needs painting—and a new floor and a new door. The old wagon has to be tied together with ropes to keep it from going to pieces, and it will go one of these days and spill the goods over the road, I daresay. And now here's the rheumatism got hold of me right in the middle of summer. I'm about tuckered out—an old man before my time.

"There's Jason Burke, three years older, and look how smart he is! They call him in his prime—as chirk as a young grasshopper—wears his broadcloth and his gold watch and chain, and I don't know what all. And here I am, limping along with rheumatism—as gray as a rat and more than half my teeth gone! Him and me was brought up on the same fodder, you may say—his father's farm and mine joined. My father's was the best, by a good sight. Now he's Judge Burke, and I'm—well, I'm nobody.

"His children are dreadful smart, they say—Joe gone to college and all that. His daughter plays the piano, sings like a nightingale, and jabbers two or three different languages, though I don't know what good that does her, or her father, either.

"And there's our Sarah Jane, no chance even of common schooling since she was twelve or thirteen years old. Had to be kept at work day in and day out! Her mother would've died if she hadn't had her help. No other way to do, in order to live. After a spell I couldn't even afford the clothes it would cost to fix her up for school. Then at last, when her mother took sick, Sarah Jane had to give up all hope of school.

"Then there's Steve. He didn't take to books—maybe he would if he'd had a chance—he went to school one whole winter and didn't learn enough to pay for the shoe leather he wore out in walking the three miles there. But he had the meanest kind of teacher. I've always thought if he'd had a different one, he wouldn't have hated his books as he appeared to. But then maybe it was lucky he didn't go on. I don't know what we'd have done with him if he'd wanted to study. I don't know what Steve does want to do. He hates the farm, and it's hard work to get him at it. I'd rather do a good stiff day's work than keep him at it half a day. Here he is, a great strong fellow, nineteen years old, and what does he know about farming? I done my best to teach him, too."

Then Mrs. Mitchell would answer, first with a sorrowful little sigh and then with a patient attempt to comfort:

"Oh, well, Father, things ain't so bad with us, but they might be worse. The farm is mortgaged, I know, and the crops are a failure this year, but maybe they won't be next. As for the children, what if Steve ain't no farmer? He don't loaf around the village or spend his time in the saloon, gambling and drinking and such. See how them Lucas boys spend their time! Steve hasn't got any bad habits, if he isn't a farmer or didn't take to books. He hadn't any books to take to, you know, Josiah. I wish Steve did take more to farming, but he don't, so what's the use?

"As for Sarah Jane, there ain't a smarter girl to do housework in the country around. She turns off more work in a day than I ever could. I wish Sarah Jane could have a chance. She's young and strong and quick about things. It 'pears to me if she could have had a chance, she might have done something. I tell you, Josiah, if we could only go to church regular, there would be some hope of things. That's the thing I worry about most."

"I know it," Josiah would respond, still in that half-sullen voice, which covered an undercurrent of disappointment. "I know all about it, Phoebe, but how can I help it? The horses are old and broken-down, just like their master. They're tuckered out with weekday work, and the roads is awful heavy and hilly. When the going's bad, you know it's almost impossible to get back and forth."

"I know you do your best, Josiah," the mother would reply in cheery tones, "and there ain't no use in worrying about any of it. You just chirk up. Something will happen next spring or next fall or sometime—things will be brighter."

As for Sarah Jane, during this interchange of confidences, she was generally upstairs in her own tucked-up, low-ceilinged room, at work, nearly always—for Sarah Jane was industrious and as "contrivin' as the next one," her mother would say. So Sarah Jane's leisure moments were spent in "contrivin' " something out of nothing. Sometimes it was a skirt ripped carefully apart, the stitches picked out and the material sponged and pressed, over which Sarah Jane bent hour after hour, contriving and cutting, without pattern or picture, except what was evolved from her own busy brain and the glimpse she'd had of the Bascome girls the last time she went to church. Her quick eyes would study details while they all stood during the opening hymn. While the morning lesson was read— wonderful words from the grand old Book—Sarah Jane would be wondering if the skirt of her blue dress couldn't be cut over to look something like theirs.

Why did Sarah Jane care whether her dress looked something like theirs or like its old-fashioned self? Who would see it, except the hens she fed every morning and the turkeys, who nearly always sickened and died before Thanksgiving, or a stray peddler or, on rare occasions, a country neighbor who came to sit for an hour on a leisure afternoon?

But her lonely life seemed no reason to Sarah Jane why she shouldn't remodel her scant wardrobe. The truth is, Sarah Jane Mitchell tingled to her fingertips with energy and hadn't enough in her stunted life to exhaust its power. She washed and ironed and baked and boiled, all the while planning an assault upon some waist or skirt or bonnet she intended to make over as soon as she had dashed off the tea dishes.

If she'd had books, she might have read them. If she'd had neighbors, she would probably have visited them. But they had no near neighbors, and the horses were always tired. And Steve hated neighbors. So they had almost no social life and no newspapers except the *Weekly Agriculture,* which, aside from the articles on carrots, beets, and potatoes and other belongings of farm life, was weakly as well.

They had almost no books at all, except the Bible, at which Sarah Jane looked reverently, respecting it always, because they read out of it at church and because it was—well, the Bible, and every decent-minded person respected it. But it was a perfectly sealed Book to her and was literally not opened by her fingers from one year's end to another, though she dusted it carefully every time she made her weekly dash upon the "best room" to put it in its dreary order. What was there left for Sarah Jane to do but rip and sponge and press and make over her clothes?

Chapter 2

On the Early Freight

On the morning in which Stephen Mitchell started on his journey into the great unknown world, Sarah Jane dashed about the kitchen "doing the dishes" and a score of other things. Her mind, meanwhile, was on the green braid she'd resolved at any sacrifice to secure.

"It'll cost only forty-five cents," she had told her mother, "and there's a bad spot in the waist and another in the sleeve it will just cover. There's that money for the eggs—you said I could have it, you know, to buy something I needed, and I need this worse than anything. I can mend my stockings and make them do, but I feel I must have it."

"Well, I would," the mother had answered in her patient, motherly voice. "The land knows you don't have much. And if you'd rather have green braid than new stockings, why, I say have it—though to my mind the dress looks nice enough fixed over to wear to a party without any braid."

No matter if it did; Sarah Jane's heart had gone out after green braid. She'd walked one morning four miles—to Farmer Bascome's place and back again—to get the information she needed and a scrap of the braid for Steve to match. It was an event for her to be looking forward to possessing something new. She couldn't keep her thoughts from it, as she worked swiftly.

"I do hope Steve won't be late tonight," she said. "It worries Father dreadfully to have him late getting home. I wonder what he thinks could happen to him between here and the village?"

"Oh, no!" said Mrs. Mitchell soothingly. The family didn't realize she was the one who had to speak most of the soothing words. "There's nothing for Father to worry about. He mustn't expect Steve home early. It's a long trip and uphill much of the way. And then there's no telling how long he may have to wait. Father told him, you know, on no account to let anybody but that Mr. Baker have the things, and of course he might not be around when Steve gets there. Oh, he'll get along all right. There's no cause to worry about Steve. We should be real thankful for that, Sarah Jane. Just suppose he was one of them boys who'd stop at the saloon and drink up all the money he got for the garden truck. And then not know enough to come home at all! That Lucas boy was reeling from side to side when he went by a while ago. Just think if you was his sister, Sarah Jane!"

"Oh, my land!" said Sarah Jane, a look of horror on her face.

Mr. Mitchell's prophecy in regard to the morning came to pass. It was very warm. Stephen shielded himself from the August sun as well as he could and let the tired old horses take their own gait up and down the long stony hills. Stephen, as a general thing, had no difficulty putting himself upon their level, so far as haste was concerned. "What's the use in hurrying?" If he'd had a motto by which to live, perhaps that might have been it. Nothing Stephen Mitchell had found in life, thus far, had seemed worth hurrying for. He was tall for his years, ungainly in form and uncouth in manners. His clothes were not only old-fashioned but much worn and badly patched. Not that his mother didn't understand patching and not that she didn't work patiently to do it neatly, but the quality of the patches has a great deal to do with their appearance when the work is done. And Mrs. Mitchell's resources, even in this respect, were so meager she sometimes produced startling effects.

On the day in question, Stephen had done what he could to make himself respectable, with indifferent success. It had been much too warm to think of wearing other than his linen coat, which was short-waisted, short-sleeved, and faded by many washings. Moreover, it was ornamented with long zigzag streaks of grass stains. His trousers were of coarse gray cloth and had a patch of bright new gray, set in a very conspicuous place. They were carefully turned up at the bottom, not because they were too long, but because they were badly frayed. He wore a loose gray shirt with a turndown collar made of the same material.

In this attire, seated on the board that was laid across the farm wagon and accompanied by potatoes, cabbages, onions, apples, beets, and, indeed, a little of everything that grows in an ordinary farm garden, he was making his way—whistling to pass the time—not only to the village which lay eight miles away, but nearly four miles farther than that, to the summer campground.

Stephen Mitchell was very much the sort of boy his father was in the habit of describing to his mother on the twilight evenings before mentioned. Nearly nineteen, freckled, blue-eyed, rough and ungainly in every way; inclined to be gruff in manner, sometimes surly, perhaps almost sullen, yet never loud-voiced or coarse; a little out of sorts with life, but utterly at a loss to know how he would have life differently arranged. Hating plowing and hoeing with all his might, yet by no means sure of anything else he'd like to do instead.

He was almost literally without education, the one winter he'd spent in school having been simply wasted. He knew how to read and, after a manner, to write, though he had ideas on orthography peculiar to him. He knew a little about figures, enough to calculate with a good degree of certainty regarding the "garden truck" he sold from time to time—though very little of this part of the work had fallen to Stephen's lot. Mr. Mitchell, thoroughly distrusting his son's business abilities, generally transacted sales and made change. But on the few occasions when Stephen had been allowed to, he'd kept his accounts square. And though the father saw him depart on this particular morning with great misgivings and gave many admonitions as to the price of the different articles and the money they should bring, Stephen had no anxieties in that direction. He had made a memorandum of his entire load, calculated the probable price, and was satisfied nobody could cheat him. Therefore he could have given his mind to other thoughts if he'd had anything to think about.

A more desolate life than Stephen Mitchell's it would seem hard to imagine. As to the stony farm he struggled over, much of the time alone—for the poor father had often days when he couldn't drag his stiffened limbs about—there wasn't a corner in it for which Stephen didn't have a fairly defined dislike. Yet day after day, with something like patience, he puttered away at his distasteful work and at night lumbered home, tired out, to sit drearily through the short evenings and get to bed almost with the chickens.

But the difficulty in the matter was that no one had come along to help him be other than the clod he was. His one teacher during the winter referred to he distinctly remembered as one he'd despised. Therefore, of course, whatever influence he had upon him was for the worse. And his father's troubles growing thicker and heavier upon him at about that time, that one teacher had been the last, so far as Stephen was concerned.

He had no intimacies with boys and girls his own age. He lived an isolated life. On the rare occasions they drove eight miles to the church in the village, Stephen stayed at home if he could. His father thought it was because he was too indolent to make the effort to get ready to go; his mother feared it was because he had no interest in such things. She, poor mother, though a Christian at heart, was a timid, unspoken one and didn't know how to help her boy have any such desires. She didn't even know how to speak to her wide-awake, energetic daughter. And neither son nor daughter knew how often her pathetic sigh was because of their manifest indifference to church and Sunday or any such thing.

Not one of the family knew that Stephen's real reason for absenting himself from church was because he recognized the infinite difference between himself and most of the other farmers' boys who would be there. It wasn't so much the matter of dress, though to even Stephen Mitchell that was important. But the other boys had a free-and-easy way: They shook hands with one another and made cheerful little speeches; they made dashing remarks to the girls, over which the girls laughed as though they were funny; they seemed to feel at home in one another's society and have plans to consider and amusements to arrange. At all these ways, Stephen Mitchell looked with amazement. How could a boy stand before a girl "all prinked out in finery" and say, "It's a pretty day," or give her a rose or maybe a pink, as he'd seen boys his age do? And do it without stammering or blushing or feeling as if he had seven pairs of hands instead of one and as though his feet were a yard long and heavy as logs? Stephen Mitchell didn't understand it or himself and got rid of his puzzling thoughts by putting them aside with his unanswerable "What's the use?"

He was determined to hold himself aloof from church people and from the few families who could be called neighbors. He met Sarah Jane's suggestions in these directions with a shrug of his ungainly shoulders and an indescribable grunt, which she knew must be translated in the negative.

This was the boy who paid his quarter at the gate of the great campground and drove his tired horses slowly in, staring about him on every side. He was filled with bewilderment, not to say dismay, over the unusual sights and sounds.

A summer encampment, holding its sessions, first for four weeks, gradually lengthening its time, from summer to summer, until now it was nearer ten weeks than four, had been in progress for years, within twelve miles of his home. Yet Stephen Mitchell looked upon the grounds this August day for the first time in his life. His father had in recent years made pilgrimages to the place, sometimes as often as once every two or three weeks, carrying with him a load of garden truck—as much as he could get ready from his worn-out and ill-tilled land. He'd discovered a ready sale at fair prices for anything fresh he could bring. But so unaccustomed was he to trusting any responsibility to Stephen that he'd never thought to send the boy in his stead, although the long, slow ride was irksome to him. But for the sudden attack of rheumatism a few unusually rainy days had developed, the paradise which suddenly opened before Stephen would still have been unknown land to him.

Very slowly the horses walked up the broad avenue. They were willing to walk slowly at all times and found the smooth road and lovely shade from the great trees, whose branches looked overhead, delightful to them. But for a warning cluck from Stephen's tongue, they'd have stopped altogether.

With some difficulty and much blushing, Stephen succeeded in asking questions to direct him to the hotel, after the Mr. Baker he sought. It was so astonishing to be driving through what he thought would be woods and find it a city with broad avenues, parks, fountains, and many cottages bright with flowers, the piazzas busy with groups of young people and the streets alive with men, women, and children hurrying to and fro. Not that he realized it was like a city or that he knew parks, avenues, and fountains by sight.

Stephen Mitchell was as far from his home this morning as he'd ever been. No knowledge of the hum and whirl of life had penetrated the stony hillside farm where he'd been reared. Had he been familiar with the Bible and the story of Eden, the grounds through which he was passing might have suggested to him that faraway, bright garden, which faded from human sight so many years ago. Indeed, had he been familiar with the Revelation and the language of the seer of Patmos, the golden city of the new Jerusalem might have almost seemed to take shape for earthly eyes. But he knew neither of those pictures well enough and at first was simply dazed, even panic-stricken.

His first desire was to get away; there were so many people. What an army of young men! Hundreds of them, it seemed, as well dressed as the detested clerk behind the counter of the one store in the village. And girls! Those creatures who had been the terror of his bashful boyhood! He felt ill-treated, deceived. Why hadn't his father told him? He looked down at his patched knees and turned-up trousers and blushed a deeper red than even the August sun had succeeded in producing. He was sorely tempted to turn his horses then and there and go back to town, dispose of his potatoes and cabbage for what he could get at the village store, and make all speed homeward, his mind in its first stage of actual rebellion against his father's authority.

His second mood was calmer. *What's the use?* he asked himself, resorting to his one philosophical sentence. *There ain't a fellow here who ever saw me before or will ever see me again. As for the girls, what do I care? Let them laugh, if they want to. Laughing won't kill me. If it would, I'd have been dead long ago. I've seen Fanny Bascome snicker right out in church when I came in. I'll just go right on and find that Mr. Baker, get rid of my load, and get out. And I'll act as though I didn't care a red cent for none of them.*

Chapter 3

More Than He Bargained For

S o thinking, he held up his head and ordered Doll and Dobbin to "go on fast!" To the best of their energies they obeyed—at least, according to their ideas of fast. But the speed wasn't so great that Stephen couldn't glance furtively at the piazzas as he passed and at the people who passed him. Much to his surprise, he seemed to attract no attention whatever. Most of the groups were busy with their books or with one another and seldom even glanced his way or, if they did, turned their eyes at once, as if he weren't important enough to arrest their attention. Nobody laughed, so far as he could discover, and two or three men actually nodded in a friendly way. After this experience, it almost seemed to Stephen as if the reddish brown hair on the top of his head stood up. Strangers bowing to him! Gentlemen dressed better than the minister!

Stephen Mitchell had never before received any courteous recognition from strangers. It gave him such a sensation that only a shy and neglected country boy, or one who has sometime occupied that position, can understand.

Mr. Baker wasn't there and wouldn't be until the two o'clock boat came in. That was the earliest hour Stephen could hope to see him, and it was now eleven. Three hours to wait. He wasn't so appalled as he would have been on his first entrance inside the gate. The people he'd seen on every side, during that brisk drive through the grounds, had roused within him a strong desire to discover what was going on—or, as he phrased it, "what all these people were about! What this thing was, anyhow?"

It was a great point with him that so far his appearance hadn't awakened a laugh. If the truth must be told, poor Stephen dreaded a laugh worse than he dreaded a pistol shot. Perhaps they were too busy to laugh at him or notice him in any way. He would find a nice place for his horses, feed them, and then saunter around and see what was to be seen. What companies of girls to look at!

"If Sarah Jane was here," he muttered, "she could find out ways enough to make all her clothes over. She'd be taking the tablecloth to make a rig like that white one. I'd just like Fanny Bascome to see it. I wonder if the Bascomes come here? If I met them, I'd sink into the ground."

He looked about him immediately in a frightened way, with a longing to be outside the gates, safe on the road again. Anything but to meet the Bascomes. They were nowhere to be seen, however, nor was any other human being he'd ever seen before. Stephen, having settled his horses, began a stroll through the grounds.

He came presently to an immense, semicircular building, or rather roof supported on pillars and filled with seats, which descended the hill in regular terraces. He stopped before it in amazement.

"It ain't a tent," he soliloquized, "and it can't be a circus. You can peek in all around, and there ain't any ring either. Ponies couldn't perform around there. But maybe they don't use ponies now, and maybe they don't shut up the sides anymore—things keep changing."

The sentence closed with a sigh, as he realized his ignorance. Stephen Mitchell hadn't even been to a circus for four years. Their circumstances were growing more and more straitened, so the half-dollars required were difficult to secure. Furthermore, he'd discovered the fashion to be for the boys to invite the girls, pay their way, and take care of them during an evening at the circus. His heart had almost ceased to beat at the thought of such a thing. He might pay for the tickets once in a season, but as for taking care of the girl—going after her and seeing her home again—he could never do it! Besides, there was nobody to take, for who would go with Steve Mitchell? And as likely as not they'd laugh at him for going alone, since most of them went with some girl. He might take Sarah Jane just once, but then none of them took their sisters. Maybe that was a thing to be laughed at, too. So Stephen had resolved to stay at home.

For all he knew, this strange wooden building, without sides and with many seats, might be a new style of circus. If so, it was evidently popular, for the seats were all down and the terraces filled, with only here and there a vacancy. A man on the broad platform was talking rapidly, while the eyes of the multitude seemed to be leveled upon him.

He ain't no clown, said Stephen to himself, stopping before an aisle with his hands in his pockets and forgetting even the crowd in his astonishment and desire to know what this thing was. *He ain't the manager of the thing, and he ain't a preacher. Anyhow, he ain't preaching now—there's no Bible or hymn-book or nothing.*

And then he turned suddenly, for a neatly dressed man touched him on the shoulder and said respectfully, "Would you care to take a seat, my friend?"

And Stephen, red-faced, stammered something, then asked a question: "What do you have to pay?"

"Nothing," said the man.

"Nothing? Is it a free show?"

"Perfectly free, sir, after you're inside the gates. Your gate ticket pays for all that goes on here during the day."

"Oh, my!" said Stephen.

The people were so busy looking at the man on the platform that they seemed to have no eyes for him. He saw no inclination toward laughter in any direction; he would take one of those empty seats and find out by his wits what this thing was and why they wanted to listen to it.

Down he went—down the incline plane as he'd seen others do, until he finally reached a seat, got out a handkerchief, mopped the perspiration on his face and neck, and settled back, prepared to listen.

He'd never heard anyone speak in Latin or Greek. If he had, he might have had a comparison by which to describe this speaker. He knew, however, there were other languages than his own and decided at first this was one of them. Then he looked about upon the absorbed audience. They weren't all foreigners. On the contrary, most of them were unmistakably Americans; he was observant enough to be sure of that. Was it possible they understood this unknown tongue? Was it an unknown tongue? Didn't he understand some of the words?

It's English, he told himself, after a few moments more of intense listening. *But it's high-and-mighty English, I suppose—them kind scholars speak. Mr. Ransom himself uses some of the words, but he doesn't speak them so outrageous fast like an express train. I wonder now if all these folks do understand him.*

The feeling of curiosity with which Stephen gazed about him began to deepen into respect, almost awe, and presently into a strange heart—longing to be one of them, to understand what that man was saying and like it as those folks evidently did. If he only could! It's the simple truth that then, for the first time in his life, Stephen Mitchell felt a longing to be other than he was. He hadn't been satisfied with himself at any time. But so far, in his unfortunate life, the idea that he might be different had never seemed to enter his mind. Nor did such an idea now—simply a vague stirring of impulses at his heart.

The next thought was a step in advance, for it took almost the form of a resolve. What if he should write down some of the words and try to find out what they meant? How would he find out, though? He thought of his father and shook his head. Mr. Ransom, perhaps—they said he had rows of books on his library shelves. Probably some of them told the meaning of words. But how would he ever get to talk with Mr. Ransom? He blushed at the thought of it.

If I'd had a dictionary, thought Stephen ruefully, *and been studying it all them long winter evenings, when I haven't known what to do with myself, I might have known most of the words he's pouring out now. Then, oh, how I should feel! I believe I'll write 'em down—a few out of the crowd—and see what'll come of it. It stands to reason I might get at the meaning of some of them somehow. It does seem kind of odd to have a lot of folks around you appear to know a thousand million things you don't. I believe I'll try for it.*

As he glanced around, with a vague idea of finding something to write on, fortune favored him. Or was it a watching Providence? On the floor at his feet lay a circular with a near-empty page. He grabbed it, got out his stub of a pencil, and commenced business.

It was hard work. He was unused to writing, and his orthography would have alarmed the speaker. But as he wrote he grew interested. It soon became his ambition to see how many of the words he could capture. They were being poured out in such a magnificent flood that the very sound of them roused within him a strange recognition of power. Words became, for the time being, tangible things.

S'pose they was apples, he inwardly chuckled, *and I was trying to catch them!* And his pencil fairly raced over the paper.

He was "catching them." A long row, reaching to the very edge of the sheet— a double row, a third one, and yet a fourth. He was reaching the end, his paper nearly exhausted, his brain in a whirl of excitement. Not a single word he'd written did he understand.

Suddenly the flow of words ceased. All unexpectedly to Stephen, the speaker had rounded out his closing period. Almost immediately the audience burst into song. The initiated knew the "Gloria" was being sung. Stephen didn't. He only knew it was music—such as that he'd never heard before. He heard the roll of a great organ and the sound of many voices and the majesty of solemn yet jubilant words: "Glory be to the Father, and to the Son, and to the Holy Ghost. As it was in the beginning, is now and ever shall be, world without end. Amen."

It seems surprising, when one thinks of it, but it was a simple fact that Stephen Mitchell was listening to the "Gloria" for the first time; and the grandeur and power of the words settled themselves within his conscience, never to be forgotten. Something had awakened within him, some power he didn't understand. But he felt, as he bowed his head with the multitude and listened to the words of benediction, that he, Stephen Mitchell, standing there, was in some mysterious way a different Stephen Mitchell from the one who had had much ado not to fall upon his face as he came down the incline. He clutched at the paper in his hand and muttered to his roused and inner self that he would *find out what some of the words meant, anyhow, before he was many days older.*

"Look at that fellow," a gentleman had whispered to his companion during the lecture. He sat only three seats behind Stephen and had been watching him intently for some minutes. "He's in the commonest farmer-boy's attire. Nothing about him indicates intellect. Yet he's been writing steadily since he first took his seat. That illustrates what I was telling you. These summer encampments are taking hold of the common mind. They're permeating the country, educating the plowman, who hasn't thought much more than the clods he's turned over. Imagine a fellow dressed in that fashion listening to a lecture like what we've had this morning, taking notes on it! I'd like to see his notes. He's a grand illustration of the progress of the times. Let's go forward and shake hands with him."

"He has a good head," said the other gentleman, as they moved slowly down among the surging mass and stood presently close to Stephen's side. The first speaker laid his hand familiarly on the country boy's arm.

"How are you, my friend?" He held out his hand and grasped Stephen's rough, red one in a cordial fashion. "Glad to see you here. Grand lecture, wasn't it? I saw you taking notes. They're worth preserving, I'm sure. It would really be a liberal education for a young man to understand thoroughly such a lecture as that."

Not a word had Stephen to say. He blushed to the roots of his hair. He opened his lips as if about to attempt a reply, but voice failed him altogether. The gentlemen, noticing and pitying his intense embarrassment, added a few more kindly words and passed on.

"He's overwhelmed with confusion, poor fellow," one said. "He thinks much more than he knows how to express, evidently. Never mind. Men are made of such stuff as he. We may meet him on the lecture platform yet."

Chapter 4

The Afternoon Accommodation

One more experience Stephen had. This time with a fellow about his age, but one very unlike him in appearance. Indeed, had Stephen realized it, he was as faultlessly dressed as the disagreeable clerk at the dry goods store. But this young man wore his clothing as though it occupied a subordinate place and had no idea of demanding attention. He came down the aisle, where Stephen still stood as if rooted to the spot, and addressed him cordially.

"Did you get good notes? I saw you writing. I tried to take notes but failed. He speaks so quickly. Do you write shorthand? No? Then I don't see how you succeeded so well—he pours out the words in such a torrent! But he's magnificent, isn't he? If I knew one-third of what that man does, I'd be vain. Did you ever hear a lecture so full of historic reference? Why, he went all over the field of literature. Ever hear him before? He's a Chicago preacher—one of the finest in the city, they say. I don't recall his name, but I'd like to hear him preach. These are wonderful opportunities, aren't they?"

And the young man, whose voice and dress and manner all showed he belonged to another world than Stephen's, smiled on him with an air of good fellowship before he sprang up the aisle and was lost in the throng.

Who shall undertake to represent Stephen Mitchell's frame of mind? He to be shaken hands with by elegant gentlemen! To be congratulated on the notes he'd taken! To be asked if he wrote shorthand—whatever that was. It was a new term to him. But glancing down at his strong red hand when the question was asked, he realized that whatever else that hand might be, it certainly wasn't short, and therefore answered in the negative.

Shorthand, he said to himself. *I wonder what kind of writing it is? Easier than mine, I daresay, or his'n either, for that matter. He thought if I did, I could write more. I mean to find out what it is.*

He drew a long quivering breath; the world had suddenly grown very large to him. There was a great deal to find out. He went mechanically through the duties which filled the next hour; found Mr. Baker and made a satisfactory trade, less embarrassed than usual—less conscious of his feet and hands and clumsy tongue than he'd ever been before when trying to transact business. More alert, also, as regarded prices and the money he received—so alert, in fact, that Mr. Baker, looking after him as he drove out of the grounds with his empty wagon, said, "That fellow knows more than he looks to at first sight. He has quite a head for business." Which remark would have astonished Stephen's father.

All the way to the village, the boy was absorbed with the new thoughts presenting themselves in such whirls before him. It cannot strictly be said he thought; there was too much chaos in his mind to dignify the process by that name. Still, he went over, in some fashion, the vivid scenes of the last two hours. He lingered with the notes, which had been carefully put away in an unused vest pocket. He felt almost afraid and wholly reverent before them. This feeling had been added to by some words he'd overheard while waiting for Mr. Baker to calculate the money due.

Two gentlemen standing near had discussed the lecture of the morning, and then one had made this astonishing announcement: "Gets a hundred dollars, I suppose, for that lecture?"

"I suppose so," said the other. "It's worth it. I'd be willing to pay my share toward another hundred to hear it again."

"A hundred dollars!" Stephen Mitchell repeated under his breath. A hundred dollars paid to a man for standing on a platform for an hour and pouring out words. Then words were dollars—many dollars! For he had brains enough to know the man could go on other platforms and repeat the same words.

Over and over again! he said to himself. *There's no end to the money he can make by them.*

As he thought of this phase of the question, he took out the precious paper and began to count the words, while Doll and Dobbin, refreshed by their long rest, trotted steadily down the hill toward the village. It filled Stephen with amusement to discover he had a hundred and three words on his paper.

"Three more dollars than he made," he chuckled. "Well, I never! I wonder what Father would think of that? Plowing, hoeing, digging, and the land knows what, from sunrise to sunset, day after day, week in and week out, to get a hundred dollars toward paying the interest on the mortgage and buying the things we've got to have. And here's a man that stands up and talks off a lot of words just as fast as he can and in about an hour makes his hundred dollars. It does beat all! I think I better learn the meaning of the words. That man said it would be an education to understand all they meant. I vow I mean to understand all of 'em! He used a lot of words I didn't get, to be sure. But after I understand a hundred and three, maybe some of the others will come to me. Anyhow, I'm going to try for it. I've got a lot of chances for thinking and planning while I'm at work. I won't tell nobody a thing about it. But I'll learn that first word and how to use it. I don't care if somebody finds out and laughs at me. I mean to do it. Whoa!"

To his surprise Doll and Dobbin had reached the village and were passing the despised corner store, where the braid was to be matched and the clerk must be endured.

"Well, my good fellow, what can I do for you today?" he asked, a superior smile on his face.

The country boy felt like doubling up his strong red fist and knocking him down. Instead, with great meekness, he produced the bit of green and struggled to discern the best color to match it.

"It 'pears to me that's it," he said at last, putting his forefinger on one of the rolls.

"Oh, no!" said the clerk, with what sounded like an ill-suppressed sneer. "I assure you—you're utterly mistaken."

Stephen's red face grew redder, but he wasn't sufficiently sure of his ground to make reply.

"Now this is a much better match," the clerk went on glibly, "and a finer article in every way. It's for your sister, I suppose? Well, you take my word for it, this is what she wants. How many yards did you say?"

And he shook off a quantity from the roll, preparatory to measuring it.

Just a little below him, selecting papers of pins of various sizes, stood a young woman, unknown to Stephen. She was of another world from that of the Bascome girls and their friends. A very quiet young woman—regarding dress and movements.

Stephen Mitchell, called upon later to tell how she was dressed, could say no more than that it was in "some pale, still stuff that looked as though it was made for her and wasn't going to wear out."

Neither was he more lucid regarding the color of hair or eyes. Both, he thought, were brown, though the eyes, he admitted under cross-questioning, might be gray. They were big, he was sure of that, and "kind of searching looking, as though they saw lots of things they didn't mean to tell anything about."

And her voice made him think of that burst of music which began, "Glory be to the Father." Yet the words she said were commonplace enough.

She turned her gray eyes at that particular moment, when the clerk was prepared to measure the green braid, fixed them for an instant on Stephen's face, then upon the clerk, and said quietly, "I don't agree with you, Mr. Pettibone. I think the young man's judgment is correct. For his sister's sake, I would suggest that the braid he selected first is the proper shade for his sample, and I'm glad to learn you don't consider it of such good quality as the other. I supposed it was higher priced. Of course it isn't so expensive then?"

It was Mr. Pettibone's turn to blush. "There's no accounting for ladies' taste," he said, with an attempt at nonchalance.

"And I'm quite sure the sister will be pleased with her brother's selection. I hope he'll insist upon it," she added, fixing her eyes on Mr. Pettibone's blushing face.

"I will," said Stephen, gathering voice. "Give me the other, three yards of it, and be as quick as you can, for I'm in a hurry."

Then he wondered if the young woman should be thanked for her help and earnestly hoped not, for certainly he could never do it. Meanwhile he gave outward attention to the clerk.

"You told me this was fifteen cents a yard," he said, picking up the discarded braid, "and that it was better than the other. How much cheaper is that?"

There was the faintest gleam of satisfaction in the young woman's eyes as she paid for her pins and left the store. It amused her to discover that the awkward country boy, whom she'd saved from making a grievous mistake, had been quick-witted enough to take advantage of the clerk's glib statements and demand a lower price for the braid which had been pronounced of poorer quality. But this wasn't quick-wittedness on Stephen Mitchell's part; it was simple honesty. He knew nothing about the quality of braids; he took the clerk's statement in good faith and was astonished to find himself obliged to pay fifteen cents a yard for what had been declared inferior.

He's sulking, he said to himself of the clerk's gruffness, as he pocketed the braid and went to his waiting horses, *because I didn't take the kind he picked out. Just as if I didn't know green when I saw it and laid it beside another piece of green.*

If Stephen had known that Mr. Pettibone had been obliged to sell three yards of braid for fifteen cents a yard, distinctly marked twenty, and make up the difference out of his own pocket, he would have understood the sulks better.

He had one more errand he hated worse, if possible, than that at the corner store. Stephen could only hope Fanny and Celia Bascome weren't at home, or at least that they would not be anywhere within speaking distance while he was waiting for the pattern.

"I don't see," he muttered, "what Sarah Jane finds in them Bascome girls. If she'd seen some of the girls I have today, she would know better than that. They don't look no more like the Bascome girls than poppies and sunflowers look like roses and white lilies, and they don't look no more like her than nothing in the world or out of it."

Comparisons were exhausted when he remembered those grave, kind eyes and the "pale, still stuff" in which their owner was dressed.

He was destined to be unfortunate. Fanny Bascome was at home—the one he disliked more, if possible, than Celia. She was not only at home, but it was her voice greeting him from the piazza.

"Why, if here isn't Stephen Mitchell! For pity's sake, Steve, where did you come from? I didn't know as you ever got so far from home nowadays. How's Sarah Jane? You want to see Ma? Come in. Ma, here's Steve Mitchell—wants to see you for something."

"A pattern?" said Mrs. Bascome, waddling in from the great farm kitchen, looking heated and tired. "Land alive! There's no need to ask me for a pattern. It's some of Fanny's folderols she wants. Why don't you tend to it yourself, Fanny? What pattern is it you promised Mis' Mitchell?"

"I didn't promise any pattern. Oh, yes, I remember! She asked me, coming out of church one day, if I couldn't lend Sarah Jane my skirt pattern. I forgot all about it. I was going to send it to her. But I never have a chance to send away out there. Dear me! I don't know where that pattern is. If you're in a hurry, Steve, you'd better go on, and I'll hunt it up and send it. Let me see— when can I send it? Won't your folks be out Sunday, some of them?"

"I ain't in any desperate hurry," said Stephen, with a dogged determination to have Sarah Jane pleased and a dim idea the skirt pattern was to go with the green braid. "I ain't in any desperate hurry. If you could look it up now, I could wait. I've got a pretty good start toward home."

It was a long speech for Stephen Mitchell to make. It involved not a little self-sacrifice on his part, for he was anxious to be on his way home and out of sight of the Bascomes.

"Well," said Fanny, with a reluctant sigh, "I suppose I may as well go and hunt it now as anytime. Only I'm all dressed. I do hate to rummage through boxes and things after I get dressed. Don't you remember seeing it, Ma?"

"No, I don't," said Mrs. Bascome shortly, "and I ain't going to leave the supper I'm cooking to go upstairs and hunt it, either. When you promise to lend things to folks you should tend to it. I suppose they've been waiting for weeks. It must be four or five weeks, at least, since Mis' Mitchell spoke about it coming out of church. I never did see such a careless girl as you, Fanny Bascome. I'd be ashamed not to do a little favor like that for a neighbor."

They were out in the wide hall now, and though their voices could be heard they didn't seem aware of it, or else they cared nothing for Stephen Mitchell's ears.

Fanny answered irritably, "Neighbor! Ma, how ridiculous! They live most five miles away. I don't care about lending my patterns anyhow. Who wants the skirts of every country girl for ten miles around made exactly like yours? I've a mind to tell him I can't find it."

"You'll have to hunt a good while first," muttered Stephen, whose energies were now roused toward the skirt pattern and who resolved to stand his ground and insist upon his ability to wait hours, if necessary, while it was being hunted. He was conscious of disliking Fanny Bascome more than ever before, but for some reason he wasn't so afraid of her as usual.

Chapter 5

Making His Report

I t's an awful nice match," said Sarah Jane, examining the green braid with interest some hours afterward. "Just exactly the shade I wanted. I don't see how clerks learn how to match women's dresses as well as they do."

"The clerk didn't match it," said Stephen, with unusual energy. "I matched it myself. I didn't take the one he wanted me to, by a long sight! He picked out the meanest match."

"Land!" said Sarah Jane, surveying him with wonder. "How did you know what it should be?"

"I guess I've got eyes. If I don't know green, why, then I don't know nothing. Don't I work among green things all my days? That stuff of your dress is just the color of the grass that grows on the south meadow—a kind of sunshine green. It makes you think of daisies and dandelions and such. Yet there ain't no yellow in it. I don't understand it exactly, but that's the kind of green it is, and the braid he was going to give me was that miserable pusley green that never looks nice by the side of the others. I knew better the minute I saw it."

Sarah Jane regarded her brother with a look of wonder and finally burst into a laugh.

"If I ever heard the like!" she said. "Who s'posed you noticed what color the grass was or anything else? But I know just what you mean. That blue green would look nice on some things, but it would look horrid on my dress. I declare, Steve—I believe you'd make a good storekeeper."

"I'll never be one," said Stephen, half-ashamed and half-angry.

Then he shuffled out to attend to Doll and Dobbin for the night.

Sarah Jane, as she revelled in the mysterious pattern and fingered the green braid lovingly, trying to determine how best to place it, gave also puzzled thought to Stephen. There was a look in his face she didn't understand. A feeling had come to her that he was in some way a different person from the Steve who went to town that morning. She chuckled over his encounter with the store clerk.

"I don't see," she said to herself, "how he ever screwed up his courage to quarrel with that fellow about which color to take. It's too funny for anything."

She reverted to the subject and cross-questioned Stephen that evening while he was eating the supper kept warm for him, laughing so appreciatively over his description of the scene that he was more communicative than usual. Up to a certain point he said nothing about the strange young woman who had sustained his decision. At last he brought her forward.

"I saw a girl, Sarah Jane, that had on a dress that to my mind went ahead of anything Fanny Bascome ever wore. I don't see why you want to shape your clothes after that girl's. I'd rather take a peacock strutting around the barnyard for a pattern than her."

Sarah Jane giggled. "So would I, but the peacock's too fine for me to match the colors. I take Fanny Bascome's patterns because I can get them, and I can't get no others. But she dresses nicer than any girl in the village, they say. Who was it you saw, Steve?"

"I don't know who it was; I saw her in the store. She ain't the Fanny Bascome kind or any others like her. She don't look like 'em or act like 'em or anything."

"How was she dressed? What did she have on?"

"How do I know? It was some pale, still stuff that slipped around her."

Sarah Jane regarded him with superiority and slight disdain.

"That's just like you, Steve. How am I going to tell anything about a dress that's made of some 'pale, still stuff' and 'slips around' on anybody? If I could have seen the girl, or if ever I could see anybody that's worth seeing, I could make my clothes look something like it. But I can't."

"No," said Stephen slowly, "I don't suppose you can."

There was no sarcasm in his voice; there was even an undertone of sadness. He watched Sarah Jane with great interest while she moved about the kitchen putting away the remains of his evening meal and reducing everything to neatness and order. He was realizing certain interesting facts. He was discovering his sister didn't look like Fanny Bascome or even like the young woman in the store, and two persons more unlike each other than Fanny Bascome and that young woman he couldn't imagine. Where, then, did Sarah Jane belong, if she had to do with neither of them?

Sarah Jane was short—some people would have called her dumpy, though Stephen didn't use that word. She had reddish hair and freckles, but her hair was soft and wavy. As he studied her pleasant face, he reflected that he'd seen a great many girls that day, and not a one was like Fanny Bascome. Nor were they like Sarah Jane and certainly not like the girl in the store. He felt puzzled and troubled. It was a bewildering world.

Suddenly he thought of his list of words. He'd thought of them more or less all the way home and studied ways of beginning his discoveries concerning them. The very first word in the list was "barbarian." He had a vague impression he'd heard it used somewhere, somehow, before today. But how or where or what meaning it was intended to convey, he couldn't determine. What if Sarah Jane knew something about it? She knew about dresses and braids and a hundred things that were out of his line. And cramped and isolated as her life was, she saw more people than he did. She went more often to church and knew girls— by name, at least. Mightn't she have heard the word "barbarian"? What harm would it do to try her? He needn't explain why he wanted to know; for that matter, he couldn't explain. He hadn't yet settled that matter in his own mind.

"Sarah Jane," he said suddenly, speaking with such energy that she almost dropped the pan of potatoes she was carrying to the sink. "Sarah Jane, do you happen to know what 'barbarian' means?"

"My patience!" said Sarah. "How you made me jump! I'd forgotten you was here. 'Barbarian'? Why, it means—barbarian, of course."

"Exactly so," said Stephen. "That's what I supposed myself."

Sarah Jane laughed.

"Well, I don't know as I can tell what it means. I can kind of think it, though. It appears as if I knew. Ain't it some kind of animal, Stephen?" She spoke timidly. She was on untried ground, and Stephen had been away all day; there was no telling what he'd learned.

"I shouldn't wonder," said Stephen in a noncommittal tone. "The question is, what kind of animal? That's what I want to know."

"What do you want to know for?"

Here came the question he had hoped to avoid.

"Well," he said reflectively, "I suppose the reason I want to know is—because I want to know." And he joined somewhat shamefacedly in Sarah Jane's laugh. After a moment's silence he added, "I heard a man use the word today."

"How did he use it?" asked Sarah Jane quickly. "If I'd heard him, I could tell pretty near what it means. I've often noticed, if you pay attention to what goes before and comes after a thing, you can pretty nearly always find out what it means."

"Yes, I guess so," said Stephen, with a shade of respect in his thoughts of her, coupled with a dim realization that had she had his opportunity that day, she'd have made more of it than he had. But he couldn't have imagined himself going up to the platform and telling the speaker he wanted to look at some barbarians. How was he to find out the meaning of the word?

"So," said Sarah Jane, "what was he saying about them anyhow?"

"That's more than I know," said Stephen humbly. "He was saying a lot of things I didn't understand, and that was one of them."

Sarah Jane washed her potatoes vigorously for a few moments and said nothing. Then she spoke, and the sentence was preceded by a little sigh, which in itself was startling, for Sarah Jane wasn't given to sighing: "I suppose you saw and heard a lot of things today, Stephen, that you didn't understand. I wish we knew about things. I'm dreadful sick of sticking here on this stony old farm and not knowing what's going on. I wish I could go to the circus. There's going to be one next week, and I'd give most anything to go to it. But there! I don't suppose it's any use."

"I'd think not," said Stephen. "I guess you forget the interest on the mortgage."

"No, I don't—and ain't likely to. Father's groaned over it more than usual today, and I've wished as much as twenty times I hadn't sent for no green braid. Though Mother was kind of bent on my having it. She said it would cover up the spots, and it will, too. But I could have got along without it."

"I guess forty-five cents won't make no great difference one way or the other," said Stephen, in a voice meant to be encouraging.

Then he arose with a weary yawn and lumbered out of the room, no nearer to discovering the meaning of "barbarian" than when he heard it spoken from the platform.

No form of prayer closed the day in the Mitchell household. The mother was the only one of the family who prayed at all, and she was so shy and quiet about it that no one besides her was sure of it. As for Stephen, he'd discarded the habit of childhood prayer when he grew too old in his estimation to say, "Now I lay me down to sleep," though why one should ever be too old to repeat that simple statement of fact and ask God's keeping power when he voluntarily relinquishes all attempts at keeping himself, it might be difficult to explain. Sarah Jane couldn't have told when she outgrew the habit.

But to all practical purposes the Mitchell family, the mother excepted, were "barbarians," as far as religious life was concerned. Yet I like to think and believe that the Shepherd was watching that night the poor foolish sheep—who had wandered out of the pasture even while he was a lamb, voluntarily giving up the Sabbath school and the church service and any attempt at being led and fed—and was calling after him, though the sheep had wandered so far away he didn't know the Shepherd's voice. The great Shepherd's heart has such great depths we cannot comprehend. And some ways of reaching wandering ones are in themselves so simple that because of their very simplicity we cannot comprehend them. The very reaching out of this blind heart after something he didn't understand and knew not where to find may have been translated in heaven as a cry for help.

But Stephen Mitchell didn't know enough to connect the next morning's experiences with his own heart-cry. He was out in the field, steadily following the plow, trying to move along in exactly the same paths he'd moved two days before and finding himself unable to do so. He'd have been astonished, probably dismayed, had someone told him he could never again find that old well-trodden path and plod on in it. As a matter of fact, it was lost to him—the footprints covered over. But this he didn't realize.

Chapter 6

Another Passenger

Stephen's father was engaged that morning with a visitor from a town about twenty miles away, who was searching for a certain breed of cattle, and Mr. Mitchell was the owner of two good cows he was very anxious to sell. As Doll and Dobbin moved with dignified steps down the long field, they came upon their master and his visitor. At sight of Stephen, the stranger wished him a genial "good morning," and the father called out some question regarding the cattle, on a point where he expected Stephen to be better posted than he was.

"Is this your son?" asked the gentleman, as he drew nearer.

"Yes," said Mr. Mitchell in a half-surprised tone. He'd forgotten anybody couldn't know Stephen was his son. "This is Mr. Meadows, Steve."

"I'm glad to meet you, sir," said Mr. Meadows, holding out his hand and giving Stephen's red one a cordial grasp.

"You're rather isolated here, aren't you, Mr. Mitchell? How many miles is it to the village?"

"Oh, it's eight good miles," said Mr. Mitchell with a sigh. "Sometimes we think, when we drag up the hills, that it's ten or twelve. Yes, we're away back from everywhere and have a miserable piece of land. It's mortgaged for all it's worth. We're seeing hard times, Mr. Meadows."

"Eight miles from any market," Mr. Meadows said reflectively. "That must make your work pretty heavy. But you have neighbors, of course—some quite near you. That little shanty, shall I call it, within a mile of you is inhabited, I noticed—very much so."

"Neighbors!" echoed Mr. Mitchell in a tone of intense scorn. "They're nobodies. The man is a miserable drunken scamp, and his sons are like him. They're as hard a lot as you can find, out of state prison, I guess. As for the women folks, I don't know much about them, except they're a rough-looking lot. They can't be anything, living as they do."

"They're perfect barbarians, I'm afraid," said Mr. Meadows. "I stopped at their gate to make some inquiries. I thought perhaps I'd lost my way. Your farm lies a little out of the main road, you know, and I interviewed three or four children there—maybe more. After I'd settled as to my way, I asked a few questions about theirs. I don't think I ever before, in a civilized land, struck such dense ignorance. It seems a pity—"

But just at this point Mr. Meadows chanced to glance at Stephen Mitchell and paused in bewilderment to note the changed expression of his face. What did that sudden flash of his eyes mean? Could he be a friend of any member of the wild family back in the woods? Did he resent his plain language? Yet the look wasn't one of indignation. Mr. Meadows was fairly puzzled. The father, meantime, had turned and was looking toward the house.

"There's my neighbor Harding, from the corners," he said. "He's stopped at our gate. If you'll excuse me a few minutes, I'll go and see what's wanted."

Now was Stephen's opportunity. The Lucas family, who lived in the cabin a mile from their house, whose children had been alternately the nuisance and the terror of his mother for the year and a half they'd occupied the cabin, were barbarians, it seemed. Why? Because of their descent from some race of that name? Because of their poverty or ignorance—or what? Stephen didn't put his thoughts into such language, but such is their translation. His question came upon Mr. Meadows almost as abruptly as it had upon Sarah Jane the night before.

"What does 'barbarian' mean, sir?"

"Oh!" began Mr. Meadows, in a somewhat embarrassed tone, thinking perhaps he'd offended by his reference to the family in the cabin. "I didn't mean exactly what I said, of course. The children struck me as uncouth and singularly ignorant of some of the commonest properties of daily life. I suppose they've had no opportunity, poor things! I fear I spoke rather rudely, in your opinion. One can't judge all family members by the children."

Stephen wasn't making headway. He didn't understand what Mr. Meadows was trying to accomplish.

"You said they were barbarians," he added, "and I was wondering why."

"Well," said Mr. Meadows, smiling, "I confess the children suggested a barbaric state."

"What do you mean by that?"

He had no indignation in his tone. The young man didn't act as though he'd taken offense; yet he seemed in earnest. Mr. Meadows was puzzled.

"I don't think I get your meaning," he said hesitantly.

"Why, all I mean is that I want to get at the meaning of 'barbarian.' " Stephen had a half-smile on his face. He couldn't help wondering whether all gentlemen who used large words found it so hard to explain them.

"You mean the derivation of the word."

And then Stephen stared; this was growing worse.

"I don't think I could go into the root meaning to your satisfaction," continued Mr. Meadows, after waiting in vain for further suggestions. "I'm not well up on philology. Of course, all I mean was a lack of civilization. It's true that even the most uncultured people we find in this country are very far from absolute barbarism—that all have more or less civilization. Schoolhouses, churches, and society in general have done much for them. How much we'll probably never realize, unless we're isolated for a while from all such surroundings and set down in absolutely barbarous regions."

Light was dawning upon Stephen's mind. It was true, as Sarah Jane had said, that you could almost guess a word's meaning if you watched carefully its immediate associates. Notwithstanding the fact that Mr. Meadows had used, in those short sentences, literally more than a dozen words the meaning of which Stephen didn't understand, he yet was gaining a fairly correct idea of the original meaning and present use of the word "barbarian." But he couldn't help letting a smile illumine his face that in struggling after the meaning of this first word on his list, he was getting deeper and deeper into mystery.

I'd have as many as twenty to take hold of, he said to himself, *if I had pencil and paper and time to catch these. I declare—if words were dollars, then everybody would get rich at this rate in a little while.*

"Much obliged," he said aloud. Then, made aware by Mr. Meadow's peculiar look that he'd been caught apparently laughing at him, his face crimsoned, and he looked about him for some subject to arrest attention and turn the gentleman's thoughts into another channel.

"I reckon this ragweed is a barbarian," he said, touching a lusty specimen of it with his foot, "and it doesn't get civilized neither. And it's as hard to get rid of as the Lucas family. Father's been trying some way to have them get out of this neighborhood ever since they came, but that isn't near as long as he's been trying to get rid of ragweed. And here it is every season as regular as if it had been planted and hoed and cultivated according to order."

"But your analogy won't hold good," said Mr. Meadows, smiling in his turn. "Earnest work by good men and women will make a great difference with the Lucas family in a few seasons. Has it ever been tried?"

"Sir?" said Stephen, bewildered in his effort to follow this line of thought.

"Have you ever tried to get hold of the Lucas family, my friend? I judge from what your father said there are young men in the family. Have you given as much thought toward getting rid of the barbarism about them as you have to getting rid of the ragweed?"

Stephen shrugged his broad shoulders.

"Tough job!" he said briefly. "The ragweed's tough enough, but we can get it out of the way for a spell, at least. But the Lucases are on hand summer and winter, and you can't take a knife or a hoe or a plow to them."

"No, 'the weapons of our warfare are not carnal, but mighty through God,' nevertheless, you know. I wonder how tools named patience and kindness would work? Perhaps you have a barbarous nation all your own to get hold of, young man—to civilize and cultivate, until they're ready to become citizens in the royal city itself. Did you ever think of that?"

But Stephen could only stare and wonder what extraordinary language the man was talking now.

"We talk a great deal about barbarism and civilization," began Mr. Meadows again, after the silence had lasted for several minutes. "But I sometimes think the only civilization worth caring for is the one that brings us into companionship with the Lord Jesus Christ Himself. We're all barbarians when it comes to that, unless we have the change only He can give. I trust you're a servant of His, my friend?"

Stephen had taken up his hoe and was working furiously. Something about these last sentences bewildered, indeed almost terrified him. What a strange man this was! He'd never met his like before. It will be remembered that he'd heard little talk from gentlemen—the minister he wouldn't go to hear preach being almost the only educated gentleman he knew.

This must be "religion," he reflected. At least, it was different from anything ever said to him before.

Truth compels me to admit that this was the first time in his life he'd been asked whether he was a Christian. He wasn't even sure this was what Mr. Meadows meant, though he'd heard sermons enough to guess it was. He didn't know how to answer the question and was relieved from doing so by his father's return. Nodding his head in response to the man's bow, he strode swiftly back to his work at the farther end of the lot. He'd certainly received a good deal of information that morning and gotten his brain into a whirl thereby.

"Sarah Jane," he said, pausing before that young woman as she was washing the tea dishes, "I've found out what a 'barbarian' is."

"Have you though?" said Sarah Jane, holding a dripping cup in her hand while she stopped to give him undivided attention. Anything discovered had its own charm for Sarah Jane. "What does it mean?"

"It means us," Stephen said with a half-laugh. "I've made up my mind I'm a barbarian. I live in a country where many folks know lots of things, and I haven't learned any of them to speak of. Haven't got what they call 'civilized,' though there's schoolhouses and churches and them things round us. You should have heard Mr. Meadows go on."

"I'd like to have heard him," said Sarah Jane emphatically. "He's the man who bought the cows and paid money down for them—the nicest man I've heard of this long time. So he put such ideas into your head, did he? Well, I wish we could get civilized. I've thought this long time it was too mean for you and me to be so different somehow from other folks. We don't go nowheres to learn things or have any company. We just have to blunder along. Can't we make things different somehow?"

"Mr. Meadows thinks we should make things different for the Lucas family."

"The Lucas family!" Sarah Jane repeated in amazement. "What in the world does the Lucas family have to do with us, or we with them?"

"He says we've got to civilize them—says we've been spending our time on ragweed, and it won't take on a decent character in spite of anything you do with it; it stays ragweed to the end of the world. But he says the Lucases could be civilized, and he thinks the neighbors have something to do with it."

"Much he knows about it," said Sarah Jane. "What could we do for them, I'd like to know? They'll drink and swear and be disgusting in every way they can think of, and who's going to help it? I can't, I know."

"I don't know as we ever tried," said Stephen, leaning against the window seat and watching the swift fingers, which were again manipulating the dishes. "I don't know as we know how to try. It's one of the things we haven't learned, Sarah Jane."

"What started you?" said Sarah Jane, looking at him curiously. "It wasn't this Mr. Meadows, because you began at 'barbarian' before he came. Where did you get the word? You told me you heard it yesterday. What else did you hear, Steve?"

"I heard a hundred and three words," said Stephen slowly, "and I wrote them down on a sheet of paper. And I don't know the meaning of one of them, except the first, which was 'barbarian.' I begin to understand a little about that."

"A hundred and three words," repeated Sarah Jane, in open-eyed wonder, "and you wrote them down—all of them? To think of your taking the trouble to write down a lot of words! What's some more of them?"

"The next one is 'emancipator,' " said Stephen gravely, "and the next one is 'champion.' I don't know how to set to work to know what either one means. But I'm going to do it. I've made up my mind, Sarah Jane, to know the meaning of every word on that page before this winter's over."

"Good for you," said Sarah Jane with emphasis. "Steve, wouldn't it be splendid if you turned out a scholar? I always thought I'd like it so much. Fanny Bascome's always talking about her brother Ned being crazy over books, and I've wished a hundred times that you loved books more than Ned Bascome did and knew more about them, too. He's awful silly. I don't believe he'll ever be smart, if he is crazy over books. But I just believe, Steve Mitchell, that you could be smart."

"Of course," said Stephen, in slow sarcasm, "there's nothing in life to hinder. And I could go to school as well as not. Suppose I start tomorrow morning and leave the old farm and the cows and Doll and Dobbin and all the rest for Father to look after? How would you like it?"

"Oh, my patience!" said Sarah Jane. "Of course you couldn't, Steve. Poor fellow! You're tied to this old farm and the mortgage. We all are. I wish we could live in the village. I believe I could sew at the dressmaker's and earn more money in one season than Father does on the farm. Well, never mind. We'll do something, you and I. Don't let's go on the same old way another day—let's be different. You've begun, haven't you? There's that list of a hundred and three words—you know the meaning of one of them already. Like as not you'll get hold of another before long. Steve, suppose I try, too? I can keep my ears open and get some of them. If you'll make me a list of your words, I'll do it. Nobody likes to know things better than I do."

Chapter 7

The Downhill Road Described

While the dishes were being put away and the house set in order, Sarah Jane laid aside all thoughts of how she should fix the ruffles on her skirt and said over, with a puzzled air, " 'Emancipator,' 'champion'— seems as if I'd heard that word before—I wonder if it has anything to do with horses? They champ. Maybe it's a horse's name. But it doesn't sound like that. I wish we had a dictionary. I wonder how much they be? Perhaps if—"

She didn't finish her sentence, but the thought in her heart was that perhaps if she'd gone without the green braid and a few other trinkets her starved life had reached after and accomplished, she might have had enough money to buy a cheap dictionary—who could tell? To such heights of self-abnegation did Sarah Jane reach that if she'd thought about it before, she declared to herself, she would have gone without green braid and the roses her soul had craved for her summer bonnet—for the sake of accomplishing such a result as that.

It's an interesting fact, although she didn't realize it, that from that moment things with Sarah Jane began to be "different." The making over of her old dresses became a secondary consideration. Steve's list of words took precedence over every other interest. His determination to know their meaning and her determination to assist him in this effort became the all-important work.

As the twilight deepened, Stephen came in from doing the chores. Doll and Dobbin were settled for the night, and everything was done. On the side piazza, or stoop, as the family called it, sat the father, much worn with his day's work, but in a more cheerful frame of mind than usual. The visit from Mr. Meadows and, above all, the substantial reminder of that visit, in the shape of several crisp bills Mr. Mitchell had in his pocket, was an event in his life. It cheered and encouraged him. Moreover, Stephen had done very well with the load he'd carried to the campground the day before. A few weeks more of such "luck" as this, and he could be prompt with the interest on the mortgage, the object for which Mr. Mitchell lived—to contrive to be ready for these semi-annual payments and so keep in abeyance that terrible fear of being sold out of house and home.

Stephen took a seat on the step below him and looked thoughtfully up at his father's worn, wrinkled face. How little he knew concerning his father's early life. It had never surprised him before, but tonight, when he thought of it, he wondered why he hadn't been told about it. Perhaps it was because he'd asked no questions. Did his father work on a farm, he wondered, and did he hate it? Were there other things he thought he could have done if he'd had a chance? Did he go to school when he was a boy? How much did he know?

Stephen had never thought about it before, but he was suddenly struck with the fact that his father talked very well and was apparently at ease with men like Mr. Meadows—yes, and with the minister. Perhaps he knew the meaning of many words; he might have learned them when he was a boy. It was barely possible he might know the meaning of some on his list. What if he tried him? No sooner thought than he put the idea into language.

"Father, what does 'emancipator' mean?"

"Emancipator?" repeated Mr. Mitchell, turning his eyes slowly away from the western sky and fixing them on his son. "Why, one who emancipates. I might call Mr. Meadows an emancipator," he added with a half-laugh. "Anyhow, he's emancipated me from the fear I'd fail altogether this time with the interest, and I feel about as pleased as a slave could with his freedom papers, I reckon. What did you want to know the word for, Steve?"

"I was thinking about it," said Stephen, an undertone of satisfaction in his voice.

This was his first day's effort, and, behold, two of the words which had so bewildered him yesterday had suddenly been made plain. Had been illustrated, indeed—one by the Lucas family, and the other by his father's own experience. And both illustrations made the meaning stand out plainly. Mightn't his father know a great many things he didn't? Had Stephen Mitchell been asked at any time during the past years if he loved his father, he would have stared in astonishment on the questioner and answered, "Of course!" But as he looked up at him this evening, he had perhaps the first dawning of respect for the old man, who possibly knew a great deal and yet plodded on, content to live day by day with those who knew little or nothing.

How astonished would Stephen Mitchell have been to know his father's thoughts then. A very strange remark had been made to the father that day— a remark which had stayed with him. Its only rival interest was that he had almost enough money in his pocket to meet the next payment due on the mortgage. The words belonged to Mr. Meadows—spoken as Stephen and his hoe had tramped hurriedly toward the far end of the lot.

"You have an interesting son, Mr. Mitchell, a thoughtful one for his years. He's studying philology, I take it—a valuable study for a young man, but somewhat unusual. Are you going to give him an education, sir?"

Strange words these to Mr. Mitchell—and about Stephen, of all persons. He a thoughtful young man—interested in the study of anything. The word "philology" was quite beyond the father. He'd wondered over it several times during the day.

He looked down at Stephen with respectful curiosity. The boy impressed other people differently, then, from what he did him. A "good boy," he always called him—one to be proud of, every time the Lucas boys were thought of. But a student, or one who would have cared to be a student, had the opportunity been his—of such an idea the father hadn't dreamed. In his earlier days he'd had dreams of having a son who would be "smart" and make amends for his own disastrous failure in life. But when Stephen made that miserable record in school, during his one winter, all such thoughts were given up, and the bare struggle for existence had ground as heavily on both father and son as to give them little time or wish to think about such things. What if he'd been unjust to his boy? What if Stephen had failed to be a student simply for lack of the right kind of help?

"What are you trying to do, Steve?" he asked, looking at him with a touch of respect in his voice. "Mr. Meadows said he reckoned you was studying 'philology.' What's that?"

"More than I know," said Stephen with a short laugh. "He used the same word to me, and I don't know what it means. I'm just trying to find out the meaning of a few words, that's all."

"Oh! That's a good thing to do. I wish you had a better chance to find them out. Folks who know the meaning of words have a pretty good education, as far as it goes. One of my troubles has been, Steve, that I couldn't give you and Sarah Jane any chances. I didn't think you cared, but Sarah Jane would have been a scholar, I guess, if she'd had a chance. And I always kind of wanted one of you to turn out that way. There used to be scholars in my family. My great-grandfather was a real, thoroughgoing scholar—understood Latin and all that, and you're named for him. I used to have my notions when I was a young man and you was a little chap, but life went hard with me. Things got wrong."

"How did they get wrong, Father? I was thinking tonight how strange it was I'd never heard anything much about you when you was a boy—what you did and all that and how you begun living."

The shadows were growing deeper about the faded house. Stephen couldn't see the look of pain on his father's face or understand the long silence which ensued or the quiver in his father's voice when he spoke again.

"There isn't much to tell, Steve. A good deal of it's better forgotten, instead of told. I went wrong in more ways than one. I threw away many of my chances. I had a great deal better than you ever had, when I was a boy, and threw them away. Then I married, and after that I went wrong again. I was a slave for a while myself, Steve. I should understand what an 'emancipator' is, if anybody does. A man got hold of me and set me free from the worst slavery anyone can have. I used to get drunk, Steve—come reeling home to your mother and pretty near broke her heart. I've always been afraid you'd inherit a taste for the stuff. I've kept you away from that the best I know how. That's why I've kept you closer sometimes than you liked."

Stephen listened as one in a dream. His father a drunkard! This was the explanation, perhaps, of their poverty and of the heavily mortgaged farm—the last explanation that had ever entered his mind. However vague and uncertain had been his teachings in other directions, they had been very pronounced on the question of rum. Both Stephen and Sarah Jane believed drunkenness to be the sin of sins. They looked down on the Lucas family with disgust and horror and had never so much as dreamed that the curse of drunkenness had touched them. Though poor, they'd prided themselves on being respectable.

Now, perhaps, but for someone his father spoke of as an emancipator, they'd have been another edition of the Lucas family. So his father had been a "barbarian" and had been "emancipated." It was possible, then, to accomplish this. Shouldn't someone accomplish it for the Lucas family? Stephen Mitchell's education was progressing. In fact, he was taking rapid strides along the journey he'd marked out for himself, though he didn't know it. While hurried thoughts like this crowded his brain, the father presently broke the silence again.

"I don't know as I should have told you about it so abruptlike, Steve. It's a hard thing for a father to have to say to his boy. Your mother couldn't bear to have you told, nohow. But when you talked about emancipation, it reminded me there was more than one kind. And there's more than one kind of slavery. Yes, we have rum to thank for most of our troubles. I guess you could've had your chance like other boys if it hadn't been for that. I got free from it, but I had to twist and turn in every kind of way to keep the old farm—heavily mortgaged at that. I had to begin life over again, you may say, and things have gone pretty hard with me ever since. I lost my health in the same way I did my money, and I've never got either back.

"No, the worst of my troubles was lived away from here. I deserted the old farm when I was young and came back to it when I found I couldn't do anything else. Folks around here don't know I ever drank. They think I'm shiftless and all that, but they seem to have a notion I've always kept respectable. And your mother took care nobody should hear about it. You see, your mother came home to my father and mother and lived here a whole year without me—she and you. That's the year you were born.

"Then my old mother died, and things were broken up here, and your mother came back to me, and I led her a life of it for a while. Then I got free from my curse—haven't tasted a drop of the stuff since—and we came back here and began life again. Mother and Father gone and the farm mortgaged for all it was worth, to save me. That's about the story of it, Steve. Your mother never wanted me to tell you. She always talks as if she'd forgotten it herself, but I know she hasn't. Sarah Jane doesn't know anything about it, of course, and I guess you'd better keep still for your mother's sake. Maybe you'll make up somehow what's been lost to you. I thought you didn't care about such things—about study and all that—but maybe I've been mistaken in you. I've been mistaken in most things in my life."

"Never mind about all that," said Stephen hoarsely. "It don't matter what I've lost. I haven't known enough to know what was lost, anyhow, not till now, at least. And I'll make it up, as you say, maybe. I believe I've been a slave to something—I don't know what. I've been dumbheaded anyhow. I'll look around and see if I can find an 'emancipator.' " He laughed in an embarrassed way to cover feelings he didn't wish to show.

A small shadow came swiftly up the starlit path leading from the gate and stood before them.

"Bless me!" said the father, startled. "Who are you?"

"If you please, I'm Timmy Lucas, and I come to see if Mis' Mitchell wouldn't come over to our house. Ma's took very bad, and Miranda and Flora Ann don't know what to do. Miranda said run and see if Mis' Mitchell wouldn't come or something."

These sentences were jerked out in an eager, frightened voice, with gasps between.

"Dear me!" said Mr. Mitchell, rising and then sitting down again helplessly. "I don't see as there's anything we can do. I guess you'll have to run on somewhere else. Mis' Mitchell isn't well herself and couldn't walk that far nohow, and she's gone to bed, I guess, anyhow."

"No, I haven't, Josiah."

Mrs. Mitchell's head was put out of an upper window, and her voice sounded down through the night.

"I haven't gone to bed yet. I was sitting here thinking. I wish I could do something for them, Josiah. People should be neighborly in sickness anyhow. But I don't know as I could walk that far; my knee's been bad today."

"Of course you couldn't," began Josiah promptly.

Then Stephen rose.

"Doll and Dobbin could, Mother. I'll harness them if you want to go."

Chapter 8

Trying a New Road

This announcement made Mr. Mitchell dumb with surprise. A patient, plodding boy Stephen had been since he'd reached the years of responsibility, but at times he showed a dogged determination to do as he pleased. One thing he'd held out against for the last two or three years was taking out Doll and Dobbin, for anything under the sun, after their day's work was completed and they were safely housed in the barn. In the privacy of their own room, Mr. Mitchell confessed to his wife he thought Steve's resolution not a bad one.

"He has streaks of being as obstinate as any balky horse I ever tried to break," reflected the father, as he bent his stiffened joints to pull off another boot. "And balky horses, when they get going, sometimes go like possessed. Since Steve has only balked about going out evenings anywhere, my notion is we'd better let him be."

This decision he presently gave to Mrs. Mitchell, adding, "If he should get a-going, there are lots of places to go to that could bring us no end of trouble."

Whereupon Mrs. Mitchell had sighed, as one who'd understood life only too well, and murmured, "Yes, indeed!" Her husband's words had started within her such terrible memories of shadowed days and shadowed nights that she couldn't hear a suggestion afterward regarding the horses being used in the evening without trembling and turning pale. And Sarah Jane, vexed at Stephen and astonished at them all, had been obliged to put aside her ambitions in that respect, as in many others, and go on in her humdrum ways.

No wonder, then, that both father and mother were amazed when Stephen made his announcement. The mother was more than amazed—she was frightened.

"Oh, dear!" she said. "Maybe we'd better not. I guess it'll do to wait till morning, Stephen. Then I can walk it as well as not."

"It won't hurt Doll and Dobbin," said Stephen. "They haven't been working hard today. I'll have them ready in five minutes, Mother. We'd better go tonight. The woman may be pretty sick."

Not a word said the father. He watched this innovation upon the established customs of his home in silence—not without a foreboding of what "a balky horse might do when once he got started." But it wasn't as strong as it would have been without the words of Mr. Meadows that morning: "You have an unusual son, sir—a very thoughtful one." Perhaps Stephen was unusual, and he'd never known it. Something about him this evening seemed new to the father's opening eyes.

As for Sarah Jane, she bustled into her mother's room and helped her put on the black dress without which she never went abroad, got out the old black straw bonnet which had seen years of service, and wrapped a worn black shawl about her with swift, skillful fingers.

"My land! What do you suppose started Steve? I thought it would take two yoke of oxen to get him out with Doll and Dobbin at night. Most ridiculous idea ever heard of, too. A boy like him sitting down in the chimney corner like an old man. He's older than Father sometimes in his actions. I'm glad he's waked up, if it is only to get to the Lucases. Now don't stay and sit up, Mother. Why, I wonder if I couldn't go instead of you? Maybe I'd do just as well."

"Oh, no—oh, dear, no, child!" said Mrs. Mitchell hastily. She felt as if the foundations of her home were being broken up. "I don't want you to go off among them Lucases. We don't know anything about them, remember—only they're a set. If the mother's sick, I'll try to do something for her, of course. They can't hurt me if they're bad. You stay and take care of your father. He won't know how to act with me out of the house. I haven't been out of the house without him for years, I do believe."

It was a desolate home upon which they entered. The father was stumbling around the kitchen dazed, only partially sober, and his second son had just staggered in, much the worse for liquor. Two other grown sons were absent, presumably at the liquor saloon at "the corners," as the miserable place was called, situated three miles away, where the roads forked. Miranda, a girl of about Sarah Jane's age, looking slatternly beyond description, appeared in the doorway with an exclamation of relief at sight of Mrs. Mitchell.

"Oh, my goodness! If I ever was glad to see anybody, I am you. Do come in and tell me whatever I'm to do. Ma's in an awful way. She tosses about and groans the whole time, and she can't tell me nothing to do, and I'm at my wit's ends. I sent Timmy off, because I didn't know what else to do. Jim, get out of the way. You great loafer, standing there right in Mis' Mitchell's way. He's so drunk he don't know what he's about, Mis' Mitchell, and Pa don't know any too much. They're a set. I dread the other boys coming home. I don't know what we'll do with them tonight. Flora Ann, why don't you put Mime and Dele to bed? I'd think you might do so much, instead of standing round here wringing your hands. What good does that do? Now you come along with me."

This last she said to Mrs. Mitchell, who presently disappeared from Stephen's sight behind a door which, though hastily closed after her, revealed a poverty he had known nothing about. The Mitchells were undoubtedly poor, but they were sober and clean.

Flora Ann, the other half-grown daughter, perhaps fifteen, whose dress was as slatternly as Miranda's, had been crying quietly while her sister talked.

"Is your mother so bad?" he said to her in a low voice, as he stood in doubt where to put himself.

"Oh! She's awful!" said Flora Ann. "I never seen her like this. She's been pretty bad a good many times, but never like this. And there wasn't nobody to do a thing. We can't get no doctor or nothing. Don't cry, Dele. You'll worry Ma."

This she said to the little girl, who despite the warning set up a loud howl, evidently taking up the chorus where she'd left off for a few minutes to stare at the strangers.

"Hush!" said Stephen sternly. "You mustn't make a noise. That'll only make matters worse." The loud howl stopped as suddenly as though the child's mouth had been sealed.

"Oh, dear!" said Flora Ann. "I'm so glad you stopped her. She's been taking on dreadful because she thought Ma was going to die. Now, Mime, don't you begin. Ma'll be better, I reckon, now Mis' Mitchell's come to see her. She'll do something for her straight off. You and Dele go over there in the corner and get into your bed. Hurry now and be awful still, because I think I hear Jake coming."

The look of apprehension both little girls wore at the mention of that name and the way they turned their eyes toward the outer door, as if in fear of someone's entering, told volumes to those familiar with a drunkard's home. Jake was the elder brother and wasn't so meek in disposition as the half-intoxicated Jim, who'd settled himself in a rickety chair in the corner and already dropped into a drunken sleep. When Jake came home the little girls didn't cry, unless he extorted screams from them by some cruel act. Frightened as they were about their mother, curious as they were about the coming strangers, they were willing to be huddled off to the corner into that miserable bundle of rags they called bed, if there was any fear Jake was coming.

Stephen retreated to the stoop and stood looking about him, busy with his own grave thoughts. What a day this had been! Into what strange positions was his list of words carrying him. These people were "barbarians." Whatever the word might mean to others, it had a sound which to Stephen's mind seemed to fit the Lucas family. He'd always thought of his own family as very low on the scale of being. Weren't he and Sarah Jane different from all the boys and girls who went to the village church or gathered in the village Sunday school or sang in the village choir? As for the Lucases, he'd thought nothing about them until their connection with the word "barbarian" had drawn him into their midst and given him a revelation. Here was poverty.

Imagine Sarah Jane looking as that dreadful Flora Ann did. Sarah Jane, whose hair, even in the early morning, was always combed. Stephen hadn't appreciated that before; he felt sure he would now forever after. Sarah Jane, whose dress, no matter how little it cost a yard or how many times it had been washed and mended, always had a trim air about it. He contrasted his sister now with both Miranda and Flora Ann, to Sarah Jane's great advantage.

He looked in at the blear-eyed, wizen-faced, disreputable old man, who sat with his hat tilted back on his head, blinking at the smoking lamp, and contrasted him with his father. What if his father were like that? In the light of the evening's revelation, how easily he might have been.

Stephen Mitchell drew his breath hard, clinched his hands, and felt there was work in the world to be done. There was a stratum of society much lower than his own, and because his surroundings were so much above the Lucas family's, he was bound to do something for them.

"Civilization will tell," he muttered to himself, going over the words of Mr. Meadows that morning. "I wonder if Sarah Jane and I haven't enough to make a difference here."

Meanwhile, the father at home waited, with a great sinking of heart, that Steve had gone into the midst of the family whose contamination he'd dreaded as he would smallpox. He would have been comforted if he'd understood his son. It was good for Stephen to go to the depths below him.

The hour of midnight was striking when Doll and Dobbin drew up before their own gateway. Much amazed were Doll and Dobbin. If they could have expressed themselves, they mightn't have had exalted views about emancipation. When before had they been called upon to do duty at the midnight hour?

Mr. Mitchell had had an exciting time waiting for his family and expressed himself with unhesitating tongue.

"For goodness' sake, Phoebe—what did you stay so for? I've been scared almost out of my wits for the last two hours. What happened?"

"Why, nothing happened, Josiah. Only there was a woman dreadful sick needing everything done for her and nothing to do it with. I had to stay—there was no other way. Such a place as it is, Josiah—you never saw the like. The idea of human beings living in such a condition. It's enough to make one sick of life. Where's Sarah Jane? I want to take a look at the child, just to comfort me after seeing them two girls. Oh, such shiftlessness! You never saw anything like it, Josiah. I never did before.

"But then, poor things, how can they help it? I thought their mother would die the first hour. It seemed as if nothing I did for her would do any good. But we got ahold of her at last. She quieted down, and I shouldn't wonder if she'd sleep pretty well. And we left them comfortable, compared to what we found them, and just as thankful! You've no idea. They have hearts anyhow. It does seem, Josiah, as though we should do something for them."

"I should think we had," said Mr. Mitchell. "Where was Steve all the while? Did you think of him, Mother?"

"Think of him? I reckon I did—and had good reason to. Steve was everywhere. He made a fire in their rickety old stove—made some wood or cut down a tree or something. I know them girls said there wasn't one stick to make a fire with, and Steve told them he'd see about that. It wasn't ten minutes before he had a fire roaring and kept it up, too. Then he got a kettle and filled it with water from the land knows where. They don't have any water near the house— have to go off down the hill somewhere. There wasn't a drop for her to drink. Oh, well! Steve did everything.

"If you'd seen him going around there giving his directions, you wouldn't have known the boy. You'd have forgot he was a boy and thought he was a grown man. He got that drunken Jim to go up a pair of rickety stairs somewhere to bed. Then by and by that oldest one, Jake, came home swearing, drunk enough to be ugly. Flora Ann wrung her hands and screamed, and Miranda groaned—she was that scared. And I was scared myself. He knocked things about so—kicked over a chair and swore and told Flora Ann to shut up, or he'd wring her neck. Oh, dear! I don't know what he didn't do. At last he took hold of the lamp and was going to stalk off with it and leave us all in the dark, with that woman sick and maybe dying. Then, Josiah, you should have seen your son. He marched up to Jake and spoke just as quiet and composed as though he was talking to me.

" 'Jake,' said he, 'that's enough. Put down the lamp and go upstairs quick! Don't wait a minute.'

" 'Who are you?' said Jake, staring at him as if he was too astonished to say anymore.

" 'That's no matter who I am,' said Steve. 'I'm somebody you've got to mind. Put the lamp down on the table and go up those stairs. I won't give you more than a minute and a half to do it in.'

"Well, Father, I never was so scared in my life. I just expected to see him throw that lamp right at Steve's head. He glared at him as though he meant to do it. And Steve looked back as composed as if it was me looking at him. He didn't appear to be the least mite afraid. I was almost scared over that, for I've seen him turn all colors and tremble when a strange woman spoke to him coming out of church. But there he stood looking at that madman, perfectly composed. I suppose it was his steady gaze maybe cowed Jake. Anyhow, he set down the lamp and swore he didn't know what all this fuss was about. Then as true as you live he went stumbling upstairs, Steve watching him till he got to the top.

"Then Steve turned around and said to Flora Ann: 'I wouldn't cry anymore if I was you. You might disturb your mother. Jake won't hurt anybody tonight. He'll be asleep in a few minutes.' And sure enough he was.

"What we'd have done without Steve I don't know. I tell you, Josiah, there's a great difference in boys. When I saw that fellow tonight raging around, swearing at us, and then saw our Steve stand up so straight and strong and brave—oh, my, but I thanked God Steve was our boy and not the other one. We have a good deal to be proud of, Josiah. Steve hasn't got education, such as you meant him to have, but he's got some other things worth having."

"That's a fact," said the father with an emphatic nod of his head. "I don't know as we've done Steve justice, for he's always been a good boy."

Chapter 9

Becoming a Champion

The next Sunday Stephen went to church. He couldn't have explained why it seemed in keeping with his new ideas to do so. Certainly he wasn't in need of more words, nor could he hope to have light thrown on his present lesson by listening to the sermon, unless Sarah Jane's idea of watching for the connection between words might be put into practice.

Whatever the motive was, he astonished that young woman by making the kitchen fire for her nearly an hour earlier than usual and announcing as he came from the cow house with a foaming pail of milk that he was going to the meeting, and she might go along if she wanted to.

"Going to the meeting!" said Sarah Jane, setting down her pan of potatoes to stare at him. "Are you really? That's awful nice in you. It's such a pretty day. I was just wishing I could go and wondering if I couldn't manage to coax you into it somehow. But I didn't expect to, because you've been dreadfully cranky lately about going to church, you know."

"The horses didn't have to work hard yesterday," said Stephen, "and I reckon it'll be good for them to take a little tramp," which was the only explanation he gave to Sarah Jane.

But she was in nowise disturbed. "Whatever took him to go," she explained to her mother, as she put herself with speed into the green dress, whose appearance did credit to her industry and skill, when one took into consideration her meager resources, "I'm awful glad he did it. Seems to me I'd fly if I couldn't go somewheres today."

Then she stopped in the middle of the delightful task of buttoning the green dress and stared thoughtfully at her mother.

"Look here, Mother," she said at last. "Why don't you go with Steve? You ain't been to a meeting in an age. I wonder I could be so mean as not to think of it. I'll help you get ready in a jiffy, and then I'll stay and tend to dinner."

"Oh, no!" Mrs. Mitchell hurried to say. "I can't go today, child. I'm all tuckered out with the extra baking and things yesterday and don't feel equal to it. I don't, honest, child, and I wouldn't have you miss it for anything. Father and I'll see to the dinner and have everything comfortable when you come home. He likes the notion of your going off together to church like other folks, as well as I do, though he doesn't say much about such things. Sarah Jane, that dress is as pretty as a picture. I declare! You do beat all for fixing over things. I wish Stephen had a better-looking coat to wear."

"So do I," declared Sarah Jane earnestly, "but don't say a word, Mother, or he'll get a fit at the last moment not to go. It isn't so dreadful-looking. I ironed it as though it had been a satin coat, instead of an old faded linen, and I turned over the collar deeper so the grass stains don't show so bad. I reckon I had a notion he'd go to church today, and that's what made me take the extra pains."

Mrs. Mitchell was at the window in Sarah Jane's room, watching Stephen as he brought Doll and Dobbin, harnessed to the old spring wagon, around to the side door. His coat was very short waisted and, for that matter, narrow chested. "It was too bad in it," the mother murmured, "to shrink like that." But then it had been washed so many times. And she could see, even from the window, that it was frayed at the wrists.

Mrs. Mitchell had a distinct mental photograph of her Stephen as he should have been dressed, had her power been equal to her loving will. He never knew how hard it was for his mother to see him driving to church dressed as he was; yet that he'd go to church at all was something to be thankful for. And the tears she brushed from her eyes as she finally turned away were born partly of regret over the outgrown clothes and partly of joy at the thought that they were "on their way to the meeting, like respectable folk."

The church was small and plain but fairly well filled with people who were in marked contrast to the Mitchells. Even as uncultured an eye as Stephen's discovered he was by far the worst-dressed person there, and Sarah Jane felt by no means so fine in her made-over green dress as she had in her own room. It took one swift glance at Fanny Bascome's new lavender suit to discover the plaits of her dress weren't in the right place, the points of her basque were too long, and her sleeves weren't the correct shape. Her face grew red as she looked and thought, and she actually had some trouble keeping back the tears. She had worked so hard and believed she'd done so well. Why try to look like other folks? Poor Sarah Jane!

At that moment the minister was reading, "Wherefore do ye spend money for that which is not bread, and your labor for that which satisfieth not?" Why, indeed? Sarah Jane didn't even hear the words, so absorbed was she in her own sorrow. Even the green braid had lost its power to comfort, for Fanny's went down the back as well as the front and crossed in some bewildering fashion she couldn't make out.

The service over, Stephen stood on the steps outside and waited for his sister. He needed patience, for she was coming down the aisle as slow as possible. Her courage had already revived. Was she, who had overcome such mountains of difficulties in the past, to be vanquished by a bit of green braid? She resolved to conquer. If somebody would only detain Fanny Bascome in the aisle long enough for her to discover where the braid crossed in the back, she felt she could succeed. Fortune favored her. Fanny was halted before she reached the door, by someone eager to make arrangements for a basket picnic, gotten up hastily in honor of some of their friends.

Sarah Jane, while she studied the braid, heard snatches of the talk and gave one regretful thought to the fact that from all such interests she was counted out. How did it feel, she wondered, to be invited to a picnic? To be asked how they'd manage this or that? To be consulted as to what she meant to take and to wear? To be, in short, one of them? The last picnic Sarah Jane had attended, the girls had ignored her and strolled off by themselves. And at lunchtime she couldn't find anyone to share her lunch. It was a Sunday school picnic, too. After that Sarah Jane hadn't wanted to go to picnics or to Sunday school.

Stephen knew nothing about the disappointment connected with the green braid, and he stood with his hands in his pockets and wondered why Sarah Jane didn't come.

"Good morning," said a clear voice beside him.

He turned quickly to meet the woman who had "gray eyes and wore some still, pale stuff." The description fitted her yet. But why should she say "good morning" to him? In his surprise and embarrassment, he forget even to nod his head in reply. But the lady didn't wait for a response.

"You're Mr. Mitchell, I believe? I'm Helen Ransom, the minister's sister. I've come to keep house for him, and I want to get acquainted with his people. You attend church here regularly, don't you?"

Stephen studied this problem for a minute, going back rapidly over his past, to discover it was nearly two months since he'd been inside the church.

"Not very regular, I reckon," he said at last, with an embarrassed laugh. "We live a long way from the church, and the roads are heavy."

"I know. But this is your church home, isn't it? Therefore we should be acquainted. Do you know my brother?"

Stephen shook his head. Mr. Ransom was a stranger, having been in the neighborhood only a few months. On the few occasions when Stephen honored him with his presence, he'd slipped away before the new minister could see him. It had never occurred to him to wait and speak to his pastor or give the pastor opportunity to speak with him. Why should he?

The church had long been pastorless, and the constant succession of "supplies" hadn't made the acquaintance of the Mitchell family.

"Then I hope you'll wait," said Helen, "and let me introduce you. He wants to get acquainted with his people as rapidly as possible. Are there others in your neighborhood he could call on when we come out to see you?"

Stephen was about to shake his head, but he gave himself to bewildered thought instead. Why should he at this moment think of the Lucas family? They were the only ones in his immediate neighborhood, it's true. But who could imagine anything so absurd as people like her and her brother visiting them? Yet the Lucases needed good done to them, if that was what she meant.

They need civilizing, he said to himself with a grim smile. *And like enough she could do it faster than Sarah Jane and I can. But of course she won't. Them ain't the kind they go to see.*

"There's folks," he said at last, speaking half-sullenly. "But they ain't the kind to be called on."

"Why not?" she asked with a genial smile. "Wouldn't they want to see us?"

"I don't know about that," said Stephen. "But they're lowdown folks that nobody ever calls on. They don't go to church. It's out of their line. They're a hard set—'barbarians,' a man called them the other day. But I don't know as they can help it. The womenfolks can't anyhow. They're poor and never had any chance, and the menfolks drink. So what can you expect?"

"Not much, certainly," said Miss Ransom in a gentle voice, "unless they get acquainted with Jesus Christ. He's the great civilizer, you know. But don't you think such people need calling upon and helping? I'm glad to find they have a champion in you."

She was as much surprised at the sudden flash in his eyes as Mr. Meadows had been. Here was his third word, which thus far had resisted his efforts to discover its meaning. Behold! There must be some sense in which he was a "champion." And the sentence connected him with the Lucas family. Life was certainly growing full of mysteries for Stephen Mitchell.

Miss Ransom hesitated in the word she was about to speak, when she saw that peculiar flash of Stephen's eyes. What had she said to bring such a look of keen, wistful intelligence into them? While she hesitated and wondered, Sarah Jane appeared, and someone from the other door claimed Miss Ransom. She turned back to bow to Stephen and assure him of her intention of coming with her brother to see them as soon as possible, but he had plunged forward into the little yard and was already lost to sight.

"I wonder who she is," said Sarah Jane, coming slowly after him with her eyes behind her. "I never did see such an elegant-looking lady in all my days."

"Who?" asked Stephen, shortly.

"Why, that woman who stood close by you when I came out. You don't say you didn't see her, Steve? That's too bad! Why, she looked like a picture. And her dress—oh, my! Wasn't it lovely? Steve, I wish I knew such people and could shake hands with them and laugh and talk and be one of them. There doesn't seem to be any folks for us to belong to—isn't it odd?"

"Only the Lucases," Stephen said. "I suppose we might laugh and talk with them as much as we have a mind to."

"The Lucases!" repeated Sarah Jane in intense scorn. "I don't see why you keep talking about them, Steve. We're poor and don't have company or chances or anything. But we're decent and clean and all that. There's a big difference between us and them."

Then Stephen, who had already gone deeper into life's problems than his sister had thought of doing, reflected that Sarah Jane from her standpoint looked down on those below her with even more vehemence perhaps than those above her looked down on her.

But she's *above us, high enough,* he told himself, with the peculiar emphasis on the pronoun which distinguished one person in his mind from all others. *And she wasn't scornful or lofty. I guess she'd have been nice to Sarah Jane. I might have introduced her, I suppose.*

So, in much humility of spirit, he climbed into the old spring wagon and was unusually silent, even for him, during the long drive home.

Chapter 10

Obstructions

Helen Ransom sat opposite her brother at the breakfast table. She studied his thoughtful, somewhat sad face before she asked her question. During the Sabbath she'd carefully refrained from questions of all sorts and soothed and ministered to the young pastor, who she felt was her special charge, to her heart's content. But now it was Monday morning, and she meant to accomplish certain things that week if possible. Moreover, she felt that if her brother needed one thing more than another, it was to be aroused to his duties and responsibilities in certain directions and to be drawn from his brooding thoughts in certain other directions. Her question was one means toward these ends.

"Maxwell, have you called near Hilton Hill?"

The minister shook his head, and his sister could see he winced at the question.

After a moment's hesitation he said, "I haven't done much calling anywhere in the country as yet. But there are very few people to reach on the Hilton Hill road. Mr. Bascome told me he didn't know of any who could be said to belong to us, and he lives where the road forks and knows all that neighborhood."

"I met someone from that region yesterday morning. He was in church with his sister. And he told me of others—one family, in particular, he's evidently become interested in. From what he said, they need others interested in their welfare. Perhaps Mr. Bascome isn't entirely reliable regarding people you'd be interested in, Max. He impresses me as a man who might gauge the importance of people by their standing in society or their bank account. I promised that young fellow we'd come out and call, this week if we could. It's going to be very pleasant today, I think. Couldn't we go this afternoon?"

"I'm afraid you'll find it hard driving, Helen. The roads are what people in the country call 'heavy.' It must be all up and downhill and through a stony part of the country."

"Ah, but I want to ride. Mr. Dunlap told me of a beautiful riding horse to be had, and I'm longing to get into the saddle again."

The minister was silent for so long that his sister, who had purposely refrained from looking at him while she was speaking, turned anxious eyes in his direction. His own were bent upon his plate, though nothing on it seemed to claim his attention. He looked up at last with a faint smile, seeming to feel the anxiety in his sister's eyes, which were bent upon him.

"Aren't you rather hard on me?" he asked deprecatingly.

She shook her head. "You're hard on yourself, Max—yes, and hard on me. Is it fair to keep me from an exercise I'm so fond of and which has been urged upon us both, because—?" There she came to a sudden pause.

"No," he said firmly, after a longer silence than before, "it isn't fair. I don't mean to do it. I intend to rise above this feeling. But I didn't think I could yet."

"But you can," she said, with the feeling of a surgeon resolved upon the importance of probing a wound at whatever pain, rather than with the air of a blunderer who didn't know he was giving pain. "Max, I know by experience that when you allow such things to trammel you, they have power to grow harder and harder. I don't believe you intend to let this sorrow hamper your life or work in any way, and I long to see you take hold of it with the strength of will you possess. I don't think I can wait any longer."

But she had to wait some minutes again before she was answered. Certainly the minister's breakfast wasn't claiming his attention this morning. He cut his steak with exceeding care, as if preparing it for a delicate child, but he left it untasted and stirred his coffee mechanically.

"I sometimes think," he said at last, clearing his voice, for its huskiness was perceptible, "that Gertrude was right. It was all a mistake, and I'm not fit for the ministry. There's work on every hand that should be done, but I can't tell you how I shrink from it. In my study and in the pulpit I can forget myself, but this mingling with people is something I feel totally unfit for. The eternal round of calls, repeating the same inane sentences from house to house, then beginning again when someone has gotten through it alive, and doing it over. The thought of all this weighs me to the ground. Sometimes, as I say, I feel Gertrude was right and I'm not called to the work."

If he'd expected to shock his sister, he was mistaken. She turned her eyes from his face and gazed out upon the lawn. So far from being shocked was she that, if she hadn't feared to pain her brother, she could have smiled over the exceeding morbidness of such a confession. Helen Ransom was the minister's twin sister and felt herself almost a part of him—his "other self," he fondly used to call her. Through babyhood, childhood, early youth, up to the time when the brother entered the theological seminary, they hadn't been separated for a day, scarcely for an hour. Even through his theological course, his sister kept such steady pace with his mental development—reading the books he read and, so far as possible, studying the books he studied—that it hardly seemed a separation. She felt she knew him thoroughly. She believed in him thoroughly. She believed that if ever a man was called of God to the work of the gospel ministry, Maxwell Ransom was that man. She knew that when his system had rallied from the shock of a heavy sorrow which had fallen upon him, he would realize his call again, as he had in the past. In the meantime she must wait patiently and plan as skillfully as she could.

"It isn't surprising you shrink from calls," she said quietly, "if that's your conception of them. Going from house to house, saying nothings, month after month and year after year, must indeed be a dreary prospect. But, Max, what if you go from house to house reaching consciences, turning wayward footsteps, holding out helping hands?"

He shook his head, the look of pain upon his face growing deeper. "I don't know," he said at last. "I don't understand myself. I seem to have lost interest in humanity. I used to have an ambition, as you well know, to reach people—help them, lift them up, as you say—but I seem to have lost it. Sometimes I almost think I don't care whether people advance or not. It's this mental condition which leads me occasionally to feel what I've just confessed to you, that I've mistaken my calling."

"Maxwell, do you care for Jesus Christ?"

There was no mistaking the questioner's earnestness or her tenderness. Her voice was as sweet as a chime of bells; yet she threw all the strength of her nature into that one brief question and waited.

He looked at her then with a startled, searching look, as if he wished to get behind the question and see what prompted it.

"Yes," he said, after a moment. "I haven't lapsed to that degree. I do care for Jesus Christ. But for Him, it seems, there are times when I couldn't live."

"That's all," said his sister. "I was sure of it, but I wanted you to remind yourself and then think of what you've been saying. Caring for Him, you're bound to care for His interests. You'd be under just as strong obligations, you know, if you were a lawyer or a bricklayer. He cared for people, and you must, because you're His servant, His steward, His lover. I'm not afraid for you, Maxwell, eventually. But I'm troubled to think how your conscience will upbraid you one of these days, when you realize you're wasting time. Can't we go to the Hilton neighborhood this afternoon?"

"Yes," he said, looking at her again, this time breaking into a smile. "We'll go to the Hilton neighborhood or anywhere else you please. And we'll ride there. I'll inquire about the horse you spoke of. Did you say Mr. Dunlap told you? And, Helen, thank you. I don't know how it is, but you seem to know just what to say and the right moment to say it. I haven't really meant to shirk, though I've felt unfit lately. You didn't come to me too soon."

He left his scarcely tasted breakfast and went to his study. His sister waited until the door closed after him, before she drew a long sigh—a sort of escape valve for pent-up anxiety—and murmured under her breath: "Poor fellow! No, I didn't come too soon."

You're not to understand that Maxwell Ransom was a sentimentalist or a misanthrope. On the contrary, he was a strong-souled, strong-nerved young man, who had given himself gladly to the work of the gospel ministry. The years of preparation had been joyful and the preparation itself conscientious. Nor was he one of those who, in their zeal to furnish the soul and mind, forget the body's needs. He'd been delighted to bring to the work a well-disciplined body, prepared by intelligent training to serve faithfully. There really wasn't a morbid streak in this young man's nature. Yet I'm aware I've presented a picture which suggests weakness, oversensitiveness, and disappointment. It becomes necessary to explain. To understand it, however, you would need to do what one can never fully accomplish—put yourself in another's place and think his thoughts.

Also, I should introduce to you Gertrude Temple—a beautiful girl, who, in addition to her beauty and grace, had about her an indescribable charm which attracted and held captive many besides Maxwell Ransom. Still, I must confess he saw in her not herself, but what he imagined her to be. If you know any such persons who would say, "This is she! My ideal—the human embodiment of all I've dreamed," and walk with blinded eyes beside her, seeing none of the imperfections plain to others, you understand to a degree what Maxwell Ransom did. Not that he expected to find perfection in human nature; not that he didn't see what he supposed should be called faults in Gertrude Temple. But he saw less in her than in others and believed time and grace could and would smooth away her imperfections.

And she was, in his estimation, so above and beyond him that he often lost himself in amazement over her choice; for she made deliberate choice of the young theological student. She was a schoolgirl when he first met her, pursuing her studies in the same town where the theological seminary was located. Both were busy—he with actual hard work, she with a thousand things having nothing to do with her standing in class but in such a pretty way as to make one think so. It would have been impossible at that stage to make young Ransom believe he was happier in the brief spaces of time he could give the lady of his choice than he would have been if he'd been at leisure to know her better. As it was, he was satisfied and royally happy, and no more sincere prayer did he offer night and morning than the one in which he thanked God for this last crowning gift—the love of a pure, true woman.

The first shadow which fell across their lives was during the Christmas holidays. Gertrude went home, of course, and the plan had been that Maxwell, as soon as he'd paid his respects to his own home, would follow her and make more intimate acquaintance of her family. But at home the theological student found work which held him. His father was the pastor of a large and important country church, and a revival was in progress. Meetings were being held twice each day, and expected help had been detained by sickness. The father, overworked and burdened in several ways, was breaking under the strain and hailed, as a father would, the relief his son's coming could bring. Duty was never plainer to Max-well Ransom than during those three weeks he was held steadily to the work in his father's parish. In a sense, of course, it was a disappointment not to make his promised visit. But in another sense he gloried in the disappointment and believed Gertrude would join him in his joy. What a blessed opportunity had been given him for gathering experiences for his life's work!

"You can understand," he wrote to Gertrude, "how, in one sense, it's anything but a trial to be held here this way. The meetings are wonderful, dear. Every night, as I go over the day's record, I say to my heart, 'Oh, if Gertrude were only here, how she'd enjoy these opportunities!' And the interest, instead of abating, as predicted it would during the actual Christmas week, seems to be increasing. Last night more than forty persons stood for prayers. Many of them were heads of families, and a number were young men whose lives have been hard and whose mothers wept and prayed over them and felt at times it was almost in vain.

"Think of it, Gertrude, what it was to see them rise for prayer and meet them afterward in the inquiry room. It was crowded to overflowing. My dear one, if you could only be with me during this blessed time, what a daily, hourly joy life would be to me.

"Along with what I've told you, I must add that my poor father, tempted the early part of the winter to overwork, is physically unable to carry on one entire meeting alone and seems unable to secure other help. So you'll understand how impossible it is for me to get away even for a few days.

"There's a side to it, Gertrude, which makes me more sorry than the words placed on paper can tell. But I needn't even try to explain. You'll understand. It's a blessing for me to remember we're one in this, as in all other things."

Chapter 11

Intersecting Lines

If he could have seen the frown on Gertrude's forehead deepening with every line she read, as she sat in morning dress in her mother's room! If he could have heard the conversation which followed!

"Well," said Mrs. Temple, "when will we see your theologue? He seems slow in coming. I wonder how you can tolerate such indifference to your charms."

"Mamma, he's not coming at all! At least, that's what I gather from his letter. Those poky old meetings, day and night! And his father's sick. I would think he'd be, having meetings all the time! And Maxwell says I'll understand how impossible it is for him to get away. I don't understand it at all."

"The idea!" said Mrs. Temple. "A three-week vacation, and he can't find time to come and see you in your own home. I must say I consider that carrying things with a rather high hand. My dear, I'm afraid he's the fanatical sort, who'll wear your life out with an eternal round of meetings, missionary societies, and Sunday schools."

"Mamma, do hush!" said the young woman. "You show you don't know what you're talking about. Maxwell Ransom is the most brilliant young man in the seminary, and he was the most brilliant one in college. A 'sense of duty' is one of his strong points. But he'll never be a country parson, Mamma, and drag me off to missionary meetings or female prayer meetings. I'm awfully sorry he can't be here for New Year's. He has odd country notions, of course— he's been brought up in the country largely—and needs to get them rubbed off. I could help him immensely in those ways. Oh! I don't mean he's awkward, Mamma. He's a perfectly exquisite gentleman everywhere. But I mean he has ideas, old-fashioned ones, you know, about dancing and matters like that. He's a bit fanatical on the temperance question, I suspect; not that I object to that in a man—only it would be awkward sometimes in city life. Oh, dear! I'm too provoked for anything. I wanted to show him off to the girls. He's handsomer than any man in our set, Mamma. If it wasn't for those horrid meetings—I don't believe in having meetings day after day, wearing people's bodies out. He'll never do it when he has a church of his own. People should be temperate in religion as in anything else, and I know I can coax him into thinking so, too. Oh! You needn't shake your head, Mamma. I have a great deal of influence over him. Why, he thinks I'm perfection."

If he could have heard all this, it might have made a difference in his immediate future. But he didn't hear it; he went on with his eager work— though it wasn't the vacation he and Gertrude had planned together—enjoying it as only one whose heart was in it could. He was ten days late at the seminary because he'd taken such hold of the work that it seemed impossible to get away before. The detention didn't trouble Gertrude, for she was more than ten days late in getting back to school.

"Sister Kate has company, and I'm sorely needed at home," she wrote Maxwell. "It seems impossible to leave just now. Mamma needs me for special reasons and thinks even a schoolgirl mustn't forget she has duties in her own home."

The young minister pondered over the sentences, wondered what the loving ministrations were and wished his darling had been more explicit. He sympathized with her in her sacrifice of those two important weeks from school. He felt and told her on paper it was like her to think of others and not of herself.

She laughed over this added testimony to her power and went on making out the list for the brilliant party her mother was giving early in the following week—other similar engagements having prevented her from getting hers in before. Certainly Gertrude was needed at home, for the party was to be the season's most elegant, planned with a special view to eclipsing all that preceded it; and Gertrude Temple was an excellent planner in all such directions.

They returned at last to the routine of study life. But they had met only two or three times before young Ransom began to feel a change had come over Gertrude. She seemed ill at ease and at times almost dissatisfied with her future prospects. She began to make suggestions, perhaps more properly called hints, concerning the trials and privations of ministerial life and to ask him if he felt sure he was called to that work and no other. What if he was theologically educated? So were college professors, authors, and men in political life. She had once heard a certain eminent lawyer say he regarded the two years he'd spent studying theology as two of the most valuable years of his preparation for his profession.

Gradually she grew more outspoken. She felt confident, she assured him, that he'd made a mistake. She couldn't believe a man of his talent was called upon to bury himself in a country village and call people who could neither understand nor appreciate him. She'd felt for some time that he was called to a higher sphere, well, not higher perhaps, she hastened to explain, noting his air of pained surprise—but different. Common-place people, she believed, could preach the gospel as well as highly cultured ones. What was there to do but point out the right road and get men to walk on it if you could?

Maxwell Ransom listened to her at first with a bewildered air. He even laughed a little over some of her bright speeches, believing she must be trying to amuse him. Such words couldn't express Gertrude Temple's real convictions. He believed life had no higher sphere than to preach the gospel. It was folly to talk about talents thrown away. Hadn't it been the joy of his life to feel that God had called him to such great honor and endowed him with powers which would enable him to be useful in that position?

"I don't understand Gertrude," he told himself wearily.

So he began patiently to explain his views, giving her occasional glimpses of the joy the future had in store for him, when he would discover that, because of his preaching and his teaching, someone came to know Jesus Christ.

There came a time when Gertrude Temple said no more—not because she was satisfied, but because she had failed.

They were very busy, living their separate lives. The closing months of study were before them. They were looking forward, not only to the day when they would graduate, but one of them, at least, thought often of that important day in the future when they would be united to separate no more. They saw little of each other during that last term. Maxwell was away nearly every Sabbath preaching somewhere. His services seemed already in demand, and the time necessarily consumed in journeying to and from his appointments straitened him somewhat in his studies and made it necessary for him to curtail his hours of rest and recreation. He thought Gertrude very patient, wise, and sympathetic over all these disappointments. He didn't for one moment imagine she was reaching that state of mind when to visit with him was becoming embarrassing and that she hailed each detention with relief. Not until they were both graduated and Gertrude had gone to her home, leaving him expecting to follow her in a few weeks to complete their arrangements for the future, did the blow fall upon him.

This, of course, was not only cruel, but cowardly. Gertrude Temple knew weeks before she graduated that she meant to tell this man to whom her hand was pledged that she'd discovered they weren't suited to each other. But no hint of this determination passed her lips. She waited until miles had divided them, that she might escape the embarrassment of being face-to-face with the misery she'd wrought. She was very kind indeed. Words failed, she assured him, to express her deep sorrow and regret. But she'd felt for a long time, and Mamma had fully agreed with her, that she wasn't fitted to be a minister's wife. All her inclinations and tastes pointed in other directions. She didn't know, she was sure, why she'd allowed herself to be drawn into an engagement. She'd always known she was a poor, worthless creature, not suited to the dignity of such a station. She supposed that, in enjoying his society, she'd forgotten the future and hadn't realized, but the beautiful winter they'd enjoyed together would always remain. Now that her eyes were really open or she'd grown older and wiser perhaps, she shrank in terror from the future he had planned.

He would bear her witness that she'd tried to explain and done her utmost to induce him to give up the ministry and devote himself to some profession in which she could hope to keep pace with him. He would remember, she was sure, how earnestly she'd talked of this matter. And of course he would remember—certainly she would never forget—how solemnly he'd assured her that nothing but the hand of God laid upon him and the voice of God calling to him to give up his work could possibly change his mind.

From that hour, she declared, she'd given up all hope of living their lives together; for of course she couldn't expect the Lord to work a miracle in her behalf, and Maxwell demanded nothing less than a miracle.

Because of her plain speaking in the past, she felt sure he must be prepared for the conclusion of the whole matter. They must just make up their minds they were foolish young people, who, enjoying each other's society so much for a few months, had blundered into the mistaken idea they were suited to each other for life. People often made such mistakes, she believed. Mamma was engaged three times before she was finally married to Papa.

She couldn't help admiring him for holding so resolutely to his purpose to preach the gospel, though she'd thought for a time it would break her silly heart. But now that all was over between them, she presumed he was right. Probably he did have a special call to that work and would serve well in it. Only she was unfitted for it, and therefore it was eminently fitting she should take herself out of his way. Perhaps she should have told him before she left college, but it seemed a pity to disturb those few last hurried minutes they had together by any disagreeable talk. So she'd resolved to wait until she reached home and could put it on paper, thus saving him a great deal of trouble.

And I'll always be interested in your welfare (the young girl's letter went on to say). *I'd like to hear you preach better than almost any other person. I hope you'll get a church somewhere near where I live or may in the future. Who knows where that will be? Isn't life strange? What if in years to come you'd be my pastor and call on me—make pastoral calls, you know—and I would be "Mrs. Smith" or "Mrs. Jones" or something? Wouldn't that be too funny for anything? Well, just such strange things as that have happened.*

I don't quite know how to finish this letter. It's such a strange letter—different from any I ever wrote you. You won't be angry with the silly little girl, will you? I was always silly, Max, and wasn't worthy of you. I knew it all the time, but you never suspected it. That was because you were good—and because you are good, you'll forgive me, won't you? And forget me, I daresay, in a month or two. So I'll send you back the pretty ring you gave me, though I can't bear to part with it, but of course that's proper. I wonder who'll wear it next? And now, wishing you a better and happier life than I could possibly have made for you, I close by signing myself,

Ever your sincere friend,
Gertrude Temple

You can imagine something of what such a letter was to Maxwell Ransom. A man who considered a pledge of any sort a sacred thing; had thought long and carefully and prayed for guidance before offering his hand to this woman and, once offering it, had surrendered himself as utterly as a true man can; had looked upon himself as, in God's eyes, a married man, waiting only for the hour when it would become his right to consummate before the world the vows which had already been taken.

Chapter 12

Sidetracks

I don't say," he explained once in answer to a question asked him by a friend in perplexity, "that engagements should never be broken. Some circumstances, perhaps, make this not only right and proper but, further, make it the only right thing to be done. But God grant that you and I may be delivered from any such experiences. I want to consider an engagement of marriage a holy thing, a pledge upon which my Master has smiled, and upon the consummation of which I have His blessing. Certainly such an engagement isn't to be entered into lightly or for any common reason broken."

And these words were spoken only a few months before his engagement was thus rudely broken. How was he engaged to be married to a person who could write such a letter as has been described? Ah! The one who could answer such a question, and so plainly that other young men and women in years to come would be open-eyed and escape the bewilderments scarring some lives, would confer almost a priceless boon upon society. It would be impossible for you to see how altogether lovely in heart and mind and person Gertrude Temple had seemed to this young man. Childish he knew she was, only nineteen, that he'd pledged himself to wait a year after graduating before claiming her as his bride. So innocent, he thought she was, that he could read her heart. So earnest in her Christian life that she was the only young lady in her class who could be induced to take her turn in leading the young people's meetings—yet so shy and modest that her voice had trembled like a frightened child's as she read the sacred Bible words, which had never before sounded so much like music in his ears.

Nor was Gertrude Temple playing a part at that time. She was sincere enough or supposed she was. Hadn't the most talented young man in the seminary chosen her? She felt honored by his preference, knew she was envied by a score of schoolgirls, and imagined she loved him. Perhaps if he could have held her steadily under his influence, she might not have discovered her mistake. But she went home to her world for vacations—a world as unlike her school life and the influences surrounding her as possible. She frolicked and frittered away the days and nights in one continual round of parties and festivities, awakening one day to the fact that this was her life, it was altogether agreeable to her, and prayer meetings and church societies and dutiful calls were quite distasteful and might grow intolerable. As for the mother, she'd had other plans for her darling. She not only sighed but shed tears, when she heard of the engagement and told her confidential friend that "poor Gertrude is throwing herself away."

She did what she could in a ladylike way to foster the girl's unrest and feeling of unfitness for the life she'd chosen. The first result, as you've seen, was to lead her to try to turn the young minister from his set purpose in life. For a time the daughter believed she could succeed; she succeeded in most undertakings. She had coaxed, wheedled, and cried her way into fulfilling all plans she had cared to carry out. Why should she fail in this, the most important one that had touched her?

But she failed and saw this as the days went by. Mr. Ransom couldn't even understand her. He gave her credit for too much principle to suppose she could be sincere in her suggestions. He convinced her that he, too, had convictions and to move him from some of them was impossible. The only alternative was to break her engagement. A minister's wife she could never be, and she shrank from it in horror. She spent some miserable weeks—sorry for Maxwell every time she met him; sorry for herself whenever she heard his name mentioned—as she frequently did—in admiration and praise.

She didn't deliberately plan to hold him as her attendant for the season and then turn him off as worthless; she made it plain to herself it would be cruel to desert him so near the close of his seminary course. The wiser way was to wait until he graduated; people could write such things better than they could speak them. Yes, it was the better way, the Christian way, indeed. So she kept her own counsel and pressed moral science and intellectual philosophy and every other high-sounding name she could into the spaces where she might have been expected to have leisure for him and bore with what gravity she could his earnest appeals to her not to overstudy.

This was the letter the young minister had taken to his room to read behind locked doors, so the joy of the next half hour couldn't be interfered with. How utterly it had dashed to the ground, without a moment's warning, the cup which had seemed brimming with hope and happiness! He wasn't crushed outwardly; strong natures such as his rarely are. Within the hour he appeared at the family dinner table much as usual, talked with his father concerning the news of the day, and gave his usual thoughtful attention to his mother and sisters. Only his twin sister, Helen, knew he was in any way different.

To her he told the whole story in time. At least, he told his side of the whole story; he couldn't have told Gertrude Temple's side. Even after this experience he didn't understand her. He hadn't admitted to his own heart that she was deliberately false; he said she was too humble, too distrustful of her own powers, and was influenced by others to adopt the idea she wasn't fitted to the life to which his profession called her.

"She has a worldly mother," he said with a sigh. "I have no doubt her mother opposed our engagement; I felt it from the first. And Gertrude, of course, was influenced by her mother. Helen, she isn't heartless. I won't have you think so. It isn't necessary to wrong her, even in thought, because she's lost to me. She's very young and less mature than girls her age often are. She depended upon her mother a great deal, I think. Of course, she didn't care for me as I do for her; we're not alike in that respect. But undoubtedly she thought she did, and she isn't to be condemned, as young as she is and under such influences as she's been all her life, because she made a mistake."

Outwardly, after that, life moved on in about the same channel as before for Maxwell Ransom. To his mother, who was a frail, suffering woman, to be shielded from possible pain and cared for and comforted in every way, he told only the surface of his story. Of course, she knew he had been engaged, and of course she must know the engagement was broken.

"It seemed wisest, Mother," he'd said with a grave smile. "I know I've held strict views on that subject, but this is one of those rare instances in which it becomes right to break one's pledge. Don't worry about it, Mother dear. 'All things work together,' you know."

And his mother, looking wistful, yet hesitating to question what he so manifestly didn't care to tell, said presently, "Well, my son, of course we're not sorry to have you all our own once more. Only—"

"Only you don't want my heart broken," he said, bending to kiss her and trying to speak lightly. "It isn't, Mother, and you don't need, I think, to be assured that I haven't been instrumental in breaking the heart of another."

It was impossible not to let his voice tremble over that sentence, and of course it told his mother a great deal. She asked no questions; but from that hour she had her own private opinion of Gertrude Temple.

Only Helen, as I said, knew all her brother could tell; and she, who had been in some respects mother as well as sister, watched him with some anxiety during the months which followed. His first step bewildered her. He declined, in a very positive manner, the unanimous call of a church in a distant city—a church she'd supposed him to be deeply interested in and one which, indeed, had apparently been waiting for him. And he had certainly encouraged them to feel he would consider their call.

"I'm distressed over that," he said, walking nervously about his room, while Helen sat at his desk. She had just been reading his emphatic refusal of the call and reminded him they would have reason to be disappointed.

"I'm very sorry I encouraged them. They'll think I have something better in mind."

"They can't think that," said Helen, "because you've been very clear in your explanation. But, Maxwell, there's a reason for your refusal. Do you mind telling me what it is?"

"No," he said, after a moment's hesitation. "It isn't worthwhile for me to mind telling you—my other self—anything, but it's a humiliating reason. Gertrude's uncle lives in that city and attends that church, and Gertrude herself will be there a large portion of the season. I couldn't become the pastor of the church under such circumstances."

"No," she said, "you couldn't, of course. I understand." But she sighed as she spoke. It was a very flattering call to a beautiful, growing city, and she had ambitions for her brother.

Not only did he decline the call to the city church, but he accepted the very next opening which came, and it happened to be to serve the plain little church in the farming village, eight miles from where Stephen Mitchell lived.

So now we've come back to the breakfast table at the manse and to Helen's plans for the afternoon. Her plans hadn't been made without careful thought; she had been installed only about three weeks as mistress of her brother's home. But it hadn't taken three weeks for Helen Ransom to discover that the experience her brother had passed through hadn't left him unscarred. He was certainly changed, and the change made her anxious. He'd been a genial young man and very interested in human nature, especially that exhibited in young people. Not only was he interested in those of his own circle, but more particularly in the struggling ones, or those from any cause disheartened. She'd often thought with pride of what a power he would be among young men.

It hadn't taken three weeks of careful study of her brother's congregation to discover that if struggling and discouraged ones weren't among them, certainly some needed elevating, to have an influence come into their lives, different from any which had yet touched them. But she'd discovered also that her brother had lost his interest, apparently, in humanity. He preached his sermons with energy and earnestness, and they were studied sermons—intellectual, cultured, wrought out with utmost care—and as cold as polished marble. They flowed smoothly over the heads of his hearers without touching their thoughts. The truth is, the young minister was trying to cover up the pain and disappointment of his life by losing himself in his books.

He was a born student, and books had a power to absorb him, so he could forget himself, his friends, and, in a sense, his work. He shrank from society. He admitted it to himself. People, especially young people, became distasteful to him; he felt out of sympathy with their interests. His sister felt this and knew the cause of it. She knew also that it would distress him someday to discover he had let precious time run to waste. She waited silently, but prayerfully, for the awakening and had reached the conclusion her brother should be roused. She had wondered during yesterday's service, as she looked frequently at Stephen Mitchell, whether possibly he was the one to help in this matter. Something about the boy greatly interested her, though she couldn't have explained why, and the reports she'd received upon inquiry hadn't been calculated to deepen the interest.

"Oh! I know who you mean," Fanny Bascome had said. "It's Steve Mitchell. He lives out on one of the crossroads, on a farm that's all rundown. It never was managed right, Pa says, and is mortgaged for more than it's worth. They're dreadfully poor. Yes, there's a father and mother. Steve's the only son, and there's one girl. She's an odd creature, always fussing with her clothes, trying to make them look like something. It would just kill you to see her. She hasn't things to do with, you know, and she makes herself into a perfect fright—trying to follow the fashions.

"Why, yes, I know them as you know people who've lived in the same neighborhood with you all their lives. They live on the old Mitchell place—

Stephen's grandfather used to own it. He was a nice kind of man—quite smart, they say. I wonder that none of his family took after him. But Josiah Mitchell, Stephen's father, has never been any account—shiftless, I guess. Anyhow, things have gone to wreck and ruin pretty generally around them.

"Oh! I never go out there! They don't have anything to do with other people. They can't, you know; they're so poor. Steve's a regular country bumpkin. The poor fellow will blush as red as a peony if a girl bows to him on the street. As for coming to church, he doesn't do it once in an age. I suppose he's a hard sort of boy. Ma thinks the mother has more to her; she went out there to see her once or twice years ago. But she never comes to church or has anything to do with other people, and I don't suppose she's much better than the rest of them.

"It's a miserable kind of neighborhood, Miss Ransom. What few people are scattered along that road don't appear to amount to anything. There's a Lucas set out there somewhere. I've heard Ned talk about the Lucas boys. They're all drunkards, and I suppose they're a terrible lot. Oh, well! As to doing anything for them, how can you? There's no way of getting hold of such people. You can't mingle with them, of course, and they won't come to church, so you can't even preach at them. I don't know whether the Lucases have ever been asked to church or not. I don't suppose anybody ever thought of such a thing. Dear me! They needn't wait to be asked. I don't know as anybody ever asked us to come." And Fanny Bascome finished the sentence with her usual little giggle.

Chapter 13

Plans for a Through Line

Nevertheless, Helen Ransom continued to be interested in Stephen Mitchell. She'd resolved, as we're aware, that his family should be called upon that very afternoon and that she and her brother would ride there for that purpose, despite the fact that she knew he hadn't been on horseback since one bright day in the early spring, when he rode with Gertrude Temple.

Helen had never seen Gertrude Temple in her life, but she had a supreme contempt for that young woman and resolved that by riding, at least, the power of association connected with her should be broken. Her brother should ride with her. She would urge it on the ground of her own enjoyment of that exercise and let him understand she considered it selfish of him to bar her from it. Those two arguments, she knew would be potent with him. He had no desire to nurse his disappointment at the expense of other people's pleasure.

"Oh, my sakes!" said Sarah Jane Mitchell, gazing from her upper window away down the road. "What a cloud of dust! Look here, Mother, quick! Here's a woman coming on horseback. My! Doesn't she ride pretty? I declare, if it ain't Mr. Ransom with her, and she's that girl I seen in church Sunday. I do wonder who she is. Don't they look nice together, Mother? If I could ride a horse like that, wouldn't it be too splendid for anything? She's got a dark blue—Mother, as true as you live and breathe, they're coming here. They've turned up our lane. Oh, land! What will I do now? Say, Mother, do go down and tend to them, won't you? It's the minister, you know, and he'll have to see you. Just think of his coming here to call on us! I'm all in a fluster. But I must put on my green dress before I can come down; this one ain't fit to be seen. Oh, good land of pity! Do hurry, Mother. He's got her off her horse, and they're coming up the stoop together."

In the wildest excitement, Sarah Jane dashed like a grasshopper about her room, putting herself with frantic haste into her green dress, twice buttoning it wrong in her hurry, and at last, very red of face and almost breathless, made her way downstairs as her mother was coming up to call her.

"I don't know how they did it," she explained to Stephen afterward, "but they hadn't been here three minutes before I felt as if I'd known them all my life. They were just as nice and easy and pleasant as if we were old friends. Mother did it up real nice, too. You'd have been proud of her, Steve. 'This is my daughter,' she said.

"And Miss Ransom got up and came over to me like a queen—oh, a great deal nicer than a queen, because she would have been stuck-up, and Miss Ransom wasn't a bit. She held out her hand and said, 'How do you do, Miss Mitchell?

I saw you in church Sunday. I'm so glad to know you.' And she kept hold of my hand and turned to the minister and said, 'My brother, Mr. Ransom, Miss Mitchell.' And then he shook hands as cordial as could be and said he was glad to meet some of his flock away out here; he hadn't known until today that his people were so far out. Then they both sat down and talked as pleasant as if they were real glad to talk to us. And Mother told them how far she was from church and how much church was to her and all that."

But one of Helen Ransom's remarks had astonished Sarah Jane.

"I hope your brother is at home, Miss Mitchell. We want especially to meet him and ask him about some people he was telling me about yesterday. And my brother wants to make his acquaintance."

"Steve?" Sarah Jane had said in bewilderment, turning a rosier red than before and looking over helplessly to her mother.

"Why, yes," said Mrs. Mitchell, who in the days past had known of pastoral calls and knew how to conduct herself, "Stephen is at home. He's digging potatoes. Sarah Jane, you run and find him, will you? And tell him the minister is here. I'm sorry my husband isn't home," the mother had continued. "He's gone up the road a ways this afternoon. He'll be real sorry not to see you."

And then Sarah Jane had gotten herself out of the room, much astonished. How well her mother conducted the conversation. How nice it was for her to say that about Father. But Steve—how would she manage about him? Ministerial calls, or any calls, for that matter, had been unknown quantities in the Mitchell family for years, and the idea of inducing Steve, with his great discomfort around women especially, to come in and receive a call wasn't to be entertained for a moment. She followed him like one dazed, as, receiving her astounding news, he dropped his hoe suddenly and walked toward the water trough to wash his hands.

"I don't look over and above respectable," he said, surveying himself ruefully. "But if you'll slip up the back stairs, Sarah Jane, and get my coat, I reckon I'll do."

"Yes," said Sarah Jane, almost breathless, "I will." And as she dashed up the back stairs, she wondered to herself if "barbarian" and "civilization" and "champion" could have anything to do with Steve's astonishing behavior.

While the minister interested himself in Stephen, Sarah Jane was lifted to the seventh heaven of delight that Miss Ransom was giving most of her attention to her. She asked her innumerable questions about the farm, the animals, the garden, the woods in the vicinity, and the wildflowers that bloomed there, and she seemed interested in her answers. Presently she roused to the fact that the minister was addressing her.

"I beg your pardon, Miss Mitchell. But may I interrupt you for a moment to ask my sister a question?"

"Helen, what would you think of waiting here for me while Mr. Mitchell pilots me to the Lucas home? He tells me that across the fields it's a comparatively short walk, and I'd like him to introduce me to the family, if it can be arranged."

Helen expressed herself as entirely willing to remain as long as necessary, and Sarah Jane forgot to be overwhelmed with delight over this new plan in her astonishment that Steve was actually going to "pilot" the minister across the fields to the Lucases'. What could have made him willing to do it? She'd never known Steve to act like that before in his life. A vague feeling that he might be going to die and that this was some mysterious process of "getting ready," such as she'd heard about, flitted through her mind. But Stephen looked exceedingly unlike a youth who was failing in health or strength; his cheeks had never been redder, and his eyes had a look in them such as she'd never noticed before.

It was a charming September afternoon, not too warm for comfort. Part of the way across the fields led along the margin of a gurgling brook, which the minister admired very much. Stephen Mitchell hadn't thought before this that it was a subject for admiration.

"I know very little about farming," said the minister, looking around him with interest and across the level fields. "I've often wished I'd had opportunities in my boyhood days to study farm life. I like the country; everything about it interests me. I believe I'd have made a good farmer if I'd begun early enough. Do you like the work?"

"No," said Stephen frankly, "I hate it."

"Do you? I'm sorry to hear that. It always seemed to me such clean, healthful, independent work. Then, too, it would be interesting to watch the constant, marvelous changes and to experiment and improve from year to year."

Stephen eyed him with a half-doubtful, half-cynical expression.

"I'd like to know!" he burst forth at last. "There ain't no changes about it, so far as I can see. It's just hoe and dig and plow and harrow and all them things, over and over till you're sick and tired of the whole of it—early and late, day after day, just tugging along."

"Oh, but you forget the harvests! Think of the pleasure of seeing things grow that your own hands have planted, watching them develop from day to day, getting stronger, moving toward maturity, moving as steadily as they can toward that for which they were created. Then there's the experimenting to see what sort of seed will produce the best results and what sort of care such-and-such seeds need and whether, by a little extra effort, you can produce a greater harvest or one better in quality than was ever produced on that piece of ground before, and so create a demand for your work in the market. Oh! I'd think it would be very fascinating work. The returns are so quick and in a sense so sure."

Stephen was silent and thoughtful. This phase of farm life had never been presented to him before. Little hints in it held his admiring thoughts. But soon he offered some of his objections.

"You can't do any of them things unless you're rich. Poor folks that ain't got anything to do with must plod along in the same old way, day in and day out, fighting with bugs and worms and all kinds of pesky things that are doing their level best to upset what little harvest you can get. This land is all run out anyhow."

"Then I would learn how to revive it," said the minister briskly. "There are ways of rejuvenating land—making it young and fresh again. I have a friend studying in that line now. He's trying to find out what changes to make in his field that will enrich the land. He's been reading and studying in that direction for some months—years, indeed, I may say. He's advanced some theories already which have upset the old ideas. And, what's better, has proved by his own experience that his theories are probably correct. No, I think you're wrong about its needing money. It's like most other things, my friend. It needs brains and perseverance and pluck in the face of difficulties. Do you intend to be a farmer, Mr. Mitchell?"

It was certainly a simple enough question; yet something about it made the blood flush to Stephen's temples. Nobody had ever asked him before in his life what he meant to be. I'm not sure he'd ever thought he could be anything in particular. He had just expected to live along somehow, getting through a day's work and getting to bed, only to get up in the morning to another day's work. This, until his ambition had been aroused about that curious list of words and where they were expected to lead, he hadn't planned. There had simply been born into his heart a desire to know the meaning of words. He looked up with sudden interest into the minister's face and found that young man's keen gray eyes fixed upon him, studying him apparently. He dropped his eyes under the gaze and half laughed.

"I don't know, I'm sure. There ain't anything else for me to be. I don't know as I ever expected to be anything. I have to work on the farm. We've got that, and we ain't got anything else. And Father can't do the work alone. I don't suppose I'd do it if I could help it. But I'm here and have to stay here. I ain't a farmer, though. I ain't anything, and I can't say I have any notion of being."

"Why don't you take hold of the farm?" said the minister, speaking with eagerness. "Put all your energies into it and your knowledge and skill and become such a farmer as people in this part of the country have never seen. Become a farmer who'll be quoted in agricultural papers as one who knows and whose opinions are to be received with respect. Lead off in new lines and make yourself a power in all these directions. I believe you could do it."

Silence again on Stephen's part, and that peculiar thrill running through his veins which reached to the ends of his toes. Perhaps what Stephen Mitchell needed, more than anything else in life, was someone to believe in him— someone to think he could be other than a blundering boy barely trusted to go to the village on weekly errands.

"The farm ain't ours," he said at last. "It's mortgaged—a big mortgage, I guess. I never asked how big, but I know it takes all the life out of Father to think of it."

"Why don't you pay the mortgage?"

Mr. Ransom said the words as composedly as if they'd been "Why don't you kick that stone out of your way?"

Stephen caught his breath and answered, "That's what he's been struggling at 'most as many years as I am old, but he ain't got it done."

"No, I don't mean your father. He's getting to be an old man and should be taken care of and treasured. I mean you. Why don't you take hold of that mortgage and get rid of it?"

"Me?"

"Certainly, you. You're just beginning life, with splendid health and strength and all your powers ready to develop in the direction you choose to push them. You're just the one to take hold of such a burden. It would take years, of course, but you have years to spare. If I were you, I'd wrestle with it."

"I don't know anything about it," said Stephen excitedly, and his voice was growing irritable—a sure sign the minister had accomplished his object and thoroughly roused the young man. He wouldn't likely drop the subject again.

His companion understood him, at least enough to answer wisely, "Of course you don't. If I understand you correctly, you haven't given the matter any thought. So you aren't prepared with how to do it successfully. But there's such a thing as learning, my friend. Find out how. Take hold of it with the energy any work worth doing deserves. Throw yourself into it, not as a lifework, but as a means toward an end."

Not as a lifework. Stephen caught at that sentence. Suppose he took hold of this farm. Given the possibility he could find out how to do it and make a success of it—even pay off in the end at least part of the mortgage—it seemed to him it would take a lifetime to do it. After he'd accomplished that, what else would he be fit for in the world?

"Not as a lifework?" he said aloud in an inquiring tone. What did the minister mean him to think about as a lifework? "Seems to me a fellow who'd do all you've been telling of would need a lifetime to do it in."

"Oh, I don't doubt that! I don't mean I wouldn't be a farmer all my life, if I considered that was my place in the world. It's a good, useful, healthful life—a grand life, if you make it that. But, after all, it is, as I've said, a means to an end. The true lifework, you know, Mitchell, is to get ready to graduate."

"Graduate!" Stephen could only repeat the words with a helpless stare.

"Yes, certainly. We're at school, you know, down here—just getting ready, educating our souls—and on graduation day we'll receive our diplomas and go Home to do the work that's been planned for us. That's the real life. This life is such a little time. It takes all our powers to get ready for commencement."

Chapter 14

Stockholders in Council

Could the man mean dying? Stephen thought over the sentences with a strange awe in his heart. He knew the word "commencement." It was a sweet morsel on Fanny Bascome's tongue; she had a cousin who had graduated. But he'd never heard the word used this way before.

"Have you taken hold of that study yet?" asked the minister, after he thought the silence had lasted long enough.

"I ain't taken hold of nothing," answered Stephen, shortly.

"Then you've lost a good deal of time. If I were you, I'd let no more wasted days pass. And about the farmwork, though I'm personally ignorant, I think I can help you get started. This friend I spoke of has piles of agricultural papers, magazines, books—everything you'd need. He'll be glad to lend them to me, and we might look over them together and see if we find the starting point. Now what about the Lucas family? How low down on the scale are they, and what have you been trying to do for them? How did you first become interested in them?"

Was he interested in them? It seemed to be taken for granted he was. In fact, he was their "champion." He remembered how those soft gray eyes had brightened as their owner used the word.

"They're as lowdown as they can get, I guess," he answered. "I never seen any folks as low before. Drink's the matter. The father and the three boys all drink—get drunk and tear around like crazy folks. The womenfolks are afraid of them. They knock the little girls around some, I guess. And of course they're poor, and they live like pigs. We ain't had nothing to do with them. Father had a horror of them coming around our place. He'd hardly speak to them when they did come—even the little chap—so's not to get them used to coming, you know.

"Then the woman got sick, and they sent for my mother. That was last week. She did for them and has been there two or three times since. Folks, when they get sick, want Mother. And the girls were awful glad over what she done. That's about the whole of it. I went with Mother; that's all I did. Oh, while I waited for her, I done two or three little things, of course, that she wanted done. But I don't know how to do anything for such folks. Mr. Meadows said they needed civilizing. There's the cabin where they live, off there to the left. You can tell by the outside of it what the folks must be. It's the worst spot, by all odds, anywhere around us. Most other folks are decent, at least—though a good many drink some."

"It's the old story," said the minister gravely. "Have you noticed how often rum is at the bottom of all sorts of troubles? Well, I'm glad, as I said, that the

Lucases have found a friend in you. I think you're mistaken in your idea that you can't help them. Living as near them as you do, you can probably do more for them than others can. My sister told me I'd find you especially interested in them and ready to help."

Whereupon Stephen made what must have seemed to the minister a very irrelevant answer.

"What's the meaning of 'champion,' sir?"

Mr. Ransom turned his eyes away from the distant hills, which he'd been studying as he walked, and studied Stephen Mitchell's face.

"Its derivation or, that is, its original meaning you refer to, of course. Why, it comes from the Latin word *campus*, which means field, and used to have exclusive reference to field battles or, rather, to persons who took part in them."

"I reckon I ain't after any such meaning," said Stephen, bewildered. "Ain't there a way in which folks use it now, different from that?"

"Oh, yes! For instance, I might use it with you and the family we've been talking about. Let's say the neighborhood looks down on them, scoffs at any effort to better their condition or reach them morally. And you stand up as their champion, explaining that circumstances have been against them, they shouldn't be left to poverty and misery, and people should take hold and help lift them. If that's the case, I might call you their champion, because you're prepared to engage in the contest that's going on about them. Do you get the idea?"

"Yes," said Stephen, and that gleam of satisfied intelligence shone for a moment on his face.

"Are you studying words?" asked Mr. Ransom, watching with interest the changing expressions on his companion's face. "May I ask what suggested the word we've just been talking about?"

"I heard a man use it one day," said Stephen evasively.

Then, after a moment's pause, he did what for him was a surprising thing. He began at the beginning and told the minister the entire story of his experience at the campground and afterward. Not only of the long list of words, but in what surprising ways the meaning of some of them had been revealed to him. He kept silent only regarding the portion of the story which referred to his father's past. Mr. Ransom listened with deep interest and ever-increasing surprise.

Stephen, his face ablaze, had time to ask himself how he could have made such a revelation to a stranger. He hadn't even told the whole of it to Sarah Jane.

"An original idea," the minister said, "and an excellent one. Do you say you have a hundred and three words on your list? Undoubtedly, by the time you reach the end, you'll have made a fair start toward self-education. So you're watching people, to see how many of the words they use and how their use suggests the probable meaning? That's an interesting plan. I'd like to help you—and myself at the same time. Won't you give me a copy of your words and let me see which ones will fit into my next sermon and whether I can use them in a sensible manner and throw light on their meaning? We use many words so vaguely that it would probably be impossible for a listener to get a correct idea of their meaning, merely from our use of them. I think I've learned something this afternoon that will help my sermons in the future. I hope I may have a copy of the list?"

By this time they'd reached the Lucas doorway, from which Dele and Mime ran like frightened deer as they saw the approach of strangers. Father and son, fortunately, were absent from home, but the frightened little woman, who had to pose as head of the family, succeeded in answering the minister's questions only with "Yes, sir" and "No, sir," getting voice once to say, "Oh, Mirandy! Don't sweep now, for pity's sake. You'll choke us to death." For Miranda, overcome apparently by the magnitude of the situation and filled with shame as to her surroundings, could find no better way to vent her feelings than to seize upon a stump of a broom, occupying a conspicuous place by the front window, and raise a whirl of dust not two feet away from where she had seated their guests.

"Well, I don't care," she said, in answer to her mother's petition. "It needs sweeping, if ever a room did. 'Tain't fit for nothing but a pigsty, anyhow. Them young ones keep it in such a muss all the time. I thought I'd just dig out a place for his chair to set."

"Oh! Don't mind me," said Mr. Ransom heartily. "I'm seated all right, my friend. I'd rather have a visit with you now than to have the room swept."

And he prided himself upon maintaining his seriousness and rejoiced in the thought that his sister was a mile away. Had she been there to exchange glances with him, he felt he would have laughed.

Thus seconded, the mother renewed her petition, and Miranda was persuaded to put the broom in the corner. But the presence of the carefully dressed stranger had succeeded in awakening in her heart such a longing after respectability as wouldn't be subdued. She seized upon Dele, who, in an unfortunate moment, thrust her head in at the half-open door, and dragged her, an unwilling victim, into the room.

"Here, you, Dele! Come along here, this minute. Flora Ann, hand me that comb up there on the shelf, behind the teacups. I'm going to have this young one's hair combed before she's a half hour older. I never did see such a fright. And company come! I'm ashamed of the whole set anyhow."

Flora Ann handed the comb in silence, and there began a vigorous onslaught on the tangled locks of the unwilling Dele. Flora Ann retreated to the doorway and began an undertone conversation with Stephen, who felt utterly out of place and bewildered.

"Who is he?"

"He's the minister down in the village—the new one. He's round making calls and getting acquainted with folks."

"What for?"

"Why," said Stephen, "that's the way they do, I suppose."

"I never heard of it," said Flora Ann, who had lived but a few miles from a so-called Christian community all the fifteen years of her life.

Helen Ransom rode home, satisfied with the result of her afternoon's experiment. It had been pleasant to talk with the eager-eyed girl at the farmhouse and watch the light of satisfaction in the mother's faded face while she did so. It had been pleasant to think of Stephen as having the benefit of a two-hour visit with her brother. But, after all, her special satisfaction was derived from the evident effect the afternoon had had upon the minister.

"We must get hold of those people, Helen," he said. "There's great work to be done. That wretched home I visited—you have no idea of it. Children growing up there who are to go out in the world and influence it for good or ill. It's only too evident it will be for ill, unless they're rescued. Intelligent faces they have, too, some of them—especially the girl of fifteen or so, and one called Mirandy also."

There followed an outburst of laughter, as he gave Helen a graphic account of the sweeping and hair-dressing scenes, turning almost immediately from its comic side to repeat with earnestness: "They must be gotten hold of. I rely upon you, Helen, to study ways and means."

"Can't Stephen get hold of them?" she asked.

"Poor Stephen," he said, "what a task he's undertaken. He's an unusual boy. I'm deeply interested in him. Yes, I believe he can, after he's learned how himself. He's already started to grow in the most original way possible."

Then he told the story of the list of words and the progress made in learning their meaning and of the list to be made for him.

"I'll have rare assistance in preparing my next sermon," he said, laughing. "I wonder how many of his words I can work in and what ideas I can give him about them."

So, talking and planning, he forgot to think his life was wrecked and that there could be only a shadowed happiness for him. He hadn't resolved to be unhappy, but in his youth and inexperience he'd thought unhappiness, or at least unhappiness in certain directions, was his heritage.

Helen, as she watched him and saw the change in his face and felt the healthful reawakening of his mental and moral nature, blessed not only Stephen and Sarah Jane in her heart, but the whole Lucas tribe as well. And she began that very afternoon her plans for getting to know them better. She had her side of the story to tell at the tea table, which was a brighter and pleasanter meal than she'd enjoyed in her brother's home.

She was especially interested in Sarah Jane—her energy, her pleasant disposition, and her gift in sewing. "Did you notice how neat her dress was? And how clean and free from dust the large, dreary parlor was, with its attempts at ornament? How can I get hold of the girl, Max, and give her a chance to imitate things worth the trouble? She's by nature an imitator—quick to feel and see what others do. That elder Miss Bascome says she makes a fright of herself in trying to copy the dresses of the girls she sees in church or on the street. I studied her dress this afternoon, and really, when you think of the complicated present style, it was a success. I was interested in it, too, for another reason—I selected the braid it's trimmed with."

"You selected it?" her brother asked with wonder in his voice. There followed a history of the scene at the corner store, and the minister laughed over the clerk's probable discomfiture.

Chapter 15

More Passengers

C an't you set her to sewing?" asked Mr. Ransom.

His sister's face brightened. "That's an idea. How quick you are at planning! I have so much sewing to be done this fall. Mamma was so distressed about your loneliness that she hurried me away before I was ready. I wonder if I could get Sarah Jane to come here and sew with me? That would be accomplishing two or three things at once. I'd get my work done a great deal sooner than if I plodded on alone, and I could teach her a hundred little things she doesn't know now. Do you suppose it will do on such short acquaintance to ask her to come?"

"I wouldn't think a long acquaintance would be needed to secure help in the sewing room. But there's another difficulty in the way. Stephen mentioned the fact that his mother isn't well and Sarah Jane did what he called the 'heft' of the work and shielded her all she could. I suspect the poor old lady needs shielding, and we couldn't begin by teaching her daughter selfishness."

"No, of course, but I wonder if there isn't a way to plan? What about that fifteen-year-old girl? She wasn't the sweeper, was she? What if it could be arranged so she could take Sarah Jane's place in the home for a week or two, to help the mother? Couldn't she learn neatness and cooking from the mother and save her drudgery, while Sarah Jane was learning other lessons here?"

"Possibly," said the minister. "That would certainly accomplish several things at once. If Mrs. Mitchell's consent can be secured, it's worth trying. As for the Lucas girl, the contrast between her place and the Mitchell home is as strong as that between earth and heaven to some of us. Her surroundings are simply terrible."

They sat late at the tea table discussing the two households and the possible changes that might be made in the near future.

The minister, on leaving the room, turned back to say, "I believe I won't study tonight, Helen. I'll go out and call on my young men. My ride has rested me so that I feel equal to it."

"I think that's an excellent plan," said his sister quietly, but her eyes danced with triumph. For this particular minister to resolve not to study, but instead to mingle with his people, was a step forward.

Two days later Mr. Mitchell, who had gone to town for needed supplies, created a sensation at the supper table. He set down his cup and fumbled nervously in first one and then another pocket for several minutes.

"I'm bound if I know what I did with the thing," he said at last. "I thought I put it away as careful as if it was made of gold. Ha! I've found it!" He produced a white envelope and held it between thumb and finger for careful study.

"A letter!" said Sarah Jane, her cheeks flushing with surprise and excitement.

"I call that a neat thing," said Mr. Mitchell. "Look at that handwriting now. Plain as print, yet full of pretty flourishes. I tell you, Sarah Jane—if you could write like that, it'd be something to be proud of."

"Where did you get it? At the post office?"

"I got it from the new minister. He came up to me in the store, bowing as polite as if I'd been the governor, and wanted to know if I was Mr. Mitchell and if I'd do his sister the kindness of taking a note to my daughter."

"To me!" said Sarah Jane. And as she reached forth her hand, Helen Ransom should have seen her eyes.

"Yes, sir, them's the words he said, and a pleasant-spoken man he is, too. He didn't start off right straight, either. He stood and talked to me for as much as five minutes. The doctor and some high-up folks came in, too, while he was there—he just bowed to them pleasant, as if he was glad to see them, and said 'Good day,' but he kept right on talking to me. Well, Sarah Jane, what have you got there? Read out. If it's as plain writing inside as it is out, you can do it."

But Sarah Jane's cheeks were glowing like damask roses, and she was apparently lost to sound, in the contents of that wonderful letter. She was seventeen, but a dainty note, written on perfumed paper, had never reached her hands before.

"Well, of all things in this world!" she said at last. "Who would ever have thought such a thing could happen?"

"How can we tell?" answered Stephen, trying to hide his own intense interest under gruffness. "We can't find out what's happened."

"Why, she wants me to come there and stay, to her house, and sew. She's got a lot of plain sewing, she says, and she saw by the way I fixed my own things that I knew how to sew, and she needs my help, and she'll give me a dollar a day and my board. Only think of that, Steve. A dollar a day for just sitting and sewing! And, Mother, she says if you can't spare me because the work is too hard for you—and she should think it would be—if you'd let the Lucas girl come over in my place and help you for a week or two, it would be a real blessing to the girl. Not the oldest one, she says, but the next one to her—that's Flora Ann, ain't it? She says she would—well, here, I'll read the letter to you, and then you'll know just what they all say."

Rarely had there been such excitement in the Mitchell house as that letter produced. "Something different" had certainly come to them. Sarah Jane invited out to sew by the day, at the enormous price of a dollar a day and her board! She was particular to add that statement whenever the terms were mentioned, and not less bewildering was the suggestion to have Flora Ann Lucas come and work for them. The Mitchells keeping hired help!

"I'd have to pay her," said Mrs. Mitchell dubiously. She'd never paid anyone for working for her, except through one week of her sorrowful life, years ago.

"Yes," said Sarah Jane, "of course you'd have to pay her something. But, land!

She'd be tickled to death to work for a dollar a week. And just think, Mother—I could earn six while she was doing it and learn a lot of things, besides, that would help me through the rest of my life. Mother, I do hope you can do it. And then you know what she says about its being a help to Flora Ann."

The minister had been wise in making that statement, and his sister had been as wise in repeating it. Both of them saw deeper into the little worn-out mother's heart than her children had. They knew the thought that the mother could help someone would be a powerful argument in Flora Ann's favor. Still, it must be confessed she shrank from the ordeal with a dread they also couldn't have understood.

"Well," she said at last, after a period of utter silence, during which she sat with folded hands, looking straight ahead at nothing at all, "well, if you'd like to go, Sarah Jane, and he'd like to have her come, why, I'll do my best about it—though I don't know as I can help her—that is, if your father thinks best."

It was a confused sentence certainly, but the Mitchell family understood it. The children turned inquiring eyes toward their father.

"I don't know as we can do anything else," he said. "They appear to want it pretty bad and have it all planned. I did want to keep clear of that Lucas set. But then the girl ain't so bad, maybe—I daresay, she ain't so bad, but she might be worse—and it'll give Sarah Jane a start, if it's the kind of start she wants."

"Well," said Mrs. Mitchell again, "I'm agreed to it. Not but what I could get along better without Flora Ann than with her. But if he thinks I could help her to be more neat, why, maybe I'd better try."

And so the momentous question was settled, with Stephen saying absolutely nothing. Not until an hour later did Sarah Jane, as she dashed about the kitchen, putting it in order, realize this fact and charged her brother with it when he came in from his good-night visit to the barn.

"Say, Steve, you didn't say one word about my going to the minister's. Ain't it an odd thing to happen to me? What do you think of it anyhow?"

"I don't know," said Stephen. "I can tell better when you come back. It's a good chance for Flora Ann, I think. She can learn lots of things from Mother. But what you can learn from them will have to be found out."

Sarah Jane faced him with a bewildered stare. "Steve, what do you mean? If they ain't high enough up to learn from, I'd like to know who is."

"That's just it," said Stephen slowly. "Maybe they're too high. When I was at the village the other day, I saw a book on the counter that somebody had been looking at. While I was waiting for the clerk to get my sugar, I took it up. Says I to myself, 'How do I know but what some of my words will be in this, with a meaning to them?' I looked the thing through from beginning to end and couldn't make head nor tail to it. I couldn't understand one word. Come to find out—the thing was Latin. So I was thinking that maybe they live in Latin at the minister's house, and you and I couldn't understand them yet a while."

"Oh, my!" said Sarah Jane. "If you don't have the oddest notions! If I don't learn a few things while I'm there, whether it's Greek or Latin or whatever, then you can set me down for a dunce. And I never believed I was one—in some things anyhow."

But perhaps, after all, the most bewildered one of all concerned was Flora Ann Lucas.

Stephen's conceit about people living in Latin and not being able to help those who lived in English might have applied better to her, if he'd known it, than to his sister. Flora Ann was only fifteen, and her family had been reduced to the lowest dregs of poverty through all the years her memory reached. An empty cupboard and a broken stove, with little or no fuel, was the basis on which the Lucas family did their housework. They had long ago fallen out of the habit, as a family, of sitting down to eat their daily portion but ate it rather by snatches, standing in the doorway or hiding sometimes in the corner closet, when Jake was heard coming. They very often went without food from early morning until late in the evening. Flora Ann, indeed, was more accustomed to this than the other family members. Whether her heart was more tender than her sister's, or whether Miranda felt the need of more food, certainly Flora Ann most often saved her portion to divide between the hungry-looking little girls, who had never, in all their miserable lives, remembered when they had all they wanted to eat.

It was Stephen who went to make the bewildering proposition to the Lucas family.

"I didn't mean he should go there," said his father, sitting at home and looking drearily into the darkening west after Stephen strode away. "I meant to keep them separate always. But I don't know what's come over the boy. He seems different somehow from what he was before. I've always told him things to do. But when he said, in that positive way, 'I'll go over there, Mother,' it seemed as if he was grown-up all of a sudden, and there wasn't anything to be said."

"I don't feel exactly afraid of the Lucas boys' influence over Steve," said Mrs. Mitchell. "They're dreadful different from him, and he don't hanker after them. And besides"—there was a little pause, and then, in a lower key, she added—"besides, he's gone on a good errand—gone to try to help them, Josiah—and it's my notion that folks get took care of that go on such errands."

"Me go over to your house!" said Flora Ann, staring. "What for? What does she want of help? Ain't Sarah Jane there? And what in time can I do to help her? I don't know how to work. I ain't had no chance to learn."

Stephen couldn't help glancing around the hopelessly dirty room, with its small-paned windows so thickly set with cobwebs and soot and flyspecks that it was scarcely possible to see out of them. He was tempted to say it looked as though "chances" were plenty. But he refrained and presented, as briefly as possible, an explanation of the mystery.

"Well, I don't know," said the mother, pausing in her work of bumping a bundle of rags back and forth, in a rickety chair without rockers, in a vain effort to get it to sleep. "I like to accommodate the neighbors, and Mrs. Mitchell was terrible good to me when I was sick. But Flora Ann ain't never been anywhere to do things, and I don't know as I could spare her very well."

Stephen drew himself up, and his face flushed. Evidently his sense of the fitness of things was jarred.

"It ain't exactly accommodation," he said with dignity. "Sarah Jane is going away, and Mother needs some help, because she ain't very strong, and is willing to pay for it. But of course if you don't want Flora Ann to come, then I can go somewhere else."

"Pay for it!" echoed mother and eldest daughter in the same breath.

And Miranda added, "Good land of pity! Ain't some folks getting big? I didn't know your mother could afford to keep hired help. Ma, do for pity's sake let her go. She ain't no account here, just standing around in the way, and I'd like dreadful well to get hold of a little money again. How much is your mother going to pay, Steve?"

"She'll give her a dollar a week," said Stephen.

"A dollar a week!" echoed Flora Ann, her tone expressing volumes. She had never as yet earned a cent.

"I say let her go," said Miranda with emphasis. "Dollars don't grow on bushes, not that I ever found. And there's her eating, besides, that counts for a good deal. Flora Ann's as willing to eat as anybody, when she gets a chance."

The dollar seemed also to have a happy effect on Mrs. Lucas, and it was settled that Flora Ann would come the next morning. She followed Stephen to the door, looking frightened.

"I ain't fit to go," she said deprecatingly. "Your ma looks so terrible nice, Steve—clean dress and her hair slick and everything. I'll be scared out of my wits; yet I'd kind of like to try it. Say, Steve, is she cross?"

"No," said Stephen, "but she won't stand no dirt, that's a fact. And you want to wash up and comb your hair before you come."

"I can comb my hair," said Flora Ann timidly. "But I ain't got no dress but this, Steve, as true as you live. And it's an awful-looking dress; it needs washing and mending. But how can I do it when I ain't got nothing else to put on? If I had as many dresses as Sarah Jane, you'd see me looking different."

"Never mind," he said kindly to the shamefaced girl, thinking how his sister would feel to know she was being envied for her dresses. "If you ain't got nothing but that, you can't help it. Fix up your hair the best you can and come along. Mother will show you how to clean up somehow, I daresay. She always contrives to make things clean. I don't know how."

Flora Ann looked after him until in the gathering darkness he was a speck in the distance. Then she reentered the house, to attack and conquer her rebellious hair. It had a reddish tint and was very curly. Stephen little understood the terrible task he had set for her.

Chapter 16

Through a New Country

When Flora Ann presented herself before Mrs. Mitchell's dismayed eyes early the next morning, her dress was an accumulation of terrors, but face and hands were reasonably clean, and her tangled mass of hair had certainly been through a terrible ordeal and must have been amazed at its own subjection.

The next few days were bewildering to Flora Ann. What they were to Mrs. Mitchell it might be hard to explain. The first time the girl set the table for the family meal, her mistress, who had been half-frightened and wholly dismayed that she was her mistress, lost self-control entirely when she came to survey the finished task and sat down on the first available chair to laugh. The tablecloth was still lying on its shelf in the closet; the table was against the side of the wall. Three plates were set in a row on one side of it, and a cup without a saucer stood at each plate.

"I'll go down to the cellar after the things, and you can set the table while I'm gone. Plates and cups and saucers, you know." Such had been the directions, with the last words added in response to Flora Ann's bewildered looks.

"For pity's sake!" said Mrs. Mitchell. "Do you call that table set?"

"You said plates and cups," answered the puzzled girl, "and I got them out. There's three of you, ain't there?"

"Why, yes, four of us, for that matter. Don't you expect to eat nothing at all? Is that the way you fix the table at your house?"

"No," said Flora Ann promptly, "it ain't the way at all. We don't fix the table. We just stand round and eat something when we can get it. But you said put the dishes on the table. Anyway, that's what I thought you meant."

"You poor thing!" said Mrs. Mitchell, checking her laugh and speaking in a more compassionate tone than she had yet used. The depths of Flora Ann's ignorance and desolation were dawning on her. But the laugh had done her good; she felt less frightened than she had before.

"I'll just show you how to do it," she said, rising briskly, "then you can do it all by yourself next time. Set them dishes back in the pantry and pull the table out into the middle of the floor. Sarah Jane is particular about having it just in the middle of the room, because we get the breeze then from both windows and are out of the way of the sunshine. Now bring the tablecloth from the lower shelf in the corner. Open it out, child, and spread it on nice and smooth. If there's anything Sarah Jane hates, it's a tablecloth put on crooked, and it does look kind of miserable and lopsided, I think myself. Now set four plates at each end and side. No, no! I don't mean four along in a row, but four in all—

like this, you know." And she briskly arranged the plates.

"Now you want knives and forks and the salt. Put the salt in the middle of the table, so we can all reach it. And the cups and saucers you want to fix to my place, so. Now get a plate for bread and another for butter and a pitcher for milk. Then set the dishes for potatoes and ham on this corner, so I can reach them handy when I come to dish up the things. Why, child, you don't want a plate for potatoes. Sarah Jane hates to see potatoes in a plate. That there platter in the corner is what we put ham on. Oh, you'll learn after a while. I supposed you knew all them things, of course—supposed everybody did. Now I'll dish up, while you go out and call Steve and his father. Then you come in and set down at the table along with the rest of us. You can set over there, and we'll have our dinner like folks."

Ten minutes more and Flora Ann sat down for the first time in her life to a civilized and reasonably well-appointed dinner table. She was helped to a generous piece of ham; she had the potatoes passed to her; she had a cup of tea poured for her and sugared and creamed; she ate such butter and such bread as had never before fallen to her lot. It's true she took a potato from the dish with her own fork and helped herself to butter with the knife she had just taken from her own mouth; but so did all the others. She copied them carefully and believed she was being as royally served and sustaining herself as well in her new position as a lady could. As for the taste of the wholesome food, properly cooked, it would be difficult to explain what it was to this half-starved girl. As a mark of progress in her education, she refused the third large potato and obliged herself to be content with four slices of bread, although she could have easily eaten more. This was her concession to what seemed to be the customs of civilization.

It was a week for Flora Ann to remember. Every step she took in this plain little home was new and bewildering. It seemed to her that she washed her hands so many times the skin would wear out; that she used soap enough to have stocked the village store; that the dishes to be washed and dried and put away in their places were so many as to be beyond her counting; and that suppertime came, and the table had to be arrayed in white again, almost as soon as she had cleared it away, so swiftly the hours passed.

"She doesn't know anything at all," Mrs. Mitchell confided to her husband in the privacy of their own room, at the close of the second day's trial. "She beats all I ever heard of. Why, Josiah, it's a burning shame to think that in this country, and just a step away from us, you may say, there's been living all these years a girl who knew so little. But then what could I have expected? I've been there and seen how they lived. But I never thought there was folks that didn't sit down to a table and eat their victuals like human beings. She broke the blue bowl. I don't know what Sarah Jane will say to that; she set great store by the blue bowl. But, dear me, the girl was so scared I couldn't say anything! She acted as if she expected me to knock her over the head with the broom I had in my hand."

"Like enough she did," said Mr. Mitchell. "That's about the way she's been treated, I guess. Old man Lucas isn't so ill-tempered when he's been drinking as some folks are. But that oldest boy of his beats all I ever heard of for raging around at such times, and the most of his time is 'such times.' They say he rules the whole family. Silas Springer was telling me today it ain't more than a couple of weeks since he knocked this girl down and kicked her."

"Oh, for the land of pity!" said Mrs. Mitchell. She had been a drunkard's wife, and it had been misery enough, though she'd never been knocked down or kicked.

"Well," she said, after a moment's silence, "I declare, I'll do what I can for the girl. I thought twenty times today I couldn't stand it. We're clean by nature, and she does lots of things that rile your stomach. But I'll make out. Did you see how nice she looked in that old dress of Sarah Jane's? We thought it wasn't fit for anything but the ragbag. But I got it out today and mended it, and, I declare, she looked real fixed up in it. Her own was so poison dirty I couldn't stand it. I'm going to have her put it into the washtub the first thing tomorrow morning. Dear me, Josiah, I thought we were poor. But I've come to the conclusion we must be rich."

As for Sarah Jane, who shall describe what this experience of life was to her? What a thing it was to occupy a room whose bed was spread in purest white, whose windows were curtained with white muslin, whose floor was covered with a neat and tasteful carpet, and whose dressing table had pretty accessories arranged upon it. Sarah Jane, as she stood before the mirror and combed and arranged her abundant hair, felt at times almost bewildered that she herself was living this charmed life.

She put on her pretty light calico dress in the early morning "just like any lady in the land," she told herself, and went down with Miss Ransom to look at the dew-washed flowers in the little garden under the dining room windows and wait there for the tinkle of the bell calling them to breakfast.

That breakfast table! If the table appointments in the Mitchell home were a revelation to Flora Ann, what shall be said of those in the manse and their effect upon Sarah Jane? Not that they were extravagant or startling. Helen Ransom would have felt astonished if she'd known how they impressed her guest. The linen was fine, but not too fine for daily use. Silver knives and forks and teaspoons at each plate were necessities of life to Helen. So also were the large, fine, carefully ironed napkins, which Sarah Jane surveyed with awe, tucked inside the pretty napkin ring, tied with ribbon. Then there were the dainty butter plates and the individual salts, the pretty breakfast service at Helen's place, the fruit plates of delicate pattern, and the vases of roses at either end—all simple and appropriate to the hour, from Helen's standpoint. From Sarah Jane's, it was a glimpse of Eden.

Then the sewing room, where she sat all day and sewed, was another revelation to her. Simply furnished, with conveniences for the work, but so dainty and fair and free from dust and disorder that Sarah Jane could hardly repress a little sigh of satisfaction in looking about. She worked well in the sewing room, and the mistress rejoiced in the great strides she was taking. For Helen Ransom, who didn't like long seams and minute details, knew how to plait, gather, puff, fold, and drape after the day's most approved fashion. And Sarah Jane, with the cunning of her fingers and her own refined taste, was quick to catch on.

"I never could guess how it was done," she said exultantly, as she folded away a finished skirt, which exactly suited its fastidious owner. "I studied them skirts time and again, going out of church and walking along the street, and how they got them to hang like that behind, and so smooth and straight before, I never could make out. But it's easy enough, now that you know how. I could make one as well as not."

"Most things are easy after you know how," said Helen, smiling. "Things like that, I mean. I sometimes wish the rule applied to the other part of us as well."

"What other part? I don't see what you mean."

"Why, I was thinking of soul education, instead of what belongs to the fingers, and of how many things we know like that which seem hard to apply. I know how to be gentle and patient and long-suffering, for instance, but sometimes find it very hard to put my knowledge into practice."

"I shouldn't think you did," said Sarah Jane, surveying her with undisguised admiration. "I think you know them things as well as the others. I know I'd been fit to fly to pieces fifty times, if I'd had anybody to teach that was as stupid and awkward as I've been. And you've been as patient as one of them lilies over there all the time."

Helen laughed. "My dear, I haven't found it hard to be patient with you. I succeed extremely well with people who try to please—who give me the best that's in them. I confess I was thinking of Nancy when I first spoke. She tries me very much, by sweeping in the middle of the room and leaving the corners and under the bed and all out-of-sight places undisturbed—'eye service,' you know. I haven't learned to be long-suffering with that. All of which reminds me to ask if you'd mind going downstairs to set the table for dinner. Nancy's late again, and I have the dessert to look after. Can you take the table arrangement into your hands?"

"I'd like it first-rate, if I could do it," said Sarah Jane, and her eyes shone with pleasure. She might be swift with her needle, but housekeeping was her forte, and her fingers had fairly longed to handle the pretty dishes and fine napery. This was after she had been in her new sphere for nearly a week.

The truth is, Helen Ransom's handmaiden was a source of unfailing satisfaction to her. She found her not only deft-handed, but keen-sighted and clear-brained, and possessing a determination to make the best of every opportunity that fell within her reach.

The mistress watched, with a smile on her face, to see her arrange the cloth in its exact position and then finger the pretty dishes lovingly, as she might have done with flowers. She arranged and rearranged, not forgetting the smallest detail of the well-appointed table, but making it in every particular as she'd seen it before. Since she couldn't have seen it in her own home or in other homes to which she'd had access, Helen decided, and told herself for the hundredth time that week, that the girl was certainly unusual.

Helen was sitting in the alcove, which was supplied with writing desk and easy chair. This was for the minister to lounge in, with the latest papers and magazines at his command, and was a corner dear to the heart of the young mistress of the manse.

"The average man, you know, can't wait comfortably for five consecutive seconds after being summoned to the dining room," Helen had written to her mother, when she described her household arrangements. "Max is no better than the rest of them, except that he pretends patience, pacing solemnly to and fro while he waits for the 'dishing up.' So I've planned a resting place, with a book or paper to occupy him during the aforesaid five seconds. Man is usually peaceable under such circumstances. Some people might wonder why I called the masculine part of my family before the final dishing up took place. But you, my dear mother, won't wonder; for you know, by a lifelong experience, how impossible it is for a man to come to breakfast or dinner when he's called. He's sure, on ninety-nine occasions, to have something important to do that will detain him 'just a minute' after the bell rings. Do you think I'll run such risks and let my dinner cool? Oh, I'm learning how to manage Max beautifully. I only hope I can educate his wife before she comes into power."

At this writing desk, therefore, sat Helen Ransom, transcribing briskly certain papers of her brother's which she knew he needed for that afternoon, but not so preoccupied she couldn't rejoice over the work going on a few feet from her.

"Sarah," she presently said, pushing the portiere a little aside to see the girl's face, "can you cut the flowers and arrange them for the table?"

Then Sarah Jane's cheeks flushed, and her eyes glowed with pleasure. Helen was well aware the girl loved flowers—the wildwood ones, in the broken-nosed pitcher on her mantel at home, had told that story. And the look, half of delight, half of awe, with which she regarded the roses and jasmine strewn lavishly about the manse, repeated it. Now the crowning delight of the hour had come to her. She was to go to the garden among the flowers and select for herself those which should adorn the table.

"Why, I'm afraid—" she said, pausing, sunbonnet in hand.

"Well," said her mistress, with a reassuring smile, "afraid of what?"

"How shall I know which you want picked and which I must let alone?"

"It isn't the question which I want picked but which you want. You're to use your own taste, with the garden before you. No restrictions are placed on any of the flowers. Gather enough for the two table vases and arrange them, please."

"Oh! I don't know how to fix them," said Sarah Jane, her face redder than before. "I never fixed no flowers in my life, but I can bring them in to you."

"I'm much too busy now, Sarah. Maxwell's papers I'm copying must be ready for him at dinner. I can trust you. Arrange the flowers as you like to see them, and they'll be right."

Chapter 17

Laying a Track

Helen laughed softly over the vases when they were finally set in triumph in their places. Bright-colored autumn flowers were beginning in all their glory, and Sarah Jane had revelled in them. Crimsons and yellows and scarlets abounded, placed in contrast to each other, as if in a sort of wild ecstasy they'd rejoiced in the display they could make. This, she found, applied to only one of the vases. The other surprised and touched her. It was placed in front of her own plate and held only a single white rose.

"It looks like you," said Sarah Jane, pointing to it. "All white things do, Miss Ransom."

"Thank you," said Helen, her voice breaking into a laugh and her tears very near the surface. It began to touch her deeply and, in a sense, to humiliate her to see the almost worship this sheltered girl bestowed upon her. *Simply because someone outside the family has treated her like a human being,* she said to herself. *How starved the poor creature's life must have been all these years! I wish I could make it up to her. I wish I could give her such a hold upon life—the true life—that she could never be starved again.*

The week was also an interesting one to the minister in his study. He worked over his sermon as never before. His list of words had puzzled him—written with Stephen's untrained hand—but he entered in with the zest of a teacher bent on winning his pupil. If from the list he could gather a theme that would speak to this young man's soul and awaken it to vigorous and healthful action, so it would become not only a soul saved but a soul in pursuit of the redemption of others, that would be an object worth living for.

"I will pursue a soul," he said exultantly to himself.

He read the list, not only with care, but with prayer. He conjectured rightly that a boy so interested in words had probably learned his list fairly well by this time. He went down the list, with pencil in hand, searching for a keynote, and marked it presently with a great deal of satisfaction: "Sun of Righteousness." After that his work was easy. A world in darkness—no, a soul in darkness—lost in an impenetrable fog. A storm gathering and the Sun of Righteousness rising to dispel it, to "rescue" the soul from "bondage." Then came the word "surrender." It was necessary in order to be rescued. Even the glorious Sun of Righteousness couldn't dispel the midnight of the soul, unless that soul willed it—free to choose to revel forever in glorious light and liberty. And "obstacles" would be in the way—for when did Satan see a soul trying to escape from bondage without inventing obstacles? He would like to picture a soul in bondage—the darkness of it, the hopelessness of it, the dire necessity for rescue.

In short, the minister was held to his study that week by a sermon more personalized and more focused than any he had ever prepared, such as he'd imagined he would preach, and hoped for more to come.

"Well," he inquired, as he grasped Stephen Mitchell's hand, having overtaken him in the aisle at the close of the next Sabbath morning's service, "how did it work, my friend?"

"I found them," said Stephen briefly, but with a significance in his voice which meant something positive, though the minister couldn't quite decide what.

"I had a feeling you were so interested in that list that no word belonging to it could escape you. Did I succeed at all in making their meaning plain?"

"Why, yes," said Stephen, "plain enough. A fellow would have to understand what you were driving at. Part of them I am, I guess."

"And the other part you need," said Mr. Ransom, catching the boy's meaning. "Undoubtedly you need rescue. All souls, except those who have been to the Sun of Righteousness for light, walk in darkness. Have you any idea how much I thought of you and prayed for you while I was preparing that sermon? If you have, you'll think about this matter, if only for the sake of comforting me." This he said with a half laugh that had a touch of sadness about it and was altogether winning.

But Stephen wasn't to be won. He was intensely interested in the sermon so far as it was connected with his list of words. He was interested in the minister—he wanted to see more of him, hear more of him, and learn words. But no ray from the Sun of Righteousness had yet penetrated his heart. On the contrary, he felt disappointed because Mr. Ransom was trying to turn his thoughts in that direction.

"I don't know nothing about religion," he said, as he drove slowly homeward alone, for Sarah Jane's work wasn't finished at the manse. "I don't know nothing about religion, and I don't want to know—not yet a while. There's lots of other things to learn first. I just wish he wouldn't pitch it at a fellow. He ain't like the other ministers. None of them ever troubled me before. I like him the best of any of them, to be sure, but I don't want to know about them things. Odd, though, how he fitted in them words—five of 'em, and he acted as if they were made to fit them places. He's a smart fellow. I wisht I knew a little corner of what he does."

"Oh, Maxwell!" his sister said, as soon as they were together in the privacy of his study. "You preached a sermon for me this morning. The kind I want and have been watching for."

"I preached for a soul," he said eagerly. "I'm fishing for a soul, Helen."

"I know—I was so glad to hear the ring of it. Didn't you notice what a different impression it made on the people? They went out more quietly than usual. Not a person told me 'what a lovely sermon that was.' But I heard Deacon Watson ask young Mr. Simmons if he couldn't begin to come to the prayer meeting again, now that the summer's hurry was over. Depend upon it, Maxwell—such sermons will bear fruit."

Such words were pleasant to the young minister's ears. He'd had many compliments for his preaching, which had been valued for what they were worth and thought of afterward with a sigh, for they emphasized to him his failure. But today he glowed with new energy; he had been preaching for results. And his prayer at family worship that evening was so earnest and pointed that his sister, at least, knew some one soul was pressing upon his heart.

He gave himself with as much earnestness to his study during the following week—only to be disappointed on the Sabbath. Stephen Mitchell, for whom he'd prepared another sermon, didn't appear in church. Soon after breakfast the next morning, Maxwell Ransom was in his saddle on his way to the Mitchell farm.

"I've brought you a package of papers," he said to Stephen, whom he'd seen in the barnyard. "They have all sorts of farm articles in them. Some of them, I'd think, would be of practical interest to anyone who was so fortunate to own a farm. That horse of yours has a very intelligent face, and he's almost a match for mine in size, isn't he?"

The two stood there together, talking about horses and pigs and other matters pertaining to farm life, until Stephen had recovered from his surprise and confusion. Then Mr. Ransom came to the special object of his visit.

"I missed you yesterday, my friend, and it was a sore disappointment. My sermon was prepared with a special view to your list. I think I succeeded in making clear some words which would have interested you. I hope no one is ill at home?"

If Stephen hadn't been trying to be polite, he would have laughed. It occurred to him as a surprising thing—a thing which marked what Sarah Jane would have called a "difference" in their lives—to be cross-questioned in this way about his nonappearance in church. Certainly none of the family had been so regular in their attendance as to have their absence awaken surprise or anxiety. On the contrary, to have appeared there for two Sabbaths in succession might have astonished the congregation. Nevertheless, there stood the minister searching for a reason. Stephen cast about him for one honest enough to meet those keen, clear eyes studying him with evident interest.

"I'll tell you the downright truth," he said suddenly. "I ain't been no hand to go to church, along back for a good many months. I said I wouldn't go no more; I didn't see no use in it. But last Sunday I was interested in my words, and I'd like to have come again. But I made up my mind it wouldn't do. The fact is, I ain't got respectable clothes. We're harder up than usual this fall, or else the clothes are harder up," he added with a grim smile. "They're wore out—I suppose that's the common sense of it. And I made up my mind, thinking it over, that it wasn't fair to go to church and sit among nice-dressed people, looking like that, and I'd stay at home."

Mr. Ransom looked and felt bewildered. Brought up in a home where, if there wasn't much wealth, there certainly wasn't poverty, he'd had whatever befit his circumstances. He tried to imagine how it would feel not to have suitable clothes.

He wasn't especially fond of clothes himself; at least, he didn't know he was. But he decided then and there that it wouldn't be pleasant not to be suitably attired. He hadn't noticed Stephen's Sunday clothing particularly. He tried to recall it now and realized it was shabby.

It was hardly worthwhile to counsel Stephen to rise above dress and come to church in whatever he had. People further advanced in Christian knowledge than Stephen Mitchell hadn't been able to rise above this thing—how was he expected to? *People should have suitable clothes to wear to church,* was this young man's conclusion. How could it be managed—not for the world at large immediately, but for this one young person before him, in whom for the time being all his interests centered? If he could put his hand in his pocket and draw forth the sum needed to furnish the boy with an entire suit of respectable clothing, that would certainly be the easiest way out of the difficulty. But he looked at the strong-limbed, rugged-faced young man, noted the lines about the mouth— which could settle into firmness or even obstinacy—remembered those flashes of feeling in the gray eyes he'd seen once or twice, and decided such a course wasn't open to him. Poor, the Mitchells certainly were. But it was a poverty which would have to be handled carefully.

Maxwell Ransom made a fairly short call and galloped home without stopping at the Bascomes', although Fanny, who had seen him pass, dusted the parlor carefully and put herself into her most becoming dress to wait for his return, certain he wouldn't pass them by.

From his study he summoned his sister to a council. "Come and help me, Helen. I'm fishing for a boy and have struck a ponderous obstacle. I want that young Mitchell to come to church regularly. I'm preaching sermons prepared especially for him, and he tells me that he has no clothes to wear." He stopped over this sentence and looked so perplexedly at his sister that she could only laugh.

"So that's your obstacle? It's a formidable one, I confess. One is always running against it in Christian work of almost any sort. Poor Stephen! I sympathize with him; his clothes really are dreadful. I thought he had a good deal of courage or an almost unfortunate indifference to come to church at all."

"Is that true? I remember he looked shabby, but I didn't consider the matter closely. It takes women to think of these things. What can we do, Helen? If I could send him to the tailor's and order the bills sent to me, the matter would be easily settled. But that's out of the question. We must think of some way for him to earn them."

"Could he come here, Maxwell?"

The minister shook his head. "Too far away—he's needed at home all day. And after a day's work for him and his horses, to think of driving into town and accomplishing anything isn't feasible. Suppose he could—what could I set him at?"

"Oh, we might think of some things if we had him here. Could he copy anything for you?"

Mr. Ransom laughed. "I'd show you his 'list,' Helen, if I didn't think it would be a breach of confidence. He's shown great ingenuity in spelling words. No—copying isn't to be thought of, for a while at least. But there must be some way we can hold out a helping hand to a young fellow like that. I feel sure there's grand material to work upon. And whether there is or not, we're bound to do our best."

"Yes," said his sister, with a bright look for her brother.

This was the brother she was used to, and he had been lost for months. If it was the Mitchell family who had brought him back to hearty interest in humankind again, she owed them a debt of gratitude. Meanwhile, her eyes roved thoughtfully about the study, taking in the rows and rows of books, shelves of pamphlets, pigeonholes lettered and numbered and filled. What in all their intellectual life could fit into Stephen Mitchell's life? Suddenly her gaze rested upon a formidable pile of papers of miscellaneous character, which refused to be arranged in orderly shapes but bulged out and overflowed the box trying to hold them.

"Max, couldn't he cut out the marked articles from those papers and place them in their envelopes? That doesn't require a great deal of literary power, and it's of an intellectual nature. Perhaps his orthography might be improved by the process. There's a good deal of work crowded into that box. It would consume a number of his evenings, I imagine, and you keep me so busy with your numerous other schemes that I don't know when I'm to get to them."

Her brother turned quickly in the direction she indicated.

"The marked papers," he said, with a relieved air. "Helen, you're a genius. That's the very thing—nothing but scissors and patience are needed. I can supply the one, and I believe he has the other, when there's something to be accomplished. I can give him a package of envelopes marked like those in the scrap cabinet, and he can make files for me. His eye may even rest on something while he works that may have an influence on his whole afterlife. Living is very interesting, Helen." He turned from his papers and gave her one of his bright looks. "It's so wonderful to think that the very next step one takes may influence a soul."

Two days later, after this conversation took place, a very interesting scene to some people might have been witnessed in the Mitchell kitchen. It was in after-supper order, neat and clean; the table was drawn into the middle of the room and had two lamps burning on it. This in itself was an unusual luxury in the family. Kerosene, like everything else, was used with sparing hand, and one small light was expected to supply the family needs, even during a long winter evening. But on this night there was rare work to be done, and Mrs. Mitchell herself had carefully filled and trimmed not only the kitchen lamp, but Sarah Jane's own, and set them both on the table.

"If Steve is going at scholar's work, he must have scholar's accommodations," she had said. "It's kind of wonderful, Josiah, that the minister picked him out of all the congregation to help him—now, ain't it?"

Mr. Mitchell didn't express his mind other than by an untranslatable sound in the throat, which apparently conveyed satisfaction to the wife's mind. She went on with putting the kitchen in extra array. Then, as carefully as if she were managing rare glass or china, she arranged the files of papers, the package of envelopes, and the sharp, bright scissors, setting forward their best chair for Stephen to occupy. When the work was fairly commenced, Mr. Mitchell drew his chair out of the chimney corner, the better to watch his son, and Mrs. Mitchell made less progress at her patching than usual, because her eyes constantly wandered to see what "great big paper Stephen was looking at now."

Chapter 18

Complications

As for Flora Ann, she hovered about the room in a restless way, unable to settle herself to anything and unwilling apparently to leave the charmed region and climb up to her own small corner of the world. The fact is, Flora Ann deserves a paragraph by herself.

Almost three weeks of civilization had wrought a great change in her. It's doubtful whether her brothers and sisters, if they'd come upon her suddenly in an unexpected place, would have recognized her. Sarah Jane's cast-off dress, being washed, mended, and altered to fit the younger girl, was such an immense improvement on anything she'd worn before, that in her own estimation it transformed her into a lady. Of her own will, after that, she combed and brushed and carefully fingered the reddish brown curls. Also, a tiny line of white had been added to her dress about the throat. "Sarah Jane always wears something white on her neck when she's dressed up," explained Mrs. Mitchell. "She says it makes her feel better." Flora Ann, examining herself in Sarah Jane's mirror after the addition, understood the statement and agreed with it.

There's really nothing more exciting, if people understood it, than these transformations in life. Such little commonplace things had been done for the Lucas girl; yet they'd started springs of hope and action within her of which she hadn't dreamed before and which would lead no one could tell where.

"She ain't Sarah Jane, not by a great ways," Mrs. Mitchell confided to her husband, "but she does real well, I must say. For a girl who knew nothing at all when she first came here, she's got along first-rate. She washes her hands now without me telling her, whenever she's going to touch a dish. And she ain't run her fingers through her hair since I told her Sarah Jane couldn't eat no dinner one day when she was sick, because Mrs. Jinks, who came in to help me, twisted up her hair when it fell down and went to cut the bread without washing her hands. I told it to her to see if it would learn her anything—'cause she was always twisting her hair and running her fingers through it. She's quick to learn. She colored up like a peony and ain't fussed with her hair since. She's slower motioned than Sarah Jane and quieter like, but she gets things done somehow, and I must say I take to her as I didn't have any notion I could. All the same, I'll be thankful to see Sarah Jane again, Josiah—I will that! There's lots of things she could teach Flora Ann."

Mrs. Mitchell had made a sacrifice in receiving this ill-kept, ill-taught, slatternly girl into her household. Mrs. Mitchell had been poorer in her life even than she was today. But she'd always been neat and clean, and, as is natural with such people, dirt was the terror. Nothing but the minister's carefully dropped seed, that by receiving Flora Ann Lucas under her care she could help cultivate a soul, had induced the mother to make the sacrifice. She'd willingly have done without her help; she'd gladly have saved the dollar a week she paid her, but for this fact. It's pleasant to know that even thus early she was reaping her bit of reward. Flora Ann was copying her and growing neat. She swept the kitchen in the corners as well as in the middle of the room; she was learning to rinse the dishes, as well as the dish towels, carefully; she was learning to cook simple food and serve it decently.

There's no telling, said Mrs. Mitchell to herself, *what good it may do her. It don't seem like she could accomplish anything in that shanty where she lives, surrounded by them drunkards. And it don't seem like she'd ever have a home of her own. I don't know how anybody ever could take a notion to her enough to want to marry her. But then things often happen odd in this world. I'll do my best.*

So Flora Ann hovered about the neat kitchen, watching the bright scissors travel slowly down the black line dividing the columns.

"Couldn't I help?" she said presently, drawing near and speaking timidly.

The magnitude of the proposition filled Mrs. Mitchell with dismay. But Stephen raised his eyes and surveyed the questioner thoughtfully. It was as if he had just noted the change in her. He said to himself that her eyes were even bigger than he'd thought them.

"Do you know how to read?" he asked suddenly.

Flora Ann nodded her head eagerly. "I learned how to read when I went to school, up at the other place where we used to live. I could read real fast, and I was in the class with bigger girls than me."

"Read that," said Stephen, pointing with his finger to a paragraph he'd just cut from the paper.

Flora Ann obeyed, her cheeks ablaze, her breath coming hard and fast, the words tumbling out on top of each other in a promiscuous heap without regard to pauses or pronunciation. But she proved her statement; she could "read" without doubt and "very fast."

"Can you read writing?" Stephen interrupted the flow of words to ask the next question.

Flora Ann paused her breath and nodded again.

"Yes, I kin; I learned writing, too, at that school. I had a writing book I made full of letters and words. Teacher said it was done real well, too. I can read them words just as plain as print." And she pointed to those written on the ends of the envelopes, in Mr. Ransom's round hand. They were really quite as plain as print, but Stephen was surprised Flora Ann could compass them. Perhaps, after all his looking down upon her, she knew more than he did. What a revelation that would be.

"Well," he said slowly, coming to his conclusion by careful steps, "I don't see why you shouldn't help do this, if you ain't got nothing else to do. Bring your chair and sit down here, and see if you can put these papers I've cut out into the places that belong to them. Here's one about 'giving.' He said I'd find the word 'giving' through the envelopes somewheres, and I was to put it in it. If you can find the word, you may as well do it."

Thus began a new era in the Lucas girl's life. With hands that trembled so she could scarcely hold the package, she searched eagerly for the word "giving"—and if she finds in searching through the years a diamond lying in her path, I doubt if it will give her the thrill of exultant joy which came over her as she drew forth the envelope with the word she was searching for at its top.

"Here it is," she said in a tone of suppressed eagerness, "right straight here. I knowed I could find it. I ain't forgot them, though it's an awful while since I've seen any writing. It was when I was a little girl, you know. I ain't been to school this four years. But here's the word, sure enough."

Stephen leaned over and surveyed it. Yes, it was the word, and he watched Flora Ann's fingers seize the slip of paper and place it with great care in the envelope—dimly conscious of having gained a victory over self in thus summoning Flora Ann to his aid.

"You, being their near neighbors, can do more for them than the rest of us can," Mr. Ransom had said. Stephen was honestly trying to do something for the Lucas girl.

Evening after evening they sat together over the papers and envelopes. It was long, slow work given them to do. Stephen was slow in finding the marked places and slow in using the scissors, unaccustomed instruments in his hands. Moreover, his eyes were often caught by a sentence to be marked and were held spellbound over it. Often he was in great bewilderment as to where certain slips really belonged. In cases where there was no definite heading, he'd been told to decide by the statements where to place them. A tremendous piece of work was this last; it often necessitated his reading the clipping from beginning to end. Occasionally he read it aloud and speculated over it, and Mr. Mitchell found himself listening and giving his opinion. On two or three occasions Flora Ann had given hers, with such success that the clipping had been consigned to the envelope she chose. All these things took time—and another Sunday came and passed before they were half-through with the first great package.

Long before this, however, both Stephen and his helper had grown intensely interested in the work. It was becoming the custom now to read out the small bits of special interest and discuss them—not only as to where they belonged, but as to the statements made. In short, the Mitchells, with the Lucas girl, were becoming a reading circle. It would be difficult to tell how much it increased Stephen's interest to discover, from time to time, certain words in his list and find their connection threw light on their probable meaning.

One evening, he and Flora Ann settled to their work before the father and mother appeared. Mr. Mitchell had gone to the cellar to examine something needing his care, and Mrs. Mitchell was in her bedroom looking through the depths of a great bandbox for certain pieces she needed to use. It was Flora Ann's opportunity to ask a question which had been haunting her all day.

"Steve, do you suppose all them things can be true that you've clipped out?"

"Of course," said Stephen indignantly. "He ain't a man that would want to cut up papers and keep a lot of things that wasn't true. And he knows what he's about—there's lots of things he ain't marked, you see."

"Well, I wish I could believe them all."

This was followed by a sigh so heartfelt that Stephen looked at her curiously. "What do you care?" he asked, in a voice which, though gruff, wasn't unkind.

" 'Cause I do. I read one of them I put up last night, and it's been following me round all day. I can't get it out of my head. It was about a man who drinked. An awful drunkard he was, and he swore awful. Just like our Jake. He had a little girl who went to Sunday school, and she took to praying for him every day—after a while he gave up drinking and got kind and went to work and was as good as he could be. And it was all along of the little girl's praying, so it said. Do you believe that?"

"I s'pose so. Folks that know about such things seem to believe in praying. And, of course, if there's any use in it, things get done by that means."

"Steve Mitchell, do you believe that if anybody prayed for Jake, say—day in and day out, like that little girl did—that he'd ever get good in this world?"

Here was a question in theology which might well have puzzled wiser heads than Stephen Mitchell's. He laid down his scissors and ran his right hand thoughtfully through his hair, considering what it would be best to say. In his heart he knew he had very little hope for Jake Lucas.

"I don't know, I'm sure. If we could find the little girl who was willing to try, we might prove whether there was anything in it or not. Maybe there's some that might be got ahold of that way, and maybe there's some that can't. I don't know about them things. I'd think Jake was about as hard a one to try on as any of 'em."

"Yes," said Flora Ann earnestly, "he is that! He's enough sight worse than the others. But I was thinking if the thing was true, I might try it. I ain't a little girl, and he ain't my father, but I wouldn't think that could make a difference, would it? There's Father. I might try with him. But he ain't bad. He drinks, but he don't knock folks around and swear, and he's kind of good-natured always. I don't feel that hard about Father that I do about Jake. It wouldn't make so much difference, either, if Father'd give it up. But Jake, oh, my! If Jake should come in sober, I guess Mother'd just about die. You see, Steve, Mother cares more for Jake than she does for the rest of us. He's the oldest, you know, and she had him to think about when she was young. She's got some of the clothes he wore when he was a baby—cries over them, if you'll believe it. She says he was a good little boy and as pretty as a picture. Folks used to stop on the street and watch her go by with him, when she got him all fixed up. She didn't have as good times with the rest of us, because we was so horrid poor and lowdown after a spell. But with Jake she had real nice times. She loves him this minute, for all he knocks her around and is horrid. I'm just a mind to try it anyhow. It couldn't do no harm, if it didn't do no good." She spoke the last sentence in lower tone and looked up timidly at her auditor as if to discover what he thought of it.

"Well," said Stephen, after a silence which could have been felt, "I don't know why you shouldn't, I'm sure. I don't know much about them things, but folks do pray, and they pray for folks, and they believe in it. The minister believes in it and thinks it should be done."

"Would he believe in praying for Jake, and me doing it?"

"Why, I s'pose so. I tell you I don't know anything about it, but I can't see why not—if there's anything in it. If Jake would let the drink alone, I s'pose he could learn to be decent. Some folks do give it up after they've been at it a good while." Stephen thought of his father, but not for worlds would he have mentioned his name in this connection.

"Well," said Flora Ann, with a little catch of the breath which was peculiar to her and indicated great and suppressed excitement, "I've been thinking about it all day and wondering if I couldn't. I made up my mind I'd ask what you thought. I could use them same words, only instead of 'father,' I could say 'Jake.' It was real short: 'Oh, Lord! Please save my father.' That's all she said—she was a little bit of a girl, you know—and I could say, 'Oh, Lord! Please save Jake.' It couldn't do no harm now, could it, if it didn't do no good?"

"I should say not," said Stephen, low-voiced and troubled. Already Flora Ann, "one of the Lucas set," was getting ahead of him to give intelligent answers. He should know how to answer her. He should be able to assure her, and from his own experience, that prayer was exactly what Jake needed. He should be able to say he would join her in praying. His conscience told him these things. The minister's sermon two weeks before had been plain. He didn't dare do other than advise Flora Ann to carry out her purpose. He wasn't willing to confess to her that he knew he should begin to pray; he wasn't willing to begin. It's true he had no sense of the power of prayer and hadn't the slightest hope, or rather expectation, that any prayer Flora Ann or, for that matter, anybody else could offer would make any difference with Jake Lucas. But he did believe praying for her brother would, in some mysterious manner he didn't understand, make a difference in Flora Ann. This far his knowledge of theology reached—that he recognized a certain power in prayer; but that it would help in the direction in which he was reaching, he didn't understand.

The little church to which Maxwell Ransom ministered had a sensation the next Sabbath. The congregation was made up of people who, to a marked extent, were posted as to their neighbors' affairs. They knew, for instance, to the fraction of a dollar what each new garment cost in which any of their number chanced to appear and where it was purchased. The minister's sister was an exception and an excitement. They didn't know where her things were bought or what she paid for them. There was a shrewd suspicion abroad that she had a great deal of money. How else could she manage such elegant costumes? For the community was largely made up of those young people who suppose elegance and refinement have only a monetary value. They were by no means through with discussing Helen Ransom's attire, and various speculations concerning the probable cost of certain articles were still rife, when Sarah Jane Mitchell helped cause the new sensation. Back of this is a story, a bit of which you should hear.

Hanging in Helen's wardrobe was a dress of soft cashmere, delicate in color and fine in texture, but somehow in wearing it she had found it ill-fitting and uncomfortable. Lately, whenever she saw the dress, she thought of Sarah Jane and mentally measured her height and shape.

I believe it would fit her to perfection, she told herself. *How pretty she'd look in it. I'd like to see her in it and a bonnet of the same color, with a slight touch of pale pink about them both. What a revelation it might make to her. I wonder if I couldn't manage to give her the dress. She needs a new one, and I've sacrificed my comfort to this long enough. I'll talk to Max about it.*

And Max had shown a lively interest in the whole matter. In fact, as he laughingly told his sister, he'd adopted the Mitchell family and meant to induce them to adopt the Lucas family, "and between us we'll civilize all of them." Then his face had grown sweetly grave, as he added, "We may do more and better for them than that. Perhaps we can bring them into intimate companionship with Jesus Christ. Helen, I'm getting in love with life again. There are such possibilities for souls."

And Helen had gone away glad and resolved to present the dress that very day.

Chapter 19

Progress

Helen had no such puzzling road to travel as Maxwell Ransom had had with Stephen. In a sense Sarah Jane was above her brother.

The girl had been with her now for more than three weeks. They had sat and sewed together through the long days and in some respects had come very near each other. Helen knew she was looked upon as a friend and that Sarah Jane had a frank, sunny nature, which could receive joyously and gratefully any tokens of kindness she might choose to bestow.

Helen had no hesitancy in saying to her, as she did an hour after reaching her decision: "Here's a dress I've borne with for some time. It doesn't fit me, and I don't like it, and as I don't need it this fall, I'm giving it to you if you'll accept it. I think that with very little alteration it will fit you, and I know it's just the color to suit your face."

Sarah Jane's face had been a lovely color just then, and her bright eyes had grown brighter as she looked at the soft, pretty folds, lying over Helen's arm.

"Oh, goodness me!" she said. "Ain't it too fine a dress for me? I never seen anything prettier, and it's soft as feathers."

"It isn't expensive goods," Helen had explained, nor was it from her standpoint. "And it wears well and washes nicely. It'll make you a very pretty dress, and it's just the right shade to go with those bits of velvet I was showing you. A piece of the cashmere trimmed with the velvet will make you a pretty bonnet. Suppose we spend this evening in seeing what we can do in the millinery line?" And Sarah Jane's face was alight with joy at the idea.

She had made great strides during her three weeks at the manse. It will seem incredible to some that such a change of manner and views had come to her in so short a time. But the grace of God can accomplish much in a human heart.

Having no books to read and no opportunity for study, Sarah Jane had never thought to read the Bible, for none of the people she came in contact with seemed to read it much. So when she entered the atmosphere of Helen Ransom's life, it was a revelation to her. Here were two people, at least, who evidently lived their lives by the Bible, referred to it familiarly, read it together daily, and stopped over the verses to discuss their meaning in a simple, interesting manner she could understand and appreciate.

When, after two or three days' acquaintance, Helen Ransom had said to her, "Sarah, have you ever considered living for Christ? You have splendid opportunities for service," she was bewildered.

"Me, opportunities for service! Me live for Christ!" She didn't understand what was meant and said so.

The conversation which followed would have astonished many ministers of the gospel accustomed to using only theological terms and talking about "conversion" and "regeneration" as though understood as matters of course. Helen, used to teaching young people, found she had to choose her words with care and go back over her sentences and simplify. But she had a listener who meant to understand, if at all possible.

An hour came when her eyes seemed to grow luminous with a new thought which had taken possession of her. The work she was doing dropped from her hands into her lap, and she sat with parted lips, as if about to speak, yet hesitating for words, and looked at Helen.

At last she said, "Why, Miss Ransom, that almost scares me. It sounds as if I could have it for the asking."

"You can, my dear," said Helen, deeply moved by this way of receiving the call. "It's His own desire. His 'Come unto Me' means all this and infinitely more. It means daily and hourly companionship and guidance, and such depths of love and tenderness and patience as you will learn about Him, for no mortal tongue can tell it."

And Sarah Jane had received the thought with the same directness and frankness with which she received her invitation to come and sew at the manse. That had been a wonderful opening to her, and she'd accepted it. Now here was another—something, it seems, she might have had all her life and never understood before.

"There's been a lot of wasted time," she had said a little while after this conversation. "I wisht I'd known it a long time ago, Miss Ransom, and I wish Steve had known it. It would have made a difference. But I'll do my part now, whatever it is. I don't understand it, of course, but I'll do my level best to find it out."

In this straightforward manner her Christian life had begun. Her first conscious prayer on her knees might have startled you; it was so unlike the ordinary forms of prayer, so simple and direct: "Oh, Lord Jesus, I've just heard You wanted me for a friend. Folks have said so in sermons, I s'pose, and it's been in Bible verses I heard, some of them. But I never understood it—I don't know why. Now, Lord, I feel in my heart that it's true, and I want to belong and do what You want me to."

So, in their separate ways, Sarah Jane Mitchell and Flora Ann Lucas, all unknown to each other, had begun to pray. Sarah Jane's Christian life from that moment was a vigorous plant. What she undertook she meant to perform. She was as resolute about her Christianity as she'd been about ripping and turning and remodeling her dresses. She took the Bible as a literalist, with no hesitancy about its meaning what it said. And when she didn't understand what it said, she went to Helen Ransom for light. Also she went daily on her knees for help from Him Who is the Light of the world and Who has promised to give wisdom liberally and upbraids not. Does anyone who understands Him need to be told that such living as this meant steady and rapid growth?

One day she took the verse about "yea and nay" to Helen in the sewing room.

"I don't think I understand it," she said. "It can't mean we're never to say anything but yes and no?"

Then followed a conversation on care in the use of language and on the value of simple words which meant what they said and weren't marred by extravagances.

All these things being taken into consideration, it perhaps isn't surprising the young girl had greatly changed, both outwardly and inwardly, in that short space of time. Three weeks of constant communion with refined and cultivated people had done much, and who shall say what companionship with Jesus Christ had done for her? Yet Sarah Jane wasn't a little startled over the picture presented to her in the mirror on the Sabbath morning when she first put on the new dress and bonnet.

Limited in her choice of colors all her life and obliged to wear what she chanced to have, whether it suited or not, she'd had no opportunity for studying harmony of color, even if she'd understood how to do it. But she would have been blind not to discover that the young girl arrayed in soft dove-like cashmere, with a neat little bonnet of the same delicate tint, made in the prevailing style, was a very different-looking person from any Sarah Jane she had ever seen before.

When she came downstairs to wait for Helen, the minister added unwittingly his commendation, by pausing with surprise and bewilderment on seeing a stranger in the hall, but recovered in a moment to say cordially, "Why, Miss Mitchell, is it you? I didn't know you at first."

I'm glad of it, murmured Sarah Jane to herself, as the door closed after him. *I'd like to begin all over again and not have anybody know me. I'd like to be somebody else—Miss Jones or Miss Jenkins or somebody—and just start afresh. Things are different, and I'd like to have them different all through. But then Steve wouldn't be my brother, I suppose, and there would be Mother and Father—no, I guess I like to be Sarah Jane Mitchell, but a different one all the way through. My! How different I'll have things when I get home.*

And so this young woman made quite a sensation, seated in the pastor's pew—the finishing touch to her wardrobe added by a pair of kid gloves that matched her bonnet. The gloves had been Helen Ransom's birthday gift to her, presented then because she couldn't resist the temptation to study their effect.

Another figure near the door required more or less study. This was none other than Stephen Mitchell in a new suit. The papers, clipped and arranged in their various envelopes, had been brought home two days before.

Stephen interrupted the hearty commendations his work had received to say, with the air of one determined to be honest at all hazards, "It ain't fair for me to get all the thanks. That Lucas girl working at our house, she helped me lots. She's a better reader than I be, a good deal, and she put the things in their places and kept them straight. I don't know as I could have got through with them if it hadn't been for her."

"I'm glad of it," said the minister heartily. "If you were able to set her to work and interest her in doing it, you accomplished more than the work itself. It's worth a great deal for a young girl like her to have her evenings employed for her in such a safe and helpful manner. So she can read and write? That's good. Perhaps she'd like to study. Why don't you start a school, Stephen, while she's with you—you and she?"

"Humph!" said Stephen with infinite sarcasm. "And me be the teacher, I s'pose."

"Yes—unless you'd like me for a teacher. Suppose I furnish the books and the suggestions, and you and she do the work? Perhaps you'll give her a start which will save her to a respectable life. Why not try it? But now to business. You haven't told me what this work is worth that you've done for me, and since I have more of the same I'd like to have done, I have a plan to talk over with you."

Then with great care he presented his plan, which was for Stephen to go with him the following morning to the city twenty miles away and select from the clothing store a neat suit of clothes fit for church all winter. The minister would pay the bill, and Stephen would work for him during the winter evenings, similar to what he'd been doing for the past weeks. There was a good deal of conversation and some opposition. Stephen was quick-witted enough to know it would take a great deal of the work he'd been doing to pay for a suit of clothes. But the minister explained he meant to furnish a great deal of work. Such matters had been accumulating in his study ever since he began his college course, waiting for leisure hours which had never come. And he'd be very glad to get his study put into systematic order.

"You can give an evening to me here, perhaps," he added, "which will be very helpful in several ways. In short, it's as reasonable a business transaction as I ever made. I could pay you in money, of course, and let you wait for the clothes until it accumulated, but I'd much rather have it as I've proposed. I like to see you in church. You're a help to me there, and I want you in my Bible class. I'm working up a class, and I want recruits from your neighborhood, and I want you to get them for me. I hope to have all three of the Lucas boys in my Bible class."

He laughed at Stephen's dismayed exclamation but tried to impress him with the fact that it might be done and that stranger things had been done in the world. He went to his library shelf and got down the great encyclopedia of illustrations and turned to one or two startling facts illustrating God's power over depraved and apparently lost human lives.

Stephen's reply was one the minister least expected to hear: "Flora Ann Lucas would like to hear them stories."

"Would she? Why?"

Then Stephen, somewhat to his own regret, had to repeat his conversation with her and her resolution to "begin that very night" to pray for Jake. "It's odd praying, I suppose," he added with a little chuckle. "She knows as much about that as I do, I guess. But it can't do no harm, I reckon."

"We can't tell what it may do," said Maxwell Ransom, with such gladness in his voice that Stephen looked at him in wonder—almost in pity. What could he expect Flora Ann Lucas to accomplish by saying over a half-dozen words about her brother Jake?

"You don't know Jake Lucas as well as I do," he said. "He's lowdown, I can tell you. He's enough sight worse than the other two—hateful and cruel when he's drunk, bad to everybody, kicking and knocking things around that ain't harming him, and swearing just awful. They're all afraid of him. The girls'll hide for hours to keep out of his sight, and his mother's afraid of him, too. She don't dare speak while he's in the house, unless he lets her. It'll take more than praying to make a decent fellow out of him. If he could get put into jail and have to stay there, maybe something could be done for the rest of the family.

"There's Flora Ann now. She's been to our house three weeks. She's afraid to go home, because she knows Jake will go on so. He hates her worse than the rest of them somehow, and yet she's a-praying for him. I kind of think something decent might be made out of her, if somebody would take hold that knew how to do it."

There was more conversation, about this and several matters, but it ended in the minister carrying off his prize in triumph the next morning to the clothing store. The result was even more bewildering than in Sarah Jane's case, for Stephen had had no ability to make the best of his own poor wardrobe. The change from the worn and patched and outgrown garments, in which he'd figured so long, to a suit of clothes which fitted him from head to foot, made a transformation which cannot be described in words.

Stephen had felt its power, though he had no mirror to look into. There was a little eight-inch glass in Sarah Jane's room, and he was tempted to slip in there before he went down. But, after reaching the door, he turned away, calling himself a fool, and went downstairs. Here his mother had been sufficient mirror, reflecting his image in her own delighted eyes, and having no hesitancy in expressing her views.

Chapter 20

Trying to Catch Up

W ell, if ever I saw the like in all my days! Why, Steve Mitchell, I wouldn't know you if I met you on the street. I'll tell you who I'd think you were, Steve. You look just like your father did as much as thirty years ago. Oh, my! But he was a handsome young man. I never knew you favored him so much. Oh, dear boy! I'm just too glad to think of your being all dressed up, as you should be, and going to church." Whereupon her emotions rose above the reserve or timidity of years, and she wound both arms around his neck and kissed his tanned red cheeks again and again.

"Huh!" he said, struggling a little, yet pleased in spite of himself. "What a fuss you do make, Mother, over a fellow's new clothes."

" 'Tain't the clothes altogether," said his mother. "It's the feeling, Steve, that that's the kind of clothes you should wear and that we meant our boy should wear, didn't we, Josiah? Only look at him. Isn't he a handsome fellow now?"

Mr. Mitchell, thus appealed to, turned and surveyed his tall, broad-shouldered son from head to foot and presently nodded his head with great satisfaction. "I guess he'll do, Mother—if he behaves as well as he looks, and I reckon he will. The fact is, he's always behaved pretty well, hasn't he? Only the clothes haven't matched. Maybe you can keep things matched now, Steve. Times seem to be a-changing with us somehow."

It was really the first hearty commendation the boy had ever received from his father in his life. He turned and went out of the room suddenly, a choking feeling in his throat. It was a new sensation to be approved. On the instant, his conscience arose, telling him of hundreds of things he could have done to have made the lives of his father and mother easier.

"And I'll do it," he murmured. "I'll learn more than words. If Father will trust me, I'll try to make things different on this old farm. I'll do the very best I know how, and I'll learn how in ways I don't know now. He'll help me." (The pronoun always referred to Maxwell Ransom.) "He said he would, and them papers will help me. I'll show Father yet what kind of boy he has."

That spirit he took to church on the day he helped create a sensation. I'm bound to confess he didn't listen to the sermon as Mr. Ransom hoped he would. Portions of it he listened to intently, but this was when he recognized some of "his words," as he still called those on the list. But between times his thoughts wandered frequently to a distant pew, where Helen Ransom and a strange young lady sat. I'm sorry to say this strange young woman discouraged him. He thought he recognized in her a being from another sphere.

" 'Tain't clothes," he said to himself disconsolately, "and it ain't knowing words. I don't know what it is. Sarah Jane now might know all the words on the list and a lot more, and so might Flora Ann, and they wouldn't either of them look like that girl no more than I look like the minister, though I've got on new clothes and do look different. Maybe it's knowing words and wearing that kind of clothes all your life that makes the difference, and folks that hasn't had them never get it."

Thus, from the state of exaltation in which he'd entered the church, he sank into the depths, all because of the strange lady from another sphere. I hope you can put yourself to a degree in his place and feel the amazement which thrilled through him as, almost with the "Amen" of the benediction, the strange young woman turned her head and let her eyes move eagerly over the church, evidently searching for someone. Behold! The eyes belonged to Sarah Jane. Stephen stood perfectly still, lost to every idea but that.

It was clothes, then, or knowing words, or it was being with the minister's family for three weeks—perhaps all three combined. How did girls make themselves so different in such a little while? He stared at Sarah Jane, his amazement growing steadily. She caught a glimpse of him, and her pleasant face broke into smiles as she nodded appreciatively. Manifestly she also saw a "difference."

She's pretty, said Stephen to himself, *as pretty as a picture. She ain't like the other one, but she's most as pretty. I never seen the like. I reckon she's learned lots of things. I wonder when she's coming home.*

"Dear me!" said Fanny Bascome. "If you'll believe it, Sarah Jane, I didn't know you at all when you first came into church. What a difference fixing up makes, doesn't it? Is that one of Miss Ransom's dresses? I never did see a woman with as many dresses. I'd think if her father was a poor minister, she'd have used up his salary long ago. But it's very becoming, Sarah Jane. So is your hat. Did she give that to you?"

And Sarah Jane was jarred. The verse the minister had recited at family worship that morning was, "Let the words of my mouth, and the meditation of my heart be acceptable in thy sight, O LORD, my strength, and my redeemer." She wondered what fitting words she could reply and found she had no answer whatever for Fanny Bascome and liked her less than usual that morning.

Nothing daunted, however, by her silence, Fanny hurried out her questions.

"Are you staying there all winter, Sarah Jane? What do you do anyhow? Housework? I didn't know you was willing to do housework. Ma would have liked your help often if she'd known it.

"How'd do, Steve?" Fanny said, for they were moving down the aisle, and Stephen had taken a few steps forward to meet his sister. "I declare, Steve, if you and Sarah Jane keep on getting fixed up, we'll need spyglasses to recognize you." She laughed at her own silly words. "I never knew before that clothes could make such a difference. Yours are brand-new, aren't they, Steve? No made-over about them. Oh, Mr. Pettibone!" She raised her voice as that gentleman slipped from a seat ahead of her. "Wait a minute, won't you? I want to see you about the sociable." And Stephen and Sarah Jane were released.

"Who's that young fellow coming down the other aisle near the door?" inquired Mr. Bascome of his pastor. "I never saw him here before."

"Oh, yes! He's been here several times. That's young Mitchell, from the Hilton Hill neighborhood, you know."

"Is it possible that's Steve? I didn't recognize him. Why, he looks much changed."

"Does he?" asked the minister, smiling, and he hastened on to reach the door so he might have a word with Stephen.

The Mitchells were thoroughly discussed that day at the Bascome dinner table.

"I must say," began Fanny, "I never saw anyone so changed in all my life by a little finery as Sarah Jane Mitchell. Half the people in the church didn't know her. Mrs. Smith nudged me while the first hymn was being sung and asked me who that pretty girl was in the minister's pew. She's quite stuck-up, too. I couldn't get anything out of her after church. I believe I asked her a dozen questions, and she didn't answer one of them."

"Steve has blossomed out, too," said Mr. Bascome. "I didn't know the fellow. I asked Mr. Ransom who he was."

"Yes, Stephen was in a spic-and-span new suit. I wonder where he got it? Mr. Ransom must have given it to him. Dear me! How they are going on. I don't see what they find in the Mitchells to attract them. Steve's always seemed like the stupidest fellow. Sarah Jane is smart enough about some things, but she don't know anything other girls do. Why, the Mitchells are nobodies, we all know— and have been for years and years. I must say Helen Ransom looks high for her friends."

The talk flowed on uninterruptedly for some time, until not only the Mitchell family, but various other persons who were in church, or were conspicuous by their absence, were discussed. Not a word was said of the sermon, on which the minister had put not only hours of study, but hours of prayer; not a word was spoken indicating that this day was theirs to help them into nearer fellowship with Him.

Sarah Jane went home by the middle of the following week. Helen Ransom had detained her until, as she told her brother, not even the semblance of an excuse remained for keeping her another day. And though he meekly suggested shirts and other masculine articles, which might be made for the indefinite future, she only laughed and shook her head, assuring him even Sarah Jane's and her ingenuity had limitations and that shirts, she must confess, were beyond her.

"We must help them," said Helen earnestly. "It would be a shame to leave them to themselves now. Sarah is an unusual girl. If she'd had even the ordinary opportunities of life, she would have shown her exceptional ability, but she's been dwarfed on every side. Really, Max, there seems to have been no one, in the church or out of it, who has thought of their neighborhood and tried to reach it in any way. I didn't know there were such left-alone portions of country, in the state, at least."

"There should be some kind of Sabbath service out there," said the minister thoughtfully. "There's that Lucas family to reach and several others in the outlying neighborhood. I wonder if I couldn't manage an afternoon service? It's some distance to go, but we might ride there. Could you go, Helen, and sing and teach and other things, if we could wake up an interest there?"

It certainly wasn't Helen Ransom's fault the idea got no further than the minister's "should." He was a young man, and so many "shoulds" pressed upon him. He did speak of the plan once to Mr. Bascome and one or two others, who assured him the neighborhood had no place for holding meetings and that the people wouldn't attend if it did.

Meanwhile, Mrs. Mitchell went about her home like one bewildered. Sarah Jane had returned, brisk, bright, full of her same breezy energy and yet different. Daily, hourly, the mother noted and studied the difference. What mysterious something had gotten hold of the girl? Not only the mother, but the father, noted it—and, most of all, Stephen. In a hundred ways her life indicated that its center was changed. Ways which perhaps wouldn't be easy to define, yet which could be distinctly felt. It wasn't her new ideas about setting the table and arranging the furniture or her new ways of expressing herself, though these were marked enough. It was something behind these changes and superior to them. Mrs. Mitchell fathomed it to its source one day.

"I don't know what's come over you, Sarah Jane," she said, looking at her in that bewildered, wistful way. "You seem so dreadful different somehow."

Sarah Jane laughed cheerily. "Don't I seem nice, Mother?"

"Oh, nice, child! That's no word for it. If you knew how glad I was to have you home again. Oh, Flora Ann did her best, poor thing! And she did a great sight better than I expected, and I'm sorry for her having to go back there to live like the pigs, as they do. She cried about it dreadful hard, poor thing, the last day, but then—oh, my!—Sarah Jane, I done my best for her the three weeks she was here. But she never was and never will be you. No, you haven't changed in any way for the worse, child. You was always industrious and faithful, and you was always good-natured and never grumbled or found fault, and yet it seems some way as if nowadays the sun was shining all the time where you are. And you look out more than usual for other folks, though you never was selfish. I don't know what it is. Don't you feel it yourself, child?"

Sarah Jane laughed again, a bright, sweet laugh.

"Yes," she said, "I feel it myself. It's true, Mother. I've got some sunshine in my heart I never had there before. I suppose if you come squarely down to it, I've been converted, though Mr. Ransom didn't use that word, and she didn't. But I was reading a book he gave me yesterday. He said it would explain some things to me that maybe I didn't understand, and it has. As near as I can make out, I've been what they call 'converted.' At first I was almost scared to think that anything so wonderful could have happened to me, but I guess it has. The more I think about it, the more I believe so."

"Bless the Lord!" said Mrs. Mitchell softly. "Here I've been praying for this thing every day of my life since you was born, and yet I didn't seem to expect it somehow. And I'm just as astonished as I can be."

Sarah Jane turned from the pan of potatoes she was carefully paring and gave her mother a curious, half-wistful glance.

"Have you really, Mother?" she said. "I wish I'd known you were praying for me. When I think about it, it does seem too everlasting foolish I've wasted so many years. If I'd known about it maybe I would have attended to it right off. But maybe I wouldn't. I suppose I knew enough all the time, if I'd thought any."

"It's likely my fault," said the mother meekly. "I never was brought up to talk about them things, and I didn't know how. I was always afraid of doing harm. It's my opinion Satan gets hold of a lot of people that way. Many times I've wished I knew how to say something to you, and I thought I couldn't do it right. But you've got it now, Sarah Jane. That just explains it—it's religion, bless the Lord!"

She pressed her old, tired hands together in delight, and her worn, homely face would have made a study for an artist.

Still it must be confessed that, as winter closed in, Sarah Jane found it hard to settle down to her meager life. She wasn't unhappy; she was simply restless, with an intense desire to reach out. The contrast between her days and those she had spent at the manse were too vivid. She wanted books; she wanted to study; she wanted a hundred things she couldn't compass. Her days were by no means spent in idleness. She relieved her mother now almost entirely of the routine of farmwork, and she'd learned many little touches which made life much pleasanter in the old house but took more time.

Long evenings held much interest now, for both Sarah Jane and her brother. They studied faithfully the few books the minister had put into their hands— among them a dictionary. And they didn't let up their interest in studying the now-famous list of words. But these glimpses into the world of knowledge made them both realize more fully what they'd lost and how much of a journey they must take before they "caught up," as Sarah Jane phrased it. She never explained in words who the persons were she was trying to catch up with, but they certainly weren't the Bascomes.

Helen Ransom had by no means forgotten her protégée. Not a week passed without a book or paper or card with an important verse on it, or perhaps a ruffle or bit of ribbon, finding its way through the mail to Sarah Jane. She began to watch eagerly for a chance to send to the post office, and Stephen, though he didn't own it in words, was as much interested in the little parcels as she was and was ingenious in planning ways and means to secure them.

Nor did Helen Ransom's interest end here; she was constantly planning how to help her friend. The Mitchell family was the subject of frequent and earnest conversations in the manse during those early winter weeks. Many projects for furthering their interests were brought forward, considered carefully and abandoned as impracticable.

Frequently Helen would remark, "I wish there was some way for them to keep boarders. I can't help feeling Sarah is talented in that direction. The mother's very neat and understands good, wholesome cookery. And Sarah would be as fine as any lady in a home of her own, if she had the means. Think what a pleasant country home it could be made into for tired city people. If we only knew the right ones to gather about them and if it were only summer."

Her brother laughed pleasantly over this statement. "It seems to me, my good sister, that you have several important 'ifs' in your plans. Since it isn't summer and we have no winter boarders to suggest to them, the question is: How can we help them more than we are now? I like the boarding scheme immensely, if it could be brought about. I see in it a way to reach the Lucas family. I suspect the Mitchell home was paradise to that poor Flora Ann, who, on the whole, is the most hopeful one in that household. I wish very much she might be kept under Mrs. Mitchell's teaching for a time."

Chapter 21

Transferred

Do you know, Max—I believe Hilary would come to the Mitchells' to board if she understood the situation? The thought came to me last night like an inspiration. I mean to write her this morning and explain the circumstances. I wonder why I didn't think of it before."

Her brother's laugh was compassionate this time, but his only reply in words was, "So that's your latest scheme, is it?"

She answered the laugh, rather than the words. "You don't approve of it, do you?"

"Oh, as to approval," he said, smiling kindly, "of course I have nothing to say. But as to the feasibility of the plan, I'm a bit skeptical. Didn't you tell me she was settled in New York for the winter—and very comfortably? By what reasoning can you expect her to break up her home and come to a dreary portion of the country, among total strangers, and live in a farmhouse? If she would be near you, that might be an inducement. But the road to the Mitchell farm isn't too inviting in the winter. I can't imagine anything more dreary, for one used to city life, than to be there and shut in, often by storm or cold."

"Ah, but, you see, you don't know Hilary. If you did, a great many of those statements would mean nothing, if she believed she could accomplish good results."

His smile was still compassionate and superior. This young man of twenty-six believed he knew the world, especially the world of women, much better than his sister—so much had Gertrude Temple accomplished for him. By his reasoning, Gertrude Temple hadn't been weak and false above others. But all women were weak by nature and shrank from unpleasant or uncomfortable situations. He had as much faith in Hilary Colchester as he had in any woman, but, as he said to Helen, what could be her motive?

"Hilary doesn't think of herself," explained Helen. "She never belonged to the class of people who put self first. That there's work to be done for the Master, which she may accomplish, will be motive enough for her."

"But, dear sister, there's work to be done everywhere. She won't let her talents in that direction run to waste while in New York. I can't see why she should put herself in unpleasant surroundings to work."

"Not if the thought was really an inspiration, Maxwell? If it was, the Lord Jesus intends it to be carried out."

Now his smile was sweet to see and had no cynical line in it. "By all means, try," he said gently, "if you feel impressed that way. It'll do no harm. The trying will benefit your own soul at least."

But he left the table with so little faith in Hilary Colchester's coming and so little interest in the matter that he forgot it entirely, although during his leisure moments that day he considered several projects, any one of which, if it could be brought about, might help the Mitchells. And Helen Ransom wrote her letter.

In a very few days came a reply so characteristic of Hilary Colchester that you shall have it complete:

My dear Helen,

It was a joy to hear from you again and such a long letter. I'm deeply interested in your friends. I both laughed and cried over Sarah Jane and Steve, and that poor Flora Ann touches my heart. But your plan fairly took my breath away for a few minutes; it was so unexpected. Were you entirely frank in your picture, my dear? Are the surroundings as dreary as you made them? If so, what a forlorn life it must have been for Sarah all these years. I'll be glad to help her out of it—no, I mean help her in it, if I may.

You're right. I'm fond of the country, though I'm fond of city life also, and I'm pleasantly situated here, but not really at work yet. No door has seemed to open for me. I wonder if it was because I was needed elsewhere. I shall so interpret it, if your friends will receive me. Make all arrangements for me if you can, and I'll leave New York as soon as I receive your letter directing me to do so.

I'm writing to catch the next mail out, after receiving yours, so there's no time for long stories, nor is there need. I have nothing to tell except the old story—that the Lord is good and His tender mercies have been great toward me. A wonderful story, truly—but you know it by heart. Of course, the joy over possibly seeing you soon is great.

The minister arched his eyebrows in evident surprise over the letter's contents and made only this comment as he gave it back: "It's direct and to the point, but I confess I'm astonished at the result. Of course you know, Helen—I hope it'll work out according to your desires."

But you have no faith in it, nevertheless, or in her, was his sister's mental comment. *You believe that all women, except Mother and possibly me, are built after the fashion of your shattered idol and amount to very little as a whole. I hope your eyes may be opened sometime.*

Perhaps her eyes held a little resentful sparkle as she indulged in these thoughts. It really was hard, with the prospect of Hilary so near her, to have such an unsympathetic and unappreciative brother.

An explanation is needed as to why this beloved friend of her youth had never come in contact with her brother. Hilary West had been Helen Ransom's roommate during her entire four years at a boarding school several hundred miles from her home. From almost the first day of their companionship they were friends, congenial in tastes and pursuits. Wonderfully unlike in outward appearance, but wonderfully alike at heart, they had grown toward each other throughout these years. Of course, the home people had heard a great deal about Helen's school friend, and many plans had been made for her to spend some weeks with Helen. But various household matters in both families had prevented this, and at last Hilary West graduated, married, and sailed for India with her husband, without meeting any of her friend's family.

Up to that point, life had been continued sunlight with her. The only child in a lovely home, surrounded by all the beauty and culture that wealth and refined taste could secure, consecrated from her early childhood by Christian parents to the Master's service, wherever He would call her, she had been given to the faraway work in India, with tender tears in which smiles intermingled. Father and mother felt their hearts breaking on parting with her; yet they were proud and glad to part with her for such a cause. She'd made a safe, pleasant journey to her faraway home and begun what she thought was her lifework, under circumstances hopeful for success.

Then the shadows began to fall. The first news from home brought word that the father had been called from them without a moment's warning. This had left the mother and the little sister, only seven years old, desolate.

"It almost seems as though Mother needed me now," the young wife had said with trembling lips, looking at her husband.

But he had kissed the lips which trembled so and said tenderly: "The Lord knows, my darling. Didn't He send you out here to work among those who need you?"

So she had thought, and her faith upheld her during the mysteries of that dark hour. She needed faith, for the darkness thickened about her. Before mastering the language to preach even one sermon to the benighted souls he came to reach—though not before he had, by his kindly ways and skillful ministrations to those in physical need, won some hearts—the young missionary succumbed to the disease which makes victims of so many in that land, and the six-month bride was a widow. Now nothing hindered her from returning to the mother she'd thought needed her; for the customs and superstitions in that heathen land were such as to make a widow all but useless as a missionary. So, as soon as Mrs. Colchester could arrange her affairs, she sailed alone for America.

After a long, weary, dangerous voyage, detained by storm, almost shipwrecked, "in perils often by land and sea," she reached New York only to learn, as the first news after she trod her native soil, that her mother, too, had gone home to God. Father and mother and husband in less than one year gathered home! Would it have been any wonder if the young spirit, whose life had been so bright, had been almost crushed? Such a result wouldn't have seemed incredible. But what to me was almost a mystery was that this young woman's faith was equal to the strain, and after the first shock of the added sorrow— indeed, while the first hours were still upon her—she cried out, "Though he slay me, yet will I trust Him," and, after a little, with lips that quivered and smiled, "It is all right—He knows." But, thank God, many such grand triumphs of faith over sorrow are on record.

Helen Ransom had gone at once to her friend, upon her arrival in this country, and had brought her to spend two precious weeks with her in her father's home, before Hilary went to take up what was now her lifework—the care and training of her little sister, Nina. But young Ransom had been hard at work in the second year of his seminary course at the time and hadn't met his sister's friend. Truth to tell, he had little interest in meeting her.

"All girls have friendships," he told his mother, in that oracular fashion in which young men are wont to talk, "and they're always perfect, while it lasts. Helen's dearest is perfect, of course. And in a few years she won't even write to her. I don't think young men have such exclusive friendships. They're more sensible in their arrangements, think enough of many nice fellows, and let it go at that. If Helen corresponds with this paragon of perfection in five years from now, I'll have some curiosity to see her."

This had been in response to a suggestion from his mother, while he was at home for the short vacations, that he should go out of his way on his journey back, a two hours' ride, to make the acquaintance of Mrs. Colchester. Only one young woman at that time did he consider worthy of taking a two hours' ride to meet, and that was Gertrude Temple.

To his mother's hint that his sister's friend was a missionary and therefore worthy of all respect, he answered: "Certainly, my dear mother, if it would do her or the missionary cause any good in life, I'd take an extra journey to shake hands with her. But she can have as little desire to see me as I have to see her, so it's an unnecessary sacrifice. She has my respect and sympathy, of course. Her threefold sorrow must have almost crushed the life out of her, and frankly I think the best thing strangers can do for her now is to let her alone."

That was two years before, and still they hadn't met. Neither was Mr. Ransom any more anxious to meet this woman than in the past. In fact, he shrank from the ordeal in dismay. If he had felt the slightest prospect of Helen's being able to carry out her scheme, he would have urged against it. He wouldn't have chosen a sad-faced, broken-spirited woman to come in contact with the Mitchell family to help them. Moreover, what did she know of life from such a standpoint? It was well to be a missionary, and it required a certain sacrifice, which he admired and respected. But she had gone out to India from wealth and elegance and returned from India to inherit the large fortune her father had left her and could surround herself with elegance still. What had she in common with the life she'd have to live? *Helen was wild,* he told himself half-irritably.

"She thinks that because a girl has spent six months in India as a missionary, she's ready to take up home mission work like this. Nothing is more absurd. She'll be miserable herself and will make their lives miserable. I gave her credit for some common sense when she declined Helen's invitation to be her guest at my house, but she must have taken leave of it now. As for Helen, I'm amazed. The whole scheme is unlike her usual good sense."

On the whole, the minister was perturbed. The improbable had happened. An attack of melancholy, he thought, had induced the rich young widow to turn her steps toward martyrdom. "To everyone's great discomfiture, I don't doubt," he muttered.

He was perverse enough to feel relieved when, all arrangements made, on the day appointed for the stranger's arrival, a telegraph summoned him to a distant town, where an old college friend lay ill. Circumstances connected with the friend's illness and death necessitated a Sabbath's absence from home and an exchange of pulpits for the Sabbath following; so that Mrs. Colchester had been domiciled in the Mitchell homestead nearly two weeks, and yet Mr. Ransom hadn't seen her.

When at last Helen's brother reached home, he was so entirely indifferent to the newcomer that Helen felt piqued and half-resolved to wait until he himself proposed a call. But after waiting four days, she meekly suggested one morning that they enjoy the pleasant weather and hard roads by riding out to the Mitchell farm. The minister assented with a grave countenance, as if he were resigning himself to a duty. Of course it was a call that must be made sometime and really should in courtesy have been made before.

Flora Ann, who had been installed as "help," admitted them, much flurried, and left them standing in the hall while she went to receive directions. Calls weren't common at the Mitchells', and Flora Ann's reign had been too recent for her to learn what was proper under existing circumstances. She had no sooner disappeared from view than Sarah Jane's head was seen leaning over the baluster.

"Oh, Miss Ransom!" she said. "Is it you? Could you come upstairs a minute? And would Mr. Ransom wait there a few minutes? I'll come down as quick as I can."

Mr. Ransom cordially signified his willingness to "wait there" any length of time, and Helen disappeared. The door leading into the Mitchell parlor stood open, and the minister, gazing into it abstractedly, not realizing he was gazing, became suddenly aware it had undergone change. He'd been in this dreary room several times during the early fall, but his glimpse of it now gave a different impression from what had lingered in his memory. It dawned upon him that the parlor must have been given up to the boarder. No sooner had he settled this than the occupant of the room appeared before him. He remembered afterward just how she looked. Quite unlike his unconscious mental picture of her. That person was tall and had steely blue eyes and tufts of yellow hair about her forehead. He couldn't have told why; no personal description of the woman for whom he had conceived an unreasoning dislike had ever been given him.

This woman was perhaps below medium height, and her hair arrangement was unlike the prevailing style but fitted the face perfectly. Her eyes were brown, like her hair, and a healthy color was on cheek and lips. A young, fair, pleasant-faced woman, in a plain black dress. She came swiftly toward the stranger as soon as she caught sight of him, her face breaking into a smile of recognition.

"Isn't this the pastor?"

She spoke the title as if nothing else was needed to win recognition and respect. As he half-confusedly bowed assent, she held out her hand cordially.

"I thought so—Helen resembles you. Come in, Mr. Ransom. We receive our friends in this room."

Chapter 22

A New Engineer

Yes, the room had been transformed. It was an old-fashioned, long, low room, capable of being pleasant. An alcove stood at the farther end. If this parlor were to become a sleeping room, the natural place for the bed was in that corner, and there it had been set. At least the minister learned afterward that such was the case. No such suggestion presented itself to him that afternoon. Heavy curtains hung before the alcove, shutting it out entirely and making the room cozier.

In the fireplace burned a great pine knot that threw a ruddy glow over every somber thing. A large table, wheeled into the center of the room, had about it an air of "systematic disorder," indicating constant and intelligent use of books and papers, pens and paperweights, and other belongings of a well-furnished study table. A bookcase occupied a niche near the south window, and behind its glass doors the minister's book-loving eyes caught the names of treasures. The common ingrain carpet, dulled by age and worn in spots, was almost covered from sight by rich rugs, lying everywhere an excuse could be found for a rug.

An old-fashioned lounge, or "settee," in the Mitchell family for generations, had been transformed by throwing a brilliant afghan, long and wide and soft, over it and piling sofa pillows high at one end ready for use. Two or three straight-backed, high, uncomfortable chairs still lingered in obscure corners of the room, ready for emergencies. But a study chair, a couple of low rockers, and a wide armchair occupied the comfortable spaces.

To complete the picture of a home, instead of being merely a room, was a tiny table with a tiny chair beside it and near the chair a dolly's crib, on which reposed the fair-faced dolly herself. A little row of shelves occupied the corner, filled with treasures dear to a child's heart. Vases on the mantel and potted plants in the window filled the room with bloom and fragrance.

In short, the clean but dreary room Mr. Ransom remembered and was always sorry to be ushered into, preferring the kitchen by far, had become both beautiful and comfortable. And the lady, who motioned him to the high-backed chair and dropped herself into the low rocker, seemed to fit her surroundings extremely well. Her very first sentence was decidedly unconventional.

"Mr. Ransom, do you know I believe Flora Ann has become a Christian?"

She had no affectation in her tone or hint that she was saying anything out of the ordinary in conversation with a stranger. Instead, she quietly assumed he was interested in Flora Ann. Having given his life to soul-saving, he would be interested in that theme above all others. In fact, the tone was so natural and the statement so surprising and intriguing that Mr. Ransom forgot conventionality—forgot he didn't quite approve of the lady who was talking to him, forgot the lady herself, and thought only of Flora Ann.

"Is it possible!" he said eagerly. "I didn't know the poor girl understood what it meant."

"I'm not sure she does. Isn't there such a thing as being a Christian without knowing it? Doesn't the mysterious change come sometimes to ignorant hearts, who don't recognize its name? This girl is very ignorant. I've never met anyone more so. She doesn't recognize Christ as a personal Savior, so far as I understand her. But she's heard of Him as a Savior, and she trusts Him and prays to Him daily, hourly—not for herself, you understand, but for her miserable brother."

"Jake?" inquired Mr. Ransom, thinking at once of Helen's reports of the horrors in the Lucas home when Jake was present.

"Yes, Jake. Humanly speaking, the most hopeless of all that family. The poor girl seems to have grasped the fact that the Lord Jesus Christ can save even him, and for this she cries to Him constantly."

"This is very strange," said Mr. Ransom, "and very touching. How did she get this much knowledge, Mrs.—"

He paused, remembering for the first time that he'd never been introduced to this lady.

"Mrs. Colchester," she said simply. "I beg your pardon. I took it for granted you knew my name, because you're Helen's brother."

"I did know it," he said humbly, ashamed of conventionality before this bright-faced, earnest woman, who had a subject of great importance to talk about.

She didn't wait to be led back to it but answered his question promptly.

"That part is strange to me, too. What information she's secured seems to have come through Stephen."

"Stephen! I didn't think he possessed enough knowledge to impart any. You don't think he's found the way?"

"Not for himself, but he's pointed it out to another. I think he knows the way, Mr. Ransom, but doesn't choose to walk in it—like so many others. But Flora Ann is different; she's simply unselfish. Hearing of Jesus Christ and His power to save, her faith has sprung entirely past herself and laid hold upon Him for her brother. I wanted you to know about it," she added, "because the poor girl should be helped. It's a peculiar case. She's so ignorant and yet so earnest that I haven't known how to teach her. And Sarah feels much the same. Sarah's a lovely Christian, Mr. Ransom, but a beginner, you know. So—well, I'm not a beginner. I've been personally acquainted with Jesus for a great many years. But I confess I don't know what to say to this young girl.

"Besides, Mr. Ransom, not only that entire Lucas family, but other families not far from us, need help. Couldn't we have a meeting? A regular evening service here, until we get hold of the people and stir them to go to church? Some are too far away and too feeble or too poor to make church practicable just now. But couldn't we have a service? Are you too busy for it?"

"Not at all," he said. "I've wanted to. One difficulty has been to find a place. Helen and I've talked it over and abandoned several plans already."

Mrs. Colchester glanced about her pretty room.

"Couldn't we have them here, Mr. Ransom? At least for a time? Or perhaps in the dining room—that's a large room, cheery and comfortable. I'm sure Mr. and Mrs. Mitchell would gladly lend it for an evening service. And Sarah and I could trim it with evergreens and make it bright and inviting. Then my piano is on its way. If it could be moved into that wide old hall one day a week, I could lead the music. Oh, I hope it can be done!"

"I'm sure it can," said the minister heartily. "You're making it so."

They heard feet flying down the stairs, and Sarah Jane entered, her face flushed.

"I was hurrying down to introduce you," she said, looking from her boarder to her guest. "But I guess you don't need it."

"No," said Mr. Ransom, smiling, "I think we're introduced."

Then he stepped aside for Helen to greet her friend. He looked on curiously while the two women, so nearly of an age, so unlike in all other respects, exchanged fond greetings. He'd known of their friendship for years, but it had never seemed reasonable until that moment.

She's very different from other people, he told himself, watching the two.

This "missionary woman," as he'd called her, forgetting her name, had known the neighborhood a few days; yet she said "we" and "us" and "our" like one who had adopted the people and meant to center her interests and influence among them. He had known her a few moments; yet they had carried on a conversation about the most important concern of humankind, as if they were friends and one in sympathy. Well, weren't they? Hadn't she evidently the Master's interests at heart? And wasn't his work in the world the same as hers? It would be foolish not to enjoy such a woman; not to meet her frankly on her own ground and take gratefully the help she was so freely offering.

Certainly work should be started in that neighborhood, if only for the Lucas and Mitchell families. Weren't they worth reaching? He regretted being so slow. He would take hold of the matter now with vigor. He dimly realized a certain amount of vigor was being breathed into him by the atmosphere surrounding him. He would show Mrs. Colchester her confidence wasn't misplaced, and he was as deeply interested in this work as she'd thought him to be.

No, he said to himself, with humility, *I'll prove that my confidence in the Lord Jesus Christ isn't misplaced and because of His life in me I'm interested in souls above else. That I'm ready to work anywhere with anybody, to take the lead or be led, as He directs. I thought I was roused some weeks ago, but certain portions of the work I've been shirking. If I know my own heart, I mean utter self-surrender now. And personal likes or dislikes shall have nothing to do with it. Jesus Christ has enough power to save even Jake Lucas, though I couldn't realize it before.*

Thoughts somewhat like these surged through his mind, with a dim awareness that it wouldn't be disagreeable to work in this portion of the vineyard.

They had intended to visit at a reasonable time and then call at the Bascomes on their way home. But they spent the afternoon—stayed to tea—and Sarah Jane, in a flutter of excited delight, served them in her best style. She'd set her table in the whitest napery, ironed until it shone; put a vase Mrs. Colchester had given her, with a single flower Helen had brought her, in the center of the table. She served gems of rare puffiness, which she learned to make at the manse; had strawberries of her mother's own canning—and Mrs. Mitchell knew how to can strawberries; had newly laid eggs, poached as even the minister rarely saw them, for some things Sarah Jane did well, because she had what her mother called "knack." In short, a tea table was rarely enjoyed as much as that one at the Mitchell farmhouse.

Stephen, who had expected to be embarrassed before Mrs. Colchester and had only half-liked the scheme at any time, had forgotten to be afraid of her after the first day and was learning to handle even his napkin with ease and a certain degree of satisfaction. As for little Nina, about whom I see I've said nothing at all, she was simply the sweetest, most winsome child of eight that ever made sunshine in a home. She'd centered herself with one bound in Mr. Mitchell's heart—called him "Grandpa" and bestowed the little attentions upon him a child of eight can give a man who looks as if he were nearly seventy. In fact, Mr. Mitchell wasn't so old by years as he looked, but he lived too hard and fast in his youth to have a genial or appropriate middle age.

Truth to tell, Mr. Mitchell had dreaded the invasion into his home as no other family member had. It might have been hard for Stephen, but it was martyrdom for his father. Yet he had surrendered his heart to Nina and already felt as if the house would be desolate without her.

Flora Ann, who sat at the table with the rest, according to local customs, kept herself in absolute quiet, but with eyes alert for anything wanted of her and ears attentive for anything said that could help her in the consuming desire of her heart. For a feeling, almost a passion, had taken hold of her regarding her brother. He was daily becoming more of a terror in his home, and her prayers were daily becoming more intense and importunate.

Mr. Ransom noticed the girl's watchful eyes and, remembering what Mrs. Colchester had said, shaped some of his conversation to encourage her heart's desire.

"Mr. Mitchell," he said, "do you know the man from town—a shoemaker by trade?"

"Oh, yes!" said Mr. Mitchell. "I know Old Roger—Smithson, his name is, though you don't often hear the last name. He used to work for the Harding brothers until they discharged him. Since that time he hasn't done much but drink and swear. He's a hard old case."

"That describes the character he's earned, and he's sustained it well for the last five or six years, they tell me. But the description won't answer any longer, sir—Old Roger is made over. People will be calling him 'Mr. Smithson' soon."

"Is that so?" exclaimed Mr. Mitchell. "Why, I haven't heard anything like that. What's happened to him?"

"The Lord Jesus Christ has met and saved him," said the minister earnestly, with an involuntary glance toward Flora Ann, whose eyes seemed fairly to grow. "He went to the city sometime ago, got intoxicated there and quarrelsome, and was arrested. He spent the night in the lockup—two days, in fact. It seems a curious place in which to reform, but that's exactly what Roger did. He came in contact with some Christian workers, who succeeded in acquainting him with Jesus Christ, the only One Who can save. He's been true to His Word again, and Roger is saved. That's the story briefly. Isn't it marvelous that the Lord can take hold of such wrecks as that and make men of them?"

Mr. Mitchell was absolutely silent. He was thinking some people gave up the drink without the help of the Lord Jesus Christ. But did it make men of them? All his life, he'd felt bowed down under the weight of his early evildoing. He had carried about with him a discouraged, disappointed heart and told himself he'd wrecked not only his prospects, but those of his children, and that there was no help for him. Yet it was years since he'd drunk a drop of liquor. His wife, who hadn't studied his face for a quarter of a century without understanding it, knew something of what he was thinking and ventured her timid response to the minister's words.

"But folks do sometimes give up the drink without His doing it for them, don't they?"

Mr. Ransom turned toward her in surprise. He didn't know Mr. Mitchell's story. Why should she be anxious to emphasize that side of the question?

"In a sense He never does it for them," he said. "That is, there's a part they must do for themselves. They must yield their wills to the power trying to save them. But I question whether a man is ever saved from liquor, or any other evil habit, except by the power of Jesus Christ. He may not recognize that power; he may not give himself afterward to the service of Christ. But by so much has he been freed from Satan's power, if he's freed from the curse of liquor, and the only One stronger than Satan is Jesus Christ."

"Then he should love Jesus just for that."

It was Nina's clear, childlike voice which took up the story.

"Yes," said the minister emphatically, "he should. He's only half a man who can receive such help as that from the Savior of the world and yet fail to own it or give Him thankful service in return."

"Grandpa wouldn't be such a man as that, would you, Grandpa?"

Mrs. Mitchell's face flushed, her eyes took on an anxious look, and Stephen's hand trembled so that he almost dropped the cup he was lifting to his lips. None of the rest knew cause for special anxiety. But Mr. Mitchell put out his wrinkled hand and touched tenderly the golden curls clustered around Nina's neck and said not a word.

Chapter 23

Blocking the Track

Before Maxwell Ransom and Helen went home that night, they had arranged that, on the following Friday evening, a religious service would be held in the Mitchells' dining room. Stephen had promised to tell any neighbor he came in contact with and give the invitation.

"It's out of my line," he said, with an awkward smile, avoiding the minister's earnest eyes, "but then I s'pose I can do it."

"I don't wonder you're fond of Mrs. Colchester, Helen," the minister said, as they rode home in the moonlight. "She's very pleasant and winning in her manner."

And Helen, like the wise woman she was, resisted the temptation to say, "I thought you would discover other women in the world beside Gertrude Temple," and held her peace.

The winter, which a few months before seemed to stretch endlessly ahead of Maxwell Ransom, passed as if by magic. Absorbed in his work, he had no time to regret the holidays when they were upon him, although he'd regretted them much in anticipation, because of the contrast in his life with that of a year ago. He even forgot the date of the last letter he wrote Gertrude Temple and was so absorbed in preparing for the Christmas tree for the Hilton Hill Sunday school that he forgot to recall how he was occupied a year before. Some chance remark of Helen's suggested that time, and then he smiled, somewhat sadly, over what he called his blighted past. But the next minute he responded to Stephen Mitchell's call for help in fastening up the evergreen over the west window and forgot all about it.

By this time, you know a Sunday school was started in the Hilton Hill neighborhood, and I may as well tell you now it was a success. Even Sarah Jane Mitchell, who thought she knew the neighborhood well, declared one day she didn't see where the children came from. They seemed to spring up in the night. As for the meetings started in the Mitchell dining room, who shall tell what they'd accomplished?

"From the first," Mr. Ransom said, speaking of them with deep feeling to an intimate friend long afterward, "the Lord seemed to smile on that effort. Do you remember how surprised we were over the number who came the first night? And what a joy it was to hear Mrs. Mitchell break the timid silence of years and pray before them all! And how wonderful it was when Flora Ann gave her life completely to Jesus."

Oh, they were weeks to remember. And the interest, instead of dying out as spring drew near, seemed to increase. Not only had the Sunday school been started, but a reading circle was organized and a young people's club with the temperance pledge for its center, which pledge was signed by some least expected to take that stand.

In short, as Fanny Bascome put it, "That stony old Hilton Hill neighborhood has become the fashion. If you don't go out there to their prayer meetings and clubs, and I don't know what all, you don't amount to anything."

But despite all the good, there was no denying the fact that some who had been prayed for earnestly, and reached after persistently, failed to be moved. Among these was Stephen Mitchell, the minister's special care and anxiety.

"I'm greatly disappointed," Mr. Ransom said to Mrs. Colchester. "In fact, I may as well admit my faith has gotten a setback. I confidently looked for him as a firstfruit. He interested me from the first time I spoke with him and seemed started on the road toward a better life even then."

"He's improving rapidly," said Mrs. Colchester. "Sarah makes good progress, and so does Flora, but they're both slow compared with him. You'd be surprised, Mr. Ransom, to see how rapidly he acquires what he sets his mind on learning, which, by the way, explains your disappointment. He's set his mind and heart on acquiring knowledge in certain directions. Something, or someone, has roused in him the determination to become a skilled farmer, and everything agricultural, or anything tending toward agricultural knowledge, is seized upon with avidity. If the book or the person, whoever it was, who started him in this direction could have laid the other foundation first, Stephen would have been won for Christ before now."

Then the minister looked at her in a startled, troubled way. He remembered his first walk with Stephen when they went across the fields to the Lucas place. He remembered distinctly their conversation. A few words he spoke for Christ then, surely. But he recalled with humiliation and pain that his special effort had been to arouse in Stephen an ambition to reconstruct the old farm, which had been for years so nearly a failure. The foundation work had been his. He knew he was responsible for starting Stephen in the direction in which he was pressing. He tried to find comfort in the sermon he'd preached, using Stephen's words. Certainly then he had tried hard to lead the young man to sense his need of Jesus Christ and make that the first ambition. Yes, but the first impression was evidently stronger. And the first impression had been made in another direction.

That evening the minister went home troubled at heart. But if Stephen Mitchell had been called as a witness and been honest with himself, he'd have admitted that enough had been said to lead him to understand the importance of choosing Christ as his Leader, in the new life journey he meant to take.

He's simply another illustration of the power at work in this world, keeping people from the road they should travel and settling their wills against the decision they should make. Stephen Mitchell couldn't have explained, even to his own satisfaction, why he was so persistent in his determination to avoid all decisions of this kind. Why he should listen to Mr. Ransom's sermons to get every bit of information they could give and shut his heart against any call to him. Why he accepted, at Mrs. Colchester's gracious hand, assistance in writing, reading, studying words, and constructing sentences and was grateful for it, but turned from her almost rudely the moment she attempted to speak a word for the Master she served. Why he met Sarah Jane halfway in her home improvements and in her future plans but told her gruffly "not to preach," when she asked him if he had read the verse on the card she given him and if he didn't think it was about something that should be looked after. He even turned coldly from his mother one night, after she prayed for her children in the prayer meeting, and told her heartlessly, when she questioned him as to what was the matter, that he didn't "care about being prayed at;" he thought "folks better keep such things to themselves."

Oh, there was no question Stephen's conscience was enlightened enough and was being worked upon. It was his stubborn will blocking the track.

"I don't understand him," said Sarah Jane frankly to Helen Ransom. "He isn't a bit as I thought he'd be. Why, the first time it dawned on me that I could have the Lord Jesus Christ for my Friend, I was happy enough to shout. Do you remember when it was? I was at your house, that first three weeks, and I wanted to come home right away and tell Steve about it. I thought I'd only have to tell him how it was and he'd take hold of it. I never thought he'd hang back for a chance like that."

Another "hung back" from all the chances that might have redeemed his wretched life—Jake Lucas. Despite all their invitations and appeals, he hadn't once attended neighborhood prayer meetings or been inside the little red schoolhouse after the Sunday services were established there. Other Lucases had been reached and in a measure helped. The little girls came regularly to Sabbath school and were learning outward propriety of behavior, at least. Miranda frequently attended the afternoon service and occasionally the midweek prayer meeting and was at least respectful when spoken to about her personal interest or responsibility. Mrs. Colchester felt sure she was thinking.

Even poor, worthless Jim had lounged in once or twice on a Sunday afternoon, when he was less intoxicated than usual, and admitted to Flora Ann the singing was "fine," and maybe sometime or other, when he felt like it, he'd come again. And the poor old mother, weighed down with many years of disappointment and ill treatment, found a refuge at last and crept into it like a bruised soul in dire need of shelter. But Jake would have none of it. Wouldn't even answer when asked to the meeting; growled at his mother and swore at Miranda for having anything to do with the "canting hypocrites;" threatened at last to "knock the breath out" of Flora Ann's body, if she ever "opens her head to me about them things again"—in short, grew worse. As the spring opened, it seemed folly to invite him to the meetings, for he was rarely ever sober enough for them to be of any use.

"I'm afraid," said the minister with a sigh, "that Jake's a hopeless case. That miserable Jim and the other one may possibly be reached. They're better natured than Jake. I even have hopes at times of the old sot of a father. But I confess it requires more faith to pray for Jake than I seem able to exercise."

"There's someone who'll pray for him as long as she has breath, I think," Helen said, with a grave smile. "The tenacity with which she holds on to that worthless brother is remarkable. He's more cruel to her than he is to the others. Mrs. Mitchell confided to me last week that she 'hated' to have the girl go home, because her brother abused her so."

It was true. Flora Ann's bloodshot eye or bruised arm often told silently and eloquently the story; yet she prayed on.

Perhaps the winter had done more for Flora than anyone else of the group. She was wonderfully changed. Enough wholesome food, eaten at regular intervals, had rounded out her form and made her less hollow-eyed and hungry-looking. Then her dress, though very poor and plain, of course, was always scrupulously neat nowadays. She'd become skilled in many little household ways, meanwhile. And Mrs. Mitchell didn't hesitate to pronounce her "real downright good help; enough sight better than I had any notion she'd ever be. She's willing to learn, and that's half the battle."

She was still quiet and reserved, speaking plainly her thoughts and feelings to no one but Stephen, whom she always looked upon as her first friend, the one who had protected her unexpectedly from Jake on that terrible midnight of her mother's sickness. Perhaps Stephen listened to her more patiently than to any of the others, because she never spoke to him of himself. Never seemed to realize, indeed, that he wasn't in all respects what he should be. It was about Jake that she poured out her anxieties.

"Why don't you let him alone?" Steve asked her roughly, though not unkindly. "He kicks you about as if you was a toad. I wouldn't stand it. He's a worthless fellow, too. Why not let him go?"

"Oh! I can't, Steve! Something here"—she laid her hand on her heart—"tells me to pray for him and pray and pray. I guess if I knew he was going to kill me, I'd pray right on. Steve, it's just an awful thing not to have him saved. He's so bad—worse than the rest, you know—worse than anybody around. I heard a man say last night, coming home behind me, that Jake Lucas was the worst fellow in the neighborhood for miles around. And it's so, and he should be saved, Steve. It would be so easy, if he only would."

Stephen didn't believe this. In his heart he even sneered at the idea of anyone caring whether Jake Lucas was saved or not, and as to its being "easy" to make a changed man of him, nothing seemed more improbable.

"Humph!" he said in reply. "I wouldn't pester him about religion, if I was you. If the fellow would get sense enough to give up his whiskey and be halfway decent, that's all I'd ask. . .and enough sight more than I expect," he added in muttered undertone as he strode away.

Nevertheless, his conscience troubled him. Hadn't he been called a "champion" of the Lucas family? How was he furthering their interests? For Flora Ann he'd begun to have a very friendly, brotherly sort of feeling. He aided her in her laborious studies to the best of his ability, and his ability was steadily growing. Still, he was well aware that Mrs. Colchester, the minister, and his sister, and even Sarah Jane were doing more for Flora Ann than he could.

As for the others of the family, he was letting them severely alone. What if he induced Jake to reform! Not to "get religion"—he had no confidence in that for Jake—but to sign the pledge and let whiskey alone.

"Father did it," he muttered to himself when in severest solitude. "Father has let it alone these many years, and he didn't sign a pledge, either. Jake could stop if he had a mind to, of course. What if I could coax him to do it?" And he half-formed a purpose to try, at the next opportunity—not without an undertone wish that the opportunity might be long in coming.

And this state of mind perhaps any of us, who've been hard-pressed by conscience, can understand, but opportunities aren't very hard to find, and very often they come unsought. Stephen's did.

Not two hours after the conversation last recorded, Jake came lumbering over from the cabin to borrow a hoe. He was more nearly sober than morning often found him, and he had a vague intention of trying to behave respectably to people who didn't belong to his own family. But if Stephen had been skilled in studying the human face, he'd have known Jake was very cross, that every nerve was tingling with a desire for the liquor he had no means of getting. The only thing Stephen thought was that here was his chance, a rarer one than had come to him for months, so far as Jake was concerned. If he actually meant business, it should be improved. He looked over toward the window of the upper backroom Flora Ann occupied and strengthened his resolution by remembering the prayer which had floated in to him from the cracks in the wall only that morning: "Oh, Lord Jesus, do please save Jake. You know You can if he'll let You. Do please do something to make him let You."

"Yes," said Stephen, "you can have the hoe if you'll bring it back. I want to use it this afternoon. And look here, Jake—if I was you, it appears to me I'd turn over a new leaf. Now's as good a time as any."

Jake turned upon him the most astonished pair of bloodshot eyes he'd ever seen but was apparently dumb with amazement.

So, taking heart at the silence, Stephen went on. "If you'd let whiskey alone, Jake, you could be a decent fellow. People would help you and your folks. They need it bad enough, and land knows it's because people are discouraged about you that they don't try to do things for the family. There's your mother, with her sick spells coming oftener, Flora Ann says. She'll go in one of them spells yet, and then how will you feel?"

Certainly Stephen had made an effort and done his best. Jake still stared at him but found voice at last to speak distinctly.

"If I was you, I'd mind my everlasting own business. You're a miserable puppy that ain't worth the salt you eat on your potatoes and that get your very clothes out of other folks—begging and fawning and whining around preachers and their set. And then you try to turn preacher yourself. You just mind your own business, will you, every time?"

And he shouldered the hoe and strode off. None too soon, perhaps, for there was a fierce light in Stephen's eyes, and his muscles were strong and firm. If Jake had known it, his would-be helper had exercised a mighty self-control to keep from knocking him down. As it was, he trembled under the excitement of temptation. He looked after Jake with dangerous eyes but took no step to follow him. In fact, he stood perfectly still until the excitement had somewhat subsided.

Then he said aloud and firmly: "Well, I've done my level best, and it's the last time. Flora Ann can pray forever, if she's such a fool to do it, for all I'll try to help—she might as well pray for that stump out there to split itself into kindling wood. It would never do it, and he'll never reform. He don't want to or mean to. I've washed my hands of all of them."

No, he didn't mean Flora Ann. He had a mental reservation concerning her. The truth is, he was separating her as far as possible from the Lucas family. She was beginning to be classed with the Mitchell family. Then this illogical young man took an axe and proceeded with strong, powerful strokes to demolish and make into kindling wood the very stump which had served him as an illustration. If he'd only understood enough of theology to realize the force of his own worked-out illustration. It was true the great stump could never make itself into kindling wood. But a power outside of and superior to itself could and did.

Chapter 24

The Wrong Road

W ithin the week something occurred that brought Flora Ann home from a visit to her father's cabin, red-eyed and miserable.

"Jake's gone," she said to the first person she met as she entered the house, and that person happened to be Stephen. "He never came home last night or the night before, and Bill says some of the boys saw him get on the train. He's tooken his things, and he never did that before. He never stayed from home a whole night in his life. Ma says so, and she says her heart is just broke." Whereupon Flora Ann sat down in a forlorn heap on one of the kitchen chairs, buried her head in her hands, and cried.

"A good riddance, I think," said Stephen brusquely. "I wouldn't take on about it, if I were you. Maybe it'll be the saving of your mother's life. She couldn't have stood the way he's going on much longer. Didn't you tell me he kicked her the last time you were home? And that was the very day I—" Then Stephen stopped abruptly. He wasn't going to own, even before Flora Ann, that he'd made an effort and failed. "If any fellow kicked my mother, I reckon I wouldn't cry because he'd taken off. Look at your wrist there, black and blue this minute, because he twisted it so the last time you saw him, when you was trying to keep him from kicking your mother, and yet you cry about him being gone. I'd have more spirit."

"It ain't that," said Flora Ann, between the sobs. "But I thought—he'd be different, and now he's run away. And the last thing he did was to kick Mother and hurt me and swear at the little girls. Oh! It's just too awful to think of him gone."

"Oh, but he hasn't gone away from God."

It was Nina's clear, astonished voice which made this startling announcement. She'd come into the kitchen with her velvet tread a few minutes before and, stopping in dismay to see Flora Ann in tears, had been absorbed in her story. Flora raised her eyes and looked at the child, the misery in her face slowly dying out.

"That's as true as a Bible verse," she said at last. "We can't get away from God, can we? I thank you for that, Miss Nina. I'll go straight on praying for him."

"I'll pray for him, too," said Nina, her own eyes full of sympathetic tears.

Then Stephen went out, slamming the door a little as he did. He was vexed with Flora Ann for being "such a fool."

It was the evening for prayer meeting in the Mitchell dining room, and Mrs. Colchester, who had heard the story of Jake's disappearance and Flora's grief from little Nina, presented his case for special prayer. It was a prayer meeting to remember. Mrs. Mitchell, having once found voice, had such joy in this prayer circle that it was coming to be a cross to spread her wants before the Lord in words her friends could hear. And she prayed for Jake that night so that his mother's heart, at least, would have been touched, had she heard it. Miranda was there and cried softly behind the corner of Flora Ann's neat white apron, which had been lent her to cover certain disreputable portions of her dress.

Then Mrs. Colchester prayed, and Helen Ransom and the minister—all for Jake.

Then little Nina, as simply and naturally as though she'd been kneeling by her bedside, bowed her head on her folded hands and said, "Dear Lord Jesus, please find Jake tonight and save him and take care of him for his mother and Flora."

Flora Ann's heart broke entirely then, and she sobbed out her cry to the Lord, for the first time in the hearing of human ears: "Oh, Lord, please do save him. We know You can if he'll let You. Oh! Do please do something to make him let You."

Mr. Mitchell coughed a good many times that evening and used his handkerchief as often for his eyes as he did any other way. He shook his head when Nina brought him the book for the closing hymn. When she looked wondering and regretful, he bent down and whispered to her that he couldn't sing tonight.

Just as the minister was about to offer the closing prayer, an electric thrill went through the hearts of the little company, for Mr. Mitchell was rising to his feet. He took hold of Nina's hand as he said: "Friends, this little girl has shown me the way to Him at last, and my poor service, such as it is, I'm giving Him for the rest of my days. I thank Him tonight for all the way He's led me, though I was blind and didn't know I was being led."

Stephen wasn't there to hear his father's voice. He had taken his lamp early and gone up to his room, shaking his head in response to Sarah Jane's petition to come down in time for the meeting. He replied gruffly that he hadn't "time for meetings;" he had a "tough lesson to get out." In the midst of Sarah Jane's joy over her father was a sigh for her brother. She was anxious for this young man, who, everybody said, was improving so rapidly. Her daily prayer for him, though perhaps not so heartrending, was as earnest as Flora Ann's for her brother.

The night was a beautiful moonlit one, and as the minister and his sister rode home they talked about the blessed meeting they'd had and the changes in such a short time in the Hilton Hill neighborhood.

"It's truly astonishing," said the minister, "that we've all been asleep so long. Why, the fields were white for the harvest. Those people listen as if for their lives. I'm sure many consciences were touched tonight. Mr. Mitchell's stand is worth a great deal. It's wonderful to see a man of his years come out squarely for the Lord. We have now another proof of the truth that 'a little child shall lead them.' "

"Hilary's been watching for this for some days," said Helen. "She told me two weeks ago that Nina wasn't going to be satisfied until 'Grandpa' prayed.

They've had long talks together, he and Nina. He's asked her many puzzling questions which she's brought to Hilary, of course, and, I suppose, has been carefully taught how to answer them—though Hilary says she's been taught of God."

"I don't doubt it," said the minister heartily. "Her sister evidently is. I think she's peculiarly a woman who is led by the Spirit."

Then the talk drifted toward Jake and the wonderful prayers offered for him that night, and they wondered where on the broad earth he was.

"Only the Listener to our prayers knows," said the minister. "Isn't it wonderful He carries the sins and sorrows of this great old world on His heart and hears the cry of every child of His, treasures up their requests, and brings to pass, through them, human impossibilities? I have faith for even Jake tonight. I don't know how many years it will be before the Lord will reach him, but it does seem to me as if those prayers tonight have been answered and that Jake is to be saved."

"That's just what Hilary said," was Helen's jubilant response. "In the hall she put her arms around me and whispered, 'Do you know—I expect to meet Jake in heaven?' "

"Did she?" said the minister, with a satisfied note in his voice. It gave him, to say the least, a not-unpleasant sensation to learn that he and Mrs. Colchester had thought alike.

In the meantime, what of Jake? If those who prayed could have seen him at that moment, their faith might have almost failed them. He was three hundred miles from his home, on a dangerous street of a large city. He was partially sober, for the simple reason that he had failed in securing any liquor since morning. He was intoxicated when he left his home and continued so during the hours in which he'd begged and stolen his way to this point.

What his plans were in going away, even he never knew. A vague idea that sometime he would run away and get rid of "the whole pack," as he called his family ties, had possessed him for months. Why he hadn't carried it out before, he couldn't have explained. Why he selected that particular night for starting, only He Who overrules all events can tell.

Half an hour before the moment in which we introduce him to you, he occupied a corner of a downtown omnibus. What we call a chance incident had given him the opportunity. He had been standing at the street corner, more utterly dreary and desolate than he'd ever felt in his life—a burning thirst for liquor in his throat and not a penny with which to gratify that thirst; not a spot to go to warm his half-frozen body; not a place where he could get a mouthful of food or a chance to sleep. Perhaps for the first time in his life, he had a dim impression that even the wretched home he'd run away from was worth something.

Two ladies descended from an omnibus which had drawn up near the curbstones. As they did so, the string confining two or three bundles in one woman's hand broke, and the bundles rolled. It was a wonder Jake Lucas thought to stoop and pick them up or, thinking, cared to take the trouble. Perhaps he had in his heart a hope for reward. At least, he gathered the packages, brushed off the filth of the street as well as he could, and carried them to their owner.

"Poor fellow!" she said compassionately, as she offered her thanks. "I haven't a cent of change. Will an omnibus ticket do you any good?"

He smiled cynically as he took the offered ticket. What good would an omnibus ticket do him? But the lady wasn't out of sight before he decided to make it useful. Why shouldn't he ride on an omnibus, since he had nothing else to do? It must at least be warmer there than on the street corner, and by the time it reached the end of its route, it might land him in a part of the city where he could get something to drink. So he hailed a passing omnibus and seated himself in the corner, drawing his hat well over his face. He paid little or no attention to the constantly changing passengers, not even glancing at a middle-aged, well-dressed man, who was quietly from time to time passing little slips of printed paper to one and another. He halted before Jake once or twice and looked at him doubtfully but, seeming to decide the man was too much intoxicated to be approached, had turned away. He was about to leave the omnibus as a couple entered it—a young, elegantly dressed lady, accompanied by a gentleman. The stranger offered his slips of paper to both of these.

"What is it?" asked the lady, as they seated themselves, and the seat she took was beside Jake.

The gentleman laughed. "It's an invitation to the midnight mission, Gertrude. Shall we go?"

"Oh, dear!" said the lady, echoing the laugh. "Do you suppose he thought us suspicious-looking characters? I wonder if mine is the same? Yes, it is. 'Come to the mission tonight and hear the song, "I was lost, but Jesus found me." ' "

"That does mean us, Charlie. We've been lost, you know. Are you sure you can find your way home now? We're certainly in a part of the city I've never seen before. Oh, Charlie! Mine is a tract on the other side—the most solemn talk you ever heard of. The idea of giving such things out in a public omnibus. What in the world made me take it? I don't want a tract. Do you suppose they ever do any good in that way, Charlie? I believe I'll try it. Here, my good fellow, don't you want a tract? You look as though you needed something like it."

"My dear," said Charlie, in warning undertone, as the pretty gloved hand reached over toward Jake, "don't speak to the fellow. He's intoxicated."

"Never mind—he won't hurt me. Take it, my man. If you'll read it and do as it says, I have no doubt you'll be improved. Oh, Charlie! We're passing the Twenty-Third Street Theater. Now I know where we are. We must take the green line of cars at this corner."

And Gertrude Temple gathered her handsome robes about her and followed her escort from the omnibus, leaving the little tract in Jake Lucas's hand.

He hadn't accepted it. He'd simply let it lie passive on his arm, where it had dropped, while he remained lost in astonishment over being addressed by an elegant woman. Presently he took the tract in his thumb and finger and held it up to the light. When Jake was a little boy the Lucas family had been almost respectable, and his early educational opportunities had been passable. He could read much better than Flora Ann. The words on the tract were very distinct to him.

> Come to the Mission on Wilmoth Street tonight and hear the song, "I was lost, but Jesus found me," and get a bowl of hot soup and a good night's rest.

Here, then, was his opportunity. The singing he cared nothing for; there was no objection, of course, to their throwing it in, if they were fools enough to do it. But the bowl of hot soup wasn't to be despised, since he couldn't get whiskey. And a place to sleep, to a man who had wandered homeless for three nights, was certainly inviting. He wondered vaguely where Wilmoth Street was and how he was expected to find it. He even muttered a curse on the people who hadn't brains enough to define the locality. Then he turned the tract over and glanced contemptuously down the other side, where the words Gertrude Temple had pronounced "solemn" were printed. While he was looking at it, the omnibus driver put his head in at the little window and called, "Wilmoth Street, change cars for Green Avenue." Jake started up at the sound of the name and lumbered out again into the night, Gertrude Temple's tract still between his thumb and finger. Now he was in the lowest and most crowded portion of the city. Saloons, gambling houses, and all kindred places of evil seemed to have headquarters here. The air was throbbing with the fumes of vile tobacco and viler whiskey. The air was pulsing with oaths.

Jake Lucas, only half-sober, burning with the desire for whiskey, stumbled on, looking in at the brightly lighted soul traps—the only cheery spots on that dismal street, luring him with sight and sound and smell. He was kept from entering only by the thought that he had no money and by knowing he would be unceremoniously kicked out of all such places, unless money in some form could be produced. He cursed the tract he still clutched in his hand, because he couldn't hope to turn it into whiskey, and stumbled on.

Chapter 25

Reviewing the Road

In due time, summer came again to the Hilton Hill neighborhood. If summer were that sentient creature poets would have us believe, she would undoubtedly have looked about her in wonder over the changes one brief year had wrought. Hints of change were throughout the neighborhood, but nowhere were they so marked as on the Mitchell farm. Stephen himself, in the midst of his busy life, occasionally took time to look about him with admiring surprise and contrast it with the June before.

Not for a single day had Stephen Mitchell lost sight of the new idea which had taken possession of him during that first walk to the Lucas cabin. It was on the way back, while the minister was trying to impress upon him other more important concerns, that he resolved to put all his strength into the old farm and see "what would come of it." He possessed certain admirable qualities for wrestling with such a task. He had always, from childhood, persevered in his endeavors, though he'd rarely been offered enough inducement to endeavor. He possessed, also, an almost exhaustless patience; so, when roused and energized by encouraging words, he put himself into the effort.

It was hard work at first. Yet soon it grew interesting to note how many opportunities for acquiring knowledge seemed to open before him. He began to listen to the chance talk he heard among farmers from time to time and discover how many things could be done on the old farm, which had been left undone. It surprised him to learn how many of these things lay within his own strength. Once realizing he was worth something in the world and could "make a difference" in life about him, he bent all his awakened energies to the work. The result wasn't large or remarkable, except to people who had for years let strength run to waste. It meant simply a mended fence here; a mended hinge there; a few panes of glass set in a certain window; a coat of whitewash in some places and a coat of paint in others; a general picking up about barnyard and farmyard, and a surprising "difference" began to manifest itself.

People driving by remarked upon it. "The Mitchell place is coming up," they said to one another.

As spring opened, and work began with such earnestness the fields hadn't known for years, the ever-ready ground responded. The dew and the rain and the sunshine of heaven blossomed things to beauty.

And people said, "What's happened to the Mitchells? Their fields haven't looked like this for years."

Then there were new things: a strawberry bed, over which both Stephen and Sarah Jane—to say nothing of one scarcely less interested, Flora Ann Lucas—

had worked and read and studied, early and late. The result was ripe strawberries before any others were heard of in the neighborhood. Potatoes fresh from the ground were on the Mitchell dinner table before their neighbors had thought of trying theirs. Green peas of a very early, choice variety were the next sensation. At a surprisingly early date, the Mitchell farm wagon was filled to its utmost capacity with fresh fruits, fresh vegetables, even fresh flowers, and started on its way to the summer campgrounds.

It's interesting to watch people adjust themselves to altered circumstances and positions. Stephen was only a year older than when he took that ride before, but it seemed to him he had lived half a lifetime since, so marked were the contrasts. He scarcely knew when his father, instead of saying with authoritative voice and manner, "Go here" or "there," "Do this" or "that"—the order always followed by a sigh for his own physical limitations and a groan over probable results—adopted the fashion of asking, "Shall we get at the potatoes today, do you think?" or "How should we plan for the south meadow?" or "What's your idea about that fence on the west side?"

Only the day before, he'd heard his father explain to a neighbor, "Steve thinks we better change the crop entirely on this lot another year. He says the ground needs the change, that it's worn out for the other crop. I don't know how he finds out, but he appears to know about many things I never heard of, and his plans turn out all right. A man was looking at his strawberry patch yesterday, and he said he didn't know any such strawberries in the country."

Doll and Dobbin may not have approved of all the changes, though nothing in their manner hinted at such a thought. They were taken better care of than ever before, more faithfully fed and groomed. But they certainly had to work faster, and loitering, on reasonably good stretches of road, wasn't permitted these days.

Stephen's start for the encampment was early, and his entire air was the alert one of a man of business. He looked around him curiously as he drove through the enchanted land, fully as beautiful as it was the year before, and was rather pleased to learn that the all-important Mr. Baker couldn't be seen until noon. This gave him a chance to go around to that remarkable spot where he'd first secured his list of words.

Apparently the same crowd was there, at least in numbers. The platform was occupied, not by the speaker he'd heard, but by one who seemed to use language with equal ease. Stephen secured a seat with a little effort and gave close attention. It chanced—as we're fond of using language—that this was "Agricultural Day" at the encampment, and the subject of the platform address had an absorbing interest for the young farmer. It was in a line he'd been reading and studying, and no more earnest or intelligent listener was in that large audience than Stephen Mitchell. Early in the hour he took notebook and pencil from his pocket, not this time to secure lists of flying words, but to note down certain points new to him. As he did so he resolved to "study them up, to see if that fellow is right."

Oh, there was no denying Stephen had made wonderful progress. He let his mind dwell a good deal on contrasts this summer day; the experiences of his first visit were such vivid memories. As he drove homeward his thoughts were busy. Perhaps no small thing marked the changes more forcefully than his stop at the corner store, where the same Mr. Pettibone still simpered behind the counter. Stephen didn't like him any better than the summer before, but he was by no means so afraid of him. He had discovered Mr. Pettibone wasn't such a grand gentleman as he'd supposed and that his opinion of persons and things was of relatively little consequence. He gave his orders with an ease and glibness which contrasted strongly with the "green braid" experience. The clerk's manner was also changed.

"How are you, Mitchell?" he said with friendly familiarity, as Stephen entered the store. And as he attended his customer's commissions, he asked if he'd been out to the encampment and whether there were crowds and if anything "nice" was going on evenings.

Then, to sharpen the contrast, Helen Ransom entered the store, and her eyes brightened with welcome as Stephen turned to meet her.

"How fortunate!" she said. "You're just the one I wanted to see. Can you call at the house a moment? I'm anxious to send Sarah a package. And my brother has a package for you, I think—some illustrated papers he says that explain those plans for the trellises you and he were talking about."

Stephen even had to call at the Bascomes'—not this time to borrow a pattern; Sarah Jane had no need of Bascome patterns these days; instead, they were delighted to borrow from her—but to leave a book Mrs. Colchester had promised Fanny.

When he'd passed in the morning it had been too early for the Bascomes; their house was closed and silent. Fanny was on the piazza when he returned, and her manner marked the contrast again. She'd decided to be very friendly with Stephen Mitchell—wasn't he on intimate terms at the manse, more at home there than she was? And there was that elegant Mrs. Colchester; he seemed to be really intimate with her. And Steve really was a nice-looking fellow, now that he wore good clothes and had found out what to do with his hands and feet.

She gave him a most cordial greeting and tried to be very genial, sending her love to Sarah Jane and her thanks to Mrs. Colchester and asking if he wouldn't bring them both out someday to see her flowers. She had some flowers she knew Mrs. Colchester would admire.

It wasn't so much what she said, as the way she said it, that reminded Stephen forcefully again of the year before. His smile was half-amused, half-cynical as he sprang into his farm wagon and hastened homeward.

"She's willing to stand Sarah Jane and me, if she can have Mrs. Colchester thrown in once in a while," he said to himself. "But she wouldn't speak to Flora Ann, not for a farm"—by which you'll discover Stephen Mitchell, though he had learned many things, hadn't learned to like Fanny Bascome.

It might have been a vague feeling that Flora Ann had been slighted which made Stephen unusually kind to her that evening. He looked at her thoughtfully as she moved around the dining room, putting the finishing touches to the table, which she'd learned to do as neatly as Sarah Jane. He was still in the mood for contrasts; he contrasted Flora Ann not only with the Bascomes, but with the many girls he'd seen that day.

She's a pretty girl, was his grave conclusion, *and she's a good girl, and she's going to be a smart girl. In some things she goes ahead of Sarah Jane.*

At that moment the subject of his thoughts stopped in front of the window near which he sat and looked wistfully down the road.

"It'll be nice moonlight," she said. "If I can get off early enough, I mean to go home. I'm kind of worried about Mother. She looked as if she was going to have one of her poor turns the last time I was there, and I haven't seen any of them for more than a week. I could stay all night, you know, and come home real early in the morning."

"There's no need for that," said Stephen kindly. "I'll go over with you. I'd as soon go as not. I haven't been working today."

Within another hour they were walking briskly down the moonlit road, talking cheerily together. The two had many subjects in common. As a scholar Flora Ann kept good pace with Stephen and had original ideas on many subjects, which surprised and interested him. His sister did her best to be interested in agricultural studies, but her tastes evidently didn't lie in that direction.

"She's quick as lightning at grammar," Stephen had explained one day to Mrs. Colchester, "and she's willing to study half the night about flowers. But when it comes to turnips and beets and cabbages, why, you can see she only reads because she thinks it should be read. She doesn't take to farming. Now Flora, if she had a chance, would make a first-rate farmer. She has ideas that surprise me."

Mrs. Colchester smiled and explained that that was an experience common to students; each had his or her specialty. She reminded him that if all the world "took to farming," there would be no teachers or merchants or preachers.

"It's very still around here," said Flora, as they neared her father's cabin. "I don't think the boys can be at home, or else—"

She didn't need to finish the sentence; Stephen understood well. The boys, now that Jake wasn't there to frighten them into silence, were rarely quiet. They weren't fierce or dangerous, as Jake had been, but hilarious, in a way which was sometimes harder for Flora Ann to bear than Jake's blows. She never neared the door of this sorrowful home without thinking of "poor Jake." She always spoke of him now with that adjective before his name. But she spoke of him frequently and made it evident she had by no means forgotten him. She still spoke more freely to Stephen than to any other person and still apparently believed he felt as she did.

"Poor Jake!" she said, her thoughts going from the boys to him. "I'm praying for him right along steady, Steve. I always will, you know, till I hear he's where he don't need it. Wouldn't it be nice to know he'd got into the right way and God had taken him where he wouldn't be tempted anymore? I'd be willing for that—I guess for Mother's sake I'd be glad for it. Mother mourns for Jake all the time. She can't get along without him as the others can. I never go home but she talks about him and cries and says she wishes she'd borne with him better. Poor thing! She used to bear with him always, but she won't believe it. The rest of us used to be cross to him."

"I guess you was never cross to him," said Stephen. "I never saw anything like it."

"Well, I wasn't much of anything to him. I was afraid; that was the trouble. It was silly in me to be such a coward. He wouldn't have killed me, I guess, if I'd tried to help him more. I wish I had."

Then she opened the door leading into the family room, and they went in. It was surprisingly still. The boys weren't there. The father was sitting in his chair, drowsing and partially intoxicated. The little girls were huddled in a corner, occupied in staring at a neatly dressed stranger, who sat with his back to the door.

"There's Flora Ann!" exclaimed the children, as the door opened.

The stranger arose and came toward them. Behold! It was Jake! Jake, with his shock of black hair neatly combed—Flora Ann never remembered seeing it combed before—and not only were his clothes whole and neat, but he had on a collar and a necktie. Moreover, his eyes, which had always been blood-shot, were clear and smiling.

"How do you do?" he said, holding out his hand, as Flora Ann still stood staring at him. "Surely you haven't forgotten me?"

"He's come home!" exclaimed his mother, unable to keep silence any longer. "He come this afternoon. I told 'em we ought to send for you. But there wasn't nobody to send; the boys ain't come yet. Don't he look nice? I wouldn't have knowed him if I'd met him in the street. Oh, yes, I would! I'd know my Jake any-wheres. Ain't it wonderful?"

But Flora Ann had no words. She was overwhelmed. This to be Jake! This man with a smile on his face!

"Things don't match, do they?" he said, the smile deepening. "I don't think they ever will again. I'm Jake, and yet I'm not Jake. No, I'll tell you how it is—I'm a new Jake."

Then he turned to Stephen. "How do you do, Steve? I remember being down-right hateful, the last words I spoke to you. And I was getting a favor from you at the same time. That was the old Jake. I know you don't lay up anything against him. The new Jake is ashamed of him."

Stephen shook the offered hand heartily but was as silent as Flora Ann. This seemed to him, indeed, to be a new Jake, or rather not Jake at all. Remember— he'd never seen him when he wasn't more or less under the influence of liquor. Now there was no sign or smell of it about him. He was thin and pale, and the marks of his hard life showed on his face. But he was quiet, with the quietness of one who had been in the battle and been wounded but had come off conqueror.

They sat late in the evening, listening to his story. He told it from the begin-ning, describing the ride in the omnibus and the elegantly dressed, silver-voiced young lady who laid the tract in his hand. Told how he got out into the night and the darkness and on what sort of corner he stopped, cursing the tract because it couldn't be turned into whiskey. Told how the little tract had seemed to lure him on, pointing out soup and a bed—although he'd have given the prospect of both for one drink of whiskey. Told how at last he found the mission and the soup. How he was offered a chance to wash and given some decent clothes and invited in to hear the singing. It was a wonderful story, though it could be put into a few sentences, and the same story is being lived over every night in our large cities.

Men and women connected with that mission held on to Jake, even though he tried his best to slip away from them and more than once fell back into the gutter, only to be sought after, reached after, and lured back to the shelter of their care. There were miserable weeks, during which Jake later realized the mission workers hadn't lost sight of him for one full day. Elude them as he would and in some cunning way get enough liquor to fire his brain and make him angry at them all—yet they followed him and brought him back to that one spot where things were clean and pure, food was wholesome, and faces were kind.

"I can't tell you about it," said Jake, breaking off in the middle of a sentence. "I don't know how to tell it. I didn't understand what made them hang on to me so. I hadn't a bit of faith in myself. I thought I was about as worthless a fellow as they could find, even in that city, and I saw some hard-looking fellows, too. But I looked to myself worse than any of them. And I felt worse. I haven't had a very high opinion of myself for a good many years, and I thought it was too late for me to do anything else."

But they wanted to hear his story. They plied him with questions and heard how at last the outraged body and brain refused to endure anymore. Fever and delirium followed, during which poor Jake raved and cursed and groaned and was watched over and cared for every day and night, faithfully, skillfully, tenderly. Following the fever were long weeks of prostration, during which he lay as helpless as a child. Then he slowly crept back to life and strength again.

Chapter 26

Other Travelers

A nd the rest of it," said Jake, breaking off again, a light on his face they'd never seen there before—"I don't know how to tell. I haven't found any words yet that tell it. One day I felt so lowdown and miserable that it seemed to me a terrible pity I'd lived. I couldn't see how I was to be any use to myself or anybody else. I thought I'd be a blot on the earth. I thought of Mother here, and it seemed to me the best news that could come to her would be that I was dead and buried. I thought of all of you here at home, and I felt as if there'd be more hope for you if I was gone. I didn't see why I'd lived. I didn't have a bit of hope for myself. I knew there wasn't any use trying to be anything but a drunken wretch. Spite of all I'd been through, the sickness and everything, there was nothing I wanted so much as whiskey, and I knew as soon as I got out on the street where it was to be had, I'd find a way to get it.

"I don't know what made me think of Flora Ann just then, but I did. You see, I knew about her praying for me, and it used to make me mad—but all of a sudden it came over me that there was a God and He must have made me, and I had a sister who'd talked to Him a good deal about me. I didn't suppose I believed in prayer, but I seemed to all of a sudden. I was alone, sitting on the side of the bed, and I just slipped down on my knees and said, 'Oh, Lord'— that's every living word I said." To have seen the look of awe on Jake's face as he repeated the word would have been a lesson in reverence. "And the reason I can't tell the rest of it is because I don't know what happened. Only He came and took hold of me, and—well, I knew I wasn't Jake Lucas inside anymore. But how can a man tell a thing like that?"

Yet Jake must have understood that his face and voice and manner told the story eloquently. He wasn't even Jake Lucas outside anymore.

There were other details. He was slow in regaining his strength. He was very much afraid of the streets at first—until he discovered the Power that had taken hold of him would "go along with him through the streets." Having come to himself—or rather having come to God—his next fixed thought was for his mother. But along with the desire to see her came an ambition to present himself before her in such garb as would fit the new man he felt himself to be. With this for an incentive, he went to work, almost before his strength was equal to the demand, and worked faithfully until he'd earned a suit of clothes and a little money in his pocket. Then he started homeward, working his way as he came, stopping at point after point, as the need arose. He worked at anything he could find to do—so his small sum of money, instead of decreasing, steadily increased.

"And so," he said at last, "I've got home."

"Yes," his mother broke in eagerly at that point, "and the first thing he did was buy some tea for me. And he bought crackers and a piece of meat and brought them home. Just to think of my Jake coming and bringing me tea."

Flora and Stephen made almost one third of the distance home in total silence that evening. They seemed unable to find words for their thoughts. At last Flora broke the silence.

"It seems too wonderful to believe, doesn't it, Steve? But I don't understand why I should feel so. You see, I've been praying and praying for him and wanting him to come home; yet it seems I didn't expect it. When I found him sitting there all dressed up and talking so nice and being good to Mother, why, I just felt as if I'd scream. One time things got all black in the room, and I was dizzylike, just because I was so astonished. I didn't expect any such thing."

"I don't wonder," said Stephen. "I wouldn't have been more astonished, it seems to me, if a stick of wood from the woodpile had walked in and sat and talked with us. It's most amazing. It doesn't seem as if he could be Jake Lucas."

"He isn't," said Flora Ann, with quiet exultation. "He's made over. Folks aren't the same after they begin to pray, Steve. I know that by myself. I'm not the same girl I used to be at all. Folks don't know it, but I'm not. I don't think the same things about people or places or doings of any kind. Oh, I ain't a bit the same! I can't describe it, as Jake says, but I understand what he means. It's all different—still there's more difference for Jake than for any of us. Oh, my! Think of Jake coming to prayer meeting and praying. Do you suppose he will? I'll faint then and miss hearing the words, and I wouldn't for anything."

It was fully as wonderful and bewildering as Flora Ann had foreseen. The first time Jake Lucas came to prayer meeting, the Mitchell dining room was crowded to its capacity, and the hall was full. Even the stairs were full up to the landing. It was such a strange sight for the neighborhood to see one who had been its terror, sitting among them, "clothed, and in his right mind." He not only prayed, but sang and talked, standing up boldly for the One Who, as he always reverently expressed it, had "made him over."

"You can all see, friends, that I ain't the same," he said earnestly. "I don't think the same thoughts or do the same things—not by a great sight. I've belonged to the devil for a good many years, and I've served him faithfully—nobody will deny that. Now I've changed owners—no, it isn't that. I didn't do it. Another owner has got me somehow. I don't know how He got me away from the devil, but you can see for yourselves He's done it. From this time forth I belong to Him, and it makes a difference."

As he sat down, Helen Ransom's clear voice took up the story:

I was lost, but Jesus found me,
    Found the sheep that went astray;
Threw his loving arms around me,
    Drew me back into his way.

I was bruised, but Jesus healed me;
  Faint was I from many a fall;
Sight was gone, and fears possessed me,
  But He freed me from them all.

The minister came into the manse sitting room one afternoon and found Sarah Jane in earnest conversation with his sister.

"Sarah has an application for board," explained Helen, when her caller had been duly greeted.

"Indeed!" said the minister with polite interest. "Who's that?"

"A Mrs. Sedgwick," said Sarah. "I have a letter from her. She wants to come for the summer and have her husband come Saturday nights when he can. She says sometimes he can't get away. She wants to get into the country for her health and be near the city where her husband's business is. She offers a very nice price for her board."

"That's a good recommendation for her," said the minister, smiling. "How did she hear of you, Sarah?"

"She says a friend of hers is a friend of Mrs. Colchester and told her where she was staying."

"What does Mrs. Colchester say?" asked the minister, rousing to deeper interest. "Would she like to have this boarder come?"

"I don't think she's anxious to have more company," said Sarah. "She's very busy all the time and never seems lonesome. But she says of course she wants us to earn all the money we can, and she thinks there's no reason why we shouldn't have this lady come, if our rooms will suit her."

Helen and Sarah Jane carried on a detailed discussion of plans. The minister lingered and offered a suggestion now and then. But he chiefly interested himself in studying Sarah Jane, contrasting her with a girl by that name who had come to them only a year before. He decided she was a somewhat remarkable study and felt he hadn't realized a human being could take such strides in a year's time.

She's a pretty, ladylike girl, he said to himself, *neatly and becomingly dressed. Helen has certainly done wonders for her. She's more changed than her brother, in some respects. When one thinks of those four people—Sarah, Stephen, Flora, and that marvelous Jake—it's enough to intoxicate one with life. To realize what the almighty power of God, with a little human effort, can do for souls, even here on earth, gives one a faint conception of what an eternity of heaven and the companionship of Jesus Christ may do for us all.*

By the time he'd reached this concluding thought, Sarah's arrangements were perfected.

In due time, the new boarder came to them.

"A sickly looking, fashionable girl," Helen said, describing the newcomer to her brother. "She doesn't look at all like a married woman or act like one. I can hardly understand what the attraction could have been in this direction. She impresses me as someone who could cordially hate the country, and there's no more affinity between her and Mrs. Colchester than there is—between Sarah and Fanny Bascome."

"Well," said the minister with a sigh, "if she pays the price for the board Sarah mentioned, there'll be some compensation at least."

The sigh was for a thought he had—that it wouldn't be so pleasant at the Mitchell farmhouse as it had been. Up to the date when the new boarder was heard of, he'd felt that no scheme of Helen's had been happier than this one of setting Sarah Jane to keeping boarders. Since that time he'd been occasionally troubled with doubts as to its wisdom.

It was two weeks before he made Mrs. Sedgwick's acquaintance. She had come on the Wednesday following the Tuesday evening prayer meeting, which had now become an institution in the Hilton Hill neighborhood. The following Sunday had proved very rainy, and although Mrs. Sedgwick was said to have expressed a strong curiosity to attend church, she wasn't inclined to brave a six-mile ride in the storm. On the following Tuesday evening the minister was called miles away in another direction, to visit a sick parishioner, and the prayer meeting had to get on without him. In this way two weeks had passed.

On Saturday evening he proposed to Helen a ride out to the farmhouse.

"I've been working very hard," he said, "and I think a canter would do me good. Besides, I shouldn't let another Sabbath pass without calling on the stranger. We can make a short call and get home in good season."

Sarah Jane saw and recognized them in the distance and came to the gate to meet them.

"I never was so glad to see anyone in my life," she said earnestly. "I've just been praying Mr. Ransom would come. I didn't know what else to do."

"What's the matter?" asked Mr. Ransom hastily, recognizing more than cordial greeting in her anxious tone.

She made her story brief: Mr. Sedgwick had arrived that afternoon, very much under the influence of liquor and growing more so every moment, with a plentiful supply in his traveling bag. Sarah Jane's eyes were wide with terror.

"He's been singing and shouting and acting like a crazy man for the last hour," she explained. "And now he's getting cross. They're in the dining room, and he won't go away or let her. I think she's scared of him, and he keeps getting so much worse. We don't know what to do. If Mrs. Colchester were here I think she could do something with him. She can with almost everybody. But she went with Flora out to her house. And Steve hasn't got home from the village, so we're just alone. Father don't know anything to do, and he won't go there at all. He says he'd as soon see a wild tiger as a drunken man. I never saw Father act as he does about this."

And Sarah Mitchell never understood why her father "acted" as he did. The loyal wife and son kept always silent about that chapter of his life.

"Mrs. Colchester's help shouldn't be expected under such circumstances," said the minister, with more severity than Sarah Jane had ever heard him speak.

"Where drunken men are is no place for her. I'll go in at once and see what can be done."

What he succeeded in doing was presently apparent. His sister and Sarah, waiting outside, heard their voices—the drunken man's loud and hilarious, the minister's firm and commanding. Presently they heard the footsteps of the two, making their way upstairs, the drunken man's unsteady and trembling. Evidently he was being half carried, and the minister was speaking quiet, authoritative words.

"Put your foot there, Mr. Sedgwick—so! You won't fall. I'll see to that. No, you're not coming back. The place for you at present is in your room. You're to go to bed as speedily as possible. Yes, you can. I'll help you. Yes, I understand," interrupting the man in his maudlin attempts at explaining he'd been "s–sud–sud–'nly ta–'on ver–ver'–s–s–sick."

"I understand it perfectly, sir. You needn't explain."

By this time they'd reached the landing above. Sarah Jane drew a long breath of relief.

"What a man he is!" she said, meaning the minister, for there was admiration in her tones. "He's like Mrs. Colchester, Miss Ransom. He can do anything with people. They both can. I don't believe he'll have any trouble getting him to bed. And she just coaxed and begged him to go on. Miss Ransom, he swore at her. Oh, dear! Such a time as we've had. And I was afraid Jake Lucas would come in every minute. It would have been awful for Jake to see a drunken man, don't you think? Miss Ransom, will you go in and see Mrs. Sedgwick? Maybe you can comfort the poor thing. I suppose her heart is almost broken."

"Perhaps she'd rather not see a stranger just now," said Helen, holding back and wondering what she could say that would comfort a drunkard's wife.

At that moment the door opened, and Mrs. Sedgwick's pale, pretty face appeared.

Good evening," she said to Helen.

"Wasn't it awful? He never was as bad as that before. He's been with some of those fast men in town, who have such a bad influence on him. Isn't it dreadful to think that men will drink and make such awful nuisances of themselves? But they all do it. I don't believe my husband has an acquaintance who doesn't take a glass when he feels like it. They're not drunkards, you know, of course. But once in a while they're overcome. I'm sure I wish my husband didn't drink at all. But he'd have to be a minister in that case. I believe they're the only men who don't indulge. You're fortunate in having one for a brother. Girls should look out for such men for husbands. It's a hard life, but there are compensations, it seems."

And she actually laughed, this silly woman! Helen looked at her in dumb dismay. She made no attempt to comfort; she'd as soon have tried to comfort a parrot.

"I'd better go upstairs," said the wife. "Or would you wait down here until Mr. Ransom gets him to bed? I've had enough of him for one night. But he'll be all right as soon as he gets to bed and has had his first sleep. He'll waken in the morning vexed with himself, poor fellow! He does dislike making a scene. I assure you, Miss Ransom—this is a rare occurrence. Gentlemen stay in their clubs in town, you know, when they find themselves overcome with liquor. But in the country, of course, they must brave the embarrassment. Sarah, I believe I'll go up to your room, if you'll let me, and wait until Mr. Ransom comes out."

And she gathered her silken robes about her and climbed up the old-fashioned staircase, with Sarah and Helen looking after her, one almost as bewildered as the other.

Mr. Ransom came down presently, pallid to a degree that startled and frightened his sister and grave almost to sternness. He was in a hurry to start home. He wouldn't go into the dining room, which, between meals, had now become the family sitting room. He declined waiting to see Mr. and Mrs. Mitchell, who had fled to the kitchen from the presence of the drunkard. He couldn't wait for the return of Mrs. Colchester and Flora or even to see Stephen, with whom he was supposed to have an errand. "Another time will do," he said; he must get home at once. He and Helen had only come out for the exercise.

He hurried Helen's last words with Sarah, and in a few minutes they were out, mounted on their horses and galloping toward home. The minister rode at almost breakneck speed, and in the moonlight his face showed pallid still, and his mouth was set in stern lines. Helen wondered and was silent. He had seen drunken men before. Why was he so moved by this exhibition? Was it sympathy for the foolish wife, who didn't seem to deserve to have such feeling wasted upon her?

But she must have talked at random, Helen said to herself, *to cover embarrassment and pain. She wanted me to think nothing very terrible had happened and talked on perhaps without realizing what she said. She probably lost her unnatural self-control when she got upstairs. I wish Maxwell would talk. How miserable he looked! If he's going to carry other people's burdens in this intense way, he'll wear out long before his time.*

They were within two miles of home before the minister spoke, other than to ask his sister if they were riding too fast and if she were comfortable. But at last he slackened rein and turned toward her. The first words he spoke struck his sister dumb.

"Helen, Mrs. Sedgwick is Gertrude Temple."

It was even so. The pretty city boarder, willing to bury herself in the country and offer a liberal price for the privilege of doing so, was the woman who, for one well-remembered year, Maxwell Ransom had looked upon as his promised wife.

His sister, who hadn't felt drawn toward the stranger, but rather repelled, and who had struggled with the feeling and chided herself for it as unworthy, now began to study the woman with a strange mingling of feelings and was obliged to pray much for grace to keep her not only from saying what might injure others, but also from thinking uncharitable thoughts. Still the curious problem presented itself: What motive could Mrs. Sedgwick have for coming away from her home surroundings and home friends, miles into the country? Unquestionably it wasn't the love of nature that had brought her. Nature, in its loveliest forms, seemed only endured by her and, when it put on its unlovely face, was positively repulsive.

Perhaps it was hardly to be expected that a woman like Helen Ransom should have understood a woman like Gertrude Sedgwick. Nothing could be much farther apart than the moral vision of the two. Yet to those who have come in contact with this type of human nature, Mrs. Sedgwick's motive will be readily apprehended. From babyhood she had pleased herself; she'd been a creature of whims and notions; she hadn't for one quiet hour in her life looked ahead and studied the consequences of her actions from the moral side of her being. Results which might be disagreeable to her she could to a degree apprehend—though even for herself she was shortsighted.

She had married, the winter before, the man whose attentions had first inclined her to feel she wasn't fitted to be a minister's wife. If Maxwell Ransom had been preparing for the bar, or if he'd been a gentleman of wealth and leisure, she would have decided for him, instead of for Charlie Sedgwick. But since she couldn't move him from his purpose and realized his profession would demand certain irksome duties from her, the scale had finally turned in favor of the man who was her husband. She was fond of him in her way, but as compared with her pleasure—even the passing pleasure of an hour—he was secondary. She had lived fast after her marriage—without regard to the laws of health or any laws except those her fancy dictated. She had treated her body as a mere machine whose business it was to do her bidding. Of course it had taken a few months to break down a body which was never strong at best. When the physician ordered rest and entire freedom from the requirements of fashionable life, Mrs. Sedgwick had looked about her for some entertainment. In doing so, she'd heard of Mrs. Colchester's departure from the city.

"Have you heard of our beautiful young widow's latest freak?" That was the way the news was communicated. "It has suited her to go to the country in midwinter and bury herself and her little sister in a farmhouse."

"There's some special attraction, you may depend upon it," Mrs. Sedgwick had said as soon as she heard this story. "Mark my words, Mrs. Sylvester—you'll hear of some interesting young man stranded in the vicinity of that country farmhouse, before the season is over."

This explanation was met with approval by some of the circle and with indignation by others. A thorough discussion of Mrs. Colchester's affairs had followed. But Mrs. Sedgwick, caring not in the least for either side, had forgotten all about it, until the conversation was recalled to her a few days later by Mrs. Sylvester.

"You were evidently right about Mrs. Colchester, my dear Mrs. Sedgwick. I'm told there's a brilliant young clergyman where she's gone, who has one or two protégés in the aforesaid farmhouse and is therefore a frequent visitor. One may always trust young widows to keep their eyes wide open."

"It speaks well for her husband that she's willing to choose another from the same profession," was Mrs. Sedgwick's light rejoinder. "What's the name of the clergyman who's brilliant enough to hold people in the country through March?"

"Why, that's an interesting part of the story. His name is Ransom, Maxwell Ransom. He's a nephew of the famous professor by the same name and has inherited all his uncle's talent, I'm told."

Mrs. Sedgwick received this piece of information in utter silence but pondered over it to such purpose that, later in the season when she was ordered to the country, she could think of no part of the world where she could be induced to go except to the Mitchell farmhouse. No, you're not to think of her as the wickedest woman on the face of the earth, but simply as a weak, vain woman, who desired to amuse herself. She couldn't help feeling it would be amusing to come in contact with Maxwell Ransom and bring her fascinations to bear upon him again. It would be very exciting to meet him and talk over old times, even sigh a little over memories of the past. Where was the harm? They'd had delightful times together.

She frankly admitted to herself that in some respects he was Charlie's superior; she'd always thought so. Sometimes she had frankly told Charlie that if she had married Maxwell Ransom, he would never so far have forgotten himself as to drink enough liquor to make him either silly or cross.

No, it was entertainment, pure and simple, Mrs. Sedgwick was after. She felt herself somewhat defrauded of entertainment at times, for her husband's temptations made her more or less nervous in society, and now her failing health had added to life's inconveniences. It was only fair she should get what enjoyment she could out of banishment. And where could more be found than in the society of a young man she knew so well and could talk freely and associate familiarly with, without being misunderstood? For he was a clergyman, and she was a married woman.

This was the extent to which her shallow little brain had planned, and Helen Ransom, in studying her, didn't do her justice. Perhaps one of her nature couldn't do justice to so small an amount of brain as was given to Gertrude Sedgwick.

The minister, reaching home, went directly to his study and was seen no more that night. The next morning he was himself again, though perhaps a bit paler than usual. He admitted to his sister he was late in retiring. But he was as deeply interested in his work as the day before and entered upon it with energy. Nor did he change his habits in the slightest degree regarding the Hilton Hill neighborhood. He went regularly to the meetings and made his regular calls as usual. Helen, who always accompanied him on these trips, watched with anxious eyes but couldn't see that he treated Mrs. Sedgwick any differently from what he would a stranger, whom chance had brought in his vicinity.

As the weeks passed, Mrs. Sedgwick also made this discovery, and it's unnecessary to confess that it annoyed her. Mr. Ransom as a theological student had been wont to flush and pale under her influence; to try in every way in his power to please her; to put himself out to gratify her whims. But it was only too apparent that this Mr. Ransom, while perfectly courteous at all times, was also perfectly indifferent regarding her. He neither sought her society nor shunned it. And the weak little woman who liked her husband less, and Mr. Ransom more, every time she saw him and thought she knew it was Mrs. Colchester who had "come between" them, as she expressed it to herself, grew daily more determined to win the attention she coveted. Or, failing in that, at least she would prevent their enjoying each other. It wasn't in Gertrude Sedgwick's nature to stand tamely by and see Mrs. Colchester accomplish what she could not.

It was a lovely afternoon in early autumn, and the Mitchell farmhouse, which had taken on many improvements during the summer, was bright with sunshine and autumn flowers. In Hilary Colchester's room, that lady, with Helen Ransom and her brother and Sarah Jane, were having what the latter called "a first-rate visit." It was Tuesday, and Maxwell Ransom and Helen had come out early that day as they always did to make a call or two in the neighborhood, take tea at the Mitchell farm, and prepare for the evening meeting. That meeting was growing in such interest and power since Jake Lucas had taken hold of it that people drove for miles in various directions to see and hear this marvelous specimen of what God could do. He was so earnest in securing allies for his new Master that he let no opportunity pass without urging people "just to try Him and find out for yourselves."

They were talking about Mrs. Sedgwick. "I invite her to my room as often as I can," Hilary Colchester had said, "because I'm very sorry for her. She's an unhappy woman. She isn't gaining in health, and her husband isn't improving his habits. He was worse at his last visit than we've ever seen him. Of course she feels very anxious about him, with an anxiety that can't be spoken of. It seems to make her nervous even to hear his name mentioned. I don't know how she bears her burden, and she's trying to bear it alone. I know," she said in response to Helen's inquiring look, "she's a member of the church, but I think she has yet to learn the first principles of vital Christianity. And she's so hard to reach, because she takes it for granted she's on safe ground, of course—hasn't she been a church member in good and regular standing ever since she was fourteen? I'm afraid for such people. They seem in far greater danger than those who reckon themselves outsiders."

Chapter 28

The Through Line at Last

At that moment Gertrude Sedgwick entered the room, and Maxwell Ransom, who had been listening to this talk—which was rather between Helen and Mrs. Colchester—after greeting the newcomer, moved away and took up a book, not to read but as a cover for his thoughts. Was it his duty to assume more friendly relations with Mrs. Sedgwick, to try to lead her into the right way? He admitted to himself that probably Mrs. Colchester was right, and there was little hope this woman he'd once thought a lovely Christian understood the first principles of personal religion. Was it his duty to try to help her? Wouldn't he be misunderstood? But even if he were, would that relieve him from his duty?

And the minister's mind was in chaos. It ended by his joining the circle, summoned there by a question Mrs. Sedgwick called out to him. For a few moments the conversation was general. Then Sarah, being called from the room, presently returned and asked Miss Ransom to come out to the dining room a few minutes, and the three were left together. Whether the spirit of maliciousness took hold of Gertrude Sedgwick to an unusual degree that afternoon will not be known; certainly she became very personal in her words.

"This is almost like old times, isn't it, Max? Dear me! What a short time ago it seems when you and I used to be very much pleased when people were called out of the room. Do you remember that Friday evening at the seminary, when the girls all stayed down in the parlor? I suppose I should say 'Mr. Ransom,' but it sounds more natural to me to call you by the name I'm used to. Mrs. Colchester, we're amazing you, aren't we, by our reminiscences? You didn't know Mr. Ransom and I were very, very old friends, did you?"

"I'm a very new friend of Mr. Ransom," said Mrs. Colchester, with a quiet smile, "and therefore have no knowledge of his friendships of long standing, of course."

"No, and our friendship wasn't of a character to be published, was it, Max?"

"I know no reason, Mrs. Sedgwick, why you shouldn't state to anyone you choose that we were formerly very intimate friends, if it pleases you to."

The minister's tone was cold as ice and his manner dignity personified. It made Mrs. Sedgwick feel more wicked still. Evidently she wasn't gaining any influence over him; then she would sacrifice him to her jealous disappointment.

It had been disappointment from the very first. She'd gone angrily over it in her mind only that day and told herself what a fool she was for her pains. How carefully she'd guarded the secret of her former acquaintance with Maxwell Ransom, on her first arrival, so she might enjoy the excitement of his and their surprise when they learned who she was. And, behold, the first meeting was when he came to help her drunken husband to bed! How hard, even after that, she had striven to get a little excitement out of it, by being an innocent child before Helen Ransom, believing her brother was too much overcome to explain who she was! It was another disappointment.

"Certainly I know you were once Miss Temple," Helen Ransom had said one day when Gertrude had resolved to make the revelation. "I've known you since the first evening my brother called here after you came. It was quite natural, of course, that he should mention it." And she'd spoken as if it were a matter of no interest for her or for her brother.

At that time the lady had concluded her story was well-known to Mrs. Colchester—for of course Helen Ransom had told it—this was Mrs. Sedgwick's idea of friendship. But later, when she came to know Helen better, she had a shrewd suspicion that silence concerning her had been maintained. When she resolved to sacrifice Mr. Ransom, she rejoiced over this. She laughed the little girlish laugh that used to be so sweet to his ears.

"Dear me, Max! Don't be so fearfully dignified. What's the use? You remind me forcibly of the times when some escapade of mine used to disturb you. I've received many curtain lectures from him, Mrs. Colchester. I used to be a sad trial to him, I suspect. He owes me a vote of thanks for refusing to victimize him all his life. What an odd minister's wife I'd have made! Can you imagine me for one minute in such a position, Mrs. Colchester?"

"No," said that lady with a grave smile, "not with your present views of life."

"That's just the trouble. My views of life were always at variance with the life planned for me. And they are yet, for that matter—I think life has treated me in a very niggardly fashion. Here I am an old married woman, sick and miserable, when I should be just a girl, enjoying myself. But I'll try to do my duty, Mrs. Colchester, and I warn you this gentleman is very set in his ways. He's a slave to a creature he calls 'Duty,' but which is really only another name for self-will. He won't hesitate to sacrifice any and everything that comes in its way. Oh, don't I know all about it? I'm one of the sacrifices. But, my dear, I don't think you need to blush so over my revelations. Having been a married woman, you know men, of course. They're all alike—fickle, I daresay. Some of them think more of books, it's true, than they do of any woman, even before marriage—but I assure you Max is quite attentive for him. Of course it's apparent you're the attraction to this old farmhouse, and you may as well enjoy it while it lasts. That's the only way to get along with life."

Said Hilary Colchester: "Nina, dear, don't try to get out of the swing alone. Wait—I'll come to you." And she stepped from the doorway near which she stood, out on the piazza, and moved swiftly toward the swing under the great old trees.

Maxwell Ransom was left alone with Gertrude Temple. She lifted her eyes to him, and actually they were full of tears.

"Oh, Max!" she said, and her voice had the old childish quiver in it which used to move him. "Have I offended you? Have I been hateful? I didn't mean to be. I don't know what I say half the time. I talk lightly to other people, but really, Max, life is very hard on me. You don't know what I have to suffer, and it hurts me so to think that you used to be so entirely my friend and now seem to—"

Then she stopped, her beautiful eyes all dim with tears. She might as well have attempted to move a marble statue with tears and tremulousness. Maxwell Ransom had risen from his chair the moment Mrs. Colchester left the room and moved to the doorway through which she'd passed. His voice was cold and stern.

"You've done no harm, I imagine, Mrs. Sedgwick, except to yourself. A woman who can forget herself and her husband and speak as you have just now is to be pitied perhaps, even more than she's to be blamed."

Then he, too, went through that open doorway and walked deliberately out to the swing under the old trees. In the near distance was Stephen Mitchell, riding in from the field on a load of corn. He shouted to Nina, and she ran happily away to ride up the long lane by his side. Her sister stood looking after her, her fingers engaged in breaking little twigs from the great tree, her face averted from Mr. Ransom, and her whole manner showing she was struggling for an outward calm which would have belied the tumult in her heart.

"Mrs. Colchester," the minister said, speaking in quick, firm tones, "you've heard several truths this afternoon. You may not be interested in any of them. Yet it becomes me as a man to own them as truths. I was engaged to be married to Mrs. Sedgwick, as she's intimated. I didn't desert her as she hints; instead, she deserted me. I would have been true to what I thought she was if she'd given me the opportunity. It's a long story you may not care to hear. It rests with you to say whether you care or not.

"She spoke other words which are also true—among them, that I'm drawn to this house to see you. I've known it for some time. I've hoped the time might come when you would let me tell you so and explain everything to do with my life. I hadn't meant to come to you in this abrupt, almost rude fashion, and assuredly I hadn't meant to subject you to insult because of me. As it is, I hardly know what to do next. You'd be justified in wishing me to leave you. Yet I don't feel willing to do so without trying to explain. I'm so hurt and grieved that you've been exposed to the venom of a cruel tongue through my influence, however remote, that I can't decide the least offensive course to take under such strange circumstances."

There was silence under the trees for what seemed hours to the minister, although it was in reality moments.

Then Mrs. Colchester gave him a view of a very sweet face and eyes that smiled. He'd never heard a gentler voice than the one which said, "My trust in you isn't shaken, Mr. Ransom. You may tell me as much or as little of your past as you choose, whenever you will. And I'm not angry at that poor woman— it's as she said: Life has used her hard—or rather she's used it hard—and there's bitterness in store for her. When I think of the contrast between her life and mine—" her voice broke, and it was a moment before she added, "I have only pity for her, Mr. Ransom."

They lingered under the trees, sitting down together on the rustic seat Stephen had made. Nina danced back from her ride and, finding them unsatisfactory company, flitted away again and went to help Sarah and Flora arrange a most delightful-looking tea table. In her room upstairs, Mrs. Sedgwick watched the two under the trees with angry eyes and brushed away from time to time certain miserable tears, saying to herself over and over again: "What a wretched idiot I've been all my life!"

Downstairs Helen Ransom sat alone, taking neat stitches in the work she was doing and giving satisfied glances occasionally out of the window—she liked the picture under the trees. In due time Nina summoned them all to that delightful tea table.

"Helen," Mr. Ransom said, as they rode home that evening after prayer meeting, "did you ever tell Mrs. Colchester anything concerning Mrs. Sedgwick and me?"

"Maxwell!"

It was the only answer he received. But he needed no other and hurried to respond: "I beg your pardon, Helen—but you are friends of such long standing and so intimate. I thought possibly—"

"Max, do you think long and intimate friendship justifies breaches of confidences made by other friends?"

"Certainly not—forgive me. I never thought you did or could do other than what was true and noble. It was only my awkward way of introducing the subject. I've told her the entire story—and I have something to tell you. Not about Mrs. Sedgwick—poor creature!—I feel only pity for her. I haven't even the heart to be indignant with her tonight—though assuredly she gave me cause this afternoon. Helen, I know it will make you glad, but will it surprise you very much to hear that your friend has promised to be your sister?"

Three months afterward, on a moonlit winter evening, Stephen Mitchell and his pastor were walking across the fields from the Lucas home, where they'd been spending the evening together under the most solemn circumstances human experience knows. "Old man Lucas," as he was known in that neighborhood for so many years, had just exchanged worlds. The marvel of marvels had taken place once more. The old, worn body, dimmed of sight, dulled of hearing, poisoned with rum and tobacco, abused and wasted beyond repair, had been left behind. The soul, stained so many years with sin, having breathed out through lips of clay curses innumerable upon its Maker and done almost all a soul can to wreck its possibilities, had toward the closing of that solemn "eleventh hour" given heed at last to the Voice which had steadily called after it.

Those waiting around the old man's bed had heard the sin-stained lips speak marvelous words, even these, "God, for Jesus Christ's sake, has forgiven my sins." At the very last, when they thought him done with earth, the dimmed eyes opened again and looked upward for a moment. The thin, pale lips took on the majesty of a smile and once more formed the words, "God, for Christ's sake—amen," and old man Lucas was gone.

"What a wonderful experience!" said Mr. Ransom, as he crushed the frosted snow under his feet. "What a privilege we've had tonight! Think what an infinite Savior we have, to take that man with his load of seventy years of sin upon him and put a new song in his mouth and stamp the clay he's left behind with such a look of a conqueror that his children stand about it in awe, saying, 'Can that be Father?' What a thing it must be for that man to enter heaven!"

They were crossing the Mitchell farm now. It lay under the snow, but both men thought of the golden harvest waving there a short time before and of the golden returns, unusual both in quality and quantity. Stephen Mitchell was going to be a farmer; nobody questioned it now. Even in such a short time he'd made his mark. Even in such a short time his father had learned to say, "Ask Steve about it—he does the planning. Steve knows what he's about." Even in such a short time they'd learned at the city market to ask for berries and early vegetables— yes, and even flowers—from the Mitchell farm.

Oh, yes! Stephen's heart was in it. The way he worked and studied and planned proved that. But the minister thought of it all sadly. He remembered their first walk together across these fields and the mistake he was convinced he'd made. Why had he started Stephen Mitchell's energies, ambitions, hopes, and plans all earthward? Even while he thought and sighed, Stephen broke the silence.

"Mr. Ransom, something else has happened today you don't know about yet. I've boarded the right train at last, sir."

"What's that, Stephen? What do you mean?"

"I mean I've been running on a sidetrack for the last year or so. It's been a pretty good road, as you know, in some respects, but you haven't been satisfied with it—I know that. And I haven't been real downright satisfied myself, though I tried to think it first-class. But I've changed roads now. I'm on the main line at last and am bound for home. I'm not a passenger, either, but a stockholder."

"The Lord be praised!" said the minister, the joy in his heart ringing in his voice as the full meaning of this quaint language dawned upon him. He grasped Stephen's hand. "I've waited and prayed for this so long, Stephen. Do you mind telling me the story—what started you on the right road at last?"

"Well," said Stephen, clearing his throat, "I've been thinking about it a good deal more than any of you know, but I really suppose it was Jake Lucas at the last who got me on the main track. It seemed so remarkable for him to board the lightning express, as you may say, and me, with the long start I had ahead of him, to be left behind. Then he was determined I should travel with him. It seemed as if nothing less would satisfy him. Then—perhaps you remember that list of words which started me in the first place?"

"I certainly do," said the minister promptly.

"Well, I kept studying them. I made up my mind, you know, to master them, and they brought me square up against the Bible one day and made me go at that if I meant to be honest."

There was a moment's pause, then Stephen cleared his throat and continued: "There's another thing, to be downright honest. I found out Flora had taken me in place of her brother and was praying for me every day, the same way she used to for him before he started. And she's had such a hard life, one way and another, that I didn't want to disappoint her."

The minister told this story over to Mrs. Colchester not long afterward.

"So it was Jake and the list of words and Flora Ann who reached him, you see," he concluded, and the faintest little sigh was in his heart as he said the words. He had prayed so long and worked so earnestly for Stephen Mitchell.

"Well, what does it matter?" he added. "Just so he's on the main line at last. It's of little consequence who took him to the train." Then, after a moment's silence, he laughed. "I remember he told me once he thought something might be made of 'that Flora Ann,' if the right person could only get ahold of her. And I really think, Hilary, the right person to help her all through her life has been found."

Mary Lou Mackey loses her best friend and confidante when her mother succumbs to illness. Grief and pain place a wall between Mary Lou and her father. Her first love rides off into the sunset, as cowboys are bent to do. And a host of caring relatives simply can't fill the void in Mary Lou's heart.

Under the shade of her favorite cottonwood trees, Mary Lou pours out her soul to her heavenly Father. She clings to precious memories of her past, but life is moving ahead on the Kansas prairie.

Slowly, she accepts the love of a gentleman, planning a future at the general store her father has maintained. But a piece of her heart still clings to dreams of a redheaded cowboy who left long ago. How can a woman possibly love two men?

The choice she makes now will forever determine the course of her life, and the lives of generations to follow. Will her heart find a home? What legacy will Mary Lou leave to posterity?

Follow this pioneer woman's story through four complete novels, all in one volume. See how great faith and love combine to build life on the Great Plains.

❤ ❤ ❤ ❤ ❤ ❤ ❤ ❤ ❤ 💙 ❤ ❤ ❤ ❤ ❤ ❤ ❤ ❤

Getaways

W hen the work piles up, the stress builds, and there seems to be no end in sight, we all could use a break from the routine and a chance to regroup. Of course, God doesn't need holidays, and eight individuals will soon learn that He is actively working in their lives—even when they are trying to escape the everyday pressures of life.

If you're ready for a break, read on. No need to pack suitcases or make travel arrangements when you can sit back and enjoy four separate *Getaways* in one terrific collection. Bon voyage!

paperback, 352 pages, 5 ³/₁₆" x 8"

♥ ♥ ♥ ♥ ♥ ♥ ♥ ♥ ♥ ♥ ♥ ♥ ♥ ♥ ♥ ♥ ♥

British COLUMBIA

The early twentieth century not only births the town of Dawson Creek, British Columbia, but changes it from a prairie village into the southern anchor of the Alcan Highway. Follow the fictionalized growth of author Janelle Burnham Schneider's hometown through the eyes of characters who hold onto hopes, dreams. . .and love.

This captivating volume combines four complete novels of inspiring love that you'll treasure.

paperback, 464 pages, 5 ³⁄₁₆" x 8"

♥ ♥ ♥ ♥ ♥ ♥ ♥ ♥ ♥ ♥ ♥ ♥ ♥ ♥ ♥ ♥ ♥ ♥ ♥

Please send me _____ copies of *British Columbia*.
I am enclosing $4.97 for each.
Please add $1.00 to cover postage and handling per order. OH add 6% tax.)
Send check or money order, no cash or C.O.D.s please.

Name_____

Address _____

City, State, Zip _____

♥ ♥ ♥ ♥ ♥ ♥ ♥ ♥ ♥ ♥ ♥ ♥ ♥ ♥ ♥ ♥ ♥ ♥ ♥

To place a credit card order, call 1-800-847-8270.
Send to: Heartsong Presents Reader Service, PO Box 719, Uhrichsville, OH 44683

Experience a family

saga that begins in 1860 when the painting of a homestead is first given to a young bride who leaves her beloved home of Laurelwood. Then follow the painting through a legacy of love that touches down in the years 1890, 1969, and finally today. Authors Sally Laity, Andrea Boeshaar, Yvonne Lehman, and DiAnn Mills have worked together to create a time-less treasure of four novellas in one collection.

paperback, 352 pages, 5 ³/₁₆" x 8"

• • • • • • • • ❤ • • • • • • • •

Daily inspiration for Women

The apostle Peter wrote that a gentle spirit, not our outward appearance, is of great worth in God's sight. In our harsh and often heartless world, gentleness is a much-needed characteristic. With an emphasis on personal spiritual development, this daily devotional for women draws from the best writings of classic and contemporary Christian female authors.

384 pages, Printed Leatherette, 4 ³⁄₁₆" x 6 ³⁄₄"

❤ ❤ ❤ ❤ ❤ ❤ ❤ ❤ ❤ ❤ ❤ ❤ ❤ ❤ ❤

Grace Livingston Hill
Collections

Readers of quality Christian fiction
will love these new novel collections
from Grace Livingston Hill, the leading lady of inspirational romance.
Each collection features three titles
from Grace Livingston Hill and a
bonus novel from Isabella Alden,
Grace Livingston Hill's aunt and a
widely respected author herself.

Collection #8 includes the complete Grace Livingston Hill books
The Chance of a Lifetime, Under the Window and *A Voice in
the Wilderness,* plus *The Randolphs* by Isabella Alden.

paperback, 464 pages, 5 ³⁄₁₆" x 8"

♥ ♥ ♥ ♥ ♥ ♥ ♥ ♥ ❤ ♥ ♥ ♥ ♥ ♥ ♥ ♥ ♥

♥ ♥ ♥ ♥ ♥ ♥ ♥ ❤ ♥ ♥ ♥ ♥ ♥ ♥ ♥